Occasions

Josep Lluís Mateo

“Whatever *time* and *space* mean, place and *occasion* mean more.”[1]

Aldo Van Eyck

Occasions refers to the specificity of our actions and puts distance between itself and the generic approach. Operating as an architect, I have to go up to phenomena; I cannot merely explain them from the distance that renders them uniform and dilute. I am interested in the viewpoint that causes experiences and ideas to materialize in a unique, special way.
In consequence, rather than proposing a practice of general, abstract, generic architecture, **Occasions** seeks to understand it and to describe it as the product of an intelligence and a specific sensibility.

Occasions points out that our work is always an **opportunity** to understand and establish active relations with the world.

Occasions distinguishes between the various **moments**: initial, middle and end. The initial or imagined possibility. The ongoing effort in the middle, the art of ending with the requisite separation that gives way to a new beginning and ending.
Occasions means enjoying the **process**, using it to improve the project.

Occasions insists on the **place** and on the **material** as central moments that are confronted by the idea.

Occasions notes, without mythification, the **archaism** underlying any architectural practice: making holes in the ground, erecting structures, covering, protecting. Our **physical** as well as our mental condition.

Occasions speaks of the experience and the action as a sum of **encounters** with things, persons and ideas. These pages follow some of their traces.

Occasions, despite its fragmentation and specificity, is **not** an inward-looking autobiographical chronicle. **Occasions** seeks to interact with what is **outside** it.

Occasions operates on the basis of the statement that in the practice of architecture, ideas are produced and come together in action. They are **not pre-existing** principles (we like to look freely), **nor** are they justifications **after the fact**; Here, we seek to describe this simultaneous interaction.

Josep Lluís Mateo

1 Van Eyck, Aldo: Writings. Sun Editions, ISBN 9789085062622.

OCCASIONS

NICE

PROPOSAL FOR THE REDEVELOPMENT OF THE PROMENADE DES ANGLAIS
Nice, France. Invited competition, 1995

Promenade des Anglais. View with the Hotel Negresco in the background

DOMINIQUE BOUDET, Director and editor in chief of *AMC* architecture magazine. Since 2004, he has worked as a freelance critic. He is currently researching new urban strategies in Europe.

JOSEP LLUÍS MATEO OR THE ART OF CONSTRUCTING THE CITY USING ARCHITECTURE

Josep Lluís Mateo is one of Spain's most influential architects and a guest in Nice at this first lecture of 2008. He is an architect with an atypical career.

The early years were devoted to promoting his fellow architects in the pages of *Quaderns d'Arquitectura i Urbanisme*, the magazine published by the COAC (Architects' Institute of Catalonia), of which he was editor from 1981 to 1990. During the same period, a few small-scale but outstanding interventions served to strengthen his own architectural stance: a modern architecture, based on great constructive delicacy, free of nostalgia but sensitive to memory.

In the 1990s, his work began to grow in scale. The projects were not of a kind to attract media attention (social housing) and the locations were thankless: usually on city limits, those shifting grounds where urban forms tend to dissolve. These apparently unfavourable conditions called for concentration on the essence. It was a hard training, but one that allowed Mateo to forge his exceptional urban *savoir-faire*: an art of constructing the city using strong, decent architecture, and forms that are compact but not without delicacy in their detail, built to consolidate territories under construction.

Complex works on a larger scale that conserve this manifest unity, such as the Barcelona International Convention Centre, led to research into the organization of volumes in order to create a genuine skyline. This phase served as preparation for larger scale urban projects such as the new neighbourhood on the embankment of the Adour in Bayonne, or the apartments in Badalona marina.

Brought together in a highly coherent whole, the volumes acquire an autonomy, volume and orientation that respond to specific situations of the context. The organization of projects into different volumes serves to create a strong identity based on the controlled interplay of the dynamic equilibrium of masses in urban space.

Presentation of Josep Lluís Mateo at "Recent work. Projets Actuels": Lecture given at the MAMAC (Musée d'Art Moderne et d'Art Contemporain) at the invitation of Nice City Council (France), on 24 January 2008.

AN URBAN SEQUENCE LINKED TO THE WIDER LANDSCAPE

In Bayonne, nature forms part of the essence of construction. The river, the trees and the mountains are materials that merge into the town and determine its specific quality, its singularity. Our proposal consists of building an urban sequence linked to the wider landscape. The buildings are set back from the main approach road, protected from noise and pollution by a generously proportioned park. We position the office building as a landmark at the end of this approach. Laid out transversally between the town and the river, the buildings free up ground, and create views and itineraries. Their implantation is also influenced by the irregularities of the urban fabric. The project works at the intermediate scale (GF + 3-4) that characterizes Bayonne. This relatively small scale helps the buildings to blend into the natural setting, enhancing the quality of life of their inhabitants. The architecture aims to be simple and modern, with the capacity to integrate domestic, personal and variable features within a unitary order.

EMBANKMENT OF THE RIVER ADOUR

First prize. Invited competition. 2006

Bayonne/France. Location: Area around the Henri Grenet bridge. Surface area: 70,000 m²

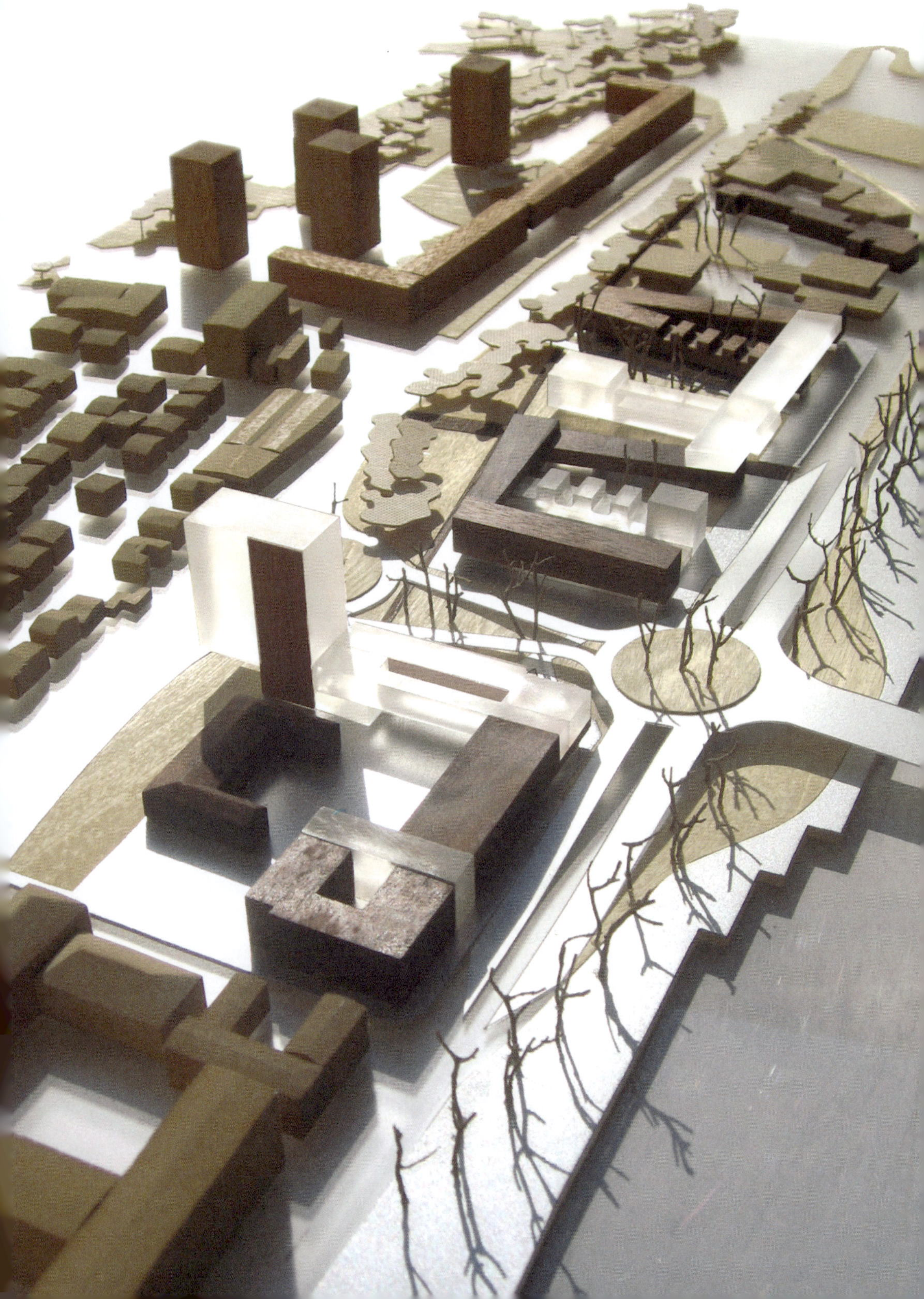

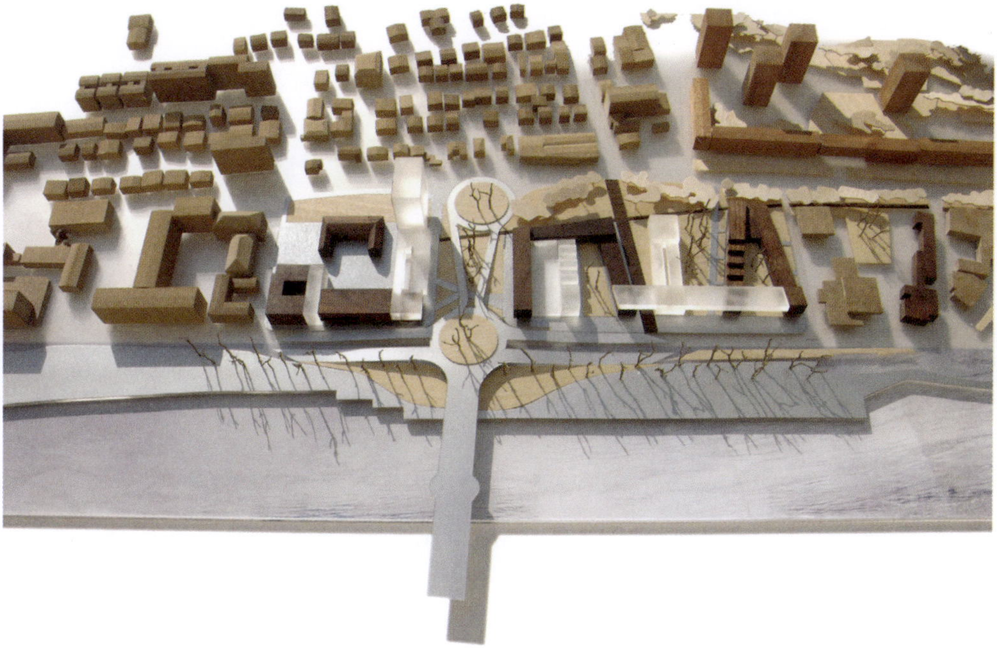

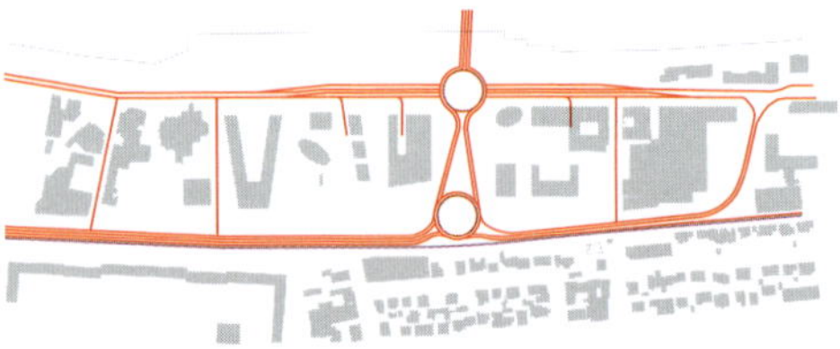

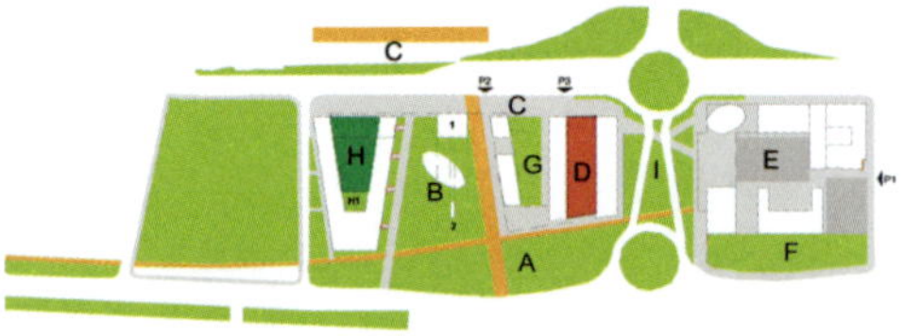

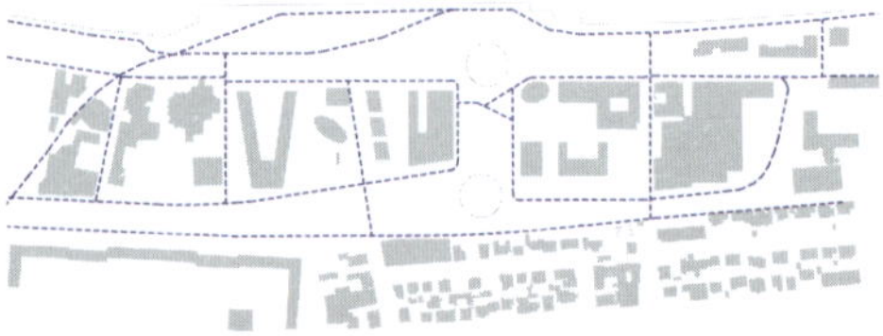

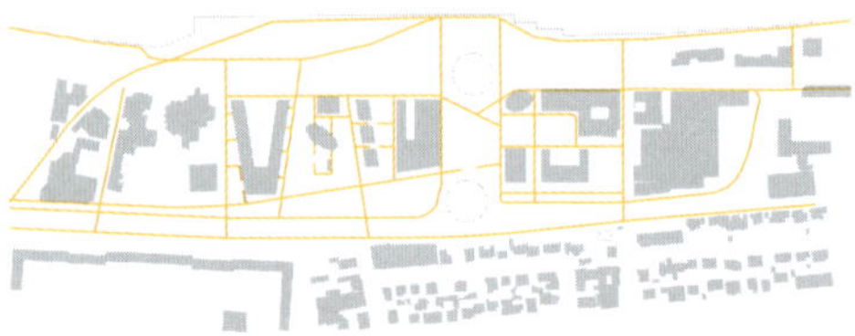

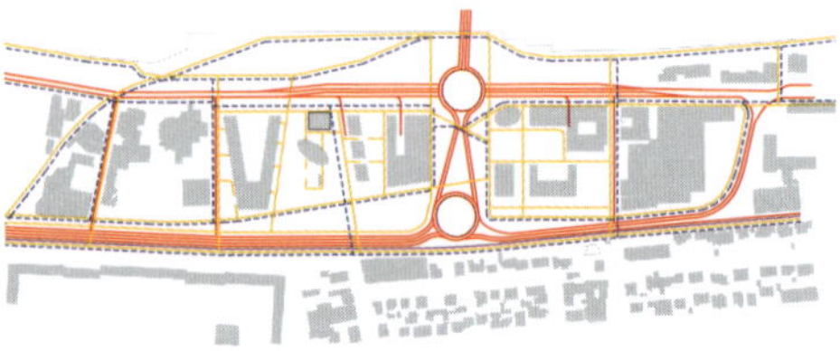

Public areas

A Green space (filter with section of dune and perspective towards the roundabout)

B Space continuing the urban axis. Green area (with no underground car park, where trees could be planted)
1. Commercial area linked to the public space
2. Building on piles

C Space linked to the course of the river

D Raised square (with views of the river), +3.00 m

E Interior square, cloister configuration

F Square with trees continuing the green axis of the dune along BAB

G Interior garden linked to the riverside space

Semi-public areas

H Interior garden linked to the riverside space

H1 Enclosed garden for children

Landscape-building

Green roof (reference to the architecture of the old fortifications)

Car park entrance

P1 Public entrance

P2 Private + public entrance

P3 Service entrance

Remodelling of the urban space between the two existing roundabouts: by separating the roads, nature and asphalt are intertwined, reducing the presence of the latter.

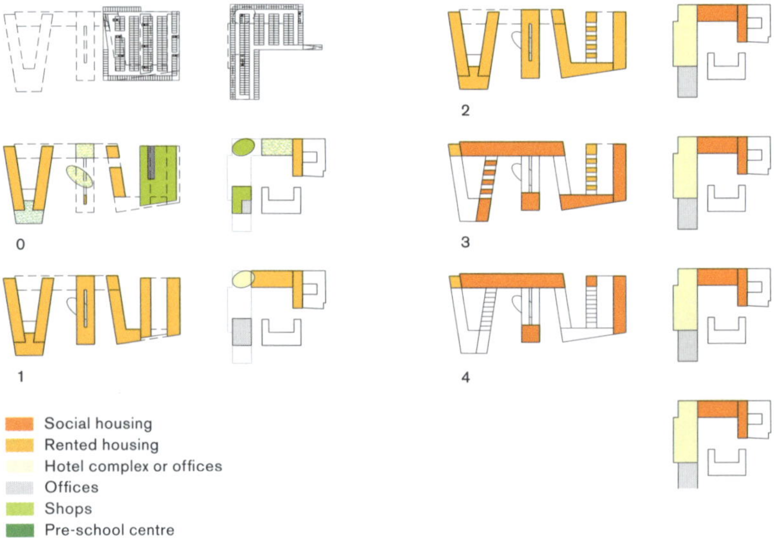

0
1
2
3
4
Social housing
Rented housing
Hotel complex or offices
Offices
Shops
Pre-school centre

CRECHE

Along the river

WHY DO YOU DESIGN LARGE PROJECTIONS?

THE BEST COLUMN IS ONE THAT IS NOT THERE

The law of gravity is one of our themes. It speaks to us of the meeting with the earth, of being rooted, of solidness and of stability. Yet at the same time we also experience the opposing force: the will to fly, to float, to break free of our weight and conquer the air. Greek mythology offers us a beautiful description: Dedalus, the first architect and builder of the thick walls that enclosed the Labyrinth, was succeeded by his son, Icarus, who tried—and almost managed—to fly. We all know how that story ended. In my case, building walls (the definitive activity of an architect) is sometimes accompanied by the aim of making them levitate. I prefer to imagine covered spaces (building roofs) rather than constructing columns. The best column is one that is not there.

Answer to a question. Intervention of Josep Lluís Mateo in "Recent work. Projets Actuels": a lecture given at the MAMAC (Musée d'Art Moderne et d'Art Contemporain) on the invitation of the City of Nice (France), on 24 January 2008.

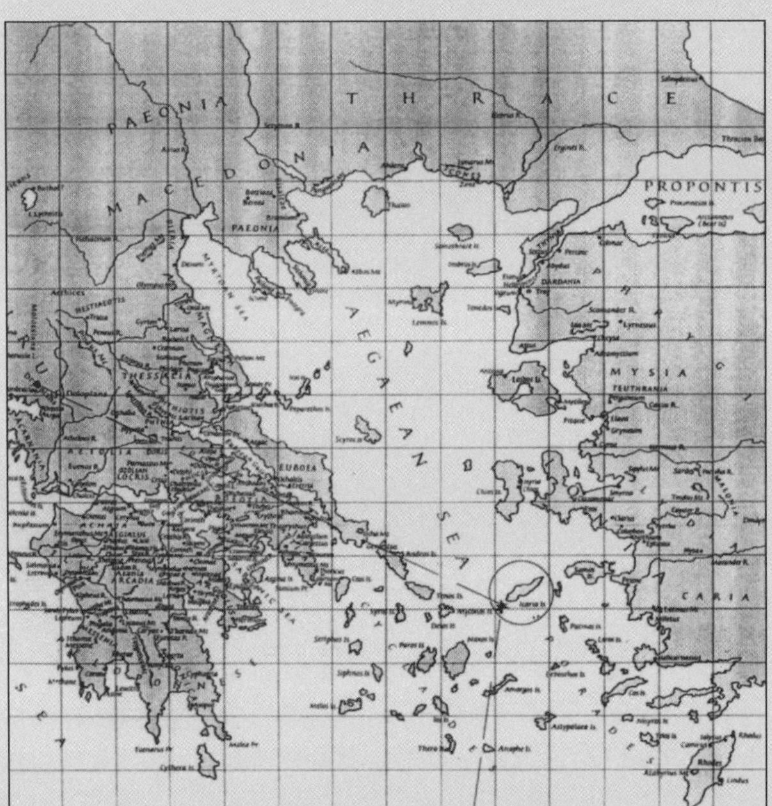

Route of the Flight of Icarus (as seen by Peter Greenaway)

URBAN SPACE

As I see it, urban space can express one of the two sides of the following duality: it is either the memory, the expression, of *pre-existing nature* (Carrer Balmes in Barcelona still contains and expresses the movement of water in the former stream; we have all been struck by the sight of raw earth in the holes dug by workmen in the streets), or it is the expression of *pure artificiality*, a film that covers a more or less sinister underworld where the greed of the contemporary city is directed towards the centre of the earth. Here, the urban space has a twofold tension: the atmospheric exterior and an interior magmatic pressure that compresses it into a hard film, like a tombstone. Naturalistic expression is easier and more complex, and pure artificiality is abstract and difficult to design. See p. 62

CASTELO BRANCO

CARLOS MANUEL REIS DE FIGUEIREDO Architect and head of the Polis Programme for Castelo Branco Town Council

CASTELO BRANCO

POLIS, a Portuguese Government programme for urban regeneration being implemented in some of Portugal's cities, has served to directly question the models of urban growth of the last 30 years and introduce new approaches.

Castelo Branco took up the challenge of addressing changes in use and function of its urban space, considerably altering its appearance, accepting a break with the past and not allowing memory to hinder these far-reaching changes. The town did, however, view the change of scale and the introduction of new paradigms of scenic spots and conceptual areas as a complex process and one that would be difficult to materialize. Primarily, we were aware that there would be resistance to any change and foresaw that the prevailing technical, social and political order would not give free rein to the agents of ideas for transforming the town centre. We therefore concluded that it was vital to find someone who would help ensure solid urban planning, incorporating an overall conception of the town and its buildings, and give the planned change of urban scale the necessary theory and authority.

That person was Josep Lluís Mateo, a colleague whom I invited in the name of the municipal corporation of Castelo Branco. The reasons for choosing him were obvious: his curriculum and built work showed that he was an architect who was capable of addressing the large and the small scale, and was conscientious in his reading of towns and cities and their buildings, manifesting his interest in a form of creative urban design that transmits new scenic force and new concepts. He was an expert in the kind of urban character we were hoping to bring to a provincial town.

Initial strategic plan 1999

- **1** Portuguese broadcasting company
- **2** Arts centre
- **3** Library
- **4** Restaurants
- **5** Council buildings (using former barracks)
- **6** Hotel
- **7** Shops and cafés

- **A** Car parking
- **B** Viewpoint
- **C** Garden – Wood
- **D** Square
- **E** Skating rink
- **F** Esplanade

Aerial photo before the intervention

Mateo quickly grasped the importance of the urban operation, the imperious need for a change of scale of public space, the creation of quality facilities and, most of all, the necessary organization of the various investments being made, ensuring that they were at all times subject to the appropriate cultural and technical control. His initial sketches and models immediately showed that he had grasped the complexity of this large public space, the various urban and traffic issues, and the cultural restrictions that the town's people were beginning to manifest publicly, calling for the conservation of certain debatable heritage values. His first sketches and models highlighted the complexity of Praça Largo da Devesa, which dominates the entire urban design. The "base" he introduces creates a beautiful formal effect. His proposed topography, moulded like a potter handles clay and shapes his sculpture, shows Mateo's sublime command of plasticity. Consequently, the square responds to major topographical problems and, like an open hand, offers refuge to a whole array of buildings designed in keeping with it. Still to be built is the splendid work of urban design that is Castelo Branco's arts centre, which will be completed as part of the 2007–2013 Community Framework Programme.

All of these plans and projects involved major problems, leading Mateo to question his continuing involvement in the process on various occasions. The structural changes being carried out in cities, particularly in Portugal, reveal exasperating levels of provincialism that clash seriously with more lucid approaches. Our ongoing collaboration with Mateo and good relations with the president of Castelo Branco's corporation, as well as the constant help of Sociedade Polis and its appreciation of the prestige and professional skill of the experts involved in this long, complex process of urban transformation, ensured that the continuing efforts of Mateo and his team paid off. For my part, I have fond memories of the best and the worst times, together with Mateo, designing a part of the town with undeniable urban and formal qualities that will remain forever in the history of Castelo Branco.

TOPOGRAPHY When building, I have sometimes felt that the work of the architect evokes a strange symmetry with that of the archaeologist. We started by making holes in the ground: foundations and the laying of tubes. We then built structures and walls that looked broken down, unfinished, until, suddenly, something complete and polished appeared. Then we withdrew. Later, the constructions once again fell down and came apart, leaving just the foundations, fields of ruins of history that speak to us of the past. Castelo Branco never reached the stage of completion. A lack of funds and organization prevented it moving beyond the fragmentation of its construction. Furthermore, Castelo Branco offered something perverse but fascinating: the radical separation between work of extraordinary excellence (for example, the paving of Portuguese setts) and examples of spectacularly poor quality. No middle ground.
The project addressed the largest public space in the town's historic centre. From the outset, it was very important to define a topography: the large plaza sloping downwards to the centre to collect water and a difference in level where the shops are situated. Higher up came the most actively urban space. The edges are important, too: a green slope continues the street above on one side, and a semi-open pergola offers protection from the street with its heavy traffic on the other. The paving, the constant object of our attention, is extraordinary. Some fun street furniture was added (moveable seating...). It is much frequented, particularly at night, in summer; when the place disappears as a tectonic presence and comes to life as a virtual space, I find it very attractive. It is as though the disappearance of the architecture as a shiny, polished, finished object allows the town's residents to appropriate it for themselves, collaborating enthusiastically in its destruction.

MARIA JOAO PIRES ARTS CENTRE AND LARGO DA DEVESA CITY SQUARE

First prize. Invited competition. 2000–2007:
Largo da Devesa square. 2000: Arts centre at the design phase
Castelo Branco/Portugal. Location: Parque da Devesa. Surface area: 6 ha

Section 1

Section 2

Section 3

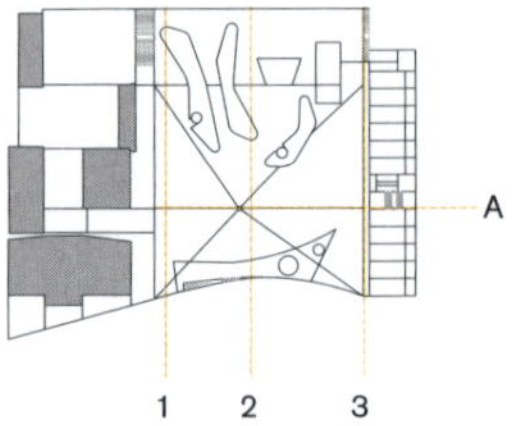

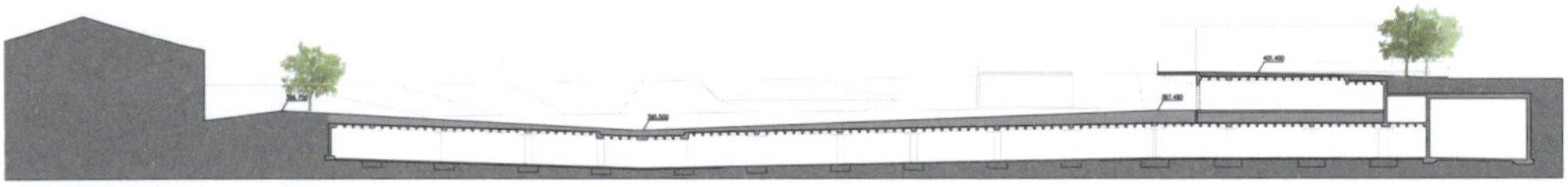

Section A

Sequence: Pergola – Green slope

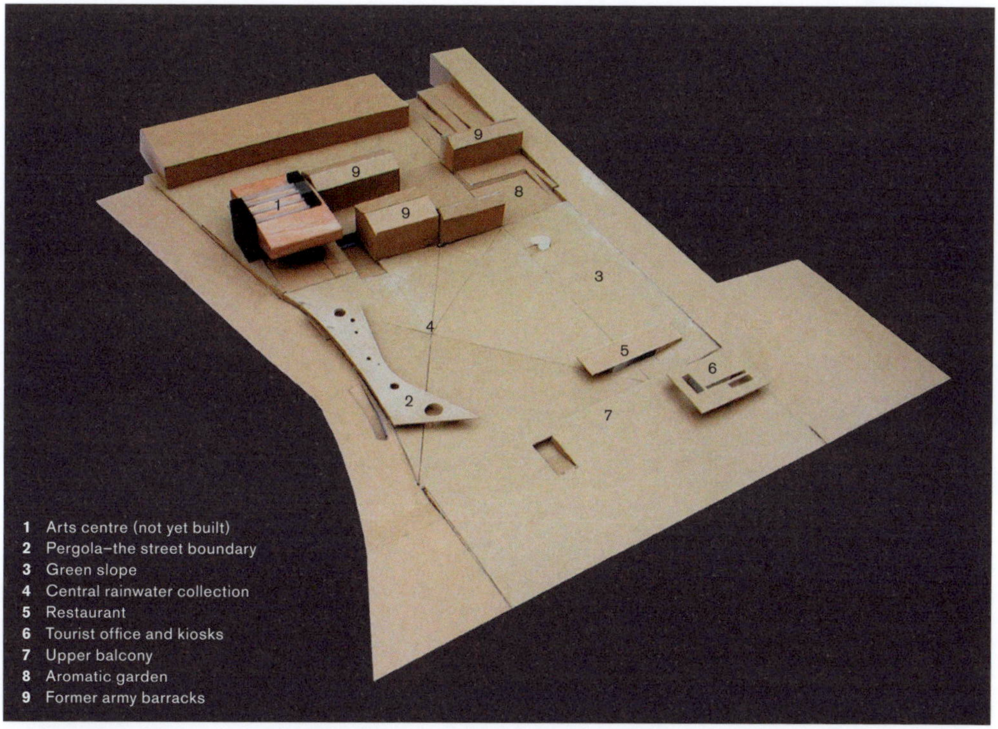

1 Arts centre (not yet built)
2 Pergola–the street boundary
3 Green slope
4 Central rainwater collection
5 Restaurant
6 Tourist office and kiosks
7 Upper balcony
8 Aromatic garden
9 Former army barracks

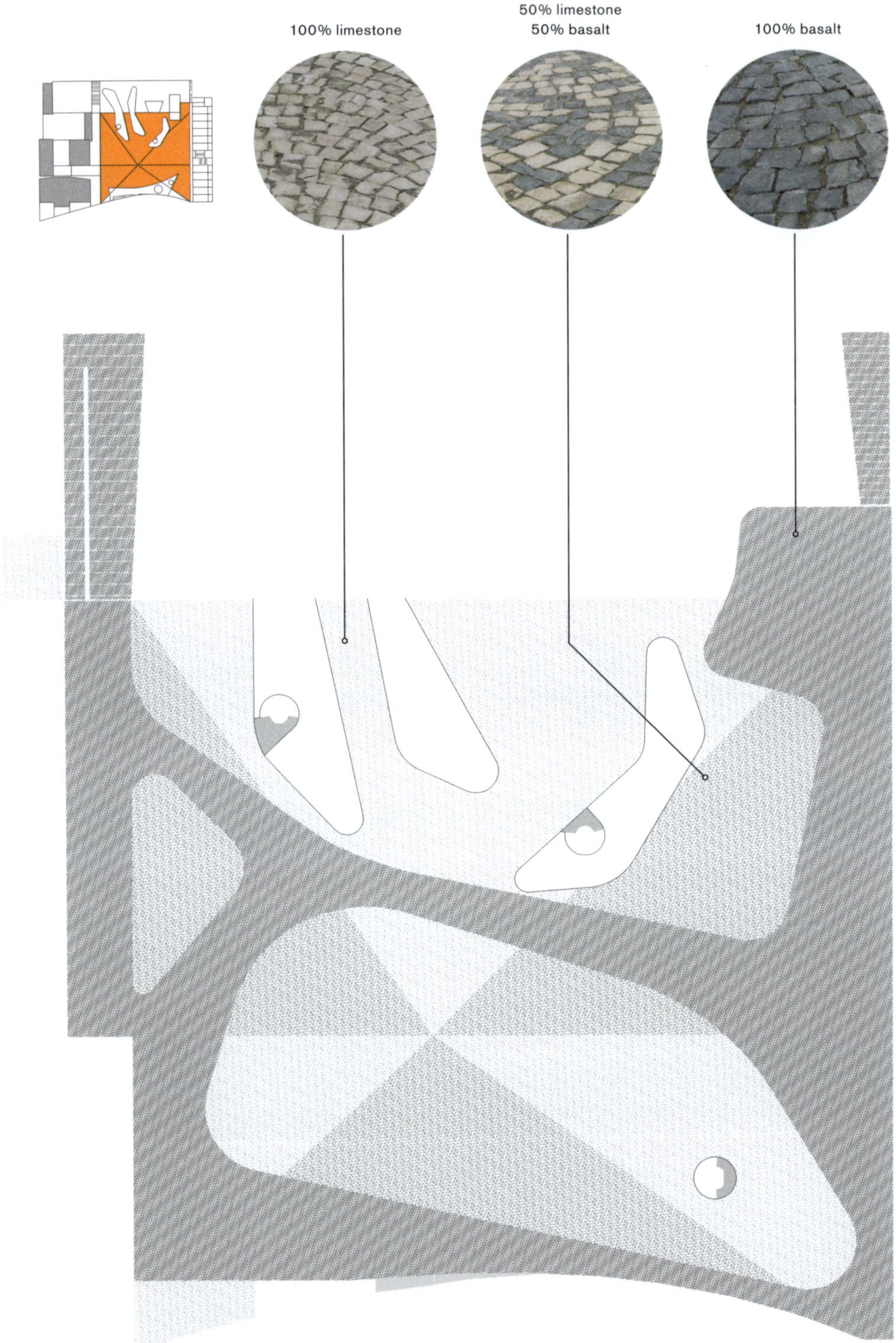
100% limestone
50% limestone
50% basalt
100% basalt

The *calçadinha*[1] comprises two types of paving sett, measuring 10 x 10 x 10 cm, in black or white. After various experiments, we discovered that the finished product was fabulous if we followed a basic pattern of growth: the *leca*, a semicircular wave that provides a geometric base for the arrangement. We also played with the colour of the stones: black, white, or a random combination of the two. These were the data with which we constructed the square.
The different planes that form the slopes to the centre are marked alternately with white stones or a mix. This produces a basic topography that is similar but not identical. On this rectilinear geometric background, we used black stones to draw out the more organic lines of habitual movement across the surface. At specific points, we introduced patterns inspired by nature (animals, wheels, etc.), of the type used by the sett-layers to enhance their work.

1 *Calçadinha*: paving used in public spaces in Portugal

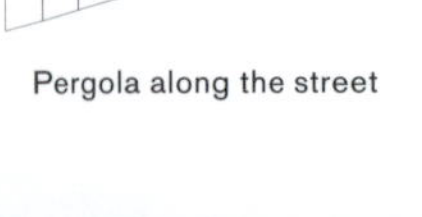

Pergola along the street

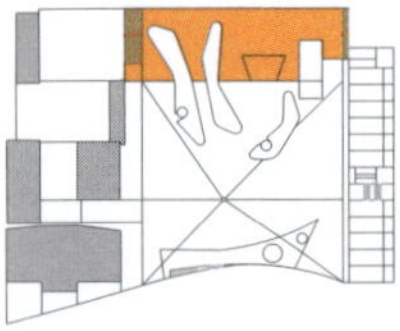

Green slope

CHAMPAGNE
Home Fashion

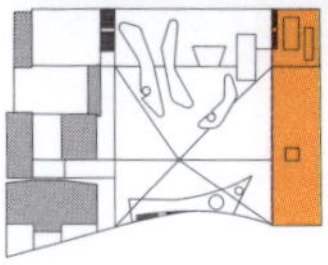

The boulevard above

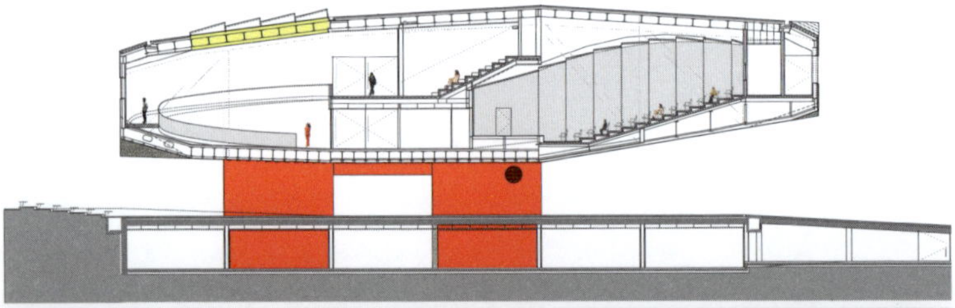

Arts centre

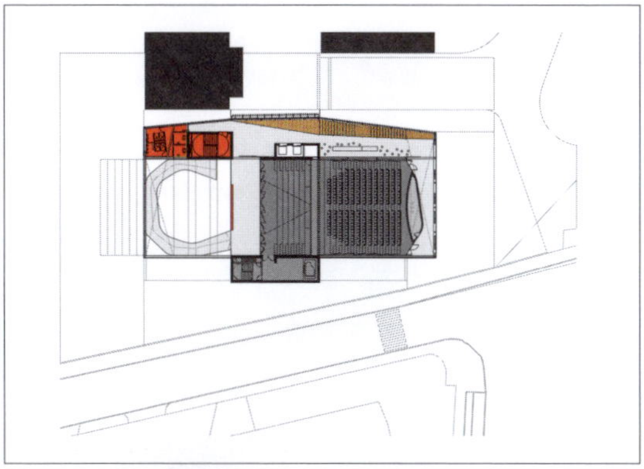

Second floor

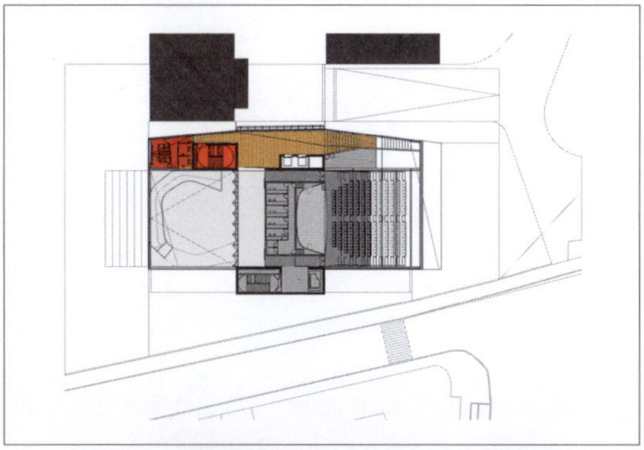

First floor

Ground floor

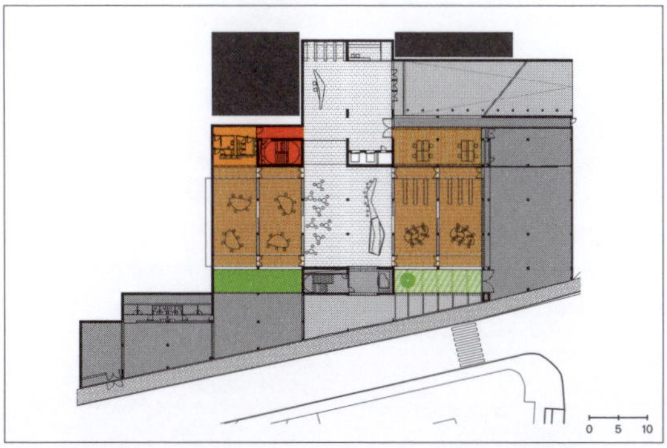

Basement

Interpretation of the arts centre project by the children of Castelo Branco's schools

IN-OUT (20/03/08–14/04/08) TIRANA: A PROPOSAL

Tirana, in its monumental historic centre, stores, formalizes and constructs part of the history of the 20th century: its harshest, most dramatic, utopian and inhuman, yet, at the same time, surrealistic and ideal aspects. Construction started in the early 20th century, in the brief reign of the self-proclaimed King Zog, and the Italian occupation introduced the great axis of *fascio*. Enver Hoxha (educated, like his colleague Pol Pot, in French culture) completed it with monuments, museums (socialist realism) and opera (with Russian architects). The axis comprises government ministries and city hall, with the university to the rear... All the symbolic representation of the new country, concentrated into a single point. Though sometimes less intensely, architecture has always operated on these terms: representing power, aspiring to an (im)possible eternity. In this respect, to see Tirana is to come face to face–brutally–with your origins, currently overlooked in business or comfortable adaptation. The presence today of all this material, seen from the outside by a foreigner with no personal history there, is memorable. This sensation is only heightened by the realization that this built delirium could very fast become one big McDonald's (I hope I am wrong; I wish them luck). The intervention in Tirana, as a cultural issue, called for a definition of the bases on which a radically transforming intervention should be effected. We propose to conserve the large scale of the space, its differential essence; to intervene on its limits (some interventions at the base of existing buildings seek to democratize them–that is, to relate them more directly with the ground, with the base) and launch a whole battery of small-scale interventions to promote a sensual, recreational use of the space that does not currently exist. We also employ irony as a criterion absent from the place (see for example the intervention around the monument to the mythical Skanderbeg, the national hero, or speaker's corner). Irony, recreation, openness and modernity were factors to be combined with the unyielding, military, grandiose, inhuman, abstract thinking that runs through 20th-century culture and is amply represented in this remote place. What we aimed to produce was a new synthesis. Like acting in the revolutions of the 1970s, when dissidents put flowers into the barrels of the army's guns.

REHABILITATION OF SKANDERBEG SQUARE

Third prize. Invited competition, 2008

Tirana/Albania. Location: Skanderbeg Square. Surface area: Built. 2,500 m^2, Urbanization 45,000 m^2

STADTPLAN von TIRANA

Ausgeführt von der
K.U.K. KRIEGSMAPPIERUNGSABTEILUNG № 7
unt. Leitung des Abt. Komdt. Hptm. v. MILIUS

SHKALLA 1 : 5000

April 1917

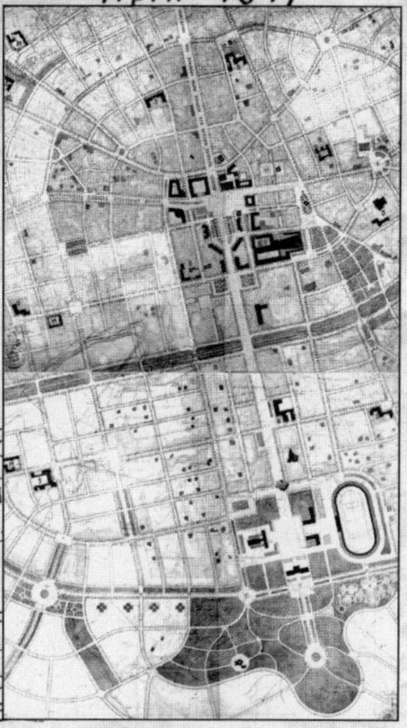

At the crossing of winding paths, the Italian occupation introduced the axis of *fascio*. Below, the stadium and the university directly formalize the fascist symbol.

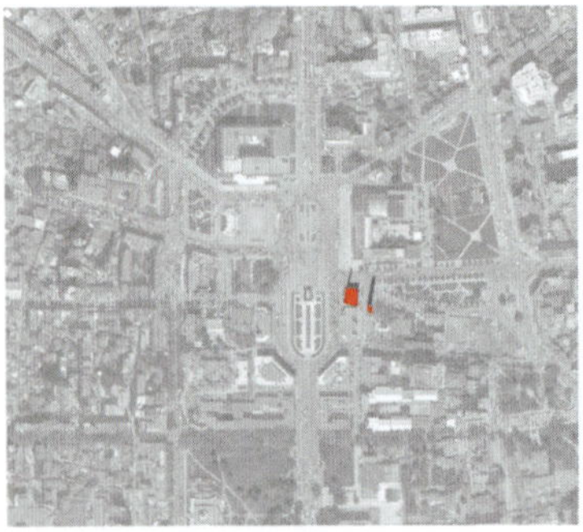

1. Et'hem Bey Mosque, 1789–1821
Clock tower, 1821–1822

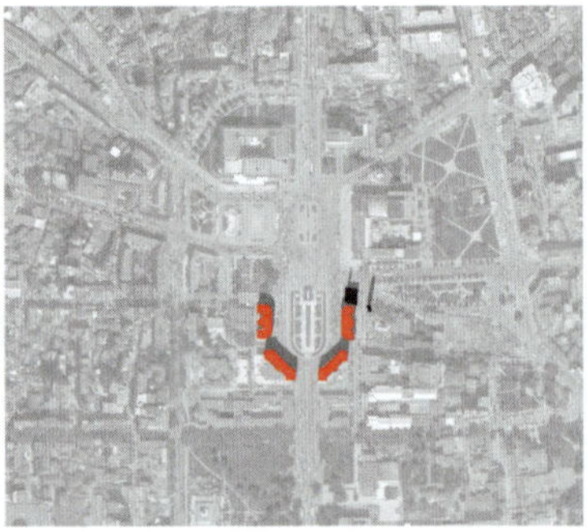

2. Palace of King Zog, 1930
Ministries

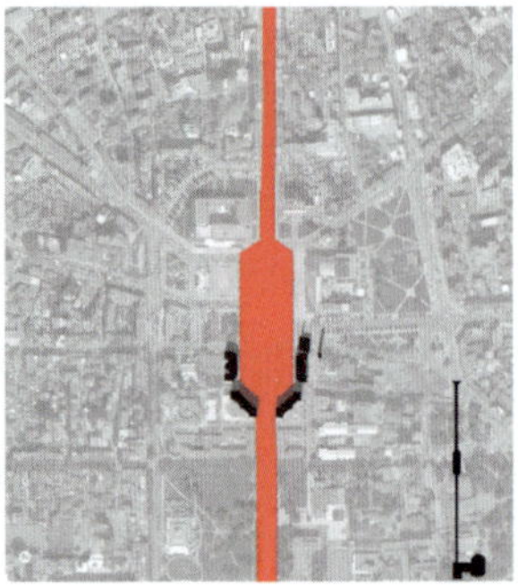

3. The axis of *fascio*, 1920s

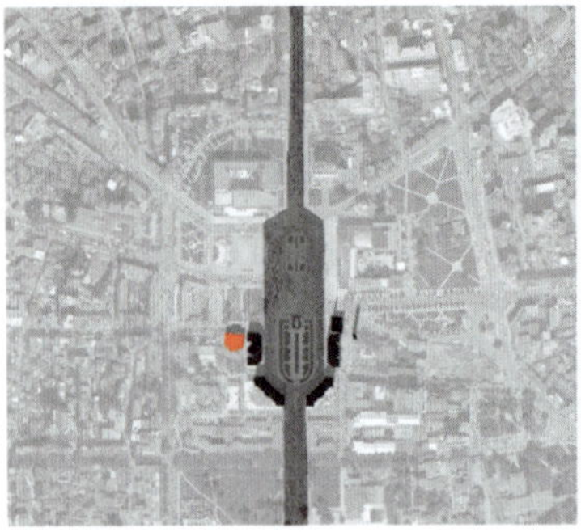

4. Former Parliament building.
Theatre

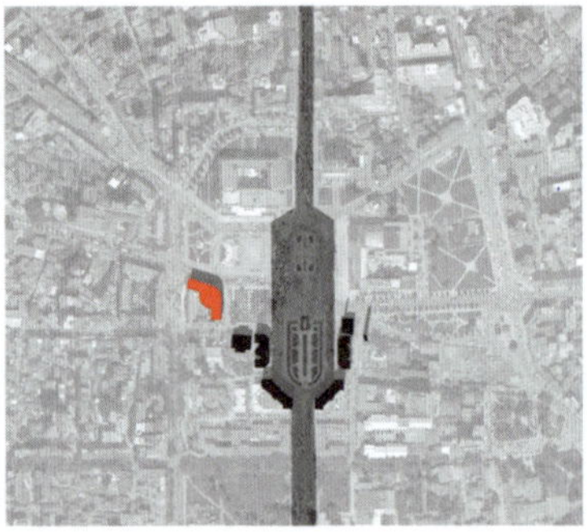

5. Bank of Italy, 1930s

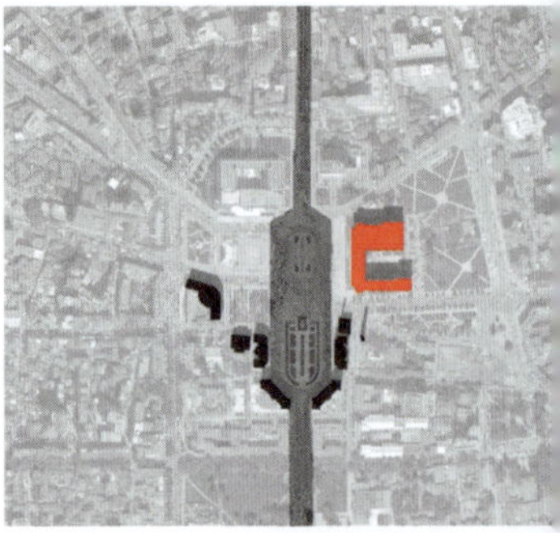

6. Palace of Culture, with the Opera and Balle
House and the National Library, 1963

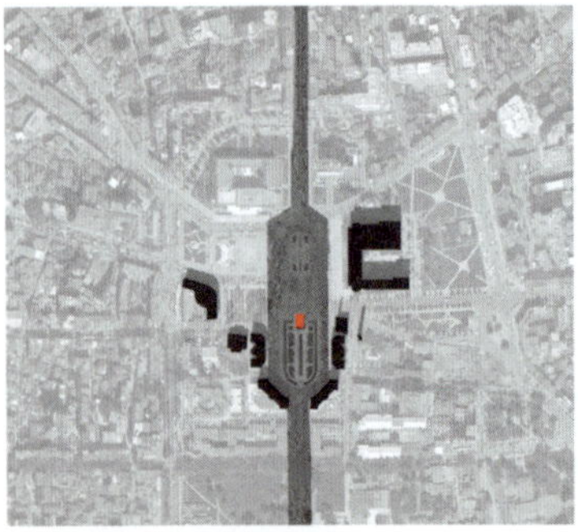

7. Skanderbeg Statue, 1968

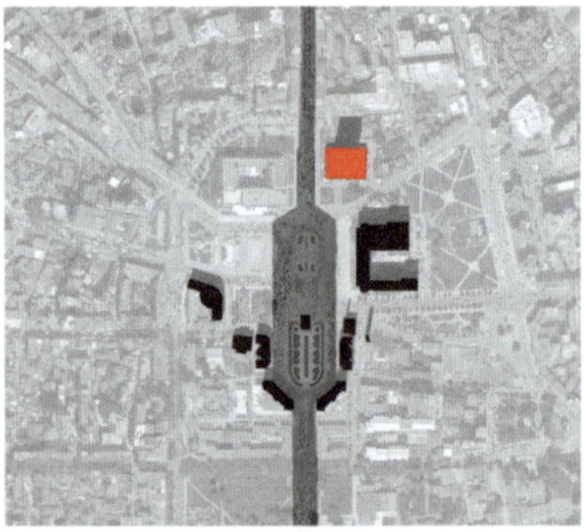

8. Hotel Tirana International, 1960s

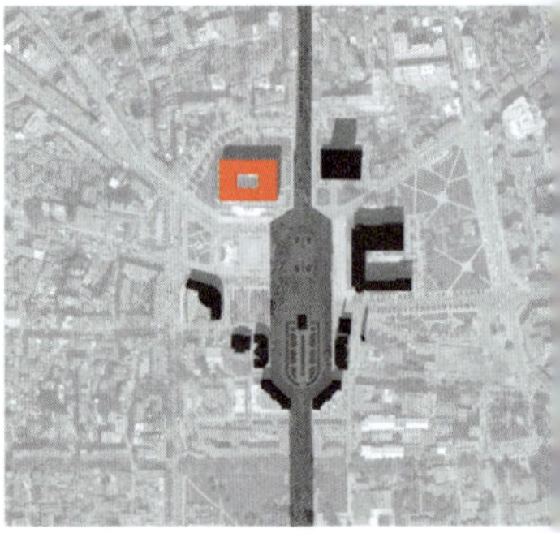

9. National Museum, 1981

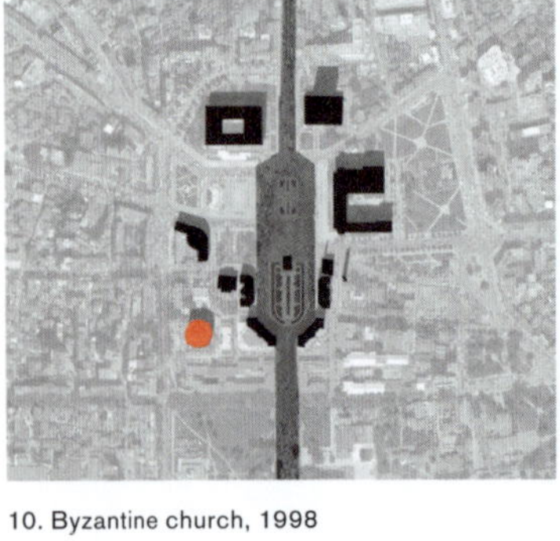

10. Byzantine church, 1998

11. Skanderbeg Square today

1

2

4

5

6

7

8

9

10

11

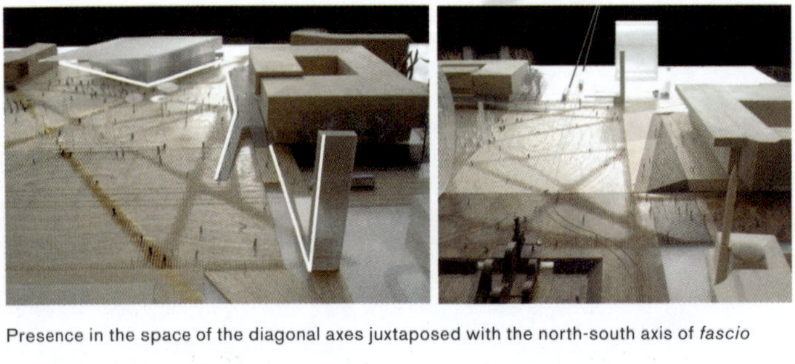

Presence in the space of the diagonal axes juxtaposed with the north-south axis of *fascio*

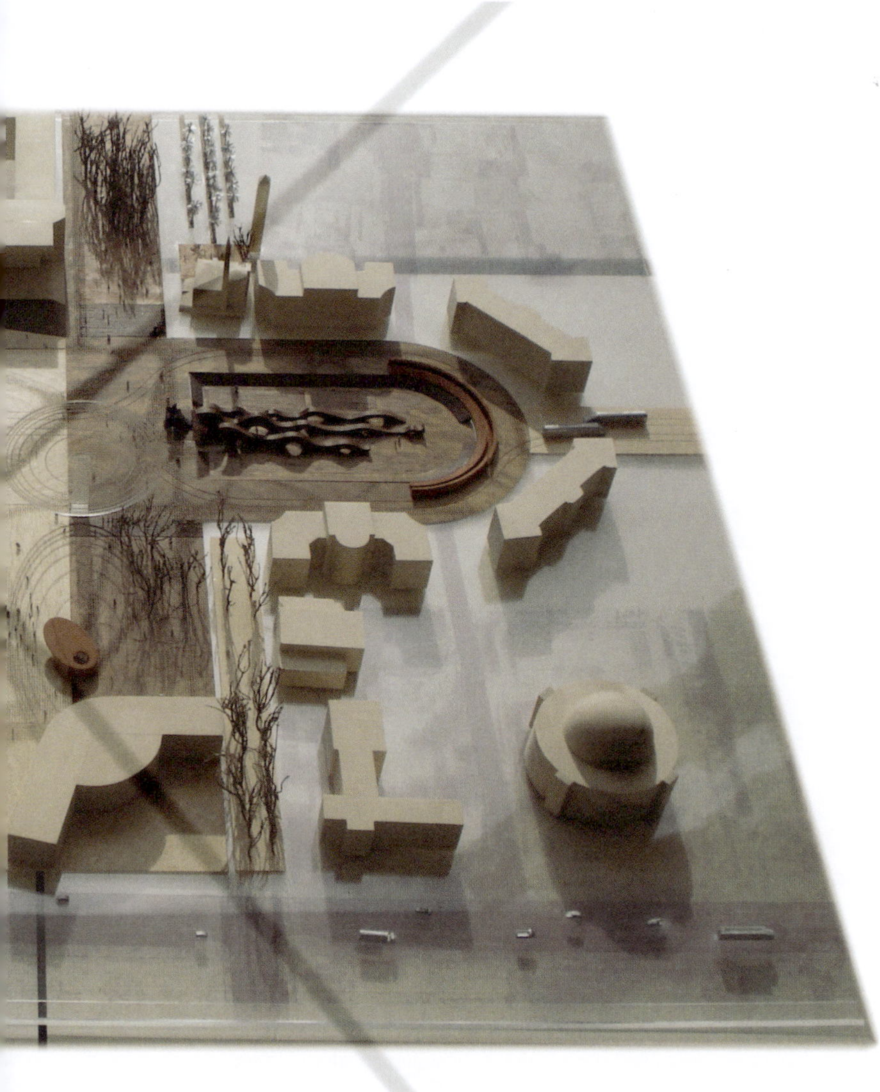

Construction on the limits. Before and after

1 Podium-entrance to the museum
2 Information tower
3 Slope with ramp (*propylaea*)
4 Green T

4

CAFE SHOPPING CENTER

Speaker's Corner as a pergola with bougainvillea

Redesign of the setting for Skanderbeg's Statue. Tall hedges continue the horse's tail.

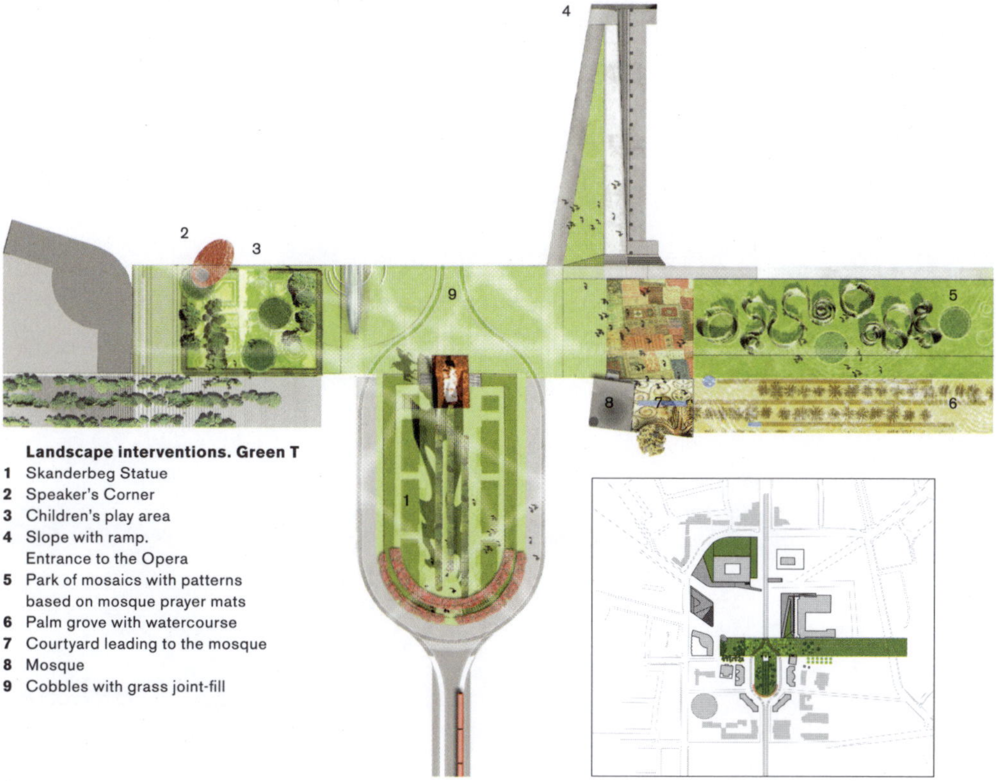

Landscape interventions. Green T

1 Skanderbeg Statue
2 Speaker's Corner
3 Children's play area
4 Slope with ramp. Entrance to the Opera
5 Park of mosaics with patterns based on mosque prayer mats
6 Palm grove with watercourse
7 Courtyard leading to the mosque
8 Mosque
9 Cobbles with grass joint-fill

IANO BAR

Activities

QUESTION TIME:

WHY DID YOU LOSE THE TIRANA COMPETITION?

It's always difficult to know. Apart from the possible, perhaps real phantasms and the underlying forces that are always present in these cases, from a design viewpoint I think that our project defended two issues that were not shared by the client.

One was a positive, affectionate appreciation of the empty space and the existing architecture. In the eyes of a foreigner, a chance visitor, past drama had left a physical mark that was memorable, singular and very special. This approach was perhaps overly romantic, though the alternative, very much present, is a vulgar "McDonaldization" of the city and its public space, now pathetically provincial and banal.

The other issue was the ironic, playful tone of our proposal, with the construction of perfumed, colourist gardens, a green tail for the horse in the monument to the mythical Skanderbeg (the country's founding father, probably non-existent), the paving around the mosque that forms stone carpets suggestive of prayer mats, etc. The idea was to introduce a familiar, sensual, slightly surrealist dimension into a space that had always been the abstract, grandiose, violent expression of power.

Presentation of the proposal to the competition jury, Tirana April 2008

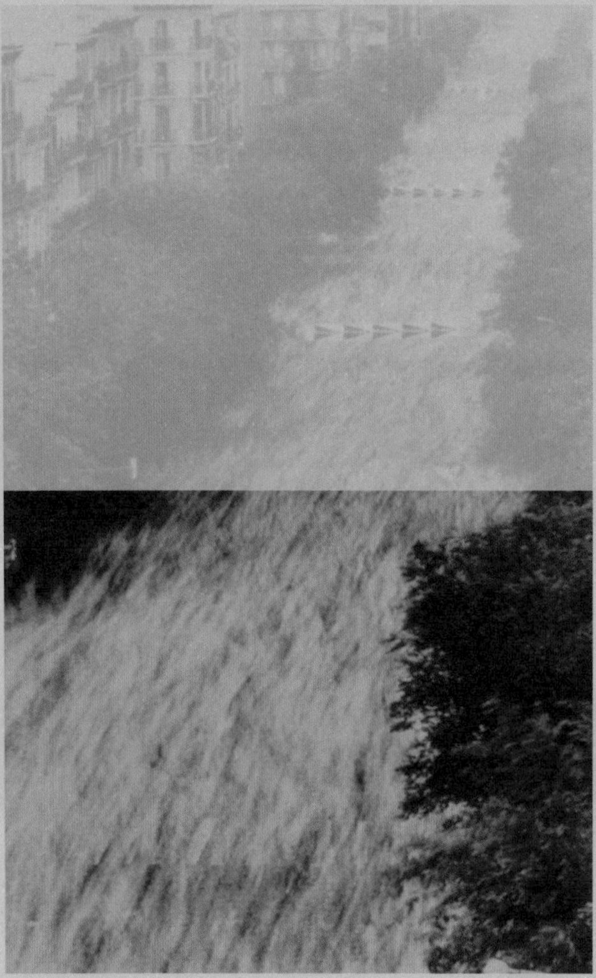

Urban space as a project means, though it may be more or less obvious, designing a *topography*. The naturalistic metaphor is not so far removed from the work of the constructor. Designing ridge roofs and eaves guttering, mountains, rivers and valleys.
People, the masses, are not just the users of the space but they also, if I may make so bold, can be seen as a construction material, as natural paving stones that give form to the space.
In his unforgettable *Crowds and Power*,[1] Elias Canetti designs urban space using words and concepts.
The flows, the movements that form patches and patterns, are often the true protagonists of the form. The constructor is left to apply all of his ambition to the task of disappearing.

Excerpts from the text "Notas sobre el espacio urbano" [Notes on urban space]. Transcription of an oral presentation at the "Skins and Eyes" Conference, April 2002, Institut Municipal del Paisatge Urbà i la Qualitat de Vida, Barcelona City Council.

1 Canetti, Elias: *Masse und Macht* (1960), Fischer Taschenbuch, Frankfurt, 1980; (English translation: *Crowds and Power*, Farrar, Straus and Giroux, 1984).

ON INVIS- IBIL- ITY

In our work for Banc Sabadell, we adopted a policy of invisibility. In old buildings worthy of conservation (for a variety of reasons), the project has to keep a low profile, sacrificing its own desire for protagonism. In all cases, our intervention is highly abstract, depersonalized, intelligent (I hope), but without the stamp of explicit authorship—one of various possible lines for future development.

Pre-existing situation

A. The flooring is a white sheet that touches the ground at either side (as a ramp or as a stairway) and floats over it at the centre.

REMODELLING OF THE MAIN ENTRANCE TO THE BANC SABADELL DIAGONAL TOWER

2006–2007

Barcelona. Location: Intersection of Avingude Diagonal/Carrer Balmes

B. The awning is effectively a large trough that collects rainwater and channels it down to the ground at either end.

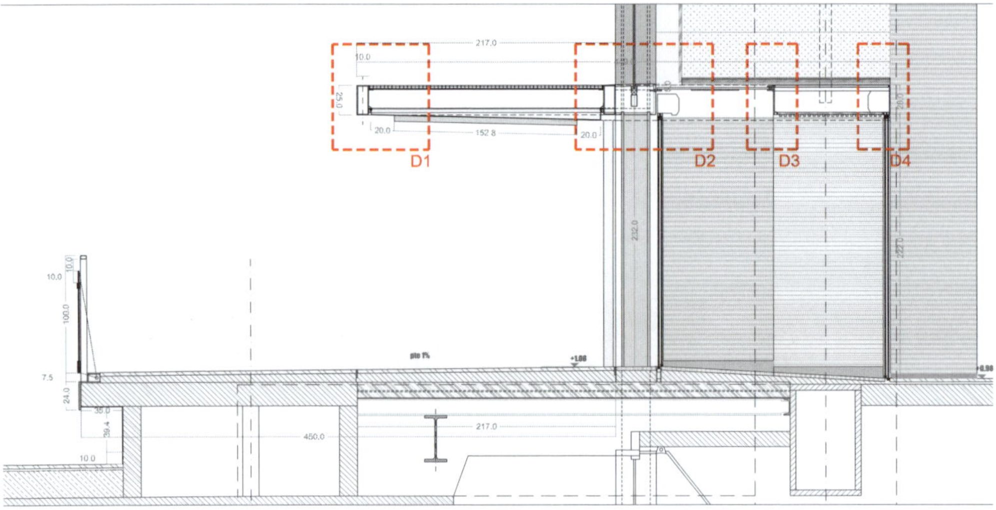

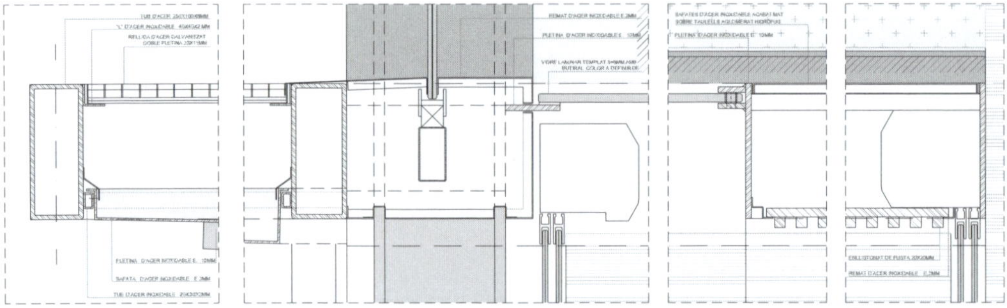

DETALL_1 DETALL_2 DETALL_3 DETALL_4

C. The finishes of the doorway (a series of mirrors, doormats and glazed surfaces) seek to break down the image of passage into independent photographic stills, highlighting the singularity of the movement: an interchange between exterior and interior.

Pre-existing situation

Banc Sabadell was originally a local bank set up in the town of the same name, close to Barcelona. It has recently received a major injection of new energy and now enjoys a broad-based presence at both national and international level. Our task was to modernize the bank's historic headquarters, the place of its birth. This raised various issues:

1. The relation between old and new. Since the building was, in its entirety, old, we had to address a complex mix of historicist conservation, functional and technical updates (with no noticeable physical presence), and new additions.
2. An interior calls for alarmingly precise detail; this was our aim.
3. It is a subtle project (it has to be). It is, however, radical in its reconsideration of space and physical characteristics: natural lighting, acoustics and transparency.

It is a project that has (that has to have) the intensity and subtlety of a Schubert sonata and does not (must not) have the grandeur and thunder of a Mahler symphony.

REMODELLING OF BANC SABADELL HEAD OFFICE

2004–2006

Sabadell/Barcelona. Location: Plaça Sant Roc. Surface area: 6,000 m²

A.D. 1881
BANC DE SABA
21

Entrance

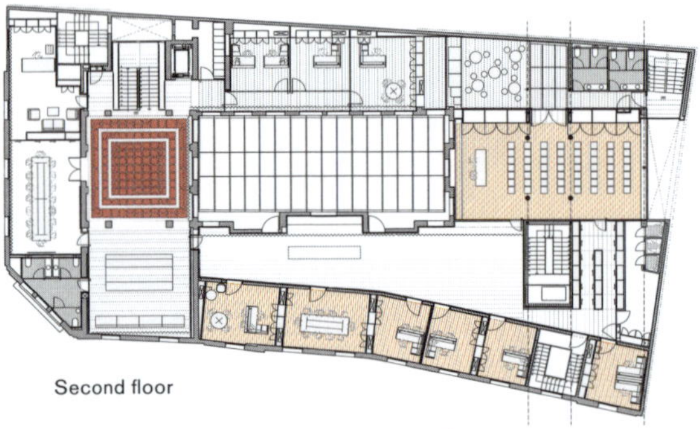

Second floor

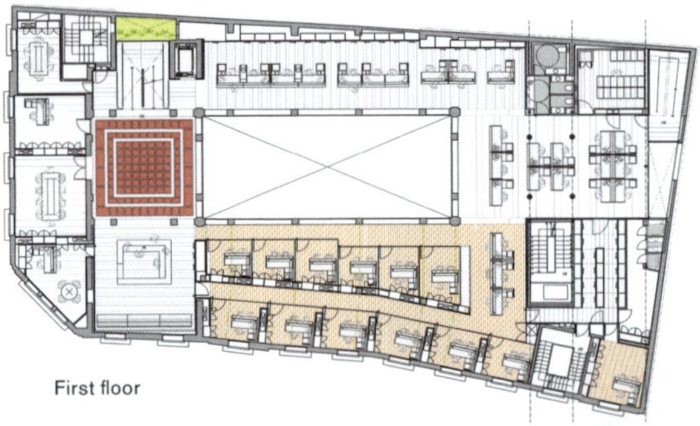

First floor

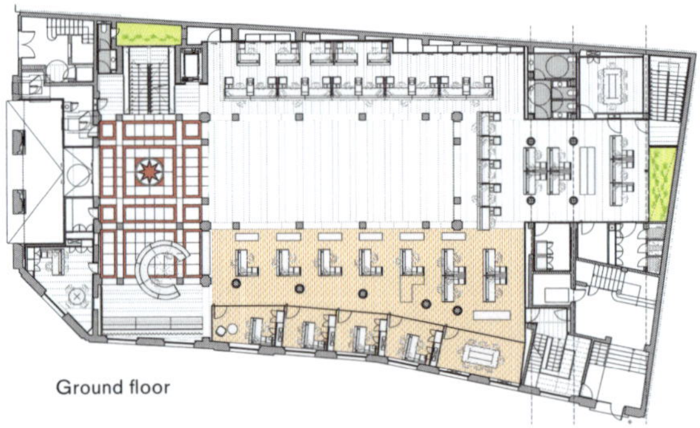

Ground floor

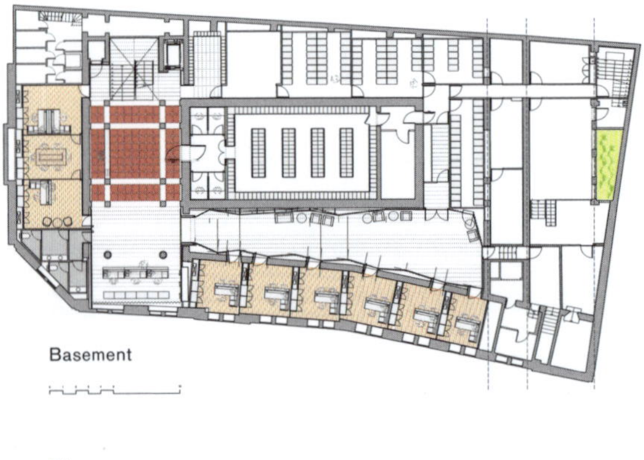

Basement

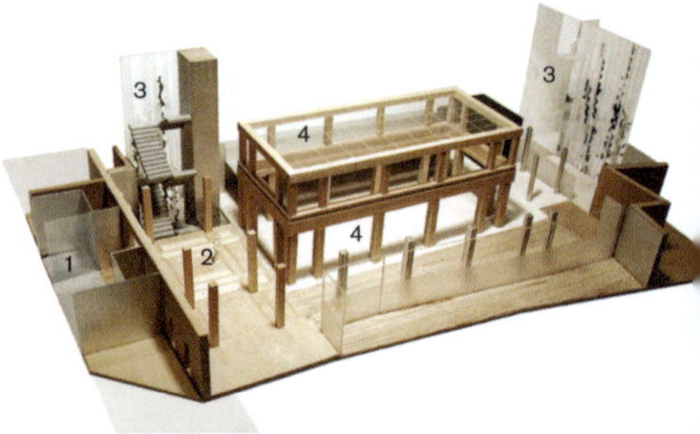

Strategy of intervention

1. Exterior: new entrance, façade rehabilitation
2. Archaeological conservation of the foyer on all floors
3. New vertical axes of light and movement
4. Transactions area: opening and lighting through the new skylight

Ceiling painted by Jordi Teixidor on the second floor, at the top of the new stairway

JORDI TEIXIDOR, Painter and artistic collaborator in the project to remodel the historic branch of Banc Sabadell

LESS PAINTING, MORE ARCHITECTURE

Whenever I am asked to take part in an architecture project, I enjoy doing so—in fact, I like architecture so much that sometimes I'm sorry I'm not an architect. The chance to make a balanced, proportional contribution to the overall project in my role as a painter is not only satisfying, it is a moral and intellectual motivation.

I try to ensure that my participation is in proportion, establishing a balanced relation between the way I see and feel the commission and the overall project, so that this fusing together does not detract from the architect's principal idea—less painting, more architecture.

In the case of the ceiling on the third floor of Banc Sabadell, my ideas quickly moved towards a basic geometrical composition.

What decided me was the repeated presence of the square that appeared in the formal structure of the building, in the layout of columns and the regular pattern of the floor. As the ceiling was rather low, I decided not to cover the entire surface, some 50 square metres, using broad strips of colour to frame it. Applied using a traditional method (oil paint on a canvas support), the colour was varied without being garish and blended in with the tones of the room's claddings and floor. Rather than competing with the colours used for furnishing and fittings, which were more forceful and definite in tone, the reference was the idea of colour as used in traditional interior decoration.

The aim was to give the right degree of emphasis to the room in keeping with its function as a space that leads to the boardroom and main office.

It was a question of respecting the overall idea of the work and its historical context by means of a proportionate pictorial intervention that visually recreates the modelling of the building's new architecture.

STAN ALLEN, Architect. Dean of the School of Architecture at Princeton University

THEORY AND PRACTICE

Meeting between Josep Lluís Mateo and Stan Allen on the occasion of "Recent work", a lecture given by Mateo at Princeton University School of Architecture, New Jersey (USA), on 15 February 2008.

Mateo: I would like to talk about the relation between theory and practice.[1] You have defended the viewpoint that recently, as opposed to other historical moments, Europe has been producing the practice of architecture while America has been generating the criteria of value and conceptual frameworks for understanding and appreciating it. This is an inversion of the classic paradigm in which Europe produced the ideas and North America built them and projected them onto the world. Could you explain this standpoint in greater detail?
What is the basis of the idea that, until now, architectural practice had its roots in Europe, whereas the theory really came from here, from America? Could we say that America provided the theory and Europe put it into practice?
Allen: As I see it, that was certainly the model in the nineties, a period when younger American architects had very little work and the architectural practice scene in Europe seemed much healthier, at least in Spain, the Netherlands or Switzerland, which were the countries we took as a reference. At that time, American schools were consolidating the change that began in the eighties in the teaching of theory of architecture.
In other words, in the eighties the field of architecture theory expanded and, specifically in the US, many people in other disciplines, such as Sanford Kwinter, Catherine Ingraham and Jeffrey Kipnis, got involved in the world of architecture. As a result, references, texts and sources became considerably more diverse, for example with Kwinter and theories of biology and of complexity, or with Catherine Ingraham and literary theory. Of course, this was the time of deconstruction, cultural studies and the rise of critical theory.
It led to a positive opening up of the theoretical discourse of architecture, with a proliferation of very interesting and productive work. This period was marked by journals like *Assemblage*, which were closely associated with these figures. In general, some positive new approaches were brought in by other disciplines, though something of the specificity of the architectural discourse was lost…
Mateo: What is the relation between the production of works and the thought on which they are based? The eternal debate about theory and practice...
Allen: It depends on the institutional structure, particularly here in the US, and more specifically on the appearance of the figure of the professional academic architect. It has to be said that, in Princeton, the first generation of historians, theorists and critics—Tony Vidler, Alan Colquhoun, Robert Maxwell, Kenneth Frampton—had a training in architecture and started out as architects before migrating to the fields of history and theory, though none of them were actually doctors in the field.
These days, there seems to be a kind of person whose career and life develop exclusively in academia. Although in many cases these people also trained as architects, they don't have such a close connection, in my opinion, with

the profession. This leads to the disappearance of the idea that reflection on the profession also forms part of the practice of an architect, and that this activity should not necessarily be given up to professional theorists or academics.

Mateo: I come from the archaic Spanish tradition in which the active architect was also a critic, so that division did not exist here. Today, the widespread trend at universities seems to be an increase in the presence of professional academics.

Allen: There is some cause for optimism, or should I say cautious optimism. On the one hand, we have to acknowledge that both the academic and the professional worlds have become much more demanding in the last 20 or 30 years. At this school, for example, the first title of Doctor was awarded to Charles Moore in 1959, with a doctoral thesis that would seem more like a master's degree thesis today.

At our level, then, the quality of work and the degree of sophistication of research are now much greater. This is both a reason for optimism and the price of specialization. At the same time, the demands of today's professional practice and the complexity of globalization and technology are far greater than they were 30 years ago. All this technology that is supposed to make life easier has actually only made things much more complicated.

If we analyse this phenomenon in full, it is important to point out that since the late 1990s—we are now almost a decade into the 21st century—a new generation has emerged. Ironically, the architects who studied at Columbia University in the early nineties did so in an environment that was saturated by theoretical discourse, and these architects now devote their time almost exclusively to practice.

So young architects, such as SHoP, Lindy Roy or Winka Dubbeldam, etc., the generation of 40-something New York architects, used their background of theory to create a different kind of practice. Evidently, they all make intensive use of digital technologies in their professional practice, but beyond that, they look at things in new ways and have even restructured certain client relations. They are much more entrepreneurial and more involved in the market. This might be seen as a simple return to practice, but they have actually incorporated some of the discoveries and analyses of theory-based work into a new operative model.

Another very important area is the contribution of thought to the field of contemporary urbanism, a type of research for which architects are particularly well qualified. As architects, we can produce maps and diagrams, we understand spatial and temporal phenomena and we have sophisticated means of graphic creativity at our disposal. This is a kind of production in which the architect is especially efficient.

To continue this argument, the kind of aptitudes and skills architects need to carry out the kind of projects assigned to them is strategic intelligence. Architecture is of course related to design, but also to funding, to local communities and to being highly creative with the programme…

If the commissioning bodies do not present architects with a specific programme, the architects must have the necessary experience to reflect and produce their own ideas on the programme, and about how to implement it. This is a necessary part of their knowledge and competencies. And, to be cautiously optimistic, this is precisely the kind of task that allows architects to prosper in their careers, and to make use of critical thinking in new ways: they have to embrace it and offer a variety of intelligences and knowledge.

Mateo: I tend to think that, recently, theory has disappeared and become pure propaganda.

During the flight, I was reading Walter Benjamin's famous text in which he speaks of the "aura" of the artwork.[2] His idea of the "aura" was so romantic, distant and from another era.

We, conversely, receive a series of images that are repeated over and over, making it difficult to believe in an inherent discourse or any motivation beyond doing business.

Allen: Maybe pragmatism is not the right word—it is too easy to think of pragmatism as a simple accession to the market, or to the needs of the client, but I always insist that a true philosophical pragmatism has nothing to do with the rejection of theory. It operates instead in the territory suggested by William James when he says that "pragmatism unstiffens all our theories, limbers them up and sets each one at work".

1 ALLEN, Stan: *Practice: Architecture, Technique and Representation*. New Edition. Routledge, London, 2009.
2 BENJAMIN, Walter: *The Work of Art in the Age of Mechanical Reproduction (Das Kunstwerk im Zeitalter seiner technischen Reproduzierbarkeit: Drei Studien zur Kunstsoziologie)*. Frankfurt: Ed. Suhrkamp Verlag, 1981, p. 107. ISBN: 3518100289

ICONOCLASTIA

In the past, buildings and other constructions representing singular moments for the community were called monuments. Their origin was expression of power, celebration of ritual or collective affirmation. They were normally solid (permanence was their rather unlikely objective). They were few, in a proportion of perhaps one to 100 (100 being a more or less homogeneous continuous mass of dwellings and services, and one being the new and special object). Despite their limited number, or perhaps because of it, they drew together the world around them; they **established relations** with their surroundings (or forced others to). Definitely terrestrial, a monument was like a rock, like a mountain that rose up to dominate the plain.

The monument had an interior: the purpose of its thick walls was to protect what was seen as a sacred space. Within those walls, the boundaries of space were tattooed and made up; it was no longer the representation of construction that was offered, as on the outside: the walls were transformed into gold and wood into pictorial representation, and light and, perhaps more importantly, dark, marked what was to be seen and what, despite existing, went unseen.

In the contemporary world, a project that aspires to be exceptionally expressive (almost all) is commonly called an Icon. An icon, etymologically, was the representation of divinity by means of painting. The presence of Byzantine icons is well known; with their highly coded style, they were venerated as the presence on earth of God and the saints.

The presence of icons in contemporary architecture is defined by a series of characteristics that I would like to examine here.
One is multiplicity: in the contemporary city, everything is potentially iconic—that is, expressively autonomous, disconnected. Walter Benjamin[1] wrote that the classical definition of the "aura"[2] of the work of art was the **"unique phenomenon of a distance"**, whereas the contemporary world changed the conditions of this **"phenomenon"**. Rather than **"distance"**, mass culture called for closeness; for repetition rather than **"uniqueness"**. In our case, iconicity may be seen to parallel repetition, copy and non-originality, and it is rarely related to "closeness". Indeed, iconic buildings are ill equipped to stand up to contact and close phenomenological analysis.
Icons do not guide, they do not create hierarchies; they declare their presence, but though they may impose it at a given moment, that moment is fleeting. Sooner rather than later, new icons will appear and erase the first (or at least try). The creator of Icons, in his energetic, unceasing travels around the galaxy, does not tend to return to what in the past was a desert, the base on which the Icon was built, now inhabited by new barbarian colleagues who perhaps reduce the effect imagined by its creator (or do they reinforce it?).
The place for the Icon is a flat base and a background. The desert is a suitable base, but water is still more highly prized: it reflects and reproduces the form. Since an Icon is, almost exclusively, form, this multiplying effect intensifies its essence.
The place is also sky: blue, with clouds. It may incorporate—in its renders, as a sensitive adaptation to the place—a particular luminosity: more intense in Dubai, colder in Moscow.
The Icon has no thickness, it is pure skin. It knows itself to be pure appearance and does not blend in. The skin must be **spectacular**

in the sense of offering spectacle; night lighting is fundamental. Local motifs are always welcome: Gaudí in Barcelona, touches of feng shui in China, references to vernacular architecture (if there is any), etc.
The Icon has no spaces, it has no interior. If an interior exists, it is of no interest.
Further, the Icon frequently serves no purpose: the museum has no collection or the auditorium has no orchestra. In this case, it is logical that acoustics simply should not exist.

The tradition of the Icon includes its antagonist; the Iconoclastic movement, which destroyed all representations of divinity, arguing that they destroyed its essence.

A rare relic of Byzantine Iconoclasm: a mosaic cross above the main narthex of Hagia Eirene in Istanbul, in the position usually occupied by the *Theotokos* (Virgin with Child) icon (c. 740)

1 BENJAMIN, Walter: *The Work of Art in the Age of Mechanical Reproduction.(Das Kunstwerk im Zeitalter seiner technischen Reproduzierbarkeit: Drei Studien zur Kunstsoziologie)*. Frankfurt: Ed. Suhrkamp Verlag, 1981, p. 107. ISBN: 3518100289

2 The aura, in Byzantine iconography, is the circular halo around the head of a person represented, denoting their divine condition. The aura is used here to mark the special quality that separates everyday objects from those that are given particular artistic transcendence.

Introductory text to the symposium of the same name organized by Josep Lluís Mateo's department at ETH-Z and published in "Iconoclastia. News from a post-iconic world. Architectural Papers IV" (MATEO, Josep Lluís *et al.*). Published by ETH Zurich-Actar. ISBN: 978-84-96954-47-2

VICENTE GUALLART, Architect and author of the Sociopolis Master Plan for the construction of a new model of affordable housing district in Valencia

BARCELONA–VALENCIA

Text of the meeting between JLLM and Vicente Guallart on the occasion of Josep Lluís Mateo's lecture at the IAAC_Institut d'Arquitectura Avançada de Catalunya, on 12 June 2008, on local projects in the framework of "glocal" culture.

Josep Lluís Mateo: What do you think of Barcelona as a brand?
Vicente Guallart: Someone recently said that it's overrated. I would add that an illusion was created to convince millions of people all over the world that Barcelona is a good place to come, though no one is quite sure what for. It is actually a good brand, associated with an idea of urbanness and the good life, but it is certainly not a place to do business, or even to create. There is too much control. In reality, Barcelona is a place that has the potential to reinvent itself, to be a creative referent for all things new.
Josep Lluís Mateo: Why did you come here? Or rather, why are you here? Why didn't you leave?
Vicente Guallart: I'm here in Barcelona because, for me, it's like being a foreigner in a place I know well.

Vicente Guallart and Josep Lluís Mateo
visiting the vegetable plots of Sociopolis, 2005

Josep Lluís Mateo: You could be in many different places, though. You have an infinite number less one to choose from.
Vicente Guallart: That's true; in fact, it's the closest thing to the place where I was born, which is some distance away, sufficiently far for me not to be there, and at the same time it's a place where, hypothetically, it is possible to do many things you can't do in other places. I like the fact that it is a crossroads of cultures, though now it is becoming something of a theme park.
Josep Lluís Mateo: Future.
Vicente Guallart: The future is that I'm buying a wood with a piece of Barcelona ... The future is a wood.

Josep Lluís Mateo: The future is a wood. OK, to close: Valencia.
Vicente Guallart: Valencia is a fantastic place with very strange collective behaviour.
Josep Lluís Mateo: Strange in what way?
Vicente Guallart: Highly irrational, but at the same time it apparently has a degree of ingenuity that allows it to invent incredible things. The thing is, this very ingenuity could destroy it, so in fact it sustains an instable equilibrium which, at the moment, I find more interesting, in one way, than Barcelona. Though of course Barcelona always has a greater capacity for reinventing itself, and doing something bigger, which is why I'm here.
Josep Lluís Mateo: Sociopolis. Why didn't you keep the market gardens and orchards going?
Vicente Guallart: Because it was literally impossible. I'm the person to have conserved the largest tract of farmland on urban land in the history of Spanish urban planning.
Sociopolis is basically an idea; as Paco Jarauta would say, it is a micro-utopia. It is a utopia made reality: the idea of building a neighbourhood where everything—the buildings, the urban design, public space, housing—is designed simultaneously, and all this in a relatively collective way, the idea of being able to invent a new way of building the city, basically by being ingenuous, by questioning, by asserting basic issues that do not seek to imitate what is going on around it. And I discovered this by reading someone, Ramon Margalef. Ramon Margalef said that what makes an organism complex is the ability to incorporate part of its history rather than destroying it. For example, a human being is a human being rather than a bacterium because it has undergone mutations and incorporated part of these mutations into its next phase. I see Sociopolis as a clear example of mutation undergone by a place that retains a high percentage of its history within and therefore leaves history open, allowing it to continue its transformation in the future.
Josep Lluís Mateo: What do you think of the architecture?
Vicente Guallart: In Sociopolis? Really, it was the product of ingenuity; I actually thought that the architecture, the architects, would be more interactive. Ultimately, the autism that characterizes the contemporary world will manifest itself there, so there will be some buildings that are better than others. Let's say that its merit lies in preparing the build-up to allow each architect to score his goal in the way that he chooses.
Josep Lluís Mateo: What do you think of our project?
Vicente Guallart: I think that your project is one of the good ones in Sociopolis. I'd say that it stretches to the limits a constructive or structural affirmation in relation to the way that social housing is built. In any case, what is important is that social housing be built, and if that is possible within the bounds of economic rationality, I think it will be one of the most outstanding buildings in the neighbourhood.

1 GENERAL In La Huerta, surrounded by fields and the remains of the agrarian culture that deserves our protection, the city advances, co-existing with an earlier world. The Sociopolis urban development plan (architect: Vicente Guallart) will be built with an open layout at the boundary between the city and the countryside, thereby continuing both.

2 ENGAGEMENT The car park bores into the ground and anchors the building. We have sought to rationalize and reduce it, and turn its top into another green space (though of course artificial) that will serve as a support, as a horizontal base for the building. In our case, the platform, the meeting point with the land, is a manifestly horizontal topography that creates a new field joining those already in existence.

3 VOLUME: DISSOLUTION OF THE MASS The rectilinear volume of the tower, in accordance with the orientation and the distributional logic of the apartments, is modified at three points. At the point of contact with the ground, part of its mass has been removed to increase the new green space. The top part has been treated in a similar manner in order to create a transition to the sky. This open courtyard is seen as a support for environmentally-friendly features (a rainwater cistern and solar panels). The mass has also been cut out at an intermediate level in order to create a garden/hothouse inside the volume.

4 CONSTRUCTION/STRUCTURE The tower comprises a system of self-supporting concrete walls that make up the façade, plus a central wall that also divides the apartments. The structure and outer walls are one and the same.
This makes it possible to operate on these walls as though they were beams with large ends that naturally form the substantial cantilevers required to remove material from the parallelepiped volume described above. The distribution of openings and solid spaces follows the logic of load distribution, giving the far from arbitrary façades a dynamic composition.
The form and final texture (concrete is relatively unsophisticated in appearance) produce an unrefined building in keeping with its peripheral position at the border between the city and the countryside, a place full of objects that are perhaps the remains of another era or unfinished promises of new possibilities. It is intriguing to imagine the building with this open and relatively matt, unfinished character.

HOUSING BLOCK IN VALENCIA

2005–

Location: Plot R01, La Torre sector, Valencia. Surface area: 12,000 m²

TERCIARIO
ZONAS COMUNES
Ground floor
1
2
3
4
5
6
7
8
9
10
11
12
13
14
15
16
17
18
19
20

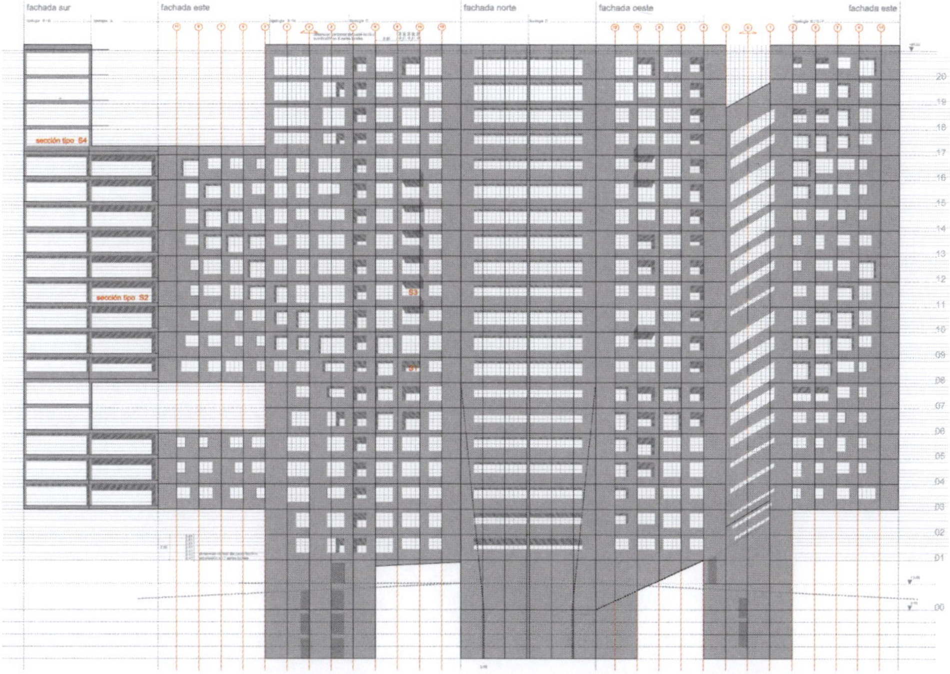
fachada sur
fachada este
fachada norte
fachada oeste
fachada este
sección tipo S4
sección tipo S2
20
19
18
17
16
15
14
13
12
11
10
09
08
07
06
05
04
03
02
01
00

A.M.R. +64.0m
20
19
18
17
16
15
14
13
12
11
10
09
08
07
06
05
04
03
02
01
PB
+6.0m
+3.0m
+0.0m

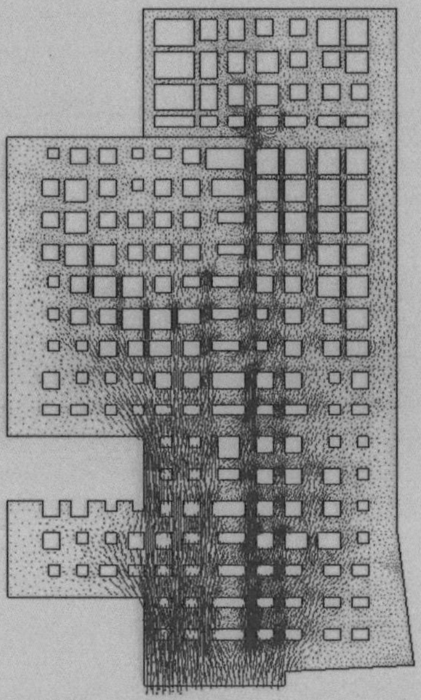

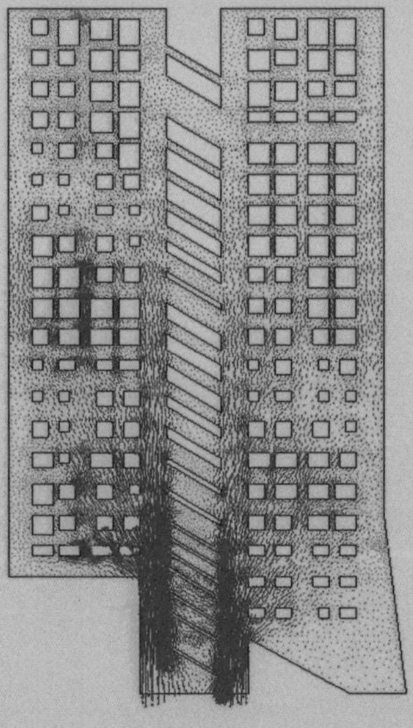

INITIAL OCCASIONS

Suspended
Ephemeral
A passionate activity compounded of great energy, great loss and the need to survive once the intense initial fire has burnt out.
But something remains, of the essence, when you are still interested in the project as an open issue, not just as a political tool to secure a commission. Then, sometimes, you uncover something there that you did not know before.

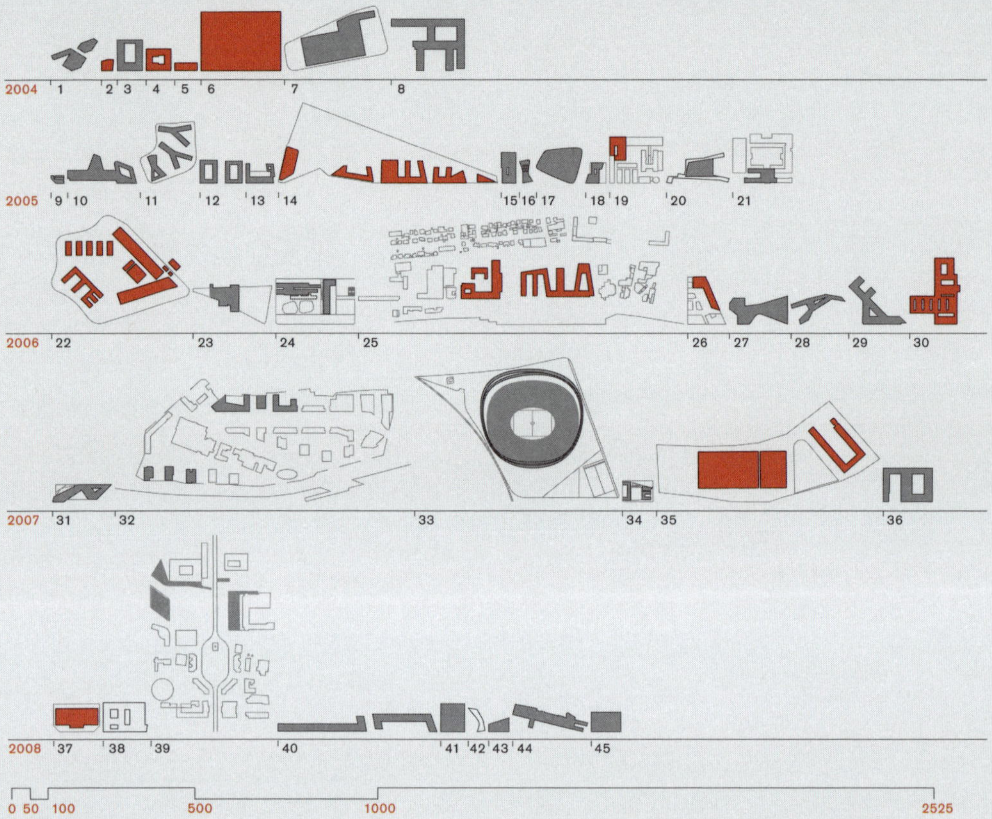

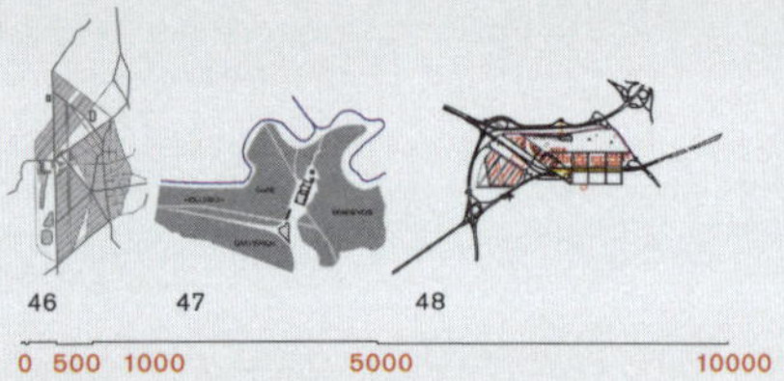

2004

1 Offices. Zurich, Switzerland. Surface area: 63,077 m²
2 Museum. Prague, Czech Republic. Surface area: 2,000 m²
3 Offices. Prague, Czech Republic. Surface area: 21,839 m²
4 Offices. Barcelona, Spain. Surface area: 15,000 m²
5 Film theatre. Barcelona, Spain. Surface area: 7,000 m²
6 Railway station. Barcelona, Spain. Surface area: 112,000 m²
7 Congress centre. Lugano, Switzerland. Surface area: 137,080 m²
8 Hotel. Shanghai-Pudong, China. Surface area: 55,478 m²

2005

9 Dwellings. Barcelona, Spain. Surface area: 8,527 m²
10 Offices–Dwellings. Tirana, Albania. Surface area: 17,790 m²
11 Dwellings. Grünwald, Switzerland
12 Offices–Dwellings. Boulogne-Billancourt, Paris. Surface area: 30,000 m²
13 Dwellings. Barcelona, Spain. Surface area: 17,734 m²
14 Development–Dwellings. Paris, France. Surface area: 19,353 m²
15 Museum. Warsaw, Poland. Surface area: 17,790 m²
16 Library. Barberà del Vallès, Barcelona, Spain. Surface area: 2,774 m²
17 Congress centre. Saragossa, Spain. Surface area: 17,819 m²
18 Offices. Tortosa, Tarragona, Spain. Surface area: 12,276 m²
19 University centre. Barcelona, Spain. Surface area: 20,000 m²
20 Town Square. Valls, Tarragona, Spain. Surface area: 3,000 m²
21 University centre. Barcelona, Spain. Surface area: 15,000 m²

2006

22 Prison. Sant Llorenç d'Hortons, Barcelona, Spain. Surface area: 40,000 m²
23 Multipurpose building. Amersfoort, Holland. Surface area: 73,755 m²
24 Development. Marseille, France. Surface area: 62,000 m²
25 Development. Bayonne, France. Surface area: 70,000 m²
26 Offices. Boulogne-Billancourt, Paris. Surface area: 15,500 m²
27 Multipurpose building. Novosibirsk, Russia. Surface area: 92,450 m²
28 University centre. Tortosa, Tarragona, Spain. Surface area: 9,880 m²
29 Offices. Sant Cugat, Barcelona, Spain. Surface area: 51,555 m²
30 Hospital. Girona, Spain. Surface area: 117,000 m²

2007

31 Hospital. Bilbao, Spain. Surface area: 31,950 m²
32 Redevelopment. Moscow, Russia. Surface area: 33,435 m²
33 Football stadium. Barcelona, Spain. Surface area: 130,000 m²
34 Museum. Mechelen, Belgium. Surface area: 20,695 m²
35 Congress centre and hotel. Oran, Algeria. Surface area: 73,863 m²
36 University centre. Barcelona, Spain

2008

37 Market. Barcelona, Spain. Surface area: 15,000 m²
38 Offices–Dwellings. Kiev, Russia. Surface area: 97,455 m²
39 Square. Tirana, Albania. Surface area: 47,500 m²
40 Offices. Igualada, Barcelona, Spain. Surface area: 69,514 m²
41 Museum. Zurich, Switzerland. Surface area: 15,000 m²
42 Dwelling. Canberra, Australia
43 Offices. Barcelona, Spain. Surface area: 14,125 m²
44 Museum. Meaux, France. Surface area: 7,212 m²
45 Offices. Zurich, Switzerland. Surface area: 15,000 m²

URBANISM

46 2005. City planning. Geneva, Switzerland. Surface area: 537,728 m²
47 2005. City planning. Luxembourg, Luxembourg. Surface area: 509,000 m²
48 2008. Town planning. El Prat de Llobregat, Barcelona, Spain. Surface area: 150 ha

MARTA POCH, Architect and editor. A regular collaborator with Josep Lluís Mateo.

48 MONTHS/48 COMPETITIONS 2004–2008

"Almost all my work is the product of competitions" [1]

As Josep Lluís Mateo says, much of his built work is the result of taking part in international competitions, both public and invited. This dynamic is clearly reflected in the last four years, in which much of the practice has been up against the deadline that is a competition. After completing its major works of 2004—the CCIB (Barcelona International Convention Centre) and the head office for Bundesbank in Chemnitz, Germany—the practice went back from constructor to designer. Since then, it has continued to formalize ideas, concepts, places... that have been reflected in a wide variety of architecture projects, from public space to housing units, from the large scale to the domestic.

Competitions have the intrinsic particularity of never quite knowing where you are treading; you often sense where you are and the possibilities at your disposal, but never with a clear, objective sense of reality. **"[...] I observe the problem, examine it and gather information. [...] This process of observation and accumulation of material frequently drives my collaborators to despair as they see time passing with no progress on the part of the project. I see it from the outside, with indifference. It is an introspective beginning that gives way to frenetic activity when the situation finally condenses and the project emerges."**[2] This is how Mateo explains that initial moment of planning based on the world of ideas.

It was a difficult time of accumulated handovers and postponed holidays: in 48 months, 48 competitions distributed irregularly along the time line. The regular competition team changed over the years, with Vicky Daroca at its head in the first phase and now jointly with Till von MacKensen. The team was also joined by collaborators with different interests and specializations to meet the needs of each competition.

This creative period saw the emergence of common IDEAS and STRATEGIES that have developed from one competition to the next, evolving in each of them. It saw the creation of design and collaboration strategies that gradually came to form part of the practice's everyday work. Some of them have materialized, and many others remain in the realm of ideas to await their time.

Supporting framework / Architectural Form (Jointly with Agustí Obiol, BOMA)

Intensity in the treatment of the building's skin, addressed in the office block in Carrer Taulat in 2004, is an argument that was picked up in both the Film Theatre of Catalonia and the MAAG tower in Zurich. In the MAAG tower, the building's primary nucleus was transferred to its perimeter, thereby allowing an exploration of the formal and functional possibilities of a radical geometric treatment of the skin. This way of working has gone on to provide the strategy for multiple projects, being materialized in the housing block in Valencia (soon to be built) and the office building in Boulogne-Billancourt, Paris. In both cases, rather than representing a tie, the structure forms part of the language of the building, giving the façades increased complexity and avoiding a configuration based on the sequential repetition of openings, as is habitual in housing blocks, or on curtain walls, as occurs in office buildings. The façades serve as great girders through which the loads are transferred diagonally or in zigzag fashion to produce the same distribution of openings in all of them. In the Film Theatre of Catalonia, the building becomes a girder-cum-wall; between the façade walls, post-tensioned girders are laid out crosswise, supporting a traditional solid floor slab to free up inner space.

This structural system evolved from a wall structure to horizontal or vertical structural slabs, first experimented with in Warsaw and later developed in Saragossa; or to the hollowing out of the structure almost to the point of dematerialization of the skin, culminating in the project for the new Camp Nou football stadium. In all cases, it is the geometric organization that governs the way of working with the structure and its components.

A dual structural principle is deployed in the Museum of History of Polish Jews in Warsaw; first, a central nucleus is constructed with a basic concrete structure, with post-tensioned slabs to reduce thickness, then the geometry of the skin is set to work as an autonomous structure that seeks maximum efficiency.

In the Congress Centre in Saragossa, conversely, which involved covering an anisotropic space, the laminar solution was utilised, folded to optimize its use and turning the slab into a corner girder or diaphragm. The structure is generated by a sheet which, as it extends, folds back on itself, alternating horizontal and vertical stretches.

In the project for Camp Nou, the skin acquires thickness, mass and weight; it is structure full of function, programme and use; the skin becomes a sculptural volume.

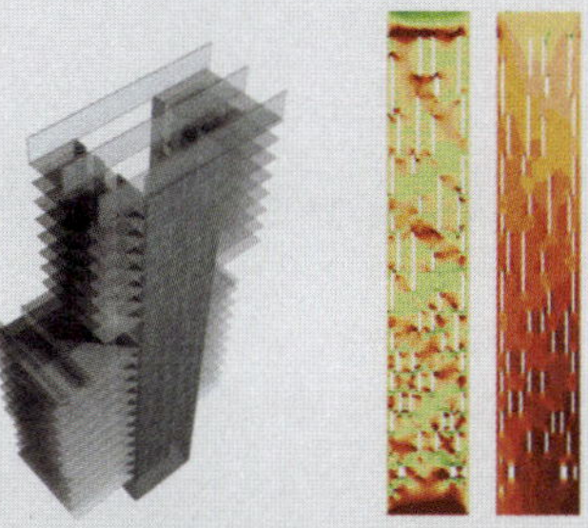

0

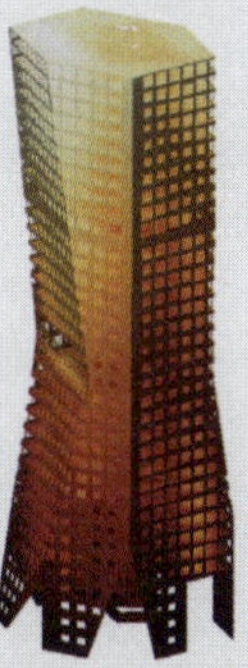

1

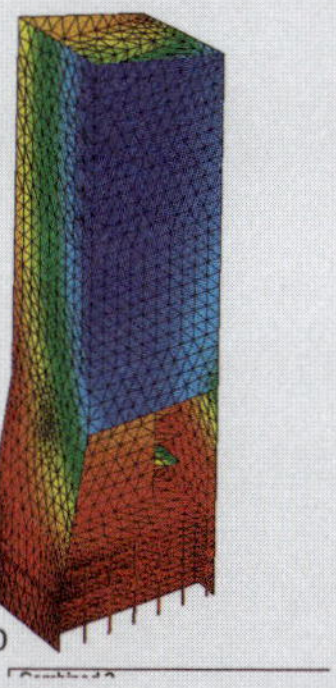

10

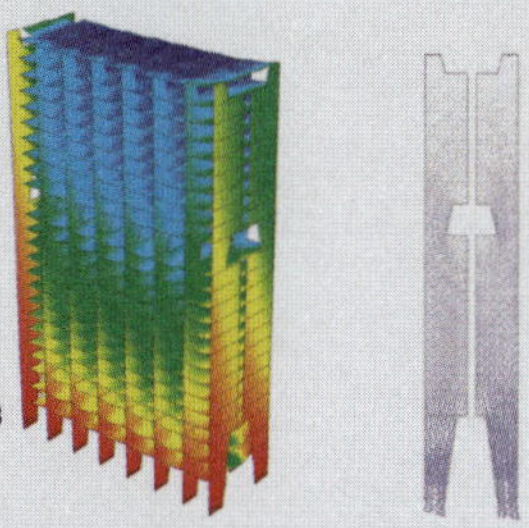

8

26

+

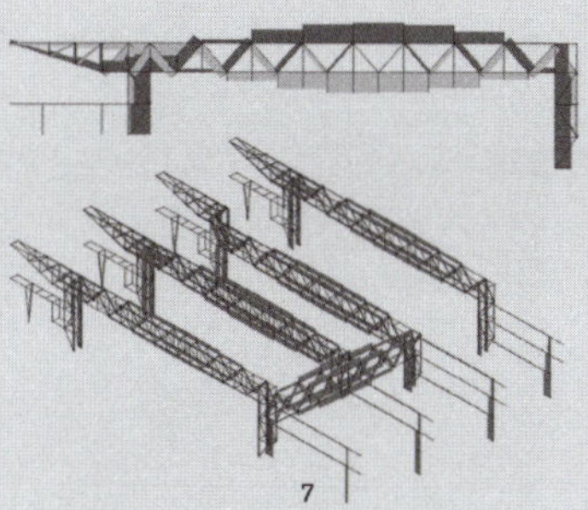

7

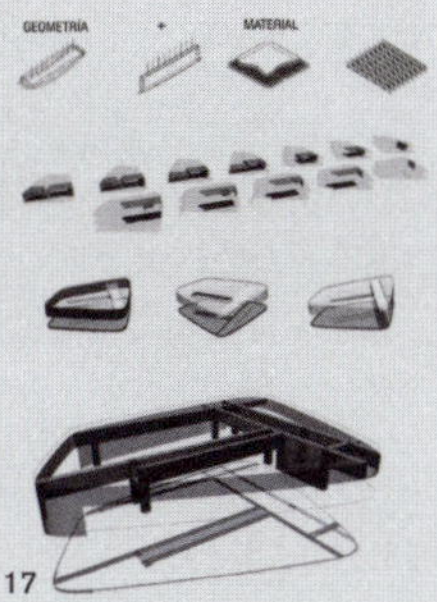

17

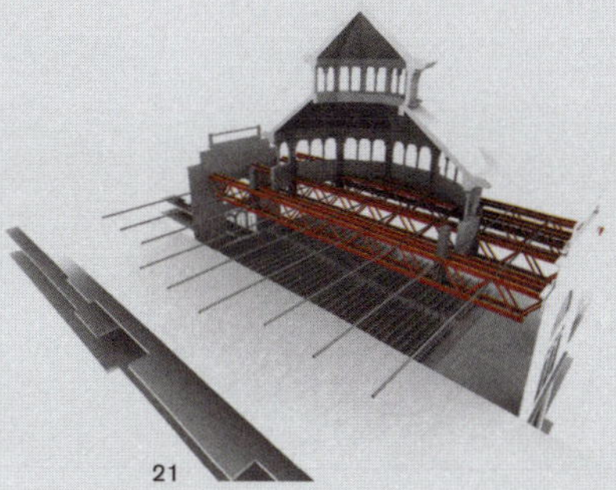

21

=

15

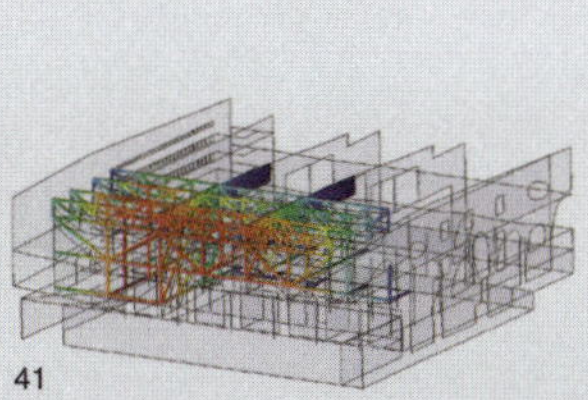

41

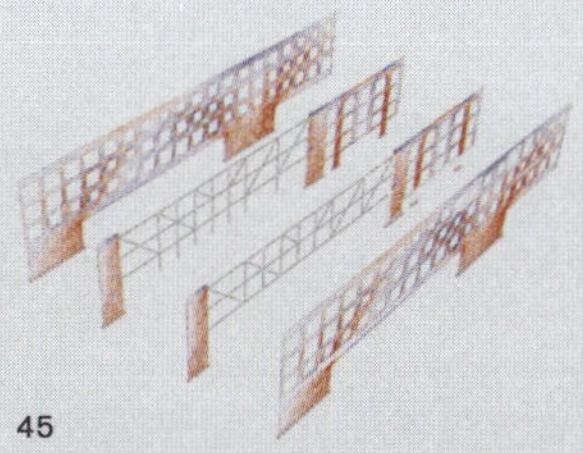

45

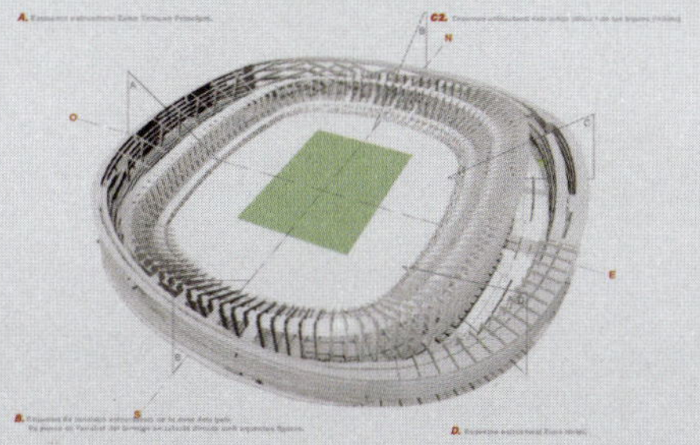

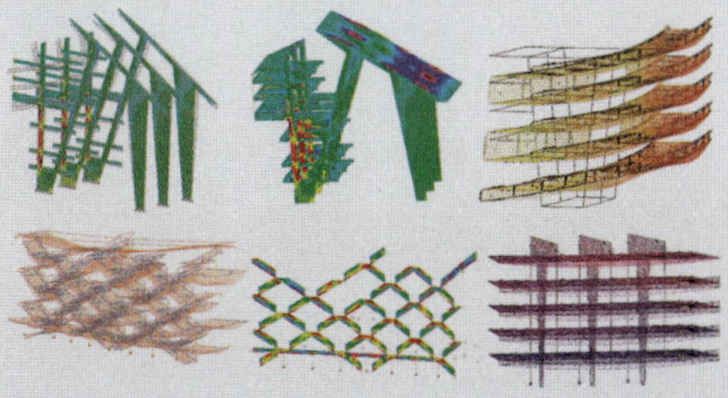

3

16

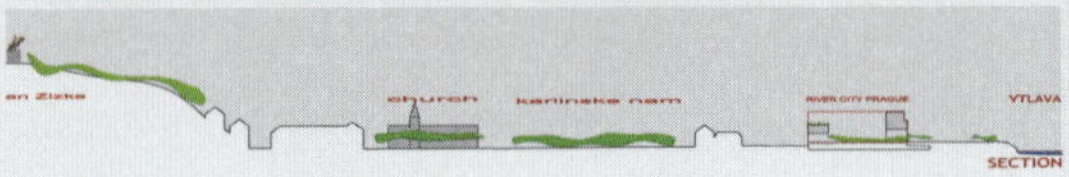

12

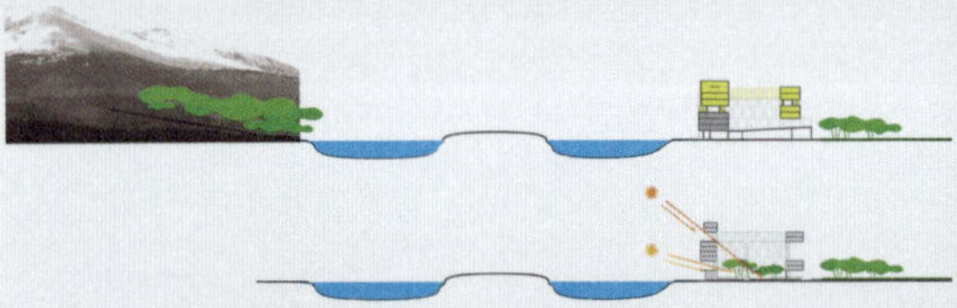

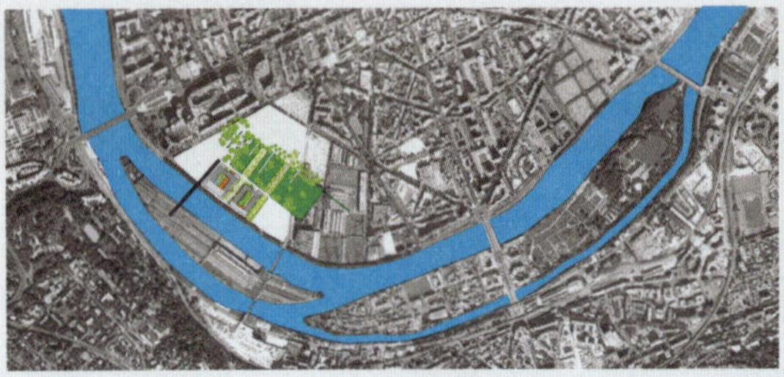

18

18

30

30

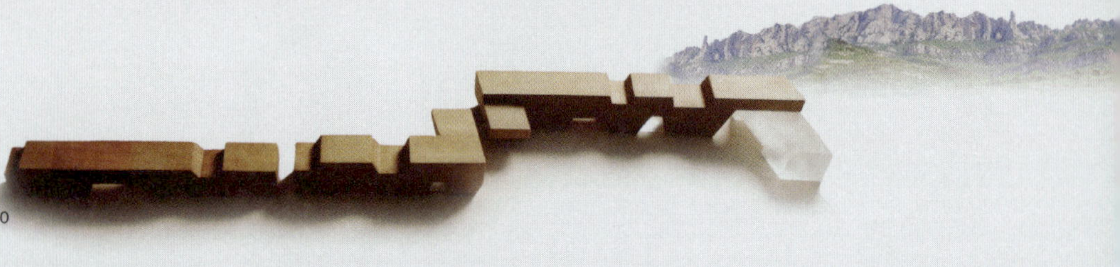

40

Place-Landscape/Architectural Form
The routines of place and landscape have been ongoing themes.
"A project explains a history of a specific place and time—a history that many do not yet know, but are waiting to hear. [...] The project foretells a world that does not yet exist, but is latent."
The reading of the place, from its physical presence to the coherence of its energy, at the starting point of design, is ever-present in the work of Josep Lluís Mateo: from the *Limit* to the *Centre*, from the *Periphery* to *Urban density*. The place as a meeting of energies, movements, flows, forces, textures, as something that is to do with life, with the life force, is also a cultural construct. The project emerges as a catalyst of all of these energies and ultimately establishes a dialogue with the real world of the context, modifying, transforming and completing it. It forms part of an established urban sequence, it follows the geometries of the place, it has no interest in the exception. Both the office building for River Amazon Court in Prague and the head office for Swiss Re are clear examples.

Many of the projects are related to nature, to the landscape in which they are set, in an essential sense, as with the women's prison in Sant Llorenç d'Hortons. Situated amid fields, it sets out to complete the surrounding woods and free up space at the centre of the project. In Doctor Trueta Hospital, the direct allusion to the landscape even forms part of the competition watchword, RIMUNTAT (RIUS-MUNTANYA-CIUTAT, or river-mountain-city). In the Great War Museum in Meaux, the aim of the project is to continue the existing park and construct the landscape, and to this end the project is excavated into the site, merging with it. In the WTC office in Igualada, the presence of the landscape is manifested in the irregular outline against sky and earth.

44

Programme / Architectural Form

"Our programmes are based on oneiric and mythical as well as quantitative data. Our task is to translate them into concrete terms, to construct them. To this aim, cool analysis is always more useful than moralizing involvement."[3] For Josep Lluís Mateo, the programme must not be subordinated to a concrete form; his architecture emerges like a three-dimensional framework from physical and mnemotechnical values.

Analysis of the programme, with all its implications, gives rise to efficient projects, as we see in the study of optimum office space. Abiding by international standards, a bar with a depth of 18 metres is used as the basic office typology; this allows a layout of the building in three strips, two exterior and one interior, with multiple planimetric and spatial possibilities. This architectural strategy, tested in various office projects such as the Business Centre in Kiev, the WTC building in Igualada, the River Amazon Court building in Prague and the head office of Banc Sabadell in Sant Cugat, using different architectural solutions, materialized in the office building in Cornellà, where the ratio of square metres of offices in relation to service space, along with other readings, won the competition.

Type 1: two corridors

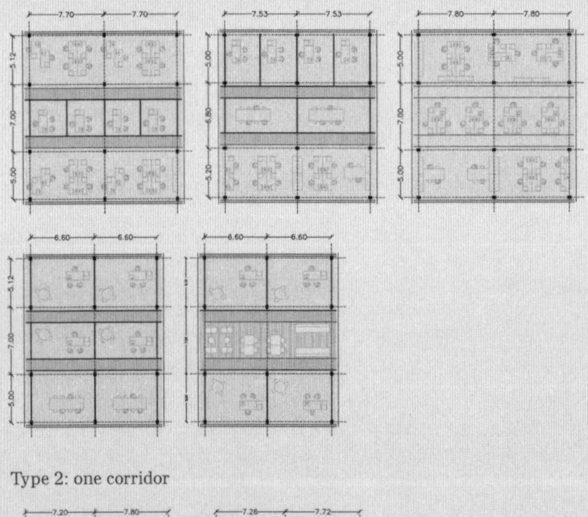

Type 2: one corridor

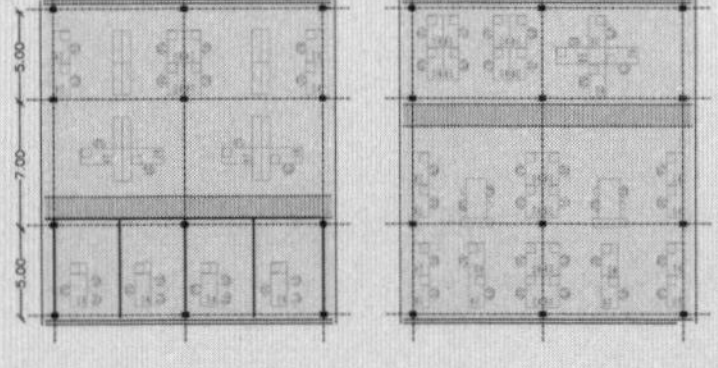

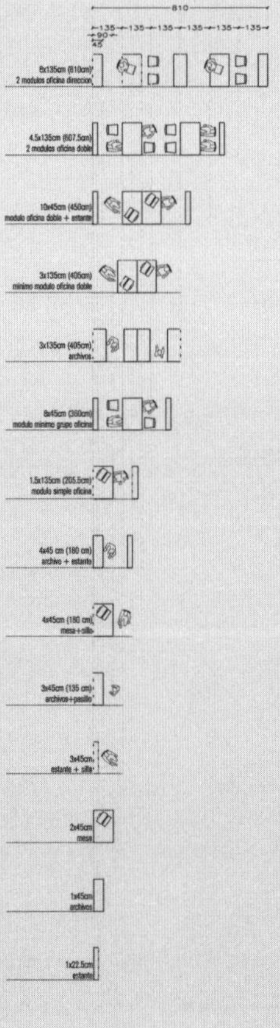

Interpretation and investigation of the programme give rise to the efficiency of the floor plan, the efficiency of the layout.
Projects are born of the sum of these ideas and strategies. When a project tells a story that is both invented and real, when it foretells a world, which, though it does not yet exist, is latent—that is when it has a real possibility of winning.
The practice continues with this dynamic, undertaking new approaches with new energy, seeking new models, always moving between the world of ideas and the world of materialization. Each new competition is a fresh challenge from which the best project could emerge.

"My best project is one that I have not seen yet, but I am preparing for it."[4]

1 MATEO, Josep Lluís: *Josep Lluís Mateo, Obras, Proyectos, Escritos.* Barcelona: Editorial Polígrafa, 2005, pp. 7-15.
2 ÁBALOS, IÑAKI and MATEO, Josep Lluís: "Conversación con Iñaki Ábalos". 2G. No. 25 (2003). Barcelona: Gustavo Gili, pp. 132–143.
3 MATEO, Josep Lluís: *Josep Lluís Mateo, Obras, Proyectos, Escritos.* Barcelona: Editorial Polígrafa, 2005, pp. 7–15.
4 MATEO, Josep Lluís: *Textos Instrumentales. Josep Lluís Mateo.* Barcelona: Editorial Gustavo Gili, 2007.
5 ÁBALOS, IÑAKI and MATEO, Josep Lluís: "Conversación con Iñaki Ábalos". 2G. No. 25 (2003). Barcelona: Gustavo Gili, pp. 132–143.

OCCASIONAL CITY

is an ideal city consisting of fragments of cities in which we have been invited to work. It is global and local, comprised of order and hierarchy (despite being fortuitous), and it organizes our responses on the occasions when we have been asked.

A Housing block. Valencia
B Urban development. Draga, Sibenik. Croatia
C Hospital. L'Hospitalet de Llobregat. Barcelona

Proposal for the installation of the same name. Galería Ras, Barcelona. September 2009.

Pattern structuring the fabric

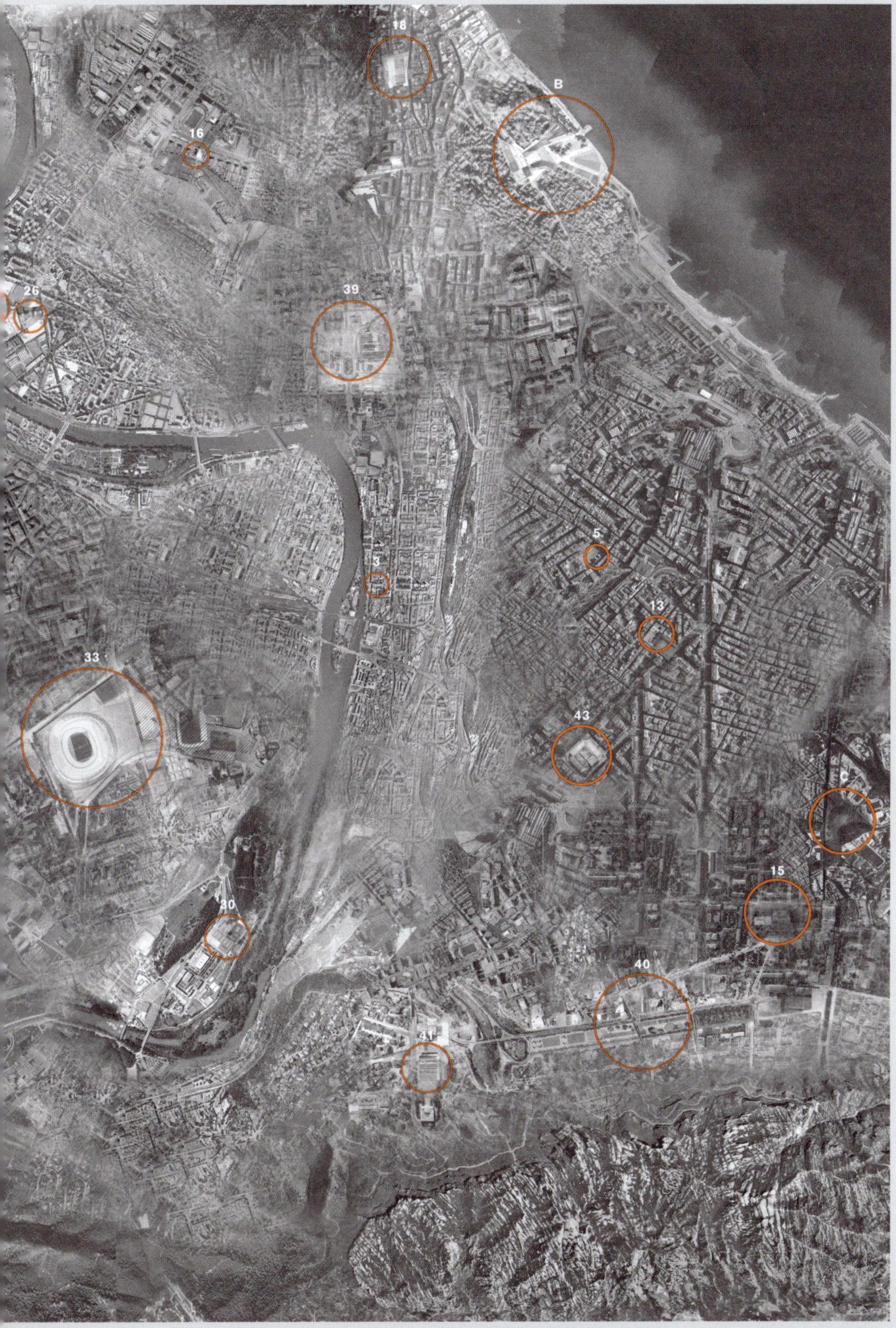
18
B
16
26
39
5
3
13
33
43
C
15
30
40
41

ZURICH 2004

The context, a metropolitan street corner and the movement around it, explains the building's volume. The dynamic manipulation of loads in the super-strength concrete façades explains its form.

MAAG AREAL SKYSCRAPER

Invited competition. 2004

Zurich/Switzerland. Location: Zurich. Surface area: 63,077 m²

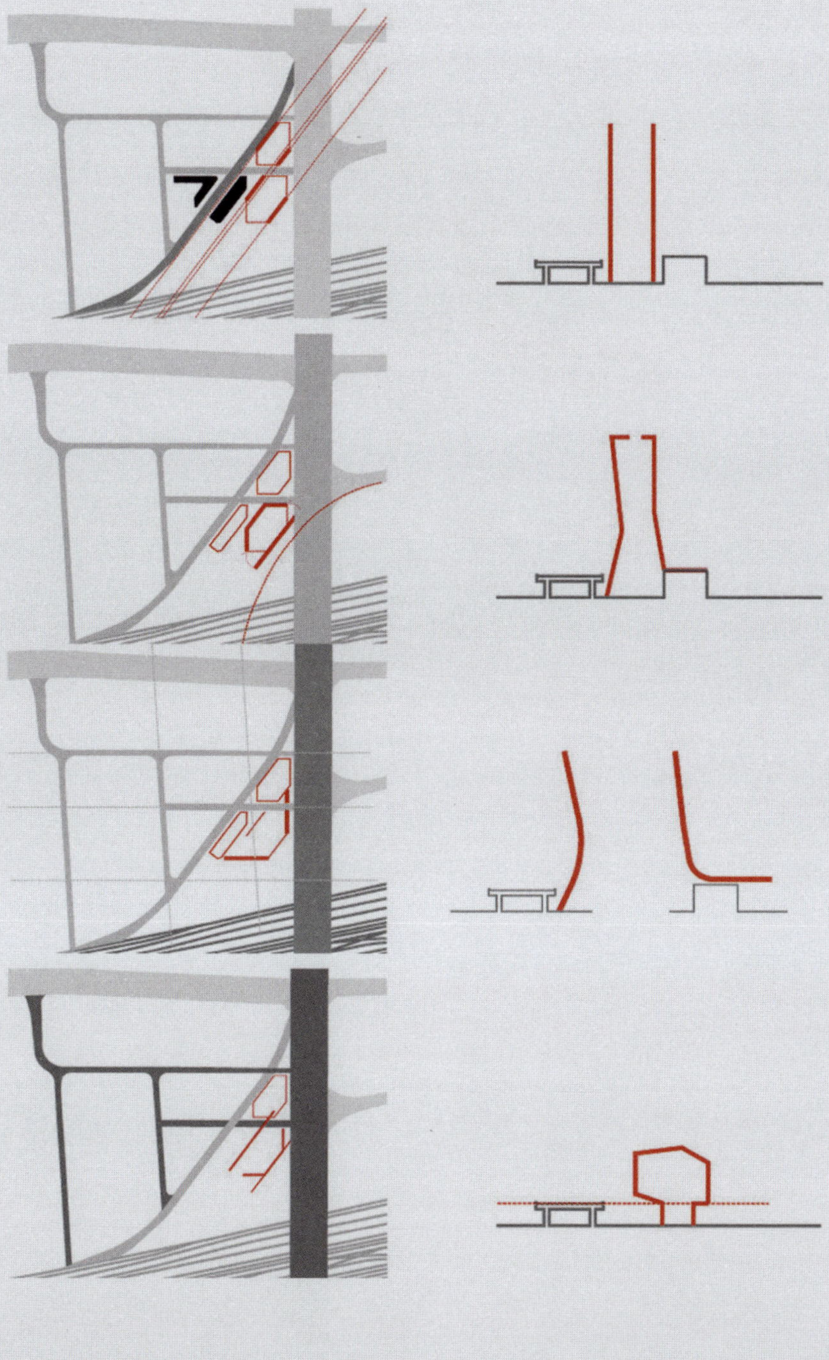

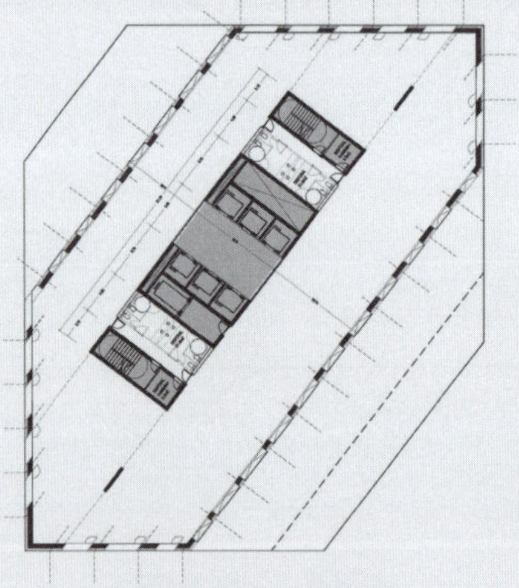

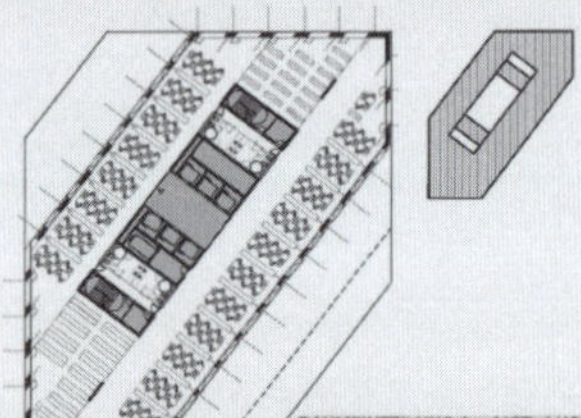

RAUMEINTEILUNG A_ MST. 1/400

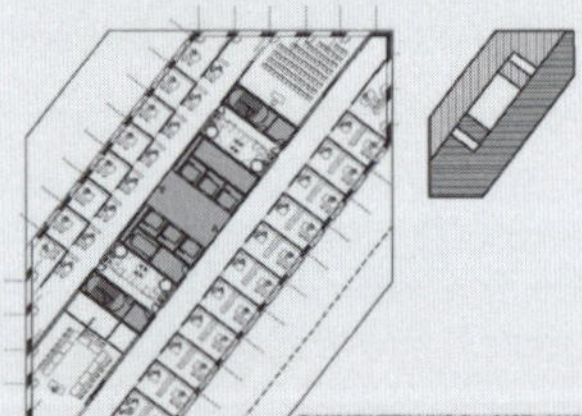

RAUMEINTEILUNG B_ MST. 1/400

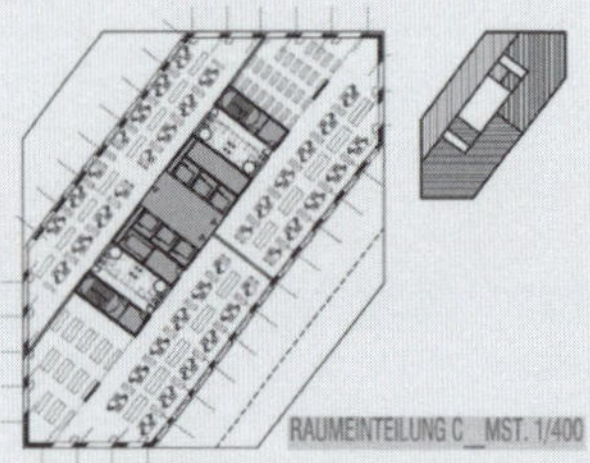

RAUMEINTEILUNG C_ MST. 1/400

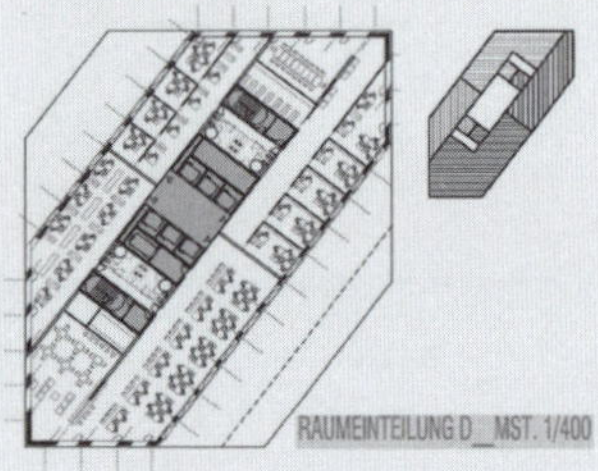

RAUMEINTEILUNG D_ MST. 1/400

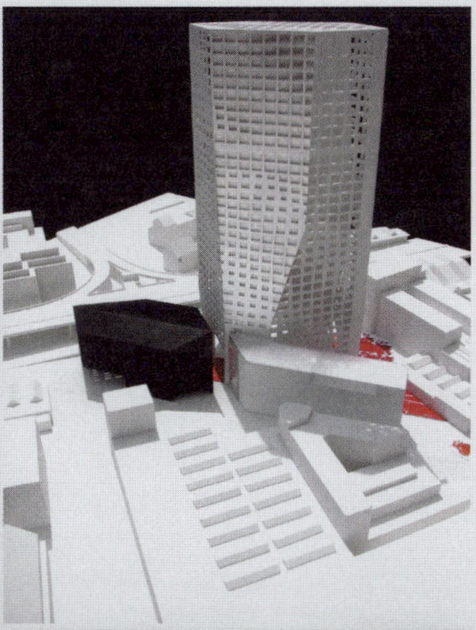

BUS

stress Nx
kein wind

frontalfassade
mst.1:1000

stress Nx
kein wind

rückfassade
mst. 1:1000

stress Ny
kein wind

frontalfassade
mst. 1:1000

stress Ny
kein wind

rückfassade
mst. 1:1000

verschiebungen
kein wind

frontalfassade
mst. 1:1000

verschiebungen
kein wind

rückfassade
mst. 1:1000

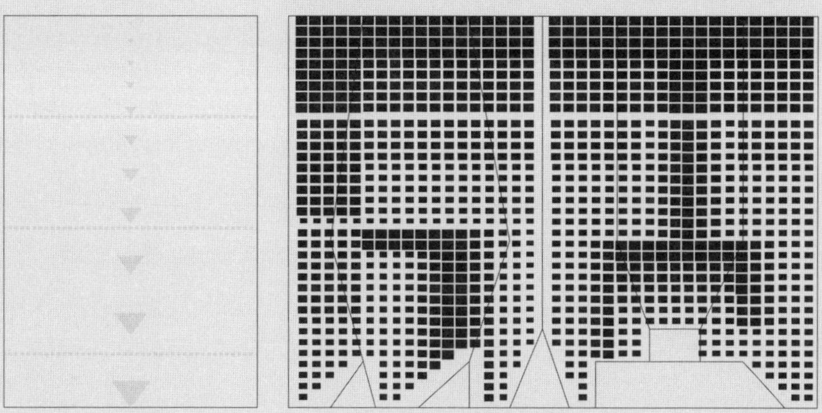

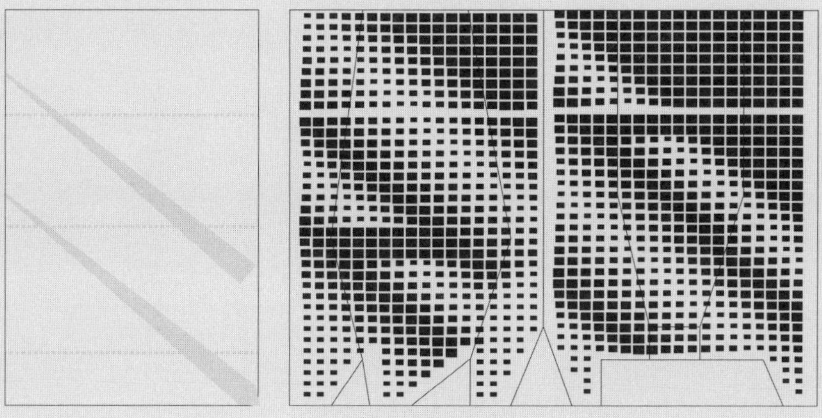

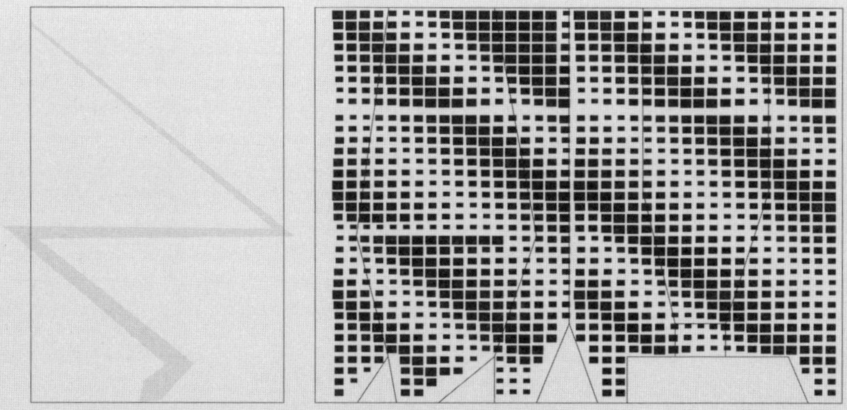

BARCELONA 2007

BONES NOT SKIN

Our project did not seek simply to add an obvious, colourist skin that would be out of date even before it was put into place. Our project seeks to establish an intelligent, sensible relation with the original building. Our project seeks to address the urban issues of the stadium's large volume. Our project seeks to construct a singular space. Our project believes not in the superficiality of skin but in the depth of the mass, the sculptural volume and the logic of the bones as figurative, solid, moving arguments.

NEW CAMP NOU STADIUM.

Invited competition. 2007

Location: Aristides Maillol, Les Corts (Barcelona). Surface area: 130,000 m²

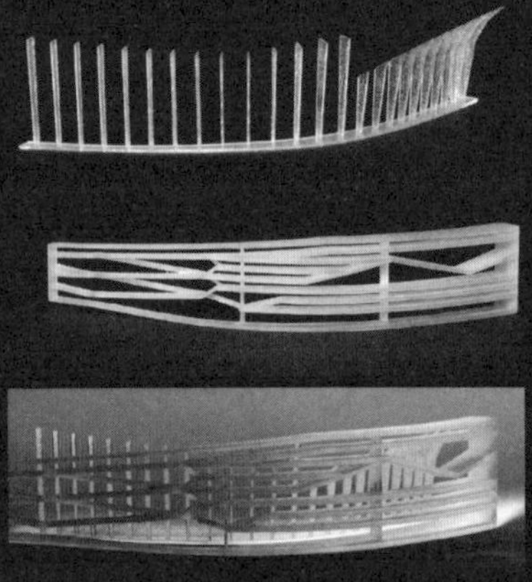

Old-new structural relations

Relation between background and envelope; the sun of the two layers is a new figure.

Olafur Eliasson. Test for Pedestrian Vibes Study, 2004
As part of his research into light waves and motion, Olafur Eliasson conducted a number of tests with a simple lamp describing a spiral, which were recorded using long-exposure photography.

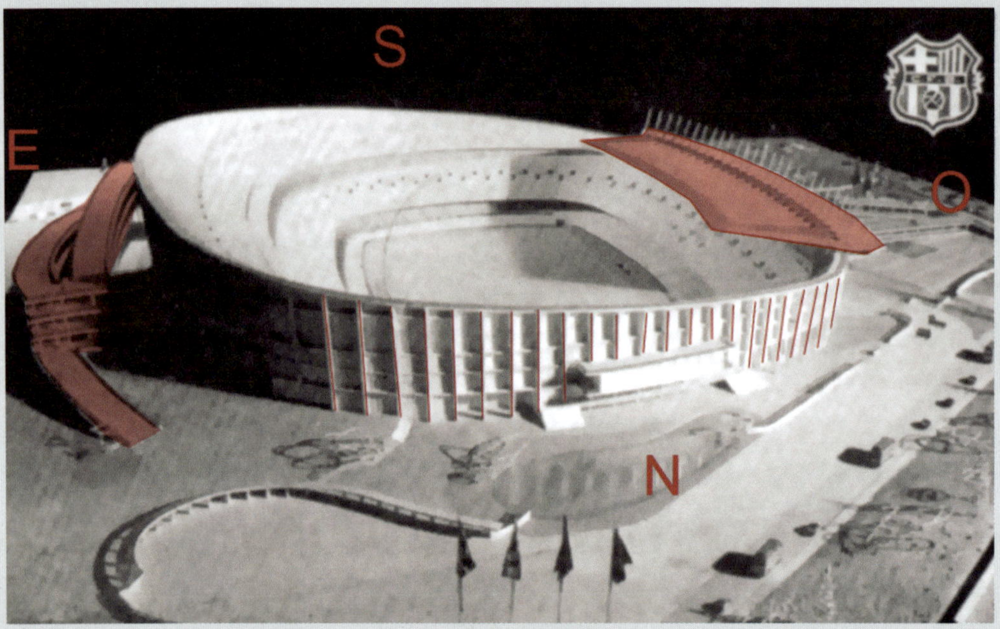

The initial project presents an **asymmetrical** stadium, with a repeated **vertical cadence of exterior supports** and a spectacular **counterpoint in the west and east façades.**
In the west side, the roof of the stands and the actual façade, with their special tectonics, give form to the main monumental entrance.
In the east façade, built much later, flows and movement around the ramps are given centre stage.

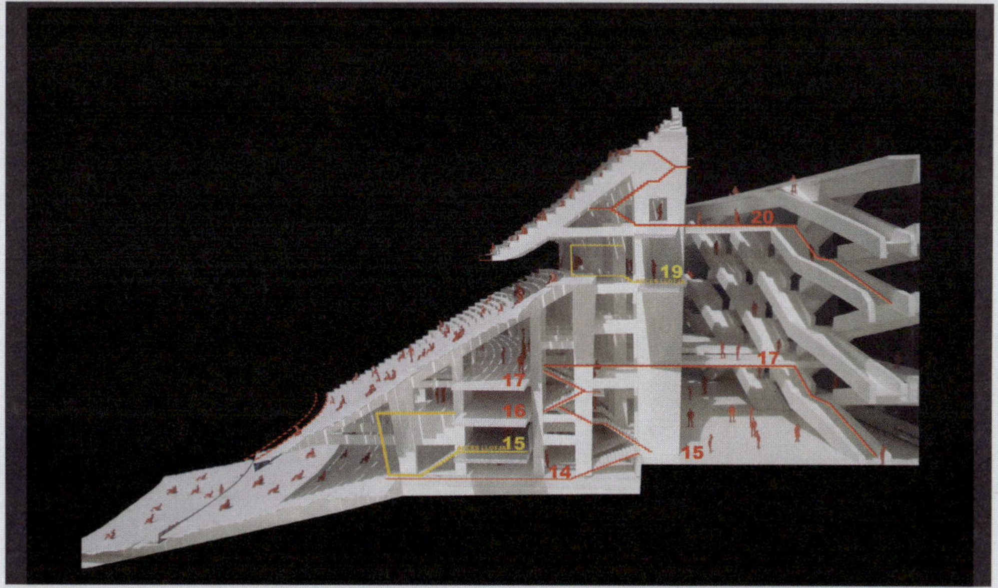

The interior of the stadium presents a lovely surrounding to the pitch. The geometrical dissymmetry of the stands gives rise to the spatial dissymmetry of the masses, introducing an extraordinary dynamic component that accompanies the movement of the game. In contrast to the order of the pitch, the spaces behind the stands, which house accesses, catering and other services, call for functional and architectural interventions to highlight this singular space with its sloping ceiling and brutalist tectonics. The latest intervention serves to insert new systems of mobility and services into the new envelope, and give the existing structure a cleaner line.

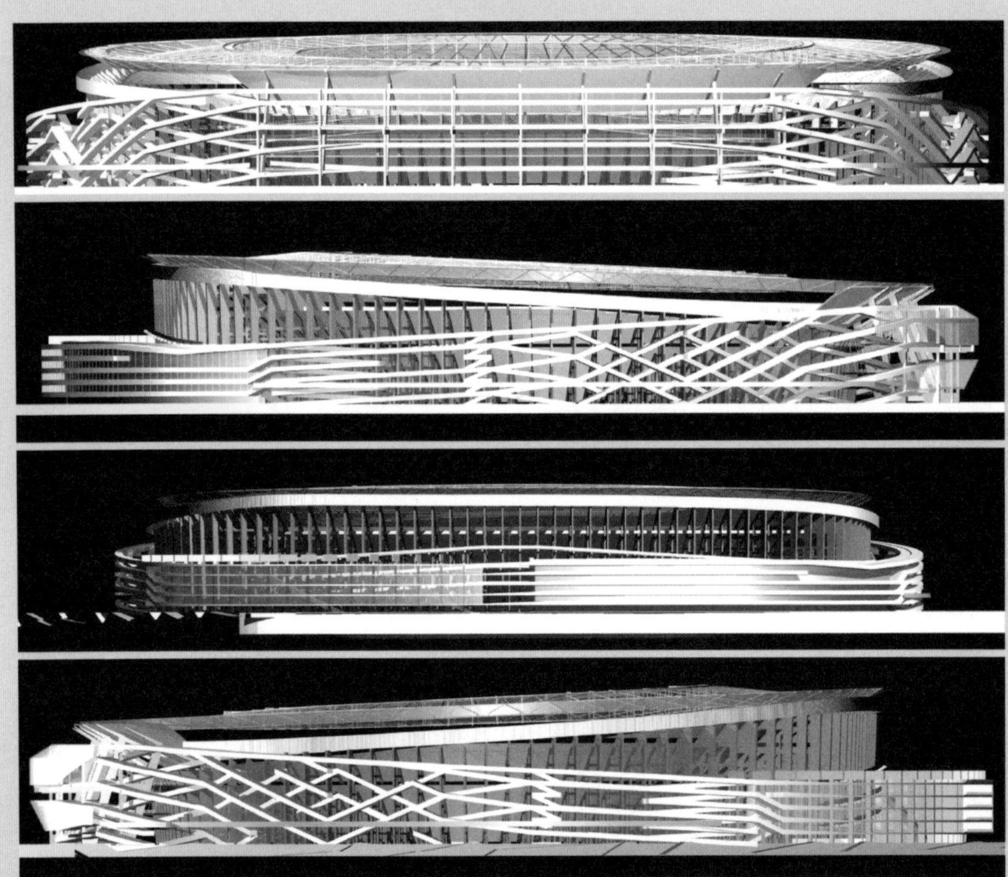

A new figure as a complementary sum of the old and the new

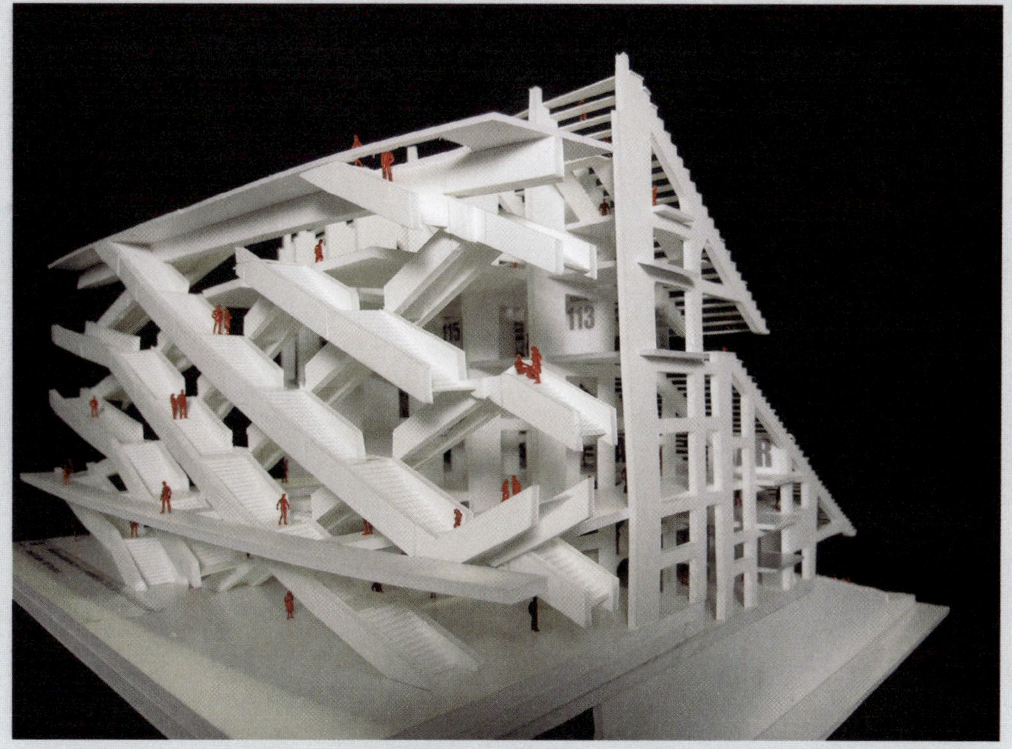

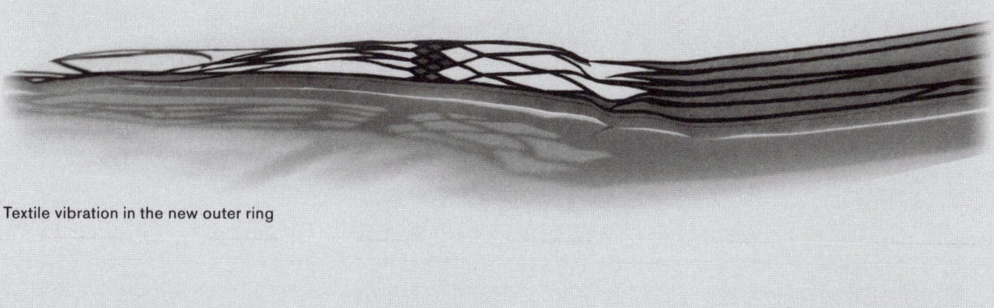

Textile vibration in the new outer ring

1

Contact of the new-old structure. Monumental neo-Gothic interior space

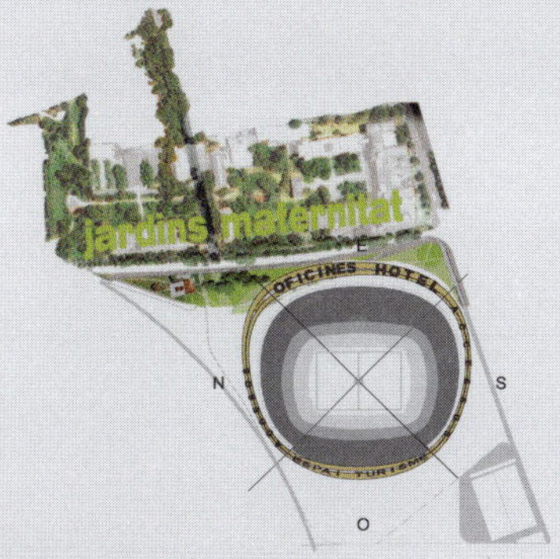

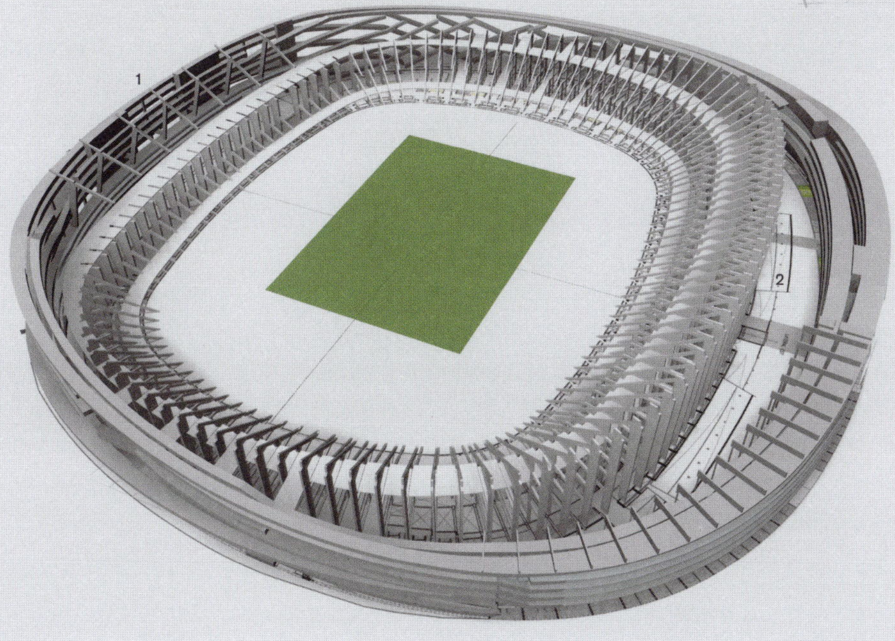

Contact of the new-old structure. Open garden in connection with the adjacent gardens of the Maternity hospital

Objets à désir: Photos of the construction of the stadium, *circa* 1955

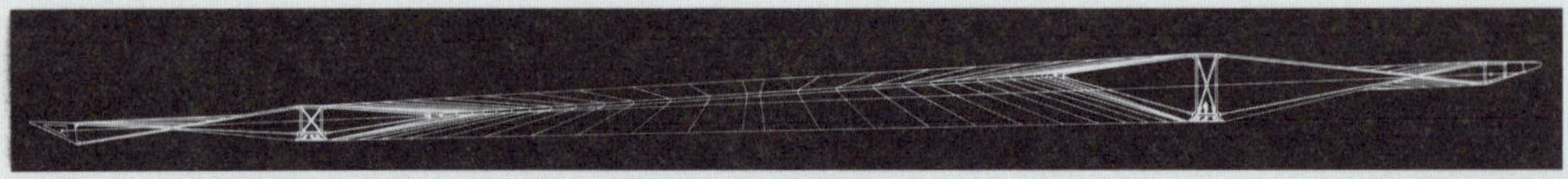

The new roof is devised as a forest of cables working under traction, covered over by a double layer of canvas: a cloud floating over the space. (Structural design: Agustí Obiol, BOMA)

ZURICH 2008

Low and flattened, it forms the base to the Kantonschule and the mountains. It is open to the plaza before it, which it draws inside. Where it borders the plaza, the building hovers, expanding it. To either side, concrete walls enclose the box. Through its rear garden (north façade), the building reaches away to the mountains.
The whole is covered by the great technological hat that is the roof.

KUNSTHAUS MUSEUM EXTENSION

Invited competition. 2008
Zurich/Switzerland. Location: Kunsthaus.
Surface area: 15,000 m²

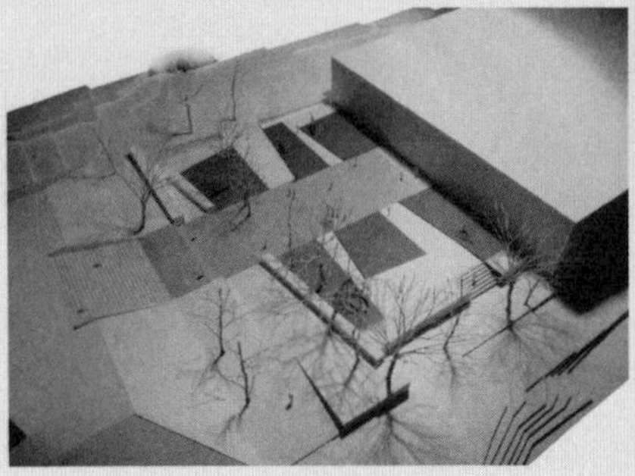

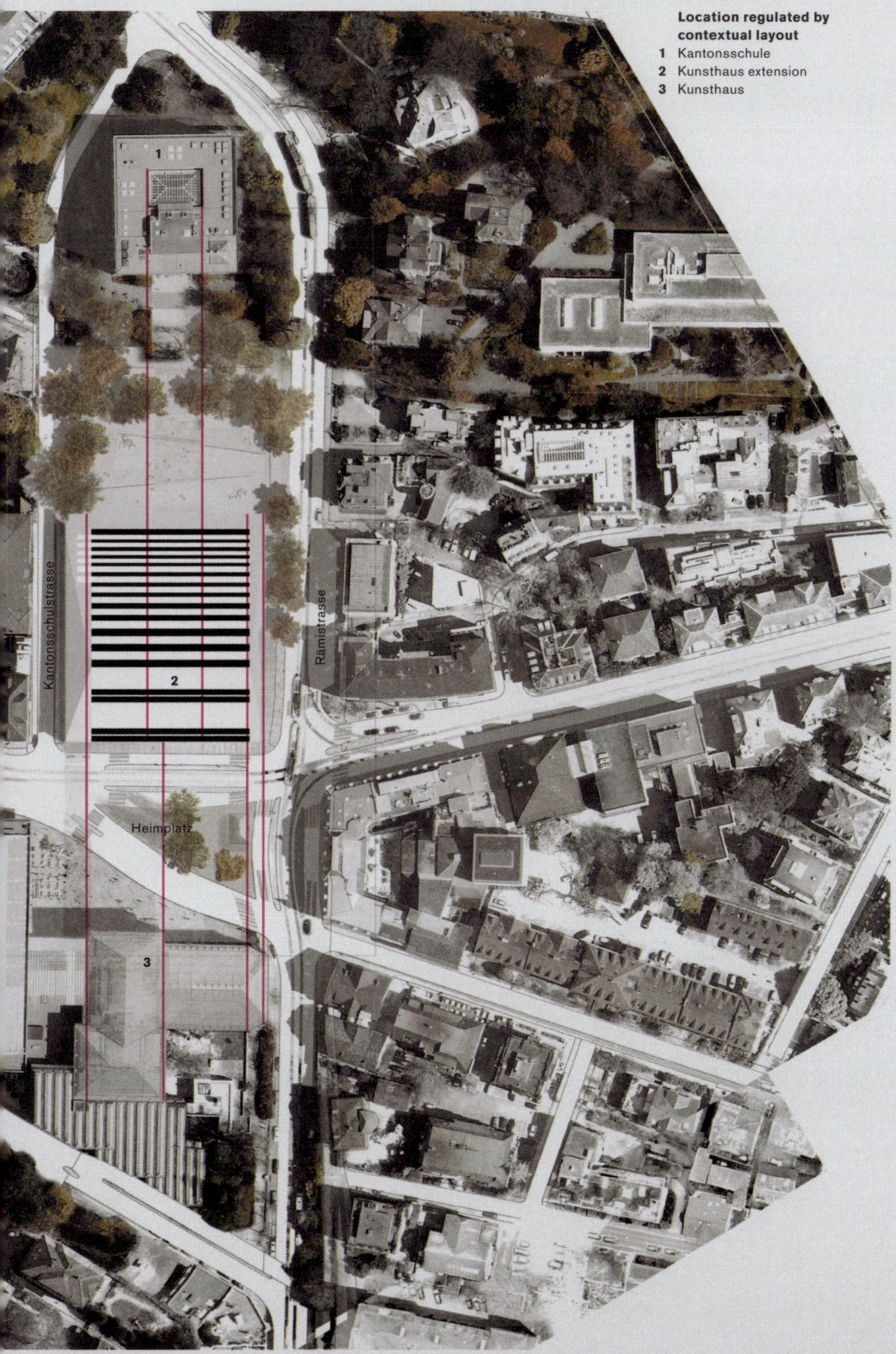
Location regulated by contextual layout
1 Kantonsschule
2 Kunsthaus extension
3 Kunsthaus
Kantonsschulstrasse
Rämistrasse
Heimplatz
1
2
3

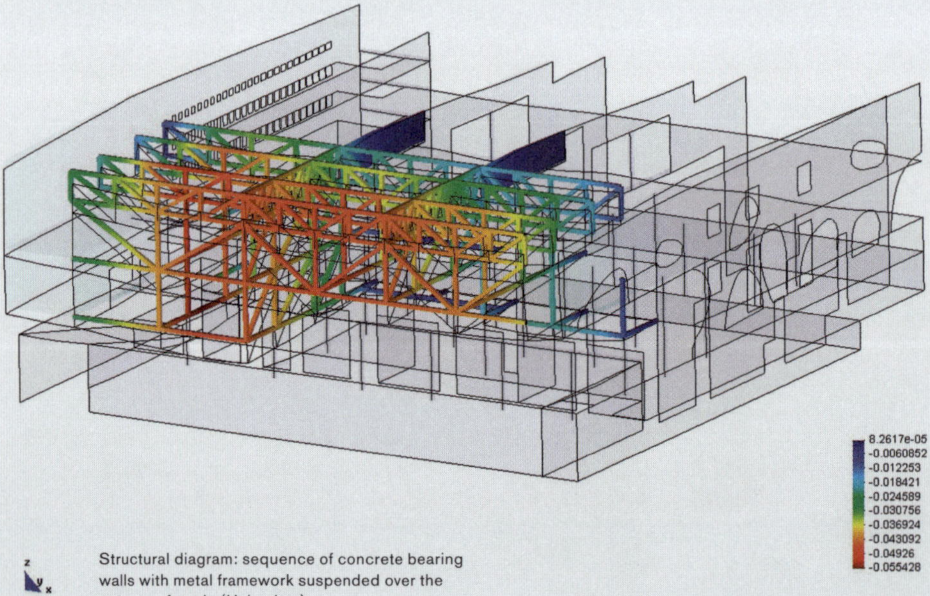

Structural diagram: sequence of concrete bearing walls with metal framework suspended over the entrance façade (Heimplatz)

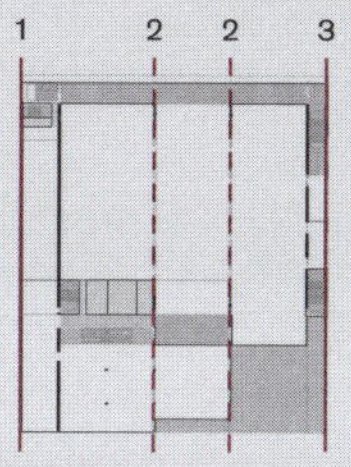

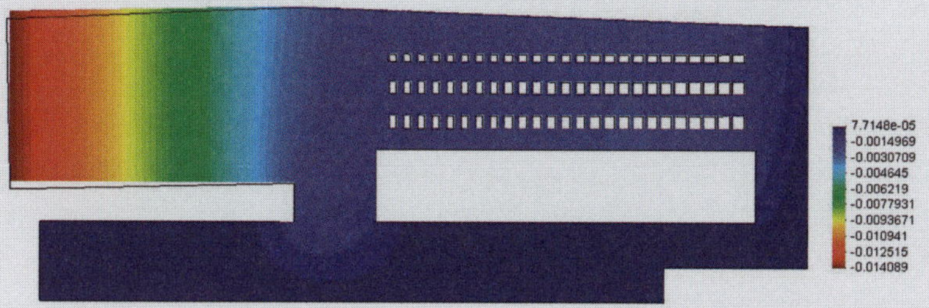

Portico-façade on Kantonsschulstrasse

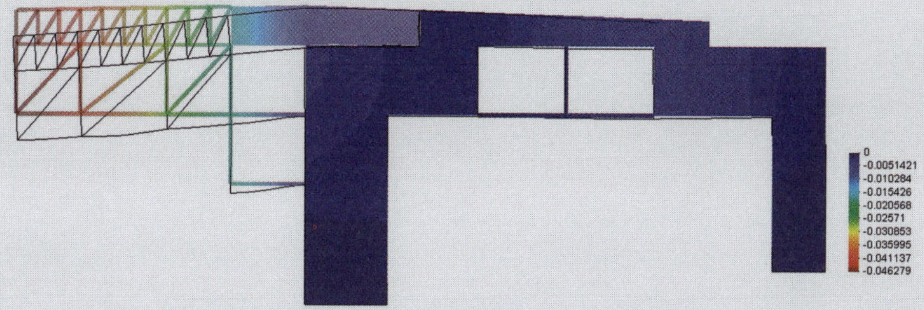

Central porticos

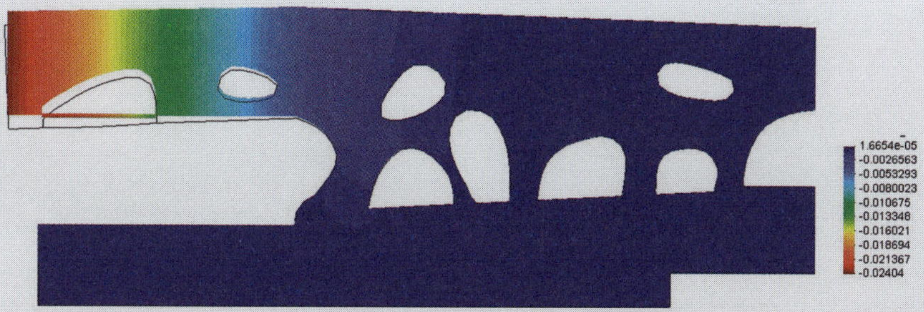

Portico-façade on Rämistrasse

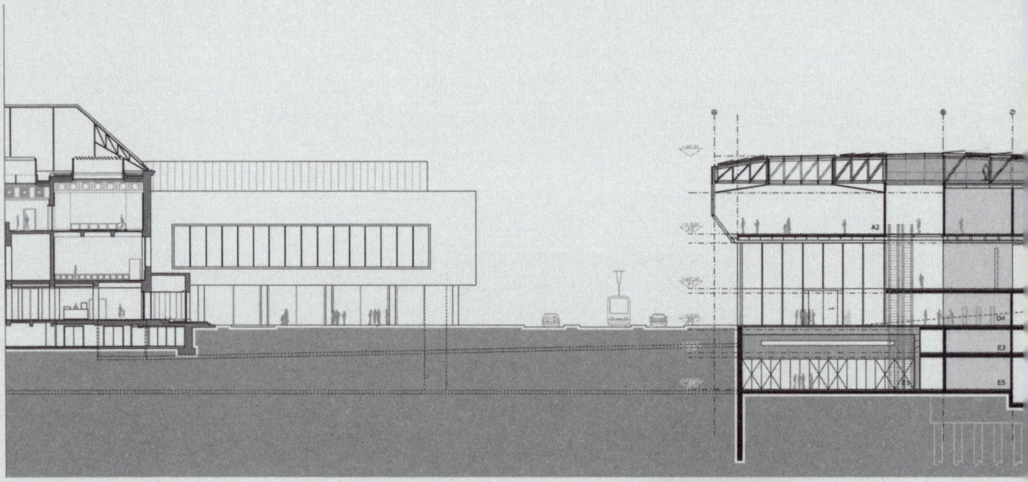
A2
D4
E3
E5

sch

A1
A4
F20
F30
B1
Verlegter Wolfbachkanal
B-B
LÄNGSSCHNITT 1:200

Klasse
17. 9. LUCIE DE BEAUNE
17. 9. TODESVARIATIONEN
BORRMAN
BEGINNT.
Reproduction

EARTH

Barcelona, October 2008:
Clay, bones and water

Zeist, November 2008:
Sand and water

Paris, November 2008:
Gravel and water

Meeting between Josep Lluís Mateo and José Luis Guerín, director of the film *En construcción* [Work in Progress], about the Raval district in Barcelona, which served as a reference for Josep Lluís Mateo's project for the new Film Theatre of Catalonia.

Guerín: I'm a very keen cinema-goer, so this will be my home, the home of cinema, *la Maison du Cinéma*. I say it in French because it was Langlois who invented the film theatre. The world's first film archive was actually Henri Langlois' bathtub, and Langlois was also very much involved in the way the Trocadero was planned. It was the first to be set up, in the France of the Occupation. He collected films and preserved them, on his own initiative, creating a great film archive in his own home. He went without a bathtub out of love for the cinema, and at that time the French state was the first to invest money in this art.

If Josep Lluís had called me before, I would have told him to visit the Trocadero film theatre. A new one has since been built. I still find it hard to accept, because the old one represented so much for our memory.

The existing one in Barcelona is rather sad and unpleasant. People don't argue about films; this may be a sign of the times, but nor is there a place that incites you to do so. The café is a vital place in this respect.

Stills from the film by José Luis Guerín, *Work in Progress*

Mateo: There are pictures of the site for the new film theatre showing machines building the piles alongside archaeologists. There was a wonderful moment when there were awnings put up, like on an Egyptian excavation site. Awnings, with huge machines moving earth beside them. They found pieces of an axe, from the Bronze Age, tiny pieces. They also found lots of pottery and a skeleton. They were very thorough, to my great despair.
Guerín: What are they going to do with the remains? What they usually do is put them in sad bags in a warehouse, where they lie in row upon row with their number tags. I should make a film in one, one day. It's like a great rubbish dump, with lampposts, statues of Franco, and so on; like a great film set, with all the useless things cast off by the city. It would be great if that vessel were placed in the building's museum. The film theatre is a space for heritage and memory, so those remains should come to rest there.
Mateo: That would be wonderful. Exhibiting them would be ideal.
Guerín: Otherwise, they'll simply be invisible. Were there any drawings on the pottery?
Mateo: No, no. They found the remains of a women's prison—it's amazing, our practice has to design one, kind of a replacement, in Sant Llorenç d'Hortons—and that was no problem, but then they found pieces of pottery, too. We thought it wouldn't take long. To our despair, they then found the axe, and then a hold-up of work was inevitable.
Guerín: So, the time sequence of this place includes an axe and a prison. There must have been things in between.
Mateo: There were fields of crops, of course; the site was inside the town walls, but outside the centre. There were wells, kilns, canals, pipes, sewers, etc.
Guerín: The place within the town walls where they couldn't build houses. Hence the name *arrabal*, a part of the town outside the centre, which produced the district's name, the "Raval".

Laying of the foundations alongside the archaeological excavations. Some of the finds

Guerín: In the new project, how far will we have to go down to get to the cinema?
Mateo: Six metres. There will be two cinemas, a large one and a smaller one.
Guerín: Isn't there a risk that films will be showing in both, and the sound from one will be audible in the other? There are cinemas where this happens.
Mateo: No. Under the mezzanine, an acoustic buffer alongside the curtains separates the two.
The problem is that it'll be like a descent into hell. The fact that you notice you're underground, the concrete, everything painted black—it'll be like falling down.
Guerín: Initially, I find it quite shocking that the cinema is practically hidden. It's dark and subterranean, and without any further explanation, it doesn't seem very logical; it seems as though what, for me, is the central, the most important space, is down with the drains.
We viewers occupy a marginal space in comparison with the workers and other spaces in the film theatre.
Mateo: The Trocadero was underground, too. I seem to recall that it was all down below.
Guerín: Yes, that's true. For us cinema-goers it was a real underground moment, it seems to me, almost an archaeological experience.
Mateo: To cheer things up a bit, there'll be light pouring down from above. There'll be a museum, spaces for processing films, the library, etc. The administrative workers will be right at the top.

Henri Langlois coming out of the Musée du Cinéma.
Trocadero, Paris.

Guerín: I was thinking about cinema venues. The first were ephemeral fairground architecture; that was where the cinema was born. Later, with the desire to legitimize it, film production companies started to think: how can we get the middle classes to go to the cinema? And that was when the iconographic names started to appear...
Mateo: Buildings for the cinema started out as a poor imitation of theatres.
Guerín: The first names chosen for cinemas were things like Capitol, Capitel, Capitolium, or Arcade in France, Arcadia (I think that's the loveliest name), Olympia, Coliseo, Coliseum...
Whichever city you go to, the signs and names are very similar. Then cinema names were associated with a notion of glamour. Take Barcelona; there are lots of cinemas with the names of luxury hotels—the Luxor, the Savoy, the Windsor—and others associated with rich countries, like the Montecarlo, the Niza, and so on.
Later, in the 1950s and '60s, the cinema came up against the problem of television. What can we do to rival that? So they emphasised the typology, and lots of cinemas changed to very long, rectangular screens. The square screen changed, and so did the way cinemas were built. I find it very rare and exceptional to see a cinema where the architect has gone to town.
Mateo: No, no. There was a time, in the fifties, when many of the cinemas that you liked—the Astoria or Balañá cinemas, for example—were designed by Antonio Bonet, who was a good architect.
Guerín: They're going strong—long may it last!
Mateo: Plus they are huge. What are really horrible are the multi-screen complexes. Or perhaps they're not horrible, just invisible.
Guerín: That's it; in my film-fanatic memory, I clearly remember at which cinemas I saw films, before. Now, on the other hand, I can't remember, because the cinemas are interchangeable.

ZANOTTI

Guerín: One thing I really like about the neighbourhood is its nooks and crannies, its irregularities. I think there is something about the human condition that won't let popular characters live in a city without odd little corners. I was thinking of Haussman's hygienist projects, with great boulevards to prevent people plotting in corners. The intrusion of a new block or a new building often attracts my attention, and I find it aggressive; it's like the imposition of a bunker that crushes this more meandering idea of little corners that I see as being so characteristic of popular memory and these neighbourhoods that have formed haphazardly over the years, creating little corners.

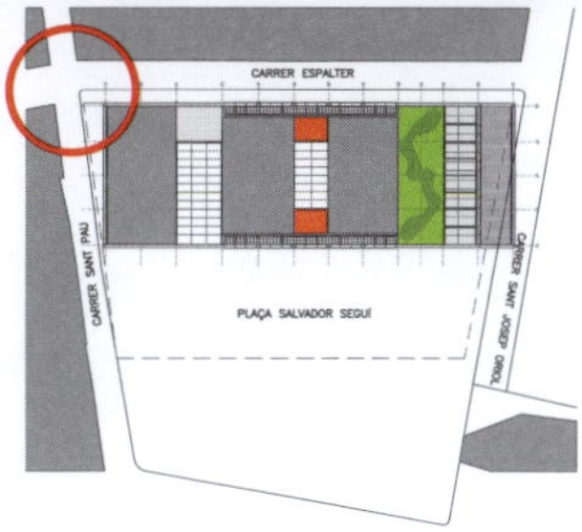

Mateo: What I find interesting are the edges and corners. The building is a more or less parallelepiped volume. The two longitudinal façades (on the street and the plaza) were obvious, but the real interest lay in the other two. One gives rise to the fourth corner with Carrer Sant Pau, and the other appears at the end of Carrer Josep Oriol.
This fourth corner covers the street with a huge projection, like a room with a ceiling. The volume dissolves at its edges.
Guerín: So, this will be a new corner within the complex. People can enter through it.
Mateo: Yes, it's a kind of porch open to the street and the plaza. The bar and the cafeteria are also supposed to open up to the plaza.
It will be a local café. Open all day, or all night, whatever the opening times are. You can go in from the outside; you won't have to go right inside the film theatre.
The structure means that it is a floating building. So you can go into the plaza or downstairs, to where the cinemas are, or upstairs.

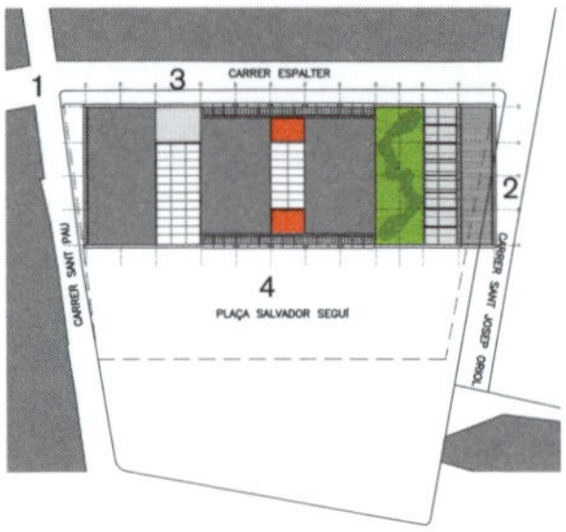

1

3

Volumetric study of corners and façades

2

4

Mateo: The library area is a fabulous space, with a huge window overlooking the plaza and the street. Its transparency is lovely; it's a space without pillars and with a window on either side, which is sort of floating and surrounded by books. At the top, which is enclosed, are the quieter work tables and the terrace. But it is a space without limits, with books and without limits in its two façades.
Guerín: Will there be curtains?
Mateo: On the outside there's a great metal blind to filter the light and nuance the views. The blind is designed to be Arabic in style, with a pattern, so it can be moved to create a space that is more closed or more open—to create a degree of opaqueness, really. So you can control the views. I'd like to work on it on site, because it's difficult to create the desired effect. There comes a point where it's very difficult to complete the details before—or, at least, five years before.
Guerín: Is it a regular pattern?
Mateo: No, it should have a rhythm, not just a single motif ...

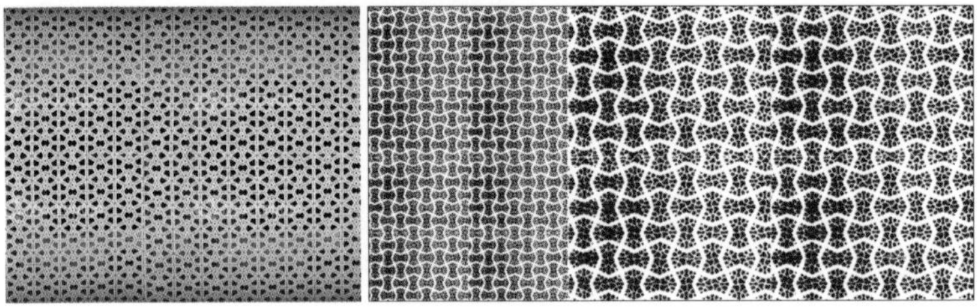

Blinds

Guerín: One idea for a motif could be film frames, breaking down movement, like in the origins of the cinema. A succession of frames was used to analyse the motion of going downstairs, step by step, or birds in flight, showing the gestation of a movement.
Mateo: From the outside, you'll see a great concrete screen with a large window, which is where the library is situated. It will be covered with this kind of bronze metal blind that acts as a kind of curtain. From the street, you'll see a building that looks like it's floating, that allows you to connect, to enter; it acts as a filter, but it is open to the plaza.
It's quite complicated to make it all bare concrete, materials, tubes, etc., with nothing hidden. There are beams supported by ties, and the structure is very curious, basically to produce a pillar-free space. It's a space like an industrial warehouse, like a bridge.
Guerín: Have you designed other buildings with these characteristics?
Mateo: Well, I like this kind of thing. It was also a way of not designing a building with decoration, of making it pure structure.

Movement in the cinema.
The movements of a bird, invisible to the naked eye - Chronophotographic images taken with the photographic gun - Étienne-Jules Marey, France, mid-1880s.

Mateo: My mother was from a village where they would bring the film in from outside. When you went to the pictures, you took your own chair. It was a kind of contract—a very interactive, community thing. Well, that kind of thing could happen here, too.
The fourth corner creates a kind of "head". This is where we suggested screening films in the summer, so it could be used as a screen that can be seen from the plaza.
Guerín: I think that's very important.
Mateo: It would be great. First, it would give the plaza meaning, too. The plaza would have people coming and going, the bar...
Guerín: Even if it's not used, I think the idea of the screen is very important. It is an outward expression of the cinema, this vocation of reaching out and communicating with the public space, the neighbourhood and the people. Otherwise, the place runs the risk of being endogamic, closed in on itself.
Mateo: In the plaza, the film would be screened on a light grey concrete surface. Two types of colour are combined. The slightly darker concrete is used at the bottom, next to the ground, which will be all grey, as usual, and we'll try to use white cement, too, to make it a bit more reflective.
Guerín: Anything that evokes a white screen is great.
Mateo: It is very difficult to produce a well-finished concrete surface. So I expect it to be slightly rough, natural and unfinished.
Guerín: Don't finish this building. The outline is always much better than the finished product. It's lovely, Josep Lluís.
Mateo: Do you think the screen is OK?

Guerín: It seems a bit marginal in relation to the building. Right now, it seems a bit far away. Perhaps it's a bit small; I'd like it to be full-screen cinema. In relation to the building, if it's possible, if there's room, the best thing would be to give this screen pride of place, because it would be the centre that establishes a dialogue with its surroundings. Cinemas used to be very special spaces. In Catalonia, we've always been too bashful; in Madrid, the cinemas on Gran Vía had great big signs and huge canopies.
The outside space, with the box office, is where people meet in the street, creating a space of relation. Of course, this is not a cinema; it's a film theatre, which makes it a cultural space, like a museum. The ticket desks are inside, not in the street, and this makes it more endogamic, so it is this screen that creates...
Mateo: I think all this bustle is great for the plaza. Because here it is closer to the street.
Guerín: That's very important; it's like the opposite of the basement. The basement is for the film buffs. It's good to create a space to remind us that the cinema was a great popular art in the 20th century, which established this relation with society and the neighbourhood—the local cinema. Even if it doesn't serve this function, the white screen is great as an architectural motif, because it can host absolutely any film. So, yes: this rectangle is very important. I personally would like the rectangle to be big. And perhaps I'd include a portrayal of the screen, with a small black frame or something like that, to make it more obvious when a film is not being screened...
Did the client ask for the façade to be used as an outdoor space for screening?
Mateo: No, that's something we came up with.

Guerín: Do you control the light? What sort of lighting will there be at night? Remember that cinema-goers rarely see the light of day.
Mateo: Of course, the lighting is fundamental.
The offices will be on the top floor. There'll be an inner courtyard, and all the machinery, like the air-conditioning, will be housed there, too. So the building won't have machinery on the roof; it'll be inside so that it doesn't change the volume or upset the neighbours. This courtyard will also provide light for the library. The skylight will draw overhead lighting into the centre of the library. It is a very large space.
Light is really magical. We are used to working with harder things, like walls, but light defines a space without using matter.
Guerín: Light is the soul of the stage. In the past, cinemas even had special lighting to ritualize the film as an event; the lights would go down, and there were still curtains, the last trace of archaeology. The idea was to make it like the theatre, even using something that film never needs, such as curtains...
Although it's something that's not up to you, I think it would be a good idea to suggest that the remains that were found on site, the ones that held up building work, be housed here. In the same way that the screen creates a link with the neighbourhood, it is important for these remains, these vestiges of the neighbourhood's earlier past, to be made visible.

One thing that architecture and interesting film have in common is shadow. It might be an idea to cast a shadow on this outdoor screen—as a reference to antiquity, caves, Plato's allegory of the cave, shadows. The cinema started out as shadow play in some cases. I'm particularly sensitive to this; I have lots of white walls at home because I have trees, and I much prefer to watch the shadows of the trees than the television. These marvellous shadows that change with the seasons are cast beautifully on walls. I even changed the layout of the library because I really liked the way the shadows of the trees formed part of it, with huge shadows cast by the leaves.
Mateo: That's very nice. Recently we did a project with a Japanese landscape designer, Miyagi, who had created a garden using shadow and light. He had to redesign or change the garden 24 times a year, every two weeks, to adapt it to the environmental conditions of the climate, light and temperature. It was a very enlightening process...
Guerín: No effort should be spared with light. The cinema is light. It's an amazing coincidence that the inventors of cinema were called Lumière, because the cinema is movement, light and shadow. Light is the soul of the cinema, and it is sometimes the soul of architecture, too.

Guerín: I'll be following the process with interest.
Mateo: We'll invite you to come on a site visit.
Guerín: Great. It's been a pleasure meeting you.

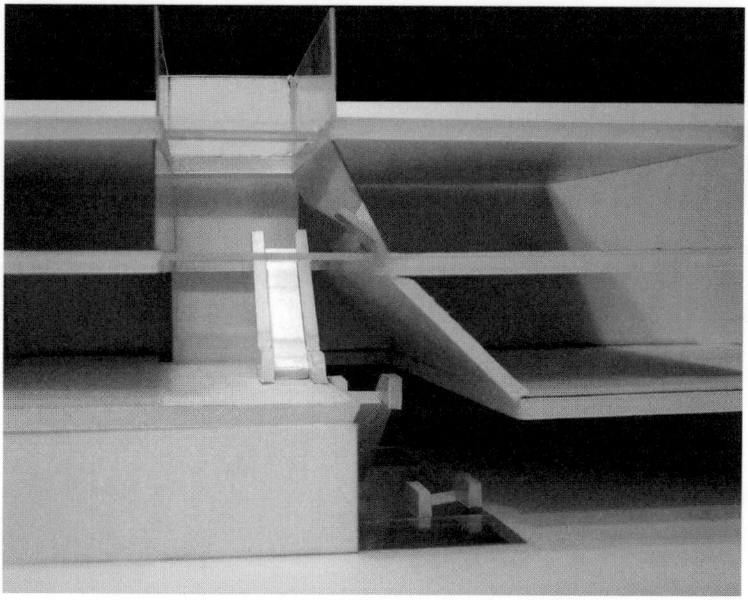

FILM THEATRE OF CATALONIA

First prize. Invited competition. 2004–2010

Location: El Raval, Barcelona. Surface area: 7,000 m²

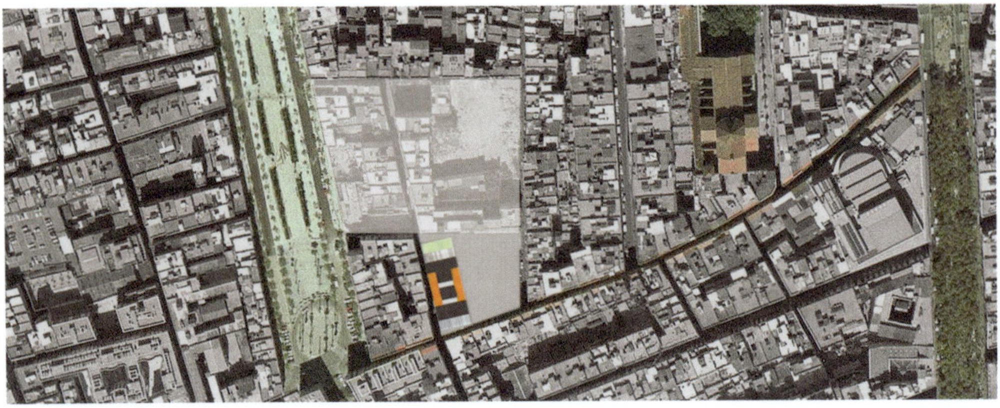

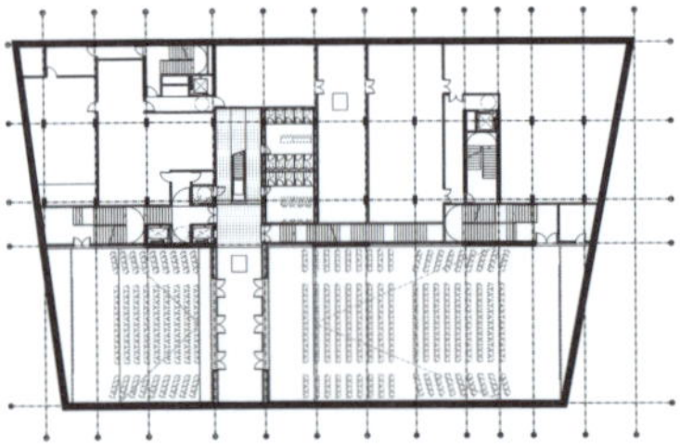

Second basement

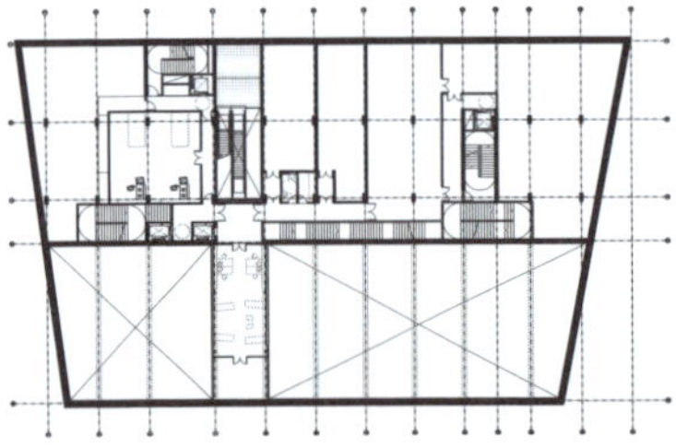

First basement

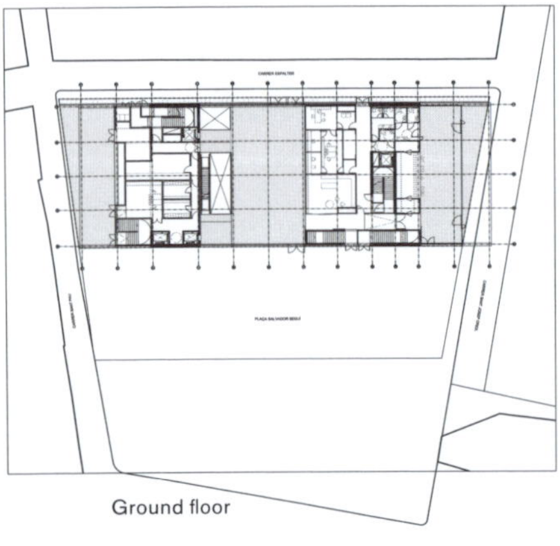

Ground floor

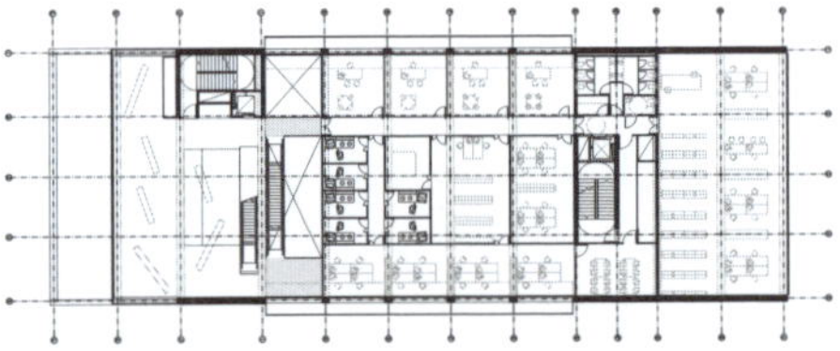

First floor

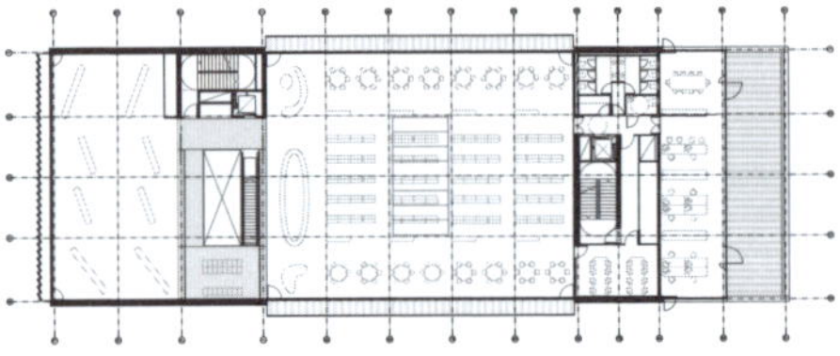

Second floor

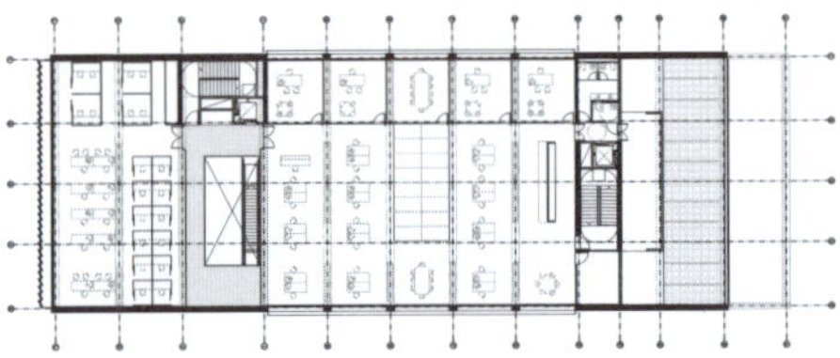

Third floor

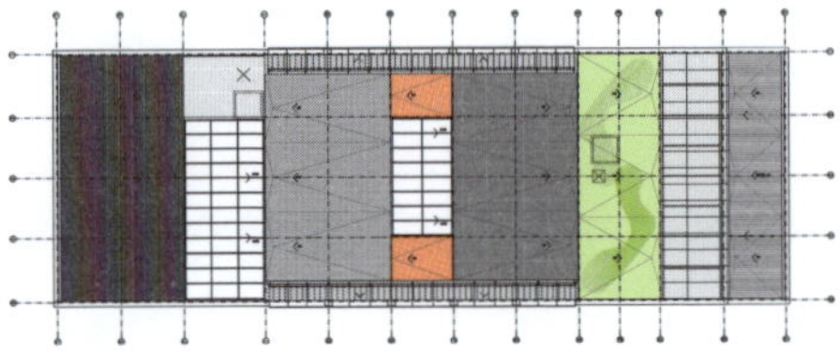

Roof

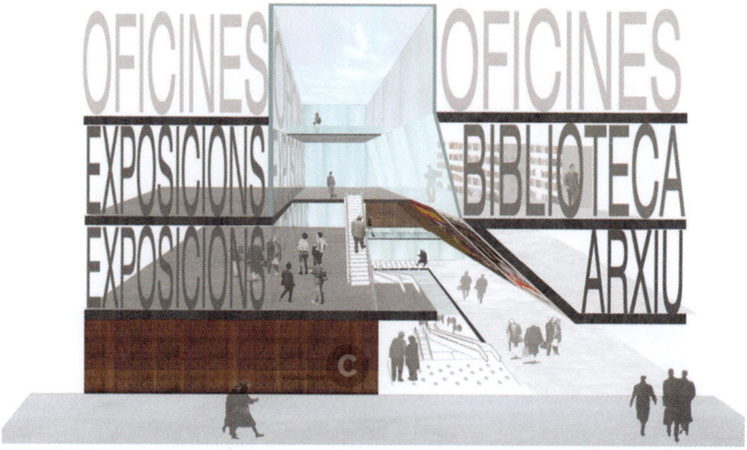
OFICINES
OFICINES
EXPOSICIONS
BIBLIOTECA
EXPOSICIONS
ARXIU

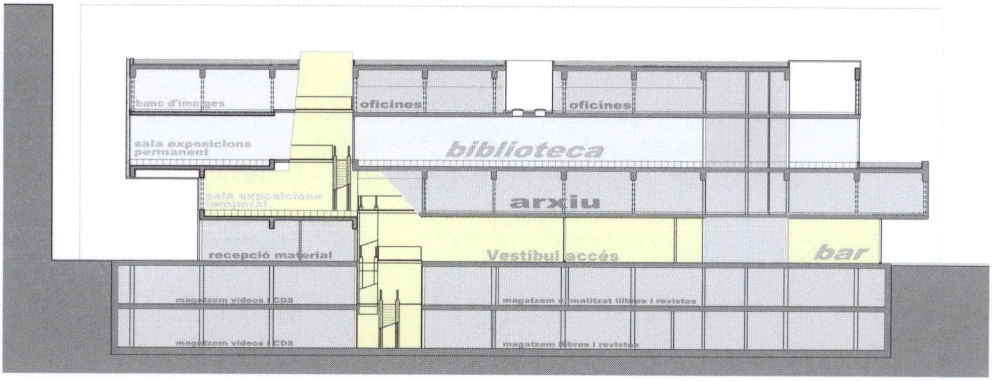
oficines
oficines
sala exposicions
permanent
biblioteca
arxiu
recepció material
Vestíbul accés
bar
magatzem videos i CDS
magatzem videos i CDS
magatzem llibres i revistes

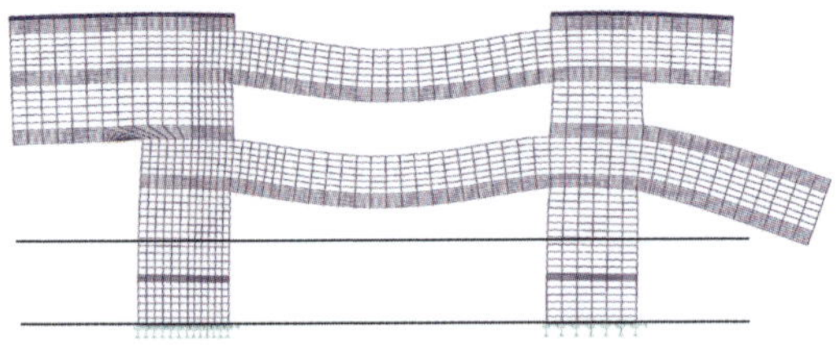

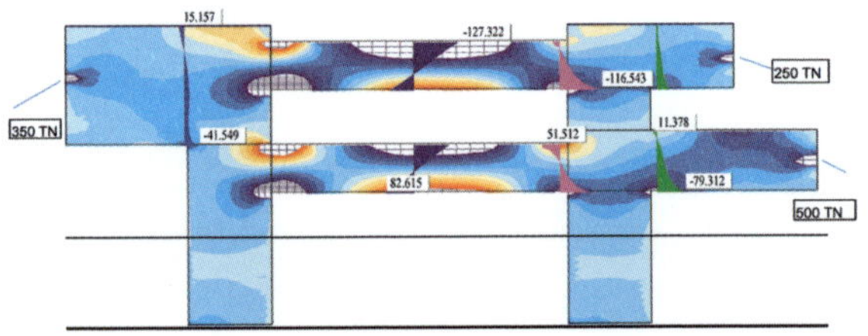

15.157
-127.322
-116.543
250 TN
350 TN
-41.549
51.512
11.378
82.615
-79.312
500 TN

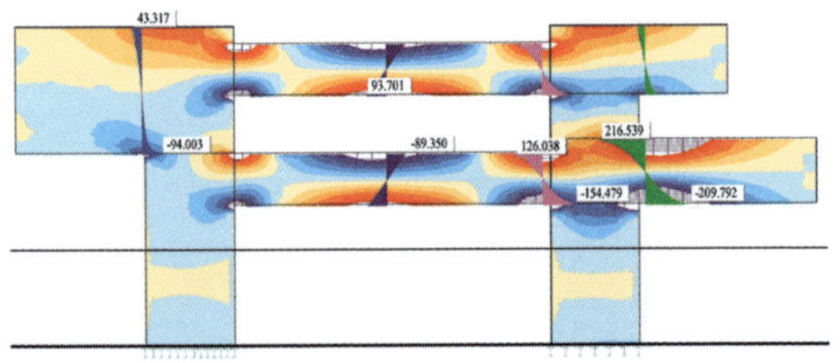

43.317
93.701
-94.003
-89.350
126.038
216.539
-154.479
-209.792

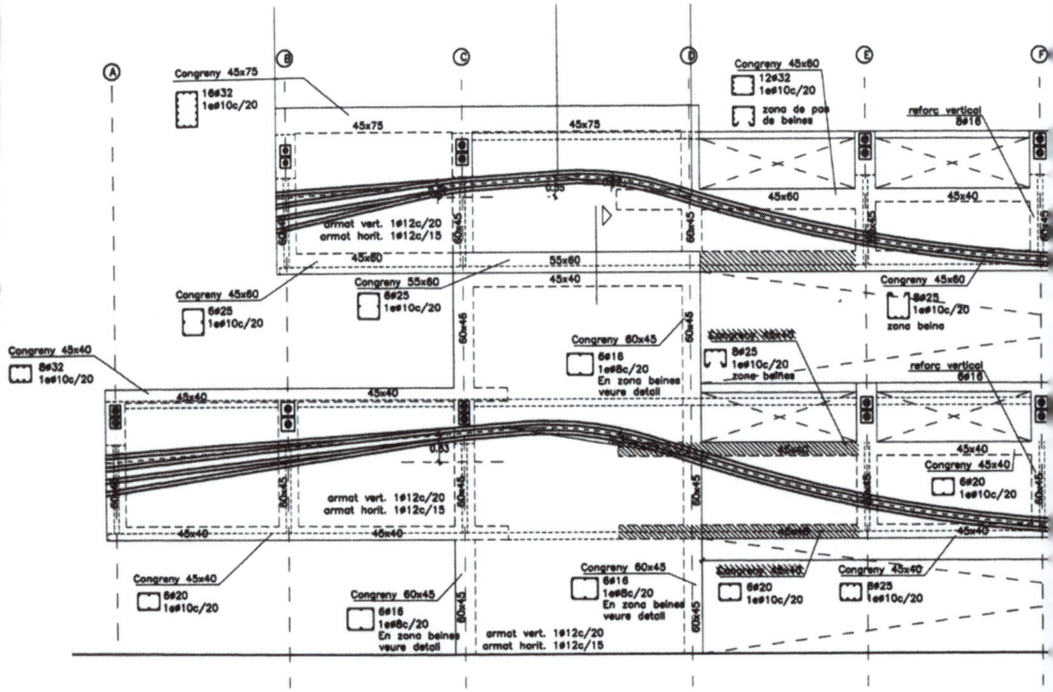

Congreny 45x75
16ø32
1eø10c/20
45x75
45x75
armat vert. 1ø12c/20
armat horit. 1ø12c/15
45x60
55x60
45x40
Congreny 45x60
6ø25
1eø10c/20
Congreny 55x60
6ø25
1eø10c/20
Congreny 45x60
12ø32
1eø10c/20
zona de pas de beines
reforc vertical
8ø16
Congreny 60x45
6ø16
1eø8c/20
En zona beines veure detall
Congreny 45x40
8ø32
1eø10c/20
45x40
Congreny 45x40
6ø20
1eø10c/20
Congreny 60x45
6ø16
1eø8c/20
En zona beines veure detall
armat vert. 1ø12c/20
armat horit. 1ø12c/15

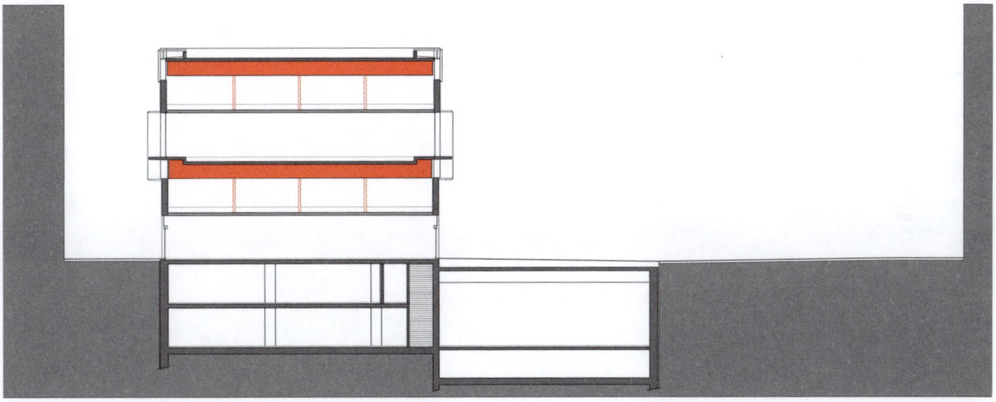

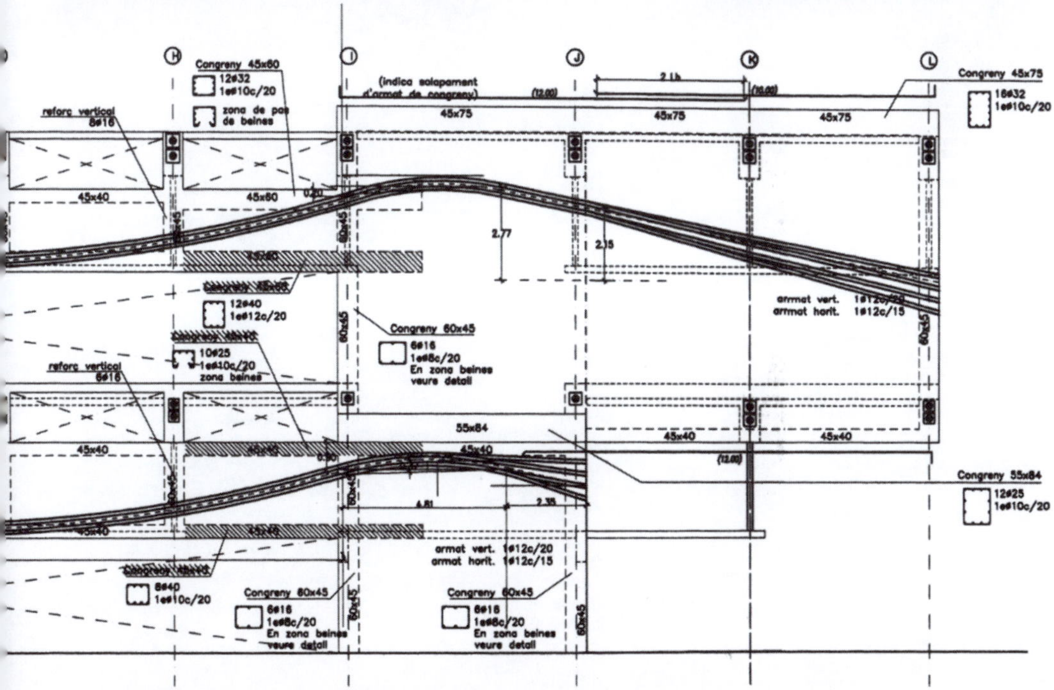
H
I
J
K
L
Congreny 45x60
12ø32
1eø10c/20
zona de pas de beines
reforç vertical
8ø16
(indica solapament d'armat de congreny)
(12.00)
2 Lb
(10.00)
Congreny 45x75
16ø32
1eø10c/20
45x75
45x75
45x75
45x40
45x60
2.77
2.35
armat vert. 1ø12c/20
armat horit. 1ø12c/15
12ø40
1eø12c/20
Congreny 60x45
6ø16
1eø8c/20
En zona beines
veure detall
10ø25
1eø10c/20
zona beines
reforç vertical
6ø16
55x84
45x40
45x40
45x40
(12.00)
Congreny 55x84
12ø25
1eø10c/20
4.81
2.35
armat vert. 1ø12c/20
armat horit. 1ø12c/15
8ø40
1eø10c/20
Congreny 60x45
6ø16
1eø8c/20
En zona beines
veure detall
Congreny 60x45
6ø16
1eø8c/20
En zona beines
veure detall
60x45

March 2007

June 2009

OFFICES AND LANDSCAPE

NEW HEADQUARTERS OF PGGM INSURANCE COMPANY

First prize. Invited competition. 2002–2010

Zeist/Holland. Location: Zeist. Surface area: 25,000 m² offices, 25,000 m² car park

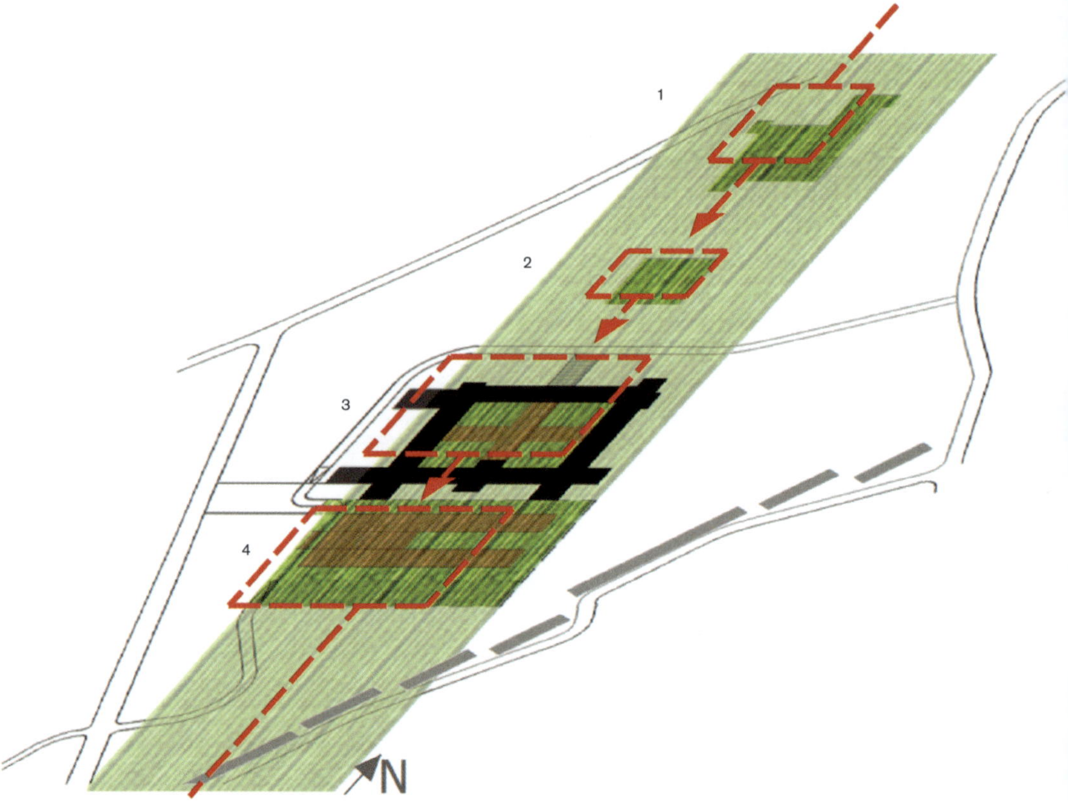

Contextual sequence

1 Monastery
2 Monks' graveyard
3 Existing cloister building, with proposed densification
4 New extension over the car park

With regard to the question in hand, two issues interested me:

- Firstly, how to expand the existing building, making it twice its current size, and
- Secondly, how to address the landscape.

At this very basic level, our ideas are to:

1. Work at the scale of the old building
2. Continue your suggestion: densifying the court (with an independent structural element) and constructing the new building in front of the existing one. We have come up with several possibilities and envisage a clear structural connection with the underground level.
3. Use greenery as a continuous layer, with the new buildings floating above it into the landscape.

We are interested in conceptual architecture but also in its precise materialization.

Josep Lluís Mateo

www.mateo-maparchitect.com JOSEP LLUÍS MATEO MAP ARQUITECTES BARCELONA SEPTEMBER 2002

Excerpt from the letter to the client on the occasion of the competition for the new headquarters of Dutch insurance company PGGM. Origin of the commission. Invited competition. First prize. The project, located in Zeist (Holland), is currently at the construction phase.

Existing situation and new landscape

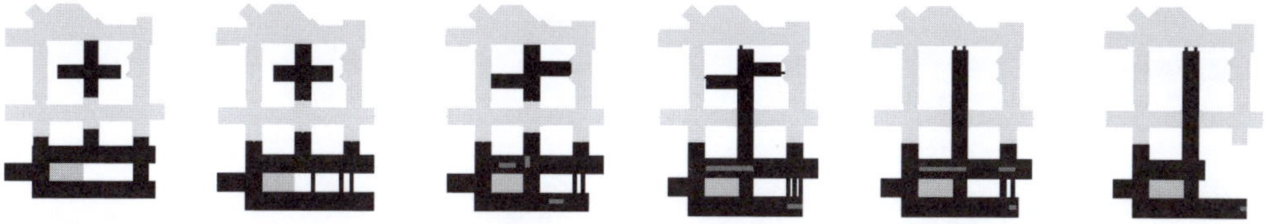

2002 2003 2003 2004 2007 2007

Evolution of the project, drawn as a Chinese ideogram

Initial model

Working in the woods

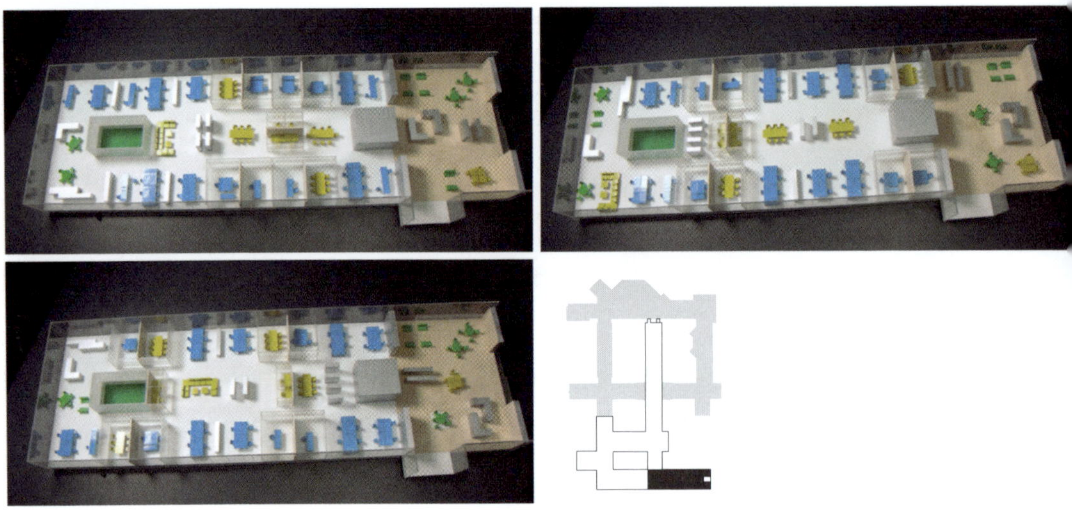

Variations in layout

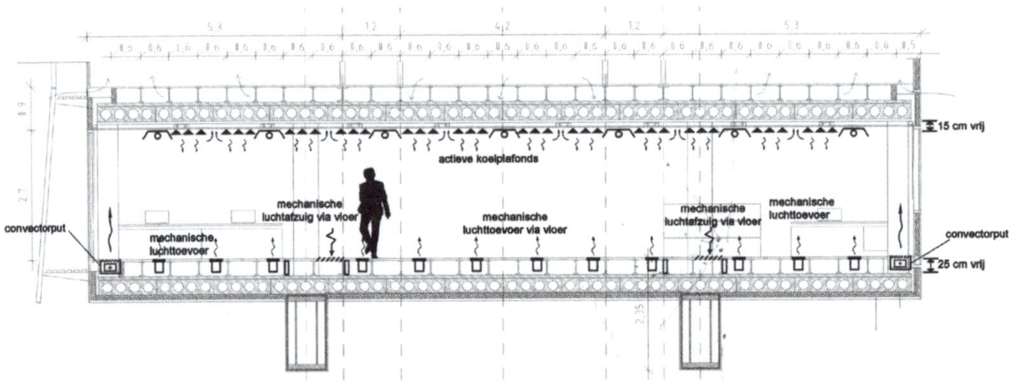

Generic office space. Floor and ceiling as energy supports

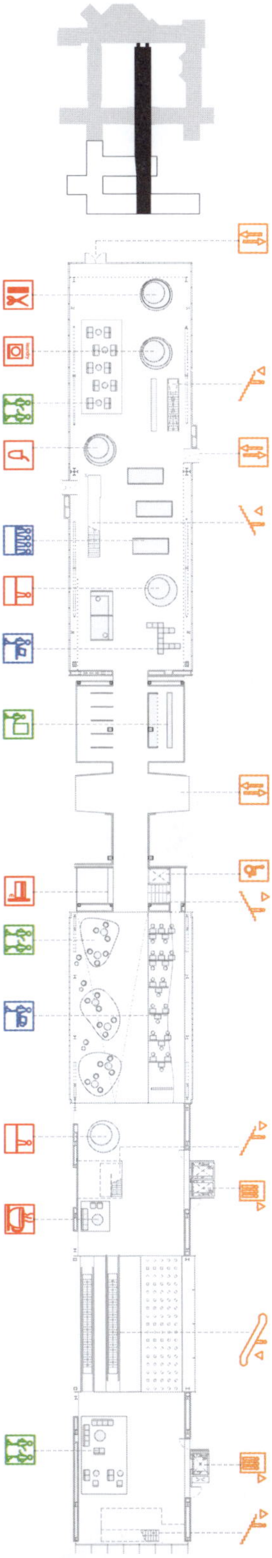

La Rambla (The boulevard) is a backbone of services and collective activities running right through the complex.

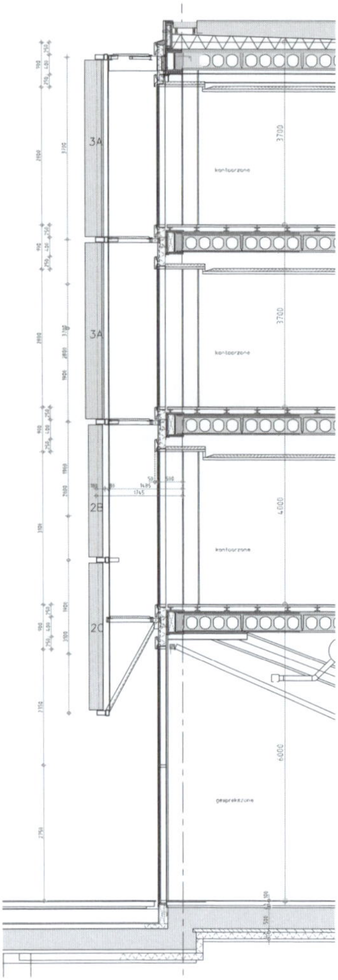

Slats 1

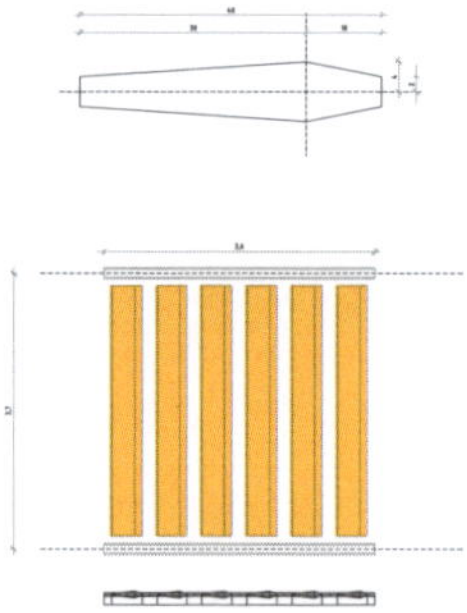

Slats 2

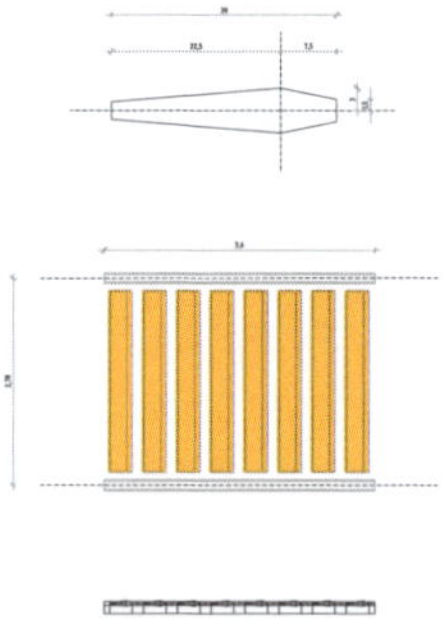

Slats 3

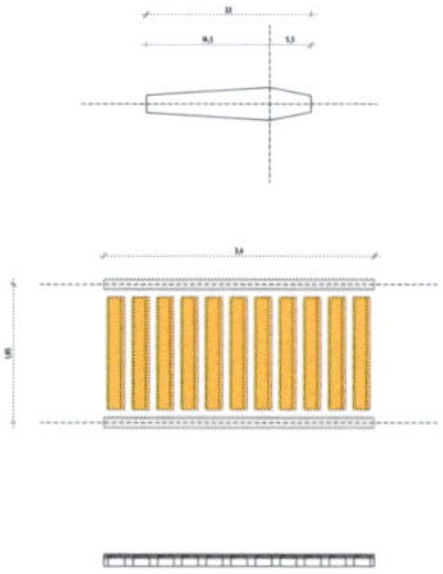

South façade overlooking the new main entrance. The slats of unvarnished copper-treated timber are motorized to follow the course of the sun.

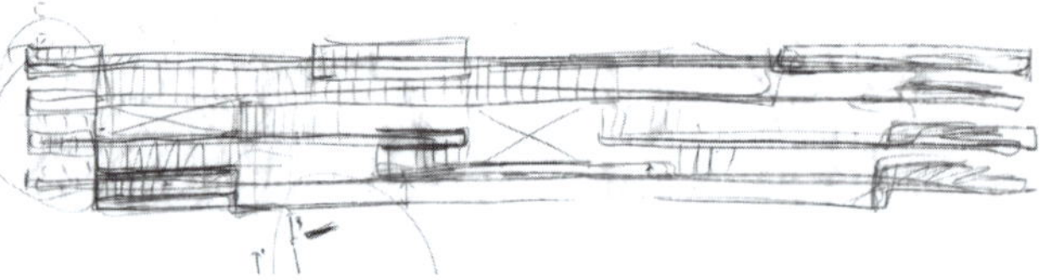

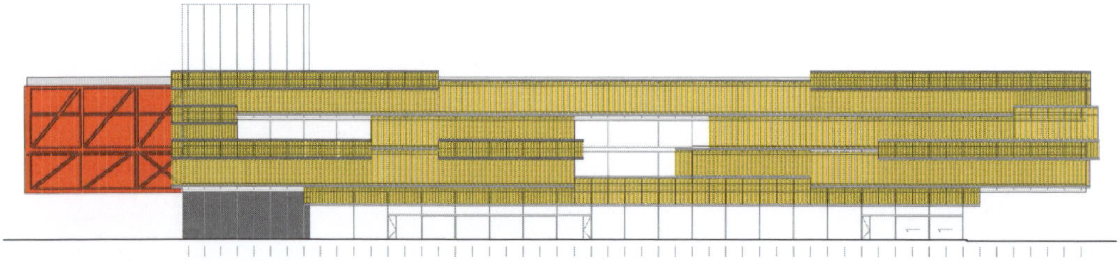

November 07

June 2009

HOW TO BUILD A CLOSED STREET BLOCK

using various disconnected pieces was the first question we had to address. The general composition, a score to be played by others, envisaged empty spaces between blocks, like great windows onto the empty green centre, and volumes with different responsibilities: one established the corner; another, taller and long, constituted the front that overlooks the large boulevard; others, pivoting on the corner, defined the sides.

We then had to build the great linear office block in keeping with our studies into the expressive capacity of concrete structural walls and the standard typological conditions of contemporary office space.

OFFICE BUILDING ON THE OLD RENAULT FACTORY LAND

First prize. Invited competition. 2006–2010

Paris/France. Location: Boulogne-Billancourt. Surface area: 15,500 m²

Floor plan (initial proposal)

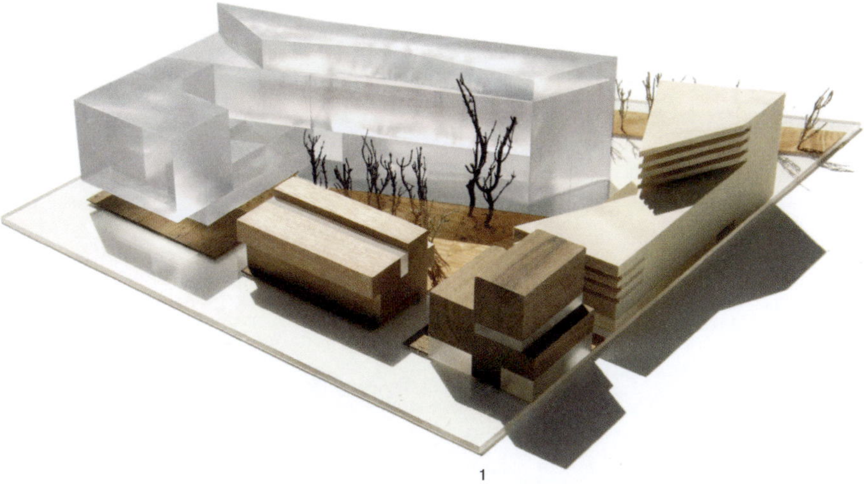

1

2

Independent volumes creating empty spaces-windows overlooking the inner space

1 First version of the street block

2 Second version of the street block. Commissioned building highlighted

3 Landscape inside the block (*d'ici et là*)

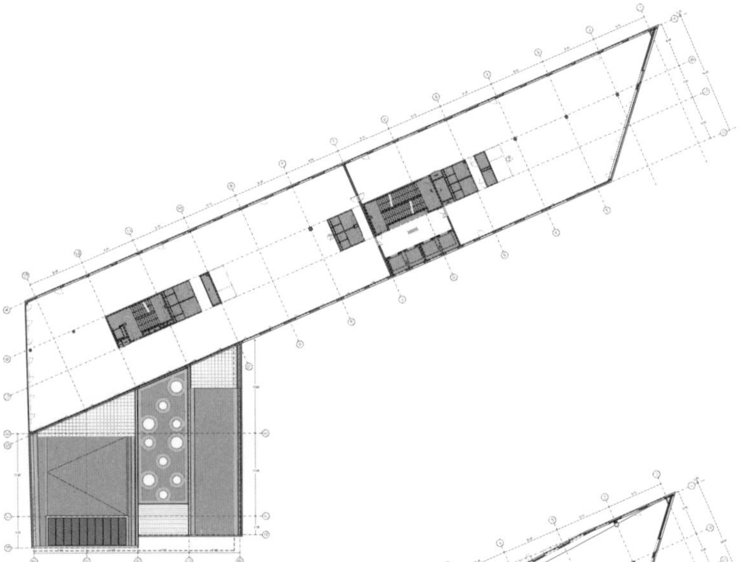

Standard floor

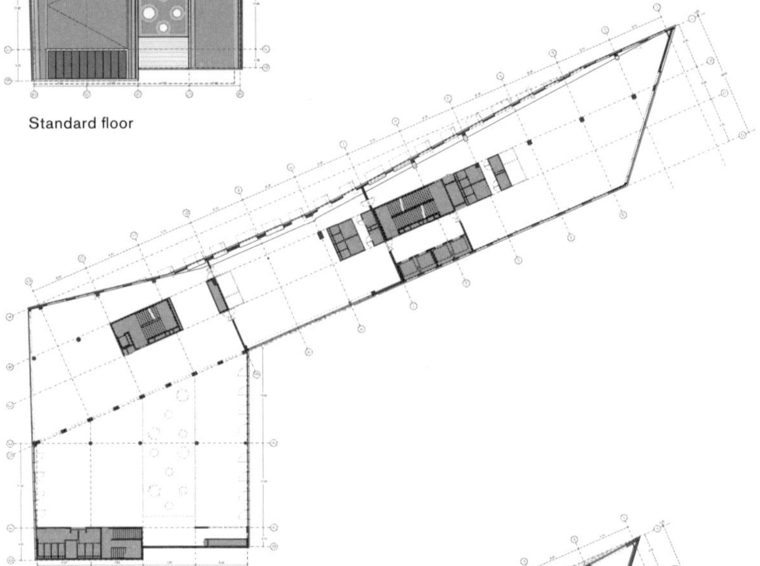

First floor

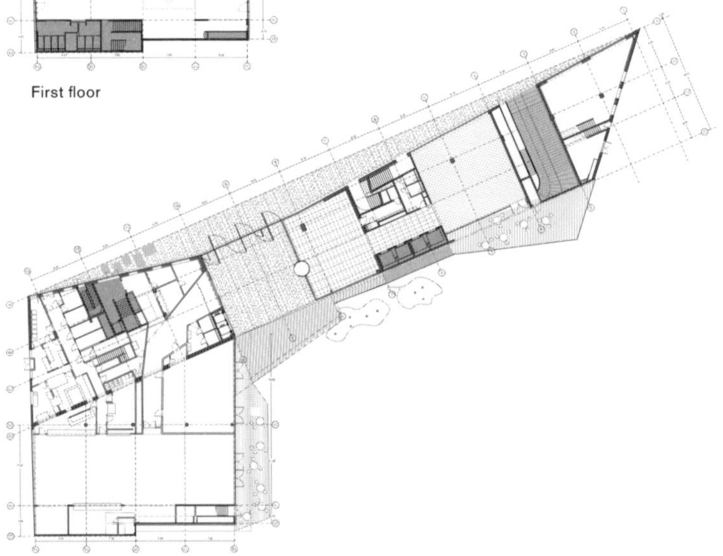

Ground floor 0 5 10 20 30

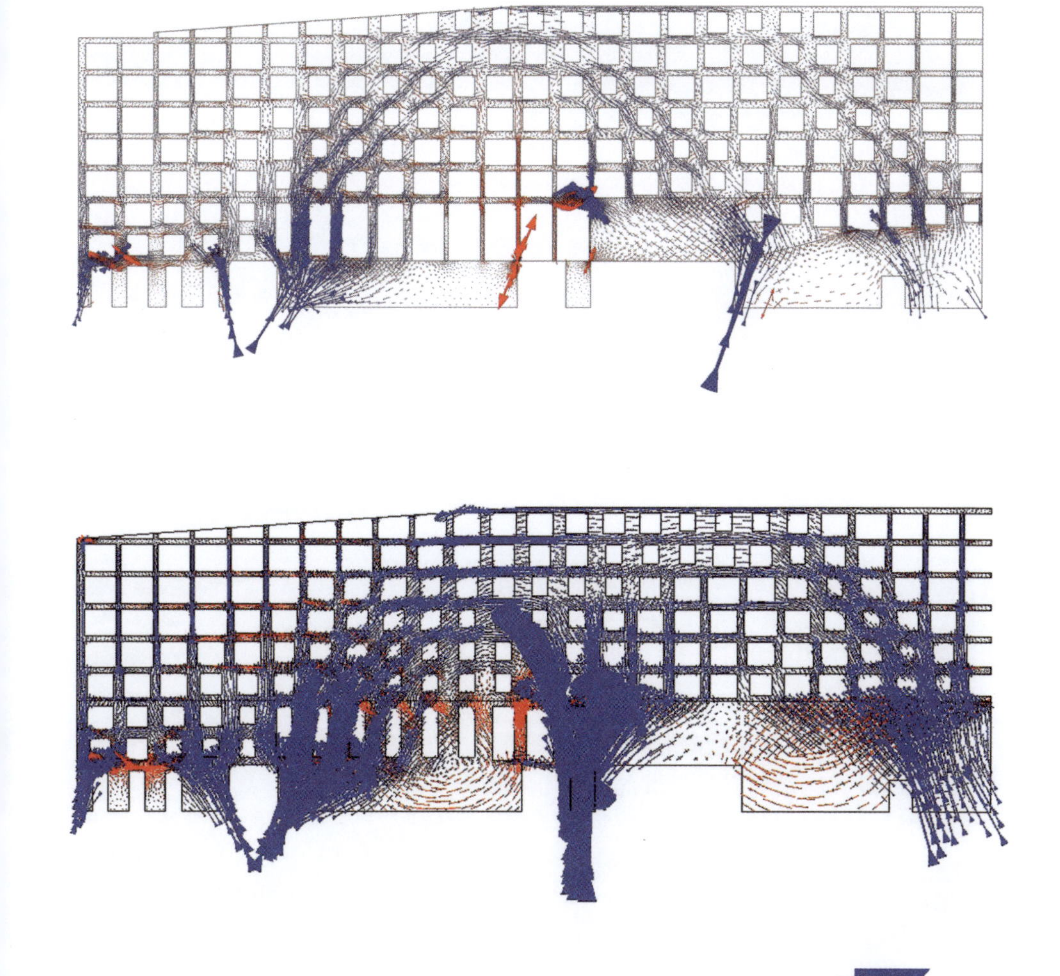

Diagrams of the structural façades

Various façade solutions: façade on Rue Émile Zola

July 2008

June 2009

Barcelona, May 2009

Zeist, March 2009

Paris, May 2009

FACTS

The art of finishing

Beginnings call for energy, joy, hope. They may seem like a game and sometimes they must be precisely that.

Endings, now without hope of **another** possibility, call for blind energy without despair.

Endings require us to control our melancholy. "When one has finished building one's house, one suddenly realizes that in the process one has learned something that one really needed to know in the worst way—before one began."[1]

The ending allows us, for a few seconds, to contemplate our work and, sometimes, to appreciate it.

The ending obliges us, immediately, to disappear, to abandon it to its fate—a necessary condition for our survival.

1 NIETZSCHE, Friedrich: *Beyond Good and Evil.* Penguin Classic, 1990.

OFFICE BUILDING

CORNELLÀ/BARCELONA

First prize. Invited competition. 2004–2007

Location: Cornellà. Surface area: 15,000 m² offices, 32,255 m² car park

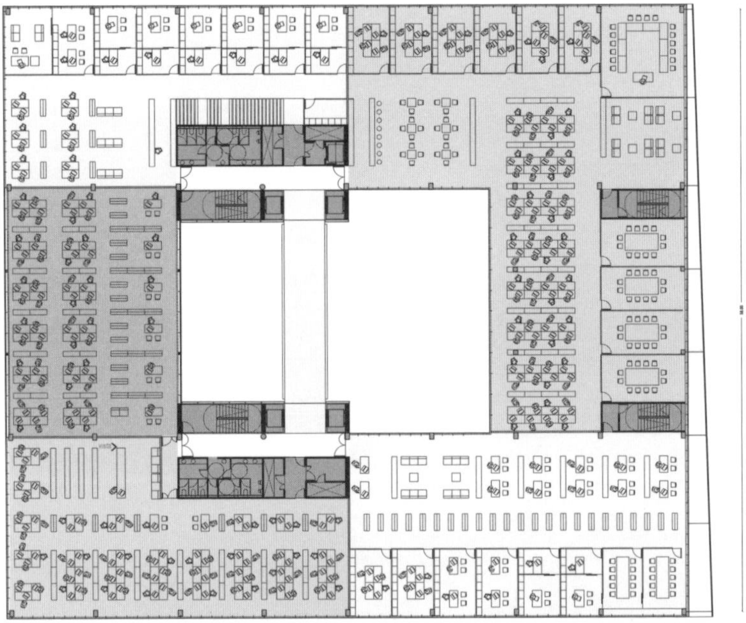

MEDITERRANEAN PATIO Emphasis on the climate, changing the role of the Northern European lobby (air conditioned) for that of the Mediterranean courtyard, protected from the sun and naturally ventilating, was a core argument in this project. Then the reaction to a setting of mainly picturesque buildings in the global corporate architecture strain explains the dryness and extreme hardness of the exterior.

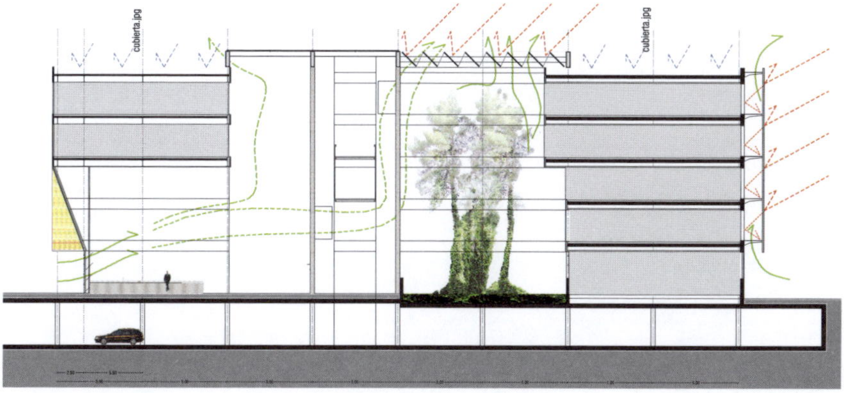

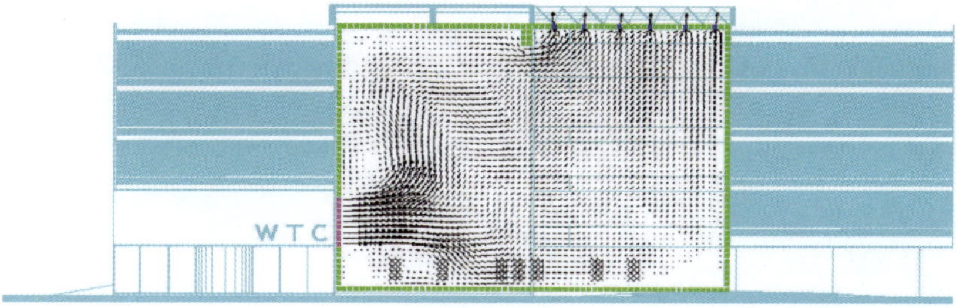

simulació de corrents d'aire
air flow simulation

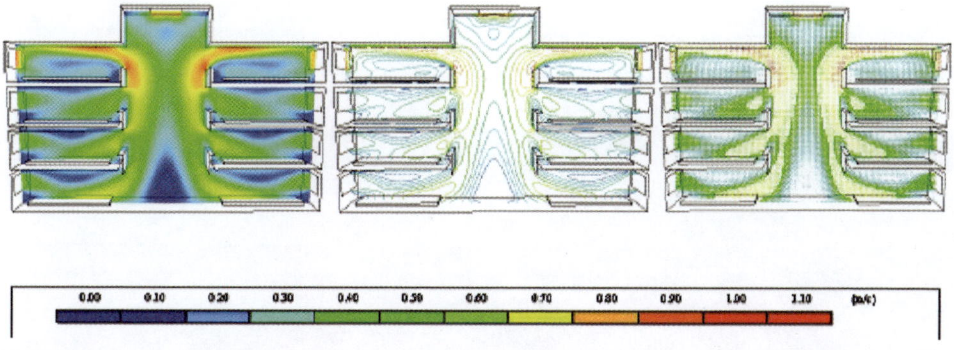

MAJOR
Col·leg
Major
Sant
Jordi

SANT JORDI STUDENTS' HALL OF RESIDENCE

BARCELONA

First prize. Invited competition. 2001–2006

Location: Avda. Sarrià. Surface area: 8,110 m²

COL·LEGI MAJOR SANT JORDI

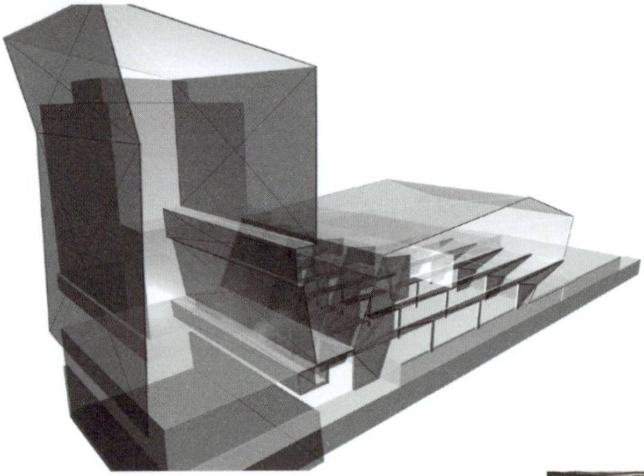

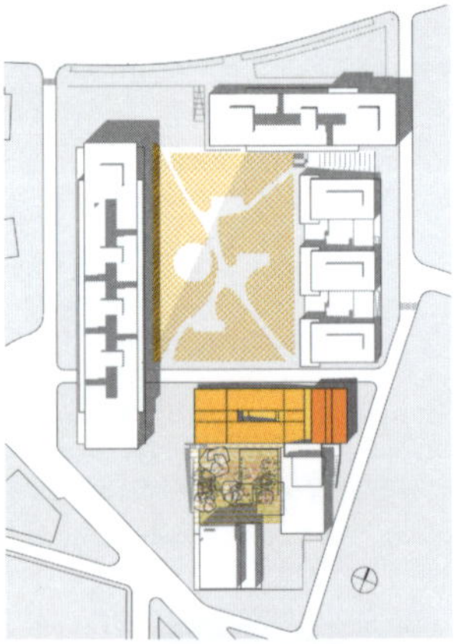

CONTEXT AND MATERIALITY We designed the final piece in a residential campus. A tall element continues the existing line of construction and a low-rise volume divides the public space in two. The project obeys the existing logics, at the same time seeking to stand out as a special element with a voice of its own to give this rather monotonous place a change and an injection of new life in keeping with its use by young people, students. The low-rise block is lightweight and translucent with a colouristic treatment. It is positioned in the middle of empty space, rejecting the idea of forming a wall that would create a drastic division. The taller building is a continuous snaking strip with a fold that constitutes the roof of the low-rise volume.

STONES An old house in the country, partially in ruins, clinging to the mountainside. The existing stone retaining wall is all that remains to organize the space and represent the force of the old in a place that is totally transformed. The stony masses are lightened by the use of gypsum board (and *vice versa*).

REHABILITATION OF MAS EL VILAR

2006–2008

Location: Sant Joan les Fonts/Girona. Surface area: 500 m²

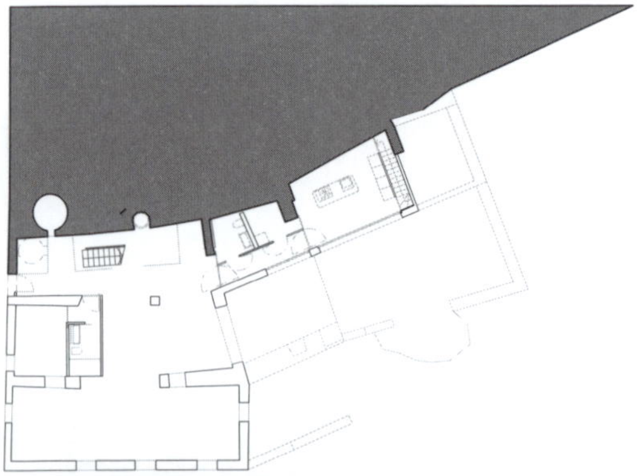

Stan Allen

Stan Allen is an architect working in New York and Dean of the School of Architecture at Princeton University. He has taught at Harvard, Columbia and Princeton, and his architectural firm SAA/ Stan Allen Architect has produced buildings and urban projects in the United States, South America and Asia. Responding to the complexity of the modern city in creative ways, Stan Allen has developed an extensive catalogue of innovative design strategies, in particular looking at field theory, landscape architecture and ecology as models to revitalize the practices of urban design. In 2007, he received a Progressive Architecture Award for Taichung Gateway Park and, in 2008, he received a Faith and Form Award for the CCV Chapel and a Progressive Architecture Award for the Yan-Ping Waterfront in Taipei. His architectural work is published in *Points + Lines: Diagrams and Projects for the City*, and his essays in *Practice: Architecture, Technique and Representation.*

Dominique Boudet

Over the last 25 years, Dominique Boudet has been closely involved in the architecture scene in France. As editor-in-chief of *Le Moniteur* weekly construction magazine, he created L'Equerre d'Argent, one of France's most coveted architecture awards. Manager and editor-in-chief of *AMC* architecture magazine, he is a committed observer of the evolution of architecture in France and in Europe as a whole. In 2002, he set up the European Architects Forum to support the emergence of a new generation of architects. Since 2004, he has been a freelance critic, contributing to European magazines. He also works in consultancy, helping private and public clients, mainly cities, to develop coherent architectural strategies. He is currently researching new urban strategies in Europe and is preparing an exhibition about the works of a young Belgian architecture firm.

Vicente Guallart

Vicente Guallart (Valencia, 1963) is the director of Guallart Architects, a practice set up in Barcelona in 1993 to develop architecture and urban design projects. He is currently working on a wide range of projects in Spain, Taiwan, Iran and Norway: social housing, eco-neighbourhoods, cultural projects, and parks and buildings for tourism. Since 2001, he has directed the Institut d'Arquitectura Avançada de Catalunya, working on research into eco-cities, self-sufficient buildings and digital manufacture. Vicente Guallart is the author of the book *Geologics. Geography, Bits and Architecture*, and co-author of numerous publications.

José Luis Guerín

José Luis Guerín (Barcelona, 1960) is a film director and lecturer in Cinematography at Pompeu Fabra University in Barcelona. His first full-length film, made in 1983, was *Los motivos de Berta*, which was awarded the Sant Jordi Film Prize for the Best Spanish Film. In 2001, he was awarded the National Film Prize and filmed the documentary *En construcción* (Work in Progress) about the demolition of the Raval district in Barcelona, which served as a reference for Josep Lluís Mateo's project for the new Film Theatre of Catalonia. This film received the Goya Prize for the Best Documentary and the Jury's Special Mention at San Sebastian Film Festival, as well as the prizes of the International Federation of Film Critics (FIPRESCI) and the Círculo de Escritores Cinematográficos. In 2003, the Architects' Institute of the Basque Country and Navarre awarded Guerín its Titanio Prize in recognition of his full-length film *En construcción*. In September 2007, Guerín released *En la ciudad de Sylvia* (In the City of Sylvia).

Marta Poch

Marta Poch qualified as an architect at the ETSAM (Madrid School of Architecture) and focuses particularly on the field of publishing. She has collaborated with Josep Lluís Mateo since 2002 as head of the Publications Department, coordinating the following books, among others: *Josep Lluís Mateo. Opere e Progetti*, Electa (Milan, 2007) *Josep Lluís Mateo. Proyectos, Obras, Escritos*, Ediciones Polígrafa (Barcelona, 2005). *CCIB. Josep Lluís Mateo. MAP Architects*, ACTAR (Barcelona, 2004). *2G. Josep Lluís Mateo, obra reciente*, Gustavo Gili (Barcelona, 2003) She has her own practice where her work centres on promoting works of architecture and photography. She collaborated in the architecture project that won first prize in Europan 8, held in Göteborg, Sweden.

Carlos Manuel Reis de Figueiredo

Carlos Manuel Reis de Figueiredo qualified as an architect at the School of Fine Arts in Porto and has been practising since 1982. A particular area of concern in his many projects is urban renewal. He has been responsible for the revitalization of various historic villages in Portugal, the General Rehabilitation Plan for the Historic Centre of Castelo Branco, which generated the rehabilitation of the city' central area (Polis Castelo Branco), and the design of various public buildings in collaboration with Josep Lluís Mateo. He is currently completing work on a museological and expository space about the discovery of Brazil in Belmonte, the birthplace of Pedro Álvares Cabral. He is a lecturer at the Coimbra School of Art, where he teaches Projects V.

Jordi Teixidor

Jordi Teixidor is a painter. He was born in 1941 in Valencia and studied at the San Carlos School of Art in the same city. From 1979 to 1981, he lived in New York, where he took part in the exhibition "New Images from Spain" at the Guggenheim Museum and was involved in the P.S.1 programme, before moving to Madrid. In 1997, the IVAM (Instituto Valenciano de Arte Moderno) hosted an outstanding retrospective of his work. His work has shown at major galleries both in Spain and internationally, and his painting is a rigorous, discerning constant in abstraction, a trend in which he is one of Spain's most representative artists. He is currently a full member of the San Fernando Royal Art Academy.

mateoarquitectura studio

Barcelona-born (1949) **Josep Lluís Mateo** graduated in Architecture in 1974 from the ETSAB and gained his doctorate (*cum laude*) at the Polytechnic University of Catalonia in 1994. He has been Professor of the Architecture and Projects Department at the Swiss Federal Polytechnic in Zurich (ETH-Z) since 2002. He has also taught at various universities and lectured at foremost international academic institutions. He was Visiting Scholar at the Jean P. Getty Center in Los Angeles from 1991 to 1992. In 2009, Josep Lluís Mateo was named President of the Board of Directors of the Barcelona Institute of Architecture.

Recent work (selection):
The head office of the Bundesbank in Chemnitz, Germany (First Prize, international competition) 1996-2004
Barcelona International Convention Centre (First Prize, international public competition) 2000-2004
Banc Sabadell: Standard office (First Prize, invited competition) 2002; renovation of the bank's historical head office in Plaça Sant Roc, Sabadell, 2004-2006; interventions in the bank's Torre Diagonal in Barcelona, 2009
Sant Jordi Hall of Residence (First Prize, national public competition) 2001-2006
Largo da Devesa park in Castelo Branco, Portugal. 2000-2007
Office building for WTC Almeda Park in Cornellà, Barcelona (First Prize, invited competition) 2004-2007
Film Theatre of Catalonia in Barcelona (First Prize, national invited competition) 2005-2010
Extension of the office building for PGGM insurance company in Zeist, Holland (First Prize, international invited competition) 2002-2010
The office building in Boulogne-Billancourt, Paris (First Prize, invited competition) 2006-2010

Exhibitions (selection):
2009 Galería Ras, Barcelona. "Occasional City"
2006 MoMA, New York. "Spain: On Site". Group exhibition. Housing block in Valencia
2004 Arkitekturgalerie Aedes, Berlin. "Organic versus Inorganic"
1998 Col·legi d'Arquitectes de Catalunya, Barcelona

Awards (selection):
- Top International Purpose-Built Venue 2008, *C&IT magazine*. First Prize for the best international building to host events, conventions and congresses. CCIB-Barcelona International Convention Centre
- 2008 Archizinc Award, First Prize. Sant Jordi Students' Hall of Residence, Barcelona
- Contract World 2006, Second Prize. AC Hotel
- 15th Award of Grupo Dragados de Arquitectura and the CEOE Foundation 2001, First Prize for the apartment building in Borneo Docks, Amsterdam (Holland)
- 1991 Santander Spanish Architecture Biennial. The remodelling of the old town of Ullastret was considered one of the best Spanish architecture projects of the '80s.
- 1991 ITALSTAT Award for Young European Architects

Publications:
Monographs (Selection):
Josep Lluís Mateo, Opere e progetti, Electa (Milan, 2007)
Josep Lluís Mateo, Works, Projects and Writings, Ediciones Polígrafa (Barcelona, 2005)
Josep Lluís Mateo, *World Architecture*, Tsinghua University (Beijing, 2003)
Josep Lluís Mateo, Recent Work, 2G, Gustavo Gili (Barcelona, 2003)
Mateo Atlas, Actar, Ministerio de Fomento and COAC (Barcelona, 1998)
Josep Lluís Mateo. Ideen und Bauten, Birkhäuser Verlag (Basel, 1995)
Josep Lluís Mateo, "Catálogos de Arquitectura Contemporánea" collection, Gustavo Gili (Barcelona, 1992)

Books (writings):
Textos instrumentales. GG (Barcelona, 2007)
Bauen und Denken. Quart (Lucerne, 2002)

Books published by the Chair of Professor Mateo (ETH-Zurich):
Iconoclastia. News from a Post-Iconic World. Architectural Papers IV. ETH-Actar, 2009
Global Housing Projects. ETH-Actar, 2008
Natural Metaphor. Architectural Papers III. ETH - Actar, 2007
Big Scale. Grossform. Architectural Papers II. ETH - Gustavo Gili, 2006
Object Laboratory. Architectural Papers I. ETH – Gustavo Gili, 2005

Further information at www.mateo-arquitectura.com

Team:

Josep Lluís Mateo, Principal
Marta Cervelló, Associate architect

Project leaders:
Anna Llimona
Vicky Daroca
Laurent Badelot
Till von Mackensen

Xavier Monclús, Technical architect

Design team:
Marc Pi
Marta Gonzalez
Pati Baztán
Marco Podesta
Victor Molina
Tian Ren

Enric Sanitjas, Model-maker

Publications Department:
Marta Poch, Architect and editor
Anabel Linares, Journalist

Administration:
Isabel Riambau
Salvador Torroja

IT consultancy:
Rabindranath Andújar, CAD Manager
Eupalinos – Cooperativa d'Arquitectes Jordi Capell

Graphic design:
Tere Guix

Our thanks to everyone who has been involved in the projects and competitions carried out by the practice since it was set up, for their participation and enthusiasm.
It is impossible to name everyone who has been involved, but we would like to acknowledge some of the people who have worked with the practice since 2005:

María Alejandre, Inés Alomar, Santi Amaro, Cristina Anglès, Pascal Babey, Marianne Baumgartner, Pedro Bento, Rafael Berengena, Boris Bezan, Andrea Brechtbühl, Maria Eugenia Canel, Iris Cantante, José Carcasés, Sara Cardoso, Alicia Casals, Mariana Castro, José Luis Cisneros, Johan Cordonnier, Lucas Echeveste, Gonzalo Elizarraras, Aitor Estévez, Co Govers, Mathias Grabbe, Ismael Heras, Mathias Hoffman, Arnoud Hulpia, François Jaubert, Markus Lauber, Enriqueta Llabrés, Victòria Llinares, José David Martínez, María Matamala, Sota Matsura, Miriam Moreno, Francisco Mouzo, Daniel Moyano, Sabrina Németh, Yolanda Olmo, Jordi Pagès, María Pancorbo, Elisabeth Parra, Adriana Porta, Joana Ramalhete, Emma Reyes, Oliver Rodríguez, Sergi Romero, Cristina Sánchez, Benjamin Scharf, Mariona Segura, Evelyn Steiner, Ana Valente, Paula Vallejo, Mathijs Van Daal, Meritxell Vilar, Bianca Von Geyr.

PROPOSAL FOR THE REDEVELOPMENT OF THE PROMENADE DES ANGLAIS (P 7)

Invited competition
1995. Nice/France

Location: Promenade des Anglais
Surface area: 40,000 m². Client: Nice City Council
Team: Silvia Alvarez, Lluís Cantallops, Jordi Espriu, Queralt Garriga, Amalia Granolleras, David Koch, Joan Magi, Florence Raveau, Anna Zubelzu
External collaborators: Landscape architect: Manuel Colominas. Engineer: José María Jofre

EMBANKMENT OF THE RIVER ADOUR (P 10)

First prize. Invited competition
2006. Bayonne/France

Location: Area around Henri Grenet bridge. Surface area: 70,000 m²
Client: KAUFMAN&BROAD-Malardeau
Team: Competition leader: Vicky Daroca
Competition team: Sabrina Németh, Pedro Duarte, Johan Cordonnier, Pascal Babey, Enriqueta Llabrés.
Project leader: Laurent Baudelot
External collaborators: Structural engineering: BOMA
Engineering: BETURE CEREC. Quality control: NORISKO
Landscaping: Michel DESVIGNE. Adviser: Dominique Boudet
Economist: IFFEC

MARIA JOAO PIRES ARTS CENTRE AND LARGO DA DEVESA CITY SQUARE (P 28)

First prize. Invited competition
2000–2007: Largo da Devesa square
2000: Castelo Branco/Portugal

Location: Largo da Devesa city square. Surface area: 6 ha
With Carlos Reis Figuereido. Arquitectos da Beira Lda.
Client: Camara de Castelo Branco, POLIS Programme
Team: Project leader: Maria Viñé. Executive manager: Victoria Llinares. Team project: Rafael Berengena, Victoria Llinares, Martin di Renzo, Nazario Branca, Daniel Guerra, Nidia Kurtin
External collaborators: Structural engineering: Manuel Arguijo
Landscaping: Manuel Colominas. Acoustic engineer: Higini Arau.
Lighting project: Ove Arup and Partners, Ing. Pinguinha
Clima Assessment: INDUS. Ing. Madeira da Silva, Engenharia Lda. Economic control: Aumedes-Embuena

REHABILITATION OF SKANDERBEG SQUARE (P 46)

Third prize. Invited competition
2008. Tirana/Albania

Location: Skanderbeg Square
Built: 2,500 m², Urbanization: 45,000 m²
Client: Municipality of Tirana
Team: Competition leader: Vicky Daroca
Team: Víctor Molina, Marc Pi, Till Von Mackensen, Johan Cordonnier, Matthias Hoffmann, Joana Ramalhete
External collaborators: Structural engineering: BOMA
Installations engineering: JG. Landscaping: Manel Colominas
Artistic advisors: Gloria Moure. Traffic advisors: DOYMO

REMODELLING OF THE MAIN ENTRANCE TO THE BANC SABADELL DIAGONAL TOWER (P 64)

2006–2007. Barcelona

Location: Avinguda Diagonal with Carrer Balmes
Client: Banc Sabadell
Team: Leader and executive manager: Ismael Heras
Team: Mariana Castro, Sara Cardoso, Miriam Moreno
External collaborators: Structural engineering: BOMA

REMODELLING OF BANC SABADELL HEAD OFFICE (P 68)

2004–2006. Barcelona

Location: Plaça Sant Roc, Sabadell
Surface area: 6,000 m². Client: Banc Sabadell
Team: Project leader: Victoria Llinares. Executive manager: Ismael Heras. Team: Xavier Monclús, Enriqueta Llabrès, Gonzalo Elizarraras, Jaume Prat, Ivan Llach, Oscar Espinosa
External collaborators: Structural engineering: OMA
Installations engineering: Grupo JG
Budget: Aumedes-Embuena, Xavier Aumedes

HOUSING BLOCK (P 88)

2005– . Valencia

Location: Plot R01, La Torre sector, Valencia
Surface area: 12,000 m²
Client: Instituto Valenciano de la Vivienda, S.A. (IVVSA)
Team: Project leader: Yolanda Olmo
Team: Ismael Heras, Paula Vallejo, Adriana Porta
External collaborators: Structural engineering: Agustí Obiol-BOMA

MAAG AREAL SKYSCRAPER (P 104)

Invited competition. 2004
Zurich/Switzerland

Location: Zurich. Surface area: 63,077 m². Client: Maag Areal
Team: Competition leader: Virginia Daroca, Yolanda Olmo, Maria Viñé. Team: Adriana Porta, Bianca von Geyr, Daniel Blum, Víctor López-Rioboo, Oscar Ko
External collaborators: General advisor: OVE ARUP, Herr Rüdiger Lutz. Structural advisors: BOMA BCN, Agustí Obiol; Zurich, Prof. Dr. Otto Künzle. Services engineering: Basler&Hofmann, Ingenieure und Planer AG

NEW CAMP NOU STADIUM (P 112)

Invited competition
2007. Barcelona

Location: Arístides Maillol, Les Corts
Surface area: 130,000 m². Client: Futbol Club Barcelona
Team: Competition leader: Virginia Daroca.
Documentation: Marta Poch, Víctor Molina, Maria Matamala
Historical documentation: Ignacio López Alonso.
Scale model: Enric Sanitjas, Adrià Maynés-Labrys, S.L.
Audiovisual: Frame a Frame audiovisuals, S.L.
Team: Till von Mackensen, Iris Cantante, Ismael Heras, Sara Cardoso, Marc Pi, Laurent Baudelot, Johan Cordonnier, Joana Ramalhete, Matthias Grabe
External collaborators: Structural engineering: Agustí Obiol (BOMA, S.L.). Engineering and Security: Grup JG Ingenieros Consultores de Proyectos, S.A

KUNSTHAUS MUSEUM EXTENSION (P 124)

Invited competition. 2008. Zurich

Location: Kunsthaus. Zurich/Switzerland
Surface area: 15,000 m^2. Client: Zürcher Kunstgesellschaft, Stiftung Zürcher Kunsthaus and the City of Zurich with the Amt für Hochbauten Stadt Zürich [Office for Construction, City of Zurich]
Team: Competition leader: Till von Mackensen. Team: Matthias Hoffman, Andrea Brechtbül, Pascal Babey, Anna Llimona, Ismael Heras, Víctor Molina
External collaborators: Structural engineering: BOMA Installations engineering: JG. Landscaping: Placemedia Acoustics: Higini Arau. Lighting: Artec Luminotecnia Artistic advisor: Glòria Moure

FILM THEATRE OF CATALONIA (P 134)

First Prize. Invited competition 2004–2010. Barcelona

Location: El Raval, Barcelona. Surface area: 7,000 m^2
Team: Project leader: Jordi Pagès, Anna Llimona
Executive manager : Vicky Daroca
Project team: Xavier Monclús, Enriqueta Llabrés, Benjamín Scharf. Competition team: Marc Camallonga, Enriqueta Llabrés, Adriana Porta, Lucas Echeveste, Ismael Heras, Daniel Blüm
External collaborators: Structural engineering: OMA, Agustí Obiol. Installations engineering: Grupo JG
Budget: Aumedes-Embuena – Xavier Aumedes
Fire protection: Francesc Labastida

NEW HEADQUARTERS OF PGGM INSURANCE COMPANY (P 152)

First prize. Invited competition 2002–2010. Zeist/Holland

Location: Zeist.
Surface area: 25,000 m^2 offices, 25,000 m^2 car park
Competition with: Luca Gazzaniga
Team: Competition leader: Markus Lauber. Project leader: Co Govers, Mathijs van Daal, Markus Lauber. Competition team: Hector Mendoza, Pilar Ferreres, Marta Poch, Michel Roschach. Project team: Till von Mackensen, Xavier Monclús, Jordi Pagès, Victoria Llinares, Héctor Mendoza, Boris Bezan, Nataly Wierenga, Enriqueta Llabrés, Arnoud Hulpia, Cristina Fernández, Emile van Vugt, Johan Cordonnier

OFFICE BUILDING ON THE OLD RENAULT FACTORY LAND (P 162)

First prize. Invited competition 2006–2010. Paris/France

Location: Boulogne-Billancourt. Surface area: 15,500 m^2
Client: VINCI Immobilier d'entreprise/NEXITY Entreprises
Competition with: Agence SAISON-MENU architecture: Isabelle Menu, Annabelle Vérecque.
Team: Competition leader: Vicky Daroca. Project leader: Laurent Baudelot (Detail design, executive project). Team: Johan Cordonnier, Pedro Duarte, Sabrina Németh, Till Von Mackensen, Pascal Babey, François Jaubert, Marianne Baumgartner
External collaborators: Structural and installations engineering: SNC Lavalin. Quality control: VERITAS. Fire protection: EURO Coord. Energy control: COTEBA Environnement

OFFICE BUILDING (P 174)

First prize. Invited competition 2004–2007. Cornellà/Barcelona

Location: Cornellà.
Surface area: 15,000 m^2 offices, 32,255 m^2 car park
Team: Competition leaders: Vicky Daroca, Victoria Llinares. Competition team: Adriana Porta, Bianca von Geyr, Jaume Prat, Daniel Blüm
Architectural project leader: Yolanda Olmo, Anna Llimona
Project team: Paula Vallejo, Maria Canel
External collaborators: Structural concept: BOMA, Agustí Obiol. Technical installations: Grupo JG
Fire protection: Francesc Labastida
Landscaping: Manuel Colominas

SANT JORDI STUDENTS' HALL OF RESIDENCE (P 188)

First prize. Invited competition 2001–2006. Barcelona

Location: Avinguda Sarrià, Barcelona. Surface area: 8,110 m^2
Client: Universitat de Barcelona. Project: 2001
Team: Project leader: Markus Lauber (preliminary design), Anna Llimona (detail design), Jordi Pagès (executive manager)
Project team: Rafael Berengena, Héctor Mendoza, Cristina Fernández, Arnoud Hulpia, Alvaro Homar, Elsa Bertrán. Competition team: Héctor Mendoza, Nacho López, Virginia Daroca, Elsa Bertrán
External collaborators: Structural engineering: Manuel Arguijo. Installations engineering: Francesc Labastida
Artistic consultancy: Silvia Hornig

REHABILITATION OF MAS EL VILAR (P 202)

2006–2008. Olot

Location: Sant Joan les Fonts/Girona. Surface area: 500 m^2
With: Dot Arquitectes (Bet Capdeferro, Ramon Bosch).
Client: Mª Dolors Dilmé
MAP collaborator: Xavier Monclús

RECONSTRUCTION OF THE HISTORIC CENTRE OF SIBENIK (P 219)

First prize. International open competition 2009. Sibenik/Croatia

Location: Draga. Surface area A: 40,000 m^2
Surface area B, urban design: 2 ha
With: Krunoslav Ivanisin
Team: Competition leader: Till von Mackensen
Team: Marc Pi, Marta González Cubillo, Victor Molina, Marco Podesta, Sota Matsura
External collaborators: Installations: Grupo JG

CREDITS

Published by ACTAR
info@actar.com
www.actar.com

Editor
Josep Lluís Mateo
Marta Poch

Editorial coordination
Marta Poch
Anabel Linares

Texts
Stan Allen
Dominique Boudet
Vicente Guallart
José Luis Guerín
Josep Lluís Mateo
Marta Poch
Carlos Reis de Figuereido
Jordi Teixidor

Graphic design
Reinhard Steger, Actar Pro
Anna Wenter, Actar Pro

Photographs
Xavier Ribas
Ferran Mateo
Pedro Pegenaute
Beat Marugg

Translation and proofreading
Elaine Fradley

Printing
Ingoprint S.A.

Digital production
Oriol Rigat, Actar Pro

ISBN: 978-84-96954-97-7
DL B-9494-09

Printed and bound in the European Union

Distribution
ACTAR D
Roca i Batlle 2
08023 Barcelona
Tel. +34 93 417 4993
Fax. +34 93 418 6707
office@actar-d.com
www.actar-d.com

Distribution USA
ACTAR D US Office
158 Lafayette Street, 5th Floor
New York, NY 10013
Tel. +1 212 966 2207
Fax. +1 212 966 2214
officeusa@actar-d.com

BONUS TRACK

DRAGA-SIBENIK

ON THE LIMITS OF THE PLACE

The empty space between the islands draws an axis that continues on dry land, on Draga. The location is marked by a geological structure that produces empty and full spaces. We choose to respect, continue and construct it. We build on the limits of the place. Volumes to either side consolidate the topography. At the far end, following the axis, our buildings construct the street, forming a gateway to the whole. The centre is empty public space that receives various treatments, moving gradually from the greater urbanness of the plaza beside the street to the increased presence of nature where the project meets the sea. (This proposal should be seen as a topographical, volumetric strategy for construction on this site. The materiality of the architecture is an open issue.)

RECONSTRUCTION OF THE HISTORICAL CENTRE OF SIBENIK

First prize. International open competition. 2009

Sibenik/Croatia. Location: Draga. Surface area A: 40,000 m². Surface area B, urban design: 2 ha

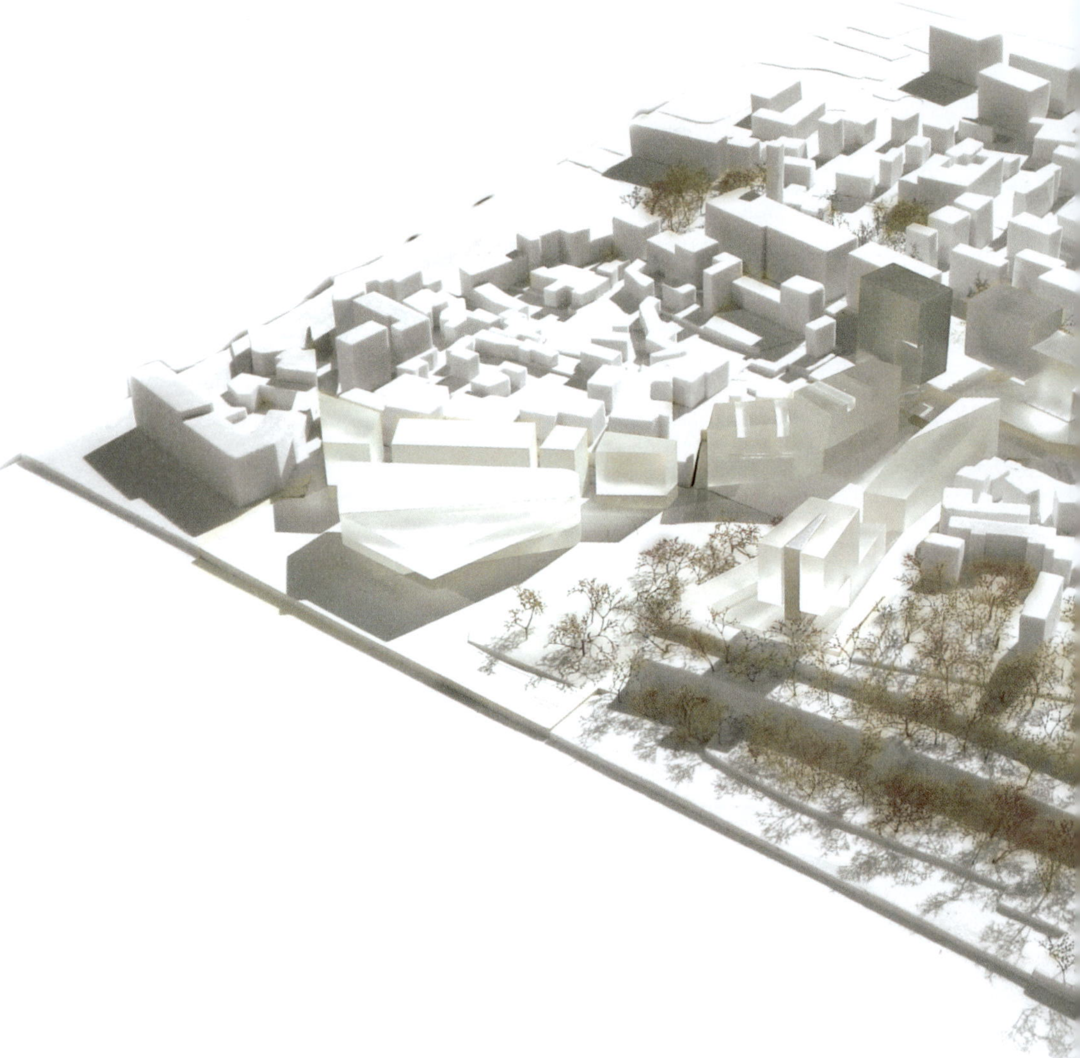

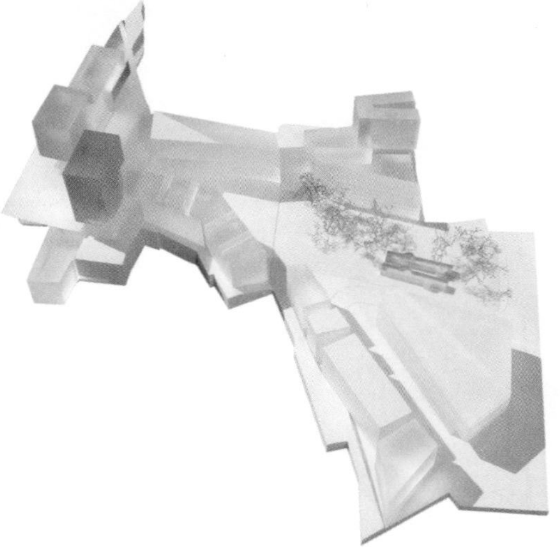

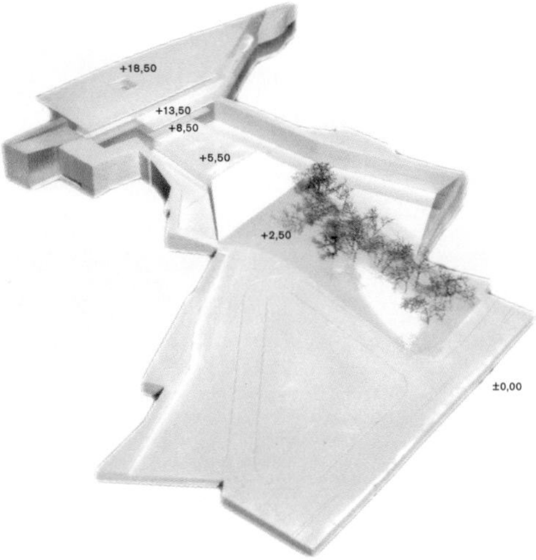
+18,50
+13,50
+8,50
+5,50
+2,50
±0,00

ANTE STARCEVICA

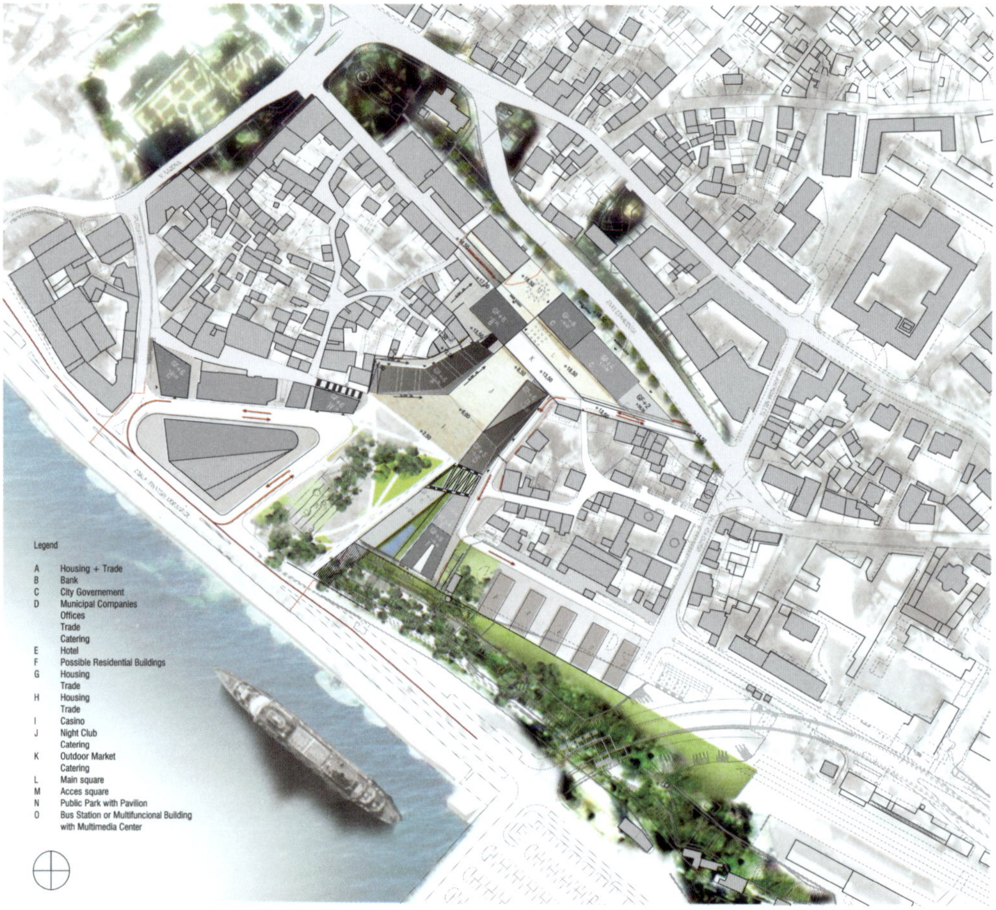
Legend
A Housing + Trade
B Bank
C City Governement
D Municipal Companies
Offices
Trade
Catering
E Hotel
F Possible Residential Buildings
G Housing
Trade
H Housing
Trade
I Casino
J Night Club
Catering
K Outdoor Market
Catering
L Main square
M Acces square
N Public Park with Pavilion
O Bus Station or Multifuncional Building
with Multimedia Center

HOTEL
BANK

BANK
BUSINESS
HOUSING
CASINO
NIGHT CLUB

BANK

Reconnaissance of the sea, the islands and the coastline

Fechner und die Folgen außerhalb der Naturwissenschaften

Gert Mattenklott

Gustav Theodor Fechner. Ein deutsches Gelehrtenleben

Gustav Theodor Fechner – Physiker, Philosoph, mystischer Theologe und Autor von Satiren – sperrt sich als Persönlichkeit gegen die Vereinnahmung durch akademische Disziplinen. Wer er »eigentlich« war, steht immer erneut zur Disposition. Der Versuch, sein Porträt zu entwerfen, hält sich nicht an die Chronologie und deren vermeintliche Logik seiner Lebensdaten. Die organisierende Frage heißt vielmehr – jenseits seiner Teilhabe an diesen oder jenen Aktivitäten, wie sie sich aus seiner akademischen Profession oder anderen Nötigungen seines Alltags ergaben –: »what made him tick?« Es gibt einen oberflächlichen Konsens darüber, dass die bedeutenden Personen zugunsten der Erfüllungsgehilfen von Funktionen mit dem Ende des 19. Jahrhunderts ausgespielt haben. Fechner lässt daran zweifeln.

In der Geschichte deutschen Gelehrtenlebens steht Fechner ohne Beispiel. Er war ohne Vorgänger, wie er denn auch ohne Nachfolger blieb, weil sein Werk und Leben – wie durch Konstruktion ermittelt – zum Kreuzungspunkt der entscheidenden wissenschaftlichen Tendenzen seines Zeitalters wurden, somit aber auch zum Schauplatz einer epochalen Krise. Traditionsfähig mochte sein, was aus ihr hervorging. Wundt und Preyer waren in diesem Sinne Fechners Schüler. Erben seiner Krise waren sie nicht, waren sie zu ihrem Glück nicht.

Schulgründer pflegen mit der Kraft zur scharfen Profilierung ihrer Erkenntnisse genügend Robustheit zu verbinden, um sich auch einseitig geltend zu machen. Fechner, so entschieden er über diese Kraft zur Gestaltung seiner theoretischen Absichten verfügte, war zur Einseitigkeit ebenso unfähig wie unwillig. So scheut er denn zwar nicht das suggestive Bild und die polemische Zuspitzung; so ist er wortmächtig genug, um den Bildern seiner inneren Anschauung den Nimbus von Visionen zu geben; und bleibt doch immer genügend er selbst, um sich und sein wissenschaftliches Pathos sogleich auch in der Gegenrichtung zu entwerfen. Nie hat er den hohen Wert positiven Wissens bestritten, und seine Experimente zur *Psychophysik* sind grundlegend für sein Fach geworden, ohne dass er ihre geistigen Voraussetzungen des Respekts vor naturwissenschaftlichem Empirismus je revidiert hätte, als er seine Philosophie der *Allbeseelung* des natürlichen und kosmischen Lebens vortrug.

Dass experimentelle Physik und Naturfrömmigkeit sich nicht widerspruchsfrei zusammenfügen können, ist ihm nicht verborgen geblieben. Doch ehe er sich zur Liquidation des einen oder anderen entschlossen hätte, riskierte er mit seiner Lehre des *Parallelismus* von Geist und Materie lieber wissenschaftlich Kopf und Kragen und geistlich den Frieden mit der religiösen Orthodoxie. Einseitigkeit hat Fechner nicht aus liberaler Überzeugung verwehrt, aus Entscheidungsschwäche oder Opportunismus. Es steckte vielmehr eine mächtige Energie dahinter, deren Richtung mit nicht zu irritierender Hartnäckigkeit aufs Ganze ging, buchstäblich und jederzeit und überall. Hier ist der Knoten von Leben und Werk dieses Mannes geschürzt.

Inwiefern? Der *Wissenschaftsbegriff* der Neuzeit ist zum einen pluralistisch. Es gibt keine *prima scientia*, sondern ein Ensemble von Wissenschaften, deren keine von ihnen das Ganze verwaltet, sie sind alle vielmehr Zuträger, weniger zu einem Begriff des Ganzen, als zum begreifenden Denken. – Zum anderen: Der Begriff des wissenschaftlichen Weltbildes ist ein Euphemismus, indem er verschweigt, dass die Zersetzung von Anschaulichkeit durch Abstraktionen seine Voraussetzung ist. Als Bild kann das Ganze nicht mehr entworfen werden. Die wesentlich abstrakte Form naturwissenschaftlicher Erkenntnisse ist dafür *ein* Grund; ein anderer die Verzeitlichung der Erkenntnis zum Prozess. Schließlich sind Partialisierung und Spezialisierung der Wissenschaften ein dritter Grund, weshalb das Ganze sich den Wissenschaften entzieht; ja weshalb diese sich ihrem modernen Begriff nach geradezu erst konstituieren, durch eine Enthaltsamkeit, für die das Ganze aus dem theologisch-philosophischen Rang einer ursprünglichen Einheit in den erkenntnistheoretischen einer regulativen Idee rückt.

So setzt sich mit der Herausbildung des neuzeitlichen *Wissenschaftsbegriffs* und seiner Verzeitlichung im Denken der späten Aufklärung auch eine sehr spezifisch neuzeitliche Regelung der Kompetenz für das Ganze durch: Neben den Religionen werden die Künste zu dessen Statthaltern. Ihnen ist konzediert, was den Wissenschaften aus Methode versagt sein muss: Bilder des Ganzen zu entwerfen, sei es als intensive Totalität des lyrischen Augenblicks, sei es als extensive der progressiven Universalpoesie der modernen Form des Epos, im Roman. »Dichters Aufgabe« heißt ein Gedicht, in dem Fechner diesen Sachverhalt zur Sprache bringt:

Der Bergmann hat aus tiefem Schacht
Wohl Gold und Demant dir gebracht;
Der Fischer aus des Meeres Gründen
Die schönsten Fische, die zu finden.
Der Seher, von des Thurmes Höhn,
Zeigt dir, wie Mond und Sonne gehen;
Der Pflanzenkenner auf den Auen,
Wie sich die schönen Blumen bauen.
Daß Jeder recht sein Werk beschickt,
Drum hat man so die Welt zerpflückt;
Wie könnt' in solchem großen Garten
Ein Jeder aller Beete warten.
Doch was tief in der Erde Grund,
Was in des Meeres dunklem Schlund,
Was auf der Sternen weiten Bahnen,
Was auf der Wiesen grünen Planen
Zum Leben einet alles Sein,
Beim Einzelwerk fällt Keinem ein;
Drum mögt ihr wohl den Dichter preisen,
Der's Jedem zeigt in seinen Kreisen. (Dr. Mises 1841, 47)

Fechner hat sein Gedicht als »Dr. Mises« geschrieben. Satiren und poetische Phantasien, in denen er sich nicht genügte, so wie denn die zitierten Verse auch eher metrisierte und gereimte Gedanken sind. Mit seiner Nüchternheit, die eher aufs Finden aus war als aufs Erfinden, und einer Natur zu prosaisch zum Phantastischen, war er sich im Wege. An Jean Paul, dem er sich im *Universalismus* seiner Bestrebungen verbunden fühlte, schreibt er als Ergebnis einer Selbstreflexion, »dass ich eigentlich das harmloseste Geschöpf auf Gottes Erdboden bin, der ein tägliches Leben wie ein Uhrwerk führt, wenigstens im Äußeren, und im Inneren selbst vielleicht manchmal nicht recht weiß, was er will, es sei denn, was ich mir in der Tat bewusst bin, dass ich überall im Einzelnen gern ein Ganzes finden oder es dazu verarbeiten möchte, nur dass ich zu letzterem leider in der Kunst, die meine Neigung der Wissenschaft vorziehen würde, der inneren Bedingungen ermangele.«[1] Nicht recht zu wissen, was er will, ist aber nur scheinbar der Pubertätszustand eines Lebens am *Kreuzweg* von Wissenschaft und Kunst. In Wahrheit kann er es gar nicht genau wissen

[1] Brief vom 6. Oktober 1825; zitiert bei Kuntze 1892, 66. Vollständige Wiedergabe des Briefes Fechners an Jean Paul siehe Beitrag von Altmann, Brief 1, in diesem Band.

wollen, sonst müsste er sich entscheiden. Stattdessen ist aber die Krise in Permanenz die geistige Voraussetzung seiner individuellen Produktivität.

Ist die Phantasie der Virus seiner Wissenschaft, oder ist sie deren Engel? Fechner durfte sich diese Frage kaum stellen, entscheiden gewiss nicht, denn ihre Offenheit ist die Voraussetzung seiner intellektuellen Existenz. Phantasie ist die Macht, durch die sein Denken aufs Ganze gespannt ist, innerer Widerstand gegen das Phantastische der Grund, weshalb er sich ästhetische Erfüllung versagt. Diese Doppelrichtung ist eine Bedingung der Entstehung seines Werks. Man sollte sie fest ins Auge fassen und daraus nicht verlieren, wenn man die Abfolge beschreibt, in der die drei wesentlichen Phasen seines Oeuvres aufeinander bezogen sind: die des Lehrstuhlinhabers für Physik von 1834 bis 1839, der seinen akademischen Ruf durch ungewöhnlich präzise galvanische Experimente zur festen Etablierung des Ohm'schen Gesetzes begründet hatte, Forschungen, auf die er auch in späteren Veröffentlichungen immer wieder zurückkommen konnte; die zweite Phase dann, in der »Nanna oder über das Seelenleben der Pflanze« erscheint und »Zend-Avesta«, das »lebendige Wort« »über die Dinge des Himmels und des Jenseits«; das eine ein Versuch, »die Pflanzen in einer allgemein gottbeseelten Natur als eines individuellen Anteils dieser *Beseelung* wieder teilhaftig erscheinen zu lassen, und insbesondere ihren Verkehr mit dem Lichtgotte Baldur zu schildern oder, kürzer und einfacher, ihnen eine eigene Seele beizulegen, und ihren Verkehr mit dem Lichte psychisch auszulegen« (Fechner 1848, VIII), das andere ein Vorschlag zur »Vereinbarkeit des Christentums mit religiösen Naturansichten, die man ohne ihre Aufhebung im Christentum freilich heidnisch zu nennen haben würde ...« (Fechner 1901, 1, X); die dritte Phase endlich, in der er eine exakte Lehre von den Beziehungen zwischen *Leib und Seele* (Elemente der Psychophysik, 1860) nach dem Ideal der Mathematik entwerfen möchte, d.h. durch Messung der Intensität von Empfindungen und deren Definition auf einer Skala von Reizstärken.

Der Schein einer Entwicklungslogik in diesem Schema einer Periodisierung trügt. Es gibt keinen Entwicklungsfortschritt in Fechners Denken derart, dass er von einer strikt empirisch-experimentellen Auffassung ins Gegenteil *metaphysischer* Spekulationen verfallen sei, um dann bei synthetischen Versuchen anzukommen. In die Zeit seiner intensivsten galvanischen und optischen Forschungen fallen Veröffentlichungen über »Rückert« und »Heinrich Heine als Lyriker« (1835) und das »Büchlein vom Leben nach dem Tode« (1836). – In den Jahren, in denen seine gesammelten »Gedichte«, »Nanna« und »Zend-Avesta« erscheinen, publiziert er auch Aufsätze »Ueber die Verknüpfung der Faraday'schen Inductions-Erscheinungen mit den Ampère'schen elektro-dynamischen Erscheinungen« (1845) oder »Ueber die physikalische und philosophische Atomenlehre« (1855). Vollends synkretistisch zusammengesetzt erscheint sein Werk in der dritten Phase, indem es die Impulse sämtlicher Lebens- und Werkphasen zugleich wirksam erkennen lässt. – Unerwähnt sind in dieser summarischen Aufzählung noch zahlreiche kleinere Beiträge zur Physiologie der Sinneswahrnehmung und seine Begründung einer »Ästhetik von unten«, d.h. aus der Reiz-Physiologie, und mehrere Aufsätze zu Holbeins »Madonna« im Baseler Museum. – Fügt man dieser Konstellation noch seine gelegentlich im Leipziger Tageblatt gedruckten Äußerungen über Volkssouveränität, die Probleme der Veteranen, den Fahnenschmuck in Leipzig oder Ausstellungseröffnungen hinzu, so wird das Spektrum vollends unübersehbar.

Dafür werden aber die Konturen eines Gelehrtenlebens deutlich, in dem – aus Treue zur Vorstellung eines Ganzen – die Gläubigkeit des Christen sich mit Theologie nicht zufrieden geben konnte; die Empfindungs- und Gestaltungskraft eines Künstlers in ästhetischer Produktion keinen allein angemessenen Ausdruck fand; das Denken des Philosophen sich systematisch nicht runden konnte; die Forschungen eines Wissenschaftlers in einem oszillierenden Verhältnis zu Wissenschaftskritik stehen. Alle diese Züge aber sind nicht in einer Logik des Fortschreitens verbunden, sondern in der Ausprägung einer Grundspannung auf den verschiedensten Gebieten und in wechselnden Konstellationen.

Fechners Gelehrtenleben trägt eine unverwechselbar deutsche Prägung wohl darin, dass es seiner inneren Widersprüchlichkeit zum Trotz auf der Totalität einer vereinheitlichenden Auffassung besteht, deren eigentümlicher Status im Niemandsland zwischen Wissenschaft und Religion, Philosophie und Belletristik den unübersetzbar deutschen Begriff »Weltanschauung« hat prägen lassen. Daran ist ein regressives Moment unüberhörbar, nicht notwendig, aber gelegentlich auch als Ressentiment gegenüber methodischer Konsistenz vernehmbar. Für »the German Weltanschauung« ist die Konzession an die logische Inkohärenz ihrer Elemente charakteristisch. Deutsch an ihr ist nicht der vage Index eines irrational gestimmten Nationalcharakters, sondern einer auch intellektuell besonders stark ausgeprägten Ungleichzeitigkeit im internationalen Maßstab sukzessiv auftretender Strategien der Wissenschaftsgeschichte. Unter den Umständen einer ewigen historischen Verspätung der eigenen Entwicklung bei voller intellektueller Präsenz der Maßstäbe auf internationalem

Niveau, entstehen bis in die Gegenwart hinein immer wieder Trends des Denkens, in denen sonst nacheinander begegnende Impulse wie in lange stehenden Momentaufnahmen zugleich wirksam sind: hier experimentelle Standards der Sinnenphysiologie, physikalisch-ästhetische Grundlagenforschung zugleich mit theologisch inspirierter Naturphilosophie und der Anwendung ästhetischer Produktionsformen als Methode wissenschaftlicher Verknüpfung.

Eine erhebliche Partie seines Werks – alle Forschungen, die auf psychophysischen *Parallelismus* zielen, aber auch die Schriften über das Seelenleben der Pflanzen und Himmelskörper, benutzen die Dynamik der Metapher zur Gedankenverknüpfung, das heißt hier zumeist *Assoziation* und *Analogie* nach dem Muster »die Sonnenstrahlen sind lange Lichtfinger«. Die Analogie ist eine gedankliche und stilistische Grundfigur in Fechners Denken, die wesentlich dazu beiträgt, die Statik, in der sein Denken weniger fortschreitet als sich räumlich ausbreitet, ins Methodische zu wenden. – Weltanschauung ist auf Gleichstoffigkeit ihrer Gegenstände nicht angewiesen. Homogenität erzielt sie durch die ästhetische Form der *Wahrnehmung*:

> Soll man nicht sagen, das ganze Pflanzenreich schlinge sich wie eine schöne Arabeske um und zwischen das Menschenreich durch. Der Mensch selbst wächst mit aller Pracht seiner Gewänder und allem kunstreichen Gerät wie halben Leibes von unten aus der Pflanzenwelt hervor; und von oben wachsen wieder Blumen und Trauben der darnach verlangenden Hand, dem verlangenden Mund entgegen. Und über all diesem schwebt der schönste Duft poetischer Beziehungen. (Fechner 1848, 398)

Gesetzt den Fall, die Sonne hätte eine Seele, oder wie sieht die Welt aus, wenn wir den Menschen als eine schlummernde Pflanze betrachten – derart bestimmt also die Wahl des Standpunkts und die Form der Verknüpfung die Anschauung der Welt, die als Weltanschauung in dem Maß ihre Beliebigkeit verliert, wie sie ihre Integrationskraft bewähren kann. Nur darauf wollte Fechner in jeder Phase seines Denkens bestehen, dass die Ergebnisse sich nicht ausschließen sollten, wenn sie auch logisch unverknüpft bleiben. Der häufige Gebrauch des Konjunktivs und von Partikeln wie »vielleicht«, »möglicherweise« sowie von Wendungen wie »warum sollte nicht [...]« ist dafür typisch.

Beredt hat er in der Einleitung des »Zend-Avesta« (1851) die Komplementarität der verschiedenen Weisen zu argumentieren, zu denken und zu sprechen in Sätzen verteidigt, die hier in extenso zur Sprache kommen mögen, weil sie eine Zusammenfassung dieses Aspekts überflüssig machen:

> Ich selbst bin weit entfernt, die Betrachtungen und Schlüsse dieser Schrift als absolut sicher anzusehen. Wer möchte überhaupt von *vollständiger* Sicherheit in Gebieten sprechen, wo nur der Ausgang von der erfahrbaren Wirklichkeit genommen werden kann, doch keine directe Bewährung darin möglich ist und die Methoden der exacten Forschung keinen Angriff finden? Auch weiß ich, dass diese Schrift kein Evangelium ist. Ja wohl manchmal habe ich mich, im Rückblick auf dieselbe und betroffen von ihrem Widerspruch gegen das, was ringsum gilt, selbst gefragt: ist nicht das Ganze doch nur ein geistiges Spiel? Lassen sich nicht Gründe für Alles finden, wenn man es darauf anlegt, solche zu finden? Hast du nicht früher, dich selbst parodirend, bewiesen, daß auch der Schatten lebendig ist; ist nicht umgekehrt die Lebendigkeit, die du jetzt beweisest, ein Schattenspiel?
>
> Aber es war diesmal nicht das Interesse der Verfolgung einer Paradoxie, sondern das uns Alle verfolgende Ungenügen der bestehenden Ansichten selbst, was darüber hinauszugehen drängte, ein Ungenügen, das ja wohl jeder, wenn auch von andern Seiten, zugiebt, und sollte er nicht auch zugeben, daß demselben mit keiner halben Ansicht wird abzuhelfen sein, welche aus Scheu, Gewohnheiten zu verletzen, eben die Consequenzen zu ziehen fürchtet, welche Abhülfe gewähren können? Und welches Mißtrauen ich auch in die Schlüsse und Resultate dieser Schrift, als menschlichem Irrthum unterworfen, zu setzen geneigt blieb, war es hauptsächlich Dreies, was mich bei mir selbst beruhigte: einmal, daß die Naturbetrachtung im obigen Sinne doch von den verschiedensten Seiten zu demselben, alle diese Seiten verknüpfenden Ziele führt, zweitens, daß sich dadurch im Grunde nur die ursprüngliche Naturansicht wiederherstellt, endlich daß den höhern praktischen Interessen des Menschen ein um so volleres Genüge dadurch geschieht, je mehr man auf den ganzen Zusammenhang derselben eingeht, während freilich ein Stück davon auf das alte Kleid nicht frommen kann. Ich gebe aber etwas auf den ursprünglichen Naturinstinkt der Menschen und glaube, daß nichts wahr sein kann, was nicht auch gut ist zu glauben, am wahrsten aber das, was am besten. Freilich auch in dem, was man für gut hält, kann man irren, aber einmal muß doch ein Punkt kommen, wo der Mensch sich selbst glaubt. (Fechner 1901, 1, XI)

Sich selbst zu glauben, d.h. in diesem Zusammenhang davon ausgehen, dass das Bedürfnis des Menschen nach einer ursprünglichen natürlichen Einheit auch einen Gegenstand in der Wirklichkeit hat, der in der Bildungsgeschichte des Bewusstseins verdrängt worden ist. Die »ursprüngliche Naturansicht«, die diesem entspricht, ist *Naturwahrnehmung* abzüglich Geschichte. Indem die historische Dimension zurücktritt, soll sich die Möglichkeit einer durch Bildung und Wissen unvermittelten Naturerschließung ergeben. Darin kommen experimentelle Physik und Naturphilosophie Fechners überein, dass sie auf Anschauung aus sind. Mit der Kindlichkeit, die sein Biograph als hervorstehenden Zug seines Habitus bezeichnet hat, gibt er diesem Anspruch auf Unmittelbarkeit eine Form; einen »Versuch, in dem mit noch kindischen Händen ein Spiel von hohem Sinn gewagt wird«, hat er selbst »Zend-Avesta« genannt (Fechner 1901, 1, 7); eine andere Form findet er im Anknüpfen an ein Stadium der Völkergeschichte, in dem er – mit dem späten Goethe und Friedrich Rückert – die menschliche Jugend zu finden glaubte: im indisch-persischen Orient.

Diese Entdeckung des inneren und des geschichtsgeographischen Orients ist durchaus eine Sache des *sentiments* – des *sentiments* für das verlorene Ganze –, obschon nicht bloß von Sentimentalität. Von den »höhern, praktischen Interessen« (Fechner 1901, 1, XI) spricht Fechner, wenn er sich den Wiedergewinn der ursprünglichen *Naturansicht* wünscht, weil lebenspraktisch die Menschen sich auf Schritt und Tritt in einer Totalität natürlicher Zusammenhänge verantwortlich bewegen und bewähren müssen, deren sie allein am Leitfaden der exakten Wissenschaften nicht inne werden können. Gerade dies ist ein besonders aktueller Gesichtspunkt seines Werks, der das Interesse an Fechner denn auch weckt, seit das Bewusstsein für Ökologie sich bildet: mit einem kräftigen Schub in den Jahren der monistischen Bewegung und wieder in der Gegenwart.

Immer war es freilich möglich, wird es möglich sein, aus Fechners Oeuvre die Elemente herauszulösen und zu benutzen, die jeweils zeitgemäß und praktikabel sind. In unserem Kontext, wo es darum geht, die Physiognomie dieses Gelehrtenlebens in relativer Unabhängigkeit seiner denkbaren Aktualität zu zeichnen, steht eher die problematische Einheit des Ganzen als die Aktualität von Einzelheiten im Vordergrund.

Kein Zweifel, diese Einheit ist tatsächlich keine von logischer Konstruktion, sondern die einer weltanschaulichen Erzählung mit einem gelehrten synkretistisch zusammengesetzten Apparat, womöglich ein anderer Divan mit Noten und Abhandlungen. Wie für dessen persisches Urbild und Goethes Nachfolge gleicherweise die *Verschriftlichung* eine bedeutende symbolische Rolle spielte, so auch für Fechner. Der narrative Zug seiner Wissenschaft hat ein Pendant in der ausschweifend geliebten Schriftlichkeit, die regelrecht seine Lebensform war. In der Verschriftlichung kommt das Lebensganze zwar zu keiner logisch-systematischen, wohl aber zu einer ästhetisch-arabeskenhaften Gestalt. Gelehrter war Fechner weniger im Lesen – sein Rezeptionsvermögen war nicht hoch – als vielmehr in der kontinuierlichen Produktivität des Schreibens, die möglichst keinen Anlass seines Wahrnehmungsfeldes ausließ. Seiner oft gerühmten Vielseitigkeit und der Ganzheit seines Denkens hat er sich in diesem Sinne buchstäblich verschrieben, wie es sein Biograph, der als der Neffe über Jahrzehnte seinen Hausstand teilte, beobachtet hat:

> Er hatte keine Passion, keine Angewohnheit, keine Prätention. Schreibend sann er, sinnend schrieb er. Das war der Rahmen, der Gang seines Lebens, eine Gelehrsamkeit strengsten Sinnes. (Kuntze 1892, 315)

Ohne zu schreiben habe Fechner »an grausamer Langeweile« gelitten, so habe er – wie wiederum der Neffe schreibt – geradezu »maschinenmäßig« geschrieben, wiewohl »ohne eine eigentliche Schaffensfreudigkeit« (Kuntze 1892, 313). Jahrzehnte verbrachte er in dieser Weise sein Leben in Leipzig, »ein Tag wie der andere, ein Abend wie der andere, nur selten durch eine kleine Geselligkeit in oder außer dem Haus unterbrochen« (Kuntze 1892, 324f.), ausgestattet mit einem Taschengeld für den einzigen Luxus, den er sich gestattete: Kaffee und einen gewaltigen Konsum von Schreibpapier, da er die Angewohnheit hatte, das einzelne Blatt nur mit wenigen Zeilen zu beschriften. Vom Ganzen, das er für sich selbst lebhaft empfand – ein *homo religiosus*, dessen Vater und Großvater Pastoren waren –, hat er ohne Not mit Wissenschaft allein kein Abbild herstellen können, und das Surrogat von Weltanschauung ist eine problematisch synkretistische Komposition. So ist vielleicht diese exzessive unablässige *Verschriftlichung* all seiner Bestrebungen der reinste Ausdruck seines Verlangens nach der Anschauung des Ganzen – nicht aufgrund des Geschriebenen also, sondern mit dem Anspruch, dass nichts der Verschriftlichung entgehen sollte.

Noch unter einem anderen Aspekt ist das *Verschriftlichen* ohne Ansehen der Größenverhältnisse von Personen und Sachen eine Symbolform seines Denkens. Fechner hat keinerlei Sinn für Hierarchie. Dem analogischen Verfahren in der Methode entspricht für die Komposition im Einzelnen wie im Ganzen die Parataxe. Die Gleichordnung von Gegenständen, die in der Tradition des Denkens in Über- und Unterordnungsverhältnissen geschieden sind, opponiert gegen eine Autoritätsstruktur im gegenständlichen Aufbau der Welt ohne Rücksicht auf ihre Wirklichkeit für die Empfindung. Über der Verschriftlichung seines Denkens am roten Faden der *Analogie* steht unsichtbar das Motto ›Was der Tag mir zuträgt‹. Das Maß von Bedeutsamkeit ist nicht mit den Sachen gegeben, sondern es liegt allein beim Menschen. Wovon hier die Rede ist, mag eine Beschreibung der *Katastrophe* in der Lebensmitte Fechners verdeutlichen. Die epochale Krise der westeuropäischen Kultur am Scheideweg des Denkprozesses der empirischen Wissenschaften einerseits und einer hermeneutischen Auslegung der Welt aus der unterstellten Gottimmanenz allbeseelter Schöpfung durch betroffene Subjekte andererseits, zieht sich zu einer dramatischen Kollision der widerstreitenden Kräfte in der Wissenschaftsbiographie des Autors selbst zusammen.

Es ging um seine *Augen*. Auf den Spuren von Goethes »Farbenlehre« und der »Phantastischen Gesichtserscheinungen« des Arztes Johannes Müller hatte Fechner methodische Untersuchungen von Ermüdungserscheinungen am Auge durch extreme Helligkeit und andere Belastungen betrieben. Noch ehe er seine Erkenntnisse über die Subjektivität von *Farbwahrnehmungen* auswerten konnte, versagten seine überanstrengten Augen den Dienst. – Während dreier Jahre fällt der Forscher nun in eine immer tiefere Nacht. Der blauen Brille folgt die schwarze Binde, dieser eine metallene Maske mit ausgetriebenen Buckeln über den Augen. Maskiert geht er durch den Garten. Eichendorff singend: »Möcht' auch spazieren gerne!« oder: »Ich kann wohl manchmal singen, als ob ich fröhlich sei«. Endlich bewohnt er eine verschlossene schwarze Kammer, in der er nur noch die Stimme eines Vorlesers durch einen Trichter in der Tür vernimmt. Ein allgemeiner körperlicher und geistiger Verfall begleitet die extreme Lichtempfindlichkeit: Auszehrung als Folge eines erlöschenden Ernährungswillens. Infantilismus in der Konsequenz von Gedankenflucht und Verwirrtheit. – Die Ärzte greifen rasch zum Äußersten: Moxen, glimmende Kegel, auf die nackte Haut gesetzt. Aus den schwärenden Brandlöchern soll das Übel entweichen. Es bleibt aber, und die Mediziner geben den Sterbenden auf. – Nun ist die Talsohle erreicht, ist die Raupe verpuppt, aus deren Kokon der Schmetterling sich entfalten soll. Aus dem gebildeten Leipzig, das schaudernd Anteil am Schicksal des berühmten Physikers nimmt, der es mit dem Licht der Aufklärung zu weit getrieben zu haben schien, kommt die Erlösung. Einer Bürgerin träumt das Rezept der rettenden Speise.

Fechner erholt sich langsam, nährt sich wie ein Neugeborenes, trinkt eimerweise Milch; vor allem aber, er schreibt nun wieder und zwar wie einer, der durch den Tod gegangen ist und dem jetzt auf der anderen Seite alle ehrlichen Dinge entgegenkommen. Erstmals fühlt er sich nicht mehr nur als Protokollant einer Wissenschaft, die, im methodischen Selbstlauf dahintreibend, den Wissenschaftler nur als ihr Medium benötigt. Stattdessen spricht er nun von seiner »geistigen Selbstmacht« (Kuntze 1892, 122). Dieses Selbst darf durch Methode nicht um seinen Anteil gebracht werden. Vom Licht lässt er sich nicht mehr nur anstrahlen und blenden. Vielmehr will er nun »dem Licht energisch entgegentreten« (Kuntze 1892, 124), ein selbst Beseelter dem Beseelenden.

Damit in eins setzt er der Eigendynamik der immer wieder wildwerdenden Denkbewegung entschlossenen Widerstand entgegen, wie es ein Nachtrag eigener Hand zum *Krankenbericht* von 1847 anschaulich schildert:

> Meinen Kopf anlangend, so hat derselbe vollkommene Klarheit des Denkens; aber immer noch fällt es mir schwer, die Gedanken zu bannen; und anstatt dass Andere die Gedanken suchen, ist es immer noch bei Spaziergängen und zu Zeiten, wo ich nicht arbeiten will, meine stete Uebung und Mühe, das Fortspinnen der Gedanken, mit denen ich mich bei der Arbeit beschäftigt habe, zu verhindern, mich immer von Neuem auf gleichgültige oder in's Leben greifende Gegenstände abzulenken, da ich theils den Nachtheil spüre, den dieses Fortspinnen der Gedanken für meine geistige Selbstmacht und Kraft hat, theils dadurch unfähig werde, an den Interessen des Lebens Theil zu nehmen. Aber trotz der täglichen Arbeit und Mühe, die ich mir in dieser Beziehung gebe, scheint es, daß ich mehr den Fortschritt des Uebels hindere, als einen wirklichen Rückschritt darin bewirken kann. (siehe Kuntze 1892, 125f.)

Das Leben hat ihn dennoch wieder, und der Rückblick auf die *Katastrophe* gibt allem Lebendigen neuen Glanz. Das Leben der Kreatur strahlt für ihn in den leuchtendsten Farben, weil er es auf dem Hintergrund seiner Erinnerung an die durchstandene Nacht wahrnimmt – in »Nanna« das Leben der Pflanzen. Daher das Sammeln von Argumenten für deren *Beseeltheit*: in den *Analogien* des vegetabilen zum animalischen Leben, im »Pflanzenschlaf« etwa; sodann in den Korrespondenzen des Pflanzenlebens mit den Tages-, Jahres- und Lebenszeiten (»Pflanzenuhr«), mit den Wettern (»Pflanzenbarometer«) – Analogien der Pflanze zum animalischen Leben sind *ein* Indiz dieser Beseeltheit; ein anderes erblickt Fechner aber auch im Gegenteil – ein leidenschaftlicher Anwalt des grünen Lebens bis zum Anschein von Rabulistik –, in der Andersheit der Pflanzen: Nicht was der Mensch von ihr habe, sondern was er von ihr *nicht* habe, mache sie zur Seele. – Die Seelen der Kreaturen vergleicht er mit den verschiedenen Instrumenten eines Orchesters. Deren jedes hat sein eigenes Recht an seinem Ort. In der Schöpfung gibt es keine Hierarchie; Nebenordnung des Andersartigen ist ihr Prinzip, nicht Unterordnung des scheinbar Niederen durch Höheres.

Gegen die Geistphilosophie Hegels, die ihm als eine Arroganz des theoretischen Bewusstseins vorgekommen sein muss, verbündet sich Fechner mit den Beseelungslehren der Alten Welt und ihren orientalischen Pendants, beruft er sich auf manichäische und hinduistische Tradition. Im Zentrum seiner Philosophie steht eine Metapher, die ihre aktuelle Reprise im Jargon der *Ökologie*- und Selbsthilfebewegung findet, von der anderen Seite eine *Analogie* zur Symbolik der *Verschriftlichung*: »Vernetzung«. In »Zend-Avesta«, seinem Versuch, die Lehren Zoroasters für die Moderne zu erneuern, stehen die Sätze:

> Menschen und Tiere sind gerade die Glieder der Erde, in denen die größte verknüpfende und mischende Kraft für die gesamten irdischen Stoffe und Verhältnisse liegt; sie sind in dieser Hinsicht vergleichbar mit den Knoten eines Gewebes, in welchen die draußen mehr einfach und verstreut verlaufenden Fäden der Stoffe und Kräfte zusammenkommen, um sich im engsten Raum zu begegnen und aufs innigste zu verschlingen, und zwar in jedem auf besondere Weise. Nun ist aber der Knoten doch nichts, was sich trennen ließe von den Fäden, die in ihm zusammenlaufen; er ist vielmehr selbst der innigste Zusammenschluss der Fäden, als Knoten freilich unterscheidbar von allen einzelnen Fäden, aber darum nicht scheidbar von ihnen. Beides verwechselt man nur zu gern. Und je mehr von den Fäden des ganzen Systems ein Knoten in sich zusammenfasst, je mehr er sie verschlingt und verwickelt, desto mehr unterscheidet er sich freilich von dem ganzen Gewebe und desto vielseitiger und fester ist er mit allen anderen Knoten verknüpft. So ist der Mensch das am besten unterscheidbare und zugleich das am wenigsten scheidbare Glied des Erdganzen. (Fechner 1901, 1, 15)

Fremd war Fechner an Hegel nicht nur dessen Hierarchisierung der Lebenswelt anhand der Stufenlehre des sich bildenden Geistes; auch das agonale Prinzip des Hegel'schen Denkens, die Entwicklung aus der Kollision von Gegensätzen, widerstrebte seinem Denken, das in jeder heftigen Selbstbehauptung auf Kosten eines anderen einen Riss im Gewebe des unendlichen Lebens zu befürchten hatte. Selbstverhaltung von Energie und Produktivität, um das sensible Geflecht wechselseitiger Abhängigkeiten nicht zu zerstören, ist das Ethos dieses Denkens, das sich darin mit der Ökonomie und der inneren Vernunft der Schöpfung einig sieht.

»Nanna« erschien im Jahr der ersten und einzigen deutschen *Revolution*. War Fechner Konterrevolutionär? Er war es weder praktisch (im Gegenteil: einige Tage ging er mit auf die Straße), noch ist er es theoretisch gewesen. Den Namen der germanischen Pflanzengöttin – anstelle der romanischen Flora – gibt er seinem Werk im Jahr 1848 vielmehr, weil er »das deutsche Wesen sich jetzt verjüngen, wieder selbstwüchsig werden« (Fechner 1848, VIII) sieht. Freilich entgeht ihm nicht, »dass die Trommel der Zeit nicht zugunsten der leisen Stimmen der Blumen gerührt wird« (Fechner 1848, IV). Charakteristisch für seine Wahrnehmungsweise ist aber die Antwort: Wie die Blumen am farbigsten in der Erinnerung an die schwarze Nacht zu blühen scheinen, so sind für ihn die leisesten Stimmen am deutlichsten, wenn sie sich gegen das turbulente Geräusch der Revolution zu behaupten haben: ein vorgegriffener Akkord von sanfter Zukunftsmusik, die für ihn aus der Grube klingt, in die mit Getöse die alte Zeit hinabfährt.

Drei Jahre später, als die alten Mächte sich doch noch als stärker, vor allem aber die neuen kompromittierbarer gezeigt hatten als vermutet, formuliert er sein gesellschaftliches Credo ganz goethesch:

> Ich glaube, dass alles Neue, was bestehen soll, nur erwachsen kann aus dem, was schon bestanden hat, nicht durch den Umsturz, sondern die Fortbildung oder die Verjüngung des Bestehenden oder Bestandenen. Ich glaube, dass in der Verjüngung nur fallen können altgewordene Hüllen, doch frischer, höher, weiter treiben muss der alte Kern. (Fechner 1901, 1, 434)

Nachdrücklich setzt Fechner diese Sätze an den Schluss des »Zend-Avesta«. So gelten sie auch für dieses eigene Werk. Auch in Philosophie und Wissenschaft soll es keinen Umsturz geben, wohl aber Verjüngung. Tatsächlich verneint er zwar gewisse Formen analytischer Rationalität der eigenen Zeit, nicht jedoch die wissenschaftliche Vernunft überhaupt – in keiner Phase. Romantische Rückfälle hinter die naturwissenschaftlichen Standards hat er mit Polemik bedacht. Zu den irrationalistischen Strömungen der eigenen Zeit hält er feste Distanz. Vom Stamme Schellings und Okens sieht er sich gefallen: herstammend aus deren *Naturphilosophie* in den Themen seines Denkens, abgefallen von der Behandlungsweise, denn selbst will er nicht spekulieren, sondern beweisen.

Seine These von der individuellen *Beseeltheit* der Pflanzen, so auch der Erde und des *Kosmos*, sucht er mit den weitest fortgeschrittenen physikalischen Erkenntnissen in Einklang zu bringen: mit der neuen *Wellentheorie* etwa, wie sie Thomas Young am Anfang des 19. Jahrhunderts für das Licht formuliert hatte und die dann durch Maxwell in den 1860er-Jahren für die Elektrizität und eine Reihe anderer Phänomene verallgemeinert worden war. Alles Seiende ist laut Fechner in ein Netz von determinierenden physikalischen Gesetzen gebunden. Die Schnittpunkte der räumlich sich erstreckenden Wellenfelder sind indessen Beispiele sowohl für diese *Determination* als auch von *Freiheit*. Sie sind nämlich asymmetrisch geknüpft. In keinem herrschen dieselben Bedingungen: In Gottes Weltordnung geschehe Unnatürliches und Übernatürliches und es würden ungewöhnliche und nie dagewesene Wirkungen durch ungewöhnliche und nie dagewesene Ursachen erfolgen. Mit anderen Worten: Gesetzmäßigkeit und Freiheit stehen nicht im Widerspruch zueinander. Das *Kausalitätsdenken* setzt Fechner dergestalt nicht generell außer Kraft, doch legt er die Feldtheorie der Wellendynamik in einer Weise aus, dass aus dem alten Gesetz die Ordnung von immer gleichen Phänomenen ebenso erklärbar wird, wie die zufällige Abweichung von individuellen. Zu Darwins Lehre der Sprünge und Mutationen in der Vererbung, mit der die Erosion der klassischen Naturwissenschaften fortschreitet, hat er sich später ebenfalls positiv gestellt.

Freiheit als oberster Gesetzgeber: in diese paradoxe Formel, vor allem aber in eine geradezu barocke Rhetorik von zitierender Gelehrsamkeit und assoziationenreicher Poesie, mathematischer Formelsprache und enthusiastischer Predigt fasst Fechner seine Einsicht, in der die Ausfälle des Zufalls im Gesetze gezähmt, der versklavende Despotismus des Gesetzes durch das Spiel von Zufällen gebrochen erscheint. Das war keine Vision eines Schwärmers, sondern der kühne Vorgriff auf Erkenntnisse von Lebensprozessen, die experimentell erst im letzten Jahrhundert gänzlich gesichert worden sind. Im naturwissenschaftlichen Weltbild der Gegenwart kommen determinierte und sich zufällig bewegende Systeme zugleich vor, eine Struktur, die für Fechner so wunderbar und unfasslich war, dass er dankbar die Formulierungshilfe der Theologie in Anspruch nahm, um den Skandal des Erkannten in eine vertraute Sprache zu fassen.

Der Doppelcharakter der *Schöpfung*, zuerst in den optischen Experimenten am Rande der Lebenskrise als ein Nebeneinander subjektiver Farbwahrnehmungen und der »objektiven« Wellenbewegung des Lichts erahnt, dann an den Pflanzen, schließlich die am Universum erörterte Duplizität von Determinismus und Freiheit, bleibt Fechners Lebensthema bis zu seinem Tode 1887.

Zumal in methodischer Hinsicht war seine Philosophie bereits zu seinen Lebzeiten heftig umstritten. So galt der *psychophysische* Parallelismus, wie er ihn in den Schriften zur »Psychophysik« (2 Bde., 1860) und in seiner »Vorschule der Ästhetik« (2 Thle., 1876) demonstrierte, rasch als überholt, weil er auf problematische Weise erst abstrakt auseinanderreißt, was dann mit Hilfe von Mathematik und Physik überbrückt werden soll. Viktor von Weizsäcker wiederholt diese Kritik noch vom Standpunkt der Gestaltpsychologie, als er 1922 zur Neuausgabe von Fechners spätem Resümé »Die Tagesansicht gegenüber der Nachtansicht«[2] ein Vorwort schreibt. Darin würdigt er aber auch die Entschlossenheit Fechners, »nicht die Wissenschaft gegen den Menschen zu schützen, sondern den Menschen vor der Wissenschaft zu retten (Fechner 1922, Vorw.).«

Das ist über Fechners Naturphilosophie, seine Lehre von der *Allbeseeltheit* und die Begründung menschlicher *Freiheit* gesagt. Deren Wirkung ist nie ganz erloschen. Sie ist bei den Haeckel-Schülern Wilhelm Bölsche, Bruno Wille und Ernst Fuhrmann zitierbar; im Kreis um Bruno Taut, Scheerbart und die »Gläserne Kette«; Fechner-Leser sind Jorge Luis Borges und Ernst Jünger; einen Schlüssel zur Eröffnung des eigenen Denkens fanden in seinen Schriften Eugen Rosenstock-Huessy, Franz Rosenzweig und Franz Kafka. Die Letztgenannten scheinen von Fechners Hartnäckigkeit, mit der er das *metaphysische* Leben aus dem profanen der geschaffenen Natur zu deuten unternahm, Zuspruch erfahren zu haben.

Dass Fechners Werk gerade für die Generation des Ersten Weltkriegs neue Bedeutung bekam, hat mit Impulsen seines Denkens zu tun, von denen erst nur beiläufig die Rede war. Seine Zuwendung zum natürlichen Leben als dem immer gleich gegenwärtigen Ursprung will über den Abgrund hinweg tragen, der sich durch eine elementare Verlusterfahrung geöffnet hatte. Die Möglichkeit, ja die Erfahrung, dass das Leben durch den Tod irreversibel zugrunde gehen kann. Der thermodynamische *Entropiebegriff* war durch Clausius zwar erst 1865 in die Physik eingeführt worden, doch in den Geisteswissenschaften drohte der Historismus längst, die Trostformeln fortzuschwemmen, die von der romantischen Naturphilosophie formuliert worden waren, um den Skandal des individuell erfahrenen Todes durch naturphilosophische Überformung hinweg zu interpretieren. Mit der Verzeitlichung des Denkens dringt die Wirklichkeit des nicht umkehrbaren Todes in das Bewusstsein der Wissenschaft ein.

In der Geistesgeschichte des 19. Jahrhunderts soll das Ideal der Bildung die Kluft zwischen der Erkenntnis der individuellen Zeitlichkeit und der Sehnsucht nach zeitloser Gegenwärtigkeit des Lebens schließen. Bildung – als Dimension der Geschichte in den Wissenschaften – ist ein Prozess, der im Fortschreiten nichts zurücklässt. Mag das Leben verfallen, so ist ihm doch im Geist ein ewiges Denkmal sicher. – Fechner hat sich mit dieser Geistwirklichkeit nicht begnügen wollen. So ist sein gesamtes Werk zwar

---

[2] Erstauflage 1879 in Leipzig.

durch den Gedanken geprägt, dass nichts wirklich verloren gehen könne, doch war nicht das Bild das Medium, in dem er das vom Fraß der Zeit Bedrohte aufgehoben sah. Die *Verschriftlichung* des Lebens ist für ihn auf ein Komplement im Leben angewiesen. Nicht in Gelehrsamkeit sah er die Gewähr für ein Überleben, darin abweichend von der Grundüberzeugung der akademischen Intelligenz des 19. Jahrhunderts, sondern in den Gedächtnisleistungen, die das Leben selbst aufbringt. Auf dessen *Beseeltheit* hat er nicht aus einer Neigung zum Erbaulichen bestanden, sondern in der Hoffnung, dass das Leben insgesamt sich treuer ist, als es der Anschein universeller Zeitlichkeit seiner einzelnen Phänomene nahe legt. Auch insofern steht sein Gelehrtenleben quer, nicht nur zu seiner Zeit, sondern zur Zeit überhaupt. – Auf den Grundsatz »Nicht was ich von ihr habe, sondern was ich von ihr *nicht* habe, macht sie zur Seele« fällt von hier aus noch Licht. Das beseelte Leben insgesamt will er für reicher halten als die einzelnen Menschen es sind. Einen Sinn kann er im Leben nur erkennen, wenn er es nicht vom Menschen her sieht. So wählt er den Standpunkt des theologischen Erzählers, um der Traurigkeit Herr zu werden, die der Anblick der Schöpfung in ihm weckt. Einige Sätze in »Nanna« enthalten diese Gedankenfigur in zitierbarer Verkürzung:

> Ja greift nicht überhaupt Leben und Sterben der Menschen- und Pflanzenwelt allwärts durch einander, und doch kennen und grüßen sich die Seelen beider Reiche nicht, wie Menschen, die eine und dieselbe große Stadt bewohnen, sich durch einander drängen und treiben, ohne einander zu kennen und zu grüßen. Ist das nicht ein traurig zersplittert Wesen im Seelenreiche. Ja wohl traurig, wenn es so ist, wie wir es uns zumeist denken. Aber ich denke, ein höheres Wesen wird's wohl geben, was der Menschen- und Pflanzen- und aller Seelen Schicksal in Beziehung miteinander denkt, ja selber in Beziehung setzt. (Fechner 1848, 395)

Die Generation des Ersten Weltkriegs hat die Kehre des Blicks, die sich in diesen Sätzen vollzieht, vielfach und mit den verschiedensten Ergebnissen vollzogen; sei es zugunsten der Sprache, deren Gedächtnis ein unerschöpflicher Brunnen der Seinserinnerung ist wie bei Heidegger, sei es zugunsten der Erneuerung der Theologie, wie im »Stern der Erlösung« bei Franz Rosenzweig. Für diesen wie für Fechner war es wichtig, dass die Kehre des Blicks keine ›ein für allemal‹ ist. Sie muss vielmehr immer neu vollzogen werden im Blickwechsel: der Augenaufschlag des selbstbewusst die Details seines Lebens erforschenden Menschen und die Selbstverhaltung des Blicks, um sich anschauen zu lassen. Ohne die Sprache der

Theologie zu benutzen, die Fechner an dieser Stelle aufgreift, und doch im Umkreise seiner Wahrnehmungswelt bleibend, kann man sagen: sehen zu lernen und dabei begreifen, dass der Mensch des Lichts nicht mächtig ist.

Literatur:

[Fechner, G. Th.] Dr. Mises, (1841): Gedichte. Leipzig.

Fechner, G. Th. (1848): Nanna oder Über das Seelenleben der Pflanzen. Leipzig.

Fechner, G. Th. (1901): Zend-Avesta oder Ueber die Dinges des Himmels und des Jenseits. Vom Standpunkt der Naturbetrachtung. 2. Aufl. in 2 Bdn. Hamburg.

Fechner, G. Th. (1860): Elemente der Psychophysik. 2 Thle. Leipzig.

Fechner, G. Th. (1876): Vorschule der Aesthetik. 2 Thle. Leipzig.

Fechner, G. Th. (1922): Die Tagesansicht und Nachtansicht. Eingeleitet und hg. von V. Frh. von Weizsäcker. Stuttgart.

Kuntze, J.E. (1892): Gustav Theodor Fechner (Dr. Mises). Ein deutsches Gelehrtenleben. Leipzig.

Michael Heidelberger

Fechners wissenschaftlich-philosophische Weltauffassung

Entgegen einer weitverbreiteten Auffassung, die in Fechners Denken starke irrationale und metaphysisch-dogmatische Ansätze sieht, wird in diesem Aufsatz ein rationaler Kern in Fechners Philosophie ausfindig gemacht und als Grundlage einer wissenschaftlichen Weltauffassung interpretiert. Fechners Panpsychismus und andere Spekulationen erscheinen auf diesem Hintergrund zwar als höchst unwahrscheinliche, aber nicht unwissenschaftliche Folgerungen. Fechners wissenschaftstheoretischer und naturphilosophischer Ansatz wird in sechs Prinzipien rekonstruiert und zusammengefasst. Die ersten vier Prinzipien liefern die notwendigen Bedingungen für eine philosophische Sicht der Naturwissenschaften, die der Biologie und Psychologie eine starke Autonomie neben der Physik einräumt. Mit zwei weiteren Prinzipien wird dann innerhalb dieses theoretischen Rahmens eine spezielle Theorie der Psychologie und Biologie formuliert, die die Autonomie dieser beiden Wissenschaften in einem speziellen nichtreduktiven Materialismus plausibel macht. Es wird gezeigt, dass Fechner zur Sicherstellung seiner Prinzipien tatsächlich keine unwissenschaftlichen Bestandteile verwendet, wie man vielleicht meinen könnte. Es liegen in seinen sechs Prinzipien sogar in nuce Möglichkeiten für verschiedene wissenschafts- und naturphilosophische Ansätze, die sich in der Generation nach Fechner in unterschiedliche Richtungen weiterentwickelt haben. Es lassen sich drei Entwicklungslinien unterscheiden: eine Radikalisierung des Fechner'schen Ansatzes im Phänomenalismus von Ernst Mach, eine Neufassung als kritischer Realismus in der neukantianisch und positivistisch ausgerichteten Philosophie von Alois Riehl und schließlich eine Umformung in den Pragmatismus von Charles Sanders Peirce, die Fechners Lehre von den Überzeugungen betont.

Wenn hier Fechners Philosophie als »wissenschaftlich-philosophische Weltauffassung« bezeichnet wird, dann soll damit gesagt werden, dass Fechner mit seiner Philosophie einen wissenschaftlichen Anspruch verfolgt hat und dass sie tatsächlich auf einem weltanschauungsfreien Fundament ruht. Ich möchte sogar so weit gehen zu behaupten, dass Fechner damit zur Tradition der »wissenschaftlichen Philosophie« des 19. Jahrhunderts zu rechnen ist, deren folgenreichstes späteres Produkt im

20. Jahrhundert der *logische Empirismus* darstellt. Der »Wiener Kreis« als die bekannteste Schule dieser Tradition bediente sich (in seinem Manifest von 1929) des Ausdrucks »Wissenschaftliche Weltauffassung«, um sich von allen spekulativen Weltanschauungen abzugrenzen.

Kann man im Ernst eine solche Ansicht vertreten, wird man fragen, wo doch Fechners Naturphilosophie in einem *Panpsychismus* gipfelt, der an weltanschaulicher Begriffsdichtung seinesgleichen sucht? Sind nicht Fechners unwissenschaftliche Spekulationen über die Pflanzenseele und die *Beseelung* der Planeten notorisch? Ist nicht der »objektive Idealismus« seiner Altersphilosophie ein gar zu metaphysisches Produkt? Die spekulative Seite der Philosophie Fechners soll keineswegs abgestritten oder verkleinert werden, aber es wird gleichwohl darauf bestanden, dass sie eine wissenschaftliche Basis hat, die durch spekulative Erweiterung nicht geschmälert wird.

Im Folgenden möchte ich zuerst Fechners Weltauffassung in *sechs Prinzipien* zusammenfassen: Die Prinzipien 1–4 sind methodologischer Art und formulieren Minimalbedingungen, die jede Weltauffassung erfüllen muss, wenn sie der Biologie und Psychologie als autonomen Wissenschaften neben der Physik gerecht werden will. Die Prinzipien 5 und 6 geben dann die Grundlagen für eine in diesem Rahmen mögliche, spezifische Theorie ab. Anschließend zeige ich, dass diese Prinzipien gut in die philosophische Diskussion der Zeit passen; ja, dass man die Auffassungen anderer Philosophen und Denker der Zeit sogar als Modifikationen von Fechners Ansicht verstehen kann. Fechners Prinzipien können als Ausgangspunkt einiger wichtiger Positionen des 19. Jahrhunderts interpretiert werden: denen von Ernst Mach, Alois Riehl und Charles Sanders Peirce. In der Schlußbetrachtung wird dann eine Bewertung des Verhältnisses zwischen wissenschaftlicher Grundlage und spekulativem Überbau versucht.

Im *ersten Prinzip* von Fechners Weltauffassung wird ein umfassender *Empirismus* formuliert: Das Fundament unseres Wissens und Vermutens ist nicht nur das, was unmittelbar in der Sinneserfahrung der Außenwelt gegeben ist, sondern auch das, was in der Innenwelt zur Erfahrung kommt, also unsere Empfindungen, Willensimpulse und geistigen Tätigkeiten. Fechner bezeichnet die Erfahrungen aus beiden Quellen als »Erscheinungen«.

Die inneren *Erscheinungen* unterscheiden sich in ihrem epistemischen Status von den äußeren dadurch, dass sie nur demjenigen direkt zugänglich sind, der sie selbst hat. Sie sind, wie Fechner sagt, »Selbsterscheinungen«. Die äußeren Erscheinungen hingegen sind solche, die auch von anderen wahrgenommen werden können; sie sind daher »Fremderscheinungen«. Fechner glaubt, mit dem Selbsterscheinungscharakter von Erscheinungen das grundlegende Merkmal gefunden zu haben, das die psychischen von den physischen Erscheinungen unterscheidet. Damit hat er eine ontologische Unterscheidung mit Hilfe eines epistemologischen Kriteriums bestimmt, also gleichsam die Epistemologie in die *Ontologie* eingebaut. Beide Arten von Erscheinungen, die psychischen wie die physischen, haben gemeinsam, dass sie »aufzeigliche Dinge« (Fechner 1879, 244) sind, d.h., durch Hinweis auf direkte Erfahrung nachgewiesen werden können. Fechner hält also das Sprechen über *Psychisches* für empirisch ebenso rechtfertigbar wie das Sprechen über *Physisches*.

Das *zweite Prinzip* betrifft die Reichweite der *Erklärungen*, die die empirischen Wissenschaften von den äußeren Erscheinungen vorlegen können. Man kann es das Prinzip von der Vollständigkeit der naturwissenschaftlichen Erklärungen nennen: Jede physische Veränderung vollzieht sich nach strenger Gesetzmäßigkeit, so dass sie sich (wenigstens im Prinzip) vollständig durch physikalische Gesetze erklären lässt. Um physische Erscheinungen zu erklären, ist es also niemals notwendig und niemals angemessen, den Bereich der physischen Phänomene zu verlassen und zu irgendwelchen wissenschaftsfremden Erklärungsprinzipien seine Zuflucht zu nehmen. Das stärkste Argument für dieses Prinzip sieht Fechner im *Energieerhaltungssatz*, den er als Garantie für die Geschlossenheit des Bereichs der physischen Erscheinungen auffasst: Physische Veränderungen können mit ihren Wirkungen weder aus dem Bereich der physischen Erscheinungen »hinausführen«, noch werden sie durch einen ihnen fremden Bereich bestimmt oder beeinflusst; der physische Bereich ist *kausal geschlossen*. Dieses Prinzip bezieht sich insbesondere auch auf die Welt der Organismen. Ihre Entstehung, Mannigfaltigkeit und Entwicklung ist durch Naturgesetze vollständig erklärbar und man muss dafür keine Zuflucht zu irgendwelchen unwissenschaftlichen Grundsätzen nehmen. Obwohl dieses Prinzip auf Erfahrung beruht und deshalb nur einen Wahrscheinlichkeitsgrad für sich in Anspruch nehmen kann und prinzipiell fehlbar ist, hat es einen so grundlegenden Charakter im naturwissenschaftlichen Theoriengefüge angenommen, dass man es als notwendige Bedingung sinnvoller empirischer Theorien behandelt. Genauso wie Beweise für ein *perpetuum mobile* von keiner wissenschaftlichen Akademie angenommen werden, ist die Vollständigkeit wissenschaftlicher Erklärung eine vernünftigerweise nicht anzweifelbare Angelegenheit.

Im *dritten Prinzip* wird das Verhältnis zwischen physischen und psychischen Erscheinungen behandelt. Man kann dieses Prinzip so aussprechen: Keine Änderung psychischer Erscheinungen ohne eine Änderung physischer Erscheinungen. Alles *Psychische* ist also durch *Physisches* bedingt, oder, wie Fechner dies auch ausdrückt, »funktional« von ihm »abhängig«. Fechner nennt dieses Prinzip auch das »allgemeinste Gesetz der Psychophysik« oder ihr »Funktionsprinzip«. Mit »Bedingtheit« wird dabei etwas Schwächeres als Kausalität behauptet. Zwar impliziert jedes Kausalverhältnis ein Bedingungsverhältnis, aber nicht unbedingt umgekehrt. (In der Philosophie der Gegenwart spricht man auch oft von »Supervenienz«, um dieses Verhältnis zu charakterisieren.) Es wird also hier von Fechner gesagt, dass *wenn* psychische Phänomene gegeben sind, es erfahrungsgemäß der Fall ist, dass auch spezielle physische Phänomene vorliegen und dass *wenn* sich ein psychischer Zustand geändert hat, auch eine physische Änderung eingetreten ist. Dasjenige Physische, das direkt (ohne Zwischenschaltung von anderem Physischen) etwas Psychisches bedingt (woran also das Psychische direkt »gebunden« ist), heißt bei Fechner das »Psychophysische«.

Fechner gibt sich die größte Mühe, dieses Bedingungsverhältnis so voraussetzungslos und so neutral wie möglich zu charakterisieren, um nicht schon dadurch einer wie immer gearteten philosophischen (also metaphysischen) *Leib-Seele-Theorie* (oder Materie-Geist-Konzeption) in irgendeiner Weise Vorschub zu leisten. Es soll damit nur ausgedrückt werden, dass wenn keine physische Veränderung auftritt, sich auch keine psychische einstellt, wobei über den Grund dieser Abhängigkeit nicht das Mindeste impliziert wird. Dieses Wenn-Dann-Verhältnis drückt den empirischen Zusammenhang aus zwischen inneren und äußeren Erfahrungen, ohne dass damit weitergehende spezielle ontologische Annahmen über Leib und Seele oder kausale Behauptungen über ihr Verhalten gemacht werden. Die *Psychophysik* ist gerade als diejenige Wissenschaft definiert, die sich all dieser weitergehenden Annahmen enthält:

> Alle Erörterungen und Untersuchungen der Psychophysik beziehen sich überhaupt blos auf die Erscheinungsseite der körperlichen und geistigen Welt, auf das, was entweder unmittelbar durch innere und äussere Wahrnehmung erscheint, oder aus dem Erscheinlichen erschliessbar, oder als Verhältniss, Kategorie, Zusammenhang, Auseinanderfolge, Gesetz des Erscheinlichen fassbar ist; [...] ohne dass auf das Wesen des Körpers, der Seele hinter der Erscheinungswelt im Sinne der Metaphysik irgendwie zurückgegangen werden wird. (Fechner 1860, I, 8)

Nach allen Erfahrungen, die die Physiologie zusammengetragen hat, sind physische Gehirnprozesse in diesem Sinne notwendige Bedingungen für unsere psychischen Prozesse. Freilich lässt sich dies nicht direkt an der Erfahrung überprüfen, da derjenige, der gerade empfindet oder denkt, nicht gleichzeitig die physiologischen Vorgänge in seinem Gehirn verfolgen kann. Aber man kann, wie in anderen Bereichen der Naturwissenschaft auch, vom Bekannten in das Unbekannte induktiv extrapolieren.

Das dritte Prinzip formuliert also auch ein Adäquatheitskriterium für philosophische *Leib-Seele-Theorien*: Jede Leib-Seele-Theorie, die Wissenschaftlichkeit für sich in Anspruch nehmen will, muss physische Veränderungen als notwendige Bedingung für psychische Veränderungen akzeptieren. Die Beschreibung des Bedingungsverhältnisses drückt also den empirischen und metaphysikfreien Kern jeder sinnvollen Leib-Seele-Theorie aus. Ähnlich wie das zweite Prinzip beruht zwar auch das dritte auf Erfahrungen. Es hat aber ebenfalls einen so grundlegenden Charakter erhalten, dass es nicht mehr als revidierbar angesehen wird, sondern umgekehrt als Kriterium der Wissenschaftlichkeit einer Theorie des Leib-Seele-Verhältnisses aufgefasst werden muss.

Das *vierte Prinzip* fasst das Verhältnis der organischen Welt zur physischen Welt allgemein analog dem Verhältnis, welches das Psychische zum Physischen hat: Es gibt keine Änderung organischer ohne eine Änderung physischer Erscheinungen. Alles *Organische* ist durch *Physisches* bedingt; Entstehung, Entwicklung und Mannigfaltigkeit der Organismen kann durch Naturgesetze vollständig erklärt werden. Wie bei der Behandlung des Verhältnisses der psychischen zur physischen Welt wird also auch bei der Behandlung des Verhältnisses der biologischen zur physischen Welt angenommen, dass empirische Naturgesetze völlig ausreichen, um die Eigenart der Biologie im Vergleich zur Physik erklären zu können. Die Wirksamkeit des Physischen muss in keiner Weise eingeschränkt werden, um der Welt der Organismen gerecht zu werden.

Bevor wir nun zu Fechners weiteren Prinzipien übergehen, schauen wir uns die bisherigen Prinzipien in ihrer Gesamtheit nochmals an. Der Einwand liegt nahe, dass diese vier Prinzipien ein viel zu materialistisches Bild von der Natur ergeben, als dass es Fechner jemals gebilligt hätte. Es lässt sich nicht leugnen, dass diese vier Prinzipien einen rigoros *empiristischen* Standpunkt einschließen, der die Zulässigkeit von Behauptungen über die Welt an ihrer Übereinstimmung mit der direkten Erfahrung misst: Empirisch nicht überprüfbare Behauptungen werden verworfen; es wird mit diesen Prinzipien gesagt, dass die Physik alle Veränderungen in der physischen Welt erklären kann – es wird also ausgeschlossen, dass unser Geist oder gar ein transzendentes geistiges Wesen aktiv oder korrigierend in den Lauf der Welt eingreift und so die Naturgesetze verletzt; es wird gesagt, dass jede psychische *Erscheinung* physisch bedingt ist (im oben erwähnten schwachen Sinne von »bedingt«) – das Geistige kann also nichts »Freischwebendes« sein, das man nach Belieben herbeipostulieren könnte. Und es wird schließlich gesagt, dass die Entwicklung der Welt der Organismen in ihrer Vielfalt und Entwicklung ganz natürlich, ohne Rückgriff auf übernatürliche Ursachen, zu erklären ist.

Tatsächlich scheint die Auffassung der Natur und der Rolle der Naturwissenschaft, die durch diese Prinzipien zustande kommt, *prima facie* schon alles zu leisten, was man üblicherweise vom reduktiven Materialismus erwartet. Ein genauerer Blick ergibt jedoch, dass dieser Eindruck trügt. Diese vier Prinzipien sind zwar mit einem reduktiven Materialismus *verträglich*, aber sie implizieren ihn *nicht*. Sie sind mit unterschiedlichen Ausgestaltungen des Verhältnisses des Psychischen zum Physischen und des Organischen zum Physischen verträglich. Mit den vier Prinzipien ist nur ein *Rahmen* für psychologische und biologische *Erklärungen* festgelegt, der im Einzelnen noch näher ausgefüllt werden muss.

Fechners Ziel im Weiteren ist es, den Rahmen so auszufüllen, dass der Reduktionismus vermieden wird und der resultierende nichtreduktive Materialismus in methodischer Hinsicht und in Bezug auf die Erklärungskraft mit dem reduktiven Materialismus gleichzieht, wenn nicht ihn sogar übertrifft. Um dies zu erreichen muss er

1. die Behauptungen über die Bedingung des Psychischen und Organischen durch Physisches zu nichtreduktiven Erklärungen vervollständigen, die mit den ersten vier Prinzipien verträglich sind, und
2. müssen die Zusatzannahmen mindestens ebenso plausibel sein wie diejenigen, mit denen der reduktive Materialismus in seinen Erklärungen derselben Verhältnisse die reinen Bedingungsbehauptungen verstärkt.

Fragen wir uns erst, wie der reduktionistische Materialismus normalerweise diese beiden Verhältnisse des Psychischen zum Physischen und des Organischen zum Anorganischen erklärt. Der reduktive Materialist fügt den vier Prinzipien ein fünftes hinzu, das besagt, dass psychische *Erscheinungen* von physischen Prozessen oder Ereignissen *verursacht* oder *produziert* werden. Als sechstes Prinzip fordert er, dass diejenigen Gesetze, die die physischen Veränderungen in der Welt erklären, dafür *ausreichen*, auch die Entstehung und Entwicklung der Organismen und der Welt im Ganzen erklären.

Diese zwei Zusatzprinzipien des reduktiven Materialisten bleiben nicht ohne Konsequenzen für die ersten vier. Es ergibt sich eine Modifikation des ersten Prinzips: Wenn die psychischen *Erscheinungen* physisch verursacht werden, dann sind sie selbst (wegen der kausalen Geschlossenheit der Welt) physischer Natur. Es ist daher nach Meinung des reduktiven Materialisten überflüssig, ja sinnlos, sich wissenschaftlich auf etwas beziehen zu wollen, was sozusagen das Physische am Psychischen übersteigt. (Psychische Erscheinungen sind für den reduktiven Materialisten höchstens das subjektive Korrelat äußerer objektiver Prozesse. Sie haben für ihn neben ihrer physischen Natur kein wirkliches oder höchstens ein epiphänomenales Sein und sind somit prinzipiell aus dem wissenschaftlichen Weltbild ohne Verlust eliminierbar.)

Weiterhin ergibt sich aus den Zusatzprinzipien des reduktiven Materialismus auch eine Erweiterung des zweiten Prinzips, demgemäß jede physische Veränderung durch physikalische *Gesetze* erklärbar ist. Wenn der reduktive Materialismus wahr ist, dann kann uns die Physik nicht nur alle *physischen* Veränderungen in der Welt, sondern überhaupt *alle* vorkommenden Veränderungen erklären, auch die psychischen oder biologischen.

Der reduktive Materialist kann seine beiden zusätzlichen Prinzipien mit guten Argumenten plausibel machen. Er verlangt ja nur, dass der Naturwissenschaftler die Erklärungsweise, über die er ohnehin schon verfügt und die er so erfolgreich handhabt, auch auf das Verhältnis zwischen Physischem und Psychischem, Organischem und Anorganischem ausdehnt. Es werden damit keine tiefgreifenden Modifikationen der vier grundlegenden Prinzipien notwendig. Außerdem schafft die Erklärung des reduktiven Materialisten Klarheit. Was soll denn das im zweiten Prinzip angesprochene Bedingungsverhältnis zwischen Physischem und Psychischem bedeuten, wenn nicht ein *Kausalverhältnis*? Und was soll die Abhängigkeit des organischen vom anorganischen Bereich denn anderes sein, wenn nicht ein Kausalverhältnis?

Um gegen den reduktiven Materialisten bestehen zu können, muß Fechner also das Kunststück fertig bringen, Zusatzprinzipien vorzulegen, die einerseits eine zum reduktiven Materialismus alternative *Erklärung* des Verhältnisses von Psychischem und Physischem, von Organischem und Anorganischem anbieten, andererseits aber mit den genannten vier Prinzipien verträglich sind, ohne dabei ihren nichtreduktiven Charakter einzubüßen.

Was bedeutet dies nun im Einzelnen? Es kommt erstens darauf an, näher verständlich zu machen, was es heißen soll, dass das faktische Bedingungsverhältnis, das zwischen Physischem und Psychischem besteht, nicht unbedingt als ein kausales aufgefasst werden muss, um die Beziehung zwischen Physischem und Psychischem zu erklären. Und zweitens muss einsichtig werden, warum es erlaubt und sogar geboten ist, neben den *physischen* Veränderungsgesetzen noch weitere *Gesetze* anzunehmen, um Entstehung, Entwicklung und Differenzierung der Vielfalt des Lebendigen in der Natur zu erklären.

Die erste Aufgabe löst Fechner durch das folgende *fünfte Prinzip*: Eine psychische Erscheinung und die in einem Bedingungsverhältnis zu ihr stehende physische sind Erscheinungen ein und desselben Gegenstands. Fechner nennt dieses Prinzip auch seine »Identitätsansicht«. Zu seiner Begründung führt er an, dass ein Gegenstand einem Betrachter (wenigstens potentiell) auf verschiedene Weise gegeben sein kann. Dinge erscheinen uns verschieden, wenn wir eine verschiedene Perspektive zu ihnen einnehmen. Wenn zwei Betrachter aus zwei verschiedenen Blickwinkeln heraus einen materiellen Prozess betrachten, etwa die Bewegung eines Körpers, so sehen sie nur *einen einzigen* Kausalprozess und nicht deren zwei, obwohl dem einzelnen Betrachter der sich bewegende Körper von seiner Warte aus anders erscheint als seinem Mitbetrachter. In analoger Weise rührt die psychische Erscheinungsweise, die man von sich selbst hat, davon her, dass man eine andere Perspektive zu sich einnimmt als zu einem anderen Menschen oder anderen Gegenstand.

Die psychische Perspektive unterscheidet sich von allen Perspektiven, die andere Menschen von einem selbst als einem physischen Wesen haben. Fechner definiert sogar das *Psychische* als dasjenige, was nur einem selbst gegeben ist. Wenn ich mir selbst auf eine Weise erscheine, wie sonst keinem anderen Menschen, dann nehme ich geistige, psychische Prozesse wahr: ich erscheine mir als psychisches Wesen. Wenn ich mir so erscheine, wie ich auch einem anderen erscheinen könnte (wenn ich z.B. in den Spiegel schaue), dann sehe ich dieselben Prozesse als körperliche; ich erscheine mir als physisches, materielles Wesen:

> Es sind im Grunde nur dieselben Prozesse, die von der einen Seite als leiblich organische, von der anderen als geistige, psychische aufgefasst werden können. Als leibliche Processe stellen sie sich Jemandem dar, der außerhalb dieser Processe selbst stehend, dieselben ansieht, oder aus Gesehenem unter Form des äußerlich Wahrnehmbaren erschließt, wie der Anatom, Physiolog, Physiker [es] thut. Ein solcher mag es anfangen, wie er will, er wird nicht das Geringste von

> psychischen Erscheinungen im Andern direct wahrzunehmen vermögen, dagegen stellen sich diese Processe wieder als psychische dar, als Gemeingefühl, Sinnesempfindungen, Vorstellungen, Bestrebungen usw., sofern eine Selbstgewahrung in diesen Processen stattfindet. (Fechner 1851, II, 320f.)
>
> Es ist im Grunde nur *ein* Wesen da, das auf verschiedenen Standpunkten verschieden erscheint. [...] [Es] greifen [auch nicht] zwei einander fremde Kausalzusammenhänge unregelmäßig in einander ein, denn es ist nur ein Kausalzusammenhang da, der in der *einen* Substanz, auf zwei Weisen, d.i. von zwei Standpunkten her, verfolgbar abläuft. (Fechner 1851, II, 347)

Versuchen wir für diese Theorie Fechners noch eine andere Formulierung zu finden: Jedes psychische Ereignis (jeder psychische Zustand) ist identisch mit einem physischen Ereignis (Zustand). Jedes Ereignis, das als ein psychisches beschreibbar ist, kann prinzipiell auch als ein physisches beschrieben werden. Da Kausalität eine Relation zwischen unterschiedlichen Ereignissen ist, wäre es also ein Kategorienfehler zu sagen, psychische Ereignisse seien durch physische Ereignisse (oder umgekehrt) verursacht. Fechner hat also durch das Erklärungsprinzip seiner *Identitätsansicht* den vom reduktiven Materialismus eingeschlagenen Weg der Verschärfung der physischen Bedingtheit zur kausalen Beziehung erfolgreich blockiert, ohne auf die methodischen Vorteile des reduktiven Materialismus verzichten zu müssen.

Hier liegt der Einwand nahe zu sagen: Wenn psychische Ereignisse identisch sind mit ganz bestimmten physischen Ereignissen, sind wir dann nicht wieder beim reduktionistischen Materialismus angelangt? Wenn Psychisches identisch ist mit Physischem, dann kann doch nach dem für Identitäten gültigen Substitutionsprinzip jeder Bezug auf Psychisches durch Bezug auf Physisches ersetzt werden. Damit ist es doch, wissenschaftlich gesehen, ganz überflüssig, einige Ereignisse auch noch als psychische Ereignisse zu beschreiben.

Darauf kann man Folgendes zur Antwort geben: Wenn alle Lungenatmer auch Herzen besitzen, Lungenatmer und Lebewesen mit Herzen also identisch sind, dann ist noch lange nicht der Besitz eines Herzens identisch mit dem Besitz einer Lunge. Übertragen auf das Verhältnis des *Psychischen* zum *Physischen* hieße dies: Auch wenn jedes psychische Phänomen ebenfalls ein physisches ist, ist noch lange nicht ausgemacht, dass in einem psychischen Zustand zu sein identisch ist mit dem Fall, in einem physischen Zustand zu sein. Dies könnten wir höchstens dann behaupten, wenn wir wüssten, dass ein und derselbe spezielle physische Zustand nicht nur hinreichend, sondern auch notwendig ist für die Realisierung eines speziellen psychischen Zustands. Fechner hat nun aber immer wieder, und meines Erachtens überzeugend, darauf hingewiesen, dass wir zwar möglicherweise im Einzelfall feststellen können, welcher physische Zustand *hinreichend* ist für die Realisierung eines speziellen psychischen Zustandes, dass wir aber nicht generell wissen können, welcher Zustand dafür *notwendig* ist. Die Beschreibung der psychischen Seite bestimmter physischer Zustände ist somit weder überflüssig noch eliminierbar. (Eine ähnliche Argumentation findet sich übrigens auch in der Lösung des *Leib-Seele-Problems*, die der sogenannte Funktionalismus in der gegenwärtigen Debatte vorgeschlagen hat.)

Wenn man die Bedeutung von »Identität« bei Fechner genau betrachtet, wird es klar, dass Fechners *Identitätsansicht* eine Erklärung des Verhältnisses von Psychischem und Physischem liefert, die den reduktiven Materialismus vermeidet, ohne die ersten vier wissenschaftsgarantierenden Prinzipien aufgeben zu müssen. Erstens kommt ein psychisches Phänomen durch eine spezielle Betrachtungsweise dessen zustande, das auch als physisch erscheinen kann. Deshalb können psychische Phänomene auch nicht als Wirkung oder Produkt physischer Phänomene gelten. Zweitens ist es unbestimmt, welche physischen Zustände für die Konstitution psychischer Zustände notwendig sind, weshalb das Sprechen über Psychisches nicht ersetzbar ist durch Sprechen über Physisches, also Psychisches nicht auf Physisches reduzierbar ist.

Nach dieser etwas lang geratenen Diskussion des fünften Prinzips steht noch die Erklärung aus für das Verhältnis vom *anorganischen* zum *organischen* Bereich, die als Alternative zu einer reduktionistischen Auffassung der Biologie dienen könnte. Erinnern wir uns, was der reduktive Materialist hier sagt. Nach seiner Auffassung können Entstehung und Entwicklung des Lebens und überhaupt der Ablauf organischer Prozesse durch solche Gesetze vollständig erklärt werden, die die einzelnen »Bewegungen der Atome« regieren, also für die mikroskopischen Veränderungen im anorganischen Bereich gelten. Dem setzt Fechner nun dieses *sechste Prinzip* gegenüber: Um die organische Welt erklären zu können, brauchen wir noch mindestens ein zusätzliches Gesetz, das von anderer Art ist als die Gesetze, die für die einzelnen atomaren Veränderungen im anorganischen Bereich gelten. Die Gesetze, die die einzelnen Bewegungen der Atome beschreiben, reichen nicht aus, um die Veränderungen der organischen Welt vollständig zu erklären; es müssen noch weitere Gesetze berücksichtigt werden.

Von welcher Art sollen diese zusätzlichen *Gesetze* sein? Beim ersten

Hören könnte man vermuten, dass dieses sechste Prinzip das vierte verletzt. Handelt es sich hier nicht um eine besonders raffinierte Form des Vitalismus, der statt von Lebenskraft nun von speziellen Gesetzen spricht? Fechner hat es sich hier nicht so einfach gemacht. Man könnte im Anklang an seine eigene Terminologie diese zusätzlichen Gesetze, von denen er spricht, »Tendenzgesetze« nennen im Unterschied zu den »Veränderungsgesetzen«. Es liegt dabei folgender Gedanke zugrunde: Auch wenn wir das Verhalten jedes individuellen Atoms auf Grund eines (oder mehrerer) Veränderungsgesetze erklären und voraussagen könnten, so könnten wir doch nicht mit der gleichen Information die *Tendenz* voraussagen (wenn es eine gibt), mit der Systeme von Atomen (oder alle Atome) gewisse Zustände einnehmen. Wir brauchen also mindestens noch ein zusätzliches Gesetz, eben ein Tendenzgesetz, das uns sagt, wie sich die Häufigkeit, mit der sich Ensembles von Atomen in einem gegebenen Zustand befinden, im Laufe der Zeit verändern (wenn sie sich überhaupt gesetzmäßig verändern). Die Veränderungsgesetze, die für den anorganischen Bereich gelten, gestatten es allein nicht, Tendenzgesetze abzuleiten.

In seiner Schrift »Einige Ideen zur Schöpfungs- und Entwickelungsgeschichte der Organismen« von 1873 stellt Fechner ein Prinzip auf, das für alle in unserer Welt gültigen Tendenzgesetze eine analoge Rolle spielen soll, wie der *Energieerhaltungssatz* für die Veränderungsgesetze. Er nennt dies das »Prinzip der Tendenz zur Stabilität, welches alle organischen Entwickelungsgesetze [wie z.B. die Gesetze Darwins] verknüpfend unter sich begreift« (Fechner 1873, IV). Ein solches *Stabilitätsprinzip* soll also notwendig dafür sein, dass es überhaupt organische Entwicklung in der Welt gibt. Es ist erfüllt, wenn sich ein abgeschlossenes System periodisch immer mehr einem Zustand annähert, den es früher schon einmal eingenommen hat, d.h. wenn es im Laufe der Zeit kontinuierlich immer stabiler wird. In Fechners eigenen Worten besteht das Prinzip der Tendenz zur Stabilität für ein geschlossenes System darin, dass es sich

> durch die Wirkung seiner inneren Kräfte ohne Rückschritt mehr und mehr einem sogenannten *stabeln* [sic] Zustande nähert, das ist einem solchen, wo die Teile periodisch, d.h., in gleichen Zeitabschnitten, in dieselben Lagen- und Bewegungsverhältnisse zu einander zurückkehren. (Fechner 1879, 209)

Für offene Systeme kann sich die Stabilität zeitweise vermindern, aber auf lange Sicht wird wenigstens eine approximative Stabilität erreicht. Das Weltall im Ganzen strebt auf lange Sicht einer absoluten Stabilität zu. Fechner bemerkt ausdrücklich, dass seiner Ansicht nach das *Stabilitäts-*

prinzip auch die Darwin'sche Evolutionstheorie mit umfasst. Darwins Gesetze der Evolution wären also ein typischer Fall für Tendenzgesetze, die dem Stabilitätsprinzip unterworfen sind.

Nach dieser Übersicht der grundlegenden Prinzipien von Fechners Weltauffassung möchte ich die Behauptung einlösen, dass sie durchaus mit dem *Panpsychismus* verträglich ist, ja, dass der Panpsychismus sogar daraus ableitbar ist, wenn man zusätzlich noch gewisse pragmatische Überlegungen akzeptiert. Die Ableitung ist freilich keine zwingende, sondern eine, die ihre Konklusionen mehr oder weniger wahrscheinlich macht. Es handelt sich, wie Fechner es ausdrückt, um eine »Verallgemeinerung durch Induction und Analogie und vernünftige Combination des von verschiedenen Seiten gewonnenen Allgemeinen« (Fechner 1851, I, XV).

Bevor wir Fechners Induktionsschluss auf die Beseelung des Universums näher behandeln können, müssen wir erst seinen Begriff des »Glaubens« einführen. Unter »Glaube« versteht Fechner »ein Fürwahrhalten dessen, was nicht durch Erfahrung oder logischen Schluß, wozu der mathematische gehört, gewiss ist« (Fechner 1863, 17).[1] Um überflüssige Konnotationen zu vermeiden, könnte man also besser von »Überzeugung« sprechen.

Von Gewissheit (im Gegensatz zum bloßen Glauben) kann man nach Fechner nur in zwei Fällen reden: beim Vorliegen von logischen Wahrheiten und beim Vorliegen von direkten Erfahrungen (und allem, was sich daraus zwingend ableiten lässt). Als *Glaube* im engeren Sinne sind dabei diejenigen Überzeugungen anzusehen, die sich durch keine neue direkte Erfahrung in Wissen verwandeln lassen. Prototyp dieser Art von Glauben ist für Fechner der Glaube an das *Fremdpsychische* (d.h. das Seelenleben des Anderen), der niemals zu einem Wissen werden kann. Wenn jemand anders als ich selbst Freude empfindet oder traurig ist, dann sehe ich zwar äußerliche Anzeichen dieser Empfindungen und Gefühle, aber ich kann keine direkte Erfahrung der inneren Verfassung des anderen haben. Ich bin auf Schlüsse aus äußeren Anzeichen des Leibes angewiesen.

Der Glaube an das *Fremdpsychische* ist für Fechner aber keine prekäre Ausnahme oder eine sonstwie besonders problematische Angelegenheit, da es viele analoge Fälle für einen solchen Glauben auch sonst in Wissenschaft und Alltag gibt: z.B. die Überzeugung, dass Naturgesetze auch

[1] Erstauflage 1863.

über das direkt Erfahrene und Erfahrbare hinaus gültig sind, dass es unbeobachtbare Gegenstände wie die Atome gibt und ähnliches mehr. Selbst der Glaube an die Existenz Gottes ist für Fechner grundsätzlich von dieser Art.

Wir Menschen werden nach seiner Auffassung zum *Glauben* im engeren Sinne sowohl durch Motive als auch durch Gründe geführt, die jeweils in drei Formen auftreten: als historische, praktische und theoretische Motive bzw. Gründe. Die historische Dimension betrifft die räumliche und zeitliche Verbreitung eines Glaubens: Je weiter er verbreitet ist, desto mehr werden wir zu ihm motiviert und desto wahrscheinlicher wird er. Das praktische Motiv betrifft die Nützlichkeit des Glaubens. Der Glaube, der uns nützt, setzt sich als Motiv durch und hat Wahrscheinlichkeit für sich. Theoretische Gründe für den Glauben ergeben sich durch *Induktion* und *Analogie* und werden dadurch auch zu psychologischen Motiven. Fechner ist überzeugt, dass ein durch das Zusammenspiel der drei Motive und Gründe etablierter Glaube »aller Metaphysik, worauf der Philosoph den Glauben stützen möchte [...] so fern wie möglich« (Fechner 1923, 137) liegt. Der Glaube muss aber selbst als »metaphysischer Abschluß« der Erfahrung angesehen werden, jedoch als der metaphysikärmste, der für einen Glauben im engeren Sinne überhaupt möglich ist.

Durch seine Theorie der Überzeugungen kann sich Fechner nun einerseits vom reduktiven Materialismus, andererseits vom Idealismus abgrenzen: Der reduktive Materialismus ist dadurch gekennzeichnet, dass er den Glauben im engeren Sinne ganz verwirft, während der Idealismus Glaubensbegründungen akzeptiert, die weit über die drei genannten Gründe hinausgehen. Der Idealismus lässt also *zu viel* Metaphysik zu, während der Materialismus *zu wenig* akzeptiert.

Als Argument für die Notwendigkeit einer rudimentären *Metaphysik* führt Fechner interessanterweise an, dass die Gründe des Einzelnen für die Existenz der Außenwelt nur darauf beruhen können, dass das Urteil anderer Personen über deren Erfahrung akzeptiert wird. Wir müssen, schreibt er,

> den Durchgang durch den Glauben an Geister außer uns [gemeint ist: Glaube an die Beseeltheit anderer] nehmen [...], um den Hallucinationen gegenüber eine theoretische *Berechtigung* für den Glauben zu finden, dass dem Scheine materieller Außendinge für jeden Einzelnen von uns auch wirklich Dinge objectiv, d.i. für Andere existierend, entsprechen. (Fechner 1879, 227)

Der *Glaube* im engeren Sinne ist also für das natürliche Weltverhältnis, das seine Wahrnehmungen im Normalfall für real hält, unumgänglich notwendig. Objektivität und Realität der Außenwelt setzt Intersubjektivität voraus und dies wiederum verlangt eben einen Glauben im engeren Sinne.

Damit ist meine Darstellung der Fechner'schen Prinzipien abgeschlossen. Man sieht, dass Fechners Weltauffassung wesentlich an seiner Behandlung des *Psychischen* und *Organischen* hängt, die sich auf subtile Weise von der Behandlung unterscheidet, die sich davon normalerweise im mechanistischen Weltbild findet. Ich möchte nun zeigen, dass die Fechner'sche Weltauffassung in ihrer Zeit durchaus auf verwandte Entwicklungen traf. Man kann sogar die Auffassungen des Physikers Ernst Mach (1838–1916), des Philosophen Alois Riehl (1844–1924) und des amerikanischen Naturwissenschaftler und Philosophen Charles Sanders Peirce (1839–1914) als Weiterentwicklungen der Fechner'schen Weltauffassung ansehen.[2]

Machs Modifikation führt in Fechners Sinne zu einem reduktiven Materialismus, da Mach jede Ergänzung von direkten Erfahrungen durch einen Glauben im engeren Sinne radikal ablehnt:

> Das Eine wollen wir aber festhalten, dass es bei der Naturforschung nur auf die Erkenntnis des Zusammenhanges der Erscheinungen ankommt. Was wir hinter den Erscheinungen uns vorstellen, existiert eben *nur* in unserm Verstande, hat für uns nur den Werth einer Gedächtnishandhabe oder Formel, deren Gestalt, weil sie willkührlich und gleichgültig ist, sich sehr leicht mit unserem Culturstandpunkt ändert (Mach 1872, 26). Die letzten Unverständlichkeiten, auf welche sich die Wissenschaft gründet, müssen Thatsachen sein oder wenn es Hypothesen sind, zu Thatsachen werden können. Sind die Hypothesen so gewählt, dass ihr Gegenstand nie in die Sinne fallen kann, also auch nie geprüft werden kann, wie dies bei der mechanischen Moleculartheorie der Fall ist, so hat der Forscher mehr gethan, als die Wissenschaft von ihm verlangt, deren Ziel die Thatsachen sind und dieses Mehr ist vom Uebel. [...] Dann sind die Molecüle nichts wie ein werthloses Bild. (Mach 1872, 33)

---

[2] Ich behaupte hier nur einen gewissen systematischen Zusammenhang zwischen Fechners Auffassungen und denen der anderen genannten Autoren. Die Frage, wie stark Fechner tatsächlich eine historische Wirkung ausgeübt hat, kann hier nicht behandelt werden. Für Mach und Peirce habe ich in diese Richtung führende Überlegungen schon in Kap. 5 und 7 von Heidelberger 1993 angestellt.

Wie dieses Zitat deutlich werden lässt, ist Mach bereit, die Konsequenzen seiner Radikalisierung der Fechner'schen Glaubenstheorie auch für das mechanistische Weltbild zu tragen. Wenn *Glaube* im engeren Sinne generell zu verwerfen ist, dann fällt damit auch der Realismus der mechanistischen Weltauffassung, der Moleküle und ähnliche unbeobachtbare theoretische Gegenstände als real anerkennt. Man kann Machs »Elementenlehre« als den Nachweis rekonstruieren, dass der »Durchgang durch den Glauben an Geister außer uns«, also die Annahme des psychischen Lebens anderer, für die Entwicklung eines Objektivitätsbegriffs der Physik nicht notwendig ist, wie Fechner dies will. Die Elementenkomplexe des Gegebenen sind je nach *funktionaler Abhängigkeit* der Elemente untereinander entweder Empfindungen oder physikalische Objekte. Das »Ich« und sinnlich angeblich unzugängliche Gegenstände wie Atome oder Moleküle sind als bloße ökonomische Zusammenfassungen von Erscheinungen zu begreifen.

Einen ganz anderen Weg als Mach ging der dem Neukantianismus nahestehende Alois Riehl, der den Gegenstandsbegriff sowohl von Fechner als auch von Mach abgelehnt hat. Weder ist der Gegenstand als gesetzlicher Zusammenhang von (gegebenen oder nicht gegebenen) Erscheinungen aufzufassen (Fechner) noch als Komplex von (gegebenen) Elementen (Mach). Vielmehr wird Erfahrung nur möglich durch den *Begriff* des (nicht direkt sinnlich gegebenen) Gegenstands als *Ursache* unserer Erscheinungen:

> So oft wir etwas als Gegenstand der Wahrnehmung auffassen, glauben wir [...], dass der Gegenstand nicht erst durch die Wahrnehmung entsteht oder mit ihr vergeht und von neuem geschaffen wird, wenn die Wahrnehmung sich erneuert. Wir glauben an die Unabhängigkeit des Gegenstandes von der Wahrnehmung [...] Dieser Glaube an die Unabhängigkeit der Objekte von ihrem Wahrgenommenwerden und an ihre Beständigkeit, ungeachtet des Wechsels der Wahrnehmungen, ist der Glaube, den wir mit dem Begriff der Substanz ausdrücken. Ohne diesen Glauben – keine Erfahrung, denn ohne ihn würde das Objekt fehlen, von dem irgend etwas ausgesagt werden könnte, das Objekt für ein Urteil über die Wahrnehmung und weil keine Erfahrung, auch keine Wissenschaft, keine Möglichkeit der Übereinstimmung der Urteile aller in Bezug auf ein und dasselbe Objekt. (Riehl 1913, 67)[3]

Riehl nennt seine Auffassung »kritischen Realismus«. Er lehnt Fechners Ansicht ab, dass der *Glaube* an das unabhängige äußere Objekt den

[3] Erstauflage 1903.

Glauben an das Fremdpsychische voraussetzt und nur dadurch gerechtfertigt werden kann. Die Überzeugung von der Existenz eines speziellen äußeren Objekts ist an die Überzeugung des Vorliegens seiner Substanz geknüpft. Substanz ist nicht als »metaphysischer Abschluß« der Erscheinungen, wie Fechner es forderte, aufzufassen, sondern als *Voraussetzung* für die Einheit der Erscheinungen im Gegenstand. Gleichwohl sind auch bei Riehl noch die Spuren des Fechner'schen »Glaubens an Geister außer uns« zu bemerken. Erfahrung heißt zwar: Beziehung einer Anschauung auf ihren Gegenstand auf allgemeingültige Art und Weise. Allgemeingültigkeit ist aber zu begreifen als »Product des gemeinschaftlichen oder intersubjektiven Denkens.« Deshalb ist für Riehl auch »die Erfahrung [...] ein socialer, kein individual-psychologischer Begriff« (Riehl 1887, 64).

Auch der *Pragmatismus* von Charles Sanders Peirce stellt sich als Weiterentwicklung von Fechners Weltauffassung dar, wobei sowohl Impulse aus Machs Positivismus als auch Riehls Realismus aufgegriffen werden. Im folgenden Zitat wird deutlich, dass Peirce (wie Fechner) mit seinem Pragmatismus eine *Metaphysik* (»gereinigte Philosophie«) für notwendig hält, die die Wirksamkeit und Berechtigung von überzeugungsproduzierenden Motiven anerkennt und den Realismus Riehls akzeptiert: Was den Pragmatismus vom Positivismus unterscheidet, ist

> erstens sein Beibehalten einer gereinigten Philosophie, zweitens seine uneingeschränkte Annahme des größten Teils unserer instinktiven Überzeugungen und drittens sein energisches Bestehen auf der Wahrheit des scholastischen Realismus (oder jedenfalls einer engen Annäherung davon [...]). [...] So gewinnt der Pragmatizist, anstatt wie andere Prope-Positivisten die Metaphysik zu verspotten, sei es durch ausgedehnte Parodien oder anderswie, aus ihr einen wertvollen Extrakt, der dazu dienen wird, der Kosmologie und der Physik Licht und Leben zu geben. (Peirce 1960 CP 5. 424)

Auf der anderen Seite nimmt Peirce jedoch eine ganz einschneidende Modifikation an Fechners Wissensbegriff vor, der gleichzeitig zu einer Ausweitung von Fechners *Glaubenstheorie* führt. Peirce lehnt die innere Wahrnehmung als Teil der Erfahrungsbasis ab. Ein Wissen von innerer Wirklichkeit kann seines Erachtens nur durch Schlüsse aus äußeren Tatsachen gewonnen werden. »Der einzige Weg, eine psychologische Frage zu untersuchen, ist durch einen Schluß aus äußeren Tatsachen« (Peirce CP 5. 249). Hier ist schon die methodische Haltung des Behaviorismus zu spüren und eine Zurückweisung der bei Fechner latent vorhandenen Billigung der Introspektion als wissenschaftlicher Grundlegung der empirischen Psychologie.

Schließlich greift Peirce in seiner Umarbeitung der *Glaubenstheorie* aber auch noch Motive des Idealismus auf, wenn er Materie als »erloschenen Geist« (»effete mind«) betrachtet und physische *Gesetze* als das Resultat psychischer Gewohnheiten auffasst. Hier zeigt sich übrigens, dass auch er nicht von panpsychistischen Versuchungen frei ist. Ein weiteres Motiv von Peirce für diese überraschende Wendung zum Idealismus scheint aber auch zu sein, dass dadurch Fechners direkter Realismus besser gerechtfertigt und mit dem Realismus von Riehl und anderen vereinbart werden kann: »Es ist ein psychisches Gefühl von Rot außerhalb von uns, das in uns das sympathische Gefühl von Rot in unseren Sinnen erzeugt« (Peirce 1960 CP 1. 311). »Woran wir denken, kann unmöglich von anderer Natur sein als der Gedanke selbst. [...] Der denkende Gedanke und das direkte Gedankenobjekt sind dasselbe Ding, das von verschiedenen Seiten betrachtet wird« (Peirce 1960 CP 6. 339). Peirce bekräftigt hier einerseits Fechners direkten Realismus (also die Auffassung, dass die sinnlichen Eigenschaften der Gegenstände, wie z.B. Farben, diesen auch wirklich zukommen und nicht nur im wahrnehmenden Subjekt bestehen) und versucht andererseits, diesen direkten Realismus mit der *Identitätsansicht* zu verbinden und als ihre Konsequenz darzustellen.

Im Vorgehenden habe ich den rationalen Kern von Fechners Weltauffassung herausgearbeitet und dann zu zeigen versucht, dass er im weiteren Fortgang der Philosophiegeschichte eine wichtige Rolle spielte. Auch wenn der Leser bis hierher mitgegangen ist, mag er trotzdem das ungute Gefühl zurückbehalten, dass die vorhergehende Darstellung irgendwie Fechners spekulativ-metaphysische Auffassungen verfehlt. Es sollte allerdings nicht behauptet werden, dass der Nachweis der Verträglichkeit von Fechners *Metaphysik* mit dem wissenschaftlichen Kern seiner Weltauffassung schon alles ist, was man dazu sagen kann. Tatsächlich klafft ein merkwürdiger *Zwiespalt* zwischen der geringen Wahrscheinlichkeit der Metaphysik Fechners im Lichte seiner Weltauffassung und der Bereitschaft, mit der Fechner diese Metaphysik vertritt. Man hat den Eindruck, dass sich Fechner systematisch und permanent über die »Sprechakte« seines eigenen Philosophierens täuscht: Anstatt seine Philosophie nur als ein System durch Argumente gestützter Behauptungen zu nehmen, behandelt er sie auch als performative Äußerungen, die weltanschauliche Bedürfnisse befriedigen sollen. Dies bringt es mit sich, dass Fechners Philosophieren immer »doppelgleisig« wirkt: Einerseits wird ein wissenschaftliches

Erkenntnisziel verfolgt, andererseits werden bestimmte, mit der wissenschaftlichen Vorgehensweise verträgliche, aber durch sie nicht unbedingt sehr plausibel gemachte weltanschauliche Elemente vertreten und zu einem umfassenden spekulativen Zusammenhang verwoben. Hier zeigt sich auf einer anderen Ebene die Kluft, die durch Fechners Charakter geht. Fechner wollte auf Biegen und Brechen zwei Dinge in seinem Leben zusammenzwingen, die nur schwer zueinander passen: das scharfe, methodisch ausgewiesene Denken des Erwachsenen über die Welt und die Wissenschaft und der mit Motiven des *Theismus* aus dem 18. Jahrhundert vermischte Gottesglaube des Kindes. Das Erstaunliche daran ist aber, dass diese versuchte Versöhnung zweier widerstreitender Charakterzüge keine rückwärtsgewandte Verneinung der Moderne beinhaltet, wie oft behauptet wird, sondern den Keim für eine Überwindung des mechanistischen Weltbildes bei Mach, bei Riehl, bei Peirce und anderen in sich trägt.

Literatur:

Fechner, G. Th. (1851): Zend=Avesta oder über die Dinge des Himmels und des Jenseits. Vom Standpunkt der Naturbetrachtung. 3 Bde. Leipzig.

Fechner, G. Th. (1860): Elemente der Psychophysik. 2 Bde. Leipzig.

Fechner, G. Th. (1873): Einige Ideen zur Schöpfungs- und Entwickelungsgeschichte der Organismen. Leipzig.

Fechner, G. Th. (1879): Die Tagesansicht gegenüber der Nachtansicht. Leipzig.

Fechner, G. Th. (1923): Über die Motive und Gründe des Glaubens. Leipzig. Hg. und erl. von W. Platz. Stuttgart.

Heidelberger, M. (1993): Die innere Seite der Natur. Gustav Theodor Fechners wissenschaftlich-philosophische Weltauffassung. Frankfurt a.M.

Mach, E. (1872): Die Geschichte und die Wurzel des Satzes von der Erhaltung der Arbeit. Prag.

Peirce, C.S. (1960) CP: Collected Papers of Charles Sanders Peirce. Hg. von Ch. Hartshorne und P. Weiss. 8 Bde. 2. Aufl. Cambridge 1960 (Bd. 7 & 8 hg. von A.W. Burks).[4]

Riehl, A. (1887): Der philosophische Kriticismus und seine Bedeutung für die positive Wissenschaft. 2 Bde. (1876–87), Bd. II, Teil 2: Zur Wissenschaftstheorie und Metaphysik. Leipzig.

Riehl, A. (1913): Zur Einführung in die Philosophie der Gegenwart (1903). Acht Vorträge. Leipzig. 4. Aufl. Berlin.

---

[4] Zitiert wird, wie üblich, nach Band und Abschnitt.

Dirk Evers

Der Fechner'sche Gottesbegriff[1]

Ausgehend von einer Rekonstruktion der Fechner'schen Tagesansicht wird ein Zugang zu Fechners Weltsicht gewonnen, in dem das Ganze seiner Philosophie sichtbar wird. Fechners Glaubensbegriff, seine Erkenntnistheorie, sein Verständnis des Verhältnisses von Körperwelt und Geisteswelt und seine kosmologischen Spekulationen kommen hier zusammen. Vor dem religiösen Hintergrund seiner Zeit stellt sich Fechner dar als ein Apologet religiöser Grundüberzeugungen, die sich eng an der Empirie der Wissenschaften orientieren, und als ein Verfechter eines freien, der Geschichtlichkeit des menschlichen Lebens Rechnung tragenden Christentums. Abschließend wird aus heutiger theologischer Perspektive gefragt, ob und inwiefern Fechners Weltsicht einen heute noch relevanten Beitrag zum Dialog von Naturwissenschaft und Religion darstellt.

1. Biographische Vorbemerkungen

Das 19. Jahrhundert, in dessen Mitte Fechner wirkte, war eine Zeit weltanschaulicher Auseinandersetzungen, die *Religion*, *Kirche* und allgemeine Volksfrömmigkeit in eine in vielem bis heute andauernde Krise stürzten. Das hatte der – oft als Kirchenvater der 19. Jahrhunderts apostrophierte – Theologe Friedrich Daniel Ernst Schleiermacher (1768–1834) schon 1829 hellsichtig gesehen. In dem bekannten Sendschreiben an seinen Freund Lücke heißt es:

> Wenn Sie den gegenwärtigen Zustand der Naturwissenschaft betrachten, wie sie sich immer mehr zu einer umfassenden Weltkunde gestaltet, [...] [so] will mir nun nichts anderes ahnden, als daß wir werden lernen müssen uns ohne vieles behelfen, was Viele noch gewohnt sind als mit dem Wesen des Christenthums unzertrennlich verbunden zu denken. Ich will gar nicht vom Sechstagewerk reden, aber der Schöpfungsbegriff, wie er gewöhnlich construirt wird [...]: wie lange wird er sich noch halten können gegen die Gewalt einer aus wis-

[1] Der Vortragsstil wurde bewusst beibehalten.

> senschaftlichen Combinationen, denen sich niemand entziehen kann, gebildeten Weltanschauung? [...] Ich werde diese Zeit nicht mehr erleben [...]. Aber Sie, [...] was gedenken Sie zu thun? Wollt Ihr Euch dennoch hinter diesen Außenwerken [gemeint sind die buchstäblich genommenen biblischen Texte] verschanzen, und Euch von der Wissenschaft blokiren lassen? Das Bombardement des Spottes, welches dann auch von Zeit zu Zeit erneuert werden wird, will ich für nichts rechnen [...]. Aber die Blokade! die gänzliche Aushungerung von aller Wissenschaft, die dann, nothgedrungen von Euch, eben weil Ihr Euch so verschanzt, die Fahne des Unglaubens aufstecken muß! Soll der Knoten der Geschichte so auseinandergehen? das Christentum mit der Barbarei, und die Wissenschaft mit dem Unglauben? (Schleiermacher 1990, 345–347)

Nein, das sollte er nicht. Fechner jedenfalls versteht seine philosophisch-religiöse Weltsicht als eine Antwort auf diese Herausforderung, hat doch die bedrängende Erfahrung, in einer Zeit zu leben, in der alle religiöse Grundlage durch die Wissenschaft zersetzt und ins Haltlose aufgelöst wird, seine eigene Biographie geprägt und ist von daher auch zur Aufgabe seines philosophischen Denkens geworden. In seiner von ihm sogenannten ›Tagesansicht‹, die er der in den Naturwissenschaften und in der Philosophie seiner Zeit, aber auch in Theologie und Kirche herrschenden ›Nachtansicht‹ entgegenstellte, fand er eine zumindest für ihn persönlich tragfähige Lösung. Werfen wir deshalb einen kurzen Blick auf seinen inneren, *religiösen Werdegang*, soweit er uns überhaupt zugänglich ist.

Wie so viele bedeutende Männer der Geistesgeschichte des 19. Jahrhunderts stammte auch Fechner aus einem evangelischen Pfarrhaus, ebenso wie schon sein Vater und seine Mutter aus Pastorenfamilien stammten. Fechners Vater wird als aufgeschlossener, von der Aufklärung bestimmter Theologe geschildert, der allerdings starb, als Fechner erst fünf Jahre alt war. Auch Fechner sollte ursprünglich Pfarrer werden, studierte dann aber Medizin, zunächst in Dresden, dann in Leipzig. Die praktische Ausbildung als Mediziner empfand er als überaus unbefriedigend, und er entwickelte geradezu eine Abneigung gegen das Fach und seine Vertreter, der er in einigen *satirischen Schriften* Luft machte. Überhaupt verhalf ihm das kleine Einkommen aus seiner literarischen Tätigkeit dazu, sich beruflich anders orientieren zu können. Im Rückblick schreibt Fechner: »Ueber meinem medicinischen Studium war ich zum völligen Atheisten geworden; ich sah in der Welt nur ein mechanisches Getriebe« (Kuntze 1892, 39). In dieser Situation entdeckt er die romantische *Naturphilosophie*.

> Da gerieth mir Oken's Naturphilosophie in die Hände [...]. Ein neues Licht schien mir auf einmal die ganze Welt und Wissenschaft von der Welt zu erleuchten; ich war wie geblendet davon. [...] ich hatte auf einmal den Gesichtspunkt einer großen einheitlichen Weltanschauung gewonnen, fing an Schelling, Steffens und andere Naturphilosophen zu studiren. (Kuntze 1892, 39)

Andererseits aber sind Fechner durch die Übersetzungen naturwissenschaftlicher Lehrbücher auch die »klaren, sicheren und fruchtbaren Resultate [...] in der Naturwissenschaft« (Kuntze 1892, 39) eindrücklich vor Augen. Damit war eine nicht unerhebliche Spannung gegeben, die Fechner in eine ernste *Krise* führen sollte. Zwar habilitierte sich Fechner in der Naturphilosophie mit der Absicht, »naturphilosophische Ideen im Schelling-Oken'schen Geist [...] vorzutragen« (Kuntze 1892, 72), doch seine Hoffnung, »nun auf dem Wege zu sein, das Geheimnis der Welt und ihrer Schöpfung zu entdecken«, erfüllte sich nicht. »Ich zerbrach mir, mißhandelte den Kopf von Morgen bis Abend und in manchen Nächten, um festen Fuß zu gewinnen, und konnte mir doch nie selbst dabei genügen« (Kuntze 1892, 100). Die *Naturphilosophie*, die ihm die Natur als Erscheinung des Geistes zeigen und ihn damit über den *Materialismus* hinausführen wollte, ließ ihn nach kurzer Zeit, wie er selber im Rückblick konstatiert, »nur um so tiefer darein zurücksinken« (Fechner 1879, 161). Fechner wendet sich nun endgültig der theoretischen und experimentellen Naturwissenschaft zu und erhält schließlich 1834 die ordentliche Professur für Physik. Er forscht hauptsächlich über Fragen der Elektrizitätslehre, des Elektromagnetismus und der Elektrochemie.

Die äußeren und inneren Anspannungen und Anfechtungen aber, unter denen Fechner existiert und die sich nicht lösen wollen, führen ihn gegen Ende 1839 in die schwere *Krise* einer über vier Jahre sich hinziehenden psychosomatischen Krankheit, die sich in heftigen Sehstörungen äußert, aber auch mit einer für Fechner kaum erträglichen Unkontrollierbarkeit seiner Gedanken und seiner Aufmerksamkeit einhergeht.[2] Im Herbst 1843 ist Fechner einigermaßen genesen; 1846 beginnt er philosophische Vorlesungen zu halten, deren Hauptgesichtspunkte er zuvor in einer kleinen Schrift dargelegt hat (Ueber das höchste Gut, 1846). Die Universität befreit ihn von allen Lehrverpflichtungen, gewährt ihm aber weiter ein bescheidenes Gehalt. Seine Professur noch auszufüllen fehlen ihm jeden-

---

[2] Fechners eigener, 1845 abgefasster Bericht über seine Krankheit findet sich bei Kuntze 1892, 105–126. Eine wirkliche Diagnose dürfte sich im Nachhinein kaum stellen lassen; vgl. den Überblick über die verschiedenen Vorschläge bei Heidelberger 1993, 70.

falls die Kräfte. Mit dem Schwinden der Krankheit löst sich aber die große innere Anspannung, die sein Leben bis dahin bestimmt hat, und er gewinnt eine neue Weltsicht, in der die verschiedenen Elemente des physikalisch-naturwissenschaftlichen Zugangs zur Welt, der *Naturphilosophie* und eine neu belebte Religiosität zu einem einheitlichen Konzept integriert werden. Diese neu gewonnene Sicht wird Fechner später als die ›Tagesansicht‹ gegenüber der ›Nachtansicht‹ des mechanistischen Weltbilds bezeichnen.[3]

Kam zuvor *Gott* allenfalls marginale Bedeutung zu,[4] so erlangt die Vorstellung eines persönlichen Gottes nun eine tragende Bedeutung für Fechners neue Weltanschauung. Er erlebt diese Wende auch als eine Rückkehr zum christlichen *Glauben*, wenn auch, wie wir gleich genauer sehen werden, in einer ganz eigentümlichen Form. Die zunächst so begierig aufgenommene *Naturphilosophie* hatte Fechner nicht nur intellektuell unbefriedigt gelassen, sie hatte ihm auch für sein persönliches Leben keine Stütze geboten. »Nur der Glaube an die Tagesansicht mit ihrer Wiedereinkehr in die christlichen Ideen von einer göttlichen Führung«, schreibt er, »ließ mich diese Stütze finden« (Fechner 1879, 162).

2. Die Tagesansicht

Wir wollen uns nach diesen biographischen Vorbemerkungen nun der von Fechner entwickelten *Tagesansicht*, in der er seine religiöse Stütze fand, genauer zuwenden und zunächst die grundlegende Einsicht Fechners rekonstruieren, auf der sie beruht. Dazu soll uns eine von Fechner selbst geschilderte Begebenheit als Illustration dienen. Zu Beginn seiner Schrift »Die Tagesansicht gegenüber der Nachtansicht« schildert Fechner, wie er eines Morgens im Leipziger Rosental auf einer Bank im hellen und warmen Sonnenschein sitzt und seine Sinne sich mit den Eindrücken der belebten Natur erfüllen – mit den Farben der Blumen, dem Tanz der

---

[3] Fechner, Tagesansicht, pass. Der Begriff der ›Nachtansicht‹ in Bezug auf die Naturwissenschaften dürfte auf die naturphilosophischen Vorträge von Gotthilf Heinrich Schubert zum Thema »Ansichten von der Nachtseite der Naturwissenschaften« (1808) zurückgehen, die zu ihrer Zeit einiges Aufsehen erregten.

[4] Im »Büchlein vom Leben nach dem Tode« (1836) werden der Glaube an Gott und der Glaube an das eigene ewige Leben schlicht gleichgesetzt, ist doch Gott ganz im Sinne der Oken'schen Naturphilosophie nur eine Bezeichnung für das Ganze der lebendigen Welt; vgl. Fechner 1950, 58.

Schmetterlinge, dem Gesang der Vögel.[5] Doch dann wird ihm bewusst, dass er als Naturwissenschaftler dieses ganze Schauspiel eigentlich als Schein ansehen müsste. Denn was der Mensch in der Natur wahrnimmt, ist ja doch im Grunde eine Illusion. Licht- und Schallwellen sind nur »blinde stumme Wellenzüge«, die sich nach mechanischen *Gesetzen* als Erregung eines Mediums durch den Raum fortpflanzen, »und erst, wenn sie an den Eiweißknäuel unseres Gehirns, ja wohl gar erst, wenn sie an einen bestimmten Punct desselben antreffen«, setzen sie sich um in wahrgenommene psychische Licht- und Schalleindrücke. Wie »durch den spiritistischen Zauber dieses Medium[s]« (Fechner 1879, 4) die Entstehung des psychischen Eindrucks vor sich gehen mag, darüber streiten sich die Philosophen und Wissenschaftler, doch über die fundamentale Interpretation ist man sich einig: alles Leuchten, Tönen und Tasten ist nichts, was den Naturerscheinungen an sich zukommt, sondern wird vom wahrnehmenden Subjekt generiert und hat den Charakter eines davon unabhängigen Scheins, einer Illusion, die unser Seelenorgan, das Gehirn produziert. In der Perspektive der Naturwissenschaften verkehrt sich die ganze leuchtende, klingende und singende Natur in finstere, stumme Nacht.

Damit hat Fechner in der Tat eine wesentliche Grundlage des naturwissenschaftlichen Weltbilds angesprochen, die sich bis auf den Gründungsvater der neuzeitlichen empirischen Physik, bis auf Galileo Galilei zurückführen lässt. In seiner programmatischen Schrift »Il Saggiatore« bezieht Galilei die messende Wissenschaft von der Natur auf eine elementare Unterscheidung, auf die Unterscheidung zwischen *primären* und *sekundären* Qualitäten. Galilei weist darauf hin, dass mit der Vorstellung einer körperlichen Substanz notwendigerweise die Vorstellung von begrenzter Ausdehnung und Form verbunden ist und dass sie sich zu einer bestimmen Zeit an einem bestimmten Ort befindet, bewegt oder unbewegt ist etc. Dies sind ihre primären Eigenschaften. »Aber dass sie weiß oder rot, bitter oder süß, tönend oder stumm, wohl- oder übelriechend sein muss, das als notwendige Begleitumstände anzuerkennen, fühle ich mich in meiner Vorstellungskraft nicht gezwungen.« Geschmack, Geruch, Farbe usw. sind »nichts anderes als bloße Namen«, sie haben ihren Sitz »allein in dem empfindenden Körper, so dass, wenn der beseelte Körper entfernt würde, auch alle diese Qualitäten aufgehoben und beseitigt wären« (Galilei 1896, 4, 347f.).

---

[5] Vgl. Fechner 1879, 3ff.

Es sind nun gerade die primären Eigenschaften, die quantifiziert und mathematisiert werden können, mit denen gerechnet werden kann. Das ist für Galilei ihr entscheidendes Merkmal gegenüber den sekundären subjektiven, den Menschen nur allzu leicht täuschenden und nicht quantifizierbaren Sinnesqualitäten, geht es doch seither in der Physik darum, die wahren Zusammenhänge der Natur in mathematischer Form abzubilden. Noch einmal Galilei im »Saggiatore«: Das Buch der Natur

> ist in mathematischer Sprache geschrieben, und seine Buchstaben sind Dreiecke, Kreise und andere geometrische Figuren, ohne diese Mittel ist es unmöglich, ein einziges Wort zu verstehen, irrt man vergeblich in einem dunklen Labyrinth umher. (Galilei 1896, 4, 232)

Alle moderne Naturwissenschaft und Philosophie (vor allem die der Aufklärung) sieht Fechner durch diese Unterscheidung geprägt. Alle sinnliche Wahrnehmung wird, von den ganz abstrakten messbaren Eigenschaften der Gegenstände (ihrer Ortsstelle, deren Änderung nach der Zeit und ihre ponderable Massivität) abgesehen, dem erkennenden Subjekt zugeschrieben, während hinter dieser Welt der Erscheinungen die eigentliche, die wesentliche und uns zugleich unzugängliche Welt der ›Dinge an sich‹ liegt als eine dunkle, unsinnliche Hinterwelt. Fechner möchte zeigen, dass es sich dabei um die irreale »Tiefe eines Schattens« handelt, »die man hinter der Tiefe der ganzen vollen lichten Welt noch sucht« (Fechner 1995, III). Die wahre Aufklärung im Sinne Fechners ist der Mut, die Welt, so wie sie uns erscheint, als die wahre Welt zu nehmen, sie gerade nicht als eine große, von uns selbst erzeugte Illusion der Oberfläche zu verstehen, hinter der wir schaudernd den mundus absconditus des ›Dings an sich‹ erahnen können, sondern als die Sache selbst.

Dann aber werden zwei Fragen virulent, die gerade die Plausibilität der von Fechner disqualifizierten *Nachtansicht* ausmachen:

1. Sind die sekundären Qualitäten nicht eben geistige Phänomene, die in der Welt der materiellen Erscheinungen nicht vorkommen, sondern ihr nur als kategorial verschieden gegenüber stehen können? und
2. Verschwinden diese geistigen Wahrnehmungen nicht, wenn das Subjekt verschwindet, und müssen sie deshalb nicht als bloß subjektive *Erscheinung* angesehen werden?

Zur Beantwortung beider Fragen bringt Fechner den Begriff *Gottes* in Anschlag, der für die Fundierung seiner *Tagesansicht* zentrale Bedeutung erhält. Zum einen sind die Wahrnehmungsqualitäten deshalb nicht von den materiellen Erscheinungen zu trennen, weil *alles* materielle Geschehen eine geistige Seite hat und dieser geistige Zusammenhang der materiellen Erscheinungen des *Kosmos* mit Gottes Geist zu identifizieren ist. Und zum anderen hat das, was wir von der Welt wahrnehmen, deshalb unabhängig von uns Bestand, weil Gottes Geist es beständig wahrnimmt.

Fechners Auffassung von der Objektivität unserer sinnlichen Wahrnehmung, sein ›direkter Realismus‹ (Heidelberger 1993, 165), der *alle* Qualitäten der Dinge als objektive Eigenschaften unabhängig von unserer Erkenntnis und Wahrnehmung auffassen will, erfordert gerade, dass auch über uns bewusst wahrnehmende Geschöpfe hinaus die ganze Wirklichkeit eine geistige Seite hat und alle sinnliche Erscheinung zusammengeschlossen und abgeschlossen wird in einer höchsten bewussten Einheit der Wirklichkeit. Die Dunkelheit der *Nachtansicht*, die die Welt nur als oberflächliche Erscheinung eines unzugänglichen, dunklen Wesens verstehen kann, wird dadurch überwunden,

> daß die sinnliche Erscheinung über uns hinaus nicht bloßer Schein, sondern objectiv durch die Welt ausgebreitet ist, und daß sie in einem einheitlichen Bewußtsein sich zusammenschließt und gipfelt. (Fechner 1879, 13)

Nun ist die Welt wirklich hell und licht, sie klingt und singt wirklich. Farben, Töne, Geruch, Geschmack, Wärme sind objektiv vorhanden, weil sie in Gott wahrgenommen werden, weil sie im geistigen Grund und Abschluss des Seins selbst begründet sind. Hatte 1872, also nur wenige Jahre, bevor Fechner seine Entdeckung der *Tagesansicht* im Rosental beschreibt, der Physiker und Physiologe Du Bois-Reymond festgestellt:

> Das mosaische: ›Es ward Licht‹, ist physiologisch falsch. Licht ward erst, als der erste rothe Augenpunkt eines Infusoriums zum ersten Mal Hell und Dunkel unterschied. Ohne Seh- und ohne Gehörsinnsubstanz wäre diese farbenglühende, tönende Welt um uns her finster und stumm (Bois-Reymond Du 1884, 17);

so gilt für Fechner, dass die *Schöpfung* Licht ist von Anbeginn, noch bevor ein geschöpfliches Auge es erblickte, weil Gott es sah und immer sieht. Nicht das Licht, die Dunkelheit wird auf Seiten des Subjekts erzeugt.

Damit ist die erste und wichtigste Bestimmung von Fechners Gottesbegriff erreicht: Alle sinnliche Erscheinung ist in Gott aufgehoben, es gibt kein Dahinter mehr. *Gott* ist der Totalbegriff der Wirklichkeit selbst. Er vertritt gewissermaßen die Stelle des ›Dings an sich‹ der klassischen neuzeitlichen *Metaphysik*.[6] Als

---

[6] Vgl. Fechner 1907b, 207: »Nachdem aber Gott das höchste Wesen über allen Dingen ist, bedürfen wir keiner dunkeln Wesen mehr hinter den Erscheinungen der Dinge.«

> Totalität des Seins und Wirkens, hat [er] keine Außenwelt mehr außer sich [...]; er ist der Einige und Alleinige; alle Geister regen sich in der Innenwelt seines Geistes, alle Körper in der Innenwelt seines Leibes. (Fechner 1922, 1, 224)

Ist *Gott* aber der alles Umfassende, dann »steht auch der Mensch Gott nicht äußerlich gegenüber, sondern ist ihm zugleich eingethan und unterthan« (Fechner 1879, 65), sein Leben ist im Göttlichen mit umschlossen. Wir sind nur Momente in Gott, »wissende und wirkende, doch immer seinem höheren Wissen und Wirken untergeordnet bleibende Momente in Gott« (Fechner 1879, 14). Unsere Wahrnehmung ist nur ein Teil von Gottes Wahrnehmung, »was wir selber von der Welt sehen und hören, ist nur die letzte Abzweigung seines Sehens und Hörens« (Fechner 1879, 5).

Damit sind die drei wesentlichen Elemente genannt, die Fechners *Tagesansicht* ausmachen, Fechner nennt sie die drei Grundpunkte:

1. es gibt keine hinter den *Erscheinungen* liegende Wirklichkeit an sich, auch unabhängig und über die Existenz wahrnehmender Geschöpfe hinaus haben die Erscheinungen eine objektive Existenz;
2. alle diese Erscheinungen finden ihren konstitutiven Zusammenhang und ihren zusammenfassenden Abschluss in einer höchsten bewussten Einheit, in *Gott*;
3. unser *eigenes Bewusstsein* ist nur ein Teil, ein Moment innerhalb des göttlichen Bewusstseins.[7]

3. Glauben und Wissen

Die in diesen drei Punkten zusammengefasste *Tagesansicht* ist natürlich keine strenge wissenschaftliche Theorie, sie ist eben eine Welt-Sicht, eine Schau des Ganzen. Fechner selbst bezeichnet sie gar als eine »Glaubenslehre« (Fechner 1879, 19). Hat sich Fechner damit nicht als der Schwärmer entlarvt, für den ihn viele halten? Hat er damit nicht gerade seinen *Realismus*, seine Rechtfertigung des Augenscheins aufgegeben zugunsten einer rein subjektiven Glaubensüberzeugung? Ist denn nicht gerade die Naturwissenschaft dazu angetreten, das bloße Meinen und Glauben zu überwinden zugunsten eines gesicherten Wissens?

---

[7] Vgl. Fechner 1879, 15 u.ö.

In der Tat, im *mechanistischen Weltbild*, in dem sich alles mit der apodiktischen Gewissheit einer mathematischen Formel vollzieht und vollkommen berechnet werden kann, ist für den *Glauben* kein Platz. Er kann nur als die defizitäre Form des Erkennens begriffen werden, die es so gut es geht zu überwinden gilt. Allenfalls in praktischer Hinsicht, für die alltägliche Lebensgestaltung und in seiner privaten Trostfunktion kann Glauben noch eine Rolle spielen, aus der Naturerkenntnis ist er völlig auszuschließen. Das Ergebnis ist eine Dichotomie von Glauben und Wissen, zu der sich eine zwischen diesen beiden Polen hin und her treibende, hilflose Philosophie gesellt. Eben diese Dichotomie zwischen Glauben und Wissen, zwischen Gott und Natur will Fechners *Tagesansicht* überwinden, und zwar auf eine Weise, die weder Glauben in Wissen, noch Wissen in Glauben auflöst, sondern Glauben und Wissen so ins Verhältnis zueinander setzt, dass beide einander nicht ausschließen oder widersprechen, sondern sich jeweils in ihrer Eigenart fördern und durch das je ihre einander bereichern und in ihrem Zusammenwirken vervollkommnen.

Doch was heißt dann *Glauben*? Fechner legt einen weiten Begriff von Glauben zugrunde und bestimmt ihn als »ein Fürwahrhalten dessen, was nicht durch Erfahrung oder logischen Schluß [...] gewiß ist« (Fechner 1923, 17).[8] Erst in einem engeren Sinne ist dann auch der religiöse Glaube an die höchsten und letzten Dinge gemeint. Dem Glauben ist auch bei Fechner das Wissen gegenüber gestellt, zu dem im strengsten Sinne aber nur dasjenige gehört, »was nach dem Satze der Identität unmöglich anders vorzustellen oder zu denken ist«, und damit alles, was »durch *unmittelbare* Erfahrung, triftigen logischen Schluß« (Fechner 1923, 21) oder durch die Verbindung von beidem erkannt wird.[9] Schon an dieser Stelle sehen wir, dass *Glauben* in die Erzeugung von *naturwissenschaftlichem* Wissen mit eingehen muss. Denn um dasjenige gesetzmäßige Wissen erzeugen zu können, das wir der Naturwissenschaft zurechnen, müssen Prinzipien der Verallgemeinerung des Erfahrenen hinzutreten, so dass aus der unterstellten Regelmäßigkeit der Naturphänomene allgemeine *Na-*

---

[8] Vgl. auch Immanuel Kant, der Glauben, Meinen und Wissen als drei Stufen des Fürwahrhaltens bestimmt (Kant 1911, 531f.).

[9] Man fühlt sich an den frühen logischen Empirismus erinnert, z.B. an Carnaps Rückführung aller sinnvollen Sätze auf zwei Klassen von Aussagen, nämlich logische Identitätsaussagen (Tautologien bzw. Kontradiktionen) und elementare Erfahrungssätze, die sogenannten Protokollsätze, vgl. Carnap 1931, 219–241.

turgesetze abgeleitet werden können. Es ist der Glaube an die Tragfähigkeit der Prinzipien der begründeten Hypothesenbildung, sei es der physikalischen, sei es der historischen Forschung, der nicht selber wieder in unmittelbares Wissen verwandelt werden kann.

> Ja, streng genommen ist alles Glaubenssache, was nicht unmittelbar erfahren ist, und was nicht logisch fest steht. (Fechner 1879, 17f.)[10]

Glaube ist also nicht bloß als das unvollkommene Wissen zu bestimmen, denn an allem »Wissen hat etwas Glaube Anteil; entziehe ihm denselben, und das Wissen selbst verfällt« (Fechner 1923, 24).

Aber ebenso, wie es irrig wäre, den *Glauben* bloß als defizitäre Form des Wissens zu verstehen, wäre es falsch, die Wissensgründe von den Bestimmungsgründen des Glaubens ganz auszuschließen. Denn das, was wir von der Welt wissen, hat einen wichtigen, entscheidenden, wenn auch oft unbewussten Anteil an unserem Glauben. Wissen und Erfahrung jedenfalls sind der Stoff, mit dem der Glauben umzugehen, den er zu interpretieren hat, von dem er sich anregen lässt. Und so gilt auch das andere, dass der Glaubende »das Wissen nicht zu sehr verachten« soll: »Sein Glaube würde ohne das zur leeren Phrase oder Blase« (Fechner 1923, 30).

4. Glaubensprinzipien

Doch entscheidend für die Rechtfertigung des *Glaubens* ist die Art und Weise, *wie* er über die unmittelbare Erfahrung hinausgeht. Fechner unterscheidet bei den Bestimmungsgründen des Glaubens »*Motive*, welche zum Glauben treiben, und *Gründe*, welche uns dazu berechtigen« (Fechner 1923, 40). Dabei entsprechen sich im rechten Glauben Motive und Grün-

---

[10] Diese Einsicht Fechners steht natürlich im krassen Gegensatz zum Vulgärmaterialismus seiner Zeit. So behauptete der vielgelesene Ludwig Büchner in den Schlussbetrachtungen zu Kraft und Stoff: »Der Realismus kämpft mit Tatsachen, welche jeder sehen und greifen kann, der Idealismus mit Vermutungen und Hypothesen. So wenig Geltung die Hypothese in den Naturwissenschaften besitzt, so wenig soll sie fortan in der Philosophie haben.« (Büchner [1932], 206) »Wer die Hypothese auf naturwissenschaftlichem Gebiete bekämpft, muß sie auch auf philosophischem bekämpfen« (Büchner [1932], 207f.). Wissenschaftstheoretisch darf die Fechner'sche Position heute als die stärkere gelten, ist doch vor allem durch Popper die Hypothese als die Grundform der naturwissenschaftlichen Aussage herausgestellt worden.

de insofern, als die Gründe die Zusammenfassung und Vervollkommnung der den Menschen zunächst antreibenden Motive sind. Sie kommen als Begründung den im Menschen angelegten Bedürfnissen sozusagen entgegen, klären und erfüllen sie. Deshalb hat auch eine Erläuterung des religiösen Glaubens der Menschen nicht mit einer abstrakten Definition der höchsten Gegenstände des Glaubens wie *Gott*, unsichtbare geistige Existenzen und *Unsterblichkeit* anzufangen, sondern den Entstehungsgrund des Glaubens, die zu ihm hindrängenden Motive aufzusuchen, um dann nach den ihnen korrespondierenden Gründen zu fragen. Fechner unterscheidet dabei drei wesentliche Arten von Motiven und Gründen; er nennt sie zusammenfassend auch Prinzipien: das theoretische, das praktische und das historische Prinzip. Das *theoretische Prinzip* geht

> vom möglichst großen Kreis des Erfahrungsmäßigen im Gebiete der Existenz aus [...], um durch Verallgemeinerung, Erweiterung und Steigerung der Gesichtspunkte, die sich hier ergeben, zur Ansicht dessen zu gelangen, was darüber hinaus in den andern, weitern und höhern Gebieten der Existenz gilt. (Fechner 1879, 77)[11]

Zum basalen Erfahrungsmäßigen gehören die Einsichten der Naturwissenschaften, aber auch die Selbsterfahrung des Menschen. Durch *Induktion* und *Analogie* wird in beiden Bereichen das Besondere verallgemeinert und das so gewonnene Allgemeine möglichst widerspruchsfrei so kombiniert, dass es noch einmal in eine gesetzmäßige Beziehung zueinander gebracht werden kann.[12] Auch für die eigentlichen Gegenstände des religiösen *Glaubens* gilt dieses Verfahren, so dass die Gewinnung von Sätzen über die

[11] Damit, so Fechner, machen wir die Philosophie zur Fortsetzung der Physik mit anderen, erweiterten Mitteln und so auch wieder zu echter Meta-Physik: »Das Neue der Metaphysik, die wir im Auge haben, denn um Metaphysik handelt sich's doch zunächst, liegt in der Tat nur darin, nach so manchen versuchten Grundlagen der Metaphysik auch einmal die Wissenschaft des Physischen (obwohl nicht ohne die des Psychischen) dazu zu machen und hiermit den Namen der Metaphysik zur Tat zu erheben, d.h., sie wirklich zu etwas *nach* der Physik, statt zu einem *a priori* oder *hinter* der Physik zu machen« (Fechner 1995, 138).

[12] »Verallgemeinerung durch Induktion und Analogie und vernünftige Kombination des von verschiedenen Seiten her gewonnenen Allgemeinen sind meines Erachtens die einzigen *theoretischen* Wege und Weisen, die uns im Gebiet der geistigen wie der materiellen Wirklichkeit zu in sich haltbaren und für die Erfahrung wieder fruchtbaren Grundlagen des Wissens über das Selbstverständnis und unmittelbar Gegebene hinaus führen können« (Fechner 1922, 1, XV).

höchsten Realitäten, Gott, Jenseits, höhere Wesen über uns, [...] hiervon am wenigsten Ausnahme [machen], indem es gerade hier der erschöpfendsten und umfassendsten, über das ganze Gebiet der Existenz hinausgreifenden Induktionen und Analogien und höchsten Kombinationen bedarf, um (so weit überhaupt der theoretische Weg hierbei ausreicht) zu Ansichten in diesem Gebiete zu gelangen, welche Lebenskraft in sich haben und Kraft für das Leben wieder entwickeln können. Nicht ein vorangestellter Gottesbegriff bestimmt Gottes Wesen, sondern was von Gott in der Welt und in uns spürbar ist, bestimmt seinen Begriff. (Fechner 1922, 1, XV)

Das *praktische Prinzip* gründet in dem Motiv, dass der Mensch das »glaubt, was ihm zu glauben gefällt, dient, frommt« (Fechner 1923, 87). Weil wir Gott brauchen, suchen wir ihn. »Denn alle Lust will Ewigkeit«, ist man versucht mit Nietzsche zu sagen, und in der Tat ist es die *Lust*, die Fechner als das höchste Gut, als den Endzweck des Menschen überhaupt bestimmt. Das ist nicht im Sinne eines egoistischen Hedonismus gemeint, sondern ganz im Zusammenhang des Fechner'schen *Realismus* gedacht, der von dem ausgeht, was wir in uns vorfinden. Und was uns zweifellos elementar bestimmt, ist, dass wir Lustgewinn suchen und Unlust meiden.[13] Die wahre und höchste Lust aber ist die der größtmöglichen »Förderung von Glück, Heil und Segen« (Fechner 1922, 1, 300). Die wahre Lust will größtmögliche und unvergängliche Gemeinschaft und zielt damit auf den Einen, auf Gott als die Einheit und den Abschluss des Seins. Und so wird das praktische Motiv des Glaubens zum Grund für den *Glauben*, weil es darauf hinweist, dass sein Bedürfnis nach Glauben »in derselben realen Natur der Dinge begründet sein [muss], welche den Menschen mit seinen Bedürfnissen selbst erzeugt hat« (Fechner 1923, 125).[14]

Bleibt noch das *historische Prinzip* des Glaubens, das Fechner folgendermaßen bestimmt: »Man glaubt, was uns gesagt wird, was vor uns geglaubt worden ist und um uns geglaubt wird« (Fechner 1923, 49). *Religion* ist in der Menschheit vorhanden, so wie die Sprache vorhanden ist, ohne dass sie sich auf ein Urdatum, eine ursprüngliche historische Erfindung zurückführen ließe. Und seitdem gilt vom religiösen Glauben: »Ein

---

[13] Fechner hat in einer kleinen Schrift auf dieses Prinzip eine ganze naturalistische Ethik begründet; vgl. Fechner 1846.

[14] Dieses praktische Argument, dass aufgrund der Annahme der stimmigen Einrichtung der Natur das Bedürfnis des Menschen nach einem Glauben an Gott nicht ins Leere gehen kann, bezeichnet Fechner auch als das argumentum a consensu boni et veri; vgl. Fechner 1922, 2, 90–95.

Mensch sagt es dem andern« (Fechner 1923, 58). So pflanzt er sich fort von Generation zu Generation und kommt durch sein Immer-schon-Gegebensein den theoretischen und praktischen Motiven zu Hilfe.

Diese drei Prinzipien des *Glaubens* sind nicht aufeinander reduzierbar und ergänzen und korrigieren einander.[15] Nur das *Wechselspiel* aller drei Prinzipien kann einen Glauben mit »Fleisch und Bein« (Fechner 1922, 1, XVIII) entstehen lassen, der nicht von einem gänzlich abstrakten und von aller unserer Erfahrung unendlich weit entfernten Begriff von Gott und den höchsten und letzten Dingen ausgeht, sondern ein realistisches und lebensvolles Ganzes darzustellen in der Lage ist.

5. Glaube und Gottesbegriff

In diesen drei Glaubensprinzipien sind die drei von uns schon genannten Grundpunkte der *Tagesansicht* (die Auffassung, dass alles Wirkliche eine geistige Seite hat, dass diese ihren Abschluss in Gott findet, und dass unser Bewusstsein einen Teil des göttlichen Bewusstseins darstellt) als gerechtfertigt begründet. Wir wollen dies zunächst anhand der theoretischen und praktischen Argumente genauer vor Augen führen. Den Ausgangspunkt bildet die Selbsterfahrung des Ich, dessen *Wahrnehmungen* unterschieden werden können in psychische Selbsterscheinungen und physische Fremdwahrnehmung.[16] Unterscheidungsmerkmal ist, ob das, was dem Wahrnehmenden erscheint, auch anderen Subjekten zugänglich ist oder nicht. Die rein privaten Aspekte von Wahrnehmungen machen die subjektiven inneren Selbsterscheinungen aus, die anderen Aspekte die objektiven, äußerlich wahrnehmbaren materiellen Erscheinungen. *Psychisches* und *Physisches*, so hält Fechner fest, stellen nicht zwei Kategorien von Wesenheiten dar, sondern gehören untrennbar zusammen, wie die konkave und konvexe Seite eines Kreises,[17] denn wie jeder an sich selbst feststellen kann,

[15] »Auf keins dieser Prinzipe hat sich der Glaube allein zu stützen. Der Mensch kann fehl gehen in Verallgemeinerung dessen, was er weiß, kann fehl gehen in dem, was er für das Beste hält zu glauben, und die Geschichte hat von jeher Fehler nach beiden Seiten begangen« (Fechner 1879, 77).

[16] Vgl. zum Folgenden Heidelberger 1993, 103ff.

[17] Siehe Fechner 1907b, 19.

> hat dasselbe Wesen zwei Seiten, eine geistige, psychische, sofern es sich selbst, eine materielle, leibliche, sofern es einem andern als sich selbst in anderer Form zu erscheinen vermag. (Fechner 1922, 2, 135)

Aus dieser elementaren Grundgegebenheit menschlicher Selbsterfahrung lassen sich durch vorsichtige Verallgemeinerung im Sinne des *theoretischen Glaubensprinzips* einige wichtige Folgerungen ziehen. In der Auffassung, dass die Natur in einer von unserer Wahrnehmung unabhängigen, objektiven Weise als Welt physischer Gegenstände erscheinen kann, steckt zunächst die Voraussetzung, dass sie eben nicht bloß uns, sondern auch anderen erscheinen, »d.i. Wirkungen in Andre wie in uns hineinerzeugen könne, welche wir von ihr als der Ursache davon abhängig machen« (Fechner 1879, 227). In unserem Selbstverständnis und in unserem sozialen Umgang miteinander nehmen wir deshalb immer schon die gut begründete und gerechtfertigte Hypothese in Anspruch, dass andere Menschen ebenso zu Bewusstsein und Erkenntnis derselben von uns unabhängigen Außenwelt fähig sind wie wir. Dies ist die Anerkennung des *Fremdpsychischen*, ohne die wir weder praktisch existieren noch theoretisch etwas erkennen könnten.

Wenn wir aber Seele und Leib, Körperliches und Bewusstsein nur als zwei Seiten derselben Erscheinung, nicht als zwei völlig verschiedene Wesenheiten anzusehen haben, dann legt es sich nahe, eine geistige Innenseite für alle materielle Erscheinung anzunehmen. Damit verschiebt sich die Fragestellung des klassischen *Leib-Seele-Problems*. Wenn alles eine geistige Innenseite hat, die sich in uns als mit Selbstbewusstsein begabten, sinnlich wahrnehmenden Lebewesen als geistiges Bewusstsein realisiert, dann ist »nicht mehr zu fragen, wo Beseelung anfängt und aufhört, sondern nur, wo und inwiefern sie sich in entsprechender Weise aus der allgemeinen Beseelung heraushebt« (Fechner 1879, 29). An dieser Stelle sind für Fechner seine Forschungen über das Verhältnis von Reizstärke und Sinneswahrnehmung, die ihn berühmt und zu einem Begründer der empirischen Psychologie gemacht haben, von entscheidender Bedeutung.[18]

---

[18] Fechner erweitert 1860 ein von seinem Freund E.H. Weber (1795–1878) aufgestelltes Gesetz zum später sogenannten *Weber-Fechner'schen-Gesetz*, welches besagt, dass zwischen der externen (S) und empfundenen (E) Reizstärke ein logarithmischer Zusammenhang besteht: $E = k \log S$, wobei k eine für das betreffende Sinnesgebiet charakteristische Konstante ist. Für den mittleren Bereich physiologischer Schall- und Lichtreize ist dies in guter Annäherung erfüllt, in der Akustik ist es z.B. die Grundlage der Dezibel-Skala. Dass es sich um eine logarithmische und keine lineare Proportionalität handelt, war für Fechner ein Erweis dafür, dass zwischen physischen und psychischen Phänomenen keine

Fechner hat in seiner »Psychophysik« 1860 u.a. die Bedeutung der *Reizschwelle* herausgearbeitet als den Punkt, jenseits dessen allererst eine bewusste Empfindung beginnt. Es zeigt sich, »daß jeder Reiz wie Reizunterschied schon eine gewisse endliche Größe erreicht haben muß, bevor die Merklichkeit desselben nur eben beginnt, d.h. bevor er eine unser Bewußtsein merklich affizierende Empfindung erzeugt oder einen merklichen Empfindungsunterschied begründet« (Fechner 1907a, 1, 237).

Bewusstsein kann also erst dann entstehen, wenn das ihm zugrunde liegende System, das anderen von außen als seine körperliche Außenseite erscheint, einen solchen Zusammenhang bildet, dass die *psychophysische* Bewegung seiner geistigen Innenseite die Schwelle für bewusste Reize überschreitet. Dies ist zum Beispiel im menschlichen Gehirn der Fall.

> Von einem engeren Seelensitze (im Gehirn) kann dann insofern die Rede sein, als man damit den nicht punktförmigen, sondern ausgedehnten Teil des Systems bezeichnet, in welchem die psychophysischen Bewegungen die Schwelle übersteigen. (Fechner 1995, 231)

Schlaf ist dann das zeitweise Sinken unter die Schwelle, während unbewusste materielle Systeme niemals diese Schwelle erreichen.

Fechner nennt seine Auffassung des Verhältnisses von *Leib und Seele* die synechologische, weil der Geist oder die Seele nur in einem komplexen, Einzelelemente zu einer Einheit verbindenden System zu Bewusstsein kommt, und grenzt sie als solche von der monadologischen Sicht der Seele ab, wie er sie bei Leibniz, Herbart oder Lotze findet, bei denen die Seele als atomares, einfaches und unteilbares Einzelwesen bestimmt wird. Zu ihrem Abschluss wird die *synechologische* Sicht nun dadurch gebracht, dass man sie auf einen Begriff des Ganzen hin erweitert. Denn alle Erscheinung enthält etwas Verbindendes, einen Zusammenhang der Erscheinungen, auf den wir uns gemeinsam beziehen können, sonst wären unsere Wahrnehmungen völlig heterogen und nicht kommunikabel. Dieser Zusammenhang ist konstituiert durch den gesetzmäßigen Zusammenhang der Welt, z.B. durch das Gravitationsgesetz, durch Erhaltungsgesetze, durch die »Kontinuität der Zeit und des Raumes« (Fechner 1922, 1, 211), d.h. durch alle die *Gesetze*, die das Grundgesetz aller

---

direkte Kausalität herrscht, also keine Wirkungen ausgetauscht werden, sondern *funktionale Abhängigkeit* besteht, bei der sich der eine Phänomenbereich mit dem andern ändert.

Wirklichkeit garantieren, das Fechner so bestimmt: Gleiche Umstände zeitigen gleiche Folgen.[19]

In diesem »Walten des obersten Gesetzes« erkennen wir »ein in sich einiges, ewiges, allgegenwärtiges, allwaltendes, allmächtiges, alle Wirklichkeit nicht nur durchwirkendes, sondern selber erst wirkendes, allen Fluß von Grund und Folge urbedingendes, Zeit und Raum, Natur und Geist in eins umspannendes und bindendes, und dabei [...] uns unser Jenseits selbstverbürgendes Wesen« (Fechner 1922, 1, 217), in dem sich die Einheit allen Seins manifestiert und das in alles überbietender und alles zusammenfassender Weise die Einzelseelen und -geister der Geschöpfe in sich als Teilmomente enthält. *Gott* steht der Welt nicht gegenüber, sondern hat »in dem Zusammenhange der Erscheinungen seine Existenz« (Fechner 1995, 106). Ebenso steht auch der Mensch Gott nicht gegenüber, sondern ist als Teilmoment des Weltprozesses und Weltbewusstseins im göttlichen Leben mit eingeschlossen. Über ihm, so folgert Fechner weiter, wird es umfassendere Systeme geben, denen man ebenso eine Seele wird zusprechen müssen, wie z.B. den Gestirnen, allen voran der Erde, und unter ihm ebenso niedrigere, ebenfalls durch ein seelisches Einheitsprinzip konstituierte Lebewesen wie z.B. die Pflanzen. So ergibt sich ein Stufenbau der Welt, in dem »Gott der absolut alles in sein Band Fassende« ist und an dessen Grund ihm als bewusstem Prinzip der Einheit diejenigen elementaren Bausteine der Wirklichkeit gegenüberstehen, die von ihm eben zur lebendigen Einheit der Welt zusammengefasst werden: »Das sind die Atome« (Fechner 1995, 78).

Damit haben wir Fechners Hauptgründe für die Annahme der Existenz *Gottes* rekonstruiert, die ihm aus der Grundeinsicht in die eigene Wahrnehmung von körperlicher und geistiger Wirklichkeit erwachsen, die durch die angesprochenen Prinzipien des *theoretischen* und *praktischen Glaubens* erweitert wird. So wie diese Erweiterung uns zunächst und ganz ungezwungen dazu führt, das Bewusstsein des menschlichen Gegenübers anzunehmen, so führt sie zuletzt zur Annahme, das Gott existiert, in dem wir leben, weben und da sind (Act 17, 28). Deshalb, so Fechner, ist Gott grundsätzlich »nicht [...] unsichtbarer als der Geist irgend eines unsrer Nebenmenschen« (Fechner 1852, 196). Der Glaube an seine Existenz

[19] Fechner formuliert in Zend-Avesta als das allgemeine Gesetz des Geschehens: »Wenn und wo auch dieselben Umstände wiederkehren, und welches auch diese Umstände sein mögen, so kehren auch dieselben Erfolge wieder, unter andern Umständen aber andere Erfolge« (Fechner 1922, 1, 210).

unterscheidet sich nicht prinzipiell von der Annahme, dass ich mich mit meinem Mitmenschen z.B. über die Farbe einer Blume sinnvoll austauschen kann. »Die Natur, wie sie dem oberflächlichen Blicke erscheint, für den reinen vollen Ausdruck von Gottes Geist halten,« so Fechner, »ist dasselbe, als das Gesicht eines Menschen für den reinen vollen Ausdruck seines Geistes halten« (Fechner 1922, 1, 261).

6. Die Bedeutung des Christentums

Haben wir nun die Funktion, Begründung und Bedeutung von Fechners Gottesbegriff in ihren Grundzügen dargestellt, so bleibt noch über die vorgestellten theoretischen und praktischen Argumente hinaus die Frage nach den *historischen Gründen* für den Glauben an die Existenz Gottes. Speziell stellt sich damit die Frage nach dem Verhältnis Fechners zum real existierenden *Christentum*, zu der Religion, in der er groß geworden ist, aus der er kommt, in die er nach längerer Zeit der Entfremdung zurückkehrt und in die hinein er auch wirken will. Über allen seinen religiösen Erörterungen jedenfalls steht sein Bekenntnis: »ich bleib' ein Christ« (Fechner 1922, 1, 314).

Dass Fechner sich in seinen Schriften auch öffentlich so intensiv mit der *Religion* und ihrer Neubegründung beschäftigt hat, liegt vor allen Dingen daran, dass er die allgemeine Krise des Glaubens spürte, die durch den übersteigerten Anspruch einer alles ›aufklären‹ wollenden, damit aber alles in die Tiefe der *Nachtansicht* mit sich reißenden Vernunft bestimmt ist.[20] Es gilt deshalb, die Religion von Grund auf neu aufzubauen. Es reicht nicht, die morschen Balken aus dem historisch gewachsenen Bau der Religion herauszuziehen. Das Bauwerk würde seinen Zusammenhalt verlieren und in sich zusammenstürzen. Stattdessen gilt es, neue, tragende Fundamente einzuziehen, der Bau muss »auf neuem Grunde, aus neuen Balken, neuen Steinen« (Fechner 1879, 59) erstehen. In seiner »Tagesansicht in ihren Grundzügen und den Principien ihres Auf- und Anbaues« sieht Fechner den idealen Neuansatz, der auch »der universalen Idee des

[20] »Ein Gefühl geht durch die Welt«, schreibt Fechner 1879, »so kann es nicht bleiben oder so kann es nicht fortgehen. Schon sucht ja die Welt fast mit Angst eine Erneuerung des Glaubens oder gar einen neuen Glauben; schon proclamirt sich sogar ein solcher als im Bunde mit dem Wissen, der aber nur der Sturz des alten Glaubens ist, und damit die Angst der Welt nicht stillen, sondern nur steigern kann« (Fechner 1879, 55).

Christenthums positive Momente eines neuen Haltes und Inhaltes für die preisgegebenen dogmatischen bietet« (Fechner 1879, 61).

Das heißt also nicht, dass Fechner das *Christentum* als Religion ablösen will. Der Kern des Christentums erscheint ihm wahr und echt und lebendig und in völliger Übereinstimmung mit seiner *Tagesansicht*. In der Heiligen Schrift findet sich die Tagesansicht im Grunde längst offenbart. Dort ist sie »durch das Wort von Oben gegeben«, während Fechners Gedanken »erst von Unten aufzusteigen suchen«. Doch findet sie sich in der Bibel ganz unsystematisch und verworren und vermengt mit vielem, was überhaupt nicht dazu gehört und nur zu Widersprüchen führt. Fechner will deshalb nur das Höchste und Beste des christlichen Glaubens übernehmen, nicht aber das Ganze. Doch dieses Höchste und Beste verspricht er so zu retten, »ehe es mit dem Ganzen selbst verfällt« (Fechner 1879, 54). Wo er etwas fallen lässt, was andere zu ihrem Christentum zählen, handelt es sich in Wahrheit um Besinnung auf den wahren Kern. Wo er über das hinausgeht, was Christus gelehrt hat, handelt es sich um organisches Wachstum von dessen Lehre.[21]

Als das zentrale Werk und die zentrale Botschaft Christi bestimmt Fechner den Gedanken,

> daß alle Menschen sich als Kinder desselben einigen, nur Gutes wollenden Gottes, als Bürger eines über dies Diesseits hinaus reichenden himmlischen Reiches und als Brüder zu einander fühlen, in diesem Sinne trachten und handeln sollen. (Fechner 1922, 1, 319)

Diese zentrale Botschaft der umfassenden Ökumene hat Christus der Menschheit ins Bewusstsein gehoben, durch sein Leben dargestellt und den Anstoß zur Verbreitung und Bestätigung dieser Lehre in seiner Gemeinde gegeben. Die zentrale Botschaft der Einigung aller Menschen durch und in Gott stellt gegen jede völkisch-religiöse Engführung das Zentrum der Botschaft Christi dar und enthält zugleich den Grundgedanken der *Tagesansicht*, dass Gott das alle zusammenfassende, einigende Band ist. Dieses einigende Moment soll sich auf allen Ebenen realisieren, über alle Konfessionen, über alle *Religionen* und alles andere Trennende hinweg sollen die Menschen sich als den einen Leib Christi verstehen. Christus hat uns nicht einen bloßen Nachlass in Form von Worten und Erinnerungen hinterlassen, die *Kirche* und *Gemeinde* ist tatsächlich sein von ihm geschaffener Leib, in dem und durch den er wirksam ist.

---

[21] Vgl. Fechner 1922, 1, 322.

Und so wie die Gemeinde als der Leib Christi mit vielen Gliedern durch das Band der Liebe zusammengehalten wird, so soll eine die ganze Menschheit umfassende Liebe die gegenseitige Einigkeit und Brüderlichkeit verwirklichen. Das ökumenische Prinzip ist sozusagen Christus selber, nicht eine gänzlich abstrakte Vernunftreligion, wie sie die Aufklärung propagierte, auch nicht das gemeinsame Gefühl allgemeiner Religiosität, zu der die Romantik hindrängte, sondern das alle vorhandene Religion nicht bekämpfende, sondern einigende und aufnehmende Grundprinzip der Tagesansicht, dass wir alle Momente der göttlichen Selbstbewegung sind. Hatte Fechner so eine neue, fest gegründete Religiosität für sich gefunden, sah er seine Aufgabe auch darin, auf dieser Grundlage den christlichen Glauben und die christliche Gemeinschaft zu reformieren, um sie damit für die Herausforderungen der Neuzeit vorzubereiten, um sie zu einer der Menschheit vorangehenden, ihre zukünftige Gestalt abbildenden Gemeinschaft zu gestalten. Doch bei der vor allem in dieser Hinsicht spärlichen Resonanz, die Fechner gefunden hat, spürt er wohl um so härter, dass es zu einem wirklichen Effekt »an dem zündenden Wort und der gemeindebildenden Kraft« (Fechner 1879, 64) mangelt. Und ihm selbst erscheint sein Bemühen in dieser Hinsicht am Ende eher gescheitert.[22]

7. Fechners Religionsphilosophie – aus heutiger Sicht

Damit sind wir am Ende unserer Darstellung von Fechners Gottesbild angelangt und wollen uns noch kurz der Frage stellen: Was sollen wir nun dazu sagen?

---

[22] »Da steht einer«, so schreibt er 1879 von sich selbst, »der eine ungeheure Last von einem Flecke, auf dem etwas wachsen möchte [...] wegwälzen möchte. Er faßt bald hier, bald da an, hebt die Last von der und jener Seite, aber sie ist zu schwer, zu tief eingedrückt, und fällt immer wieder auf die hebende Hand zurück. Die Umstehenden sehen stumpf zu, schütteln den Kopf oder lachen; einige, die auf der Last stehen und sie vermehren helfen, wollen nicht herabgeworfen werden und schelten. Hier und da klingt wohl eine ermunternde Stimme, aber niemand greift mit an. Ueber diesen Versuchen ist er alt geworden, fühlt, allein vollbringt ers nicht, thut noch einen letzten Ruck und wartet nun auf die neue Kraft. Sie wird es leichter haben; denn der innerlich morsch gewordene Stein fängt schon von selbst an zu zerbröckeln; und endlich wird die Geschichte nur noch die Brocken fortzukarren haben« (Fechner 1879, 64).

Die Hauptproblematik des Fechner'schen Gottesverständnisses wird man wohl vor allem darin zu bestimmen haben, dass seine Auffassung der Verbindung, ja der *Identität* von Gott und Welt allzu eng ist, den Erfahrungen der Geschichte kaum standhält und die Differenz von Schöpfer und Geschöpf auf gefährliche Weise verwischt. Auch sein Zutrauen darauf, dass die Menschheit sich gerade im Blick auf Gott und seinen Geist als Gemeinschaft von Schwestern und Brüdern entdeckt, erscheint, vor allem mit Blick auf das vergangene Jahrhundert, doch allzu optimistisch, ja geradezu naiv. Die *Existenzphilosophie*, schon zu Fechners Zeit mit Kierkegaard anhebend, in der Theologie bald etwa von Troeltzsch aufgenommen, und dann erst recht der Existentialismus des beginnenden 20. Jahrhunderts, der in der dialektischen Theologie sein Pendant hat, sie haben hier sicher bald tiefer gesehen. Das 20. Jahrhundert hat dann in Abgründe geblickt, die Fechner trotz allen persönlichen Ringens und allen selbst erfahrenen Leidens und auch trotz seines doch so ausgeprägten Gespürs für die ambivalente Signatur seiner Zeit so nicht erlebt hat.

Alles Weltgeschehen nur ein Moment der Selbstbewegung Gottes? Die beiden Weltkriege, Auschwitz, der Gulag, die hungernden Massen in weiten Teilen der Erde, die von Menschen gemachten Katastrophen, die die Schöpfung an den Rand des Abgrunds zu bringen drohen, alles Momente im Wachstumsprozess der göttlichen Selbsterfahrung? Es fehlt etwas im pantheistischen *Gottesbegriff* Fechners, es fehlen die urreligiösen Grundkategorien von Schuld und Sünde, es fehlt die christliche Kategorie des Kreuzes, in dem Gott selbst die Erfahrung der Gottesferne aufnimmt. Denn, so hat man mit Blick auf das 20. Jahrhundert festgestellt, ohne

> die Erkenntnis des Leidens der unerschöpflichen Liebe Gottes kann es kein Pantheismus und auch kein Pan-en-theismus in dieser Welt des Todes aushalten. Sie würden alsbald zum Pannihilismus führen. (Moltmann 1991, 226)

Man wird gegen Fechner gerade auch dies festhalten müssen – und die ganze biblische Tradition kann nicht nur ein Lied davon singen, sondern auch manche Geschichte dazu erzählen –, dass Welterfahrung und Gotteserfahrung sich nicht unbedingt entsprechen müssen. Abraham als Empfänger einer aller Realität Hohn sprechenden Verheißung Gottes, das hungernde Volk Israel in der Wüste, der klagende, ungerecht leidende Hiob, Jesus zwischen Verbrechern am Kreuz mit dem Schrei der Gottverlassenheit auf den Lippen, Paulus im Gefängnis ... sie alle, und viele Glaubende nach ihnen, erfuhren eine Wirklichkeit des Lebens, die nicht voller

Schönheit, Licht und Harmonie war und auf ihren geistigen Abschluss hinwies, sondern ihren *Glauben* gerade in Frage stellte.

Es fehlt bei Fechner deshalb auch das, was die Theologen die *eschatologische* Dimension des Glaubens nennen, die Kraft, mit der der Glaube auch der Realität zu widersprechen, die Welt zu überwinden oder ihr zumindest mehr zuzusprechen sucht, als sie von sich aus zeigt. Es fehlt über Glaube und Liebe hinaus die Dimension der Hoffnung angesichts von Erfahrungen, die Glauben und Liebe widersprechen. Der Glaube ist ja nicht nur das gerechtfertigte Fürwahrhalten von Dingen und Gegebenheiten, die man nicht sieht. Das ist er als fides quae creditur auch, vor allem aber ist er, um es mit einem poetischen Bild zu sagen, ›der Vogel, der singt, wenn die Nacht noch dunkel ist‹.

Das alles, und sicher noch manches mehr, wäre kritisch zu Fechner zu sagen. Und doch – wie schön! Wie schön ist die *Tagesansicht* des Gustav Theodor Fechner, der in ihr, und das wird jeder den Zeilen abspüren, mit denen er sie beschreibt, seinen *Gott* und eine lichte helle Welt gefunden hat. Und wie sympathisch ist es, dass dieser gelehrte Mann und Wissenschaftler die Sache mit Gott, die Sache des Glaubens, die Frage der Vollendung des Lebens, die Frage nach dem, was über das Messbare und Berechenbare hinausgeht, nicht wie so viele seiner Zeitgenossen hat auf sich beruhen lassen: ignoramus, ignorabimus. Dagegen setzt Fechner sein mutiges, bestimmtes und zugleich so irenisches: credo, credam.

Und dann wirkt er in seiner *Hermeneutik*, in seiner Verschränkung von Welterfahrung und Gotteserfahrung erstaunlich modern, ohne in fideistische Beliebigkeit zu verfallen. Als hermeneutische Leitlinien – nicht für das Gewinnen eines Glaubens*fundamentes*, sondern zur Begründung von realistischen *Glaubensaussagen* sind seine drei Motive und Gründe überaus hilfreich und der Religion und der Sache des Glaubens durchaus angemessen, treffen hier doch begrifflich-logische, situativ-pragmatische und empirisch-historische Aspekte zusammen. Vielfach hat es die Theologie zu lernen noch vor sich, dass die Gewissheit des Glaubens nicht mit einem absoluten Standpunkt letzter Sicherheit verwechselt werden darf.

Fechner zeigt, wie alle menschliche Erkenntnisbemühung im hypothetischen Entwerfen und durch Kontrollierbarkeit und Überprüfbarkeit an den Phänomenen sich vollzieht und bewährt. Die Theologie sollte von ihm lernen, auf Letztbegründungsversuche und damit auf die Suche nach unhintergehbaren Gegebenheiten, letzten Identitäten und unhinterfragbaren außertheologischen Sachverhalten ganz zu verzichten. (Dalferth 1991, 49)

Es gibt in den Fragen der Orientierung und Sinnbestimmung des Menschen keine zwingenden letzten Gründe, »sondern nur relative, interne und lokale Kriterien« (Dalferth 1991, 49). Diese aber immerhin gibt es, und es ist die Aufgabe von Wissenschaft, Philosophie und Theologie, das »uns theoretisch und praktisch im Gebiete der Existenz zu orientiren Geeignete zu sichern« (Fechner 1879, 229).[23]

Eindrucksvoll und lehrreich für die *heutige Theologie* scheint mir deshalb die Art und Weise zu sein, wie Fechner Naturwissenschaft und Glaube ins Verhältnis setzt. Hier hat die Theologie bis heute viel versäumt. Schleiermacher hatte schon in seinen zu Beginn angesprochenen Sendschreiben von 1829 die These geäußert,

daß jedes Dogma, welches wirklich ein Element unseres christlichen Bewußtseyns repräsentirt, auch so gefaßt werden kann, daß es uns unverwickelt läßt mit der Wissenschaft. (Schleiermacher 1990, 351)

Das war und ist vielfach die Lösung, wie sie die Theologie im Gegenüber zur Naturwissenschaft propagiert hat: alle Antworten des Glaubens so zu formulieren, dass sie ihn unverwickelt lassen mit den Naturwissenschaften.

Doch das kann für die *Theologie* auf Dauer keine Lösung sein. Denn die Naturwissenschaften, und dafür ist Fechner ein leuchtendes Beispiel, waren und sind nicht nur die Antipoden der Theologie, sondern haben bis heute auch das Interesse an der um ihrer selbst willen interessanten und reichen *Schöpfung* bewahrt. Die Entdeckerfreude des Naturforschers, die Ehrfurcht vor den Geheimnissen der Natur, die Disziplin und aufklärerische Helle der mathematischen und empirischen Methoden, die nach den authentischen Antworten der Natur auf unsere Fragen unter Absehung eigener Vorurteile suchen, die großartigen, Offenbarungen gleichenden Durchbrüche zu neuer Erkenntnis an den Nahtstellen der Wissenschaftsgeschichte, all das gehört zur Geschichte der Naturwissenschaften, und für all das steht auch Gustav Theodor Fechner.

---

[23] Das ist jedenfalls allemal besser, »als die fehlende Möglichkeit absoluter Gewißheit der Erkenntniß mit absolut fehlender Erkenntnißmöglichkeit zu verwechseln, und in dieser Verwechslung sozusagen das Fundament philosophischer Weisheit zu sehen« (Fechner 1879, 229).

Die *Theologie* wäre schlecht beraten, diese Grundhaltung des wissenschaftlichen Zugangs zur Welt achtlos zu übergehen, ist ihr doch darüber vieles, und vor allen Dingen viel *Realismus*, abhanden gekommen, wie umgekehrt den Naturwissenschaften mitunter das Ganze, vor allem das Ganze der menschlichen Existenz aus dem Blick geriet. Auch wenn man ihm in vielen seiner Spekulationen nicht zustimmen mag, manche seiner Bestimmungen in religiöser und theologischer Hinsicht unbefriedigend bleiben und im Blick auf die gelebte Religion und Kirche naiv erscheinen mögen; Fechners Entwurf ist eine Mahnung, dass die Theologie mit der empirischen Wissenschaft zum besten beider Teile gerade nicht unverwikkelt bleiben, sondern sich mit großer Aufmerksamkeit darauf beziehen sollte.

Literatur:

Bois-Reymond, E. Du (1884): Über die Grenzen des Naturerkennens. Die sieben Welträthsel. 6. Aufl. Leipzig.

Büchner, L. [1932]: Kraft und Stoff. Einleitung und Anmerkungen von W. Bölsche. Leipzig. Neudruck der Urausgabe von 1855. (Kröners Taschenausgabe 102)

Carnap, R. (1931): Überwindung der Metaphysik durch logische Analyse der Sprache. In: Erkenntnis 2, 219–241.

Dalferth, I.U.(1991): Subjektivität und Glaube. Zur Problematik der theologischen Verwendung einer philosophischen Kategorie. In: Neue Zeitschrift für Systematische Theologie 36, 18–58.

Fechner, G. Th. (1846): Ueber das höchste Gut. Leipzig.

Fechner, G. Th. (1852): Ueber die Erkenntniß Gottes in der Natur aus der Natur. In: Zeitschrift für Philosophie und philosophische Kritik, N.F. 21, 193–209.

Fechner, G. Th.(1879): Die Tagesansicht gegenüber der Nachtansicht. Leipzig.

Fechner, G. Th.(1907a): Elemente der Psychophysik. 2 Bde. 3. unveränd. Aufl. Leipzig.

Fechner, G. Th. (1907b): Über die Seelenfrage. Ein Gang durch die sichtbare Welt, um die unsichtbare zu finden. 2. Aufl. Hamburg; Leipzig.

Fechner, G. Th. (1922): Zend-Avesta oder über die Dinge des Himmels und des Jenseits. Hg. von K. Laßwitz. 2 Bde. 3. Aufl. Hamburg; Leipzig.

Fechner, G. Th. (1923): Die drei Motive und Gründe des Glaubens. Stuttgart.

Fechner, G. Th. (1950): Das Büchlein vom Leben nach dem Tode. Mit einem Geleitwort von W. Wundt. Wiesbaden (Insel-Bücherei 187).

Fechner, G. Th. (1995): Über die physikalische und philosophische Atomenlehre. Hg. von E. Bonk. Wien; New York.

Galilei, G. (1896): Opere. Bd. VI. (Edizione Nazionale). Florenz.

Heidelberger, M. (1993): Die innere Seite der Natur. Gustav Theodor Fechners wissenschaftlich-philosophische Weltauffassung. Frankfurt a.M.

Kant, I. (1911): Kritik der reinen Vernunft. 2. Aufl. Kant's gesammelte Schriften. Hg. von der Königlich Preußischen Akademie der Wissenschaften. 1. Abth.: Werke, 3. Bd. Berlin.

Kuntze, J.E. (1892): Gustav Theodor Fechner (Dr. Mises). Ein deutsches Gelehrtenleben. Leipzig.

Moltmann, J. (1991): Der Geist des Lebens. München.

Schleiermacher, F.D.E. (1990): Über die Glaubenslehre. Zwei Sendschreiben an Lücke. Kritische Gesamtausgabe. Hg. von H.-F. Traulsen. Abt. 1. Bd. 10. Berlin; New York.

Schubert, G.H. (1808): Ansichten von der Nachtseite der Naturwissenschaften. Dresden.

Rüdiger Thiele

Fechner und Zöllner. Die Einschränkung der realen Welt auf Mathematik und ihre Erweiterung in eine Geisterwelt. Ein Vergleich zweier Raumauffassungen

Am Beginn der Menschwerdung steht eine bewusste Orientierung in Raum und Zeit, aus der die naturwissenschaftlichen Konzepte von Raum und Zeit hervorgegangen sind. Ein kurzer historischer Durchlauf stellt die Auffassungen Fechners und Zöllners in diese Tradition. Während der Psychophysiker Fechner einen subjektiven Wahrnehmungsraum untersuchte und dabei durchweg formale objektive mathematische Begriffe zur Beschreibung der Wahrnehmungen benutzte, begann der Astrophysiker Zöllner anfänglich, die objektiven kosmischen Dimensionen ebenso zu erfassen, überschritt aber schließlich eine sachliche mathematische Beschreibung und endete im subjektiven Spiritismus. Obwohl eine vierdimensionale Welt in jenen Tagen eigentlich nur den Naturwissenschaftlern als ein formales Konzept geläufig war, dem keine tiefere inhaltliche Bedeutung zugewiesen wurde, bemächtigten sich antirealistisch und antipositivistisch eingestellte Bewegungen in ihrem Bemühen, wissenschaftliche Bewusstheit durch Poesie, Mystik, Magie oder Esoterik zu ersetzen, auch des Begriffs des vierdimensionalen Raumes (z.B. der französische Symbolismus in der Literatur, der belgische Symbolismus in der Malerei). In gewisser Weise schlägt Freuds »Traumdeutung« (1899) eine Brücke zwischen Bewusstsein und Unbewusstem.

Vor diesem Hintergrund betrachten wir aus wissenschaftshistorischer Sicht die Raumkonzepte Fechners und Zöllners sowie deren Folgen. Der Beitrag endet mit Betrachtungen über die physikalische Realität einer vierten Dimension.

Wenn Skepsis und Sehnsucht sich begatten,
entsteht Mystik. (Nietzsche 1980, Aph.71)

Das Thema, über das ich sprechen möchte, betrifft den Vergleich zweier Raumauffassungen: einer mathematischen und einer spiritistischen, exemplifiziert am Psychophysiker Gustav Theodor Fechner (1801–1887) und am Astrophysiker Karl Friedrich Zöllner (1834–1882). Von der mathematischen Ordnung, die Fechner dazu diente, Seelisches zu physikalisieren, bis zu jenem *vierdimensionalen Raum*, aus welchem heraus die Geister Zöllner und seine Zeitgenossen mit »Klopfen, Trommeln und schlechtem Englisch unterhalten« (Schubert 1892), ist es ein gewaltiger Schritt.[1]

Lassen Sie mich zunächst etwas zur Einteilung dieses Vortrags sagen. Ich werde mit einigen Bemerkungen über Raumauffassungen und ihre Geschichte beginnen sowie Fechner und Zöllner in diese Tradition stellen. »Ein mystischer Schauer ergreift den Nichtmathematiker, wenn er vom ›vierdimensionalen Raum‹ hört, ein Gefühl, das dem vom Theatergespenst erzeugten nicht unähnlich ist,« konstatierte Albert Einstein (1879–1955).[2] Vor der Vorführung des mathematischen Films über den vierdimensionalen Würfel möchte ich daher kurz die Frage erörtern: Was ist Raum? Anschließend diskutiere ich Fechners psychophysischen Raumbegriff und Zöllners spiritistische Raumauffassung. Ich werde mit Überlegungen zur Frage enden, in welchem Sinn es eine vierte Dimension geben kann.

1. Einiges über Raumauffassungen und ihre Geschichte

Einerseits mag uns für einen kurzen Überblick als wissenschaftstheoretische Richtschnur eine nüchterne Einstellung willkommen sein, wie sie der angelsächsische Philosoph John Anderson (1893–1962) in seinen »Studies in Empirical Philosophy« einnimmt und die ihn zu der allgemeinen Folgerung kommen lässt,

> that all objects of science, including minds and goods, are things occurring in space and time [...] and that we can study them in virtue of the fact that we come into spatial and temporal relations with them. (Anderson 1963, 14)

Anderson verwirft mithin alle Ideale, Endgültiges, Symbole, Wirkungen und Ähnliches, letztlich gibt es für ihn nur Tatsachen, d.h. Ereignisse in Raum und Zeit.[3] Andererseits würde uns eine derartige skeletthafte Darstellung die Raumauffassungen der Vergangenheit, insbesondere deren Vielfalt und Wirkung, weitgehend verbergen, so dass wir unsere Untersuchungen mehr aus einer wissenschaftshistorischen Perspektive führen,

---

[1] Siehe auch Schubert 1909, 3, § 10.

[2] Siehe Einstein 1969a, 46.

[3] And therefore all ideals, ultimates, symbols, agencies and the like are to be rejected, and no such distinction as that of facts and principles, or facts and values, can be maintained. There are only facts, i.e occurrences in space and time (Anderson 1963, 14).

uns allerdings dabei der Vergangenheit nicht als ein »rückwärts gekehrter Prophet« (Friedrich Wilhelm Schelling, 1775–1854) zuwenden wollen.

Am Beginn der Menschwerdung steht eine bewusste Orientierung in *Raum* und *Zeit*. Welche theoretischen Konzepte haben sich dabei herausgebildet? Am schnellsten wird uns deren Mannigfaltigkeit an den kosmologischen Entwürfen unserer Vorfahren deutlich. Kosmogonische Mythen standen am Anfang, ehe jüdischer und griechischer *Rationalismus* auf der Szene erschienen.[4] »Als droben der Himmel nicht genannt war, drunten die Feste einen Namen nicht trugen, als die Götter nicht existierten [...]« (Thiele 1993, 136);[5] so beginnt der babylonische Schöpfungsmythos, und er fährt mit einer verwirrenden Fülle von Götternamen fort, bis schließlich der Götterheld Marduk triumphiert.

Ganz anders die philosophische *Kosmogonie* der Griechen, die nicht nach einem lebendigen Gott, sondern nach dem Unwandelbaren, das hinter den flüchtigen Erscheinungen steht, sucht: die platonische Ideenlehre. Das griechische *Universum* ist räumlich endlich, die Zeit aber unendlich.[6] Die patristischen Philosophen lehnten sich an diese Anschauungen an; da aber aus christlicher Sicht Schöpfung und Jüngstes Gericht die Zeit beschränken, ist diese nun wie der Raum endlich. Auch für Johannes Kepler (1571–1630) und Nikolaus Kopernikus (1473–1543) bleibt das noch so: das All und die Zeit sind endlich. Allerdings hatte in der Antike schon Lukrez (ca. 96–55 v.Chr.) ein unendliches Weltall behauptet, in der Neuzeit tun dies 1440 Nikolaus Cusanus (1401–1464), 1567 Thomas Digges (?–1595), 1584 Giordano Bruno (1548–1600) sowie schließlich 1700 Isaac Newton (1642–1727), und dieses Universum hatte eine *euklidische Geometrie*. Die mathematische Möglichkeit nichteuklidischer Geometrien wird in den 30er-Jahren des 19. Jahrhunderts entdeckt (Carl Friedrich Gauß, 1777–1855; János Bolyai, 1802–1860; Nikolai Iwanowitsch Lobatschewskij, 1792–1856), und bereits zwei Jahrzehnte später wird deren Anwendung in der *Kosmologie* erwogen, von Zöllner 1870, und sie ist schließlich von Albert Einstein sowie David Hilbert (1862–1943) um 1917 erfolgreich ausgeführt worden.[7]

---

[4] Vgl. Thiele 1993, 125–148; Thiele 1997, 103–126.

[5] Vgl. auch Beltz 1978, 39.

[6] Euklids Parallelenpostulat (I, 5) verlangt allerdings die Möglichkeit einer unbegrenzten Verlängerung einer Strecke im (mathematischen) Raum gemäß Postulat I, 2; siehe Euklid 1933, 2–3.

[7] Siehe hierzu etwa Zöllner 1878, 1, 16–288.

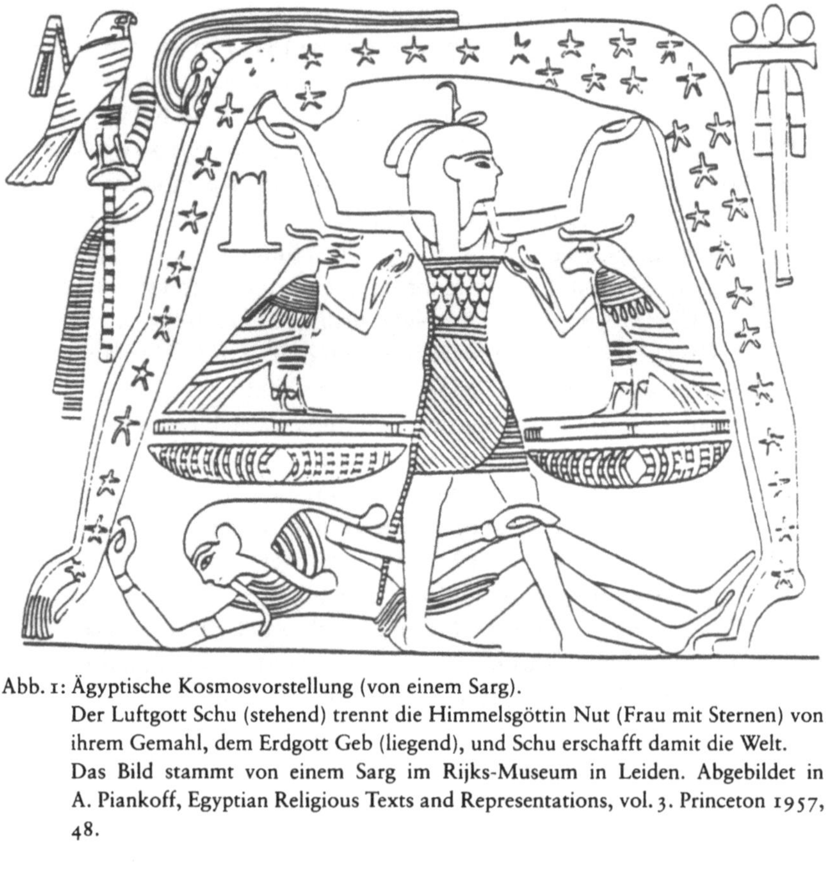

Abb. 1: Ägyptische Kosmosvorstellung (von einem Sarg).
Der Luftgott Schu (stehend) trennt die Himmelsgöttin Nut (Frau mit Sternen) von ihrem Gemahl, dem Erdgott Geb (liegend), und Schu erschafft damit die Welt.
Das Bild stammt von einem Sarg im Rijks-Museum in Leiden. Abgebildet in A. Piankoff, Egyptian Religious Texts and Representations, vol. 3. Princeton 1957, 48.

Vor einer Veranschaulichung von *nichteuklidischen Geometrien* oder – gleich allgemeiner – von Riemann'schen Geometrien steht die Barriere der Mathematizität. Man kann sie durch einen Trick teilweise umgehen, indem man diese Geometrien in die vertrauten euklidischen Räume einbettet. Beispielsweise läßt sich eine sphärische zweidimensionale nichteuklidische Geometrie als Kugeloberfläche in einen dreidimensionalen euklidischen Raum einbetten, allerdings auf Kosten einer höheren Dimensionalität des benutzten Raumes. Aber es ist wichtig, darauf hinzuweisen, dass ein solches Vorgehen nicht in der Natur der Sache liegt.

Wir haben jetzt den Zeitraum erreicht, aus dem die Raumanschauungen von Fechner und Zöllner kommen. Philosophisch befinden wir uns in der Periode der romantischen Naturphilosophie von Friedrich Wilhelm Schelling, Carl Gustav Carus (1789–1869) und Johann Wolfgang von

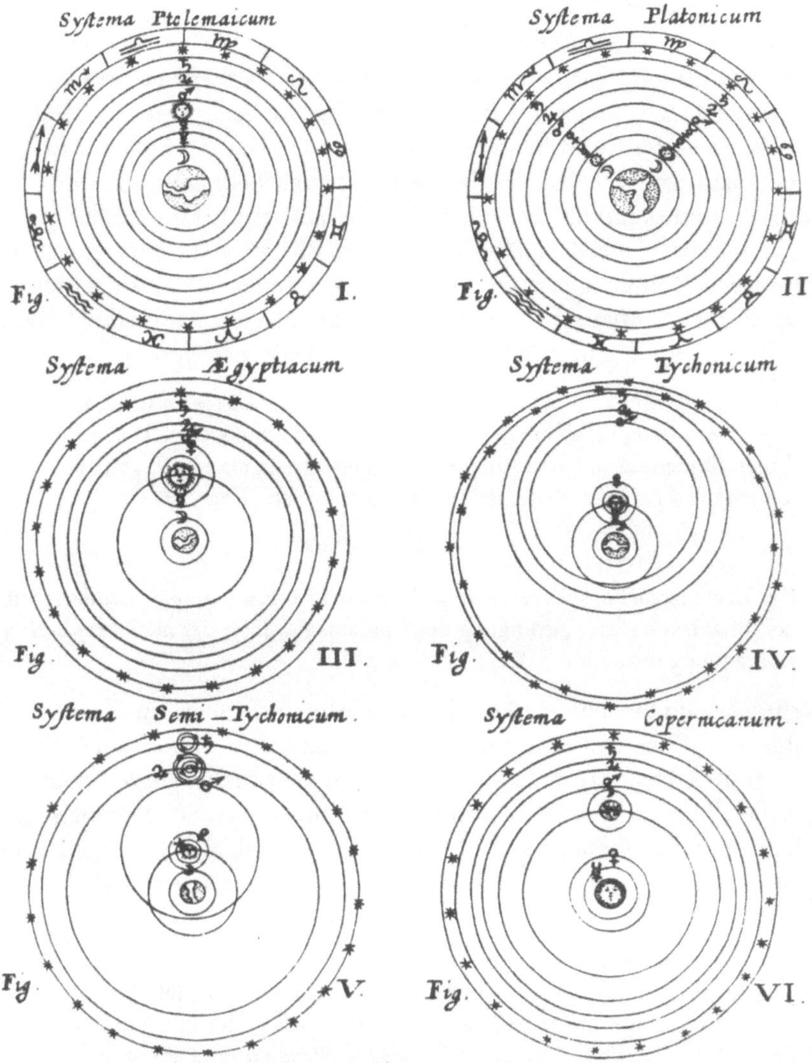

Abb. 2: Zusammenstellung verschiedener Planetensysteme aus Athanasius Kirchers »Iterexstaticum coeleste« (1660).
I. Ptolomäisches System, II. Platonisches System, III. Ägyptisches System, IV. Tychonisches System, V. Semi-Tychonisches System, VI. Kopernikanisches System.

Goethe (1749–1832); der Schelling-Schüler Lorenz Oken (1779–1851) betrachtete beispielsweise die Welt als eine sich drehende Kugel, die gleichzeitig Gott repräsentierte. Dominant ist aber immer noch Kants Auffassung, dass *Raum* und *Zeit* notwendige Vorstellungen a priori sind, also keine empirischen Begriffe bezeichnen, die von der äußeren Erfahrung abgezogen wurden, sondern im Gegenteil Bedingungen der Möglichkeit von Erkenntnis sind. Denn in jeder äußeren Erfahrung kann von allem abgesehen werden, aber nicht davon, dass diese Erfahrung stets in Raum und Zeit gemacht wurde. Damit ist Geometrie als Wissenschaft vom Raum synthetisch und doch a priori möglich. Immanuel Kant (1724–1894) selbst hierzu in seiner »Kritik der reinen Vernunft«:

> Der Raum stellt gar keine Eigenschaft irgend einiger Dinge an sich, oder sie in ihrem Verhältnis auf einander vor, d.i. keine Bestimmung derselben, die an den Gegenständen selbst haftet, und welche bliebe, wenn man auch von allen subjektiven Bedingungen der Anschauung abstrahierte. (Kant 1781, A 26)

oder

> Der Raum ist nichts anderes, als nur die Form aller Erscheinungen äußerer Sinne, d.i. die subjektive Bedingung der Sinnlichkeit, unter der allein uns äußere Anschauung möglich ist. (Kant 1781, A 26)

Neben der Philosophie des 19. Jahrhunderts muss noch ein Aspekt der zeitgenössischen Naturwissenschaft hervorgehoben werden, um Fechners und Zöllners Einstellung zu verstehen: die zunehmend *materialistische* Deutung naturwissenschaftlicher Ergebnisse, die entweder Geistiges schlechterdings leugnete oder es auf Materielles reduzierte. Einige Ereignisse der Naturwissenschaft bzw. einige solcher Deutungen sind:

1828 Friedrich Wöhler (1800–1882) stellt den organischen Harnstoff aus anorganischen Stoffen her;

1842/47 Robert Mayer (1814–1878) bzw. Hermann von Helmholtz (1821–1894) formulieren den Satz von der Erhaltung der Energie;

1847 Karl Vogt (1817–1895) stellt Geist als Produkt des Gehirns dar, gewissermaßen als ein Exkrement desselben;

1854 Auf der 31. Versammlung Deutscher Naturforscher und Ärzte in Göttingen bricht der »Materialismus-Streit« aus;

1855 Ludwig Büchners (1824–1899) Werk »Kraft und Stoff« erscheint;

1859 Charles Darwin (1809–1882) entwickelt seine Evolutionstheorie;

1899 Ernst Haeckel (1834–1919) veröffentlicht die »Welträtsel«.

Abb. 3: Un missionnaire du moyen âge raconte qu'il avait trouvé le point où ciel et la terre se touchent. (Ein mittelalterlicher Botschafter berichtet, dass er den Punkt gefunden hat, wo sich Himmel und Erde berühren.)
Abbildung im Stil alter Meister aus C. Flammarion »L'atmosphère« (1888).

Rationalität, die natürlich im Materialismus zu finden ist, und Spiritualität sind polare Haltungen, zwischen denen weltanschauliche Auffassungen pendeln. Spiritistische Traditionen gab und gibt es überall, denken Sie nur an Schamanentum, Hexerei, esoterische Lehren usw. England und die USA haben hier ebenfalls eine ausgeprägte Tradition, die auch literarisch auffällig ist.[8] Ich erinnere an die Amerikaner Edgar Allan Poe (1809–1849), Ambrose Bierce (1842–1913?) oder neuerdings Howard Phillips Lovecraft (1890–1937) und Stephen King (geb. 1947). Die angelsächsische Wissenschaft und Philosophie ist andererseits für ihre Nüchternheit und ihren *Pragmatismus* bekannt, und es verwundert daher nicht, dass im Umfeld eines solchen auf Rationalität eingeengten Den-

[8] Siehe Schenkel 1994.

kens das geistige Pendel leicht zum *Spiritismus* ausschlug, auch oder gerade bei den Amerikanern, denen bereits für Spukgeschichten u.ä. Englands klassische Traditionen gänzlich fehlt.[9] Eine solche Gegenbewegung zum Rationalismus, in der die wissenschaftliche Bewusstheit durch Poesie, Mystik, Magie oder Esoterik ersetzt oder komplementiert wurde, gab es auch im französischen Sprachraum in der Form des Symbolismus in Literatur und Malerei (Josephin Péladan, genannt Le Sar (1859–1918), Paul Claudel (1868–1955), Maurice Maeterlink (1862–1949) und Gustave Moreau (1826–1898), Odilon Redon (1840–1916) oder Alphonse Osbert (1857–1939)). Gabriel Fauré (1845–1924) bringt in seiner Orchestersuite »Pelléas et Mélisande« (1898) diese Stimmung zum Klingen.

In gewisser Weise schlägt Sigmund Freuds (1856–1939) »Traumdeutung« (1899) eine Brücke zwischen Bewusstsein und Unbewusstem, zwischen Rationalem und Irrationalem. Aber der wissenschaftliche Erkenntnisgewinn ist in dem Sinn polar, dass jeder Zuwachs mit einer Einengung des Problems verbunden ist. Sowohl die zunehmende Einschränkungen auf die Ratio als auch die damit wachsende Kompliziertheit des Denkens sowie die damit verbundenen Schwierigkeiten, diesem Denken zu folgen, beeinträchtigen fraglos die Ganzheitlichkeit des menschlichen Daseins. Die Welt wird so als unvollständig und ergänzungsbedürftig erlebt. Daher erzeugt ein eingeschränktes Anliegen wie das des Erkennens der Welt allein aus naturwissenschaftlicher Sicht, das dem umfassenden Wissensdrang des Menschen widerspricht, zwangsläufig irrationales Verhalten gegenüber wissenschaftlichen Alleinvertretungsansprüchen. Das äußert sich im Aufleben des Aberglauben, der Esoterik, der Phantasterei usw.[10] Neben solchen verbreiteten fragwürdigen Kompensierungen wird jeder Wissenschaftler über seine fachliche Arbeit hinaus das (*metaphysische*) Bedürfnis haben, seine Ergebnisse in einen allgemeinen Zusammenhang zu stellen, sie in eine Weltanschauung, in eine Ersatzreligion oder in eine theologische Sicht einzuordnen. Eine Einschränkung der menschlichen Bedürfnisse allein auf wissenschaftliche Erkenntnisse verengt nicht nur die menschliche Natur, sondern verkennt sie. Matthias Schramm (geb. 1928) beendet sein Buch »Natur ohne Sinn« mit folgenden Worten:

> Die Natur soll mehr sein als das, was uns schlechthin fremd gegenübertritt, mehr auch als ein neutrales wissenschaftliches Objekt. Es verlangt uns nach ei-

---

[9] Einen kurzen Überblick zur Geschichte des Spiritismus gibt z.B. Henneberg 1902, 3ff.; vgl. auch Meinel 1991, 37ff.

[10] Vgl. das der Arbeit vorangestellte Motto.

> nem Rückhalt, und wir suchen nach einem Sinn in ihr. Doch wir haben verlernt, das unbegreifliche Wunder zu würdigen, das uns die Natur [...] unablässig vor Augen stellt. (Schramm 1985, 188)

Man kann solche Haltungen je nach eigener Einstellung als mit den naturwissenschaftlichen Richtungen, neben diesen oder gegen sie herausgebildet verstehen, wobei von der erscheinenden Leichtgläubigkeit bis zur philosophischen Bearbeitung eine erhebliche Spannweite besteht, und die in ihr verorteten Gesichtspunkte sollte man nicht ohne weiteres als Gegenentwürfe auffassen. Verfährt man so, dann desavouiert man von vornherein jegliche ernsthaften Bemühungen, das über das wissenschaftlich begründbare Hinausgehende zur Kenntnis zu nehmen, und man favorisiert in unbegründeter Weise einen problematischen »szientistischen« Standpunkt, den man dann gegenüber allen anderen Auffassungen, die schlechterdings als Gegenkulturen empfunden werden, zu behaupten hat.[11]

Gerade im Hinblick auf Fechner und Zöllner sind solche grundsätzlichen Überlegungen wie die eben angestellten angebracht. Fechner ist diese Problematik durchaus gegenwärtig, denn, wenn er mit einer *Metaphysik* über die Physik hinausgehen will, ist ihm bewusst, »dass ich die Metaphysik für keine so exakte Wissenschaft halte, als die mathematische Physik« halten kann, und er gesteht daher solchen metaphysischen Betrachtungen »ein Moment der Unsicherheit zu« (Fechner 1864, IX), wiewohl er sie für unverzichtbar hält. In diesem Geiste bemerkte er in dem Vorwort zur ersten Auflage der »Atomenlehre«:

> Will man einmal mit einer Metaphysik über eine Physik hinausgehen, und ich meine, es ist [dies] wirklich ein Bedürfnis des Menschen, [...] so halte ich dafür, dass die dort [im zweiten Teil des Buches] aufgestellte Ansicht die wahrscheinlichste ist. (Fechner 1864, VIII)[12]

---

[11] Beispielsweise geht Meinel apodiktisch von kulturellen Gegenentwürfen aus, so dass die aufgewiesenen Widersprüche (selbst) programmiert sind, und Meinel folglich, da Zöllners Denken sich nicht allein auf wissenschaftliches Überlegen beschränkt, zu der fragwürdigen Feststellung gelangt, dass sich die Wissenschaftsgeschichte mit Zöllner schwer tue (wo?) und dass die Grundlinie zwischen der Wissenschaftskultur und ihrer Gegenkultur in Deutschland weniger als anderswo durchlässig gewesen sei (Meinel 1991,56). Snows in ähnlichem Zusammenhang entstandene (angelsächsische) Begrifflichkeit ist neutraler und spricht von den »two cultures« (Cambridge Lecture 1959), ohne dabei die Differenzen zu kaschieren.

[12] Bereits beide Adjektive im Titel des Buches »Ueber die physikalische und philosophische Atomenlehre« umreißen klar Fechners Einstellung.

2. Über Fechner und Zöllner

Trotz vieler Gemeinsamkeiten unterscheiden sich Fechner und Zöllner in der Auffassung vom *Raum*. Einige Worte sollen daher der Gegenüberstellung der beiden Leipziger Professoren dienen und den eingangs erwähnten gewaltigen Schritt verständlicher machen.[13]

Fechner hatte zunächst Medizin studiert, arbeitete aber bis zu seiner schweren Erkrankung 1840 als Experimentalphysiker mit guten mathematischen Kenntnissen. Eine existentielle *Lebenskrise* führte ihn, was häufiger der Fall ist, dann zur Psychologie und Philosophie. Fechners *naturphilosophisches* System, in dem der Mensch kein abgespaltenes Gegenüber der Natur ist, fußt in religiösen und mystischen Vorstellungen einer durchgängig *beseelten* Natur. Wilhelm Windelband (1848–1915) charakterisierte Fechners Philosophie als eine der Anschauung und des Gefühls, weniger der begrifflichen Analyse.[14] Allerdings stellte die von Fechner begründete *Psychophysik* die Beziehungen von objektivem Reiz und subjektiver Empfindung auf empirisch-experimenteller Grundlage in mathematischer Form dar. Seelisches erhielt ein physikalisches Maß.

Zöllner, etwa eine Generation jünger als Fechner, hatte Physik, aber auch Mathematik und Chemie studiert. Er erkannte sofort, dass Robert Kirchhoff (1824–1887) und Gustav Bunsen (1804–1876) mit der *Spektralanalyse* (1860) die entscheidende Basis für neue astronomische Erkenntnisse geschaffen hatten, die über die herkömmlichen himmelsmechanischen Arbeiten hinausgehen und die eine neue Disziplin konstituieren würden, welche er Astrophysik nannte. In der Astronomie war Zöllner um 1870 – ein Menschenalter vor Hermann Minkowski (1864–1909) und Albert Einstein – durch theoretische Fragen auf die Anwendung *nichteuklidischer Geometrien* sowie die Verwendung der *vierten Dimension* geführt worden,[15] die spiritistische Interpretation folgte erst ein Jahrzehnt später (ab 1878). Ein Englandbesuch (1875) brachte ihn in Kontakt mit dem Physiker und Chemiker William Crookes (1832–1919) und dessen Untersuchungen von spiritistischen Phänomenen, die den unvoreingenommenen Zöllner stark interessierten, so dass er auch Kontak-

---

[13] Zur Biographie vgl. Kuntze 1892; Laßwitz 1896, 1902; Arendt 1999; Koerber 1899; Hermann 1982; Hamel 1977; eigenhändiger Lebenslauf Zöllners (1864) in: Hermann 1974.

[14] Heimsoeth 1935, 555.

[15] Siehe etwa Leihkauf 1983, 29–33.

te zur Dialectical Society der Londoner Spiritisten aufnahm. Zöllners kritische Einstellung zum *Spiritismus* schwand jedoch rapide, als das umstrittene Medium Henry Slade (1840–1904), das russische Spiritisten nach Deutschland vermittelt hatte,[16] schließlich 1877 nach Leipzig kam, da es in Berlin bei Hermann von Helmholtz (1821–1894) und Rudolf Virchow (1821–1902) auf Ablehnung gestoßen war. Slade stellte sich dem neugierigen und spekulativ veranlagten Zöllner für ca. 40 spiritistische Versuche zur Verfügung, die am Ende Zöllners wissenschaftliche Reputation ruinieren sollten. Nachdem später Slade endgültig als Betrüger entlarvt wurde, war es immerhin noch Sir Arthur Conan Doyle (1859–1930), der meinte, ihn verteidigen zu müssen.[17] Es wäre falsch, Zöllner für einen leichtgläubigen Wissenschaftler zu halten, der nur zu bereitwillig dem Spiritismus auf den Leim gegangen sei. Zöllner war sowohl ein skeptischer Denker als auch kritischer Beobachter. Es sei nur an die bekannte optische Zöllner'sche Täuschung erinnert, die Zöllner in seinem »Cometenbuch« (1872) aufgedeckt hatte.

Als Ausgangspunkt ihrer Forschungsprogramme haben beide Leipziger Professoren die Physik, aber sie bewegen sich jeweils in unterschiedliche Richtungen: Zöllner strebt in die unermesslichen Weiten des Alls, Fechner sucht im menschlichen *Wahrnehmungssystem* das eben noch Messbare zu erfassen; Zöllner entwirft hypothetische mathematische Theorien, die er schließlich mit *spiritistischen* Experimenten zu bestätigen glaubte; Fechner erfasst den hoch subjektiven Bereich der menschlichen Empfindungen mit mathematischen Methoden, ohne diese auf Metaphysik zu gründen.[18] Gemeinsam ist beiden eine verwandte Überzeugung vom Vorhandensein einer Geistigkeit in der Welt, die letztlich Grundlage ihrer Arbeiten gewesen ist. Wenn auch nicht alle Arbeiten der beiden in ihrer Bedeutung überdauert haben, so schlagen die Begründer der *Psychophysik* und *Astrophysik* am Ende des 19. Jahrhunderts Themen an, die immer noch zum Bestand der entsprechenden Disziplinen gehören bzw. Gegenstand der heutigen Forschung sind.

---

[16] 1874 war die erste deutsche okkultistische Zeitschrift »Psychische Studien« durch den Russen Aksakow gegründet worden.

[17] Vgl. Doyle 1926; mehr über Slade in: Mulholland 1938.

[18] Vgl. auch Lennig 1994.

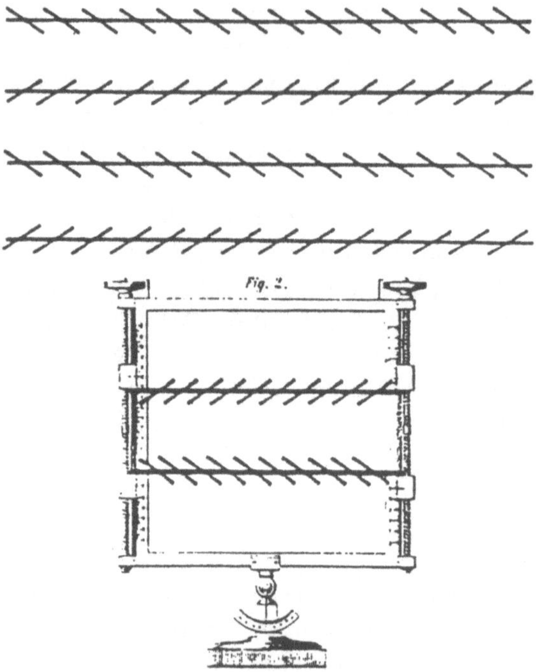

Abb. 4: Die Zöllner'sche Täuschung.
»Die horizontalen Linien sind vollkommen gerade und parallel« (Zöllner 1872). Fraser hat anstelle solcher paralleler Geraden die Zöllner'schen Linien zu konzentrischen Kreisen gefügt, wodurch eine noch beeindruckendere Täuschung entsteht, die eine Spirale anstelle von Kreisen erscheinen lässt.
Die Abbildung stammt aus F. Zöllner, Ueber die Natur der Cometen. Leipzig 1872.

3. Was ist Raum?

Das »Deutsche Wörterbuch« der Brüder Jacob und Wilhelm Grimm (1785–1863; 1786–1859) führt an, dass das Wort *Raum* allen germanischen Sprachen eigen sei, um dann dessen Bedeutung in 14 Abschnitten zu erläutern, ohne dabei auf seinen mathematischen Gehalt einzugehen.[19] Das ist ein unübersehbarer philologischer Hinweis auf die Vielschichtigkeit des Begriffs. Systematisch wurde in der Mathematik und in der naturwissenschaftlichen Philosophie der Raumbegriff erst mit Beginn des letzten Jahrhunderts untersucht, der einschlägige Grimm-Band datiert bereits von 1893.

[19] Grimm 1893, VIII, 275–283.

OX 1

Übersicht über einige Raumformen

Denkraum	
	kontinuierlich
abstrakte (mathematische) Strukturen	
	diskret
	IDEAL
Anschauungsraum	
	euklidisch (intuitiv R^1, R^2, R^3)
geometrisch	nichteuklidisch
	[mehrdimensional (> 3)]

Empfindungsraum (nicht homogen, nicht isotrop, Ferne schrumpft)	
	optisch
psychologisch/physiologisch	akustisch
	sensorisch
	⋮
	REAL

Wahrnehmungsraum
physikalisch
(klassische Beschreibung:
homogen, isotrop, unbeschränkt [ggf. unendlich],
zum Teil mittels Konventionen)

In den »Sprüchen des Confucius« (1795) beschrieb Friedrich Schiller (1759–1805) die mathematische Raumauffassung klassisch noch so:

> Dreifach ist des Raumes Maß.
> Rastlos fort ohn Unterlaß
> strebt die Länge fort ins Weite;
> endlos gießet sich die Breite;
> grundlos senkt die Tiefe sich.
> (Schiller 1915, 164)

Heinrich Heine (1797–1856) wiederum erlebte offenbar die Welt subjektiver, denn er fürchtete, dass mit Einführung der neuen Raumerfahrung durch die Eisenbahn die räumliche Distanz vernichtet werde. Für das Handy, also die Abwertung der Zeit, steht ein zeitgenössischer Dichter noch aus.

Naturwissenschaftlern dient der *Raum* zur Ordnung der Dinge. Für das Ordnen von Dingen ist die Möglichkeit des Messens nicht erforderlich, aber zur Vereinfachung der nachfolgenden Überlegungen wollen wir sie durchweg als möglich ansehen.[20]

Nach Euklid (ca. 330–260 v.Chr.) ist der *Punkt* dasjenige im Raum, was keine Teile und keine Ausdehnung hat. Der geometrischen Abstraktion eines Punktes entspricht daher in der Physik das Atom. Punkte kann man sich nur denken, aber nicht vorstellen. Trotzdem dient häufig der Punkt als Grundelement, um geometrische Räume aufzubauen: Durch Fortbewegung des Punktes entsteht eine Linie, durch deren Bewegung eine Fläche, sodann ein Raum. Weiter trägt dieses anschauliche Konzept nicht. Eine *Gerade* wird als Träger der auf ihr liegenden Punkte begriffen. Die Lage eines Punktes P auf einer Geraden kann nach Festlegung eines Bezugspunktes O durch den Abstand von P zu O, also durch *eine* Maßzahl (seine Koordinate), beschrieben werden. Man nennt daher die Gerade eine eindimensionale Mannigfaltigkeit; entsprechend wird eine Fläche zweidimensional genannt, da ein Punkt auf ihr durch zwei Maßzahlen, seine Koordinaten, festgelegt werden kann. Ein bekanntes Beispiel: die geographische Breite und Länge auf der Erdkugel, die beispielsweise für Leipzig 51° 11' 24'' N und 12° 12' 60'' O beträgt.

---

20 Wir werden gleich Konsequenzen der unterstellten Messmöglichkeit im Hinblick auf die Dimension aufzeigen. Der spätere Abschnitt über die Struktur des psychophysischen Raumes wird eine weitere Seite der Messproblematik andeuten.

Formal können drei, vier oder mehr Zahlenangaben als Koordinaten eines *Punktes* in entsprechenden drei-, vier- oder höher dimensionalen Räumen angesehen werden. *Vierdimensionale Räume* können wir uns bekanntlich nicht mehr vorstellen, aber dass sie mehr als eine Spielerei sind, zeigt eine physikalische Deutung: Werden jedem Punkt eines physikalischen Raumes R^3 noch Temperatur, Druck oder ähnliche physikalische Größen zugeordnet, so bewegen wir uns formal in einem Raum von mehr als 3 Dimensionen. Bereits seit den Zeiten von Lagrange haben Physiker in derartigen Phasenräumen gearbeitet, ohne dass *Spiritisten* hiervon Notiz genommen haben. Hermann Schubert schrieb 1892 treffend:

> In der Hand der Mathematiker war die Ausdehnung des Raumbegriffs nur ein Mittel, um auf bequeme Weise Wahrheiten [...] zu formulieren, die sich [...] auf mehr als drei Variabeln beziehen. Da aber kamen die Spiritisten und bemächtigten sich des vierdimensionalen Raumes, indem sie dieses [...] Forschungsmittel als etwas Wirkliches ansahen. Die Spiritisten waren in großer Verlegenheit darüber, wo sie die Geister der Verstorbenen wohnen lassen sollten. Es ging doch nicht gut, ihnen in der unseren Sinnen zugänglichen Welt einen Platz anzuweisen. [...] Der Wohnsitz der Geister mußte außerhalb des Geltungsbereichs der Naturgesetze liegen, mußte etwas Mystisches sein, wohin der menschliche Verstand nie vordringen konnte. Diese Eigenschaft aber besaß der vierdimensionale Raum der Mathematiker. (Schubert 1892, 9)

Klagend vermerkte daher Wilhelm Busch (1832–1908) über den Dichter in »Balduin Bählamm«, dass dieser in die Poetendimension, die fünfte ziehe, »da die vierte jetzt, von Geistern ohnehin besetzt« (Busch 1883, Kap. 1).

Allerdings ist die Dimensionszahl des *Raumes* in der Mathematik von dem Grundelement abhängig, aus dem der Raum aufgebaut wird. Handelt es sich beispielsweise um Untersuchungen in einem *Strahlenbüschel*, das sind alle *Geraden* der Ebene, die durch einen gegebenen Punkt O gehen, so wird man zur Koordinatenbestimmung dieser Geraden am besten einen Winkel nehmen, womit eine Koordinate zur Beschreibung ausreicht bzw. das Büschel hat die Dimension 1. Der Trägerpunkt eines solchen ebenen Büschels muss daher als eindimensional angesehen werden; als Element einer Geraden behält er natürlich die Dimension null. Geht man jetzt im Raum zu den Geraden durch einen festen Punkt über, so wird man zwei Winkel benötigen, um eine beliebige Gerade in dem ›Bündel‹ genannten Geradensystem zu charakterisieren (was man über die geographischen Koordinaten der Erdkugel sofort einsieht, wenn der Trä-

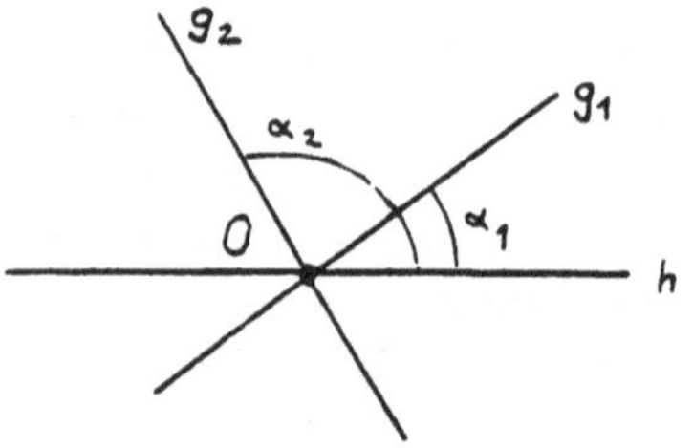

Abb. 5: Punkt- und Linienkoordinaten

a) Ein eindimensionaler Bereich (Gerade bzw. Büschel).

Die Gerade *g* mit der üblichen Maßbestimmung zur Festlegung eines Punktes *P* vom Ursprung O. Der Abstand *OP* ist die Koordinate des Punktes *P* auf *g*.

Ein Geradenbüschel der Ebene mit dem Trägerpunkt O ist eindimensional, da lediglich der Schnittwinkel α_i benötigt wird, um die Lage der Geraden g_i im Büschel festzulegen. Die Winkel α sind damit Koordinaten der Geraden *g* im Büschel.

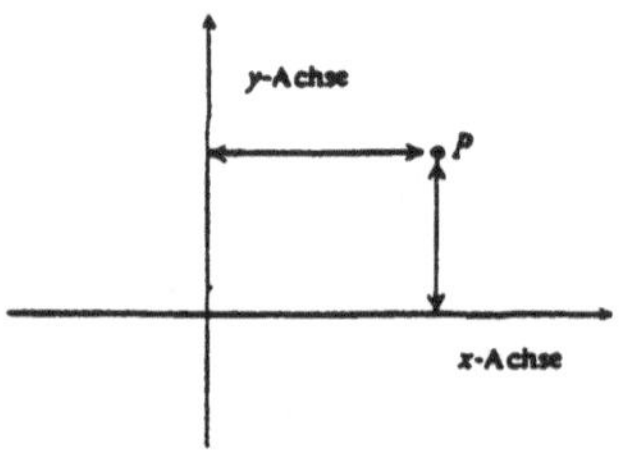

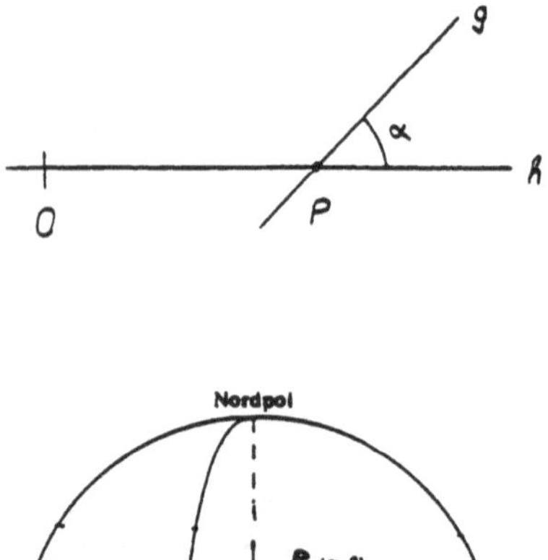

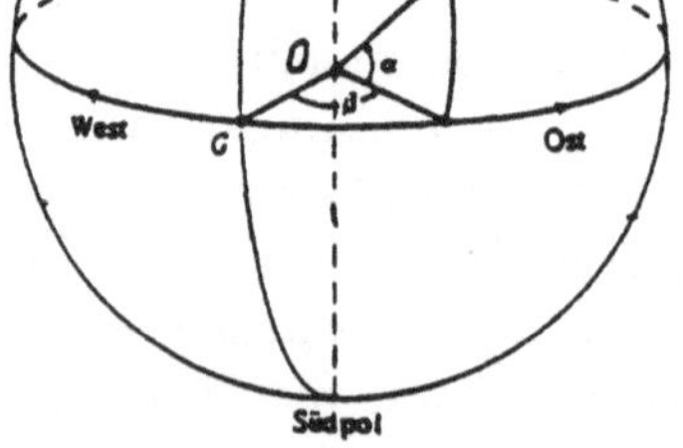

b) Ein zweidimensionaler Bereich (Ebene, Fläche). Grundelement der Ebene *E* soll der Punkt sein. Zur Festlegung eines beliebigen Punktes *P* wird auf jeder Koordinatenachsen eine Angabe benötigt (insgesamt zwei Koordinaten *x* und *y*).

Grundelement der Ebene soll die Gerade sein. Zur Festlegung einer beliebigen Geraden *g* werden zwei Angaben (Koordinaten) benötigt: der Abstand *OP* auf einer festen Geraden *h* sowie der Winkel α zwischen *g* und *h* (vgl. die in a) genannten Fälle).

Zur Festlegung eines beliebigen Punktes *P* auf der Kugeloberfläche (Erdoberfläche) werden zwei Winkelangaben benötigt: die geographische Breite α und die geographische Länge β (geographische Koordinaten). Die Kugeloberfläche ist folglich zweidimensional. Alle Geraden des Raumes, die durch den Kugelmittelpunkt O gehen, bilden ein Geradenbündel mit dem Träger O. Jede Gerade des Bündels trifft die Kugeloberfläche der nördlichen Halbkugel in genau einem Punkt *P*, und ihre Lage im Bündel ist daher durch die (geographischen) Koordinaten von *P* zu erfassen. Das Bündel ist damit zweidimensional.

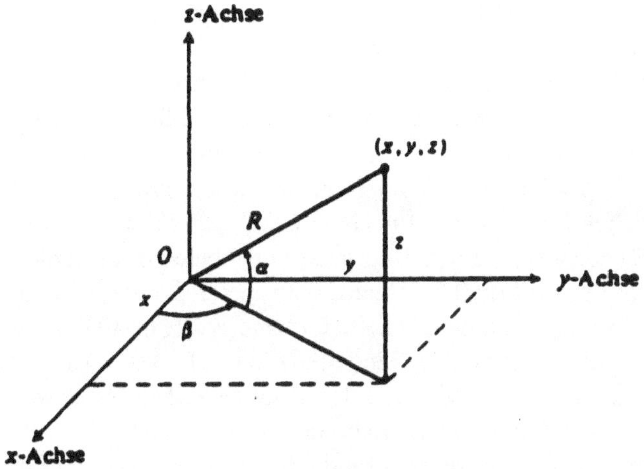

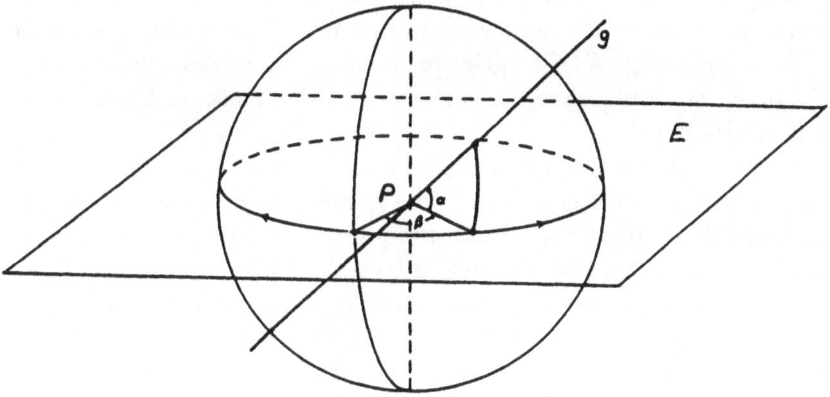

c) Der Raum als drei- bzw. vierdimensionaler Bereich in den jeweiligen Koordinaten. Grundelement soll der Punkt sein. Zur Festlegung eines beliebigen Punktes *P* des dreidimensionalen Raumes benötigt man in einem kartesischen Koordinatensystem drei Angaben: *x*, *y*, *z*. Der gleiche Punkt kann ebenfalls in sphärischen Koordinaten durch zwei Winkel *α* und *β* (geographische Länge und Breite) sowie seinen Abstand *R* vom Koordinatenursprung O bestimmt werden

Grundelement soll die Gerade sein. Zur Festlegung einer beliebigen Geraden *g* des Raumes benötigt man vier Koordinaten! Das ergibt sich so: Der Schnitt einer Geraden *g* mit einer Ebene *E* erfolge im Punkt *P*. Die Lage dieses Punktes *P* in der Ebene *E* lässt sich durch zwei Koordinaten erfassen (erste Fall in b)). Die Gerade *g* kann nun als eine Gerade in dem Bündel mit dem Trägerpunkt *P* betrachtet werden, womit zur Festlegung ihrer Lage im Bündel zwei Koordinaten (Winkelangaben) erforderlich sind (der letzte Fall in b)).

gerpunkt der Erdmittelpunkt ist und man eine Gerade des Bündels durch einen Punkt auf der »Erdoberfläche« fixiert). Das Geradenbündel im R^3 bzw. sein Trägerpunkt sind mithin zweidimensional.

Nichtmathematikern mögen diese Büschel und Bündel von Geraden etwas gekünstelt erscheinen. Verwendet man jedoch als Element des *Raumes* anstelle des Punktes die *Gerade*, so werden nun gegenüber den drei erforderlichen Koordinaten für einen beliebigen Punkt bereits vier Zahlenangaben benötigt, um die Position einer beliebigen Gerade festzulegen. Mit Hilfe von Bündeln erkennt man diesen Sachverhalt so: Jede Gerade des Raumes muss eine beliebige Ebene E, die in diesem Raum liegt, in einem Punkt P schneiden. Ein jeder solcher Punkt P kann nun durch zwei Koordinaten in der Ebene E lokalisiert werden. Da er weiterhin als Träger eines Geradenbündels angesehen werden kann, das nach dem obigen Überlegungen zweidimensional ist, braucht man zur Lagebestimmung einer beliebigen Geraden im Raum insgesamt vier Koordinaten. In Linienkoordinaten ist der Raum vierdimensional. Wenn Sie die mathematischen Geraden mit physikalischen Lichtstrahlen identifizieren, sehen Sie, dass wir in der Tat ein interessantes mathematisches Modell vor uns haben. Die Menge aller Kugeln im R^3 erfordert zu ihrer Beschreibung ebenfalls vier Zahlenangaben: drei für den Mittelpunkt und eine für den Radius der Kugel.

Wenn Sie jedoch den *Raum* durch Kugelwellen erzeugen wollen, d.h. aus konzentrischen Kugeln mit einem gemeinsamen festen Mittelpunkt, so reicht die Angabe des Radius, mit anderen Worten, dieser Raum ist eindimensional. Signale, die von einer festen Lichtquelle in den Raum ausgehen, bilden zu jedem Zeitpunkt solche Kugelwellen. Wenn sie andererseits die von der Lichtquelle ausgehenden Strahlen zum Grundelement machen, ist der Raum zweidimensional. Wenn ein Physiker den Raum durch Kräfte konstituieren will, was beispielsweise durch Gravitationsfelder nahegelegt wird, so benötigt er vier Koordinaten zur Beschreibung einer Kraft: drei für die (gerichtete) Wirkungslinie und eine für die Größe der Kraft. Ein anderes physikalisches Beispiel: Die *Spektralfarben* bilden einen eindimensionalen Raum, da diese Farben durch Angabe der Wellenlänge festgelegt sind. Nimmt man in der Theorie von Helmholtz die Mischfarben hinzu, so benötigt man zwei Angaben, um den Farbraum zu charakterisieren. Der farbige *Fernsehbildschirm* ist also ein *vierdimensionaler Raum*, zwei Koordinaten bestimmen die Lage des Farbpunktes am Schirm, zwei weitere Koordinaten legen seine Farbe fest. Ein mathematisches Beispiel mag die Auswahl der Beispiele beenden: Eine Gleichung zweiten Grades zwischen den Größen *x, y* und *z* besitzt neun unabhängige Koeffizienten. Deutet man eine solche Gleichung als Fläche im kartesischen *x, y, z*-Koordinatensystem und denkt sich den Raum durch solche Flächen erzeugt, dann ist er als neundimensional zu betrachten. Einen speziellen Fall unter diesen Gleichungen bildet die Kugelgleichung, die zur sogenannten Kugelgeometrie führt, in der der Raum als vierdimensional zu betrachten ist.

Wenn wir den geometrischen *Anschauungsraum* als intuitiv gegeben betrachten (durchaus im Sinn von Kant als apriorische Möglichkeit der räumlichen Vorstellung), so zeigt sich, dass die jeweils gewählten Elemente dieses Raumes und die damit verbundene Art des Messens zum einen die Definition einer Dimension des mathematischen Raumes überhaupt erst möglich machen, dass aber zum anderen diese Dimension keine Invariante des anschaulich gegebenen Raumes ist, sondern von unserer Art, ihn zu erfassen, abhängt. Wenn wir im gewöhnlichen Leben von den *drei Dimensionen* des Raumes sprechen und andere Dimensionszahlen als unmöglich betrachten, so mag das daran liegen, dass wir uns daran gewöhnt haben, uns selbst stets als Bezugspunkt im Raum zu betrachten und damit Gegenstände bzw. den Raum beständig von (Stand)Punkten zu erfassen.[21] Diese »Voreingenommenheit« ist uns nicht bewusst. Sie wird durch die übliche Lehrweise der Descartes'schen analytischen Geometrie verfestigt. Es war vor allem Julius Plücker (1801–1861), der diese einseitige Auffassung des Raumes durchbrach, indem er beispielsweise die oben erwähnten Linienkoordinaten einführte.

Mathematiker arbeiten inzwischen in unendlich dimensionalen *Räumen*, in denen beispielsweise Funktionen »aufeinander senkrecht« stehen. Gleichfalls benutzen Mathematiker seit einigen Jahrzehnten sogar gebrochene Dimensionen. Beide Sachverhalte will ich nicht näher erläutern. Mathematische Räume sind lediglich denkmögliche Ordnungen, physikalische Räume hingegen entsprechen Erfahrungen. Erst beides konstituiert Physik als Wissenschaft. Sehr schön hat dieses Zusammenspiel schon Leonardo da Vinci (1452–1519) in dem Bild ausgedrückt:

> Die Wissenschaft ist eine zweite Schöpfung mittels des Verstandes, gleichwie die Malerei eine zweite Schöpfung mittels der Phantasie ist. (nach Gierer 1998, 119)

---

[21] Die drei Kränkungen des Menschen (Freud), nämlich der Verlust der zentralen Stellung seines Wohnortes Erde im Planetensystem, der Verfall der Einmaligkeit durch den biologischen Entwicklungsgedanken sowie die Einschränkung des Ichs gegenüber dem Es sowie Überich, beruhen auf der gleichen Selbstbezogenheit unseres Denkens.

Bei Henry More (1614–1687) diente im »Enchiridion metaphysicum« (1671) die *vierte Dimension*, die er nicht im mathematischen Sinn verstand, sowohl der Unterbringung des menschlichen Geistes als auch der von Geistern. Die Aufmerksamkeit der *Spiritisten* für den R^4 wurde vermutlich durch veranschaulichende Vergleiche geweckt, etwa solche, dass ein vierdimensionaler Chirurg noninvasiv operieren könnte oder dass es möglich sei, problemlos den Inhalt eines (dreidimensionalen) Banksafes aus dem R^4 zu entnehmen.[22] Um »Verschwinden und Erscheinen« von Dingen im dreidimensionalen Raum zu rechtfertigen, bedarf man nicht unbedingt eines vierdimensionalen Raumes, was bekannte mathematische Taschenspielertricks wie der vom Verschwinden bzw. Auftauchen von Zwergen beim Umordnen ebener Zeichnungen zeigen oder solche vom Lösen scheinbarer *Gordischer Knoten* im dreidimensionalen Raum. Schließlich wäre auch das *Möbius'sche Band* zu erwähnen, das beim Zerschneiden nicht in zwei getrennte Bänder zerfällt.[23]

Aus meiner Sicht sind jene Veranschaulichungen des R^4 im R^3 die überzeugendsten, die Wesen benutzen, die ganz in einer Fläche leben, von denen bereits Gauß gesprochen hatte und als welche letztlich auch die Schatten in Platos (428–347 v.Chr.) berühmten Höhlengleichnis angesehen werden können.[24] Einem dreidimensionalen Lebewesen ist beispielsweise der Blick auf ein Gemälde als Ganzes sofort möglich, während ein solches Flächenwesen sich diesen Überblick erst durch Erkundungen in der Zeit verschaffen muss.[25] Vergleiche, bei denen mechanische Vorgänge (wie beim medizinischen Operieren) erscheinen, hinken insofern erheblich, als man Dinge niederer Dimension nicht »anfassen« kann; auch

---

[22] Biblisch schon im apokryphen Nikodemus Evangelium (sog. Pilatus-Akten), 15: »Und er [Jesus] nahm mich [Joseph von Arimathia] bei der Hand und versetzte mich in mein Haus, dessen Türen doch verschlossen waren« (Pfabigan 1990, 41). E. Mach, für den nur der dreidimensionale Raum ein wirklicher Fall war, hatte in seiner Geschichte der Mechanik spöttisch geschrieben: »Ein Accoucheur, der eine Geburt durch die vierte Dimension bewerkstelligt hätte, ist bisher noch nicht aufgetreten.« (Mach 1901, 524)

[23] Ein Möbius'sches Band kann man sich herstellen, wenn man einen langen Papierstreifen vor dem Verkleben der kurzen Enden um 180° verdreht. Schneidet man dann dieses Band längs auf, ergibt sich nur ein in sich verdrehtes Band. – August Ferdinand Möbius (1770–1868), Leipziger Astronom und Geometer.

[24] »Wir können uns, sagte er [Gauß], etwa in Wesen hineindenken, die sich nur zweier Dimensionen bewusst sind; höher über uns stehende würden vielleicht in ähnlicher Weise auf uns herabblicken.« (Sartorius von Waltershausen 1856, 81).

[25] Diese Möglichkeit hat auch Zöllner beeindruckt, der aber daraus u.a. auch auf die Möglichkeit des Hellsehens schloss (Zöllner 1879, 3, 96).

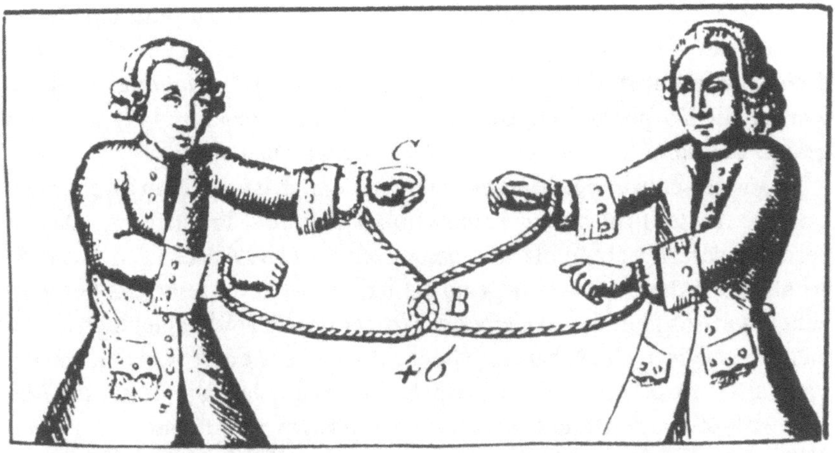

Abb. 6: Ein Fesselungsspiel aus einem italienischen Spielebuch des 18. Jahrhunderts. Eine Entfesselung im vierdimensionalen Raum wäre problemlos. Die scheinbar unauflösbare Verschlingung lässt sich jedoch bereits im dreidimensionalen Raum beheben, ohne dabei die brachiale Methode Alexanders zu bemühen.
Wiedergabe nach Konrad Haase, Rüdiger Thiele: Teufelsspiele. Leipzig, 1998, 51.

wir dreidimensionalen Lebewesen können keinen *Punkt* aus einer Ebene herausnehmen, sondern nur körperliche Dinge bewegen. Von den *Spiritisten* ist übrigens nie die Frage in Betracht gezogen worden, warum wir als dreidimensionale Wesen nicht in gleicher Weise wie die vierdimensionalen Spirits auf unseren Raum aus dem R^3 in den R^2 wirken können. Über die genannte Unzulänglichkeit einer Einflussnahme, die meines Erachtens bereits diese Richtung des Spiritismus zu Fall bringt, helfen im veranschaulichenden räumlichen Beispiel am ehesten noch »imponderable Vorgänge« wie etwa das Sehen hinweg, da Oberflächen von Körpern den Weg von Lichtstrahlen verändern.

4. Zum Film über den vierdimensionalen Würfel[26]

Nach diesen Überlegungen sind wir auf den angekündigten mathematischen Film von Thomas Banchoff (geb. 1938) und Charles Strauss (geb.

[26] An dieser Stelle des Vortrages wurde der Film »Hyperwürfel« von Th. Banchoff und Ch. Strauss gezeigt; vgl. Abb. 9.

1938) vorbereitet. Er behandelt drei Themen: Zunächst wird eine Möglichkeit des Verallgemeinerns eines Quadrates in der Ebene über einen dreidimensionalen Würfel zum Hyperkubus des R^4 aufgezeigt. Danach werden die Körper gedreht bzw. Schnitte durch Würfel und Hyperkuben gelegt, um diese Körper besser zu veranschaulichen.

Sie mögen einwenden, dass es schlecht möglich ist, auf dem zweidimensionalen Bildschirm den *vierdimensionalen Raum* darzustellen. Das ist bereits insofern richtig, als wir niemals eine solche Anschauung vom R^4 erhalten werden, wie wir sie vom R^3 haben. Aber andererseits verdeutlichen wir uns ja in der Malerei oder in der darstellenden Geometrie, namentlich beim technischen Zeichnen, dreidimensionale Körper am Papier, also im R^2. Zweidimensionale Darstellungen dreidimensionaler Körper lassen sich als (ebene) Schatten von Körpern auffassen. Der zweidimensionale Schatten des Kantenmodells eines Würfels ist in Abbildung 7 gezeigt.[27] Wir werden versuchen, in Bezug auf den R^4 diese Projektionsmethode analog im R^3 zu verwirklichen. Da wir dabei aber gleichzeitig die in Rede stehenden Körper noch bewegen können, ist diese Veranschaulichung sogar noch besser als die übliche der darstellenden Geometrie.

Schließlich möchte ich noch erwähnen, dass die Problematik der geometrischen Veranschaulichung nicht mit dem R^4 beginnt, sondern bereits im Begriff des *Punktes* steckt. Resignierend ist dieser von Mathematikern in einschlägigen Vorlesungen als dreidimensionaler Kreidehaufen bezeichnet worden oder von Oskar Perron (1880–1975), einem der bedeutenden Mathematiker des 20. Jahrhunderts, wie folgt definiert worden: Ein Punkt ist das, was sich jeder vernünftige Mensch darunter vorstellt. Und er hat hinzugefügt, dass die Definition der Geraden ebenso laute. Wilhelm Busch wiederum befand, wer sich keinen Punkt denken könne, sei nur zu faul dazu. Moderne axiomatische Theorien der Geometrie lassen mit David Hilbert (1862–1943) seit 1899 die Frage völlig offen, was

---

27 Die einfachste geometrische Figur der Ebene ist durch drei Punkte bestimmt (Dreieck), im Raum ist ein weiterer Punkt erforderlich, um das dem Dreieck entsprechende räumliche Tetraeder mit vier Eckpunkten festzulegen, während im vierdimensionalen Raum offenbar fünf Punkte für den einfachsten vierdimensionalen Körper mit fünf Ecken benötigt werden. Die Projektion (der ebene Schatten) dieses Körpers in den R^2 ergibt das Pentagramm oder den Drudenfuß. Das Pentagramm wird aus den fünf Diagonalen eines regelmäßigen Fünfecks der Ebene gebildet; die Bezeichnung Drudenfuß weist auf die magische Bedeutung dieses Symbols hin, das bereits die Pythagoreer benutzten und das in diesem Sinn in Goethes »Faust« (I, Studierzimmer, V) erscheint.

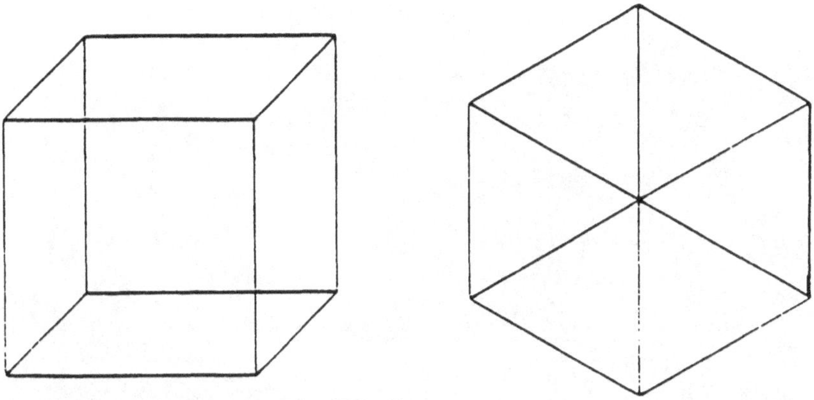

Abb. 7: Perspektivische Darstellung eines Würfels
a) Allgemeine Ansicht eines Würfels, die ein gutes räumliches Bild vermittelt (das allerdings nicht eindeutig ist ›Necker'sche Täuschung‹);
b) Spezielle Ansicht des Würfels, die jedoch im allgemeinen nicht als räumlich, sondern lediglich als symmetrische eben Figur wahrgenommen wird. Der Anteil des Betrachters bei der Bildentstehung wird hier besonders augenfällig.

ein Punkt, eine Gerade usw. sei, sondern beschäftigen sich nur mit den zwischen solchen Objekten bestehenden Beziehungen.[28]

Das Drehbuch zum folgenden Film hätte von Fechner geschrieben werden können, wie Sie aus den folgenden Zitaten, die ich aus seiner *satirischen* Arbeit »Der Raum hat vier Dimensionen« nehme, ersehen werden. Trotz der ironischen Grundhaltung greift Fechner auf solide Kenntnisse der mehrdimensionalen Geometrie zurück.

> Eine vierte Dimension des Raumes, wird man sagen, ist das fünfte Rad am Wagen. Nein erwidere ich, sie ist vielmehr eben das vierte Rad am Wagen, ohne das er wenig nutze wäre. [...], man wird sehen, dass die vierte Dimension dem Raume denselben Nutzen [wie dem Wagen] leistet. Von vornherein darf ich freilich nicht hoffen, die Ansicht von vier Dimensionen des Raumes bei zwei Klassen von Personen durchzusetzen, bei denen, die nichts glauben, als was sie sehen, und bei denen, die nichts sehen als was sie glauben. Unter den erstern verstehe ich die Naturforscher, die nur auf ihre Sinne bauen, unter den letztern die Philosophen. (Fechner 1875, 254f.)

Zur Veranschaulichung der *vierten Dimension* des Raumes benutzt Fechner die *Zeit*, d.h. er vermischt mathematische und physikalische Vorstellungen:

---

[28] Siehe Hilbert 1899.

Abb. 8: Projektionen reduzieren die Dimensionen eines Körpers, wodurch jener als Projektion anschaulich wird.

a) Mechanische Vorrichtung zur Erzeugung der Projektion eines Körpers in die Zeichenebene. Das Projektionszentrum befindet sich am Ende der in der Wand befestigten Schnur. Links werden mit dem anderen Ende der Schnur die Körperpunkte festgelegt, die »Durchstoßpunkte« der Schnur mit der im Bildrahmen gedachten Zeichenebene sind die Bildpunkte. Diese werden dann mit Hilfe eines Koordinatensystems auf die neben dem Rahmen befindliche reale Zeichenebene übertragen (A. Dürer, Underweysung der Messung, 1525).

> Ich nehme die Fläche, worin ein Scheinmännchen [Flächenwesen] sich befindet, und führe sie durch die dritte Dimension hindurch, so erfährt das Scheinmännchen Alles, was in dieser dritten Dimension ist [...]. Freilich hat das Männchen niemals ein Stück der dritten Dimension auf einmal und glaubt also in jedem Augenblicke immer noch blos in seinen zwei Dimensionen zu sein; es faßt von der ganzen Bewegung blos das zeitliche Element und die vor sich gehende Aenderung auf. Aber factisch durchmißt es doch die dritte Dimension und Alles was darin ist. (Fechner 1875, 264–265)

Auch Ideen von Oken, die sich natürlich bis in die Antike zu Parmenides (540–480 v.Chr.) zurückverfolgen lassen, werden aufgegriffen:

> [...] unsere Welt von drei Dimensionen ist eine ungeheure Kugel, die in eine Menge einzelner Kugeln zerfällt. Jede von diesen läuft; also wird die große Ur-

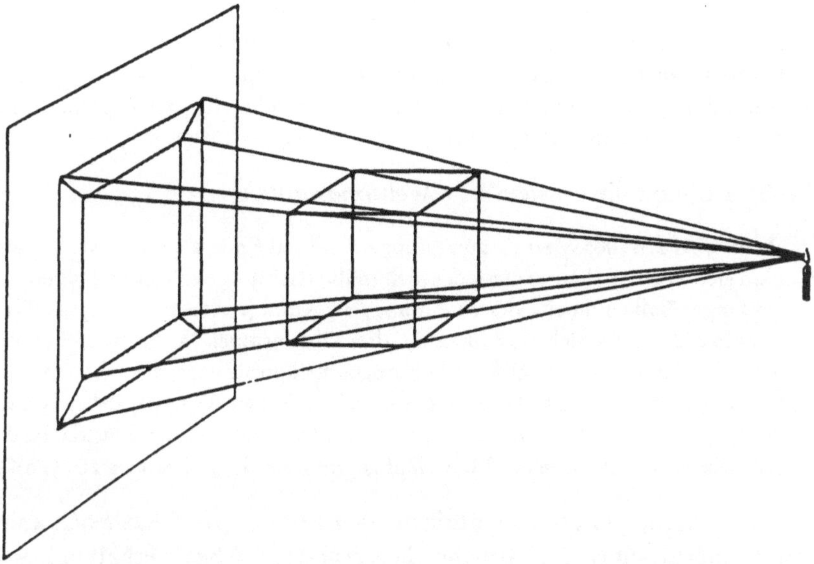

b) Projektion der Kanten eines dreidimensionalen Würfels (Kantenmodell) auf eine zweidimensionale Ebene. Gegenüber dem Dürer'schen Verfahren befindet sich die Bildebene nicht zwischen Projektionszentrum und Körper, sondern hinter dem Körper.

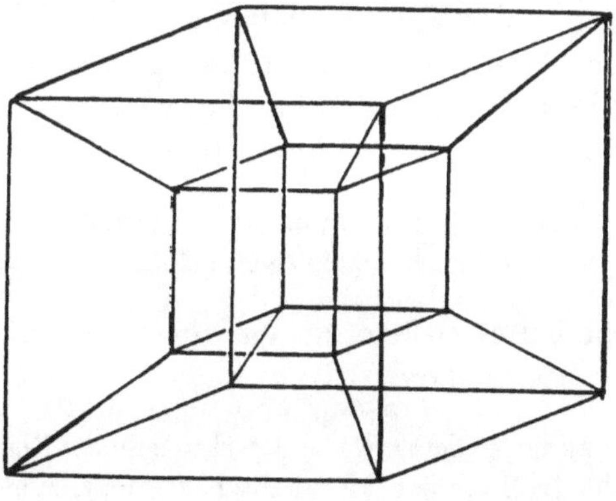

c) Projektion eines vierdimensionalen Würfels in eine zweidimensionale Ebene. Die Projektion der Kanten eines vierdimensionalen Würfels erfolgt zunächst in den dreidimensionalen Raum, wobei das so erhaltene räumliche Kantenmodell weiter in die zweidimensionale Zeichenebene projiziert wurde.

> kugel wohl auch laufen; aber wo sollte sie hinlaufen, wenn es nicht eine vierte Dimension gäbe. Indem sie aber selbst durch die vierte Dimension läuft, laufen natürlich auch alle Kugeln in ihr und Alles, was auf diesen Kugeln lebt und webt, durch die vierte Dimension mit durch [welche offenbar zeitlichen Charakter hat]. (Fechner 1875, 265)

Fechner nimmt die Einstein'sche *Weltlinie* vorweg:

> Wenn also z.B. der Mensch zu Anfange Kind, zu Ende als Greis ist, [...] hat man sich vorzustellen, es erstrecke sich in die Richtung der vierten Dimension ein langer Balken hinein, der zu Anfange als Kind, [...] zu Ende [...] als Greis gestaltet ist, von welchem Balken die drei Dimensionen im Fortschreiten immer so viel abschneiden, als in jedem Augenblick in sie geht, das gibt dann den Menschen, der in diesem Augenblicke lebt. [...] [So] wird von der Lebensstange des Menschen in jedem Augenblick durch die fortschreitende Schnittfläche der drei Dimensionen ein neuer Mensch abgeschnitten, [...]. (Fechner 1875, 266)

Ein Verfahren, das Fechner übrigens den Militärs zum Ausheben empfiehlt. Interessant ist die Tatsache, dass Fechner den Sachverhalt in Erwägung zog, dass bei mehreren Lichtquellen im R^4 vierdimensionale Körper mehrere dreidimensionale Schatten besitzen können. Er veranschaulichte diese Möglichkeit über verschiedenfarbiges Licht, das von einem Lichtpunkt in unterschiedliche Richtungen im Hinblick auf die Zeitachse ausgeht. Eine *satirische* Wirkung erzielte Fechner bei seinen Betrachtungen schließlich dadurch, dass er die *vierte Dimension*, die er bislang zeitlich gedeutet hatte, nun stillschweigend als rein räumlich unterstellt, so dass jegliche Bewegung in der Welt verschwunden ist und der *Raum* sich in völliger Ruhe und Harmonie befindet. Der gleiche Sachverhalt wurde 1917 von Einstein in der Arbeit »Über die spezielle und die allgemeine Relativitätstheorie« nüchterner so konstatiert:

> Die Physik wird aus einem *Geschehen* im dreidimensionalen Raum gewissermaßen ein *Sein* in der vierdimensionalen ›Welt‹. (Einstein 1969a, Anhang 2, 96)

An anderer Stelle hatte Einstein die *Vierdimensionalität* des physikalischen Raumes so beschrieben:

> Nicht der Raumpunkt, in dem etwas geschieht, nicht der Zeitpunkt, in dem etwas geschieht, hat [vollständige] physikalische Realität, sondern nur das Ereignis selbst. [...] Von diesem Standpunkt aus haben wir x_1, x_2, x_3, t als die vier Koordinaten [3 Raumkoordinaten und 1 Zeitkoordinate] eines Ereignisses im vierdimensionalen Kontinuum des Geschehens zu betrachten. (Einstein 1969b, 33f.)

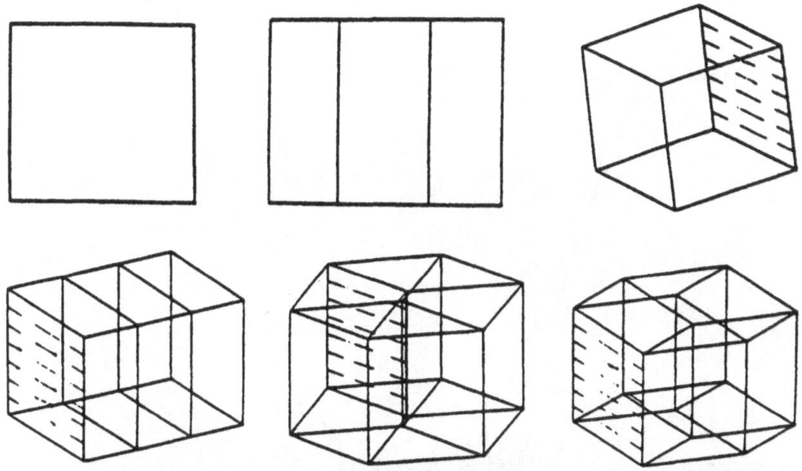

Abb. 9: Ansichten eines Hyperwürfels, der sich auf verschiedene Weise durch einen dreidimensionalen Raum bewegt. Die Bilder zeigen, wie uns dabei die Ecken und Kanten des Hyperkubus erscheinen. Die ersten zwei Zeichnungen lassen sich auch als Drehung eines dreidimensionalen Würfels interpretieren. Die Abbildungen sind dem Film über den Hyperwürfel von Th. Banchoff und Ch. Strauss entnommen, der inzwischen als ein Klassiker unter den mathematischen Filmen angesehen werden kann und 1979 auf einem Brüsseler Festival mit dem Prix de la Recherche Fondamental ausgezeichnet wurde.
(Mit freundlicher Genehmigung von Th. Banchoff und Ch. Strauss, Brown University, RI.)

Das wiederholt Minkowskis Anschauung, dass man es in der Welt nur mit Ereignissen im raumzeitlichen Geschehen zu tun hat. Hermann Minkowski (1864–1909) hatte erstmals die Relativitätstheorie als vierdimensionale Weltgeometrie formuliert.[29]

5. Fechner und sein psychophysischer Raumbegriff

Jedes einschlägige Lexikon verzeichnet das *Weber-Fechner'sche Gesetz*. Worum geht es hierbei? Modern gedeutet basiert das Gesetz darauf, dass jeder Zustand des Bewusstseins auf einem *psycho-physischen* Geschehen

[29] Vgl. seinen berühmten Vortrag auf der Naturforschertagung 1908 in Köln (s. Minkowski 1909 und 1920).

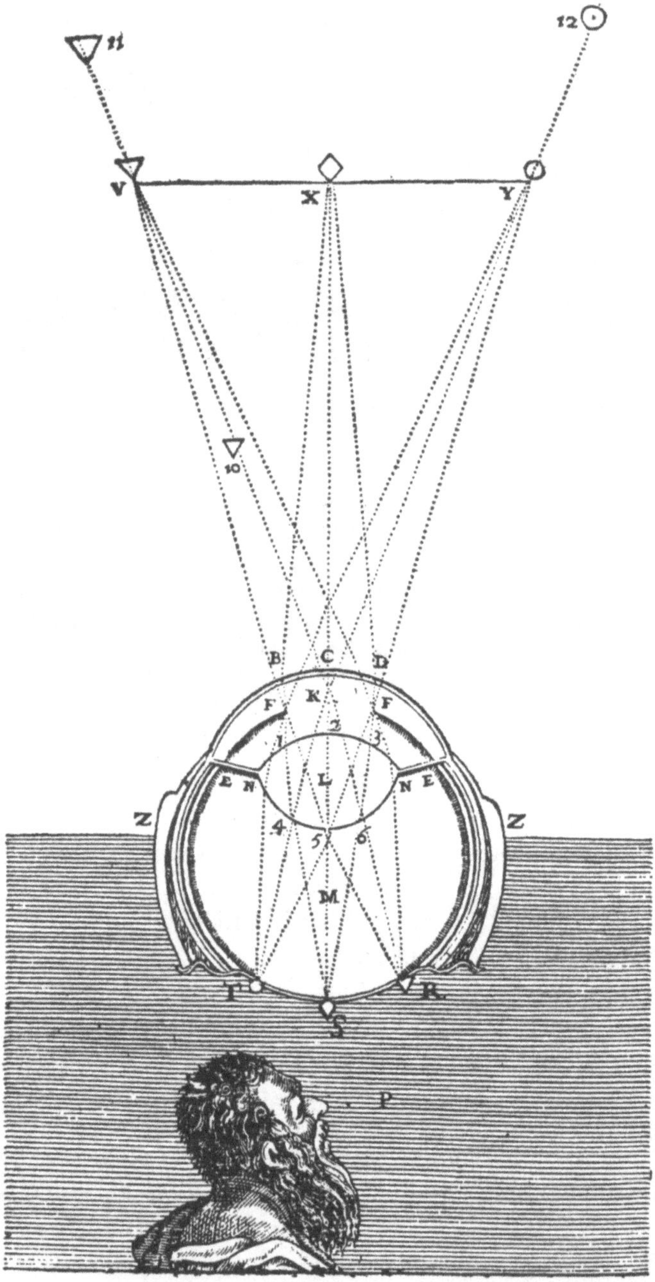

Abb. 10: Skizze zu einem Experiment über die Bildwahrnehmung im Auge von Descartes. Aus: Discours de la methode. La dioptrique. Leyen, 1637. Wiedergabe nach dem von Fayard herausgegebenen gleichnamigen Reprint. Paris 1987, 126.

beruht, wobei diese Korrespondenz von Wahrnehmung und Empfindung (kortikale Erregung) messbar ist.

Der Physiologe Ernst Heinrich Weber (1795–1878), dessen Bruder Wilhelm (1804–1891) 1843 die Nachfolge Fechners als Physiker in Leipzig antrat, hatte 1834 experimentelle Untersuchungen über den Tastsinn ausgeführt, bei denen sich Folgendes ergab: Der von einer Versuchsperson eben noch bemerkte Unterschied ΔI zwischen zwei Gewichten I_1 und I_2 steht in einem näherungsweise konstanten Verhältnis,

$$\frac{\Delta I}{I} = \text{const} \qquad (\text{const} = 0{,}025 = 1/40),$$

d.h., beispielsweise sind Gewichte von 40 und 41 Gramm gerade noch zu unterscheiden. Fechner hat dieses Gesetz als ein in der Psychologie allgemeingültiges unterstellt und dabei den Zuwachs ΔE der Empfindungsintensität proportional zum Weber'schen Verhältnis angesehen:[30]

$$\Delta E = k \frac{\Delta I}{I} .$$

Integration führt sofort auf: $E = k \ln I + C$.

Einer Reihe von im *geometrischen* Verhältnis ansteigenden Reizen entspricht jeweils nur eine Reihe *arithmetisch* wachsender Empfindungen.

Wie sieht die Struktur des Fechner'schen *Wahrnehmungsraumes* aus? Seien *A*, *B* und *C* drei Messungen, wobei *A* und *B* sowie *B* und *C* noch als gleich wahrgenommen werden. Im mathematischen Denken folgt dann logisch, dass auch *A* gleich *C* sein muss:

$$A = B, B = C \Rightarrow A = C;$$

aber im Fechner'schen Wahrnehmungsraum kann entgegen allem formalen logischen Schließen *A* sehr wohl von *C* verschieden sein:

$$(*)\ A = B, B = C \Rightarrow A < C,$$

nämlich immer dann, wenn *C* gegenüber *A* messbar geworden ist, ohne dass dies für die Messung *B* sowohl gegenüber *A* als auch gegenüber *C*

---

30 C.F. Gauß hat sich hierzu kritisch geäußert: Wenn Fechner vom Mangel an genauen Messungen spreche, so wäre es schon gut, wenn man grobe Messungen hätte, man habe aber gar keine. Wo man aber nichts messen könne, wisse man auch nichts. Fechner hätte sich auf die vom ihm als »spezielle Phänomene« bezeichneten konzentrieren und den Rest »in's Kehricht werfen« sollen; siehe Wagner 1975, 154f.

der Fall sein muss. Im Weber'schen Versuch wäre das für die Gewichte von 40g, 40,5g und 41g der Fall. Rückt man von dem realen menschlichen Wahrnehmungsvermögen ab und denkt sich die Messungen gradweise (instrumental) verbessert, so lassen sich weitere Messwerte zwischenschalten, für die sich immer wieder der gleiche Sachverhalt (*) ergibt. Die Struktur des Fechner'schen pschophysischen Wahrnehmungsraumes, in dem Reize, die sich nur geringfügig unterscheiden, als gleich empfunden werden, ist also ziemlich kompliziert, zumindest im Vergleich mit dem idealisierten mathematischen Raum (das durch reelle Zahlen messbare eindimensionale Kontinuum). Bei hinreichend genauer Messbarkeit, also bei sehr kleinen *Unterschiedsschwellen*, weicht die Fechner'sche Struktur praktisch nur wenig von dem Kontinuum der reellen Zahlen in der Mathematik ab, und im Grenzfall exakter Messmöglichkeit lassen sich beide als übereinstimmend ansehen. Mit anderen Worten, die idealisierte, aber offenbar einfachere mathematische Struktur lässt sich in der *Psychophysik* verwenden. Beim praktischen Messen sind Genauigkeitsforderungen jedoch prinzipielle Grenzen gesetzt, so dass der Grenzübergang ein fiktiver Fall bleibt. Fechner selbst hat die mathematische Struktur, die er implizit der Psychophysik zugrunde legt, nicht aus seinen Annahmen abstrahiert.[31]

Im Vorübergehen erwähne ich, dass die eben praktizierte Konstruktion des Kontinuums der Maßzahlen auch in der intuitionistischen Mathematik benutzt wird, in der der logische Satz vom ausgeschlossenen Dritten (tertium non datur) nicht mehr gilt. Ebenfalls gibt es Beziehungen zur Nichtstandardanalysis. Wenn man zu einem Messwert A alle weiteren Messwerte schlägt, die nicht von ihm unterschieden werden können, oder mehr mathematisch ausgedrückt, wenn man die Messwerte modulo der *Schwellenwerte* betrachtet, so gelangt man auf diese Weise zu einem nichtarchimedisch geordneten Zahlkörper. Auf gewissen nichtarchimedisch geordneten Zahlkörpern lässt sich die Infinitesimalmathematik besonders einfach und elegant ausführen, was dieser Struktur in neuerer Zeit Aufmerksamkeit eingebracht hat.

Die abstrakte Fassung der empirischen Gegebenheiten zeigt sehr schön, wie eine naiv genommene Wirklichkeit zerbröselt: die Frage nach der exakten Länge eines materiellen Gegenstandes ist offenbar physikalisch nicht sinnvoll, während die idealisierte mathematische Konstruktion der reellen Zahlen eine formale Antwort ermöglicht. Ein anderes Bei-

[31] Man sehe seine hierzu gehörigen Auffassungen in: Fechner 1864, 251f.

spiel: Mathematisch lässt sich zwar der physikalische Bewegungsbegriff behandeln (in der Epsilontik), aber nicht präzise erfassen, worauf bereits die frühen Paradoxien von Zenon (336–264 v.Chr.) hinweisen (z.B. Unmöglichkeit des Ankommens, Achilles und die Schildkröte). Im *Mikrokosmos* weicht die Unschärferelation von Werner Heisenberg (1901–1976) das klassische Verständnis von Ort und Geschwindigkeit auf, was sich auf die Kausalität auswirkt. Bei diesen Andeutungen will ich es belassen, um aufzuzeigen, wie problematisch das Verhältnis von abstrakten mathematischen Modellen zur Realität des jeweiligen *Raumes* ist.

Für den Naturwissenschaftler Fechner war es gewiss, dass hinter der wahrgenommenen Wirklichkeit eine weitere liegen müsse, die mit der naturwissenschaftlichen Forschung in Einklang stehe, genauer, die aus ihr abstrahiert wird. Allerdings war Fechner trotz aller *spiritistischen* Neigungen letztlich *Naturwissenschaftler*. Ich zitiere hierzu aus seiner Schrift, die sich kritisch mit der *Odlehre* Karl von Reichenbachs (1788–1869) auseinandersetzte und die den bezeichnenden Titel »Erinnerungen an die letzten Tage der Odlehre und ihres Urhebers« trug:

> Nur läßt sich ohne weitere Untersuchungen nicht entscheiden wie viel [Wahres in ihr ist], und die guten Körner vom großen Wuste scheiden. (Fechner 1876, 6)[32]

Gehen wir in diesem Zusammenhang nochmals auf die Korrespondenz von Geistigem und Physikalischem bei Fechner zurück. Er erweitert das individuelle Geistige in ein universelles, in ein kollektives Bewusstsein. Alles in der Welt ist *beseelt*, ist göttlich. Eine vierte Dimension des Raumes als tragende Grundlage des Seelischen zog Fechner dabei nicht in Betracht. In seinem »Büchlein vom Leben nach dem Tode« (1836) finden wir:

> Die Geisterwelt in ihrer Vollendung wird daher nicht eine Versammlung, sondern ein Baum von Geistern sein, dessen Wurzel in dem Irdischen eingewachsen ist und dessen Krone in den Himmel reicht. [...] Es gibt keinen Himmel und keine Hölle im gewöhnlichen Sinn der Christen. (Fechner 1906, S. 13, 41)

---

[32] Reichenbach war zur Darlegung seiner Odlehre 1867 nach Leipzig gekommen, konnte aber Fechner während seines Aufenthaltes, den Reichenbachs Tod in Leipzig beendete, nicht überzeugen. Die Odlehre handelt von einem imponderablen Agens (ähnlich der Elektrizität oder dem Magnetismus), das zwar in allen Körpern vorhanden sei, aber nur von sensitiven Menschen in unterschiedlichen Graden wahrgenommen werde.

Die letzte Aussage ist auch eine klare Absage an vierdimensionale räumliche Vorstellungen für die Verortung der Hölle.[33] Kritisch ließe sich aus heutiger Sicht fragen, ob der Fechner'sche Gedanke der *Beseelung* der Natur der Descartes'schen *res cogitans* verwandt sei und ob in diesem Falle Fechner sich nicht selbst hintergehe, indem er in seinem Denken Eigenschaften der Raumkategorie, d.h. Vorstellungen der Descartes'sche *res extensa*, auf solches unräumliches Seien übertrage? Der jeder Kritik gegenüber sehr aufgeschlossene Fechner, für den die *Analogie* ein wichtiges Erkenntnismittel war, wäre hier vermutlich weniger beunruhigt, als wir es sind.[34]

6. Zöllner und die spiritistische Dimension

In seiner Kometentheorie (1870) erwog Zöllner die Idee eines nichteuklidischen *Universums*, in dem nur eine endliche Menge an Materie verteilt ist. Bei einem solchen Verständnis des Universums meinte Zöllner, die keinesfalls triviale Frage (Olber'sches Paradoxon) beantworten zu können, weshalb es nachts dunkel werde.[35] Allerdings sind, wie wir heute wissen, die von Zöllner gemachten Annahmen über die Beschaffenheit des *Raumes* für die Lösung dieser speziellen Frage ebenso überflüssig wie die von Zöllner allgemein angenommene Einbettung eines nichteuklidischen dreidimensionalen Raumes in einen euklidischen vierdimensionalen Raum. Für die mathematische Erklärung eines *nichteuklidischen*, allgemeiner eines Riemann'schen Raumes ist ein einbettender euklidischer Raum *nicht* notwendig. Diesen Sachverhalt hat erstmals Gauß in der Flächentheorie (theorema egregium) herausgestellt. Der einbettende euklidische Raum dient lediglich der Veranschaulichung und geht nicht mit einer Vereinfachung einher, denn ein nichteuklidischer Raum der Dimensionen zwei, drei oder vier bedarf zur Einbettung in einen euklidischen Raum bis

---

33 In einer Nachschrift aus dem Jahre 1875 zur Arbeit »Der Raum hat vier Dimensionen« bemerkte Fechner, dass Zöllner ihm »eine sehr sinnreiche Weise der Erklärung von Wundern [...] durch Hineinspielen von Kräften aus einer vierten Dimension« mündlich zur Kenntnis gebracht habe; vgl. Fechner 1875, 276.

34 Vgl. den Vortrag von Dirk Evers in diesem Band. – Zur Offenheit Fechners gegenüber berechtigter Kritik vgl. dessen »Revision der Hauptpunkte der Psychophysik« (1882), insbesondere das Vorwort.

35 Siehe Vollmer 1993, Kapitel 4; Richter 2001.

zu drei, sechs oder zehn Dimensionen (allgemein erfordern n nichteuklidische Dimensionen bis zu $n\,(n + 1)\,/2$ euklidische Dimensionen).

Zöllner hat die dreidimensionale Welt als eine Projektion des *vierdimensionalen Raumes* betrachtet. Wie er diese Ansicht stützen wollte, darauf werden wir gleich eingehen. Wie spekulativ er aber mit dieser Hypothese umging, mag seine Deutung des Hellsehens mit Hilfe der *vierten Dimension* zeigen. Die Seele erhebe sich aus dem dreidimensionalen Raum in den vierdimensionalen und löse sich so vom Schattendasein des R^3 (s. Zöllner 1879, 3, 96). Für entsprechend Begabte wäre es möglich, durch einen Blick in die vierte Dimension zeitliche Vorhersagen zu machen, da sich das raumzeitliche Geschehen unserer Welt im vierdimensionalen Raum als statisches räumliches und damit auf einen Blick erkennbares Sein darstellt.

Unter den von Zöllner gegebenen Gründen für die tatsächliche Existenz einer vierten Dimension im physikalischen Raum sind zwei besonders interessant. Das erste Argument geht auf Kant zurück, der in den »Prolegomena« 1783 gefragt hatte:

> Was kann wohl meiner Hand oder meinem Ohr ähnlicher und in allen Stücken gleicher sein als ihr Bild im Spiegel? (Kant 1913, 40)

und festgestellt hatte, dass man die eine sinnliche Erscheinung nicht an die Stelle der anderen setzen könne, obwohl in ihr vom Verstand keinerlei innerer Unterschied bemerkt werden könne.[36] Zöllner sah in der Möglichkeit, solche sogenannten enantiomorphen Körper des R^3 durch *Spiegelung* im vierdimensionalen Raum ineinander überführen zu können, die physikalische Realität des vierdimensionalen Raumes als gesichert an. Herbert Georg Wells (1866–1946) hat dieses Thema in seiner »Plattner Story« literarisch behandelt.[37] Gottfried Plattner gerät versehentlich bei einem misslungenen chemischen Versuch in den *vierdimensionalen Raum*, aus dem er nach einiger Zeit wohlbehalten wieder in den dreidimensionalen zurückkehrt, allerdings gespiegelt: er hat nun das Herz am »rechten« Fleck und schreibt mit der linken Hand Spiegelschrift.

Zöllners *Spiegelargument* überzeugt nicht, denn auch im vierdimensionalen Raum gäbe es wieder zueinander spiegelbildliche Körper, für deren Ineinanderüberführen ein fünfdimensionaler Raum benötigt würde,

---

[36] Georg Cantor hat am sphärischen Dreieck diesen Unterschied von logischer und anschaulicher Erscheinung erläutert; siehe Kant 1892, Anhang.

[37] Wells 1952.

a)

b)

Abb. 11: Spiegelungen ebener Figuren.

a) Lewis Carroll, Through the looking-glass (1871). »In another moment Alice was through the glass ...« Zeichnungen von John Tenniel aus der Erstausgabe.
Alice – von hinten und vorn gesehen – durchquert den Spiegel *unverändert;* trotzdem hat der Zeichner Tenniel hintersinnig seine Signatur am rechten Bild gespiegelt (nicht aber der Graveur Dalziel).

b) Spiegelbild der Rückansicht von Alice.
Das Spiegelbild kann man auch mechanisch durch »Umklappen« im Raum erzeugen. Dabei werden sowohl Tenniels als auch Dalziels Signatur gespiegelt.

usw.[38] Der Philosoph Hermann Lotze (1817–1881) hatte in seiner »Metaphysik« (1879) moniert:

> Was hätten wir denn für ein Gut gewonnen, wenn wir uns mit dem Umklappen symmetrischer Raumfiguren beschäftigen könnten, und was geht uns jetzt ab, da wir es nicht können? (nach Kracke 1970, 239)

Interessanter ist Zöllners Argument, dass auf der Netzhaut des Auges lediglich ein zweidimensionales Bild der Welt entsteht, das von uns unter Einbeziehung der Tiefenschärfe irgendwie zur dreidimensionalen Sicht komplettiert wird. Dieser Vorgang kann auch heute noch nicht in befriedigender Weise erklärt werden.[39] Zöllner erwartete 1878, dass im nächsten Jahrhundert die menschliche *Wahrnehmung* sich soweit entwickeln werde, dass sie auch den vierdimensionalen Raum einbeziehe:

> Wir würden uns die Vorstellung eines Raumes von vier, fünf oder mehr Dimensionen bilden können, wenn uns von Jugend auf *alltägliche* Erscheinungen umgeben hätten, die zu ihrer widerspruchsfreien, d.h. verstandesmässigen, Auslegung und Deutung einen solchen vierdimensionalen Raum erforderten. Es folgt hieraus, dass die *reale* Existenz eines vierdimensionalen Raumes nebst Objecten in demselben nur durch die *Erfahrung*, d.h. durch beobachtete *Thatsachen* entschieden werden kann. (Zöllner 1879, 1, 725)

Die Zöllner'sche Vorhersage hat sich nicht erfüllt, aber es gibt eine Reihe von Mathematikern, die sich durchaus im *vierdimensionalen Raum* orientieren können. Von meinem Lehrer Ott-Heinrich Keller (1906–1990) behauptete der bereits erwähnte Oskar Perron, dass sich Herr Keller im vierdimensionalen Raum offenbar so gut auskenne wie er (Perron) sich in seiner Wohnstube.[40] Zöllner hat über gute mathematische Kennt-

---

[38] Zöllner selbst stellte jedoch ein solches Problem für den vierdimensionalen Raum in Abrede. Die tatsächliche Existenz kann nur durch Erfahrung bewiesen werden, und die »blosse Denkbarkeit entscheidet hier offenbar nichts über die reale Existenz derartiger Objekte und jeder Einwand, dass eine solche Erklärung [...] auf einen progressus in infinitum führe, beruht auf einem gänzlichen Missverständnis der wesentlichen Prämissen« (Zöllner 1878, 1, S. 218ff., 245f.).

[39] Seinerzeit hatte sich etwa H. Helmholtz mit dem Sehen beschäftigt; siehe Helmholtz 1896; auch Zöllner griff das Thema auf und sprach von »unbewußten Verstandesoperationen«; s. Zöllner 1872, 175–225.

[40] Perron schrieb 1940 über Arbeiten von Keller und anderer, die *n*-dimensionale Räume betrafen: »Jedoch muß ich gestehen, daß ich [...] irgendwo an eine Stelle oder mehrere

nisse verfügt, so dass er den fatalen Hinweis, den ihm sein späterer Leipziger Kollege Felix Klein (1849–1925) gegeben hatte, dass sich nämlich im R^3 geknüpfte *Knoten* im R^4 lösen, nicht nur inhaltlich erfassen konnte, sondern in ihm eine Möglichkeit sah, die Existenz des vierdimensionalen Raumes experimentell zu bestätigen.[41] Ich zeige Ihnen hier einen solchen 1880 von Reinhold Hoppe (1816–1900) erdachten Knoten in der von Heinrich Durège (1821–1893) korrigierten Form. Bewegt man den Knoten gemäß den angegebenen Formeln im R^4 (die Einzelheiten – etwa dass die Kurve doppelpunktfrei bleibt – sind hier nicht von Interesse), so geht die Schnur schließlich in einen in einer Ebene gelegenen Kreis über, sie ist also nicht mehr verschlungen (siehe Box 2).

In einer spiritistischen Sitzung hat Slade einen von Zöllner vorgelegten *Knoten* »auflösen« können. Bei diesem und anderen Experimenten ist Zöllner bedauerlicherweise dem Taschenspieler Slade aufgesessen, d.h. er betrachtete die Ergebnisse der Séance wie das Lösen von Knoten oder materielle Manifestationen als »experimentelle Bestätigung der Realität einer vierten Dimension des Raumes«[42] (Existenznachweise für den R^4). Im Gegensatz zur allgemeinen Gemeinde der Spiritisten, die kaum Kenntnisse der elementaren Geometrie, geschweige denn der Riemann'schen Geometrie hatte, warf Zöllner, der stets für Meinungsfreiheit eintrat und gereizt gegen vermeintliche Vorurteile anging, sein ganzes mathematisches Können in den Streit. Er entwickelte dabei eine fieberhafte Tätigkeit (in den letzten Lebensmonaten täglich einen Druckbogen!) und sorgte so dafür, dass die *spiritistische* Thematik schnell zum Tagesgespräch in Deutschland geriet, womit er aber schließlich seinen wissenschaftlichen Ruf ruinierte. Kurd Laßwitz (1848–1910, übrigens heute vor 154 Jahren geboren), der sich kritisch über Zöllner äußerte, verfasste eine Scherzdichtung, die den hübschen Titel trägt:

Prost. Der Fausttragödie (-n)ter Teil.
Von Herrn von Goethe, Excellenz,
durch astrophysikalische Vermittlung aus der vierten Dimension in ein von

---

Stellen gekommen bin, wo ich den Gedankengang des Autors nicht mehr folgen kann, so daß ich nicht recht weiß, wieweit die Sache wirklich bewiesen ist. Zum Teil, aber nicht ganz, liegt das daran, daß ich vom *n*-dimensionalen Raume nicht die geringste anschauliche Vorstellung habe, mit der andere begabt zu sein scheinen« (Perron 1940, 2).

41 Siehe Klein 1926, 169f.

42 Zitiert nach Zöllner 1878, 2, 909; spiritistische Experimente siehe Zöllner 1878, 1, 726ff.; 1878, 2, 909ff.

BOX 2

Das Auflösen eines in einer Schnur (Kurve) befindlichen Knotens bei einem Durchgang durch den vierdimensionalen Raum R^4

Die vier Gleichungen

$$x = \tfrac{1}{2} \cos u \,\{3 \cos u\,(1 + \cos t) + 3 + \cos t\}\, f(t),$$
$$y = \tfrac{1}{2} \sin u \,\{5 \cos u\,(1 + \cos t) + 1 - \cos t\}\, f(t),$$
$$z = \tfrac{1}{2} \sin u\,(25 \cos^2 u - 1)\,(1 + \cos t)\, f(t),$$
$$w = \tfrac{1}{2}\, h \sin u \sin t\, f(t), \qquad (h \neq 0),$$

stellen für jeden festen Wert von t und veränderlichem u ($0 \leq u \leq \pi$) eine geschlossene Kurve (Schnur) K im vierdimensionalen $xyzw$-Raum R^4 dar. Die variable Größe u stellt den Parameter der Kurve dar, während man einen festen Wert von t als Zeitpunkt deuten kann. Läßt man die Größe t laufen, so wird die Kurve im R^4 gemäß obiger Gleichungen bewegt. (Die Funktion $f(t)$ ist beliebig und kann so gewählt werden, daß die Länge der Kurve K bei der Bewegung stets gleich l ist.)

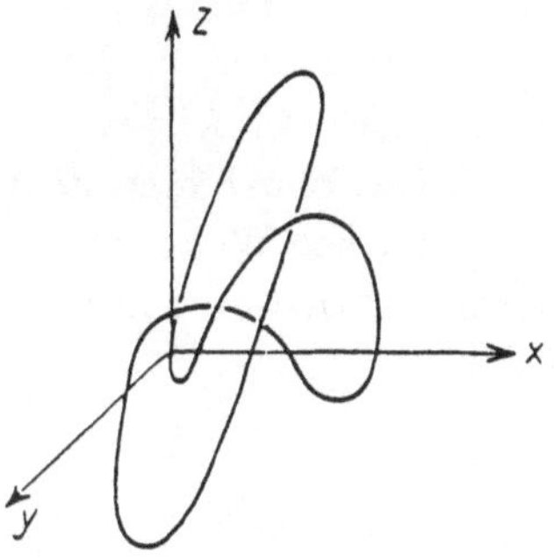

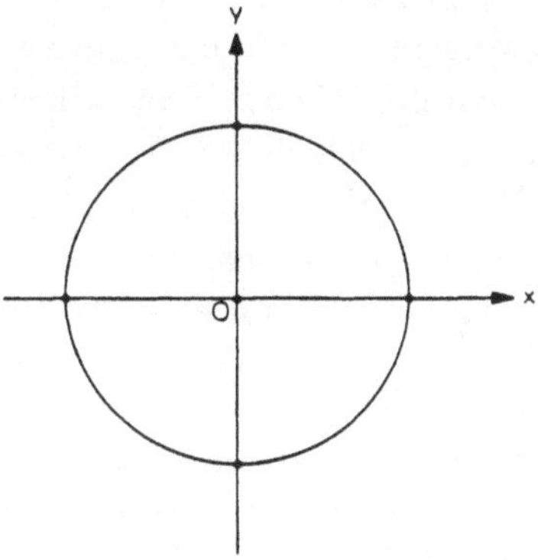

Für $t = 0$ liegt die Kurve K ganz im dreidimensionalen xyz-Raum des R^4 (d.h. $w = 0$) und hat die Gleichungen

$$x = \cos u\,(3 \cos u + 2),$$
$$y = 5 \sin u \cos u,$$
$$z = \sin u\,(25 \cos^2 u - 1).$$

Für $t = \pi$ liegt die Kurve K ganz in der xy-Ebene des R^4 (d.h. $w = z = 0$) und hat die Gleichung

$$x^2(u) + y^2(u) = \{\cos^2 u + \sin^2 u\}\,[f(\pi)]^2 = [f(\pi)]^2.$$

(Siehe R. Hoppe 1879, 224; H. Durège 1880, 135–146.)

allen Seiten verklebtes Buch aufgezeichnet. Im spirituösen Auftrage des Mathematischen Vereins zu Breslau aufgeschnitten und herausgegeben von Dr. Kurd Laßwitz.[43]

Auch Wilhelm Wundt (1832–1920), den Zöllner nach Leipzig geholt hatte und der einigen Versuchen beigewohnt hatte, äußerte sich zu Zöllners Ärger ablehnend. Der Experimentator Wundt übte sachliche Kritik an den undefinierten Umständen der Experimente, witzelte aber auch über die Kleidung der *Spirits*, die ganz nach der Mode kämen und im R^4 offenbar auch keine besseren Schuhmacher als in Leipzig hätten, und er hob schließlich spöttisch die armselige Lage der Spirits hervor, die physisch durch ihr Medium versklavt würden und zwecklose mechanische Leistungen auszuführen hätten, die intellektuell stets niederen Blödsinn produzieren müssten, aber wenigstens durch ihre gutmütige Bereitwilligkeit moralisch als harmlos eingeschätzt werden könnten.[44]

Da unser Blick auf die spiritistische Phase in Zöllners Leben eingeschränkt ist, soll nachdrücklich betont werden, dass der spekulativ veranlagte Zöllner ein bedeutender Naturwissenschaftler gewesen ist, der am Ende seines Lebens in das Fahrwasser des *Spiritismus* geriet und dessen Opfer wurde.[45] Durch seine Überschätzung der Idee des R^4 war er zu leichtgläubig gegenüber den sogenannten spiritistischen Experimenten und ihren Ergebnissen, die nüchternere Beobachter wie Wundt als fragwürdig ansahen. Zöllner hat allerdings durch seine Isolation und Verlust der Reputation hierfür einen hohen Preis gezahlt.

---

43 Siehe Laßwitz, 1883.

44 Wundt richtete diesbezüglich einen offenen Brief an Ulrici; siehe Wundt 1879. Ulrici war Herausgeber der »Zeitschrift für Philosophie und philosophische Kritik« und unterstützte Zöllners Spiritismus, in dem er den Wunder wirkenden Gott tätig sah. Dieser Punkt hatte insbesondere den Widerspruch Wundts hervorgerufen, dem Wundergläubigkeit und Wissenschaftlichkeit unvereinbar waren.

45 Es ist interessant, Zöllners Lehrtätigkeit in Leipzig thematisch zu betrachten. In von den 35 Leipziger Semestern vom Professor für Astrophysik gehaltenen Vorlesungen gehörten 43 % zur Astronomie, 22 % zur Mathematik und Physik sowie 14 % zur Philosophie, davon die Hälfte über Kant'sche Philosophie; vgl. Hamel 1983. – Auch Parapsychologen berufen sich auf Zöllner; vgl. »Zeitschrift für Parapsychologie und Grenzgebiete der Psychologie« 1977, H. 19, 195–226. F. Engels' vernichtende Urteile in seiner Arbeit »Die Naturforschung in der Geisterwelt«(1878), das auch Zöllner »die allerplatteste, alle Theorie verachtende, gegen alles Denken mißtrauische Empirie« unterstellte, was so gewiß nicht zutrifft, wenden sich letztlich gegen die eigene Aufgeschlossenheit, die in der »Deutschen Ideologie« der Naturwissenschaft entgegengebracht wurde, nämlich »Ohne exakte Wissenschaft ist Philosophie nicht mehr denkbar« (Engels 1878, 341).

7. Gibt es die vierte Dimension?

Wir haben die historischen Versuche verfolgt, Argumente für die Existenz eines realen vierdimensionalen Raumes zu finden. Bislang ist man in der Physik, selbst in der Quantenphysik mit dem alten dreidimensionalen *Raum* ausgekommen, und das ist auch in den anderen Naturwissenschaften so. Selbst wenn sich z.B. gewisse stereochemische Tatsachen im vierdimensionalen Raum klar wiedergeben lassen, reicht letztlich bereits der dreidimensionale Raum R^3 hierfür. Wenn nun im physikalischen Raum nur wenig für eine *vierte Dimension* spricht, können wir vielleicht etwas dagegen anführen?

Die Tatsache, dass wir nur drei Dimensionen wahrnehmen bzw. bisher wahrgenommen haben, lässt sich nicht als zwingendes Argument benutzen. Schon Georg Christoph Lichtenberg (1742–1799) hatte gefordert, Gottes Welt nicht nach der unsrigen zu beurteilen.[46] Setzen wir aber voraus, dass unser Sonnensystem schon hinreichend lange in einem R^4 existiert hat (wofür die 4,6 Milliarden Jahre eigentlich sprechen), dann müsste es bereits zusammengebrochen sein, weil im R^4 zufolge der Himmelsmechanik auf lange Zeitdauer keine stabilen Bahnen möglich sind; auch die klassischen Vorstellungen von Atomen und Molekülen hätten damit keinen langen Bestand, also letztlich auch wir selbst.[47] Das Huygens'sche Prinzip der Wellenausbreitung gilt für vier Raumdimensionen nicht. Die Wellengleichung läßt im R^4 nur Lösungen zu, die stets mit Nachhall und Verzerrungen einhergehen, Konversation und Musik wären in dieser Welt erschwert.[48] Natürlich könnte man sich im *vierdimensionalen Raum* auch eine andere Physik denken, als wir sie aus dem dreidimensionalen Raum kennen. Allerdings wird es problematisch sein, bekannte und bewährte Naturgesetze des R^3 aufzugeben bzw. zu verändern. Im R^4 verlieren etwa Ketten ihren Zusammenhang und damit ihre aus dem R^3 vertraute Eigenschaft. In diesem Zusammenhang ist beispielsweise Hans Reichenbachs (1891–1953) Nachweis wichtig, dass das Nahwirkungsprinzip der Naturwissenschaft zwar im R^3 gilt, aber sich nicht auf

---

[46] »Bist du Elender, denn der Richter von Gottes Werken?« (Lichtenberg 1972, 3, 272).

[47] Vgl. Whitrow 1955; Barrow 1983; Vollmer 1999.

[48] Auf diesen Sachverhalt – offenbar erstmals von V. Volterra bemerkt – hat J. Hadamard (Lectures on Cauchys Problem, 1923) hingewiesen. Das Prinzip drückt aus, dass ein scharf definierter Anfangszustand auch später ein scharf begrenzter Effekt bleibt; bei vier Dimensionen bleibt dieser Effekt jedoch nicht scharf begrenzt, sondern hallt nach, wenn er einmal eingeführt worden ist; vgl. Courant; Hilbert 1937, 169ff., 395, 438.

den R^4 übertragen läßt, so dass dort ausschließlich mit Fernwirkungen zu arbeiten wäre.[49]

Diese kleine Argumentation legt es nahe, dass zumindest der uns zugängliche Teil des *Universums* in der Tat dreidimensional ist. Allerdings muss man, wie Carl-Friedrich von Weizsäcker (geb. 1912) bei einer ähnlichen Gelegenheit bemerkt hat, mit Überraschungen rechnen.[50] Gerade hat der Garchinger Kosmologe Gerhard Börner (geb. 1941) die gegenwärtige Situation so resümiert:

> ›Ich weiß, dass ich nichts weiß‹, soll Sokrates gesagt haben. Die Kosmologen heutzutage wissen nicht einmal so viel mit Sicherheit. Denn es ist alles andere als klar, ob wir viel oder wenig über das Universum wissen. (Börner 2001)

Neuere physikalische Auffassungen wie die *Superstring Theorie*, die man durchaus als Experimente mit Ideen bezeichnen könnte, basieren auf einer Welt von 10 bis 26 Dimensionen, wobei jedoch – abgesehen von den uns bekannten Raum-Zeit-Dimensionen – die Größenordnungen der Dimensionen in einer Größenordnung von 10^{-33} erscheinen, also unmessbar klein und daher experimentell unentdeckt sind.[51] Eine Version der Theorie erlaubt zur Erklärung von verborgenen Massen sogar eine Schattenwelt, die nur über Gravitationswirkungen mit der unseren verbunden ist.[52] Gilt hier die von Max Born (1882–1970) sowie Niels Bohr (1885–1962) gestellte Frage, ob diese Theorien schon genügend verrückt seien, um die Welt erklären zu können?

8. Ein Ausblick

Treten wir einen Schritt zurück, um mit Abstand auf die Dinge zu blicken. Wir erkennen dann unsere Ausführungen zu Fechner und Zöllner als eine Variation der alten Pascal'schen Frage »Was ist der Mensch in der Natur?« Die Dinge entwachsen dem Nichts und ragen bis in das Unendliche. Wiederholen wir Blaise Pascals (1623–1662) berühmte Feststellung, dass wir sowohl unendlich weit davon entfernt sind, das All als auch das Nichts (les deux infinies de sciences) zu begreifen, sondern dass wir ledig-

[49] Siehe Reichenbach 1928, § 45.
[50] Über Wurmlöcher und andere fantastische Auffassungen siehe z.B. Khalili, al 2001.
[51] Siehe Polchinski 1998.
[52] Diese Auffassung ist ein moderner Widerschein der Theorie der Physiker Stewart und Tait aus Cambridge; siehe Stewart; Tait 1874.

lich in ewiger Verzweiflung aus deren Mitte einen Schein der Dinge wahrnehmen.[53] Wie sich jeder dieser »Verzweiflung« stellt, d.h. welche Philosophie er wählt, das hängt nach Johann Gottlieb Fichte (1762–1814) vom Charakter des Einzelnen ab. Bei aller Gemeinsamkeit hinsichtlich der Grundlagen ihrer Auffassungen liegt hier ein wichtiger psychologischer Grund für Fechners und Zöllners unterschiedliche Haltungen gegenüber dem *vierdimensionalen Raum*, dem wir aber im Rahmen unseres Vortrages nicht weiter nachgehen können.

Ich beschränke mich auf einige Hinweise, etwa den, dass Zöllner ein phantasievoller, an Neuem und Unbekanntem höchst interessierter Mensch war, der zudem mit seiner heftigen Natur leidenschaftlich für durch Mode oder Tradition unterdrückte oder scheinbar bedrohte Meinungen und Auffassungen konsequent einstand. Seine spekulativen theoretischen Entwürfe bedurften sowohl der experimentellen Absicherung als auch irgendeiner darüber hinausgehenden sinngebenden Bestätigung. Die Faszination der *spiritistischen* Fragen, aber auch der zu überwindende Widerstand in der Öffentlichkeit versetzten Zöllner in höchste Erregung und trübten seine Kritikfähigkeit. Fechner hingegen begriff sich stets als ein Teil des *beseelten* Universums, in dem er sich aufgehoben fühlte und dessen Sinn nicht in Frage gestellt war. Gegenüber Zöllner war er weniger ein spekulativer Theoretiker, sondern in seiner Philosophie – ich erinnere an Windelbands Einschätzung – eher der Anschauung und der *Analogie* verhaftet. Henri Poincaré (1854–1912) hat einmal gesagt:

> Die Gebilde des Hyperraumes lassen sich ebenso wie die des gewöhnlichen Raumes bestimmen und vermögen wir sie uns auch nicht vorzustellen, so können wir sie doch verstehen und erforschen. Wenn also zum Beispiel die mehr als dreidimensionale Mechanik als gegenstandslos verdammt werden muß, so gilt das nicht für die Hypergeometrie. (nach Maeterlink 1928, 34)

Die Mathematik ist das Gerüst, mit dem das Gebäude der Naturwissenschaft errichtet wird. Je tiefer wir in das Verständnis der Natur eindringen, desto mehr werden wir in die Welt der Mathematik hineingezogen. Man darf aber das Gerüst nicht für das Gebäude ansehen. Die Mathematik ist jedoch der Schlüssel, die Türen dieses Gebäudes zu öffnen. Aber die Mathematik sagt uns nicht, was sich hinter diesen Türen befinden wird.

---

[53] Pascal 1913, II, No. 72.

In einem Germanistischen Institut ist es angemessen, den Vortrag mit einem Literaten zu beenden. Bei mir soll der Nobelpreisträger von 1911, Maurice Maeterlink (1862–1949), das letzte Wort haben:

> Die Metageometrie ihrerseits sucht nach dem Jenseits unseres Raumes, die Natur desjenigen Raumes oder derjenigen nicht mehr subjektiven und konventionellen Räume, die uns umgeben und nur unsichere Beziehungen zu dem Raum haben, der von uns geschaffen ist oder sich in uns geschaffen hat; und sie will uns dadurch helfen, etwas von den Erscheinungen des Weltalls zu verstehen oder so zu tun, als ob wir es verstünden. [...] Auch sie besitzt nur Anfänge von Beweisen über die wesentlichen Punkte. Aber es hat wohl den Anschein, als entsprächen ihre so sicheren, so logischen und so entscheidenden Beweisführungen etwas Wirklichem, das sie sich jedoch nicht vorstellen kann, und das sich vielleicht nicht notwendigerweise in dem Raum befindet, in den sie es verlegt, sondern möglicherweise im Menschen selber, der dank der neuen Wissenschaft glaubt, aus sich herausgehen und endlich den Grenzen seines eingebildeten Ichs entweichen zu können. (Maeterlink 1928, 108f.)

Literatur:

Anderson, J. (1963): Studies in Empirical Philosophy. Syndey.

Arendt, H.-J. (1999): Gustav Theodor Fechner. Ein deutscher Naturwissenschaftler und Philosoph im 19. Jahrhundert. Frankfurt a.M.

Barrow, J.D. (1983): Dimensionality. In: Philosophical Transaction of the Royal Society London A 310, 337–346.

Beltz, W. (1978): Das Tor der Götter. Berlin.

Börner, G. (2001): Die Quintessenz des Universums. In: Süddeutsche Zeitung, 8.5.2001.

Bresch, R. (1882): Der Chemismus, Magnetismus und Diamagnetismus im Lichte mehrdimensionaler Raumanschauung. Leipzig.

Busch, W. (1883): Balduin Bählamm. München.

Carroll, L. (1871): Through the looking-glass. London.

Courant, R.; Hilbert, D. (1937): Methoden der mathematischen Physik. Bd. 2. Berlin.

Durège, H. (1880): Über die Hoppe'sche Knotenkurve. In: Sitzungsberichte der Österreichischen Akademie der Wissenschaften 82, 135–146.

Cranz, C. (1890): Gemeinverständliches über die sogenannte vierte Dimension. In: Sammlung gemeinverständlicher Vorträge. Hg. von R. v. Virchow et al. N.F. 5, H. 112/113. Hamburg, 1–70.

Doyle, A.C. (1926): History of Spiritualism. Doran.

Dürer, A. (1525): Underweysung der Messung. Nürnberg.

Einstein, A. (1969a): Über die spezielle und die allgemeine Relativitätstheorie. 21. Aufl. Braunschweig.

Einstein, A. (1969b): Grundzüge der Relativitätstheorie. 5. Aufl. Braunschweig.

Engels, F. (1878): Die Naturforschung in der Geisterwelt. In: Marx-Engels Werke (MEGA). I/26,1. Berlin 1985, 155–164; 335–344.
Euklid (1933): Euklids Elemente. In: Ostwalds Klassiker. Bd. 235. Hg. von C. Thaer. Leipzig.
Evers, D. (2000): Raum-Matrie-Zeit. Schöpfungstheologie im Dialog mit naturwissenschaftlicher Theologie. Tübingen.
Fechner, G. Th. (1864): Über die physikalische und philosophische Atomenlehre. 2. verm. Aufl. Leipzig.
[Fechner, G. Th.] Dr. Mises (1875): Kleine Schriften. Leipzig.
Fechner, G. Th. (1876): Erinnerungen an die letzten Tage der Odlehre und ihres Urhebers. Leipzig.
Fechner, G. Th. (1882): Revision der Hauptpunkte der Psychophysik. Leipzig.
Fechner, G. Th. (1906): Das Büchlein vom Leben nach dem Tode. 6. Aufl. Hamburg.
Freud, S. (1899): Traumdeutung. In: Gesammelte Werke. Hg. von A. Freud. Bd. 2–3. Frankfurt a.M.
Gierer, A. (1998): Die gedachte Natur. Hamburg.
Grimm, J. und W. (1893): Deutsches Wörterbuch. Bd. 8. Leipzig.
Hadamard, J. (1923): Lectures on Cauchy's Problem. New Haven.
Hamel, J. (1977): Karl Friedrich Zöllner. Versuch einer Analyse seiner philosophischen Position. Berlin.
Hamel, J. (1983): Zöllner als Hochschullehrer in Leipzig. In: Schriftenreihe für Geschichte der Naturwissenschaften, Technik und Medizin (NTM) 20, 35–43.
Heidelberger, M.(1993): Die innere Seite der Natur. Gustav Theodor Fechners wissenschaftlich-philosophische Weltanschauung. Frankfurt a.M.
Heimsoeth, H. (1935) (Hg.): Windelbands Lehrbuch der Geschichte der Philosophie. Tübingen.
Helmholtz, H. (1896): Über das Sehen des Menschen. In: Vorträge und Reden. Bd. 1. 4. Aufl. Braunschweig, 85–117.
Henneberg, R. (1902): Über die Beziehungen zwischen Spiritismus und Geistesstörung. Berlin.
Hermann, D. (1974) (Hg.): Zöllner. Mitteilungen der Archenhold-Sternwarte Berlin-Treptow. H. 97. Berlin.
Hermann, D. (1982): Karl Friedrich Zöllner. Leipzig.
Hilbert, D. (1899): Grundlagen der Geometrie. Kommentierte 14. Aufl. hg. von M. Toepell. Stuttgart 1999.
Hoppe, R. (1879): Gleichung der Kurve eines Bandes mit unlösbarem Knoten nebst Auflösung in der vierten Dimension. In: Archiv für Mathematik und Physik. Hg. von Grunert. 64, 224.
Kant, I. (1781): Kritik der reinen Vernunft. Riga.
Kant, I. (1913): Prolegomena zu einer jeden künftigen Methaphysik, die als Wissenschaft wird auftreten können. 5. Aufl. Leipzig. (Philosophische Bibliothek Meiner. 40).
Khalili, J. al (2001): Schwarze Löcher, Wurmlöcher und Zeitmaschinen. Übers.a. d. Englischen. Heidelberg.
Klein, F. (1926): Vorlesungen über die Entwicklung der Mathematik im 19. Jahrhundert. Bd. 1. Berlin.
Koerber, F. (1899): Karl Friedrich Zöllner. Berlin.

Kracke, H. (1970): Aus eins mach zehn. Hamburg.

Kuntze, J.E. (1892): Gustav Theodor Fechner (Dr. Mises). Ein deutsches Gelehrtenleben. Leipzig.

Laßwitz, K. (1883): Scherzdichtung. In: Zeitschrift für mathematischen und naturwissenschaftlichen Unterricht 14, 312–318.

Laßwitz, K., (1896): Gustav Theodor Fechner. Stuttgart.

Leihkauf, H. (1983): Zöllner und der physikalische Raum. In: Schriftenreihe für Geschichte der Naturwissenschaften, Technik und Medizin 20, 29–33.

Lennig, P. (1994): Von der Metaphysik zur Psychophysik. Frankfurt a.M.

Lichtenberg G. Ch. (1972): Uber Physiognomik. In: Schriften und Briefe. Hg. von W. Promies. Bd. 3. München, 256–285.

Lotze, H. (1879): Metaphysik. Leipzig.

Mach, E. (1901): Die Mechanik in ihrer Entwicklung. 4. Aufl. Leipzig.

Maeterlink, M. (1928): Die vierte Dimension. Berlin.

Meinel, C. (1991): Karl Friedrich Zöllner und die Wissenschaftskultur der Gründerzeit. Berlin.

Minkowski, H. (1909): Raum und Zeit. In: Jahresbericht der Dt. Mathematiker-Vereinigung 18, 75–89.

Minkowski, H. (1920): Raum und Zeit. In: Das Relativitätsprinzip. Hg. von H.A. Lorentz; A. Einstein; H. Minkowski. 3. verb. Aufl. Leipzig, 54–71.

More, H. (1671): Enchiridion metaphysicum. London.

Mulholland, J. (1938): Beware Family Spirits. New York.

Nietzsche, F. (1980) : Böse Weisheit. In: Sämtliche Werke. Hg. von G. Colli; M. Montinari. München.

Pascal, B. (1913): Pensées. London.

Perron, O. (1940): Über die lückenlose Ausfüllung des n-dimensionalen Raumes durch kongruente Würfel. In: Mathematische Zeitschrift 46, 1–26.

Pfabigan, A. (1990) (Hg.): Die andere Bibel. Frankfurt a.M. (Die andere Bibliothek).

Polchinski, J. (1998): String Theory. 2 vols. Cambridge.

Reichenbach, H. (1928): Philosophie der Raum-Zeit-Lehre. Berlin.

Richter, P. (2001): Das Olber'sche Paradoxon. In: Neue Welten. Olbers und die Naturwissenschaften um 1800. Hg. von G. Biegel. Braunschweig, 102–113.

Sartorius von W. (1856): Gauß zum Gedächtnis. Leipzig.

Schenkel, E. (1994): Geometrie und Geisterreich. Literarische Streifzüge durch das Spiegelland und die vierte Dimension. In: Frankfurter Allg. Zeitung, 20.8.1994.

Schiller, F. (1915): Sprüche des Confuzius. In: Schillers Gedichte (Auswahl). Hg. von H. Löschhom. Bielefeld, 164.

Schindler, H. (1857): Das magische Geistesleben. Breslau.

Schramm, M. (1985): Natur ohne Sinn? Das Ende des teleologischen Weltbildes. Graz.

Schubert, H. (1892): Die vierte Dimension in mathematischen und in spiritistischen Köpfen. In: Hamburgischer Correspondent. Morgenausg., 30.6.1892.

Schubert, H. (1909): Mathematische Mußestunden. 3. Bd. 3. Aufl. Leipzig.

Snow, C.P. (1959): Cambridge Lecture.

Stewart, B.; Tait, P.G. (1875): The Unseen Universe. London.

Tischner, R. (1921): Einführung in den Okkultismus und Spiritismus. München.

Thiele, R. (1993): Schöpfungsmythos und Naturwissenschft. In: Duisburger Mercator-Studien. Bd. 1. Hg. von M. Büttner; R. Dirven. Bochum, 125–148.
Thiele, R. (1997): Ist die Kosmographie eine vergessene Wissenschaft? In: Forschungen zur Physikotheologie. Bd. 3. Berliner Kongress zur Wissenschaftsgeschichte 1996. Hg. von M. Büttner; F. Richter. Münster, 103–126.
Vollmer, G. (1993): Wissenschaftstheorie im Einsatz. Stuttgart.
Vollmer, G. (1999): Unterwegs in neuen Dimensionen. Die Entdeckung des Raumes durch die Physik. In: Richtungen im Raum. Hg. von Rickheit. Wiesbaden, 5–35.
Vries, H. de (1926): Die vierte Dimension (aus dem Holländischen). Leipzig.
Vries, H. de (1905): Die Lehre von der Zentralprojektion im vierdimensionalen Raum. Leipzig.
Wagner, R. (1975): Gespräche mit Gauß in den letzten Monaten seines Lebens. In: Nachrichten der Akademie der Wissenschaften in Göttingen. Hg. von H. Rubner. 6, 143–171.
Weitzenböck, R. (1956): Der vierdimensionale Raum (1929). Erweiterte Neuauflage. Basel.
Wells, G.H. (1952): Science fiction Stories. Dover. Dt. Übersetzung in: Das Kristallei. Leipzig 1979, 54–72.
Whitrow, G.J. (1955): Why physical space has three dimensions. In: British Journal of Philosophical Science 6, 13–31.
Wundt, W. (1879): Der Spiritismus. Eine sogenannte wissenschaftliche Frage. Offener Brief an Hrn. Prof. Dr. Herm. Ulrici in Halle. Leipzig.
Zöllner, F. (1872): Ueber die Natur der Cometen. Beiträge zur Geschichte und Theorie der Erkenntnis. 2. unveränd. Aufl. Leipzig.
Zöllner, J.C.F. (1878;1879): Wissenschaftliche Abhandlungen. 3 Bde. Leipzig 1878, Bd. 1 und 2; 1879 Bd. 3.
Zöllner, J.C.F. (1881): Naturwissenschaft und christliche Offenbarung. Populäre Beiträge zur Theorie und Geschichte der vierten Dimension. Leipzig.

Uta Kösser

Fechners Ästhetik im Kontext

Jubiläums-Konstellationen sind zufällig – wie etwa die, dass wir in diesem Jahr den 200. Todestag von Novalis und den 200. Geburtstag von Fechner begehen. Es ist also zufällig, dass Fechner in dem Jahr geboren wurde, als Novalis starb. Solche Konstellationen können jedoch etwas verdeutlichen, nämlich, dass Fechners Ästhetikverständnis ein anderes sein muss als das der Romantik – und dies, obwohl er Schüler Schellings war: Nicht die spekulative ästhetische Konstruktion, sondern die experimentelle Analyse dessen, was gefällt, scheint angesagt, nicht ›Ästhetik von oben‹, sondern ›von unten‹, nicht Metaphysik, sondern Psychophysik.

Ungewöhnlich ist, dass ein Professor für Physik Ästhetikvorlesungen hält und dass seine Überlegungen nicht nur zur Differenzierung der Ästhetik am Ende des 19. Jahrhunderts beitrugen, sondern auch kulturwissenschaftliche Nachwirkungen hatten. Um dieses Ungewöhnliche zu erhellen, möchte ich *zuerst* Fechners Verständnis von Ästhetik und ästhetisch darlegen, das sich einerseits einordnet in die Traditionen dieser Disziplin seit dem 18. Jahrhundert, andererseits durch eine Fundierung auf Experimente neue Akzente setzt und damit sowohl den Begriff von Ästhetik ausweitet und im Sinne einer aktuellen Forderung »Ästhetik außerhalb der Ästhetik« (Welsch 1996, 135ff.) betreibt. Zugleich wird dabei das traditionelle Ästhetikverständnis bedient.

Weiterhin möchte ich – mehr kursorisch – auf Anregungen verweisen, die sich aus seiner Psychophysik für erkenntnistheoretische Fragen und für die genauere Bestimmung von Wahrnehmungsprozessen nicht nur für seine Zeitgenossen wie Büchner, Haeckel, Lange, Mach ergeben haben, sondern auch für bedeutende Vertreter der modernen Kulturphilosophie wie Simmel, Freud und Cassirer. Am Ende zeige ich an einem Beispiel, dass wir heute auch ›Ästhetik von unten‹ betreiben, selbst wenn wir das nicht so nennen.

1. Fechners Ästhetik-Auffassung

Fechner befasst sich intensiver mit ästhetischen Fragen etwa seit 1864; 1876 erscheint seine »Vorschule der Ästhetik«, auf die ich mich vor allem beziehe. Bereits 1871 stellt er jedoch eine »exacte Untersuchung« der Ästhetik in Aussicht, die er als Teil der Psychophysik fassen will, und die sich nach seiner Erklärung mit den »Massbeziehungen zwischen Reiz und Empfindung oder allgemeiner zwischen äusseren körperlichen Anregungen und inneren psychischen Folgen zu beschäftigen hat« (Fechner 1871b, 557). Ein Programm, dem seine Experimente folgen, in deren Ergebnis er seine sechs Prinzipien aufstellt, nach denen nach seiner Meinung die *ästhetische Wahrnehmung* funktioniert.

Ästhetik befand sich – wie andere Geistes- oder Kulturwissenschaften auch – im 19. Jahrhundert in einem Differenzierungsprozess: die idealistische Tradition, die den Gegenstand dieser Disziplin auf Kunst und Schönheit konzentrierte, obwohl durch Hegel und vor allem durch die Modernisierungsprozesse die »schöne Kunst« problematisiert worden war, hielt an. Gleichzeitig gab es lebensphilosophische (Nietzsche und Simmel), soziologische (Simmel) und materialistische Versuche (Marx und am Ende des Jahrhunderts die Kunstdebatten in der Sozialdemokratie), ästhetische Fragen zu reflektieren, und eben den Trend, Ästhetik exakt zu fundieren, d.h. sie auf Naturwissenschaften zu gründen.

Diese Entwicklungen haben u.a. damit zu tun, dass Ästhetik seit ihrer Begründung durch Baumgarten mit einem zwiespältigen Ruf belastet war: einerseits bewusst als dritte philosophische Disziplin neben Logik und Ethik gesetzt, andererseits auch deswegen gegründet, um das rational zu betrachten, was bisher keinen Platz im neuzeitlichen rationalistischen Weltbild hatte:[1] Phantasie, Einbildungskraft, Geschmack, Schein, Täuschung, Genuss, oder das einer Reflexion zu unterziehen, was die rationalen Wissenschaften beiseite ließen: Unfassbares, Maßloses, Inkommensurables oder Chaotisches.[2] Mit exakten Wissenschaften schien dies nichts zu tun zu haben, eher mit Spekulation. Aber diese Spekulation begründete zugleich auch eine starke Funktion des ästhetischen Feldes innerhalb der Moderne. Es wird immer wieder bis heute gegen Rationalität oder, genauer, gegen eine als rationalisierte und damit als einseitig begriffene Moderne gesetzt und gedacht, mit dem Versprechen oder der Hoff-

---

[1] Vgl. Schröder 1985, 18.

[2] Vgl. Cramer; Kaempfer 1992, 16.

nung, ein Gegengewicht zur Verfügung zu stellen und diese Einseitigkeit, wenn nicht zu überwinden, so doch zumindest zeitweise auszugleichen. Dem geht eine ab der zweiten Hälfte des 19. Jahrhunderts charakteristische Tendenz parallel: der Versuch, Ästhetik auf Naturwissenschaften zu fundieren oder, was es vielleicht genauer trifft, sich an die Faktizität des *Empirischen* zu halten. Dieser Prozess beginnt in den Künsten bzw. in den Kunstprogrammatiken. Das ästhetische Programm des *Naturalismus* beruft sich ausdrücklich auf die ›modernen Wissenschaften‹, auf Positivismus, Darwinismus, Psychologie und Soziologie. Als Beispiel wäre Wilhelm Bölsche (1861–1939) zu nennen, ein Vertreter des *Friedrichshagener Literatenkreises*, der in seiner Schrift von 1887 »Die naturwissenschaftlichen Grundlagen der Poesie. Prologomena einer realistischen Aesthetik« eine Anpassung der Poesie an die modernen naturwissenschaftlichen Erkenntnisse – lies Darwinismus und Psychologie – propagiert.[3] Er beruft sich explizit auf Fechner und geht von dessen Position einer *Allbeseelung* der Materie aus, die es ihm erlaubt, eine solche ›naturwissenschaftliche‹ Fundierung der Kunst selbstverständlich mit dem Begriff des Ideals zu verbinden[4] – eine doppelte Sicht, wie sie bei Fechner vorgedacht war, der ebenfalls die Untersuchung von *Wahrnehmungsprozessen* mit ethischen Idealen verbindet. Arno Holz, ein weiterer Vertreter des Naturalismus, sucht nach einem »Gesetz«[5] in der *Kunst* und glaubt so, die Ästhetik auf Soziologie fundieren zu können. Der Ästhetizismus fordert einen ›kalten wissenschaftlichen Blick‹, der das Zustandekommen ästhetischer Reize und die Konstituanten eines verfeinerten ästhetischen Genusses analysieren soll. Anatole Baju fordert die *decadents* auf, »All-Wissenschaft« zu betreiben und die »mathematischen Gesetze« festzustellen, die den ästhetischen Genuss »determinieren« (Baju 1980, 259). Der Konstruktivismus beruft sich um die Jahrhundertwende auf die nichteuklidische Geometrie, um die *vierte Dimension* für die Kunst zu erschließen.[6]

Nun ist Fechner von solchen avantgardistischen Ambitionen frei, aber auch er sucht nach Gesetzen, er will *experimentell* das Zustandekommen sinnlicher *Wahrnehmung* und ästhetischer Urteile untersuchen, d.h. er ordnet sich in diesen Trend ein und beeinflusst ihn entscheidend. Dieses Modell von Ästhetik bezeichnet er als ›Ästhetik von unten‹, die er in sei-

[3] Vgl. Bölsche 1987, 98–113.
[4] Vgl. Bölsche 1987, 112.
[5] Vgl. Holz 1987, 140–151.
[6] Vgl. Ferry 1990, 255ff.

ner »Vorschule der Ästhetik« von 1876 begründet. Der Titel ›Vorschule‹ ist bereits ein Programm: Vorschule ist etwas, was der eigentlichen Schule vorausgeht. Der Begriff hat eine gewisse Tradition im 19. Jahrhundert; Jean Paul hatte ihn ironisch mit seiner »Vorschule der Ästhetik« von 1804 eingeführt, indem er die mittelalterliche Bedeutung der Vorschule, das *Proscholium*, als Platz, wo der Vorschulmeister den Zögling auf die eigentliche Schule vorbereitet, übernimmt.[7] Der Titel »Vorschule der Ästhetik« findet sich auch bei anderen und bedeutet bei Fechner, dass er eine Ästhetik ›von unten‹ zu den »wesentlichsten Vorbedingungen einer Aesthetik von Oben« rechnet, die er als »Sache der Zukunft« betrachtet (Fechner 1897, 1, 4).

Diese ›Ästhetik von unten‹ geht empirisch vor. Sie versucht, über Messungen ästhetische Gesetze aufzustellen, sie will durch Besucherbefragungen – Fechner führt Besucherbücher bei Kunstausstellungen ein – ästhetische Urteile quantifizieren; sie benutzt den Vergleich von Rezeptionshaltungen, um zur Klärung der Aechtheitsfrage der *Holbein'schen Madonna* beizutragen,[8] oder sie unternimmt Versuche – wie im Falle der Auseinandersetzung mit Zeisings Theorie des *Goldenen Schnitts* –, eine Grundform der Schönheit aufzustellen.[9] Letzteres ging so vor sich, dass Fechner Versuchspersonen unterschiedlichen Alters, Geschlechts und sozialer Herkunft durch die »Methode der Wahl, der Herstellung und Methode der Verwendung« (Fechner 1897, 1, 190) verschiedene Rechtecke auswählen lies, um die Frage zu klären, »ob gewisse Dimensionen und Abbildungsverhältnisse der Gegenstände einen *Vorzug der Wohlgefälligkeit* vor andern haben, und im Falle der Bejahung welche es sind [...]« (Fechner 1871b, 558). Im Ergebnis muss er feststellen, dass die Bevorzugung des Goldenen Schnitts von denjenigen Personen vorgenommen wurde, die auch sonst einen »guten Geschmack« haben (Fechner 1897, 1, 198). Das bedeutet, dass nicht nur die Reize des Objekts entscheidend für das Wohlgefallen sind, sondern eben auch das Subjekt mit seinem erworbenen Geschmacksniveau. Es wird also im Grunde die Kulturalität unserer *Wahrnehmung* deutlich. Positiv formuliert ist es dass, was Dilthey an dieser Entwicklung der Ästhetik zur experimentellen Wissenschaft kritisch angemerkt hatte, nämlich, dass diese »nur eine Erfahrung über eine erworbene Gewöhnung« (Dilthey 1978, 6, 264) aufdecken könne.

---

[7] Vgl. Barck, Fontius u.a. 2000, 340.

[8] Vgl. Fechner 1870; Fechner 1871.

[9] Vgl. Fechner 1897, Kap. XIV, 184–189.

Diese Ästhetik ›von unten‹ grenzt sich ab von einer Ästhetik ›von oben‹, also von der traditionellen Ästhetik, deren Methode darin besteht, Begriffe der *Kunst*, des *Schönen*, des Erhabenen, Hässlichen, usw. zu bilden, um dann – wie Fechner formuliert – »von der Höhe solcher Allgemeinheiten« in »das irdisch-empirische Gebiet des einzelnen, des zeitlich und örtlich Schönen« herabzusteigen und alles »Einzelne am Massstabe des Allgemeinen« zu messen (Fechner 1897, 1, 1).

Mit der Unterscheidung einer ›Ästhetik von unten und von oben‹, reflektiert Fechner also eine *Methode*. In diesem Kontext gehört Fechner daher auch zu den Vorläufern jener Diskussionen am Ende des 19. Jahrhundert, die um die spezifischen Gegenstände und Methoden der Kulturwissenschaften kreisen; verwiesen sei auf Namen wie Rickert, Windelband und Dilthey.[10] Die Besonderheit von Fechner – etwa im Unterschied zu Dilthey – liegt darin, dass er nicht die Abgrenzung der Natur- und Kulturwissenschaften forciert, sondern ihre Einheit bzw. ihre Beziehungen betont und praktiziert hat. Denn er kritisiert zwar die bisherige Ästhetik ›von oben‹, weil sie die empirische Feststellung von ästhetischen Gesetzmäßigkeiten »durch eine solche aus Begriffen und Ideen zu ersetzen statt zu *ergänzen*« (Fechner 1897, 1, 5) gesucht habe, setzt aber auf die Wechselwirkung beider Methoden, da er sowohl die *philosophische* wie die *empirische* Ästhetik für notwendig hält, denn beide »durchmessen dasselbe Gebiet – nur in entgegengesetzter Richtung; und überall ergänzt sich die Möglichkeit der Bewegung in einer Richtung durch eine solche in entgegengesetzter Richtung. Es haben aber beide Wege ihre besonderen Vortheile, Schwierigkeiten und Gefahren« (Fechner 1897, 1, 2). Die bisherige philosophische Ästhetik habe nur um Begriffe gestritten – so Fechner weiter – »über die richtige Begriffsbestimmung der Schönheit, [...], des Stils, [...], der Kunst, der Kunstschönheit und Naturschönheit« – mit der Folge, dass die Unterordnung des Einzelnen unter diese Begriffe die »Eintheilungen des gesamten ästhetischen Gebietes« den »Hauptinhalt der Darstellung« (Fechner 1897, 1, 5) bildeten. Diesen deutlichen begrifflichen, *rationalen* Zugriff der Ästhetik kritisiert Fechner nicht zu Unrecht, da sie ja eigentlich begründet wurde, um sowohl die Sinnlichkeit aufzuwerten, den Wert der sinnlichen analog der rationalen Erkenntnis deutlich zu machen, als auch zu fragen, wie diese sinnliche Erkenntnis denn funktioniert. Fechner stellt daher fest, dass mit der alleinigen Orientierung auf Begriffe »die Aufgabe der Aesthetik« nicht erschöpft sei.

[10] Vgl. u.a. Rickert 1899; Dilthey 1910.

> Denn bei Allem, was uns ästhetisch angeht, wird die Frage nicht blos die sein: welchem Begriffe ordnet es sich unter, an welchem Platz stellt es sich im System unserer Begriffe – man hat das allerdings zu fragen, es gehört zu klaren Orientirung in unserm Erkentnissgebiete; – aber die am meisten interessirende und wichtigste Frage wird doch immer bleiben: *warum* gefällt oder missfällt es, und inwiefern hat es Recht zu gefallen oder zu missfallen; und hierauf lässt sich nur mit Gesetzen des Gefallens und Missfallens unter *Zuziehung der Gesetze des Sollens* antworten. (Fechner 1897, 1, 5; Hervorh. U.K.)

Diese Wendung ist von Interesse: Betonung der empirischen Erfahrung, der Sinnlichkeit, Kritik an der alleinigen begrifflichen Tendenz oder rationalistischen Herangehensweise, die heute von Befürwortern einer Aisthesis – allerdings ohne auf Fechner zu verweisen – viel schärfer als Entsinnlichung[11] der Ästhetik formuliert wird. Dann die Erklärung: man müsse die Gesetze des Sollens heranziehen oder die Ästhetik mit der Ethik verschwistern. Bei Kant hieß dies »das Schöne ist das Symbol des sittlich Guten«. Fechner spricht dagegen vom *eudomänistischen Prinzip*.

Mit dieser *methodischen* Unterscheidung in ›unten‹ und ›oben‹ ist Ästhetik jedoch noch nicht inhaltlich bestimmt, denn es muss ja auch gesagt werden, was empirisch oder vom Begriff her bestimmt werden soll. Eine solche *inhaltliche* Bestimmung nimmt Fechner auch vor: Ästhetik ist für ihn die Lehre vom *Gefallen* und *Mißfallen* oder von *Lust* und *Unlust* (Fechner 1897, 1, 33ff.). Hier finden sich Anklänge an Kant. Fechner geht jedoch nicht transzendental vor, sondern empirisch. Er bestimmt ästhetische Urteile nicht ausschließlich subjektiv wie Kant, der davon ausging, dass mit ihnen »gar nichts im Objekt bezeichnet werde«, sondern dass beurteilt werde, »wie das Subjekt sich fühlt« (Kant 1793, § 1), während Fechner – seiner *Psychophysik* folgend – auch am Objekt empirische Gesetze auffinden will, die ästhetische Urteile messbar werden lassen.

Damit kann für Fechner auch das Schöne im Mittelpunkt seiner Ästhetik bleiben, aber er fragt und versucht mittels Experiment festzustellen, ob und welche Eigenschaften eines Objekts eine schöne Empfindung, ein Wohlgefallen im Subjekt auslösen. Philosophische Ästhetik interessiert der Begriff des *Schönen*; sie legt also ›von oben‹ fest, was schön ist und daher *zu gefallen* hat. Für Fechner stellt sich die Frage andersherum: was *schön ist* und insofern *gefällt*. Für ihn ist aus dieser Perspektive die Frage nach dem Schönen erst zu beantworten, »wenn man von »Erfahrungen über das, was gefällt und missfällt« (Fechner 1897, 1, 1) ausgeht, wenn

[11] Vgl. Welsch 1992; Welsch 1996.

man also weiß, was gefällt. Dies verlangt sowohl eine statistische Erfassung der gefallenden Objekte als auch eine empirische Untersuchung der *Wahrnehmungsgesetze*. In Zeiten, wo sich die Ästhetik dem Problem stellen muss, dass ihr ein Schönheitsbegriff abhanden gekommen sei – ein Zustand, der nicht nur von Adorno in seiner »Ästhetischen Theorie« reflektiert wurde, sondern in den 90er-Jahren auch von Agnes Heller oder von Vilém Flusser konstatiert wird – könnte dies ein Weg sein, dennoch auf einen Kernbereich ästhetischen Reflektierens nicht zu verzichten.[12]

Bestätigt wird dieser mögliche Weg auch durch die Diskussion in der Ästhetik seit Ende der 80er-Jahre des 20. Jahrhunderts, die eine »Rückkehr der Ästhetik zur Aisthesis« verlangt.[13] Auch Fechner beruft sich bereits auf die Anfänge der modernen Ästhetik. Er nennt Baumgarten, der »Ästhetisch auf das sinnlich Wahrnehmbare oder Formen der sinnlichen Wahrnehmung« (Fechner 1897, 1, 32) bezogen habe, aber – so fährt er bedauernd fort – die Ästhetik sei dem in der Ausführung nicht gefolgt, und zwar deswegen, weil es nicht allein um den Akt der sinnlichen Wahrnehmung gehe, sondern auch um die Wahrnehmung von Sinn. Es geht ihm also darum, zu klären, *wie* wir *Sinn* wahrnehmen. Fechner reduziert Ästhetik daher nicht auf eine einfache Wahrnehmungslehre, sondern will das Verhältnis von *Sinnlichkeit* und *Sinn* als Kernpunkt *ästhetischer Wahrnehmung* und ästhetischer Urteile verdeutlichen. Wenn Ästhetik nur Lehre von der sinnlichen Wahrnehmung wäre – so sein Argument –, dann müsste sie allein den physiologischen Akt der Wahrnehmung untersuchen und »Göthe's Faust und die sixtinische Madonna« und all das, »was den *Sinn* rührt«, wäre nicht der ästhetischen Betrachtung zu unterziehen« (Fechner 1897, 1, 33). Er setzt mit dieser Argumentation nachdrücklich darauf, dass unter ästhetisch nicht nur die sinnliche oder *aisthetische* Komponente, sondern auch die *Sinnkomponente* zu fassen ist:

> Also versteht man jetzt unter ästhetisch überhaupt, was sich auf Verhältnisse unmittelbaren Gefallens und Mißfallens an dem bezieht, was durch die Sinne in uns eintritt, ohne aber blos die rein sinnliche Seite davon im Auge zu haben, da vielmehr Verhältnisse des Sinnlichen, wie in der Musik, und Associationsvorstellungen, die unmittelbar mit dem Sinnlichen verschmelzen, wie mit den Worten in der Poesie und den Formen in den bildenden Künsten, endlich Verhältnisse dieser Vorstellungen, insoweit sich an alles das Gefallen oder Missfallen knüpft, mit in das Bereich des Aesthetischen gezogen werden. (Fechner 1897, 1, 33)

[12] »So wenig ist das Schöne zu definieren wie auf seinen Begriff zu verzichten, eine strikte Antinomie.« (Adorno 1990, 82); siehe Heller 1996,333–348; Flusser 1995, 184–189.

[13] Vgl. Barck u.a. 1990; Welsch 1990.

Ästhetik ist also für Fechner nicht nur ›Ästhetik von oben‹ *und* ›von unten‹, sondern auch Kunst- *und* Wahrnehmungsästhetik, und damit auch *Alltagsästhetik;* letzteres belegen vor allem seine Experimente. Davon ausgehend scheint ihm ein gewisser ›enger‹ Gebrauch von ›ästhetisch‹ legitim, weil es auch *Wahrnehmungsprozesse* gibt, die man nicht ohne weiteres mit einem ›höheren‹ Sinn verbinden kann: etwa

> den wohlgefälligen Eindruck, den ein reiner voller Ton, eine tiefe gesättigte Farbe, der Wohlgeruch einer Blume, der Wohlgeschmack einer Speise ohne alle Vorstellungsverknüpfung zu erwecken vermag. (Fechner 1897, 1, 33f.)

Die bisherige Ästhetik hatte solche ästhetischen Erfahrungen und Wahrnehmungen unter dem Angenehmen verbucht oder unterschied – wie Kant – Sinnenurteil und Reflexionsurteil. Nahsinne wie Geruchs-, Geschmacks- und Tastsinn werden normalerweise ausgeklammert. Für Fechner gehören diese elementarästhetischen Verhaltensweisen zum Untersuchungsgebiet einer ›Ästhetik von unten‹.

Andererseits nimmt seine Ästhetik auch die traditionelle Beziehung zur Ethik auf; diese formuliert er im *eudomänistischen Prinzip.* Wenn Ästhetik nach Lust und Unlust, nach Gefallen und Missfallen fragt, dann muss sie nach Fechner auch fragen, *warum* Lust oder Unlust, Gefallen oder Missfallen erzeugt wird; sie hat dann nicht nur nach den formalen Qualitäten der Objekte, sondern auch nach den moralischen Motiven der Subjekte zu fragen. Daher plädiert Fechner für eine Verbindung von Ethik und Ästhetik:

> Unsere Bezugsetzung der ästhetischen zu den ethischen Kategorien und folgweis der Aesthetik zur Ethik ist aus einem eudämonistischen (Glück, Lust als Ziel setzenden) Gesichtspuncte geschehen, und ich wüsste nicht, wie sie zugleich klarer und sachgemässer geschehen könnte. (Fechner 1897, 1, 38)

Hier ist anzumerken, dass erstens die Beziehung zwischen ›schön‹ und ›gut‹, in der Regel noch ›wahr‹, in der Ästhetik eine lange Tradition hat. Diese Auffassung wird im 19. Jahrhundert abgebaut. Der *Ästhetizismus* verabsolutiert das Schöne und trennt es strikt vom Guten. Fechner macht diesen Trend nicht mit und beharrt auf der engen Beziehung von ethisch und ästhetisch, von Sinn und Sinnlichkeit, was ebenfalls belegt, dass er ›Ästhetik von oben‹ *und* ›von unten‹ praktizieren will. Zweitens ist die Formulierung des *eudomänistischen* Prinzips auch einzuordnen in den Kontext einer disziplinären Bestimmung. Immer dann, wenn definiert wird, was Ästhetik sei, muss man sich auch zu anderen Disziplinen in Beziehung setzen. Baumgarten setzte sich in Beziehung zur Logik, in dem er den Wert des sinnlichen Erkenntnisvermögens hervorhob; Kant entwickelte in Unterscheidung zur theoretischen und zur praktischen Philosophie seine »Kritik der Urteilskraft«; Fechner setzte sich in Beziehung zur Ethik und zur Psychologie, weil ihn das Gefühlsmoment und die Antriebe interessierten. Was ist aber nun der konkrete Inhalt dieses eudomänistischen Prinzips? Woran ist Glückseligkeit gebunden? Dazu Fechner:

> Nun ruht das hier vertretene eudomänistische Prinzip in nichts Anderm, als dass es dasselbe, was eines Jeden bewusste Antriebe nothwendig ihrer Richtung nach bestimmt, auch als Ziel dieser Antriebe in Beziehung auf *das Ganze* vor Augen stellt, und die Erziehung der Antriebe aller auf möglichste Erfüllung dieses Zieles zu richten gebietet. Dies unter Geltendmachung der *Solidarität*, in welcher sich das *Wohl des Einzelnen mit dem des Ganzen* um so mehr zeigt, je vollständiger das Princip erfüllt, und je weiter es in seinen Consequenzen verfolgt wird. (Fechner 1897, 1, 40; Hervorh. U.K.)

Mit anderen Worten bedeutet dies die Ausrichtung auf das Gemeinwohl und auf Solidarität als ein Prinzip, das ästhetisch *Lust* oder *Gefallen* bewirkt. Das ist durchaus kantisch gedacht und vergleichbar mit Kants Fundierung des ästhetischen Urteils auf Gemeinsinn, erwächst aber bei Fechner aus seiner Ethik, in der die Lust das höchste Gut darstellt.[14]

Fechners Ausgangsfrage war nicht: was schön sei, sondern warum etwas als schön erklärt werde. Aus der Sicht der ›Ästhetik von unten‹ analysiert er die Objekte und die psychologischen Prinzipien der Wahrnehmung. Aus der Sicht einer ›Ästhetik von oben‹ bleibt er bei der überlieferten Verbindung von ›gut‹ und ›schön‹, indem er das Individualwohl mit dem allgemeinen Wohl als Antrieb für Lustempfinden in Beziehung setzt. In diesem Sinne wäre Fechners *eudomänistisches Prinzip* ein übergreifendes geistiges Prinzip, während er die ästhetische *Wahrnehmung* selbst und die Auslösung der Empfindung von Lust und Unlust durch eine Reihe anderer Prinzipien, die aus der Wechselwirkung von wahrgenommenem Objekt und wahrnehmendem Subjekt resultieren, erklärt.

Grundlage für die ästhetische Wahrnehmung ist das »Princip der ästhetischen Schwelle«, die sowohl vom Objekt (Reizstärke) wie vom Subjekt (Reizempfindlichkeit) überschritten werden muss, damit eine »Einwirkung für unser Bewußtsein spürbar wird« (Fechner 1897, 1, 49). Es wird ergänzt durch das »Princip der ästhetischen Hülfe oder Steigerung«

[14] Siehe Fechner 1846; Heidelberger 1993, 73.

(Fechner 1897, 1, 50), das auf das Übereinstimmen der Teile bezug nimmt. Dahinter steckt auch die Erfahrung, dass das Ganze mehr ist als die Summe seiner Teile – eine grundlegende Annahme der Gestaltpsychologie,[15] die sich auch auf Fechner beruft. Dem folgen die drei obersten Formalprinzipien, das der einheitlichen Verknüpfung des Mannichfaltigen, das Prinzip der Widerspruchslosigkeit oder der Wahrheit und das der Klarheit. Das Prinzip der *Einheit des Mannigfaltigen* verweist auch auf eine andere Gesetzmäßigkeit unserer Wahrnehmung, die sich dann bei Cassirer findet und die uns heute sehr interessiert: die symbolische Prägnanz. Darunter verstehen wir den auch empirisch belegbaren Sachverhalt, dass wir, wenn wir etwas wahrnehmen, dies über bestimmte Prägnanzkriterien tun. Uns reichen etwa zwei bis sechs solcher Prägnanzkritierien, um ein Objekt wiederzuerkennen oder auch darzustellen.[16] Fechner formuliert folgendermaßen: »Bei einer sehr kurz dauernden Beschäftigung aber reicht schon eine sehr geringe Mannichfaltigkeit hin, den Geist Genüge und selbst positives Gefallen finden zu lassen« (Fechner 1897, 1, 55).

Das 6. Prinzip – das der *ästhetischen Assoziation* – ist Fechners Hauptprinzip. Es beschreibt eine komplizierte ästhetische Wahrnehmung, die nicht nur über die entsprechenden Objekte die Sinne anregt, sondern auch Gefühle, Erfahrungen, Erlebnisse des Subjekts ins Spiel bringt – also reflexiv wird. Kant hatte daher das ästhetische Urteil als Reflexionsurteil bestimmt; Fechner unterstützt diesen transzendentalen Befund von Kant durch eine psychologische Fundierung. Ästhetisch ist nicht das bloße Sehen, Hören, Riechen, Schmecken – das wäre aisthetisch –, sondern es findet über die Sinneswahrnehmungen zugleich auch eine Assoziation von Sinngehalten statt: Selbstreflexion und Reflexion über die Welt. »Wir sehen einen Tisch, im Grunde nur einen viereckigen Fleck. Aber auch alles, wozu ein Tisch gebraucht wird, und das macht den viereckigen Fleck erst zu einem Tisch« (Fechner 1897, 1, 93). Wir sehen nicht nur mit dem sinnlichen, sondern auch mit dem geistigen Auge, heißt es dann weiter. Daher ist *Assoziation* für Fechner nicht nur ein wesentlicher Bestandteil der Phantasie, sondern sie wurzelt in der persönlichen Erlebnisgeschichte, in der Erinnerung und in der sozialen Erfahrung. Sie ist also kulturell determiniert.

---

[15] Vgl. Goldstein 1997, 169.
[16] Vgl. Köhnke 2000, 91–103.

Ästhetik hat demnach – so könnte man Fechners Position zusammenfassen – auf verschiedenen Ebenen wie Kunst und Alltag zu untersuchen, warum Gefallen und Missfallen auftritt. Fechner betont sowohl die Rolle der Sinnlichkeit wie die der Sinnhaftigkeit und fragt nicht mehr, *was* ist schön, sondern *warum* etwas als schön empfunden wird. Er versucht eine empirische Untersuchung der Gründe des ästhetischen Urteils durch die Aufstellung von *Wahrnehmungsprinzipien*, die sowohl sinnliche wie sinnhafte Elemente der ästhetischen Wahrnehmung bedenken – und daher auch für die aktuelle Ästhetikdebatte von Bedeutung sind.

2. Zu den Nachwirkungen

Fechner wird zum einen sehr deutlich eine Neigung zu einer Ästhetik ›von unten‹ zugeschrieben. Das zeigt sich schon in der Kritik von Zeitgenossen oder unmittelbaren Nachfolgern. Vertreter der philosophischen Ästhetik sahen durch seine Experimente »die Stellung der Philosophie im Leben der Hochschulen bedroht« (Allesch 1987, 312). Das diesbezügliche Argument von Eduard von Hartmann lautete, »die Aesthetik als solche fängt erst da an, wo über diese Grundlage der blossen Erfahrung hinaus und zur Erklärung derselben fortgeschritten wird« (v. Hartmann 1886, 329). Eine weitere Einordnung schlägt ihn der psychologischen Ästhetik zu; zu nennen wäre hier Christian G. Allesch, der ihm ein Kapitel in der »Geschichte der psychologischen Ästhetik« widmet. Das ist nicht unbegründet, denn Fechner hat diese Richtung sehr nachhaltig beeinflusst. So referierte Oswald Külpe bereits 1906 auf dem 2. Kongress für experimentelle Psychologie unter dem Motto, dass »Fechners Saat aufgegangen« (Külpe 1906, 55) sei;[17] zu verweisen wäre ebenfalls auf Karl Gross oder auf Carl Langes »Beiträge zu einer sensualistischen Kunstlehre« sowie auf Auswirkungen auf den ästhetischen Diskurs in den USA, Frankreich und England.[18] Fechner wird ebenso bei der Diskussion erkenntnistheoretischer Fragen herangezogen. Zu nennen wären z.B. Ludwig Büchner, der in »Kraft und Stoff« (1855) mehrfach auf ihn verweist, Ernst Mach, der in »Erkenntnis und Irrtum« »besonders die von Fechner beschriebenen Erscheinungen des Sinnengedächtnisses« (Mach 1917, 158) erwähnt, Ernst Haeckel, der in den »Welträtseln« zwar die Exaktheit der

---

[17] Vgl. auch Barck, Fontius u.a. 2000, 376.
[18] Vgl. dazu Barck, Fontius u.a. 2000, 1, 375ff.

Fechner'schen Gesetze bezweifelt, aber würdigend hervorhebt, dass sie »prinzipiell insofern hohen Wert« haben, »als dadurch die strenge Geltung physikalischer Gesetze auf einem, wenn auch nur sehr kleinen Gebiete des sogenannten »Geisteslebens« dargetan wurde« (Haeckel 1919, 151). Lange nimmt Fechners Ästhetik in der »Geschichte des Materialismus« als Beleg, »daß selbst eine schwärmerische Philosophie den Geist wahrer Forschung nicht immer vergiftet«, widmet ihm einige Sätze, die seine *Psychophysik* anerkennen, um zugleich polemisch anzumerken, »daß Fechner jeden Philosophen hinter der Ofenbank sucht, hinter welcher er selbst gesteckt hat« (Lange 1974, 2, 639ff.)

Die Vielseitigkeit Fechners erlaubt sicher viele Zuordnungen. Wir betrachten ihn heute als zu der Tradition der Leipziger Kulturwissenschaften gehörig, d.h. wir sehen ihn in einer Reihe mit den wissenschaftlichen Leistungen solcher Angehöriger der Leipziger Universität wie Lamprecht, Wundt oder Ratzel.[19] Das tun wir nicht nur aus Lokalpatriotismus, sondern vor allem deshalb, weil in den »klassischen« kulturwissenschaftlichen Texten immer wieder auf ihn verwiesen wird, was auf seine Nachwirkung verweist und zeigt, dass Fechner für uns ein ›Vordenker‹ war.

So geht Wilhelm Dilthey auf Fechner nicht nur in seinem Aufsatz von 1892 zu den »Drei Epochen der modernen Ästhetik« ein, sondern erwähnt ihn bereits 1883 lobend in der »Einleitung in die Geisteswissenschaften«:

> An der Grenze der Naturwissenschaften und der Psychologie hat sich ein Gebiet von Untersuchungen ausgesondert, welches von seinem ersten genialen Bearbeiter als Psychophysik bezeichnet worden ist und welches sich durch das Zusammenwirken hervorragender Forscher zu dem Entwurf einer physiologischen Psychologie erweitert hat. (Dilthey 1914, 1, 34ff.)

Über einen Schüler namens Preyer hatte Fechner eine vermittelnde Wirkung auf den jungen Simmel, wie Köhnke in seiner akribischen Arbeit zum jungen Simmel nachweist.[20] Simmel zitiert Fechner beispielsweise sowohl in seiner Dissertationsschrift wie in »Psychologische und ethnologische Studien über die Musik«.[21] Sigmund Freud lobt an Fechner, dass dieser sehr deutlich »die Wesensverschiedenheit von Traum- und Wachleben« (Freud 1988a, 199) betont habe und hebt dessen Verständnis von

---

[19] Vgl. Geier; Homann 1993.
[20] Vgl. Köhnke 1996, 239.
[21] Vgl. Simmel 2000.

ästhetisch als »bezüglich Empfindung und Wahrnehmung« hervor und charakterisiert ihn als einen »tiefblickenden Forscher« (Freud 1988b, 6f.).

Und schließlich bezieht sich Ernst Cassirer in der »Logik der Kulturwissenschaften« – erstmals 1942 in Göteborg publiziert – auf einen wichtigen Ansatz Fechners, um das spezifische Denken in den Kulturwissenschaften zu beschreiben. In dem Abschnitt seiner Logik, der von den unterschiedlichen *Wahrnehmungsweisen* in Natur- und Kulturwissenschaften handelt, wird die Verbindung zu Fechner deutlich: die Naturwissenschaften haben mit *Ding*wahrnehmung, die Kulturwissenschaften mit *Ausdrucks*wahrnehmung zu tun. Cassirer erwähnt dabei lobend Fechner, da dieser in der Bestimmung dieses Unterschieds Vorleistungen erbracht habe. Es sei

> äußerst lehrreich, die Methode zu verfolgen, deren Fechner sich hierbei bediente. Sie bestand in nichts anderem als darin, daß er von der Ausdruckswahrnehmung ausging und diese wieder in ihre vollen Rechte einsetzen wollte. Diese Art der Wahrnehmung kann nach Fechner nicht nur nicht trügen, sondern sie ist im Grunde das einzige Mittel, durch das wir uns aus dem Bannkreis abstrakten Denkens befreien und uns der Wirklichkeit nähern können. (Cassirer 1994, 47f.)

Von Cassirer führt eine direkte Linie zu unseren heutigen Forschungen. Ästhetik als Kulturwissenschaft, die einerseits davon ausgeht, dass ästhetische Theorien die jeweilige Kultur reflektieren, und andererseits auch gegenwärtige Kulturphänomene untersuchen will, bedarf sowohl des Herangehens ›von unten‹ wie ›von oben‹. Sie braucht empirische Untersuchungen, um zur Theoriebildung über moderne Phänomene zu kommen, und das schließt eine *Alltagsästhetik* ein.

Auch wir betreiben insofern ›Psychophysik‹ als wir Wahrnehmungsprozesse untersuchen. Das folgende Beispiel sei mir abschließend gestattet, um die Nähe zu Fechner zu verdeutlichen. Im Rahmen des Sonderforschungsbereiches: *Regionale Identifikationsprozesse.* Am Beispiel Sachsen werden *Sachsen-Bilder* und Bildvorstellungen untersucht. Es wird gefragt: Welche bildlichen Darstellungen sollen Sachsen repräsentieren? In welchem Verhältnis stehen diese Bilder zu den ihnen beigegebenen Bilderläuterungen? Und was lässt sich über Kontinuitäten oder Diskontinuitäten von ›Sachsen-Bildern‹ seit dem 19. Jahrhundert ausmachen?

Dazu wurde eine umfangreiche Datenbank von *Sachsen-Bildern* angelegt; wir wollten also zunächst wissen, was gefällt, denn es handelt sich um massenhaft produzierte und nachgefragte Bildwerke. Diese Bilder wurden quantifiziert, vermessen und nach Motiven und beigegebenen Erzählungen untersucht. Im Ergebnis haben wir eine bildliche Konstruktion der Region festgestellt, die sich von ihrer geographischen Beschaffenheit insofern unterscheidet, als es einen Kanon, d.h. eine bestimmte Anzahl von Motiven gibt, die in allen Bildbänden zu Sachsen immer wiederkehren. Ebenso gibt es eine bestimmte Anzahl von Motiven zur Sächsischen Schweiz, einem Gebiet, dem eine empirische Teilstudie gewidmet ist.

Der Blick auf die Motive verdeutlicht, dass *Sachsen* bildlich über seine Sehenswürdigkeiten repräsentiert wird: Zwinger, Schloss Moritzburg, Schloss Pillnitz und den Meißner Dom, und über typische Produkte, vor allem das Meißner Porzellan. Da wir es mit Wahrnehmung von Räumen und deren Darstellung zu tun haben, kann dieser Kanon mit Hilfe der *Wahrnehmungskategorien* Prägnanzbildung, Ästhetisierung und Visualisierung interpretiert werden. Hier zeigen sich Bezüge zu den Fechner'schen Prinzipien.

Die bildliche Definition der Region über bestimmte Motive ist ein Vorgang von *Prägnanzbildung;* durchaus vergleichbar mit Fechners Prinzip der *einheitlichen Verknüpfung des Mannigfaltigen* wie der *Klarheit*; denn es sind wenige prägnante Motive, über die die Wahrnehmung und Wiedererkennung des Konstruktes ›Region‹ geleistet wird. Prägnanzbildung zielt auf *Identifizierung* von Region. Oder mit Fechner gesagt: *was schön ist und insofern gefällt,* wird hier zunächst erfasst. Denn wenn es richtig ist, dass unsere Wahrnehmung mit Prägnanzen arbeitet und wir nur bestimmte Strukturen erfassen (müssen), um das ganze Bild zu erkennen oder es als erkennbares Bild wiederzugeben, dann liegt es nahe, dass die sinnlich-bildhafte Konstruktion eines nicht wahrnehmbaren Ganzen wie einer Region sich ebenfalls auf prägnante Strukturen beschränken muss. *Dass* eine Region bildlich über einen Kanon von Bildern bestimmt wird, ist also aus der Beschaffenheit unserer Wahrnehmung erklärbar. *Wie* sie durch diesen Kanon bestimmt wird und *welche* Bilder den Kanon ausmachen, erklärt sich zum einen über das wirkliche Vorhandensein prägnanter Objekte und zum anderen semantisch durch Vorstellungen von der Region und Erzählungen über sie, und durch bestimmte Zielstellungen in Bezug auf diese Region.

Der Kanon gibt auch Auskunft über *Visualisierungen*, und zwar weil nicht nur die tatsächlichen regionalen Gegebenheiten wie Landschaften, Schlösser, Burgen, Sehenswürdigkeiten usw. abgebildet, sondern auch jeweilige Vorstellungen von der Region ins Bild gebracht werden. Zum anderen stehen die häufigsten Motive des Kanons auch als Teil für ein Ganzes. Dass ein Teil für ein Ganzes stehen kann, ist *eine* Methode der Visualisierung.[22] Fechner reflektierte das Verhältnis von Teil und Ganzem im »Princip der ästhetischen Hülfe und Steigerung«. Sowohl beim Kanon wie bei den gängigen Motiven wird *Sachsen* als Ganzes oder Objektkomplex im wesentlichen über Einzeldinge (Zwinger) oder Einzelwesen (August der Starke) visualisiert, die in der Erinnerung bzw. im kulturellen Gedächtnis einen Wert für Sachsen darstellen.

Und schließlich gibt die bildliche Definition der Region auch über *Ästhetisierungen* Auskunft, die nun nicht mit dem *Dass* des Kanons, sondern mit seinem *Wie* verbunden ist. Es handelt sich um ganz bestimmte Bilder – im hohen Maße um schöne Landschaften, Schlösser und Burgen –, die vor allem im restaurierten Zustand als schöne Sehenswürdigkeiten präsentiert werden – so schön, wie sie es in ihrem historisch lebendigen Zustand wahrscheinlich nie waren. Der Kanon der *Sachsenbilder* repräsentiert so offensichtlich auch eine bestimmte Erzählung von Sachsen – die Erzählung von »Sachsens Glanz«.[23] Er arbeitet also auch hier mit dem »Assoziationsprinzip«. Für die Sächsische Schweiz wurde optisch wie semantisch eine andere Erzählung festgestellt – eine deutliche Romantisierung, resultierend aus ihrer Entdeckungsgeschichte.

Zurück zu Fechner: Mit diesem Exkurs zu unserer aktuellen Forschung[24] versuchte ich deutlich zu machen, dass sich einige der Anregungen von Fechner aus seiner ›Ästhetik von unten‹ und ›von oben‹ auch heute bestätigen, weniger im Detail als der Intention nach; und das macht ihn für uns, für die Kulturwissenschaften von heute, wertvoll.

Literatur:

Adorno, Th. W. (1990): Ästhetische Theorie. 10. Aufl. Frankfurt/M.

Allesch, Ch. G. (1987): Geschichte der psychologischen Ästhetik. Göttingen; Toronto; Zürich.

Baju, H. (1980): La littérature de demain (1891). In: Der Untergang der romantischen Sonne. Asthetische Texte von Baudelaire bis Mallarmé. Leipzig; Weimar 257–260.

---

[22] Siehe Gaede 1992, 104ff.

[23] Anspielung auf einen Titel eines Fernsehfilms in DDR-Produktion: »Sachsens Glanz und Preußens Gloria«, der die barocke Lebensführung am sächsischen Hof und die preußische militärische Tradition konfrontierte.

[24] Vgl. genauer Köhnke; Kösser 2001.

Barck, K. u.a. (Hg.) (1990): Aisthesis, Wahrnehmung heute oder Perspektiven einer anderen Ästhetik. Leipzig.

Barck,K.; Fontius, M.; Schlenstedt, D.; Steinwachs,B.; Wolfzettel, F. (Hg.) (2000): Ästhetische Grundbegriffe. Historisches Wörterbuch in sieben Bänden. Stuttgart; Weimar.

Bölsche, W. (1987): Die naturwissenschaftlichen Grundlagen der Poesie. Prologomena einer realistischen Ästhetik. In: Naturalismus. Manifeste und Dokumente zur deutschen Literatur (1880–1900). Hg. von M. Brauneck; Ch. Müller. Stuttgart, 98–113.

Büchner, L.(1855): Kraft und Stoff. Empirisch-naturphilosophische Studien. Frankfurt a.M.

Cassirer, E. (1994): Zur Logik der Kulturwissenschaften. Fünf Studien. Darmstadt.

Cramer, F. ; Kaempfer, W. (1992): Die Natur der Schönheit. Zur Dynamik der schönen Formen. Frankfurt a.M.; Leipzig.

Dilthey, W. (1910): Der Aufbau der geschichtlichen Welt in den Geisteswissenschaften. Berlin.

Dilthey, W. (1914): Einleitung in die Geisteswissenschaften. In: W. Dilthey, Gesammelte Schriften. Hg. von B. Groethuysen u.a. Bd. 1. Leipzig u.a. 9–29.

Dilthey, W. (1978): Die drei Epochen der modernen Ästhetik. In: W. Dilthey, Gesammelte Schriften. 6. Bd. 6. Aufl. Stuttgart, Göttingen, 242–284.

Fechner, G. Th. (1846): Ueber das höchste Gut. Leipzig.

Fechner, G. Th. (1870): Der Streit um die beiden Madonnen von Holbein. In: Grenzboten 29, 41–58,1.

Fechner, G. Th. (1871a): Ueber die Aechtheitsfrage der Holbein'schen Madonna. Leipzig.

Fechner, G. Th. (1871b): Zur experimentellen Aesthetik.Thl. 1. In: Abhandlungen der Kgl.-Sächs. Gesellschaft der Wissenschaften zu Leipzig, Math.-phys. Cl. Bd. 9. Leipzig, 553–635.

Fechner, G. Th. (1872): Bericht über das auf der Dresdener Holbein-Ausstellung ausgelegte Album. Leipzig.

Fechner, G. Th. (1897): Vorschule der Aesthetik. 1. Thl. 2. Aufl. Leipzig.

Ferry, L. (1990): Der Mensch als Ästhet. Die Erfindung des Geschmacks im Zeitalter der Demokratie. Stuttgart; Weimar.

Flusser, V. (1995): Schönheit im Diminutiv. In: Der Flusser-Reader zu Kommunikation. Medien und Design. Mannheim, 184–189.

Freud, S. (1988a): Vorlesungen zur Einführung in die Psychologie. In: Freud, Essays II 1915–1919. Hg. von D. Simon. Berlin, 121–402.

Freud, S. (1988b): Jenseits des Lustprinzips. In: Freud, Essays III 1920–1937. Hg. von D. Simon. Berlin, 5–73.

Gaede, W. (1992): Vom Wort zum Bild. Kreativ-Methoden der Visualisierung. 2. verb. Aufl. München.

Geier, W. Homann, H. (Hg.) (1993): Karl Lamprecht im Kontext. Ein Kolloquium. Leipzig.

Goldstein, E.B. (1997): Wahrnehmungspsychologie. Eine Einführung. Heidelberg; Berlin; Oxford.

Haeckel, E. (1919): Die Welträtsel. 11. Aufl. Leipzig.

Hartmann, E. v. (1886): Die deutsche Aesthetik seit Kant. Erster historisch-kritischer Theil der Aesthetik. Leipzig.

Heidelberger, M. (1993): Die innere Seite der Natur. Gustav Theodor Fechners wissenschaftlich-philosophische Weltauffassung. Frankfurt a.M.

Heller, A. (1996): Was ist mit dem Begriff des Schönen geschehen? In: Sinn und Form. Beiträge zur Literatur. Hg. v. d. Akademie der Künste. 3. H. Berlin, 333–348.

Holz, A. (1987): Die Kunst. Ihr Wesen und ihre Gesetze. In: Naturalismus. Manifeste und Dokumente zur deutschen Literatur (1880–1900). Hg. v. M. Brauneck und Ch. Müller. Stuttgart, 140–151.

Kant, I. (1793): Kritik der Urteilskraft. 2. Aufl. Thl. 1–2. Berlin.

Köhnke, K. Ch. (1996): Der junge Simmel in Theoriebeziehungen und sozialen Bewegungen. Frankfurt a.M.

Köhnke, K. Ch. (2000): Die Prägnanz von Bildvorstellungen. In: Dialektik. Zeitschrift für Kulturphilosophie, 91–103.

Köhnke, K. Ch.; Kösser, U. (2001): Prägnanzbildung und Ästhetisierung in Bildangeboten und Bildvorstellungen. Leipzig (Leipziger Studien zur Erforschung von regionenbezogenen Identifikationsprozessen).

Külpe, O. (1907): Der gegenwärtige Stand der experimentellen Ästhetik. In: Bericht über den II. Kongreß für experimentelle Psychologie in Würzburg vom 18. bis 21. April 1906. Hg. von F. Schumann. Leipzig, 1–57.

Lange, F.A. (1974): Geschichte des Materialismus und Kritik seiner Bedeutung in der Gegenwart. Hg. u. eingeleitet von A. Schmidt. 2 Bde. Frankfurt a.M.

Mach, E. (1917): Erkenntnis und Irrtum. Skizzen zur Psychologie der Forschung. 3. durchgesehene Aufl. Leipzig.

Rickert, H. (1899): Kulturwissenschaft und Naturwissenschaft. Ein Vortrag. Freiburg i.B.

Schröder, G. (1985): Logos und List. Zur Ästhetik in der frühen Neuzeit. Königstein.

Simmel, G. (2000): Gesamtausgabe. Hg. von O. Rammstedtr. Bd. 1. Hg. von K. Chr. Köhnke. Frankfurt a.M.

Welsch, W. (1990): Ästhetisches Denken. Stuttgart.

Welsch, W. (1992): Zwei Wege der Ästhetisierung. Saarbrücken.

Welsch, W. (1996): Ästhetik außerhalb der Ästhetik – Für eine neue Form der Disziplin. In: Welsch, Grenzgänge der Ästhetik. Stuttgart, 135–177.

Monika Ritzer

Bild und Sinn.
Fechners Ästhetik und ihre Rezeption im 19. Jahrhundert

Fechners Ästhetik galt bislang als Versuch zur Formulierung einer ästhetischen Erfahrungswissenschaft oder als Begleitprojekt zur Psychophysik. Demgegenüber entwickelt der Aufsatz ihre Position im historischen Spannungsfeld von subjektiven und objektiven Bestimmungen. Hervorgegangen aus dem persönlichen Bemühen, Gefühl und Gegenstandsbezug in der literarischen Wertung zu verbinden, und intendiert als Beitrag zur aktuellen Idealismus-Realismus-Debatte in der bildenden Kunst, erstellt Fechners *Vorschule* Kriterien zur Beurteilung der ästhetischen Synthese von sinnlicher Wahrnehmung und Bedeutungszuweisung, der wiederum ontologische Strukturen in seinem Wirklichkeitsbegriff entsprechen. Die Rezeption Fechners durch die jungen Naturalisten zeigt, wie sehr die in seiner Ästhetik angelegte Verbindung von ›Natur‹ und ›Geist‹ den Nerv der Epoche an der Wende zum 20. Jahrhundert traf.

In der Rezeption Fechners nimmt die Ästhetik, neben Psychologie und Philosophie, einen festen und zugleich sehr fixierten Platz ein. Es besteht Konsens darüber, dass die ›Ästhetik von Unten‹, die Fechner im ersten Kapitel seiner »Vorschule der Ästhetik« vorstellt und zum Programm erhebt, einen »Paradigmenwechsel« in der Geschichte der Disziplin eingeleitet habe. Mit der Wendung zum Messbaren ende die spekulative *Schönheitslehre* des Idealismus und es beginne die Ästhetik als ›Erfahrungswissenschaft‹; in den Handbüchern zu Ästhetik und Kunstphilosophie erhält Fechner daher stets ein entsprechendes Kapitel.[1] In der Regel beschränkt sich die Analyse der »Vorschule« aber auf diese wissenschaftsgeschichtlich relevante Kategorie, und dies nicht zuletzt deshalb, weil hier zugleich die Beziehung zu der in der Fechner-Rezeption noch immer dominanten *Psychophysik* deutlich wird. Weitgehend unbeachtet bleiben demgegenüber andere zentrale Aspekte seiner Ästhetik, wie die Theorie der Synthese von *Wahrnehmung* und Deutung oder das *Realis-*

[1] Siehe Schneider 1997, 126; vgl. auch den Fechner-Artikel von Ch. G. Allesch in: Nida-Rümelin; Betzler 1998, 266–269.

mustheorem. Gerade diese Aspekte können jedoch zum historischen Verständnis der »Vorschule« beitragen, sowohl was deren Position im kunsttheoretischen Diskurs der Zeit, als auch was den Rezeptionsprozess anbelangt. Darüber hinaus bieten jene Aspekte die Möglichkeit einer Verbindung zu Fechners Philosophie – jenem Synkretismus von naturphilosophischer Spekulation und positivistischer Naturwissenschaft, mit dem Fechner auf die bewusstseinsgeschichtlichen Bedingungen der postidealistischen Restaurationszeit reagierte und die, erweitert um neue Bereiche der Naturlehre (wie Astronomie und Atomistik), genau wie die Ästhetik am Ende des Jahrhunderts eine ungeahnte Renaissance erfuhr.

Die folgenden Überlegungen wollen daher über die psychologischen Momente hinaus zu einem zweiten Blick auf Fechners *Ästhetik* einladen, der ihren Eigenwert im Kontext der Zeitgeschichte erschließen soll. Dabei geht es zunächst um die Genese des *Kunstbegriffs* und seine aktuellen Bezüge, in einem zweiten Schritt dann um die Ansatzpunkte und Interessen der theoretischen wie künstlerischen, speziell literarischen Rezeption.

1. Zur Genese und Intention von Fechners Ästhetik

Fechners Interesse an den Künsten reicht in die 30er-Jahre zurück und galt zunächst, in den eigenen künstlerischen Versuchen wie in der kritischen Auseinandersetzung, der Literatur. 1835 veröffentlichte der (selbst im lyrischen Metier dilettierende) Naturwissenschaftler zwei *Essays* über moderne Poesie: »Friedrich Rückert« und »Heinrich Heine als Lyriker«. Beide Aufsätze sind unverkennbar emotionsgeladene Reaktionen auf die Lektüre der Gedichte. Sie zeigen den Rezensenten als sensiblen und im Wortsinn ›angeregten‹ Leser, der mit der ganzen Beweglichkeit seiner Vorstellungskraft auf die in den Werken gestalteten Gegenstände antwortet. »Mein Herz ist eine harte welsche Nuß, doch hat man die rechte Stelle getroffen, liegt der weiche Kern auf einmal offen«, heißt es in einem der formal anspruchslosen, im Gestus bekenntnishaften Gedichte Fechners[2] – und die Lyrik, auch Rückerts und Heines, findet offensichtlich diesen Zugang. Dabei fehlt es in Fechners Kritiken nicht an substantiellen Äußerungen zur künstlerischen Attitüde, zu Technik, Qualität und Aktualität

[2] Siehe Fechner: Herzensverse. Zugänglich über das *Projekt Gutenberg*: http://gutenberg.aol.de/fechner/gedichte/herzensv.htm.

des jeweiligen Werks. So stand für den Zeitgenossen Heines »Subjektivität« ebenso zur Debatte wie seine modische »Zerrissenheit«;[3] Rückerts formale Virtuosität wurde ebenso klar bezeichnet wie seine Grenzen an Aussagekraft und Originalität. (En passant reflektierte Fechner über die Möglichkeiten, die sich der Dichtung jenseits der lyrischen Konventionen mit einer gleichsam »flüssig gewordenen Sprache« eröffnen könnten.)[4] Insgesamt aber überwiegt der Reichtum an sinnlich opulent ausgestalteten Bildern und Vergleichen, die nicht nur die poetisch initiierten seelischen Erlebnisse, sondern gleichermaßen Begriffe und Urteile in anschauliche Szenerien umsetzen.[5] Mitunter gewinnen diese Szenerien so sehr an Eigendynamik, dass der Unterschied zwischen poetischer Fiktion und rezeptiver Phantasie verschwimmt. Gefühl, heißt es entsprechend in einem Fechner-Gedicht, sei ein »reg' Gewühl, ein wunderbares Leben, wo nichts sich scheiden will«.[6]

Fragt man nach dem dichtungstheoretischen Aspekt der Kritiken, dann zeigt sich, in der Rezeptionsweise wie im Kunstverständnis, eine für die Restaurationszeit nicht untypische Spannung zwischen Objekt und Subjektivität. »Der Gegenstand soll dem Subjekt Gestalt und sinnliche Kraft leihen«, heißt es im Heine-Essay, »und dafür Seele, Gefühl und Empfindung von ihm erhalten«. Sinnliche Gestalt und ›Seele‹ artikulieren sich gemeinsam im Gedicht, das in dieser Relation wiederum eine »lebendige Wirkung« auf das Gemüt des Lesers ausübt. Dichtung meint also eine emotional produktive und künstlerisch freie Gestaltung von gegenständlicher Wirklichkeit mit den Mitteln der Sprache – von ›Verrückung‹, anormaler ›Verknüpfung prosaischer Verhältnisse‹ ist in den Aufsätzen die Rede –, die Faktisches, im kreativen Prozess der Darstellung wie in der Aufnahme, in eine Welt der Empfindung, der »Gefühle und Bilder« über-

[3] Siehe Fechner 1835a; (http://gutenberg.aol.de/fechner/essays/Ohtmldir.htm).

[4] Siehe Fechner 1835b; (http://gutenberg.aol.de/fechner/essays/Ohtmldir.htm).

[5] Schillers Lyrik »erscheint wie ein kunstvoll gebautes Pantheon voll Götterstatuen, zu denen man erst voll heißer Anbetung tritt, aber zuletzt kühl hinausgeht«. Demgegenüber »tritt man in Goethes Lyrik wie unter einen klaren blauen Himmel, unter dem die menschlichen Originale dieser Götterstatuen lebendig wandeln«. Heines Lyrik gleicht »eine[r] Wetterwolke, halb von der Sonne prachtvoll vergoldet, halb blitzend und schwarz, von heulenden Stürmen gejagt, Gespenster und Engel, die sich wie aus einem Schiffbruche darauf zusammengefunden haben, zugleich tragend, und mit ihren Blitzen das Pantheon treffend [...] und die Anbeter hinaustreibend, die nun mindestens für einen Augenblick die Erscheinung des Göttlichen in dem lebendigen aber verderblichen Naturwunder zu erblicken glauben« (Dr. Mises 1835, 758).

[6] Siehe auch: (http://gutenberg.aol.de/fechner/gedichte/gefuehl.htm).

setzt.[7] Damit realisiert sich in der Kunst eine Verbindung von materiellem und ideellem Aspekt, wie sie dem Naturwissenschaftler Fechner in dieser zunehmend sachlicher werdenden Zeit bereits zum Problem geriet.

Nach dem werkbiographischen Einschnitt in den 40er-Jahren und nicht unbeeinflusst vom Szientismus der 50er- und 60er-Jahre ging Fechner an die wissenschaftliche Begründung jener ästhetischen Transformation von Objektivem in Subjektives. Nach eigenem Bekunden setzte seine Beschäftigung mit ästhetischen Fragen 1861 ein.[8] Die äußeren Umstände, die den Anlass zu den Fragestellungen gaben, sind gut dokumentiert.[9] 1858 wurde auf Betreiben des *Leipziger Kunstvereins* das Museum für bildende Künste am Augustusplatz eröffnet, dessen innenarchitektonische Ausstattung den kunstsinnigen Kreis der Vereinsmitglieder aus Verlegern, Kaufleuten und Professoren, darunter Fechner, ausgiebig beschäftigte. Dass sich die Diskussionen zunächst um die Wandfresken drehten, für die der konservativere Teil der Mitglieder mythologische Themen, der progressivere Teil eine Landschaftsdarstellung befürwortete,[10] verwundert nicht. Denn gerade über diese Frage nach dem Wirklichkeitsbezug der Kunst verlief die Auseinandersetzung zwischen den ›Idealisten‹ und den ›Realisten‹, die in den 40er-Jahren einsetzte und mit neuen Vorzeichen die 50er- und frühen 60er-Jahre bestimmte.

Schon im Jahr 1842 hatte der bekannte Ästhetiker Friedrich Theodor Vischer in seinen Betrachtungen zur zeitgenössischen Malerei eine »allgemeine Unsicherheit in der Wahl der Gegenstände« konstatiert, weil sich der Kunst, gewohnt an die akademische Tradierung von Sujets, nun erstmals »die nächste, unmittelbare Wirklichkeit« als Stoff darbot (Vischer 1975, 2, 19f.). Damit begann, in der Theorie wie in der Praxis, die Auseinandersetzung zwischen der »alten« Kunst und einer »neuen«, in der – so der Ästhetiker und Literaturtheoretiker Hermann Hettner 1846 – »das Reale« und ein »naturalistischer Stil« überwiege, ohne dass sie damit, wie zunächst von der Gegenseite kritisiert, in einen »platten Naturalismus« und das »mechanischen Copiren« von kontingenter Empirie abgleite (Hettner 1975, 2, 13). Diese Abgrenzung gegen einen künstlerischen Empirismus, wie er für die Frühphase des *Realismus* in der Restaurationszeit nicht untypisch war, gehört fortan zum Vokabular jeder inten-

[7] Siehe Dr. Mises 1835, 761.
[8] Siehe Fechner 1978, 2, 556.
[9] Siehe Arendt 1999, 169–202.
[10] Siehe Arendt 1999, 171.

tional realistischen Kunsttheorie; ein Reflex dessen findet sich auch in Fechners Ästhetik (s.u.).

Nach 1848 hatte sich die Situation zwischen den Kritikern und den Befürwortern der »neuen« *Kunst* zunächst etwas entspannt; die politische Ernüchterung führte auch in der Kunst zu einer neuen Distanz gegenüber geistigen Entwürfen. »Die Welt ist des Spekulierens müde«, schrieb Theodor Fontane 1853 in einem Essay, und verlange in allen Sparten der Kultur nach einem »Realismus«, wie er für Fontane ohnehin das Ferment aller Kunst bildete (Fontane 1979, 28, 38). Wenige Jahre später führte allerdings die von den Naturwissenschaften, speziell der Physiologie ausgehende weltanschauliche Provokation, die »Materialismus« zum vielzitierten Schlagwort machte, zu einer Neuauflage des Dilemmas. Von der verschärften »Differenz zweier extremer Richtungen« berichtete 1858 Max Schasler, der Herausgeber der »Dioskuren« (Hauptorgan der deutschen Kunstvereine), in seinem Artikel »Ueber Idealismus und Realismus in der Historienmalerei«. An Bildern von Schwind und Menzel suchte er zu demonstrieren, wie einerseits »der berechtigte Idealismus« der Kunst »zum abstrakten *Spiritualismus*«, andererseits »der berechtigte Realismus zum *Materialismus*« degeneriert sei. Die Zukunft der Kunst lag für Schasler in einer Vermittlung beider Tendenzen, wobei, wie er erklärte, die idealistische Komponente für die »Wahrheit«, die allgemeine Bedeutung der Darstellung, die realistische Komponente dagegen für ihre »*Natur*wahrheit«, den Wiedererkennungswert zu stehen habe (Schasler 1975, 2, 35). Diese Vorstellung der Vermittlung von Idee und Gegenständlichkeit entsprach den Konventionen der zeitgenössischen Ästhetik, wo sich diese nicht zu einem neuen Kunstbegriff durchrang.

Fechners *Ästhetik* findet zunächst im Kontext dieser Debatte ihren historischen Ort. Der Wissenschaftler – der im Streit um die Museumsfresken zunächst gegen die Mythen und für die Landschaft plädiert, sich dann aber der Mehrheit angeschlossen hatte – wollte jene leidige Streitfrage nach der künstlerischen Legitimität einzelner Gegenstände übergreifen. Mit den ihm zur Verfügung stehenden Mitteln suchte er vielmehr Aufschluss zu gewinnen über den Kunstcharakter der motivlich differierenden Darstellungen und begann mit wissenschaftlichen Untersuchungen zu ihrer spezifisch ästhetischen Wirkung. Für den Psychophysiker lag es ohnehin nahe, den Begriff des *Kunstschönen* vom Objekt abzulösen und über die Analyse des ästhetischen Urteilens, genauer: der sinnlich-geistigen Reaktion, zu bestimmen. Fechners Ansatzpunkt bildete dabei das »Gefallen«: Es besaß einen »objectiven Factor« in den »ursächlichen

Bedingungen der Lust« und zugleich einen »subjectiven Factor« in der Organisation des Rezipienten.[11]

Fechners erste Überlegungen zielten freilich noch auf reine Formverhältnisse und -gesetze. 1863 hielt er im *Kunstverein* einen Vortrag »Über das ästhetische Gesetz des Goldenen Schnitts«. 1864 begann er mit der Abhaltung von Ästhetik-Vorlesungen. 1865 gab ihm der Streit um die Echtheit zweier Holbein zugesprochenen *Madonnenbilder* und deren gemeinsame Präsentation in Dresden eine Möglichkeit zur empirischen Feldforschung: Durch Publikumsbefragung hoffte Fechner, die ästhetische Wirkung des echten Bildes nachzuweisen. 1871 erschien die Schrift »Zur experimentalen Ästhetik«, in der er erstmals seine neue ästhetische Theorie einer empirischen *Schönheitslehre* vorstellte. Es könne nur erwünscht sein, heißt es im Vorwort, wenn für ein Gebiet, das »sich bisher einer exacten Untersuchung zu entziehen schien«, weil es »fast blos eine Sache philosophischer Speculation und künstlerischer Aperçus« war, nun »Angriffspuncte« für eine »exakte Behandlung« durch »Experiment, Maß und Rechnung gefunden« würden (Fechner 1978, 2, 556f.). Gegenstand dieser Berechenbarkeit war die Lustempfindung, mit der ein Rezipient auf ästhetische Reize reagiert. Insofern war die *experimentelle Ästhetik*, wie Fechner schrieb, zunächst nur »ein Zweig der äusseren Psychophysik«. Für die »höhere Ästhetik« habe die Untersuchung der »Formwohlgefälligkeit« eine noch untergeordnete Bedeutung; doch verspreche die Fragestellung eine »fruchtbare Fortentwicklung« (Fechner 1978, 2, 557).

Diese Erweiterung präsentierte Fechner in seiner 1876 in zwei Bänden erschienenen »Vorschule der Ästhetik«. Der in Anlehnung an Jean Paul gewählte Titel bezeichnete zum einen den Systemverzicht des Projekts, das allgemein ästhetische Fragen nach dem »Schönen« ausklammerte, zum andern die Fundamentalität der Vorgehensweise. Wie in seinen anderen Schriften, etwa der »Atomenlehre«,[12] zog Fechner einen Trennungsstrich zwischen dem »philosophischen« und einem »empirischen« Zugang.[13] Dabei blieb zwar die Philosophie in ihrer Sinndimension das erklärte Ziel; um jedoch Apriorismus und Spekulation zu vermeiden, die

[11] Vgl. hierzu Fechner 1978, 1, 89 und 110.

[12] Siehe Fechner 1855.

[13] Fechner erwartet »eine philosophische Aesthetik höheren Stiles über der empirischen [...], wie es eine Naturphilosophie über der Physik und Physiologie geben kann« (Fechner 1978, 1, 4).

ihr Fechner – in der Tradition der restaurationszeitlichen Idealismuskritik[14] wie in Reaktion auf zeitgenössische Extensionen des Philosophiebegriff[15] – zuordnete, sollte sie eine positive Basis erhalten.

Das Resultat bildete Fechners programmatische Abgrenzung gegen die idealistisch-deduktive »Aesthetik von Oben«, die er ohne jede Unterscheidung Kant, Schelling und Hegel unterstellte. Nahmen diese ihren Anfang noch von »allgemeinsten Ideen und Begriffen« über das *Schöne* und die *Künste*, so ging nun die neue »Aesthetik von Unten« induktiv vor – im Zug der von John Stuart Mill entwickelten Wissenschaftstheorie[16] –, indem sie mit der Analyse der »irdisch-empirischen«, das heißt der elementar sinnlichen Bedingungen begann. Gegenstand waren die »ästhetischen Thatsachen und Gesetze« in den »Erfahrungen« dessen, »was gefällt und mißfällt« (Fechner 1978, 1, 1). Das Ergebnis bildeten »quantitative« Gesetze des ästhetischen Empfindens, wie das (aus der Psychophysik bekannte) Gesetz der *Schwelle*[17] oder das der *ästhetischen Hilfe*,[18] und »qualitative« Gesetze, die ideeller Art waren, wie die Registrierung von *Einheit in der Vielheit*[19] oder von Identität im Widerspruch.[20]

Diese selbstverständliche Expansion vom *Physischen* ins *Psychische* lässt erkennen, dass Fechners Interesse nicht allein auf die neurologischen Bedingungen der Lust gerichtet war. Wilhelm Bölsche stellte später fest, die »Vorschule« begänne eigentlich nicht ›unten‹, sondern ›in der Mitte‹, da die Naturwissenschaft nach Meinung Fechners gar keinen Aufschluss gebe über die Prinzipien der Empfindung. Das stimmt, und man sollte

---

14 Die Trennung zwischen Naturwissenschaft und Naturphilosophie (vgl. Anm. 13) impliziert einen spätidealistischen Philosophiebegriff, wie ihn bereits Lange 1876 an Fechner kritisierte. Vgl. Lange 1974, 2, 639.

15 Fechner unterzog in dieser Zeit Eduard von Hartmanns »Philosophie des Unbewußten« – die im Synkretismus von Positivismus und Spekulation seiner eigenen Position gefährlich nahe kam – einer eingehenden Kritik.

16 Siehe Mill 1868.

17 »Es ist [...] ein allgemeines, nicht blos für Empfindung von Lust und Unlust [...] gültiges Gesetz, dass zum Bewusstwerden derselben ein gewisser Grad dessen gehört, woran sie innerlich und äusserlich hängt [...]. Je nach Rücksicht auf die äusseren oder inneren Bedingungen des Gefallens oder Missfallens kann man von einer äußern oder innern Schwelle sprechen« (Fechner 1978, 1, 49).

18 »Aus dem widerspruchslosen Zusammentreffen von Lustbedingungen, die für sich wenig leisten, geht ein [...] oft viel grösseres Lustresultat hervor, [...] als dass es als Summe der Einzelwirkungen erklärt werden könne« (Fechner 1978, 1, 51).

19 Vgl. Fechner 1978, 1, 53–80.

20 Vgl. Fechner 1978, 1, 80–84.

dies nicht nur als Eingeständnis von vorläufigen, sondern auch von bewusst gezogenen Grenzen lesen. Schon im Blick auf die zeitgenössische Materialismus-Debatte der Physiologen, wohl aber auch in Hinsicht auf die philosophischen Anforderungen, die Fechner selbst an eine ›Vorschule der Ästhetik‹ stellte, wollte er sich auf eine bloße Empfindungsanalyse nicht beschränken. So verstand er *Lust* und *Unlust* nicht als rein neurologische Phänomene, sondern als »Mitbestimmungen«, als »Funktionen andrer Seelenbestimmungen«, deren Geltung entsprechend von einfachen, durch »sinnliche Eindrücke« erzeugten »Gefühlen« bis zu komplexen inneren Prozessen reicht (s. Fechner 1978, 1, 8).

In mehrfacher Weise greift die Ästhetik so »durch das niedere und höhere Gebiet zugleich durch« (Fechner 1978, 1, 37), um physische und ideelle Aspekte zu verbinden. Dazu gehört auch, dass ästhetische Empfindungen eine normative Komponente besitzen. Bereits auf der ersten Seite stellte Fechner fest, dass die ästhetische Reaktion auf »allgemeine Gesetze des Sollens« zu beziehen sei, »denen die des Gefallens immer untergeordnet bleiben« (Fechner 1978, 1, 1). In der Linie dieser Argumentation neutralisierte er dann konsequent alle deterministischen wie auch relativistischen Implikationen. Zwar führt die Frage, »warum gefällt oder mißfällt es«, zu einer ebenso strikten Gesetzmäßigkeit wie die Frage »warum bewegt sich ein Körper so und so« (Fechner 1978, 1, 5). Doch kommt dieser mechanistische Aspekt in der »Vorschule der Ästhetik« ebenso wenig zum Tragen wie das Problem der Relativität, das aus der Konkretisierung des Kunsterlebens folgt. Indem die ›Erfahrungswissenschaft‹ sich dem »Einzelnen« zuwendet, wird ja »das Schöne« zum »zeitlichen und örtlichen«, kulturell oder gar individuell bedingten Phänomen. Diese für die Rezeption der »Vorschule« im Naturalismus wichtige Relativierung des *Kunstbegriffs* – die Fechner mit Positivisten wie Hippolyte Taine verband[21] – wurde zwar benannt, letztlich aber aufgehoben im Begriff einer allgemeinen psychologischen Organisation. Die gleiche ideelle Aufwertung erfuhren die Bedingungen der ästhetischen ›Lust‹. So entdeckte Fechner als anthropologische Basis dieser scheinbar hedonistischen Reaktion eine therapeutische »Heilsamkeit«, die er ebenso wenig rein physisch verstand wie das Glücksstreben (das die Lust des Betrachters auf Kunst motiviert) und daher weder biologistisch noch vitalistisch begründet wissen wollte.[22]

---

[21] Siehe Taine 1987, 32f.

[22] »Manche suchen [...] den Grund der Lust darin, dass Alles, was unsere Kraft vermehrt,

Der Wille zur Synthese von physischen und psychischen Reaktionsformen prägt Fechners »Vorschule« auch und gerade dort, wo es um mentale Reaktionen geht und die Ästhetik damit für die Literatur relevant wird.[23] Mentales kommt nun dadurch ins Spiel, dass sich zur »directen« (sinnlichen) *Wahrnehmung* ein »associirter« (seelisch-geistiger) Eindruck gesellt, der dem Gegenstand »Bedeutung« verleiht.[24] Man könnte von einer semantischen Qualifizierung sprechen, die das visuell oder akustisch Wahrgenommene zunächst in rein sachlicher Weise identifiziert (›dieser gelbe Kreis ist eine Orange‹/›das Lautbild ORANGE meint Orange‹) und insofern ein primär lebensweltlich geschultes »Verstehen« voraussetzt. Dazu kommt nun die für Fechner eigentliche Bedeutungszuweisung durch *Assoziation* (Südfrucht = Italien), die sich aus dem persönlichen wie kulturell vermittelten »Umgang« mit derartigen Gegenständen speist. Er beschrieb die so assoziierten »Vorstellungen« als »Resultante« (Fechner 1978, 1, 113) aus Erfahrung, (unbewusster)[25] Erinnerung und kultureller Tradition,[26] die auf charakterlichen, anthropologischen und sozialen Faktoren basiert und daher typologisch geprägt ist. In erkenntnistheoretischer Hinsicht bestimmte Fechner den Komplex aus Wahrnehmung und Assoziation als eine Interaktion von objektiver Gegebenheit und subjektiver Reaktion,[27] der eine Projektion oder »Abspiegelung un-

---

unseren Lebensprocess erhöht, [...] Lust gibt«. Fechner distanziert sich von dieser Erklärung, indem er Lust und Unlust nicht als quantitative, sondern als qualitative Bestimmungen versteht (Fechner 1978, 2, 265 und 266).

[23] Fechner bezog die ›Poesie‹ zunächst nur über die lustvolle Wirkung der rhythmisch-metrischen Form in seine Untersuchungen ein.

[24] »Direct« ist der »Eindruck eines Gegenstandes, insofern er subjectiverseits von der angeborenen oder [...] durch Uebung im Verkehr mit Gegenständen gleicher Art entwikkelten [...] innern Einrichtung abhängt, associativ, insofern er von einer Einrichtung abhängt, die dadurch entstanden ist, dass sich der Gegenstand wiederholt in Verbindung und Beziehung mit gegebenen Gegenständen anderer Art dargeboten hat« (Fechner 1978, 1, 121).

[25] »Es ist überall der ins Unbewusstsein gesunkene [...] Nachklang dessen, was je im Bewußtsein war, und durch [...] äussere oder innere Anlässe, in dieser oder jener Combination, wieder ins Bewußtsein treten kann.« Fechner spricht von einem bewusstseinskorrelierten »Unterbewußtsein« im Unterschied zu Hartmanns metaphysischer »Ur-Unterbewusstheit« (Fechner 1978, 1, 113).

[26] »Jedes Ding, mit dem wir umgehen, ist für uns geistig charakterisirt durch eine Resultante von Erinnerungen Alles, was wir je bezüglich dieses Dinges und selbst verwandter Dinge äusserlich und innerlich erfahren, gehört, gelesen, gedacht, gelernt haben« (Fechner 1978, 1, 93).

[27] »Jeder directe wie associative Eindruck hängt zugleich ab von der Beschaffenheit des

seres eigenen Wesens und Thuns« (Fechner 1978, 1, 109) vorausgeht. Theodor Lipps hat diesen ästhetischen Prozess dann präziser als »Einfühlung« definiert und beschrieben.[28]

In solch »einfühlender« *Wahrnehmung* und *Gestaltung* gründete für Fechner die bildende Kunst wie auch die Poesie. Der Künstler aktiviert und optimiert den Bedeutungsaspekt der gegenständlichen Welt, indem er die in ihr vorhandenen »Anknüpfungspuncte der Associationen« durch künstlerische Mittel (wie die Komposition der Gegenstände oder die Multimedialität der Darstellung) intensiviert, und erzielt dadurch eine ›lustvollere‹, also ästhetische Auffassung von Wirklichkeit. Diese Bestimmung liefert zugleich die Voraussetzungen für den Übergang zum zweiten Hauptteil der Ästhetik, der Fechners eigene Stellungnahme im aktuellen Streit um Idealismus und Realismus, sowie im ›Vorzugsstreit zwischen Kunst und Natur‹ enthält.

Fechners kunsttheoretische Prämisse ist explizit realistisch: *Kunst*, lautete sein Grundsatz, hat prinzipiell Natur zum Gegenstand. An einigen wenigen Beispielen aus der Kunstgeschichte wies er nach, dass die »Nachahmung der Natur«, also die »naturalistische oder realistische« Auffassung, von jeher die Grundintention der Kunst gebildet habe und somit die ursprüngliche sei (Fechner 1978, 2, 37ff.). Verbunden damit war eine klare Absage an jede idealistische Forderung nach Transzendierung der Wirklichkeit, die Fechner gleichwohl beim Publikum wie bei den Fachkollegen noch immer überwiegend vertreten sah.[29]

Fechners Bekenntnis zur ›realistischen Auffassung‹ bedeutet freilich nicht, dass das Kunstwerk sachlich oder formal zur Darstellung der realen Dinge verpflichtet wäre. Der »Realist«, der nichts als eine solche ›Abspiegelung‹ intendiert, vergisst vielmehr die ästhetische Funktion gegen-

---

Gegenstandes [...] und der innern (physisch-psychischen) Einrichtung des Individuum, auf welches der Eindruck gemacht wird, kurz von einem objectiven und subjectiven Factor« (Fechner 1978, 1, 121).

[28] Schönheit »ist nicht eine Eigenschaft des Objektes«, sondern dies, »daß in dem Objekt ein Akt der ästhetischen Wertung begründet liegt.« Impuls der Wertung ist die formale Angemessenheit des Objekts an die Natur des ästhetisch wertenden Subjektes, die dieses in (lustvolle) Tätigkeit setzt. Der »Inhalt« kommt durch die »Einfühlung« des erlebenden Subjekts in die Objekte hinein; »was ich in der Außenwelt finde, ist nur einfach tatsächliches Dasein und Geschehen« (Lipps 1907; 1; 349f., 355, 357).

[29] »Was habe der Mensch davon, die gemeine Wirklichkeit durch die Kunst noch einmal wiedergegeben zu sehen; vielmehr gelte es, von den Dingen der Wirklichkeit zum Ideal derselben aufzusteigen [...]. In diesem Übersteigen der Natur durch die geistige Thätigkeit des Künstlers [...] liege die Aufgabe der Kunst« (Fechner 1978, 2, 38f.).

ständlicher Darstellung und unterbindet damit den Genuss, der gerade aus der Gestaltung von Wirklichkeit resultiert. Beides, Gegenständlichkeit und Gestaltung, sind gleich wichtige Momente der Rezeption. Kunst ›weicht‹ als solche, nicht nur »wegen der Unzulänglichkeit ihrer Mittel«, von der »Naturwahrheit« ›ab‹. Aber sie bezieht sich stets formend auf Wirklichkeit, und diese Bezugnahme bleibt konstitutiv für ihre ästhetische Wirkung. Denn der Rezipient hat ein ureigen menschliches Vergnügen an der Nachahmung als einer Aneignung von Wirklichkeit. Er sucht in der Kunst das Bild seiner Welt, und er ›genießt‹ das künstlerische Bild, weil es ihm diese Welt ›schön‹, das heißt sensuell fasslich, intellektuell geordnet, emotional bedeutungsvoll oder ideell werthaft präsentiert. Visuelle Verschönerung oder moralische Aufwertung sind damit nicht gemeint; es geht einzig um Aktivierung und Intensivierung des real vorhandenen Bedeutungspotentials. Die Verfahrensweisen, durch die der Künstler die konkrete Wirklichkeit zum ›abweichenden‹ Bild formt – Stilisierung, Idealisierung und Symbolisierung –, bringen durch Auswahl, Konzentration oder Repräsentativität diese autochthone Bedeutung der Realität zur Darstellung.[30]

Indem Fechner so durch seine ›Abweichungstheorie‹ die Bedingungen des künstlerischen Wirklichkeitsverhältnisses festlegte, fand er eine Möglichkeit zur Vermittlung der Extrempositionen, ohne dabei in die Vagheit der gängigen Redeweisen (»das ideale und reale Element sollten sich im Gleichgewicht durchdringen«) zu verfallen. Jene Theorie legitimierte nämlich einerseits die künstlerische Gestaltung: Fechner gestand dieser formal wie gegenständlich weitgehende Freiheiten zu, solange sie »im Sinn der Natur« und nicht gegen sie agiert (Fechner 1978, 2, 57).[31] Andererseits wurde dadurch die Priorität der Wirklichkeit für die Kunst bestätigt, die Fechner stets gegen den zeitgenössischen *Kunstbegriff* zur Gel-

---

30 »Die Natur bietet uns Vieles, was durch [...] ideelle Beziehungen [...] verknüpft ist, so in Zeit und Raum auseinanderliegend oder [...] durch Zufälligkeiten und Nebendinge gestört dar, dass diese Beziehungen sich in der Anschauung nicht leicht [...] geltend machen können. Insofern es aber [...] einen Werth für die Menschen haben kann, sich dieser Beziehung der Wirklichkeit geistig zu bemächtigen, kann die Kunst dadurch, dass sie die Gegenstände der Wirklichkeit [...] zusammenzieht, von Hindernissen der Anschauung, störenden Zufälligkeiten, unwesentlichen Nebendingen [...] frei darbietet, jenem Bedürfnisse entgegenkommen« (Fechner 1978, 2, 56).

31 Der Künstler darf mit mythologischen oder religiösen Objekten arbeiten, wenn es die künstlerische Aussage verlangt; er hat sie aber »in den Formen und nach den Bedingungen der Wirklichkeit darzustellen« (Fechner 1978, 2, 40).

tung brachte. Kunst sollte prinzipiell »aus der natürlichen Welt herauswachsen« – die für Fechner eben schon Form und Bedeutung enthielt[32] –, und sie sollte, durch allseitige Teilnahme an den Interessen der Welt, auch wieder »in sie zurückzugreifen« (Fechner 1978, 2, 153). Jede Forderung nach Autonomie der Kunst lehnte Fechner strikt ab.[33]

2. Die Renaissance der ›Vorschule‹ im Naturalismus

Wenn Fechners »Vorschule der Ästhetik« in ihrer Zeit nicht die erhoffte Resonanz fand, so hatte dies verschiedene Gründe. Es lag an der Heterogenität der teils modern ›exakten‹, teils mit konventionellen Begriffen argumentierenden Untersuchung – aber auch daran, dass der erzielte Kompromiss, obgleich er manches auf den Punkt brachte, keine besondere historische Brisanz besaß. Das Bekenntnis zur Priorität der Wirklichkeit entsprach der künstlerischen Doktrin des *Realismus*, wie er sich zumindest in der Literaturtheorie seit den 50er-Jahren etabliert hatte. Das gleiche gilt von der Bestimmung der realistischen Gestaltung als ideeller ›Klärung‹ der realen Verhältnisse; »Läuterung« nannte es Theodor Fontane 1853, um, wie Fechner, die so erzielte Wahrheit des künstlerischen Bildes zu betonen (Fontane 1979, 28, 43).

Dazu kam, dass sich von der anderen Seite her bereits eine erneute *Rückbesinnung* auf das autonom Künstlerische abzuzeichnen begann, die nicht mehr, wie im *Idealismus*, auf das ideelle Moment rekurrierte, sondern auf das formale. Es ist kein Zufall, daß 1876, im gleichen Jahr wie die »Vorschule«, in Leipzig die Schrift von Conrad Fiedler »Über die Beurteilung von Werken der bildenden Kunst« erschien. Fiedler, Jurist und Kunstmäzen, plädierte für ein neues Kunstverständnis und wandte sich dabei explizit nicht nur gegen die Gehaltsästhetik des Idealismus, sondern auch gegen die psychologische Ästhetik, weil, so Fiedler, Kategorien wie »Lust und Unlust«, »Geschmack« oder »Genuß« nicht zum Ei-

---

32 Alle je durch Gedichte erweckten Gefühle sind »Abklänge derer, welche das Leben [...] zu erwecken vermag«. Freilich verlernen wir »zwischen unsern Geschäften, [...] Akten, Dampfmaschinen«, daß es auch eine ›Poesie des Lebens‹ gibt. Wir »glauben, Poesie sei nur in den Büchern [...] von Göthe, Schiller, Uhland, Heine; doch haben auch diese aus der Poesie des Lebens geschöpft« (Fechner 1978, 2, 150).

33 »Je mehr die Kunst sich vom übrigen Leben ablöst, desto mehr verliert sie von natürlichen Stützen und geräth in Gefahr, [...] in ihren eigenen Interessen zu versumpfen« (Fechner 1978, 2, 155).

genwert des Kunstwerks führten (Fiedler 1977, 28f.). Fechner setzte sich mit Fiedlers Schrift in einem Zusatz auseinander, fand darin aber nichts wesentlich Neues und diagnostizierte eine bloße Neuauflage des Streits zwischen Inhalts- und Formästhetik.

Wenige Monate vor Fechners Tod wurde dann allerdings eine junge Künstlergeneration auf die »Vorschule der Ästhetik« aufmerksam, weil diese ihren nun progressiv verstandenen realistischen Interessen entgegenkam. 1887 veröffentliche der 26-jährige Wilhelm Bölsche einen durch Friedrich Theodor Vischers Tod veranlassten Artikel über »Vischer und Fechner als Ästhetiker«, der das Interesse der jungen naturalistischen Dichter – die sich selbst als ›konsequente Realisten‹ bezeichneten – auf Fechners Werk lenkte. Bölsche, Literat und Publizist, war seit seiner Schulzeit am naturwissenschaftlichen Weltbild interessiert und hatte eben, von einem einjährigen Aufenthalt in Paris zurückgekehrt, seine Programmschrift »Die naturwissenschaftlichen Grundlagen der Poesie. Prolegomena zu einer realistischen Ästhetik« (1887) veröffentlicht, die er in Berlin in dem avantgardistischen Verein ›Durch‹ zur Diskussion stellte. Wenig später bildete Bölsche mit Bruno Wille – der Fechner später als Figur in einem seiner Romane auftreten ließ – und den Brüdern Hart den *Friedrichshagener Literatenkreis*.

Bölsche nannte seine Ästhetik »realistisch«, weil sie, »unserem gegenwärtigen Denken entsprechend«, nicht ›metaphysisch‹, sondern vom Standpunkt »vorurtheilsfreier Forschung« vorgehe (Bölsche 1976, 1). Vorbild war Émile Zola, dessen naturwissenschaftlich geschulte Charakterologie wie experimentell-analytische Methode er der modernen Literatur empfahl.[34] Was Bölsche von Zola trennte, war der optimistische Grundzug, den die deutschen *Naturalisten* im Prinzip mit den *Realisten* der Jahrhundertmitte, wie etwa Gottfried Keller, teilten – den sie nun aber mit ihrem verschärft szientistischen Weltbild vereinen und gegen ein dezidiert naturwissenschaftliches Weltverständnis verteidigen mussten. Bei expliziter Beschränkung auf das naturgesetzlich bestimmte Dasein bekannte sich Bölsche zu einer potentiellen Harmonie, die er in den ideellen Strukturen des realen Geschehens begründete: »Wir haben gebrochen mit der Metaphysik«, den »Kinderträumen von Willensfreiheit« und »Unsterblichkeit der Seelen«; aber »das Ideale geben wir damit doch nicht auf«. Der Mensch ziehe es aus allem, »was er sieht« und was sich ihm in Natur und Geschichte darbiete; allenthalben erkenne er Ord-

---

[34] Siehe Bölsche 1976, 20.

nungsformen (»Gleichmaß«, »Zustand des Normalen«), denen die Prozesse der Natur, im Geistigen wie im Materiellen, notwendig zustrebten (Bölsche 1976, 49).

Komponenten dieser Weltanschauung, vor allem die Hypostasierung der Naturgesetzmäßigkeit zum Prinzip universaler Ordnung, hätte Bölsche durchaus bei Fechner finden können. In der 1873 veröffentlichten Schrift »Einige Ideen zur Schöpfungs- und Entwicklungsgeschichte der Organismen«, in der Fechner Darwins Deszendenztheorie und Haeckels biogenetisches Grundgesetz mit der eigenen Lehre abglich, wies er den Prozessen der organischen Natur Richtung und Sinn durch das »Princip der Tendenz zur Stabilität« zu.[35] Doch war dies nur einer von vielen zeittypischen Versuchen, den wissenschaftlich begriffenen Lebensphänomenen ontologische Sinnprinzipien zuzuordnen. Wahrscheinlich hatte Bölsche die *Naturphilosophie* Fechners damals noch nicht zur Kenntnis genommen; eher kam Haeckel in Frage, den er auch erwähnt. Die Entdekkung Fechners verlief wohl tatsächlich über die Ästhetik, die, wie wir sahen, eine ganz ähnlich geartete Verbindung von Phänomen und Sinnstiftung anbot.

In Bölsches Essay von 1887 erscheint Fechner zunächst als willkommener Antipode zu dem eben verstorbenen Hegelianer Vischer. »Die Ästhetik, wie sie Vischer zurückläßt, ist eine mächtig aufstrebende Wissenschaft«, schrieb Bölsche, und die »besten Materialien« habe Fechner geliefert.[36] Sein *Stil* sei etwas altertümlich, aber er denke »frisch und modern«, schon indem er mit seiner »Vorschule« kein System mehr anpeile, sondern nur Prolegomena liefere. Vor allem sei Fechner »Naturforscher« – darin liege der »Kernpunkt«. Statt »mit metaphysischen Dingen« anzufangen, knüpfe seine »Aesthetik ›von unten‹ [...] an die einfachen, naturwissenschaftlichen Gesetze des Empfindens von Lust und Unlust an«. Zwar werde enttäuscht, wer »Orakel« erhoffe; denn der Forscher nehme sich nur Einfachstes vor, wie das Gesetz der *ästhetischen Schwelle*. Einen Kritikpunkt bilde auch, dass die der modernen Biologie gemäße »genetische Methode« zu schwach ausgeprägt sei. Gleichwohl liege »ein grandioser Fortschritt für die Aesthetik« in der Konstatierung solch fundamentaler *Gesetze* für die Lust- und Unlusterzeugung.

Bezeichnend für die Rezeption der »Vorschule« im Naturalismus ist nun aber, dass der so szientistisch gesonnene junge Bölsche nicht nur

---

[35] Vgl. hierzu Fechner 1978, 2, 268.
[36] Siehe Bölsche 1887, 215–217.

Fechners Wissenschaftlichkeit hervorhob, sondern zugleich dessen ästhetische Synthese von faktischer Wahrnehmung und geistiger Deutung. So würdigte er gerade das *Assoziationsprinzip* als den »Höhepunkt des ganzen, reichen Buches«, weil es den Beweis für die »Vergeistigung« des primär physikalisch bedingten Sinnenbildes liefere. Fechners Ästhetik markiere so nicht nur den zeitgemäßen »Wendepunkt vom Geiste zur Natur«, sondern verhelfe auch – wie nun offensichtlich wieder gefordert – »dem Geiste zu seinem Rechte« (Bölsche 1887, 217). Man betrete »gleichsam einen neuen, festen Boden«, der, gleich weit entfernt vom »leeren Himmel der Speculation« wie von den »Klüften der Verknüpfung von Geist und Mechanismus«, in einer »ruhigen, durchsichtigen Mitte« liege (Bölsche 1887, 216). Später wird Bölsche, als Essayist wie als Herausgeber, Fechners philosophische Schriften gerade wegen dieser Vermittlungsfunktion propagieren, die er offensichtlich zunächst an der Ästhetik erkennt.

Wie bei Bölsche richtete sich das Interesse der anderen jungen Naturalisten in der ersten Phase der Fechner-Rezeption zunächst freilich auf den erklärten *Empirismus* und den Gestus wissenschaftlicher Exaktheit. »Die Ästhetik befindet sich seit einigen Jahren in einem außerordentlichen Umgestaltungsprozeß«, schrieb Julius Hart in einem Beitrag des »Kritischen Jahrbuchs« von 1889. Die »gewaltigen Entdeckungen auf naturwissenschaftlichem Gebiete«, die »fortschreitende Erweiterung unserer Weltkenntnis« und nicht zuletzt die »Umgestaltung unsrer Weltanschauung« lenkten sie auf neue Bahnen. Noch schwanke sie in der Zielsetzung, doch wäre die generelle Richtung klar. Mit Bestimmtheit lasse sich feststellen, dass »die ältere, spekulative und systematische Ästhetik«, wie sie Hegel, Vischer und Carrière vertreten, zusammenbreche. Dafür komme Fechner zu Ehren, »der schon vor langem die Wissenschaft der Kunst auf die Erfahrung gründen wollte«. Statt nebulöser Begriffe des Schönen verspreche die *neue Ästhetik* als Erfahrungswissenschaft ein »echtes und allgemeineres Kunstverständnis«, das zweifellos zur Erkenntnis »von ganz festen Kunstgesetzen«, sowohl des Geschmacks wie des Kunstschaffens, gelangen werde. Da diese Gesetze als natürliche »auf unumstößlicher Wahrheit beruhen«, hätten sie nichts zu tun mit externem »Regelzwang«; sie würden das künstlerische »Genie« daher nicht »einschnüren«, sondern seine »freie Entfaltung als erste Notwendigkeit fordern«. Im Endeffekt werde »eine wahrhaft empirische Poetik« ebenso zu positivem Wissen von *Kunst* führen, »wie die Naturforschung über die Naturphilosophie zu einer Naturerkenntnis emporgewachsen ist« (s. Hart 1889, 29–30).

Eine ähnliche Würdigung erfuhr Fechners *Ästhetik* in den »Zwölf Artikeln des Realismus«, die Conrad Alberti 1889 mit dem Untertitel »Ein litterarisches Glaubensbekenntnis« veröffentlichte. Begeistert begrüßte Alberti schon den grundsätzlichen Wechsel vom Gegenstand zum Subjekt der künstlerischen Wahrnehmung. Ästhetik meine nun nicht mehr ›Wissenschaft vom Schönen‹, sondern Analyse der »Empfindungen« (Meyer 1973, 153); ›schön‹ sei die Reaktion einer Person auf einen gegebenen Gegenstand.[37] Damit adaptiere die Ästhetik ein »induktives« Verfahren, wie es schon der genetische Aspekt der Kunst fordere. *Kunst*, schrieb Alberti in seinem ersten Artikel, sei »ein natürliches und notwendiges Erzeugnis« der mentalen Organisation des Menschen und seiner kulturellen Bedürfnisse. »Ursprünglich [...] zur Erfüllung realer Zwecke geschaffen«, werde sie im Progress der menschheitsgeschichtlichen Entwicklung zu einem »Teil der menschlichen Kultur« und sei damit dem Gesetz der »organischen Fortentwicklung« unterworfen. Wenn sich Kunst aber mit der Zeit und dem Kulturkreis, dem sie angehöre, verändere, so gebe es keine überzeitliche Kunstlehre mit allgemeingültigen Begriffen, Regeln und Wertkriterien (Alberti 1987, 49). »Irreführend« nannte Alberti daher die Methode der prä-realistischen Ästhetik, Kunst mit Schönheit zu identifizieren und von einer Idee des Schönen auszugehen, die man als »etwas Unveränderliches, ewig Feststehendes, Absolutes« voraussetzte (s. Brauneck, Müller 1987, 155). Die »neue Ästhetik« arbeite empirisch und vermeide so diesen Fehler. Alberti sah hierin zugleich eine Chance zur naturgesetzlichen Durchdringung der Ästhetik. Es stand für ihn zu erwarten, dass die *Kunst* sich allen aus der Biologie wie der Physik bekannten *Gesetzen* zugeordnet zeigen würde: Kampf ums Dasein und natürliche Auslese, Konstanz der Materie und Gesetz des kleinsten Kraftmaßes etc. Prinzipiell waren für Alberti *ästhetische Gesetze* nur als Anwendung allgemeiner Naturgesetze auf die Bedingungen der Kunst denkbar.

Dass diese Verwissenschaftlichung der Kunst nicht zum *Determinismus* führte, hatte mit der spiritualistischen Komponente des naturalistischen Naturbegriffs zu tun, die sich bei Alberti ebenso fand wie bei den Harts oder Bölsche. Die *Naturgesetze* bildeten für Alberti Erscheinungs-

[37] »Gegenstand und Empfindung sind tatsächlich voneinander untrennbar. Die Schönheitsempfindung setzt einen realen Gegenstand voraus, an dem sie haftet, und eine Person, die sie wirklich hat – die alte Ästhetik aber kennt weder die Mannigfaltigkeit der empfindenden Naturen noch die Mannigfaltigkeit der Gegenstände, welche Empfindungen hervorrufen« (Alberti 1973, 154).

formen einer höheren Vernunft, die der »unbewußt schaffenden, aus sich selbst fortentwickelnden Natur« quasi als »göttlicher Hauch« immanent war (Brauneck; Müller 1987, 51). Da Kunst prinzipiell Natur darstellt – dieses Theorem der Fechner'schen Ästhetik wurde im Naturalismus radikalisiert[38] –, macht sie jenes ideelle ›Naturgesetz‹ (das »natürliche Gesetz, der Geist, der [den Stoff] beseelt«) (Brauneck; Müller, 1987, 54) anschaulich. Diesen weltanschaulichen Synkretismus hatten die Naturalisten, wie gesagt, mit Fechner gemein; aber er entstammte kaum einer unmittelbaren Lektüre. Wie sehr sich Alberti dabei im Einklang mit den bewusstseinsgeschichtlichen Tendenzen seiner Zeit zu wissen glaubte, zeigt seine universalisierende Gesamtschau. So plante er, »die Fundamente einer induktiven Kunstlehre« zu errichten »unter Benutzung der neuesten Studien Hartmanns, der verstorbenen Fechner, Scherer und Anderer, auf dem Grunde der darwinistischen Weltanschauung« (Brauneck; Müller 1987, 55).

Dass man gleichwohl gezielt auf zentrale Aspekte der Fechner'schen Ästhetik, wie das *Assoziationsprinzip*, zurückgriff, zeigt der Essay Bölsches von 1890 »Die Poesie der Großstadt«. Der Autor ging darin von dem Vorurteil aus, dass eine moderne Großstadt wie Berlin »baar aller Poesie« sei. In der Tat wären der »wilde Strudel« in den verkehrdurchwogten Straßen, die Nervosität, das auch den Dichter erfassende »große Rad der Lohnarbeit« keine poetischen Motive; erhebe man sie zum »Stimmungsgehalt«, so entstünden nur schlechte Romane. Suche man andererseits die Poesie der Großstadt mit den romantischen Augen Eichendorffs, dann werde nur der Mangel spürbar und es bleibe Melancholie. Demgegenüber entwarf Bölsche nun aber eine andere Sicht der Dinge, die Realbild und poetische Qualität verbinden sollte. Denke man nämlich beim Blick auf die moderne Großstadt zugleich an die damit verbundene »Großtat der menschlichen Kultur«, assoziiere man also »das *Motiv der Größe,* der Erhabenheit, der überwältigenden Herrlichkeit«, dann empfände man die Kulisse Berlins, obwohl sie dem traditionellen Schönheitsideal weniger entspräche als die Roms oder Paris', dennoch als »groß, erhaben schön«. Bölsche fügte erläuternd hinzu, dass dieses »Assoziative«, das die konkrete Wahrnehmung durch den »Gedanken an den

---

[38] Während Fechner noch mythologische Darstellungen (in natürlicher Gestalt) zum Zweck der künstlerischen Aussage zuließ, akzeptieren die Naturalisten dies nicht. Alberti: »Wir halten Engel nicht mehr für wirklich, also dürfen wir sie nicht darstellen« (Brauneck; Müller 1987, 53).

idealen Gehalt und Zweck« ästhetisch anreichere, »seit Fechner in der vernünftigen Ästhetik anerkannt« sei.[39] Die über das einzelne Beispiel hinausführende kunsttheoretische Intention wird deutlich, wenn Bölsche das *Assoziationsprinzip* an anderer Stelle zur Schlichtung des zeitgenössischen »Kampfes zwischen Idealismus und Realismus« heranzieht. So geselle sich, wie es in einem Aufsatz heißt, jedem realistisch gezeichneten »Lebensbild« ein (geistiges) Idealbild zu, das »durch eine Art Reaktion im *Hörer*« erzeugt werde.[40] Unverkennbar geht es hier darum, im dezidierten Rückgriff auf Fechners Ästhetik den Realismus der modernen Kunst zu propagieren – ohne sich in die Niederungen des physisch-materiellen Aspekts zu verlieren, gegen den auch die Naturalisten zunehmend allergisch wurden.

Mit dem Ende der programmatischen Phase änderte sich auch die Haltung zu Fechner. Auf der einen Seite findet man dann einen Autor wie Arno Holz. Der literarisch wie theoretisch konsequenteste Naturalist stellte in seinem 1891 erschienenen Buch »Die Kunst. Ihr Wesen und ihre Gesetze« die naturalistischen Kernpunkte – Gesetzmäßigkeit und Zeitlichkeit der *Kunst* – bereits ohne Rekurs auf Fechner dar, obgleich gerade das vielzitierte Holz'sche »Grundgesetz«, dass die Kunst »die Tendenz [habe], wieder die Natur zu sein«, durchaus an die Argumentation der *Vorschule* erinnert. Doch lag das spezifisch Künstlerische nun eben nicht mehr, wie bei Fechner, in den Praktiken der Stilisierung oder Symbolisierung. Für Holz, der sich an Zola, Taine oder Spencer orientiert und jedes weltanschauliche Moment ausklammert, galten nur noch die technischen und soziologischen Bedingungen der Reproduktion.[41]

Auf der anderen Seite steht ein Autor wie Julius Hart. 1905 veröffentlichte er ein Buch mit dem programmatischen Titel »Revolution der Ästhetik als Einleitung zu einer Revolution der Wissenschaft«, das noch einmal die »Entscheidungsschlacht zwischen einer alten und einer neuen Weltanschauung« (Hart 1905, 1, 5) versprach. Doch zählten zum ›Alten‹ nun nicht mehr, wie in der ersten Phase naturalistischer Programmatik, nur der *Idealismus*, sondern gleichermaßen die moderne Wissenschaft.

---

[39] Vgl. Brauneck; Müller 1987, 255–259.

[40] Während die ältere idealistische Kunst die »Wirklichkeitsdinge« direkt in das Ideal verwandelt habe, bestehe das Raffinement des modernen Realismus darin, »dass diese Ideale vom Hörer unwillkürlich als Kehrseite ›erschlossen‹ werden, *ohne* dass sie plump in Worten ausgedrückt oder gar in die Dinge hineingeworfen sind« (Bölsche 1987, 156).

[41] Siehe Holz 1925. – Zum Thema vgl. Möbius 1980.

Beiden stellte Hart die sinnlich unmittelbare Natur- und Lebenserfahrung gegenüber – wobei er sich freilich wieder auf Fechner, nun allerdings auf die weltanschaulich akzentuierte späte Philosophie, beziehen konnte. Mit unverkennbarem Anklang an Fechners Differenzierung zwischen der naturwissenschaftlich-materialistisch pessimistischen ›Nachtansicht‹ und einer sinnlich leuchtenden ›Tagwelt‹[42] kontrastierte Hart zwei Sphären: Dort die Welt, die uns Philosophie und Wissenschaft als die vernünftige und daher wahre darstellen, obgleich sie uns (via Materialismus) zu Skepsis und Weltabkehr führt;[43] hier »die Welt unseres naiven Realismus, der sinnlichen Erscheinungsfülle, der vielen und mannigfaltigen, verschiedenen Formen«, »unsere Naturwelt«. Falle die Binde von den Augen, so strahlten »Leben und Natur, Künste und Wissenschaften in Herrlichkeit« (Hart 1905, 1, 13 und 15).

Dass Hart diese weltanschauliche Kehrtwendung mit einer »Revolution der Ästhetik« verbinden wollte, hat mit dem zivilisationskritischen Impetus seiner Streitschrift zu tun, der, typisch für die Jahrhundertwende, in eine Feier der schöpferischen Kräfte mündete. So hoffte Hart auf die Wiedergeburt des »neuen Menschen, der vor allem ein Schaffender und ein Künstler ist« (Hart 1905, I, 73). Revolution der *Ästhetik* bedeutete daher eine Abkehr von der gesamtem Kunstwissenschaft, insofern sie mit Abstrakta wie ›Kunst‹ oder ›Schönheit‹ handelte. Die Ablehnung betraf nicht mehr nur die »metaphysisch-spekulative« Ästhetik, die »unter dem Ansturm der naturwissenschaftlichen Geistesströmung« zusammengebrochen war, sondern ebenso die folgende »reine Erfahrungswissenschaft«, wie sie Fechner begründet und Lipps fortgeführt hatte. Auch die *Experimentalästhetik* war für Hart im Kern ›Kunstwesenlehre‹ und arbeitete mit dem ästhetischen Prinzip der ›Einheit in der Vielheit‹, das er im Kontext seiner Rationalismuskritik geradezu perhorreszierte.[44] Ohne Fechner zu nennen, übte Hart daher indirekt Kritik, wenn er nun »eine neue Ästhetik tatsächlich von unten auf« (Hart 1905, 1, 59) errichten wollte. Was er sich darunter vorstellte, blieb allerdings unklar, da er noch schwankte zwischen dem Bekenntnis zu einer Ästhetik, die dem ›wirkli-

---

42 Vgl. Fechner 1879.

43 Zur Verbindung von Rationalismus und Pessimismus vgl. Hart 1905, 1, S. 22 und 313.

44 Hart zeigt an Theodor Lipps, wie auch die psychologische Untersuchung immer das Wissen von der Kunst voraussetzt. »Was ist das Wesen der Kunst? [...] Gleichmäßig tönt es aus beiden Lagern hervor und beide Konfessionen, die idealistisch-metaphysische wie auch die naturwissenschaftlich experimentellen Ästhetiker sagen zuletzt nur: Einheit in der Vielheit« (Hart 1905, 1, S. 142, 145ff.).

chen, organischen Leben‹ der Kunst gewachsen sein sollte, und dem Verzicht auf jede Ästhetik. Fechners wissenschaftlicher Duktus erwies sich jedenfalls als nicht mehr zeitgemäß.

Mit den Autoren wandelte sich also die Rezeption Fechners, der ja, da er in seinem geistigen Habitus Wissenschaftlichkeit und Weltanschauung verband, von beiden Seiten Kritik auf sich ziehen,[45] aber auch Interessen entgegenkommen konnte. In dem Maß, wie die Kultur der Zeit die Wissenschaftsgläubigkeit des 19. Jahrhunderts hinter sich ließ und *metaphysische* Bedürfnisse wiederentdeckte, verlagerte sich das Interesse an Fechner von der Naturforschung auf die *Naturphilosophie.* ›Was wir dagegen wirklich brauchen‹, konstatierte Bölsche »aus der Schneegrube« (so der Titel der später in Buchform veröffentlichten Aufsatzsammlung) einer szientistisch erkalteten Welt, sei ›Ein Mann wie Fechner‹.[46] Schließlich habe dieser die wissenschaftliche Erkundung der Natur von Beginn an begleitet, ohne je ihren Wert »in einem optimistischen, unser Sehen beruhigenden Sinne« aus den Augen zu verlieren. »Und dieser Fechner ist es, der uns heute«, nach der mehr als fünfzig Jahre währenden Krisis des Naturbegriffs, »wieder interessiert« (Bölsche 1903, 228f.).[47] Damit beginnt, teilweise noch im Kreis der Naturalisten, eine zweite Phase der Fechner-Rezeption, die um die philosophischen Schriften kreist und sich in weltanschaulich akzentuierten Romanen niederschlägt. Aber das wäre ein neues Kapitel.

Literatur:

Alberti, C. (1987): Die zwölf Artikel des Realismus. Ein litterarisches Glaubensbekenntnis (1889). In: Theorie des Naturalismus. Manifeste und Dokumente zur deutschen Literatur 1880–1900. Hg. von Th. Mayer. Stuttgart, 49–58.

Allesch, Chr. G. (1998): Gustav Theodor Fechner. In: Ästhetik und Kunstphilosophie. Von der Antike bis zur Gegenwart. Hg. von J. Nida-Rümelin; M. Betzler. Stuttgart, 266–269.

Arendt, H.-J. (1999): Gustav Theodor Fechner. Ein deutscher Naturwissenschaftler und Philosoph im 19. Jahrhundert. Frankfurt a.M.

Bölsche, W. (1887): Vischer und Fechner als Ästhetiker. In: Die Gegenwart. Berlin 40, 215–217.

---

[45] Zur wechselvollen Rezeption Fechners als »Phantast« oder »Materialist« vgl. Bölsche 1901, 285f.

[46] Die Formulierungen erscheinen als Kapitelüberschriften in Bölsche 1903.

[47] Den weltanschaulichen Optimismus Fechners akzentuiert Bölsche nochmals in seinem Vorwort in: Fechner 1918, 24.

Bölsche, W. 1987: Die Poesie der Großstadt. In: Naturalismus. Manifeste und Dokumente zur deutschen Literatur 1880–1900. Hg. von M. Brauneck; Ch. Müller. Stuttgart 253–259.

Bölsche, W. (1901): Hinter der Weltstadt. Friedrichshagener Gedanken zur ästhetischen Kultur. Leipzig, 259–347.

Bölsche, W. (1903): Aus der Schneegrube. Gedanken zur Naturforschung. Dresden.

Bölsche, W. (1976): Die naturwissenschaftlichen Grundlagen der Poesie. Prolegomena einer realistischen Ästhetik. Hg. von J.J. Braakenburg. Tübingen.

Bölsche, W. (1987): Die sozialen Grundlagen der modernen Dichtung. In: Naturalismus. Manifeste und Dokumente zur deutschen Literatur 1890–1990. Hg. von M. Brauneck; Ch. Müller. Stuttgart, 151–161.

Brauneck, M.; Müller, Ch. (Hg.) (1987): Naturalismus. Manifeste und Dokumente zur deutschen Literatur. 1880–1900. Stuttgart.

Bucher, M.; Hahl, W.; Jäger, G. ; Wittmann, R. (1975): Realismus und Gründerzeit. Manifeste und Dokumente zur deutschen Literatur 1848–1880. 2 Bde. Stuttgart.

[Fechner, G. Th.] Dr. Mises (1835a): Heinrich Heine als Lyriker. In: Blätter für literarische Unterhaltung. Leipzig (Nr. 182–185), 749–750; 753–754; 757–758; 761–762.

[Fechner, G. Th.] Dr. Mises (1835b): Friedrich Rückert. Bei Gelegenheit der jüngst erschienenen Sammlung seiner Gedichte. In: Blätter für literarische Unterhaltung. Leipzig (Nr. 60–63), 245–247; 249–250; 253–254; 257–258.

[Fechner, G. Th.] Dr. Mises (1841): Gedichte. Leipzig.

Fechner, G. Th. (1855): Über die physikalische und philosophische Atomenlehre. Leipzig.

Fechner, G. Th. (1879): Die Tagesansicht gegenüber der Nachtansicht. Leipzig.

Fechner, G. Th. (1918): Die Tagesansicht gegenüber der Nachtansicht. Angeb. Das Büchlein vom Leben nach dem Tode. Ausgwählt und eingl. von W. Bölsche. Berlin (= Deutsche Bibliothek 124).

Fechner, G. Th. (1978): Vorschule der Ästhetik. 2 Bde in e. Bd. Beigeb.: Zur experimentellen Ästhetik. Nachdr. d. Ausg. von 1925 und 1871. Hildesheim; New York; Ols; Wiesbaden.

Fiedler, C. (1977): Schriften über Kunst. Mit einer Einleitung von H. Eckstein. Köln.

Fontane, Th. (1979): Unsere lyrische und epische Poesie seit 1848. In: Theodor Fontane. Werke und Schriften. Hg. von W.K. Keitel; H. Nürnberger. Bd. 28: Aufsätze und Aufzeichnungen. Hg. von J. Kolbe. Frankfurt a.M., 38–62.

Hart, J. (1889): Eine schein-empirische Poetik. In: Kritisches Jahrbuch. Hamburg 1. Jg. (1889) H. 1, 29–39.

Hart, J. (1905): Revolution der Ästhetik als Einleitung zu einer Revolution der Wissenschaft. 1. Buch: Künstler und Ästhetiker. Berlin.

Hartmann, E. v. (1989): Philosophie des Unbewußten. Versuch einer Weltanschauung (1869). Nachdruck Hildesheim.

Hettner, H. (1975): Drangsale und Hoffnungen der modernen Plastik. In: Realismus und Gründerzeit. Manifeste und Dokumente zur deutschen Literatur 1848–1880. Hg. von M. Bucher u.a. Bd. 2. Stuttgart, 9–18.

Holz, A.(1925): Die neue Wortkunst. Eine Zusammenfassung ihrer ersten grundlegenden Dokumente. Berlin.

Lange, F.A. (1974): Geschichte des Materialismus. Hg. von A. Schmidt. 2 Bde. Frankfurt a.M.

Lipps, Th. (1907): Ästhetik. In: Systematische Philosophie. Die Kultur der Gegenwart. Hg. von W. Dilthey; A. Riehl; W. Wundt u.a. Teil I, Abt. VI. Berlin 349–387.

Mayer, Th. (1973): Theorie des Naturalismus. Stuttgart.

Mill, John Stuart (1868): System der deductiven und inductiven Logik. Eine Darlegung der Principien wissenschaftlicher Forschung, insbesondere der Naturforschung. 2. Bde. Deutsch von J. Schiel. 3. Aufl. Braunschweig.

Möbius, H. (1980): Der Positivismus in der Literatur des Naturalismus. Wissenschaft, Kunst und soziale Frage bei Arno Holz. München.

Nida-Rümelin, J.; Betzler, M. (Hg.) (1998): Ästhetik und Kunstphilosophie. Von der Antike bis zur Gegenwart in Einzeldarstellungen. Stuttgart, 266–269.

Schasler, M. (1975): Ueber Idealismus und Realismus in der Historienmalerei. In: Realismus und Gründerzeit. Manifeste und Dokumente zur deutschen Literatur 1848–1880. Hg. von M. Bucher u.a. Bd. 2. Stuttgart, 34–38.

Schneider, N. (1997): Geschichte der Ästhetik von der Aufklärung bis zur Postmoderne. Eine paradigmatische Einführung. 2. Aufl. Stuttgart.

Taine, H. (1987): Philosophie der Kunst (1865, dt. 1866). Hg. von A. Silbermann. Berlin.

Vischer, F. Th. (1975): Die Aquarell-Copien von Ramboux in der Gallerie zu Düsseldorf. In: Realismus und Gründerzeit. Manifeste und Dokumente zur deutschen Literatur1848–1880. Hg. von M. Bucher u.a. Bd. 2. Stuttgart, 19–21.

Ingo Warnke

Gustav Theodor Fechners Assoziationsbegriff im Licht konnektionistischer Bedeutungstheorien

Fechners »Vorschule der Ästhetik« darf für die moderne kognitionslinguistische Bedeutungstheorie als einschlägige Vorarbeit gelten. Die Darlegungen zur Assoziation und ihre prinzipielle Beschreibung sowie ästhetische Erfassung weisen vielfältige vortheoretische Parallelen zu gegenwärtigen Vorstellungen über die Verarbeitung sprachlicher Bedeutung im mentalen Lexikon auf. Der Beitrag verortet die Fechner'schen Vorstellungen aus linguistischer Perspektive. Dabei erfolgt eine Bezugsetzung der Darlegungen Fechners zu sprachwissenschaftlichen Kategorien wie Referenz, Prototypizität und Interpretantenwissen.

1. Vorbemerkung

In der vorliegenden Abhandlung sollen ästhetische Konzeptionen Gustav Theodor Fechners (1801–1887) aus linguistischer Perspektive betrachtet werden. Fechner gilt nicht nur als bedeutender Vertreter der Physik und experimentellen Psychologie des 19. Jahrhunderts, respektive als Begründer der Psychophysik,[1] sondern er ist zudem als breit interessierter Gelehrter seiner Zeit mit Fragen der Ästhetik nachdrücklich beschäftigt.[2] In seinen Abhandlungen zu ästhetischen Fragen bündeln sich kulturgeschichtliche Überlegungen mit den Interessen des experimentell arbeitenden Psychophysikers auf nach wie vor bedeutsame Weise. Kumuliert erscheinen die ästhetischen Konzeptionen Fechners in seiner »Vorschule der Ästhetik«, die 1876 zweibändig in Leipzig erscheint. Diese umfangreiche Reflexion über Gegenstände der Ästhetik ist ein Alterswerk Fechners; er war zum Zeitpunkt des Erscheinens bereits 75 Jahre alt. Dieses

[1] Siehe Dupéron 2000; Geissler & Müller 1990.

[2] Eine hervorragende Gesamtdarstellung zu Fechner verfasste Hans-Jürgen Arendt (s. Arendt 1999).

Faktum ist für die Einordnung des Werkes keine Quantité négligeable. Gert Mattenklott kann gefolgt werden, wenn er Fechner als Schwärmer einordnet und in diesem Zusammenhang den Fechner'schen Phantasmagorien Rationalität abspricht, da philosophisches Schwärmertum »zur Pathologie des Denkens« (Fechner 1984,169) gehöre. Dies gilt in besonderer Weise für das Spätwerk Fechners. Zu berücksichtigen ist jedoch, dass die »Vorschule der Ästhetik« kein geschlossenes Werk der 1870er-Jahre ist, sondern Fechner hier vielmehr »eine Reihe Aufsätze ästhetischen Inhalts ohne systematische Folge« (Fechner 1876, 1, III) versammelt. Die einzelnen Kapitel der Fechner'schen Ästhetik gehören verschiedenen Phasen seiner Biographie an, sie sind zudem teilweise unabhängig voneinander und sehr unterschiedlich in Umfang und Stringenz der Argumentation. So gehen insbesondere Fechners ausführliche Darlegungen zum ästhetischen *Assoziationsprinzip* auf einen Vortrag zurück, den Fechner bereits 1866 im *Leipziger Kunstverein* gehalten hatte. Doch bereits um das Jahr 1850 publiziert Fechner unorthodoxe Schriften, wie etwa die radikalempiristische Abhandlung »Zend-Avesta« aus dem Jahr 1851 oder 1848 die Abhandlung »Nanna oder Über das Seelenleben der Pflanzen«. Es handelt sich mithin bereits bei Fechners Arbeiten aus der mittleren Lebensphase um oft ungewöhnliche Ansätze, die im Spannungsfeld seiner außergewöhnlichen Individualität zu betrachten sind, im Kontext seiner »Begier nach den zerronnenen Evidenzen« (Fechner 1984, 180).

Der Versuch einer kognitionslinguistischen Perspektivierung der Fechner'schen Ästhetik und sonderlich seines *ästhetischen Assoziationsprinzips* könnte daher nicht ganz zu Unrecht als eine inkompatible Näherung beurteilt werden: Als Objekt der Betrachtung ein vernunftkritischer Gelehrter und nicht selten Sonderling des 19. Jahrhunderts, als Betrachtungswinkel die Konsensauffassung der rational durchstrukturierten Kognitionslinguistik und -psychologie. Bei eingehender Beschäftigung mit Fechner zeigt sich jedoch recht schnell, dass die Fokussierung Fechners aus dem Blickwinkel heutiger hochdifferenzierter Fachwissenschaft durchaus lohnend ist, da trotz der Spannung zwischen dem »Grenzgänger der Wissenschaft« (Waldrich 1993) und den wissenschaftlichen Konsensbegriffen des 21. Jahrhunderts eine Reihe von signifikanten Parallelen ausgemacht werden können. Es muss in diesem Zusammenhang jedoch ganz deutlich gemacht werden, dass die in Betracht kommenden *Analogien* nicht überstrapaziert werden sollten. Wenn in den folgenden Darlegungen Übereinstimmungen oder Verwandtschaften behandelt werden, also Felder der konzeptionellen Nähe zwischen Fechner und heutigen Bedeutungsauffassungen der kognitiven Linguistik, so heißt das nicht, dass die Divergenzen im theoretischen Gehalt nicht gewichtig wären. Doch die Abweichungen zwischen heutiger Bedeutungstheorie und Fechners Vorstellungen zur Bedeutungskonstitution im Rahmen einer experimentellen Ästhetik sind wohl weniger verblüffend als ihre Übereinstimmungen. Folglich ergibt sich eine Konzentration auf Gleichförmigkeiten in den ästhetischen Entwürfen Fechners und den linguistischen Auffassungen zur Bedeutung. Dies ist als mögliche Lesart, als *eine* Perspektive auf Fechners Darlegungen aufzufassen. Im Mittelpunkt der Erörterungen zu Fechner wird das *ästhetische Assoziationsprinzip* stehen und dessen Abgleich mit konnektionistischen Bedeutungstheorien. In Hinführung darauf soll zunächst die ästhetische Prinzipienlehre Fechners in toto umrissen werden.

2. Fechners ästhetische Prinzipienlehre

Fechner vertritt eine induktive Ästhetik, deren Voraussetzung schlechthin die Forderung nach empirischer Rückbindung jeglicher Schönheitsurteile ist. Fechner löst dieses Gebot durch empirische Fundierung aller wesentlichen Aussagen über ästhetische Kategorien ein. Damit begegnet Fechner explizit jeder philosophisch deduktiven Ästhetik, wie sie in der Tradition Kants, Schellings oder Hegels als diskursive Norm gesetzt waren. Während für Hegel die tradierte Beschäftigung mit ästhetischen Urteilen vorrangig nach dem Begriff des *Schönen* und nachrangig nach seiner Manifestation in der Erscheinungswelt fragt, setzt er selbst eine *Ästhetik von unten* an. Philosophie und Psychologie erscheinen hier als Konkurrenten in der Ästhetik.[3] Erkenntnisleitend ist bei diesem induktiven Ansatz die Bestimmung von Gründen des konkreten Gefallens und Missfallens von Erscheinungen. Erst im weiteren Schritt, also im induktiven Schluss, werden Gesetze des *Gefallens* bzw. des ästhetischen Prozesses der *Wahrnehmung* aufgestellt. Es geht Fechner mithin um die empirischen Bedingungen des Gefallens.

Bereits hier zeigt sich eine nicht unwesentliche Parallele zur Neuformulierung linguistischer Theoreme in der jüngsten Vergangenheit. Stand das

---

[3] Siehe Drue 1983, 3–36.

strukturalistische Paradigma der Linguistik des 20. Jahrhunderts ganz in der Verpflichtung auf ein deduktives Kategoriensystem sola ratione – in besonders deutlicher Ausprägung ist dies im taxonomischen Strukturalismus der Fall –, so sucht die Psycholinguistik respektive Kognitionslinguistik nach den faktischen Vorgängen der Sprachverarbeitung. In Entlehnung der Fechner'schen Formulierung könnte diese Ausprägung der Sprachwissenschaft durchaus als Linguistik *von unten* bezeichnet werden.

Bevor die *ästhetischen Prinzipien* Fechners in Vorbereitung auf eine eingehendere Beschäftigung mit dem ästhetischen Assoziationsprinzip kurz zusammengefasst werden, soll zunächst noch eine beiläufige Einlassung zu Fechners ästhetischen Vorbegriffen *Gefallen, Missfallen/Lust, Unlust* erfolgen. *Lust* ist eine Leitvokabel der Fechner'schen Ästhetik und hat als solche den Rang des empirisch zu verifizierenden Katalysators ästhetischer Prozesse überhaupt. Das *Schöne* wird bei Fechner nicht bezogen auf abstrakte Eigenschaften der Anmut etc., sondern ganz im Sinne einer *Ästhetik von unten* auf das Gefallen und Missfallen beim Rezipienten. Fechner führt aus, dass das Gefallen ein grundsätzlich lustvolles Erleben sei, wohingegen das Missfallen immer mit Unlust in Verbindung stehe. So sei eben schön, was Gefallen erweckt (Fechner 1876, 1, 15), also Lust auslöst, gut sei entsprechend das, was »mehr Lust als Unlust« (Fechner 1876, 1, 19) bedeutet und das Wahre schließlich sei der allgemeine »Grund der Lust« (Fechner 1876, 1, 31). Die Lustorientierung der Fechner'schen Ästhetik ist jedoch nicht als Hedonismus zu verstehen, sondern vielmehr als Konzentration der ästhetischen Kategorien auf das Subjekt und dessen affektive Bewertungen des Schönen bzw. Nicht-Schönen. *Lust* meint bei Fechner also nicht das triebgesteuerte Verlangen nach etwas, sondern ganz im Sinne des Allgemeinbegriffs im 18. und 19. Jahrhundert meint Lust die »Äußerung der anschauenden Erkenntnis des Angenehmen«.[4] Die Adelung'sche Formulierung verdeutlicht, dass Lust zum einen eine Form der anschauenden Erkenntnis ist, folglich den Prozess der Sinneswahrnehmung betrifft und nicht rational aktiviert wird, dass Lust aber andererseits auch auf den angenehmen Gegenstand bezogen ist, auf ein ästhetisches Objekt also, welches qua Existenz positive Resonanz findet. Mit Fechners Rückbindung der Kategorie des Schönen an die Äußerungen der anschauenden Erkenntnis des Angenehmen, an die Lust des

[4] Siehe Adelung 1796, 2, Sp. 2134.

Rezipienten, ist eine pragmatische Dimension der Ästhetik thematisiert, insofern das Verhältnis von ästhetischem Objekt, also Zeichenträger, und ästhetischem Rezipienten, also Zeichenbenutzer, ins Spiel kommt. Die Grundlagen der Fechner'schen Ästhetik sind pragmatischer Art und werden im so genannten *eudämonistischen Prinzip* klar formuliert.[5] Danach erfolgt die Zuerkennung von *Schönheit* aus einer Haltung, die Glück und Lust als Ziel des Handelns setzt. Schön ist also nicht das, was per se schön ist, sondern was als Zeichenträger in einem Zeichenbenutzer Glück- und Lustempfindungen auslöst. Damit wird die Ästhetik zu einer Beschäftigung mit eben jenen auslösenden lustmotivierenden Momenten, die mental im Zeichenbenutzer aktiviert werden.

Im Zentrum dieser innersubjektiven Vorgänge der Lustempfindung stehen nach Fechner die *Assoziationen*, sodass das *ästhetische* Assoziationsprinzip den Drehpunkt bei der Zuerkennung von Schönheit darstellt. Der Bezug auf das Subjekt und die mentalen Prozesse der affektiven Bewertung weist zahlreiche Schnittstellen zu modernen Theorien der Zeichendeutung auf, so zum Begriff der konnotativen Bedeutung. Bevor dies dargelegt wird, soll zunächst die Gesamtheit der ästhetischen Prinzipien bei Fechner angeführt werden.

Fechner selbst möchte nicht von ästhetischen Gesetzen sprechen, sondern bevorzugt die Bezeichnung ›Prinzipien‹, was durchaus zeitgemäß ist und unsere heutige Bedeutung von wissenschaftlichem Gesetz impliziert. Folglich werden sechs *ästhetische Prinzipien* benannt, wobei die Prinzipien (3) bis (5) als oberste Formalprinzipien bezeichnet sind:

(1) Prinzip der ästhetischen Schwelle
(2) Prinzip der ästhetischen Hilfe oder Steigerung
(3) Prinzip der einheitlichen Verknüpfung des Mannigfaltigen
(4) Prinzip der Widerspruchslosigkeit
(5) Prinzip der Klarheit
(6) Prinzip der Assoziation

Das Prinzip der *ästhetischen Schwelle* besagt, dass ein Reiz ausreichende Intensität besitzen muss, um überhaupt Aktivationen auszulösen. Diese Annahme Fechners, die bereits den experimentalpsychologischen Zuschnitt seiner Ästhetik verdeutlicht, entspricht dem heutigen Basiswissen der Wahrnehmungspsychologie, wonach die Reizenergie stark genug sein muss, um Wahrnehmungsschwellen zu erreichen.

---

[5] Grundlagen dieses Prinzips formuliert Fechner bereits 1846; siehe Fechner 1846.

Das *Prinzip der ästhetischen Hilfe oder Steigerung* besagt, dass die Kombination von Lustbedingungen die Lustresultate steigert unter der Voraussetzung, dass die Lustgefühle bei der Rezeption von ästhetischen Objekten untereinander widerspruchslos sind. Bereits hier spielen implizit die Begriffe der reziproken Aktivation bzw. Hemmung eine Rolle, die auf das sechste Prinzip, das der Assoziation, verweisen. Fechner geht von einem Netzwerkmodell der Emotionen aus, bei dem die mentale Aktivation infolge der Betrachtung eines ästhetischen Objektes in Beziehung zu den psychischen Dispositionen des Zeichenbenutzers steht. Je stärker der kombinatorische Bedeutungsgehalt eines ästhetischen Zeichens ist, umso stärker fällt seine Wirkung aus. Bedingung dafür ist eine semantische Kohärenz der Lustempfindungen, denn andernfalls könne das Resultat nur eine innere Zerstreuung unzusammenhängender Empfindungen sein.

Das Prinzip der *einheitlichen Verknüpfung des Mannigfaltigen* besagt demnach, dass man Gefallen an dem findet, was eine ›einheitlich verknüpfte Mannigfaltigkeit‹ positiver Emotionen auslöst. Der Begriff der ›einheitlichen Verknüpfung‹ verweist nochmals darauf, dass der ästhetische Prozess an Bedingungen der semantischen Identität von Wirkungen gebunden ist. Auch hier sind Parallelen zu modernen Bedeutungstheorien der kognitiven Linguistik zu erkennen, auf die noch eingegangen wird.

Nicht anders verhält es sich mit dem *Prinzip der Widerspruchslosigkeit*, wonach die ›Widerspruchslosigkeit‹ von Wahrnehmungsobjekten Lust verschafft. Die semantische Kohäsion ist folglich eine Bedingung positiver Erfahrungen, da nur die Rückführung von Wahrnehmungsinhalten auf eine »übereinstimmende Vorstellung« (Fechner 1876, 1, 82) eine konfliktfreie mentale Verarbeitung bzw. Decodierung von Information ermöglicht.

Was im *Prinzip der Widerspruchslosigkeit* auf den Rezipienten bezogen ist, wird im Prinzip der *Klarheit* auf den ästhetischen Gegenstand gemünzt. Nur bei Klarheit des Objektes, das heißt bei ausbleibenden Störfaktoren der Wahrnehmung, kann eine einheitliche Verknüpfung des Mannigfaltigen erfolgen und eine widerspruchslose Decodierung ausgelöst werden.

Es ist offensichtlich, dass die Prinzipien (1) bis (5) auf die empirischen Bedingungen der Schönheitszuweisung zielen. Bereits für diese ergeben sich zahlreiche Schnittstellen einer modernen Lesart Fechners, doch ganz im Sinne der Fechner'schen Ästhetik sollen die mannigfaltigen Schnittstellen zu Theorien der Bedeutung gebündelt werden. Die einheitliche

Verknüpfung des Mannigfaltigen soll also auch in dieser Abhandlung eingelöst werden; die Ausführungen mögen insofern bestenfalls Lustgefühle begründen. Im Weiteren wird also das *ästhetische Assoziationsprinzip* näher behandelt, das die Prinzipien (1) bis (5) gewissermaßen umfasst.

3. Das ästhetische Assoziationsprinzip

Während Fechner auf die ästhetischen Prinzipien (1) bis (5) eher kurz eingeht, nimmt die Behandlung des *ästhetischen Assoziationsprinzips* breiten Raum ein. Wenngleich das Prinzip der Assoziation in der Psychologie längst bekannt sei, so müsse es doch als vernachlässigt in der Ästhetik gelten. Diese Aussage Fechners gründet in der Kritik an der philosophisch-deduktiven Ästhetik, die der Assoziation des Subjektes keinen Rang einräumt, da diese jenseits der präskriptiven Schönheitskategorie erst einsetzt. Fechners Distanzierung gegenüber derart objektivierenden Aussagen über das Schöne wird offensichtlich, wenn er beklagt, das Assoziation ein eher negativ gepolter Begriff sei, wie Kants Abgrenzung zwischen *reiner Schönheit* und *anhängender Schönheit* deutlich zeige. Die assoziativ bedingte Schönheit wird vor Fechner oft als lediglich anhängend eingeordnet und insoweit gegenüber einer den Dingen eigenen Schönheit marginalisiert. Da Fechner um eine empirische Grundlegung der ästhetischen Kategorie des Schönen bemüht ist, richtet sich sein Interesse auf eben diese subjektiv bedingte Schönheitszuschreibung. Was in der spekulativen Ästhetik philosophischer Prägung zum Anhängenden wird, zur akzidentiellen Eigenschaft von Objekten – neben Kant ist als Vertreter dieser Position auch Herbart zu nennen –, ist bei Fechner das Eigentliche: die subjektiv-konkrete Wirkung eines ästhetischen Objektes. Diese Wirkung gründet Fechner zufolge substantiell im assoziativen Gehalt eines ästhetischen Eindrucks. Eine prosaische Fassung dieses *ästhetischen Assoziationsprinzips* gibt Fechner wie folgt:

> Eine Frau, die ihren Mann sehr liebte, sagte zu ihm: wie freue ich mich, dass du einen so hübschen Namen hast. Der Name war nicht sehr hübsch, aber sie liebte den Mann, darum gefiel ihr der Name. (Fechner 1876, 1, 91)

So sei auch der ästhetische Reiz der *Orange* gegenüber dem einer gleichfarbigen Holzkugel dadurch begründet, dass die Orange ein anderes assoziatives Potential enthalte als eine Holzkugel:

> Der Vorzug der Orange kann nur darin liegen, dass wir eben eine Orange, aber keine Holzkugel in ihr sehen, dass wir die Bedeutung der Orange an ihre Form und Farbe knüpfen. Die Bedeutung der Orange aber liegt freilich zum Theil selbst mit in Form und Farbe, doch keineswegs allein, vielmehr in der Gesamtheit dessen, was sie ist und wirkt, insbesondere in Beziehung auf uns selbst ist und wirkt. (Fechner 1876, 1, 88f.)

Die Bedeutung der *Orange* ist an Form und Farbe geknüpft, geht aber über diese hinaus, denn sie ist die Gesamtheit dessen, was sie ist und wie sie wirkt. Wir haben es hier mit einem modularen Modell der Bedeutung zu tun. Unterschieden werden einerseits in trivialer zeichentheoretischer Differenzierung Zeichenträger und Zeichenbedeutung, wobei dem Zeichenträger nicht arbiträre Attribute der Schönheit beigemessen werden. Modular ist diese Vorstellung aber andererseits in Bezug auf die Vorstellung von der Gesamtheit dessen, was die Orange als ästhetisches *Zeichen* ausmacht und wie es als solches wirkt. In der Sprachwissenschaft wird unterschieden zwischen denotativer und konnotativer Bedeutung. Die *Denotation* ist die kontextunabhängige Grundbedeutung, während die *Konnotation* eines Zeichens alle individuellen Spielarten der Bedeutung umfasst, die kontextuell sind. Nicht umsonst wird die konnotative Bedeutung auch häufig als assoziativer Gehalt bezeichnet. Auf eben diesen konnotativen Gehalt von ästhetischen Objekten zielt Fechner. Die Bedeutungszuweisung ist dabei als Vorgang einer subjektiven, stark assoziativ gestalteten Aktivierung von Konnotationen vorgestellt. Fechners *empirische Ästhetik* ist insofern im Kern pragmatisch, denn die Konnotation bezieht sich auf das Verhältnis von Zeichen und Zeichenbenutzer. Während die Denotation Teil der *Semantik* ist, hat die Konnotation als Teil der *Pragmatik* zu gelten.

In diesem Zusammenhang kommt der Modellierung des *Zeichens* durch den amerikanischen Pragmatisten Charles Sanders Peirce eine erklärende Funktion zu. Nur am Rand sei darauf verwiesen, dass zwischen Fechner und Peirce einige Parallelen zu ziehen sind.[6] Nach Peirce verweist das Representamen als Zeichenträger auf ein Objekt bzw. einen Referenten. Diese Zuschreibung erfolgt in der Semiose durch Aktivierung des Interpretanten, der unter anderem als assoziativer Gehalt eines Zeichens die Gesamtheit der Welterfahrung und begrifflich-emotionalen Kategorien des Zeichenbenutzers umfasst. Der Interpretant steuert also die Richtung der Semiose:

---

[6] Siehe Heidelberger 1993, 316–321.

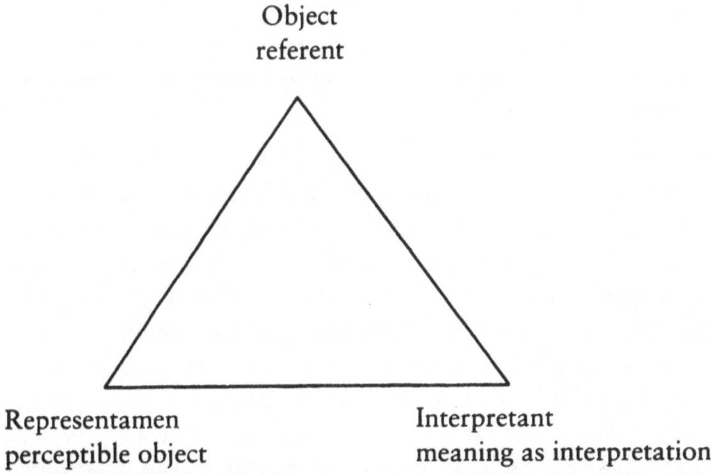

Während die strukturalistischen Bedeutungstheorien den konnotativen Gehalt von *Zeichen* marginalisieren, kommt in einer kognitionslinguistischen Theorie der individuellen Markierung von Bedeutung im mentalen Lexikon eine große Bedeutung zu. Fechners Aufwertung des *ästhetischen Assoziationsprinzips* kann aus dieser Blickrichtung also gleichsam bestätigt werden.

Zur Unterscheidung des denotativ-kollektiven Bedeutungsgehaltes und des konnotativ-individuellen Assoziationspotentials von *Zeichen* sei als Beispiel der Begriff ›Tiger‹ mit Verweis auf I. Warnke angeführt.[7] Die denotative Bedeutung von ›Tiger‹ ist im »Deutschen Universalwörterbuch« (DUW 2001) paraphrasiert: »(in Asien heimisches, zu den Großkatzen gehörendes) sehr kräftiges, einzeln lebendes Raubtier von blaßrötlichgelber bis rotbrauner Färbung mit schwarzen Querstreifen« (DUW 2001, 1579). Dies ist die klassische Erfassung von *Denotationen* im Genus proximum-differentia specifica-Modell. Die *konnotative* Bedeutung hingegen ist durch ihre assoziative Bindung uferlos, entgrenzt Bedeutung und vermittelt der Möglichkeit nach alles mit allem. Als Beispiel sei dafür die universelle Kategorisierung nach Jorge Luis Borges Erzählung »Die Inschrift des Gottes« angeführt:

> [...] sagt man »der Tiger«, so sagt man zugleich die Tiger, die ihn zeugten, die Rehe und Schildkröten, die er verschlang, die Weide, von der die Rehe sich nährten, die Erde, deren Mutterschoß die Weide hervorbrachte, der Himmel,

---

[7] Siehe Warnke 1999, 223–240.

> der der Erde Licht spendete. Ich bedachte, daß in der Sprache eines Gottes jedes Wort diese unendliche Verkettung von Tatsachen verkünden würde, und zwar nicht implizit, sondern explizit, nicht fortschreitend, sondern unmittelbar. (Borges 1992, 102f.)

Michel Foucault spricht im Vorwort seiner Schrift »Die Ordnung der Dinge« von der Befreiung des Wortes durch derartig entgrenzende Kategorien, die assoziativ generiert sind.[8] Fechner setzt eben an diesem Punkt an, wenn er darauf verweist, dass jedes Ding mental assoziiert ist mit Erinnerungen bzw. Erfahrungen. Diese »Resultante von Erinnerungen« (Fechner 1876, 1, 93) ist bedeutungskonstituierend. Und damit sind wir am entscheidenden Punkt, der Frage nach den Regeln der Assoziation, denn diese sind nun keineswegs willkürlich, sonst könnte Fechner auch nicht vom *ästhetischen Assoziationsprinzip* sprechen. Wenn die Bedeutung eines ästhetischen Objektes tatsächlich aus der Gesamtheit der assoziierten Erinnerungen folgt, und diese Erinnerungen wiederum auf die Grundkategorien von Gefallen und Missfallen zu beziehen sind, so stellt sich die Frage, welche Steuerungsprinzipien eine intersubjektive Kohärenz in der Beurteilung des *Schönen* herstellen. Mit derartigen Fragen beschäftigt sich nicht nur Fechner, solche Problemstellungen sind auch Gegenstand der gegenwärtigen kognitionslinguistischen Bedeutungstheorien. Fechner führt aus:

> Wir sehen einen Tisch, im Grunde nur einen viereckigen Fleck, aber in dem viereckigen Flecke Alles, wozu ein Tisch gebraucht wird; das macht den vierekkigen Fleck erst zu einem Tisch. (Fechner 1876, 1, 93)

Heute bezeichnet man die Bedeutungskonstitution über die Gesamtheit der situativen Einbindung von Objekten als *Frame*. Thematisiert Peirce mit dem Begriff des Interpretanten die Semantisierung des Zeichens als Aktivation von Welt- und Sprachwissen im Allgemeinen, so geht die Framesemantik von der kognitiven Komplexität semantischen Wissens im Rahmen begrifflicher Netzwerke aus. Das beim Individuum gespeicherte Weltwissen ist danach eine kategorisierte Größe mit komplexen internen Strukturen und steht bei der Semantisierung von Zeichen zur Verfügung. In den neueren Theorien werden diese strukturierten Wissenskomplexe als Schemata bzw. Frames bezeichnet. Nach S.-O. Tergan repräsentieren sie »Konzept-Wissen über Objekte, Situationen, Ereignisse, Folgen von Ereignissen, Handlungen und Handlungsfolgen« (Tergan 1986, 104).

---

[8] Siehe Foucault 1971, 17ff.

Dies gilt allgemein bei allen *Zeichen*, auch im Verlauf des Alltagsverstehens von gesprochener Sprache. Die angemessene Decodierung von sprachlicher Information setzt folglich Rahmenwissen voraus, das oft situativ gegeben ist. Die Frames beinhalten notwendiges Vorwissen für das angemessene Verstehen von sprachlichen Äußerungen. Die Parallele zu Fechner ist unschwer zu erkennen, denn Schönheitszuschreibung erfolgt nach Fechner eben über die *Assoziation* positiver Empfindungen, die als Vorwissen bei der Semantisierung ins Spiel kommen.

Fechner selbst nennt Steuerungsmechanismen bei der Bildung von Assoziationen, die heute als Bedingungen der Aktivation von semantischen Netzwerken zu verstehen sind:

(a) Assoziation durch Ähnlichkeit
(b) Ergänzende Assoziation
(c) Assoziationen durch Verstandes- und Gefühlsurteile

Wird die Ausprägung von *Assoziationen* als Aktivierung von individuellem Vorwissen im Sinne der Frametheorie verstanden, so entspricht dies den konnektionistischen Netzwerkmodellen der Kognitionspsychologie und -linguistik. Und in der Tat weist Fechners Assoziationsprinzip im Rahmen seiner *Ästhetik von unten* markante Parallelen zu den heutigen Ergebnissen experimenteller Analysen auf.

Sprachverarbeitung ist als Teil der kognitiven Informationsverarbeitung zu verstehen; R. Jackendoff versteht »language as a window on thought« (Jackendoff 1996, 184). Das Denken folgt dabei spezifischen Regeln. Nicht die 1:1-Relation von Zeichen und ihren Bedeutungen ist das Grundprinzip der Informationsverarbeitung, wie dies der Symbolismus lange Zeit annahm, sondern vielmehr ist nach den heutigen Erkenntnissen der experimentellen Psychologie, der Neurobiologie und der kognitiven Linguistik die Informationsverarbeitung ein Prozess der parallelen Interaktion zahlreicher Elemente. Man spricht in diesem Zusammenhang von *konnektionistischen* Netzen. Im Konnektionismus hat man nicht mehr die veraltete Vorstellung von der Computerarchitektur des Gehirns, sondern orientiert sich am Aufbau von Nervenzellen im Rahmen eines Brain-Style-Modells, dass Fechners Vorstellung einer *Ästhetik von unten* recht gut entspricht. So ist Assoziation in den neueren Gedächtnistheorien auch als Aktivation von *semantischen* Netzen erklärt.

Konnektionistische Netze bestehen aus einer großen Zahl einfacher Verbindungselemente, so genannten Quasi-Neuronen, »die sich wechselseitig über Verbindungen (Konnektionen) aktivieren oder hemmen können« (Roth & Prinz 1996, 381). Konnektionistische Netze können lernen, sie sind also erfahrungsdeterminiert: »Lernen beruht dabei darauf, dass die Verbindungsgewichte zwischen den Verarbeitungseinheiten [...] modifiziert werden« (Roth & Prinz 1996, 381). Nichts anderes meint Fechner der Sache nach, wenn er die *Assoziation* als »Resultante von Erinnerungen« (Fechner 1876, 1, 93) bezeichnet. Im Konnektionismus geht man davon aus, dass die Eingabe eines Musters, Reizes etc. direkt ähnliche oder assoziierte Muster mitaktiviert (vgl. Roth & Prinz 1996, 384) und auch hier sehen wir eine Parallele zu Fechner, der Assoziationen durch Ähnlichkeit (Fechner 1876, I, 96f.) eigens erfasst. Fechner folgt damit übrigens einer tradierten Vorstellung; schon Aristoteles geht davon aus, dass die Erinnerungen bestimmt sind »von Ähnlichem oder Gegenteiligem, oder von dem, was nah zusammen ist: durch all das entsteht Erinnerung« (Strube 1984, 34).

In folgender Graphik, die eine vereinfachte Form des *konnektionistischen* Modells von J. McClelland darstellt, sind verschiedene Quasineuronen dargestellt, die Klassen von Merkmalen, Lebensräumen etc. von Tieren aufweisen und semantische Einheiten zur Bezeichnung von Tieren.[9] Es ist zu erkennen, dass sich Elemente innerhalb einer Gruppe wechselseitig hemmen, was nicht eigens markiert ist, während die Pfeile zwischen den Elementen verschiedener Gruppen erregende Verbindungen darstellen. Werden die Einheiten ›Fleischfresser‹ und ›Meer‹ als Input aktiviert, so breitet sich die Aktivierung zur assoziierten Einheit ›Hai‹ aus; andere Einheiten hingegen werden gehemmt, es liegt also eine inhibitorische Verbindung vor.

Der Vorgang der Aktivierung von verschalteten Bewusstseinsinhalten ist stark erfahrungsabhängig und umfasst das gesamte Spektrum der *konnotativen* Bedeutung. In diesem Zusammenhang ist darauf zu verweisen, dass pathologische Assoziationsketten bei Schizophrenen als Hyperaktivation neuronaler Netze beschrieben sind, was den engen Zusammenhang zwischen Assoziationen und Aktivationszuständen im Cortex deutlich macht. Fechners Assoziationismus ist damit nichts anderes als die Behandlung der Abhängigkeit zwischen objektiven Reizen und ihrer subjektiven Verarbeitung, die individuelle Erfahrungen umfasst. Fechner argumentiert mithin antisymbolistisch, denn die Verarbeitung ästhetischer Reize ist keine Bezugsetzung von ästhetischen Objekten zu objektiven Kategorien des Schönen, sondern eine potentiell grenzenlose Verschaltung von assoziierten Elementen. Folgerichtig betont Fechner, dass *Asso-*

[9] Abbildung aus G. Roth & Prinz 1996, 383.

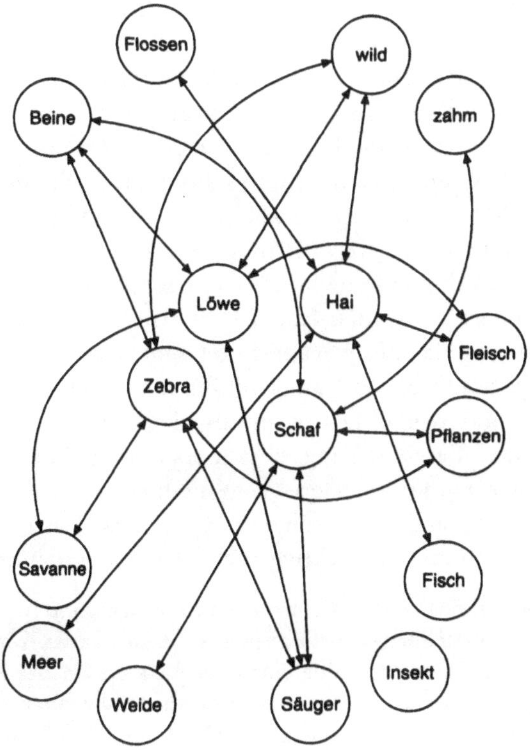

ziationen sukzessive ausgebildet werden (Fechner 1876, 1, 114f.), das Assoziationspotential also im Verlauf der individuellen Entwicklung erlernt wird. Und hier greift dann durchaus ein normativer Aspekt der Ästhetik, da in bestimmten Kulturen historisch variable Assoziationsmuster gesetzt sind. Es wurde bereits auf Fechners Beispiel vom Tisch, der in der Aufsicht an und für sich nichts anderes als ein viereckiger Fleck sei, eingegangen und der Bezug zu *Frames* deutlich gemacht, die als komplexes Konzeptwissen zu verstehen sind. Dieses Konzeptwissen ist kulturabhängig und so sind auch *konnotative* Bedeutungsspektren nicht gänzlich individuell, sondern gebunden an normierte emotionale Muster, an Stereotype, an typische Erfahrungen.

Fechner beschreibt also die *ästhetische* Signalverarbeitung als doppelpoligen Prozess, als den direkten Eindruck einerseits und den assoziierten Eindruck andererseits. Das Wohlgefallen an Dingen beruhe im Wesentlichen »auf der Erinnerung an Wohlgefälliges« (Fechner 1876, 1, 121) und betrifft mithin nicht den apperzeptiven Gedankenverlauf, den wir als kategorielle semantische Zuweisung beschreiben können, sondern den assoziativen Gedankenverlauf. Dieser ist nach heutigen Erkenntnissen als Aktivation von *konnektionistischen* Netzen zu erklären. Es ist interessant, dass auch Fechners *Lustprinzip* als Motor der positiven Assoziation und Zuweisung von Schönheit aus neurophysiologischem Blickwinkel bestätigt werden kann. Man weiß heute, dass affektiv positiv besetzte Responses mit einer Beschleunigung der Verarbeitungszeit gemessen werden können.

Fechner hat mithin eine nicht ganz unbedeutende Stellung unter den frühen Wegbereitern *mentaler Netzwerkvorstellungen* und in diesem Zusammenhang mag der Hinweis gestattet sein, dass sich die symbolistischen Modelle des Strukturalismus mit ihren distinktiven 1:1-Relationen aus heutigem Blickwinkel fast schon als überholtes Intermezzo in einer kontinuierlichen Beschäftigung mit Assoziationen und semantischen Netzen seit dem 19. Jahrhundert bis in die hochspezialisierte Forschung der Gegenwart darstellen. Ich folge G. Roth & W. Prinz, die aus experimentalpsychologischer Perspektive Fechner wie folgt einordnen:

> Obwohl Fechner den Begriff der mentalen Repräsentation (traditionell ausgedrückt: der »Vorstellung«) nicht thematisiert hat, verdanken wir ihm eine wichtige Voraussetzung für eine einstufige Konzeption der Repräsentation: den Gedanken, dass »Erinnerungen« in Form von Resonanzmustern gespeichert sind, die durch neue Sinneseindrücke automatisch reaktiviert werden, wobei diese an die schon vorhandenen Muster angeglichen werden. (Roth & Prinz 1996, 111)

Eben dies ist die Auffassung auch der *konnektionistischen* Modelle zum mentalen Lexikon und der diesbezüglichen semantischen Netzwerkmodelle.

4. Schlussbemerkung

Eingangs wurde darauf verwiesen, dass Fechners »Vorschule der Ästhetik« im Kontext seiner Begierde nach den zerronnenen Evidenzen zu sehen ist und es folglich bei wissenschaftlicher Lektüre seiner Ausführungen keinesfalls um die Herstellung von ungebrochenen Analogien zur Gegenwart gehen kann. In gewisser Weise sind Fechners Ideen einer *Assoziationsästhetik* mit den heutigen Erkenntnissen kognitiver Forschung natürlich auch nicht vergleichbar. Doch sind die Übereinstimmungen im Erklärungsansatz von *semantischen* Verarbeitungsformen auch weit mehr als zufällig. Es ist hier wie dort eine Modellierung der mentalen Bedeutungsverarbeitung zu erkennen, die ein holistisches und parallel arbeitendes System annimmt, das lernfähig ist und auf dem Boden der Erinnerung funktioniert. Fechners induktiver Ansatz überzeugt insoweit aus heutiger Perspektive durchaus.

Literatur:

Adelung, J. (1796): Grammatisch-kritisches Wörterbuch der hochdeutschen Mundart mit beständiger Vergleichung der übrigen Mundarten, besonders aber des Oberdeutschen. 2., verm. und verb. Ausg. Bd. 2, F-L. Leipzig, Sp. 2134.

Arendt, H.-J. (1999): Gustav Theodor Fechner. Ein deutscher Naturwissenschaftler und Philosoph im 19. Jahrhundert. Frankfurt a.M. et al.

Borges, J. (1992): Die Inschrift des Gottes. In: Das Aleph. Erzählungen. Frankfurt a.M., 100–105.

Drue, H. (1983): Philosophie und Psychologie als Konkurrenten in der Ästhetik. In: Kunst und Kunstforschung. Beiträge zur Ästhetik. Hg. von Wolandt. Bonn, 3–36.

Dupéron, I. (2000): G.T. Fechner. Le parallélisme psychophysiologique. Paris.

DUW (2001): Deutsches Universalwörterbuch. Hg. von der Dudenredaktion. 4., neu bearb. und erw. Aufl. Mannheim; Leipzig; Wien; Zürich.

Fechner, G. Th. (1846): Ueber das höchste Gut. Leipzig.

Fechner, G. Th. (1848): Nanna oder Über das Seelenleben der Pflanzen. Leipzig.

Fechner, G. Th. (1851): Zend-Avesta oder über die Dinge des Himmels und des Jenseits, vom Standpunkt der Naturbetrachtung. 3 Theile. Leipzig.

Fechner, G. Th. (1876): Vorschule der Ästhetik. 2 Bde. Leipzig.

Fechner, G. Th. (1984): Das unendliche Leben. Mit einem Nachwort von G. Mattenklott. München.

Foucault, M. (1971): Die Ordnung der Dinge. Eine Archäologie der Humanwissenschaften. Frankfurt a.M.

Geissler, H.; Müller, M. (Hg.) (1990): Psychophysical explorations of mental structures. Toronto; Lewiston; Bern; Göttingen; Stuttgart.

Heidelberger, M. (1993): Die innere Seite der Natur. Gustav Theodor Fechners wissenschaftlich-philosophische Weltauffassung. Frankfurt a.M.

Jackendoff, R. (1996): Patterns in the mind. Language and human nature. New York.

Roth, G.; Prinz, W. (Hg.) (1996): Kopf-Arbeit. Gehirnfunktionen und kognitive Leistungen. Heidelberg; Berlin; Oxford.

Strube, G. (1984): Assoziation. Berlin.

Tergan, S.-O. (1986): Modelle der Wissensrepräsentation als Grundlage qualitativer Wissensdiagnostik. Opladen.

Waldrich H.-P. (1993): Grenzgänger der Wissenschaft. München.

Warnke, I. (1999): Wortartenübergreifende lexikalische Kategorien. Prototypensemantik vs. Merkmalsemantik. In: Usus linguae. I. Warnke. Hildesheim; New York, 223–240.

Ulla Fix

Fechners »Vorschule der Ästhetik« und heutige zeichenbezogene Stilauffassungen

Fechners Äußerungen zu Zeichen und Zeichenwahrnehmung in der »Vorschule der Ästhetik« lassen drei auch heute noch wesentliche und anregende Problemkreise erkennen:

Man findet Grundideen der Eco'schen Theorie von den Zeichen, also Vorstellungen der Semiotik. Gemeint ist die Fechner'sche Auffassung von den ›Assoziationen‹, die sich mit der heutigen von ›Konnotationen‹ stark berührt, sowie die Idee, dass uns alles in einer Kultur etwas zu sagen hat. Da wir heute Stil als Konnotationspotenzial von Texten betrachten, stehen auch moderne zeichenbezogene Stilauffassungen in Beziehung zu Fechner.

Zweitens lassen sich Vorgriffe auf den erkenntnistheoretisch-pragmatischen Zweig der Informationstheorie erkennen, in dem es um das Maß für die pragmatische Information geht, das bezogen ist auf den Wert, den die Nachricht für den Empfänger hat, und auf das pragmatische Gelingen der Kommunikation überhaupt. Wieviel Neues muß eine Äußerung enthalten, um unsere Aufmerksamkeit zu wecken und zu erhalten?

Und drittens greift Fechner der Ethnomethodologie des Sprechens vor, einer aus der interpretativen Soziologie abgeleiteten Forschungsrichtung, die diejenigen Formen, Muster und Mittel untersucht, die Mitglieder einer kulturellen Gemeinschaft entwickelt haben, um ihr Alltagsleben organisieren und aufrechterhalten zu können. Die Ausdrücke, die eine Gemeinschaft für Bezeichnungen des Ästhetischen entwickelt, gehören in diesen Kontext. Auch sie sind Mittel, mit denen sich Mitglieder einer Gemeinschaft über gemeinsam Interessierendes verständigen können.

Die Form, das Aussehen, die Gestalt einer
Sprachhandlung eines Textes ist ihr/sein Stil.
(Püschel 1987, 143)

1. Ausgangsüberlegungen

Der Beitrag geht im Bereich der Sprachwissenschaft dem nach, was Gert Mattenklott die »Präsenz Fechners im Denken unseres Jahrhunderts« (Mattenklott 1984, 189) genannt hat, angeregt dadurch, dass sich einige der grundsätzlichen Ideen Fechners aus der »Vorschule der Ästhetik« (1876) auch in Auffassungen moderner Sprachwissenschaft wiederzufinden scheinen. Freilich wird in den wenigsten Fällen der Bezug zu Fechner auch hergestellt. Diese also eher »verborgene Präsenz« Fechner'scher Ideen kann man in Zusammenhängen entdecken, in denen es um kognitions- und bedeutungsorientierte Fragestellungen geht. Darüber hinaus kann man Fechner als Vordenker auch dort sehen, wo er mit seinen diesbezüglichen Gedankengängen, über Sprache hinausgehend, bereits den *semiotischen* Charakter kommunikativer Phänomene in *interdisziplinärer* Betrachtungsweise voraussetzt. Seine Überlegungen betreffen Fragen der Zeichenbedeutung im Allgemeinen – semiotische Aspekte also – sowie Fragen der Wortbedeutung im Besonderen, die *Semantik*. Und sie betreffen Probleme des Stils als ästhetischer und pragmatischer Kategorie. Um zu zeigen, worauf ich mich beziehe, soll erst einmal Fechner zu Wort kommen mit Äußerungen aus dem IX. Kapitel der »Vorschule der Ästhetik«, in dem es um das »aesthetische Associationsprinzip« geht. Zunächst beziehe ich mich auf das Beispiel der Orange, in der seine Zeitgenossen, so Fechner, »ganz Italien« sehen.

> In der That, sieht denn der, der eine Orange sieht, blos einen runden gelben Fleck in ihr? Mit dem sinnlichen Auge, ja; geistig aber sieht er ein Ding von reizendem Geruch, erquickendem Geschmack, an einem schönen Baume, in einem schönen Lande, unter einem warmen Himmel gewachsen, in ihr; er sieht so zu sagen ganz Italien mit in ihr, das Land, wohin uns von jeher eine romantische Sehnsucht zog. Aus der Erinnerung an all das setzt sich die geistige Farbe zusammen, womit die sinnliche verschönernd lasiert ist; indess der, der eine gelbe Holzkugel sieht, eben blos trocknes Holz hinter dem runden gelben Fleck sieht [...]. (Fechner 1978, 89)

Die Bedeutung von Begleitvorstellungen, *Konnotationen*, die *Zeichen* erst ihren Sinn geben,[1] wird hier zur Sprache gebracht. Die Stilbedeutung eines Textganzen nun beruht auch darauf, dass Wörter ihre Konnotationen und Assoziationen in einen Text einbringen bzw. im Text neue entwickeln und ihm so – durch ihren Bezug aufeinander – eine zweite Sinnebene geben.[2] Das ist der erste mir wichtige Gedanke, den ich mit Blick auf die Fechner'schen Äußerungen nennen möchte.

Fechner ergänzt das Orangenbeispiel durch andere, ebenso einleuchtende: Warum gefällt uns eine rote Wange, aber nicht eine rote Nase? Wann und warum finden wir einen Namen für einen Menschen »hübsch«? Was empfinden wir heute beim Klang des Posthorns im Gegensatz zu dem, was Menschen früher empfunden haben mögen? Was sagt das Gefühl, das man hat, wenn man, d.h. in Fechners Beispiel »der Perser«, gekochten Reis zwischen den Fingerspitzen hält? Semiotischer als in Fechners Beispielen kann es nicht zugehen. Wo bleibt aber (außer beim Eigennamen) das Verbale? Es wird durchaus – zum Vergleich – herangezogen. »Die Sprache der Worte« und die Sprache der »dinglichen« *Zeichen* (der »sichtbaren« Worte) werden von Fechner in der Hinsicht gleichgesetzt, dass alle Kodes Bedeutung vermitteln.

> Jedes Ding, mit dem wir umgehen, ist für uns geistig charakterisiert durch eine Resultante von Erinnerungen an Alles, was wir je bezüglich dieses Dinges und selbst verwandter Dinge äusserlich und innerlich erfahren, gehört, gelesen, gedacht, gelernt haben. Diese Resultante von Erinnerungen knüpft sich eben so unmittelbar an den Anblick des Dinges, wie die Vorstellung desselben an das Wort, womit es bezeichnet wird. Ja Form und Farbe des Dinges sind so zu sagen nichts als sichtbare Worte, welche uns die ganze Bedeutung des Dinges unwillkürlich vergegenwärtigen; wir müssen freilich diese sichtbare Sprache eben so gut erst gelernt haben, um sie zu verstehen, wie die Sprache der Worte. Wir sehen einen Tisch, im Grunde nur einen viereckigen Fleck, aber in dem viereckigen Flecke Alles, wozu ein Tisch gebraucht wird; das macht den viereckigen Fleck erst zu einem Tische. (Fechner 1978, 93)

Und die zweite wichtige Überlegung: Schlussfolgerungen über das Ästhetische werden, wie das folgende Zitat zeigt, auf *alle Zeichenarten* bezogen.

> Also versteht man jetzt unter *ästhetisch* überhaupt, was sich auf Verhältnisse unmittelbaren Gefallens und Missfallens an dem bezieht, was durch die Sinne in uns eintritt. (Fechner 1978, 33)

---

[1] Dezidiert bei Eco 1972, 19ff.; 1987, 99ff.

[2] Siehe Lerchner 1981, 1984; Fix 1986; Coseriu 1994.

Fechner nennt solche Verhältnisse:

> *Verhältnisse* des Sinnlichen, wie in der Musik, und *Associationsvorstellungen*, die unmittelbar mit dem Sinnlichen verschmelzen, wie mit den Worten in der Poesie und den Formen in den bildenden Künsten. (Fechner 1978, 33)

Ein dritter, für meine Überlegungen relevanter Gedanke Fechners ist, dass er von der Konventionalität der *Zeichen* und damit zugleich von der kulturellen Gebundenheit der *Assoziationen* ausgeht, z.B. wenn er sagt:

> Vielmehr, wie schon gesagt, will die Bedeutung der Formen so gut erlernt sein, als die der Worte, und wird uns nur auf demselben Wege geläufig; das ist der Weg der Assoziation. (Fechner 1978, 115)

Die Feststellung, dass *Konventionalisierung* nötig ist, wenn wir uns mithilfe von *Zeichen* verstehen wollen, gilt ebenfalls für alle Zeichenarten, die er im Blick hat. Das erinnert stark an Ecos Vorstellung von Zeichen als kulturellen Konventionen,[3] eine Vorstellung, die voraussetzt, »daß unter jedem Kommunikationsprozeß diese Regeln – oder Kodes – existieren und daß diese auf irgendeiner kulturellen Übereinkunft beruhen« (Eco 1972, 20).

Als Viertes sei noch ein Ausschnitt aus den Ausführungen zum »Prinzip der äesthetischen Hülfe oder Steigerung« zitiert, um am Text zu zeigen, wie Fechner über die einzelnen Zeichen hinaus deren *Zusammenwirken* im Blick hatte.

> Zum wohlgefälligen Eindrucke eines Kunstwerkes [...], das wir schön nennen, tragen im Allgemeinen verschiedene Momente bei, die sich durch Analyse sondern lassen; nicht leicht bringt es eins davon für sich zu einer bedeutenden ästhetischen Wirkung; und um uns von der Grösse des Totaleindruckes Rechenschaft zu geben, müssen wir daher im Allgemeinen das Princip ihrer wechselseitigen Hülfe zuziehen. (Fechner 1978, 52)

Der Begriff vom »Totaleindruck« des Ästhetischen, die Vorstellung von der »Einstimmigkeit aller Momente«, lässt an die Auffassung von Stil als intendierter Einheitlichkeit denken (s.u.). Die durch die Zitate angedeutete Leistung Fechners – kurz zusammengefasst: die Betrachtung des Zusammmenwirkens von *Zeichen* und *Zeichen-Wahrnehmung* – hat in der Sprachwissenschaft bisher noch wenig Beachtung gefunden. Dem soll nun im Hinblick auf Stilfragen abgeholfen werden. Ich werde zunächst erläutern, was man im Gegensatz zu traditionellen Auffassungen in der

[3] Siehe Nöth 2000, 129.

gegenwärtigen Diskussion unter Stil versteht, um zeigen zu können, von welcher Bedeutung dieser Begriff ist – nicht nur für die Sprachwissenschaft, sondern auch für andere Disziplinen, u.a. für Kunstwissenschaft, Literaturwissenschaft und Soziologie. Was ich herausarbeiten möchte, hat also von vornherein einen *interdisziplinären Aspekt.*

Das eigentlich Aufschlussreiche zu *Stil* ist nun bei Fechner nicht, wie man erwarten könnte, im Kapitel »Stil und Stilisieren« zu lesen. Es findet sich vielmehr genau dort, wo es um das Wesen des Ästhetischen als Auslöser ›sinnlicher Lust‹ und wo es um ›ästhetische Prinzipien‹ geht, vor allem um das ›ästhetische Assoziationsprinzip‹.

2. Stilauffassungen heute

Zunächst – kurz – ein Wort zu traditionellen Stilauffassungen: Immer noch bezieht man sich heute vielfach auf die aus der Rhetorik stammende Vorstellung von *Stil* als Kleid des Gedankens oder als Schmuck der Rede, was bedeutet, dass man sich Stil als etwas Entbehrliches denkt, das zum Gesagten hinzukommen kann, das aber nicht unbedingt vorhanden sein muss. Und was auch heißt, dass man sich ein Nacheinander von Formulieren und Stilbilden vorstellt. Stilanalyse heißt dann: das Finden und Bestimmen von Stilfiguren. Deutlich schimmern hier von den fünf Teilen der Redevorbereitung, die die rhetorische Lehre ansetzt, die ersten drei durch: Inventio, Dispositio, Elocutio. Inzwischen wissen wir aber als Ergebnis der Erforschung von Textproduktionsvorgängen – eigentlich aber schon seit Kleists Idee von der »allmählichen Verfertigung der Gedanken beim Reden« –, dass sich die Formulierungsvorgänge als ein Miteinander von Gedanken- und Sprachfindung vollziehen, und wir wissen zudem, dass Stil nicht nur Schmuck – also Äußerliches –, sondern auch Aussage, – also »Innerliches« –, Inhalt ist. Stil wäre demnach also ein Mehr an Bedeutung. Was genau nun ist dieses Mehr? Ich spreche im Folgenden von einer semiotisch-pragmatischen Stilauffassung und meine damit, dass man mit Stil erstens die Vorstellung von *Sinn* verbindet, zweitens die von formgebendem, d.h. gestaltgebendem *Handeln.*

Zunächst zur Vorstellung von *Sinn* – dem *Mehr.* Als Funktion von Stil gilt grundsätzlich, dass ein Was, ein Mitgeteiltes, durch ein Wie, die *Gestalt,* im Hinblick auf ein Wozu, einen Zweck, ausgedrückt wird. Mit dem Attribut ›semiotisch‹ benenne ich nun meine Auffassung, dass Stil Zeichencharakter hat, was heißt, dass auch das Wie, auch die *Gestalt,* Informationen vermitteln kann. Es handelt sich dabei um spezifische, nämlich rezeptionssteuernde Informationen. Die Gestalt des Textes gibt Hinweise darauf, wie der Text gelesen werden soll. Anders gesagt: Stil gibt immer etwas zu verstehen. Was ist es, das er uns mitteilt? Zum einen sind es *pragmasoziale* Informationen: Ein bestimmter Sprachgestus oder auch ein bestimmter Kleidungsstil verweisen auf den Wunsch des Produzenten, sich »lesbar« zu machen, d.h. individuelle oder auch soziale Identität auszudrücken. Hier liegt das soziologisch orientierte Stilinteresse, das in unserem Zusammenhang weniger von Bedeutung ist.

Zum anderen vermittelt *Stil* aber auch ästhetische Informationen. Gemeint ist, daß man durch das *WIE* etwas aussagt über den Wert, den man der *Form selbst* beimisst: Man wird an den hedonistischen Wert des »reinen« Gefallens denken. Es handelt sich aber auch um *pragmaästhetische* Werte, nämlich erstens um die Potenz des Ästhetischen, *Rezeption zu lenken,* d.h. es geht um Fragen wie die folgenden: In welcher Stimmung/Atmosphäre, unter den Aspekten welcher Textsorte/Gattung soll man den Text lesen? Es geht weiter um die Potenz, *Rezeptionslust zu fördern,* z.B. durch Rhythmus, Proportionen, Verhältnis von Einheitlichkeit und Wechsel. Drittens kann die *Rezeption* durch die Textgestalt *vertieft werden.* Ich erinnere an das ästhetische Vergnügen bei der Entschlüsselung von Bildlichkeit, die den Zweitsinn eines Textes tragen kann. Und es handelt sich schließlich viertens um die heuristische Funktion, *Erkenntnis zu befördern.* Erinnert sei an die kognitive Potenz, die in durch Vagheit und Bildlichkeit erzeugtem Zweitsinn liegt.[4]

Zusammenfassend sei gesagt: Ein Text hat neben seiner Primärbedeutung – also neben dem, was zum Textthema gesagt wird – eine zweite Bedeutungsebene, die durch die *Gestalt*, das Wie, vermittelte pragmasoziale und/oder pragmaästhetische Sekundärbedeutung, die Stilbedeutung, den Zweitsinn. Dass man hier an Fechners *Assoziationsprinzip* und andere ästhetische Prinzipien anknüpfen kann, liegt auf der Hand; denn Zweitsinn wird durch im Text angelegte Konnotationen (Assoziationen) hergestellt. Und er kann nur in der Einheit des Mannigfaltigen entstehen. Ich komme darauf zurück.

---

[4] »Das Stilistische gehört [...] der Klasse selektiv-pragmatischer Informationen an. Es ist zu verstehen »als der Äußerung inhärente Information über die spezifischen kommunikativen Parameter eines kommunikativen Ereignisses« (Lerchner 1981, 89); vgl. auch Fix 1990, 305f.; vgl. Kainz 1948, 529. Er unterscheidet zwei Arten von Ästhetischem: Formästhetik und Gehaltsästhetik. Einheitliche, prägnante intendierte Darstellung wäre demzufolge ausreichende Voraussetzung für Ästhetisches im Sinne einer Alltagsästhetik.

Mit dem Attribut ›pragmatisch‹ wird der Blick auf den Handlungscharakter von *Stil* gerichtet. Stil wird im Handeln hergestellt und ist so gut durch dessen Bedingungen bestimmt wie er sie auch beeinflussen kann. Das, was der Produzent mit der Form seines Textes als Zweitsinn anbietet und was der Rezipient zu »entschlüsseln« hat, das relativ Feste, woran sich im Verlauf der Kommunikation beide halten, ist eben die *Gestalt* des Textes. Der handlungsbezogene Ansatz moderner Stilistik trifft sich hier mit der Fechner'schen rezeptionsbezogenen, von der *Wahrnehmung* ausgehenden Denkweise.

Freilich ist der übliche undifferenzierte Begriff des *Handelns* (nach Luckmann 1986, 617) im Hinblick auf stilistisches Handeln zu spezifizieren: Sprachliches Handeln schlechthin ist gerichtet auf außersprachliche Ziele, z.B. kann man mit einer Äußerung jemanden INFORMIEREN, ÜBERREDEN, ERHEITERN, BEEINDRUCKEN wollen, alles Ziele, die außerhalb der Sprache liegen. Stilhandeln dagegen als spezielle Form sprachlichen Handelns, man kann sie Gestalten nennen, ist gerichtet auf ein innersprachliches Ziel, nämlich auf das Herstellen der sprachlich-stilistischen Form, der Einheitlichkeit eines Textes, die erst Stil ermöglicht – das »Zusammenwirken [...] in ihrem Füreinandersein anschaulich plausibler Teile« (Kainz 1948, 621).[5] Der Zweitsinn eines Textes kann nur entstehen, wenn sich alle Elemente der Textoberfläche in dieser Weise aufeinander beziehen, wenn sie ihre jeweilige Bedeutung durch diesen Bezug erhalten und so gemeinsam Sinn konstituieren.[6] Gestaltgebendes Handeln ist also mit Soeffner (1986) auf *Einheitlichkeit* und auf *Wahrnehmbarkeit*[7] gerichtetes und insofern ästhetisierendes Handeln. Dessen Resultat ist als *Überhöhung* zu verstehen.[8]

---

[5] In soziologischen wie strukturalistischen Arbeiten zu Stil (Soeffner 1986; Luckmann 1986; Hahn 1986; Jakobson 1965, 1972, Riffaterre 1973; Enkvist 1976) gilt Einheitlichkeit als unbedingte Voraussetzung für Stilisierung.

[6] »Stil ist Teil eines umfassenden Systems von Zeichen, Symbolen und Verweisungen für soziale Orientierung« (Soeffner 1986, 318).

[7] »Innerhalb der menschlichen Gesellschaft, die immer schon eine Gesellschaft von Beobachtern ist, wird Stil produziert, um beobachtet zu werden. Stil repräsentiert und präsentiert in sozialer Interaktion die Einheit von Präsentation und Beobachtung. In dieser Hinsicht kann ›Stilisierung‹, das ›Styling‹, begriffen werden als Bündelung beobachtbarer Handlungen, die ausgeführt werden, um eine einheitlich abgestimmte Präsentation zu erzielen« (Soeffner 1986, 319). Vgl. auch Hahn 1986, 606: »Beobachterperspektive«.

[8] » [...] im Gegensatz zu alltäglicher Typenbildung enthält jeder Stil zusätzlich eine ästhetische Komponente – eine ästhetisierende Überhöhung – des Alltäglichen« (Soeffner 1986, 319).

>Stil zu haben< ist also das Ergebnis gezielter Handlungen in Richtung auf eine >kulturelle Überhöhung< des Alltäglichen. *Es ist eine sichtbare, einheitsstiftende Präsentation, in die jede Einzelhandlung und jedes Detail mit dem Ziel eingearbeitet ist, eine homogene Figuration oder >Gestalt< – den Stil – zu bilden und darzustellen.* >Stil zu haben< – in diesem Sinne – bedeutet fähig zu sein, bewußt für andere und auch für das eigene Selbstbild eine einheitliche Interpretation anzubieten und zu inszenieren. (Soeffner 1986, 319; Hervorh. U.F.)

Der Stil einer Person, einer Gruppe, eines Kunst- oder Gebrauchsgegenstandes, eines Textes bindet alle wahrnehmbaren Details seines jeweiligen Trägers zu einer darstellbaren Sinnfigur zusammen. [...] *In jedes Detail des Stils und der stilisierenden Aktionen ist für einen konkreten oder möglichen Beobachter* (auch für den Designer des Stils als Beobachter seiner selbst) *ein Interpretationshinweis auf die Sinnfigur als ganze eingearbeitet.* (Soeffner 1986, 320; Hervorh. U.F.)

Überall, wo im gesellschaftlichen Zusammenleben sich die Notwendigkeit ergibt, eine Handlung, Sache oder Funktion hervorzuheben, auf sie aufmerksam zu machen und sie von unerwünschten Zusammenhängen zu lösen, erscheint die ästhetische Funktion als Begleitfaktor. (Mukařovsky 1982, 33)

Den Bezug zu Fechner sehe ich in seiner Vorstellung von der *Einheitlichkeit im Mannigfaltigen* und von der (implizit vermittelten) kulturellen Gebundenheit der *Assoziationen*, mit deren Hilfe wir einem Text nicht nur Farbe, sondern auch Sinn geben können.

3. Fechners Auffassungen vom Ästhetischen als »von Aussen erweckte Vorstellungen und Empfindungen« (1978, 37) im Verhältnis zu heutigen Stilauffassungen

Ich knüpfe an die Feststellung an, dass Stil als eine Beobachtungskategorie gilt, d.h. dass er für die Wahrnehmung der anderen produziert wird und an das Sichtbare, die *Gestalt* gebunden ist. Für meine Überlegungen ist es kein Hindernis, dass Fechner – wie anfangs schon gesagt – viele seiner Gedanken nicht am sprachlichen Material, sondern vor allem an Beispielen aus der bildenden Kunst und, was überraschen mag, aus dem Alltagsleben entwickelt hat (Orange, rote Nase, Haltung des Körpers, Schönheit des Fußes, Essen von Reis). Fechner denkt *semiotisch*. Das erleichtert die Vorstellung eines überdisziplinären Stilbegriffs.

Ich greife mir nun aus den möglichen Bezügen zu Fechner zwei heraus: Ich will zum einen den Zusammenhang zwischen der Kategorie der *Vorstellungsassoziationen* und der der *Konnotationen* (Eco 1972; Lerchner 1981, 1984) zeigen, weil Stil in seiner Sinnhaftigkeit heute als Konnotationspotenzial von Texten angesehen wird. Grundlage dafür ist die Betrachtung des Prinzips der »einheitlichen Verknüpfung des Mannichfaltigen« (Fechner 1978, 53ff.), das übergreifend für alle neueren Stilauffassungen gilt. Zum anderen wende ich mich (nur andeutungsweise) am Beispiel der Stilistik von Riffaterre dem Prinzip der *ästhetischen Schwelle* (Fechner 1978, 49) zu, das in strukturalistischen Stilauffassungen von zentraler Bedeutung ist. Schließlich werde ich knapp auf den ethnographischen Ansatz Fechners hinweisen.

3.1. Prinzip der einheitlichen Verknüpfung des Mannigfaltigen

Die Existenz von *Einheit in der Vielheit* (»Mannichfaltigkeit«, Fechner 1978, 53ff.) ist natürlich keine Idee, die Fechner in die ästhetische Diskussion erst eingebracht hätte. Die Reihe derer, die sich dazu geäußert haben, reicht von Aristoteles bis Kant, Leibniz, Schelling, Hegel u.a. Insofern könnte man sich fragen, ob das Prinzip eigentlich noch der Erwähnung bedarf. Hinzu kommt, dass die Vorstellung von Einheitlichkeit im Sinne von Homogenität, Kohärenz und Totalität seit der Moderne ohnehin so unhinterfragt nicht aufrechterhalten werden kann. Mein Anspruch ist auch nicht und kann es nicht sein, mich in die grundsätzliche Diskussion dieser Fragen einzuschalten. Den Bezug zum Prinzip der Einheit in der Vielheit jedoch muss ich herstellen, um das Vorhandensein von *Stil/Gestalt* erklären zu können. Zu den Wesensmerkmalen, die *Stil* grundsätzlich zugesprochen werden, gehört, dass er als Einheit verstanden wird, die mehr ist als die Summe ihrer einzelnen Teile.[9] Die verwendeten Mittel werden erst durch ihren Gebrauch zu Stilelementen. Indem sie sich aufeinander beziehen und miteinander wirken, stellen sie das Stilganze, die Stilgestalt mit ihrer spezifischen Information her. Das geht so weit, dass Wörter, die außerhalb des Textes bereits konnotiert sind, im Text eine andere *Konnotation* erhalten können. Ein als ›gehoben‹ markiertes Wort kann in einem umgangssprachlichen Kontext z.B. die Färbung der Ironie erhalten. Das Zusammenwirken der einzelnen Elemente erhält seinen

---

[9] Vgl. Grundgedanken der Gestaltpsychologie, so z.B. in Katz 1948.

Sinn im Handlungszusammenhang, d.h. in Relation zur Situation, zum Thema, zur Funktion.[10] Dabei ist alles verwendbar, was es an sprachlichen und parasprachlichen Mitteln gibt, auch das, was miteinander konkurriert oder sich zu widersprechen scheint.[11] Die Einheitlichkeit des Stils kann demnach auf mehreren Ebenen und mit sehr verschiedenen Mitteln hergestellt werden. Aus dem Kontext gerissen, verlieren die Mittel ihren stilistischen Wert wieder. Einheitlichkeit ist hier also in dem Sinne aufzufassen, dass alle Elemente eines Ganzen einem einheitlichen Stilwillen dienen, und dass, wo dies nicht gegeben ist, kein Stil existiert. Ein Bruch des im Text einmal eingeführten Stils kann (und soll häufig) einen Überraschungseffekt zur Folge haben.

Der Begriff des Ästhetischen bei Fechner nun hat mit der eben beschriebenen Vorstellung von *Stil* als ›Einheitlichem‹, als ›Gestaltetem‹ zu tun, das auf Beobachtbarkeit hin angelegt ist und dessen Voraussetzung das Einzelne im Mannigfaltigen ist. Die als modern geltende Einsicht, dass Stil – im Sinne von *Einheit in der Mannigfaltigkeit* – funktionsbezogen ist, hat Fechner auch schon, wenn er nämlich von der »Uebereinstimmung der Theile eines Ganzen zu einem gewissen Zweck, einer gewissen Idee« (Fechner 1978, 54) spricht.[12]

> Was wir einheitlich verknüpfte Mannichfaltigkeit nennen, übersetzt sich näher zugesehen in eine Uebereinstimmung des Mehreren nach gewisser Beziehung bei Abweichung nach andern. Diese Uebereinstimmung braucht nicht in qualitativer Gleichheit zu beruhen, sondern kann auch in Uebereinstimmung der Theile eines Ganzen zu einem gewissen Zweck, einer gewissen Idee oder in Causalverknüpfung der Momente eines Geschehens, (die stets eine Abhängigkeit von demselben Gesetze voraussetzt,) liegen, und aus niederem oder höherem Gesichtspunkte statt finden. (Fechner 1978, 54)

Strukturalistische Stilauffassungen sind ebenso wie soziologische, wahrnehmungsbezogene auf die Kategorie der ›Einheitlichkeit‹ angewiesen.

---

[10] Vgl. Sandig 1986; Fix 1996.

[11] Sandig verweist darauf, dass ein Stil, um identifizierbar zu sein, Konsistenz bezüglich der verwendeten Stilmittel aufweisen muss (Sandig 1986, 115).

[12] Fechner setzt zudem Einheit in der Mannigfaltigkeit gegen Identität. Hier herrscht weniger das philosophische als das gestaltpsychologische Denken: ›Gestaltqualitäten‹ sind Eigenschaften, die nur an der durchorganisierten Gestalt und nicht an den einzelnen Teilen festgestellt werden können. Eine Melodie besitzt z.B. Qualitäten, die nicht in den einzelnen Tönen enthalten sind.

3.2. »Vorstellungsassoziation« – Konnotation, Stil

Indem Fechner das Ästhetische als Phänomen der Wahrnehmung bestimmt, hat er die für die heutige Stilbetrachtung entscheidenden Kategorien ›Sichtbarkeit‹ und ›Beobachtbarkeit‹ vorausgenommen wie auch die Vorstellung, dass Stil Handeln ist, das sich erst in der Rezeption im Sinne einer ›Stilwirkung‹ erfüllt. Stil ist für Beobachter Gemachtes und hängt von deren Rezeption ab.

Beobachtbar ist das *über die Sinne* Wahrnehmbare. Fechner macht deutlich, dass er die sinnliche Wahrnehmung ausdrücklich auf das »Aussen«, also auf die Formseite bezogen sehen will. Die Form, und nicht die intellektuelle oder wie auch immer geartete Verarbeitung, sondern das, was direkt Lust oder Unlust hervorruft, interessieren ihn.[13]

> Die Ästhetik nach unsrer Fassung nun bezieht sich auf die Seite der Lust und Unlust, sofern solche ***unmittelbar an von Aussen erweckten Vorstellungen und Empfindungen hängt***, greift aber durch das niedere und höhere Gebiet zugleich durch, insofern die höheren Bezüge dieser Empfindungen und Vorstellungen nach ihrem Lust- und Unlustgehalt mit in ihr Bereich fallen. (Fechner 1978, 37; Hervorh. U.F.)

Wichtig ist demnach zum einen die Trennung von *Innen* und *Außen*, die Fechner vornimmt. Das Gute erweckt inneres Wohlgefallen, das *Schöne* äußeres, ich nenne es ›gestaltbezogenes‹.

Für meine Überlegungen entscheidend ist aber zum anderen, dass er dem *Schönen* im engeren Sinne die Eigenschaft zuschreibt, eine »höhere als blos sinnliche Lust doch unmitttelbar aus Sinnlichem schöpfen zu lassen«, was »sei es durch Auffassung innerer Beziehungen des Sinnlichen oder durch Vorstellungsassociation an das Sinnliche möglich ist« (Fechner 1978, 15). Es geht ihm über die *Wahrnehmung* durch unsere Sinne hinaus darum, dass dem Wahrgenommenen ein *Sinn* zugeschrieben wird. Ich nenne ihn ›stilistischen Sinn‹. Fechners Assoziationsbegriff nun (»der associierte Eindruck«, Fechner 1978, 94) schließt ein, dass wir nicht nur mit dem »sinnlichen« (Fechner 1978, 93), sondern auch mit dem »geistigen Auge« (ebd.) sehen. Anders gesagt: Alles, was wir wahrnehmen, ist

---

[13] »Hiernach heisst schön *im weitesten* Sinne, der zugleich der gemeinste ist, Alles, woran sich die Eigenschaft findet, *unmittelbar*, nicht erst durch Überlegung oder durch seine Folgen, Gefallen zu erwecken, insbesondre, falls es diese Eigenschaft nicht in zu geringem Grade und falls es sie verhältnismäßig rein besitzt.« (Fechner 1978, 15).

durch ›Begleitvorstellungen‹, die er »Resultanten von Erinnerungen« (ebd.) oder »geistige Farbe« (ebd.) nennt, charakterisiert.

In der heutigen Sprachwissenschaft fasst man dieses Phänomen der Begleitvorstellungen unter dem Begriff der ›Konnotation‹ und erläutert sie als die mit einem lexikalischen Element verbundene negative oder positive Bewertung bzw. Assoziation (Lutzeier 1995, 160). Eco geht mit seinem Konnotationsbegriff darüber hinaus, indem er *Konnotation* als die »Summe aller kulturellen Einheiten« bezeichnet, »die das Signifikans dem Empfänger institutionell ins Gedächtnis rufen kann« (Eco 1972, 108). In seinem Denksystem bezieht sich dies selbstverständlich nicht nur auf *sprachliche Zeichen.* So auch bei Fechner in der bereits zitierten und hier gekürzt wiederholten Äußerung:

> Jedes Ding, mit dem wir umgehen, ist für uns geistig charakterisiert durch *eine Resultante von Erinnerungen an Alles, was wir je bezüglich dieses Dinges und selbst verwandter Dinge äusserlich und innerlich erfahren, gehört, gelesen, gedacht, gelernt haben.* Diese Resultante von Erinnerungen knüpft sich eben so unmittelbar an *den Anblick des Dinges, wie die Vorstellung desselben an das Wort, womit es bezeichnet wird.* (Fechner 1978, 93; Hervorh. U.F.)

Damit kommen das kognitive und, wie Fechners Beispiele zeigen, auch das kulturelle Moment ins Spiel.

1. Das kognitive Moment: Unsere Wahrnehmung ist von *Erfahrungen* und *Erwartungen* geprägt, die (nach Fechner als ›Vorstellungsassoziationen‹, nach Eco als ›Konnotationen‹) teils mehr, teils weniger fest gleichermaßen an die *Dinge* als Zeichen wie an die *Worte* als Zeichen gebunden sind.
2. Das kulturelle Moment: Wahrnehmung ist *soziokulturell* gebunden. Vom kulturellen Hintergrund hängt es ab, in welche Richtung unsere Aufmerksamkeit gelenkt wird, welche Assoziationen wir gemeinsam haben.

Während Eco mit seinem kulturbezogenen Begriff von *Konnotation* das Psychische ausdrücklich ausschließt,[14] ist bei Fechner nun sogar beides im Blick: die physiologisch-psychische Fähigkeit des Wahrnehmens wie die kulturelle Gebundenheit der Rezeption, in dem Sinne, dass wir mit der kulturellen Verfügbarkeit, die Bildern, Musik, Worten, aber auch All-

---

[14] Die Konnotation ist für Eco die »Summe aller kulturellen Einheiten, die das Signifikans dem Empfänger institutionell ins Gedächtnis rufen kann. Dieses ›kann‹ spielt nicht auf psychische Möglichkeiten an, sondern auf kulturelle Verfügbarkeit« (Eco 1972, 108).

tagsphänomenen (Tisch, Wange, Gerüche, Speisen, Vorhänge, Teppiche usw.) eigen ist, rezeptiv umgehen können.

Auch zwischen dem Fechner'schen Begriff der ›Lust‹ als ›Mitbestimmung‹ bzw. ›Resultante‹ und dem Eco'schen Begriff von axiologischen *Konnotationen* kann man Übereinstimmung sehen. ›Globale axiologische Konnotationen‹ sind nach Eco das wertende Schlussglied einer »Kette von Konnotationen, die für den Empfänger positiven oder negativen Wert annehmen kann« (Eco 1972, 111). Eine solche Kette könnte, wenn man ein Fechner'sches Beispiel in Ecos Denkweisen »übersetzt«, sich an das Wort oder die Sache ›Reis‹ anschließen, der Reis, dessen Güte der Perser schon mit seinen Fingern fühlen könne. Reis – als Ding oder Wort – kann in Fechners Beispiel die Konnotationskette ›körnig‹ = ›locker‹ = ›sich gut anfühlend‹ = ›schmackhaft‹ = ›angenehm‹ = ›verlockend‹ haben, an die sich eine positive axiologische Konnotation anschließt, also eine grundsätzlich positive Wertung von ›Reis‹, die an Fechners *Lustprinzip* erinnert.

Zieht sich nun – und damit komme ich wieder zum Stil- und Textthema – die Verwendung solchermaßen konnotierter Wörter durch den ganzen Text, führt dies zum Aufbau eines den Text bestimmenden Konnotationspotenzials.

Dies kann erstens dadurch geschehen, dass Wörter in Textzusammenhängen eine spezifische *inhalts*bezogene Wertung aufbauen. Sie wenden sich an unser »geistiges Auge«, indem sie positive oder auch negative Wertungen des *Inhalts* vermitteln und damit möglicherweise *Lust oder Unlust* erzeugen. In dieser Richtung könnte z.B. die Verwendung der Wörter *Frieden*, *Ausgeglichenheit*, *Ruhe* und ähnlicher Elemente eines möglichen Wortfeldes *Harmonie* im Textzusammenhang wirken; sie beeinflussen uns über ihre Inhalte, nicht über die Form.[15]

Der Aufbau eines Konnotationspotenzials kann sich zweitens über die Verwendung sprachlicher Mittel vollziehen, die durch ihr Angebot an das »sinnliche Auge«, also durch ihre *Form/Gestalt*, positive sprachbezogene Wertungen hervorrufen: z.B. bewirken ausgefallene Wörter, bewirken Rhythmus, Reim, Metrik u.a. nicht nur Aufmerksamkeit und Gefallen, sondern auch Kohärenz. Hier haben wir es bereits mit Fragen des *Stils* zu tun.

Bei Fechner taucht dieses Phänomen unter dem Stichwort ›Princip der ästhetischen Hülfe oder Steigerung‹ (1978, 50ff.) auf. Er weist auf die stüt-

---

[15] Ecos axiologische Konnotationen siehe Anmerkung 14.

zende Funktion von Versmaß, Rhythmus und Reim, um nur einige Beispiele zu nennen, in einem Gedicht hin. Diese Phänomene haben zwar für sich

> sehr geringen ästhetischen Wert, doch verlieren die schönsten Gedichte allen oder fast allen Reiz, wenn man ihren Inhalt in prosaischer Redeform wiedergiebt, indem der Sinn ohne Versmass, Rhythmus, Reim ebenfalls nicht die Schwelle der Lust übersteigt. (Fechner 1978, 51)

Sowohl das inhaltsbezogene als auch das formbezogene *Konnotationspotenzial* eines Textes kann sich darin erschöpfen, dass die Wirkung der Wörter durch die gemeinsame Verwendung in einem Textzusammenhang addiert wird. Nun haben wir auf einer höheren Ebene aber einen dritten Fall der Wirkungsweise von Konnotationen, den nämlich, wo die Verbindung, die zwischen den einzelnen Elementen besteht, nicht als schlichte Summierung betrachtet werden darf, sondern wo sie mehr – und anderes – ergibt, als die Summe der einzelnen Teile. In einem solchen Fall haben wir es mit Stil als sinnstiftender Größe zu tun. Ich erinnere daran, dass im Zusammenhang mit dem *Gestaltbegriff*, den ich ja mit dem Stilbegriff gleichsetze, bereits von der pragmasozialen und pragmaästhetischen Funktion von Stil die Rede war. *Konnotationen/Assoziationen* fungieren hier als

> aussage- bzw. sinnkonstituierende Funktionsmerkmale, die durch den Bezug der Zeichen aufeinander und auf die Ganzheit der Textgestalt [...] emotional-assoziative Bewußtseinsprozesse auslösen. (Lerchner 1984, 44)

Die Konnotationen entstehen in einem solchen Fall erst im Text. Sie bringen eine zweite Ebene des Textes hervor, deren Sinn es ist, als Kodierungen für

> Handlungsanweisungen zu fungieren, Handlungsanweisungen zu subjektiven, emotionalen, evaluativen und/oder präskriptiven Interpretationen des Textinhalts und damit als ›sinnkonstituierende Faktoren‹. (Lerchner 1984, 45)

Deren Zusammenwirken auf der Textebene wird dem Text seinen Zweitsinn geben. Damit wird Stil als »spezielle[m] Fall von Textsemantik« (Lerchner 1981, 91) semiotische Qualität zugesprochen. Dass ein Zusammenhang mit dem *Assoziationsbegriff* Fechners besteht, wurde sicher deutlich.

3.3. Ästhetische Schwelle – Rezeptionsangebot, Rezeptionshilfe, Rezeptionslust

Es gibt Vieles, was uns gleichgültig lässt, indess es doch seiner und unserer Natur nach wohl geeignet wäre, Gefallen oder Missfallen zu wecken, andermal auch wirklich erweckt. Das hängt allgemeingesprochen daran, dass sei es die Stärke der objectiven Einwirkung oder der Grad unserer Empfänglichkeit dafür oder unsere Aufmerksamkeit darauf nicht die sogenannte *Schwelle* übersteigt, das heisst den Grad, von dem an die Einwirkung erst für unser Bewusstsein spürbar wird. (Fechner 1978, 49)

Das Prinzip der *ästhetischen Schwelle* beruht also auf der Erfahrung, dass ein Gegenstand, um unsere Aufmerksamkeit zu wecken und uns zu *Lust*- oder Unlustgefühlen zu veranlassen, nicht nur ein Reizangebot an sich darstellen darf, sondern dass dieser Reiz von einer bestimmten Intensität sein muss.

Es ist nämlich ein allgemeines, nicht *blos* für Empfindung von Lust und Unlust, aber *auch* für sie gültiges Gesetz, dass zum Bewusstwerden derselben ein gewisser Grad dessen gehört, woran sie äusserlich und innerlich hängt; die Qualität der Bedingung reicht nicht aus, sie muss sich durch die erforderliche Quantität, den erforderlichen Grad ergänzen. So lange nun dieser Grad nicht erreicht ist, sagen wir von den Bedingungen der Lust und Unlust wie von diesen selbst und dem davon abhängigen Gefallen und Missfallen, dass sie *unter der Schwelle* bleiben. (Fechner, 1978, 49)

Fechner sieht die Relativität dieser Zusammenhänge. Vor allem scheint es in unserem Zusammenhang wichtig zu sein, dass er die Bedingungen der *Lust* in einen quasi strukturalistischen/systembezogenen Zusammenhang einordnet. Er erkennt, dass mehrere Bedingungen der Lust, die jede für sich allein nicht ausreichen würden, die *Reizschwelle* zu übersteigen, dies in ihrem Zusammenwirken sehr wohl erreichen.

Eine Bedingung der Lust oder Unlust, die für sich unter der Schwelle ist oder sein würde, wenn sie für sich bliebe, kann in Zusammensetzung mit anders gearteten Bedingungen der Lust oder Unlust, die ihrerseits für sich unter der Schwelle sein würden, ein Lust- oder Unlustresultat geben, was die Schwelle übersteigt, wovon das [...] Princip der ästhetischen Hülfe mit abhängt. (Fechner, 1978, 50)

Ein Bezug zur Idee von der Einheitlichkeit und zum Gestaltganzen lässt sich hier mühelos herstellen. Ähnliche Gedankengänge, vor allem hinsichtlich der *ästhetischen Schwelle*, finden sich in moderner Artikulation in den Grundideen der »Strukturalen Stilistik« von Michael Riffaterre (1973) wieder.

Die Voraussetzung für die Vergleichbarkeit der Fechner'schen Idee mit dem Ansatz Riffaterres ist, dass beide von der *Wahrnehmung* ausgehen. Riffaterre will eine Methode entwickeln, die »die Beschreibung der kritischen Wahrnehmung des Lesers und des Funktionierens des ›künstlerischen‹ Stils [erlaubt]« (Riffaterre 1973, 16). *Stil* wird von ihm als Information verstanden, genauer »als Emphase (expressiver, affektiver oder ästhetischer Natur) [...], die zu der durch die linguistische Struktur übertragenen Information hinzukommt, ohne den [deren U.F.] Sinn zu verändern« (Riffaterre 1973, 30). Mit dem Zusatz »ohne den Sinn zu verändern« unterscheidet er deutlich zwischen Erstsinn (Themenbezug des Textes) und Zweitsinn (Stilbedeutung): »Das bedeutet letztlich, daß die Sprache ausdrückt und der Stil hervorhebt« (Riffaterre 1973, 31). Stil entsteht nach seiner Auffassung durch Sprachverwendung im Kontext, ist also eine textbezogene Größe. Hier wird der *strukturalistische Ansatz* bereits deutlich. Aus diesem Ansatz folgt für ihn, dass das, was als stilistisch »normal« zu gelten hat, kontextbestimmt ist. Der Text bildet seine eigene Norm. Die stilistische Wirkung eines Textes wird durch das Wechselspiel zwischen vorhersehbaren, »normalen« (kontextuellen) und nichtvorhersehbaren, vom »Normalen« abweichenden (kontrastierenden) Elementen hervorgerufen. Nun der Gedanke, der uns zu Fechner führt. In seiner wahrnehmungs- und rezeptionsbezogenen Herangehensweise fragt Riffaterre, wie man einen – schriftlichen – Text so gestaltet, dass er die Aufmerksamkeit des Lesers weckt und aufrechterhält; denn anders als in mündlicher Rede hat man die Möglichkeit der Rückkopplung nicht und muss von vornherein Sorge um die Aufmerksamkeit seines Publikums tragen. Das geschieht, indem Mittel verwendet werden, die die *Wahrnehmungsschwelle* des Rezipienten zu überschreiten geeignet sind. Solche Mittel sind immer die unerwarteten. Eine angemessene Mischung aus Erwartetem (Kontext) und Unerwartetem (Kontrast) scheint für Riffaterre daher die Lösung zu sein. Sie wirkt auf den Leser anregend, weckt und belebt seine Aufmerksamkeit. Wenn sich aber solche Kontraste im Sinne unvorhersehbarer Elemente häufen, wenn also »Kumulation« eintritt, kann sich die »Wahrnehmungsschwelle« (Riffaterre 1973, 57) erhöhen. Dasselbe kann auch im Laufe der Lektüre *eines* Textes allein durch Gewöhnung eintreten. Man empfindet die betreffenden Mittel dann als nicht mehr neu und nicht mehr expressiv genug, als dass sie auffallen würden. Andere Kontraste müssen an deren Stelle treten oder andere Mischungen von sich gegenseitig stützenden Mitteln müssen gefunden werden, um die Aufmerksamkeit zu erhalten bzw. neu zu gewinnen, um, mit Fechner gesagt, »die Schwelle zu übersteigen«. Übereinstimmungen zwischen Fechners Prinzip der *ästhetischen Schwelle* und Riffaterres Konzept der Kontext-Kontrast-Beschaffenheit von *Stil*, die sich aus dem gemeinsamen Aspekt der Wahrnehmung ergeben, sind hier also zweifelsfrei festzustellen.

3.4. Ethnomethodologischer Ansatz

Fechner nimmt bei der Auseinandersetzung mit dem Wesen des Ästhetischen und im Zusammenhang mit seiner Begründung der Ästhetik von unten einen ethnomethodologischen Ansatz vorweg. Auf das Phänomen des *Alltagswissens*, wie wir es heute in der Soziologie behandelt finden,[16] stützt sich auch schon Fechner. Alltagswissen ist hier zu verstehen im Sinne von Kenntnissen, Erfahrungen, Vorstellungen, Handlungsmustern, die Mitglieder einer Gemeinschaft gemeinsam kennen und mit denen sie gemeinsames Handeln und ihre Wirklichkeit konstituieren. Zu diesem Wissen gehören auch die Wörter und Wendungen, mit denen wir gemeinsam umgehen. Fechner zieht die Wörter heran, die seine Zeitgenossen für die Beurteilung des Ästhetischen verwenden, und leitet daraus Grade und inhaltliche Differenzierungen von Ästhetischem ab. Dies ist ein Vorgehen, das für ihn zweifellos zur Ästhetik von unten gehört.

> Auch in der Weise der Begriffsabstimmungen selbst aber unterscheidet sich der Weg von Oben von dem hier einzuschlagenden Weg von Unten. In letzterem Wege kommt die begriffliche Bestimmung blos darauf zurück, den Sprachgebrauch festzustellen, und, wo er schwankt, sich über Wahl und Weite desselben zu erklären, so dass man wisse, um was es sich bei der sachlichen Untersuchung handelt, ohne aber in der Begriffsbestimmung das Resultat solcher Untersuchung vorwegzunehmen oder in Wesensbestimmungen vorweg einzugehen, womit es leicht ist, Klarheit und Allgemeinverständlichkeit zu erzielen; indess der Weg von Oben die Wesensfrage gleich aus dem Begriffe und im Begriffe zu beantworten sucht, hiermit aber die Schwierigkeit einer klaren Feststellung der obersten Begriffe auf alle abgeleiteten Begriffe überträgt. (Fechner 1978, 6)

Er folgt konsequent dem »Prinzip, begrifflich überall von Erläuterungen des Sprachgebrauchs auszugehen« (Fechner 1978, 15), also darauf zu sehen, »wie der lebendige Sprach- und Begriffsgebrauch den Begriff der

---

[16] Siehe Schütz; Luckmann 1975, 1984.

Schönheit fassen mag« (Fechner 1978, 17). So stellt er dem Ausdruck ›schön‹, der im weitesten und zugleich im allgemeinsten Sinne gebraucht werde,[17] die »formulierungskommentierenden Ausdrücke« (Antos 1982) ›angenehm‹, ›ansprechend‹, ›hübsch‹, ›anmuthig‹, ›niedlich‹, ›erhaben‹, ›prächtig‹ usw. gegenüber und schlussfolgert aus dem Vergleich der Ausdrücke miteinander, dass sie geeignet sind, verschiedene Grade und Intensitäten »oft mit sinnlicher Nebenbedeutung« (Fechner 1978, 15) zu bezeichnen. In dieser Art deduziert er Gedankengänge aus Begriffssystemen oder, genauer gesagt, er leitet sie ab aus dem Gebrauch, den Menschen von den Begriffen machen.[18] Auch hier entdecken wir in Fechner einen Vordenker für heutige Erkenntnismethoden.

4. Fazit

Am Ende meines Ausflugs in Fechners Gedankenwelt, soweit sie *Zeichen* und *Zeichenwahrnehmung* betrifft, lässt sich resümierend sagen, dass in seiner Arbeit »Vorschule der Ästhetik« Grundideen der Eco'schen Theorie von den Zeichen, also zur *Semiotik*, zu finden sind. Weiter lassen sich Vorgriffe auf den erkenntnistheoretisch-pragmatischen Zweig der Informationstheorie erkennen, in dem es um das Maß für die *pragmatische Information* geht, das bezogen ist auf den Wert, den die Nachricht für den Empfänger hat. Schließlich greift Fechner der *Ethnomethodologie des Sprechens* vor, einer aus der interpretativen Soziologie abgeleiteten Forschungsrichtung, die diejenigen Formen, Muster und Mittel untersucht, die Mitglieder einer kulturellen Gemeinschaft entwickelt haben, um ihr Alltagsleben organisieren und aufrechterhalten zu können.

Literatur:

Allesch, Ch. G. (1988): Gustav Theodor Fechner als Wegbereiter der psychologischen Ästhetik. In: Internationales Gustav Theodor Fechner Symposium. Passau 12. to 14. June 1987. Hg. von J. Brožek; H. Gundlach. Passau, 207–215.

---

[17] Siehe Fechner 1978, 15.

[18] Für eine genauere Ausführung der Beziehungen, die dieses Vorgehen für ›Ordinary Language Approach‹ (Austin, Searle) hat, ist hier nicht der Platz. Genannt werden sollte dieser Bezug wenigstens.

Antos, G. (1982): Grundlagen einer Theorie des Formulierens. Textherstellung in geschriebener und gesprochener Sprache. Tübingen.

Coseriu, E. (1994): Textlinguistik. Tübingen und Basel.

Eco, U. (1972): Einführung in die Semiotik. München.

Eco, U. (1987): Semiotik. Entwurf einer Theorie der Zeichen. München.

Fechner, G. Th. (1978): Vorschule der Ästhetik. 2 Bde. in e. Bd. beigeb.: Zur experimentellen Ästhetik. Nachdruck der Ausg. von 1925 und 1871. Hildesheim; New York.

Fix, U. (1986): Das Wort als Zeichen im poetischen Text. In: Interdisziplinäres germanistisches Praktikum. Pädagogische Hochschule. Potsdam,116–134.

Fix, U. (1990): Die Sprachgestalt von Sachtexten – ein vernachlässigtes Element der Rezeptionsförderung. In: Leser und Lesen in Gegenwart und Zukunft. Beiträge e. internationalen wissenschaftl. Konferenz. Karl-Marx-Universität 1989. Hg. von Jutta Duclaud u.a. Leipzig, 301–309.

Fix, U. (1996): Gestalt und Gestalten. Von der Notwendigkeit der Gestaltkategorie für eine das Ästhetische berücksichtigende pragmatische Stilistik. In: Zeitschrift für Germanistik. N.F. 2, 308–323.

Gumbrecht, H.U.; Pfeiffer, K.L. (Hg.) (1986): Stil. Geschichten und Funktionen eines kulturwissenschaftlichen Diskurselements. Frankfurt a.M.

Hahn, A. (1986): Soziologische Relevanzen des Stilbegriffs. In: Stil. Geschichten und Funktionen eines kulturwissenschaftlichen Diskurselements. Hg. von H.U. Gumbrecht; K.L. Pfeiffer. Frankfurt a.M., 603–611.

Kainz, F. (1948): Vorlesungen über Ästhetik. Wien.

Katz, D. (1948): Gestaltpsychologie. 2., erw. Aufl. Basel.

Lerchner, G. (1981): Stilistisches und Stil. Ansätze für eine kommunikative Stiltheorie. In: Beiträge zur Erforschung der deutschen Sprache 1, 85–109.

Lerchner, G. (1984): Konnotative Textpotenz. In: Beiträge zur Erforschung der deutschen Sprache 4, 39–48.

Luckmann, Th. (1986): Soziologische Grenzen des Stilbegriffs. In: Stil. Geschichten und Funktionen eines kulturwissenschaftlichen Diskurselements. Hg. von H.U. Gumbrecht; K.L. Pfeiffer. Frankfurt a.M., 612–619.

Lutzeier, P.R. (1995): Lexikologie. Ein Arbeitsbuch. Tübingen.

Mattenklott, G. (1984): Nachwort. In: Das unendliche Leben. (Texte von Gustav Theodor Fechner). München, 169–199.

Mukařovsky, J. (1982): Kapitel aus der Ästhetik. Frankfurt a.M.

Nöth, W. (2000): Handbuch der Semiotik. 2., vollst. neu bearb. und erw. Aufl. Stuttgart; Weimar.

Püschel, U. (1987): GESTALTEN als zentrales Stilmuster. In: Perspektiven der angewandten Linguistik. Hg. von Kühlwein, W. Tübingen, 143–145.

Riffaterre, M. (1973): Strukturale Stilistik. München.

Sandig, B. (1986): Stilistik der deutschen Sprache. Berlin; New York.

Schütz, A.; Luckmann, Th. (1975; 1984): Strukturen der Lebenswelt. Bd. 1. Darmstadt 1975; Bd. 2 Frankfurt 1984.

Sprung, H.; Sprung, L. (1988): Gustav Theodor Fechner als experimenteller Ästhetiker – zur Entwicklung der Methodologie und Methodik einer Psychophysik höherer kognitiver

Prozesse. In: Internationales Gustav Theodor Fechner Symposion. Passau 12. to 14. June 1987. Hg. von J. Brožek; H. Gundlach. Passau, 217–277.

Sturm, H. (1979): Ästhetik und Umwelt. In: Ästhetik und Umwelt. Hg. von H. Sturm. Tübingen, 77–95.

Welsch, W. (1993): Ästhetisches Denken. Stuttgart.

Siegfried Grosse

Die Tagebücher Gustav Theodor Fechners (1801–1887). Beobachtungen zum Sprachgebrauch eines Gelehrten im 19. Jahrhundert.[1]

Fechners umfangreiches Tagebuch ist eine vorzügliche Quelle, um den beruflichen und familiären Tageslauf eines angesehenen, vielseitigen Leipziger Universitätsprofessors kennenzulernen. Seine erstaunliche sprachliche Gewandtheit dokumentiert das Ausdrucksvermögen der deutschen Sprache im 19. Jahrhundert außerhalb der Literatur und seine Andersartigkeit im Vergleich zur heutigen Gegenwartssprache: es zeigen sich viele Unterschiede in der Morphologie und Syntax, in der Phraseologie, Wortbildung und im Lexikon.

Ein Tagebuch enthält Aufzeichnungen aus dem Tagesverlauf und Gedanken darüber, mit denen der Schreibende versucht, in regelmäßigen Notizen aus seiner Sicht Ereignisse zu schildern und zu kommentieren und in Verbindung damit persönliche Eindrücke, Erlebnisse und Gefühle festzuhalten, also all das, was nach seiner Meinung im Ablauf des alltäglichen Lebens bemerkenswert erscheint und aus dem flüchtigen Strom der schnell vergehenden Zeit herausgehoben und vor dem Vergessenwerden bewahrt zu werden verdient. Es handelt sich um kurze oder auch längere subjektive Gedächtnisprotokolle mit historisch reflektierender Funktion.

Notizen über das Tagesgeschehen sind vermutlich so alt wie die Schrift, denn das Sammeln, Aufheben und Erinnern liegt in der Natur des Menschen. Deshalb haben Tagebücher in allen Sprachen ihre Tradition. Sie sind eine elementare Textsorte mit besonderen sprachlichen Eigentümlichkeiten, die sich im Laufe der Zeit verändern. Oft werden sie mit kleinen Skizzen, Fotografien und heute auch mit Tonbeispielen versehen, damit auch andere Wahrnehmungssinne das Gedächtnis reaktivieren können. In jüngerer Zeit sind die Grenzen zu Selbstzeugnissen und zur Autobiographie offen.

---

[1] Die Transkription der Tagebücher wurde von I. Altmann und A. Meischner-Metge zur Verfügung gestellt.

Heute werden tägliche Notizen vermutlich auch maschinell fixiert und auf Disketten gespeichert, um die Lesbarkeit zu erhöhen und Platz zu sparen. Ob die Menge an Tagebüchern zurückgeht, weil die optischen und maschinellen Informationen und ihre Verfügbarkeit immer weiter expandieren, dürfte sich kaum feststellen lassen, da die Niederschrift täglicher Bemerkungen eine private, nicht öffentliche Angelegenheit ist und dem Datenschutz unterliegt.

Die Qualität und Dichte der Eintragungen hängen von unterschiedlichen Faktoren ab; zunächst einmal vom Autor selbst, so etwa von seiner Aufgeschlossenheit und wachen Neugier gegenüber der nächsten und weiteren Umgebung; dem Grad seiner Wahrnehmungsfähigkeit und Beobachtungsgabe; seinem differenzierten Reflexionsvermögen; von der Fähigkeit zur kurzen, präzisen und nachvollziehbaren sprachlichen Darstellung des Wahrgenommenen; von der Gabe, Wesentliches vom Unwesentlichen unterscheiden zu können, und nicht zuletzt von der beständigen, nicht nachlassenden Energie, die täglichen Gedanken fortlaufend zu notieren und keine Lücken entstehen zu lassen.

Ort und Anlass prägen die Form der Niederschrift. Auf Reisen und bei Besichtigungen ist die Zeit knapp, und deshalb bleibt die Notiz kurz und stichwortartig, so dass die Entschlüsselung oft nur dem Schreibenden möglich ist. Gespräche können erst später in aller Ausführlichkeit aufgezeichnet oder protokolliert werden. Und schließlich ist zu fragen, ob die Eintragungen ein spontanes persönliches Memorandum sind, oder ob die Schreibenden an eine spätere Veröffentlichung denken, also die Notizen im Hinblick auf die Lektüre Dritter vornehmen.

Fechners Aufzeichnungen sind ohne den Zwang terminlicher Bedrängnis in seinem Leipziger Wohnzimmer, in seiner Studierstube oder in der Wohnung Härtels entstanden, ein großer Teil während der langwierigen Augenerkrankung, während der er auf die Lehre, die eigene Lektüre und auch die Forschung hat verzichten müssen. So bleibt ihm Zeit für die Textgestaltung und für überdachte längere, durchformulierte Sätze, wie sie für Tagebuchtexte nicht charakteristisch sind. Stichwortartig schnell hingeworfene Eintragungen sind selten.

Die Notizen sind stets persönlich reflektierte Konzentrate eigener Beobachtungen. Er sagt einmal von den Gesprächen, die er oft und gern mit den Besuchern führt:

> Was ich von Unterhaltungen dieser Art aufschreibe, ist überhaupt immer nur das Wesentliche der zur Sprache gebrachten Gesichtspuncte und Gegenstände.

[...] Wenn ich hier das letzte Wort zu behalten scheine, ist es natürlich nur, weil ich es bin, der das Gespräch aufschreibt, und es in meinem Sinn wirklich behalte. (3.8. 1845)

Zwischen edierten Tagebuchaufzeichnungen bekannter Persönlichkeiten und den Niederschriften von Unbekannten bestehen erhebliche Unterschiede, das heißt: die gedruckten Texte sind von den Schreibenden oft schon während ihrer Entstehung mit dem Plan einer späteren Veröffentlichung und damit einer möglichen Rezeption durch fremde Leser verfasst und deshalb sorgsam überarbeitet worden, wodurch sie mit der Wendung nach außen den intimen Charakter des Ich-Bezugs verlieren. Wenn aber Erben und Nachlassverwalter die Publikation verantworten, dann werden die Texte vor dem Druck zwar meist nicht inhaltlich, wohl aber formal nach den Normen der Schriftsprache eingerichtet. Die Herausgeber meinen, mit dieser falsch verstandenen ›Sprachpflege‹ dem Autor einen Dienst zu erweisen. Das ist bedauerlich; denn die besondere Eigenart eines Tagebuchtextes liegt gerade in seiner spontanen, unkorrigierten Fixierung, die in der Kürze und Schnelligkeit, mit der sie meist erfolgt ist, die Regeln der Norm außer Acht lässt und damit der gesprochenen Diktion näher kommt. Das gilt auch für die oft individuelle Interpunktion.

So können Stichworte statt vollständiger Sätze erscheinen; als eingeklammerter Zusatz erhalten sie die Funktion eines Kommentars. Individuelle Kürzel werden verwendet und Redundanzen nicht getilgt. Lange und zusammengesetzte Sätze oder gar Perioden werden vermieden, Satzbrüche oder Anakoluthe sind möglich, wie auch die unkorrekte Schreibung von Orts- und Personennamen. Spitz- oder Übernamen werden gebraucht. Der Wechsel der Stilebenen ist häufig. Unterstreichungen und Satzzeichen (Frage- und Ausrufezeichen) heben Besonderes hervor.

Aber keines dieser Merkmale, die in gängigen Tagebucheintragungen üblich sind, kennzeichnet das Diarium von Gustav Theodor Fechner. Seine Aufzeichnungen sind ein Zeugnis der geschriebenen Bildungssprache des 19. Jahrhunderts. Vermutlich hat er als vielseitiger und im Vortrag geübter Universitätslehrer nicht anders gesprochen, als er im Tagebuch schreibt. Die Diktion folgt der Standardsprache (mit geringfügigen Einsprengseln sächsischer Mundart). Sie ist klar, verständlich und von durchsichtiger, nachvollziehbarer Argumentation. Sie hat nichts von der Hast eines unruhigen gehetzten Tagespensums. Es gibt relativ wenige Korrekturen. Ab und zu sind interlinear oder am Rand kleine Ergänzungen eingefügt.

Ich halte es durchaus für möglich, dass Fechner bei großen Teilen der Niederschrift an spätere Leser, entweder an eine selbständige Veröffentlichung oder an eine teilweise Eingliederung in andere Publikationen gedacht hat. Dafür gibt es Hinweise: mehrere Male stellt er seine große, für den Außenstehenden unübersichtliche, weil personenreiche Familie vor, deren Mitglieder im Tagebuch meist nur mit dem Vornamen genannt werden. Er nennt nun Vor- und Familiennamen und erläutert das Verwandtschaftsverhältnis, den Familienstand, die Ausbildung, die Kinderzahl und die Berufstätigkeit der einzelnen Verwandten. Das sind bei der großen Familie hilfreiche Orientierungen für jeden fremden Leser oder für den, der die entsagungsvolle Aufgabe übernimmt, ein kommentiertes Namensregister anzulegen. Aber der Schreiber des Tagebuchs selbst und seine familiäre Umgebung brauchen diese Erläuterungen nicht.

Ein weiteres Indiz sind die oft längeren Diskussionen über wissenschaftliche und kulturelle Themen, die in direkter Rede aufgezeichnet sind, so dass sich die Argumente auf die einzelnen Sprecher verteilen. Es gibt z.B. ein mehrseitiges Gespräch über die sprachlichen Veränderungen und Besonderheiten in den Schriften Martin Luthers (24. 10. 1866), das Fechner mit drei Personen führt. Die direkte Rede wird auf vier Sprecher aufgeteilt. Solche für ein Tagebuch ungewöhnliche Textarten sind keine rasch hingeworfenen Skizzen, sondern Protokolle, die nach Beendigung der Gespräche mit allen Argumenten sorgsam rekonstruiert, gegeneinander abgesetzt und vermutlich auch ergänzt worden sind. Vielleicht bestand die Idee, sie in spätere Publikationen einzubeziehen.

Es gibt immer wieder ausführliche szenische Darstellungen, die den Rahmen einer Tagebuchnotiz sprengen. Die Schilderung eines Unfalls im Garten zeigt die genaue Rekonstruktion des Vorfalls, den Fechner, was den ersten Teil betrifft, nicht als Augenzeuge mit erlebt, sondern berichtet bekommen hat:

> 7. August [1842].
>
> Heute Abend, kurz nach 7 Uhr, spielt Alfred [Volkmann, Anatom und Physiologe, Bruder von Clara Fechner, mit seiner Familie aus Dorpat zu Besuch in Leipzig] mit seinem Sohn Edmund im Garten. Adele [Volkmanns Frau], meine Frau, Härtels saßen in der Nähe am Tische, Julius mit seiner Frau war bei den Aeltern, ich bei meiner Mutter. Da traf es sich, daß der Ball auf einen Baum flog. Erst wollte Edmund hinaufklettern, um ihn wiederzuhohlen; da dieß nicht gelang, so versuchte es sein Vater. Indem er sich aber an einem morschen Zweige hinaufschwingen will, bricht dieser, er stürzt kopfüber hinab, und bleibt ganz besinnungslos liegen. Die Schreckensbetäubung, in welche die Ge-

> sellschaft durch diesen Unfall versetzt ward, weicht schnell dem Antriebe zur Hülfsleistung. Meine Frau läuft schnell zu dem nachbarlich wohnenden Dr. Sachse, was freilich ein alter pumplicher Mann ist; aber das Erste erschien zunächst als das Beßte; Edmund, ohne recht zu wissen, was er thut, läuft ihr schreiend nach; dieß und die Eile und Verstörung, die sich an meiner Frau kund giebt, macht, daß sich die Leute auf der Straße vor der Hofthür sammeln. Der Doctor ist nicht gleich aufzufinden. Härtel fährt mit einem Fiacer nach einem Chirurgus; weder Günther, noch Walther, noch Kohlrusch ist zu treffen. Endlich wird doch letztrer aufgetrieben. Adele mit ihrem gewöhnlichen resoluten Wesen hat indeß vor dem Anlangen jeder ärztlichen Hülfe ihrem Manne schon auf eigene Hand Umschläge von kaltem Wasser um den Kopf gemacht, durch deren Wirkung er bald wieder zur Besinnung kommt. Er steht sogar selbst auf, wird in das Haus geführt und aufs Bett gelegt. Als ich, ungefähr 1 Stunde nach dem Vorfall, nach Hause kam, liefen mir beim Eintritt in den Garten die Kinder gleich entgegen und berichteten in verworrener Weise das Geschehene; meine Frau kam dazu und vervollständigte die Erzählung, doch so, daß ich noch das Schrecklichste voraussetzen mußte. (1842, Bl. 29–31)

Fechner ordnet die einzelnen, ihm bruchstückhaft berichteten Ereignisse und verbindet sie mit wechselnden Tempora zu einer lebhaften, sachlichen und von Emotionen freien Erzählung, die über den zitierten Abschnitt noch weiter fort läuft. Der Wechsel vom harmlosen Spiel zu einem schweren Unfall ist Anlass für die Ausführlichkeit. Die einzelnen Sätze werden nicht mit Punkten abgeschlossen. Kommata und Semikola rücken die Mitteilungen eng aneinander, ohne dass es zur stichwortartigen, schnell hingeworfenen Notiz kommt. Im Zeitalter von Handy, Notruf und Rettungsfahrzeugen können wir uns kaum vorstellen, dass bis vor etwa 100 Jahren Pferd und Bote die schnellsten Fortbewegungsmittel und Kommunikationsträger gewesen sind. Fechner hebt den simplen Entschluss Adelens hervor, der mit dem kalten Umschlag sehr viel mehr bewirkt, als die ratlosen drei anwesenden Ärzte vermögen. Mit seinem Eintreffen, eine Stunde nach dem Unfall, übernimmt er wieder die Position des Augenzeugenberichterstatters.

Das umfangreiche Tagebuch ist eine vorzügliche Quelle, um den bürgerlichen Alltag des 19. Jahrhunderts aus der Sicht eines Leipziger Universitätsprofessors kennen zu lernen, wie man sie in dieser Authentizität und diesem ergiebigen Detailreichtum kaum ein zweites Mal finden dürfte. Da es nicht möglich ist, den Inhalt der rund 1000 Tagebuchseiten eines gedanken- und reflexionsdifferenzierten Lebens auch nur kurz zu umreißen, so sollen wenigstens die zentralen Themenkreise genannt werden, denen in regelmäßiger Abfolge die Aufzeichnungen gelten:

Da ist zunächst als durchgehende Grundierung die engste Familie zu nennen. Der Ort der Handlung ist meist das Wohnzimmer, das wie ein Bühnenbild beschrieben wird (28. 10. 1842). Wichtigster und ständiger Gesprächs-, Zuhör- und während der Augenkrankheit auch Vorlesepartner ist die Ehefrau Clara, geb. Volkmann (1809–1900), mit der Fechner seit 1833 verheiratet ist. Er redet sie in den Gesprächen mit *Frau* an, sie ihn mit *mein lieber Mann*. Sie ist eine gebildete, fein fühlende, in späteren Jahren an Rheumatismus und einem Halsleiden kränkelnde Frau. Ohne Klagen steht sie dem besucherreichen und gastfreien Haushalt vor, obwohl sie nicht gern kocht und plant (13. 10. 1842). Ihre ursprüngliche Fröhlichkeit scheint im Laufe der Jahre durch die Sorgen um die langwierige Krankheit ihres Mannes einem Hang zur Schwermut gewichen zu sein (27. 9. 1842; 7. 11. 1842). In einem Brief an Karl Ludwig von Reichenbach schildert Fechner seine Frau, die dieser gern als Versuchsperson für seine odischen Pendelexperimente gewinnen möchte (27. 10. 1866).

Die starke Verminderung der Sehfähigkeit Fechners, die mit heftigen Kopfschmerzen verbunden ist und zeitweise Lehre und Forschung unmöglich macht, führt zu den verstärkten akustischen Wahrnehmungen der Gespräche und des Vorlesens, deren Niederschrift das Tagebuch entstehen lässt. – Die Mutter Johanna Dorothea Fechner, geb. Fischer (1774–1859), seit 1806 verwitwet, zieht 1824 nach Leipzig und wohnt bis zu ihrem Tod in der Nähe, so dass ihr Sohn sie, besonders während der Augenkrankheit, fast täglich besucht und sich von ihr vorlesen lässt. Von den vielen Freunden besteht die engste Verbindung zu dem gleichaltrigen Philosophen Christian Hermann Weiße (vgl. Eintragung am 21. 6. 1866, an Weißes Todestag).

Das kinderlose Ehepaar hält seine in- und extensive Hilfe bei der Pflege, Erziehung und Ausbildung der Kinder in der Familie und Bekanntschaft, die einen Elternteil verloren haben, für eine selbstverständliche Verpflichtung. Sie verfolgen die physische und psychische Entwicklung ihrer Schützlinge mit aufmerksamem Interesse und tauschen sich darüber in ausführlichen Gesprächen aus.

Die Verbindungen innerhalb der verzweigten Verwandtschaft und zum ausgedehnten Freundeskreis (Kollegen, Verleger, Musiker, Buchhändler, Freundinnen Claras) werden sorgsam gepflegt. Anlässe dafür sind: Geburtstage und Weihnachtsfeste, Taufen und Hochzeiten (Beschreibung der Geschenke); gesellige Abende mit Tanz, musikalischen Darbietungen, Scharaden und Spielen; Karneval und Kostümfeste; Theater- und Konzertbesuche; regelmäßige Kränzchen im Kollegen- und Freundeskreis mit

Berichten und Diskussionen; häufige, oft tägliche gegenseitige Besuche mit Gesprächen, Einladungen zum Kaffee, Essen oder Punsch.

Das eigene Kopf- und Augenleiden und die immer wieder akute Halskrankheit Claras werden ohne Klagen registriert und beschrieben. Die Anteilnahme am Verlauf von Krankheiten anderer führt zu Gesprächen über Ärzte, Heil- und Kurverfahren (mit entsprechenden Ratschlägen) und Todesfälle.

Reisen, Wanderungen, und gemeinsame Ferienaufenthalte mit Verwandten und Freunden werden ausführlich beschrieben. Ab und zu kommen die eigenen bescheidenen finanziellen Verhältnisse zur Sprache, aber stets ohne Klage. Bei dieser Vielzahl breit gefächerter Themen fehlen natürlich auch nicht der Klatsch und die Erörterung von absonderlichen Nachrichten aus der täglichen Zeitung, Kapitel ›Vermischtes‹, z.B. die Frage, ob Brünette oder Blonde besser kochen können (12. 11. 1869).

Eingebettet in diese farbige, von Familie und Freundschaft geprägte soziale Situation sind Betrachtungen, die Alltäglichkeiten aus ihrem unscheinbaren Rahmen herauslösen und ihre sinnvolle Einbindung in größere Zusammenhänge des Lebens zu zeigen versuchen. Das führt zu den zahlreichen lebhaften, teils kontrovers geführten Diskussionen mit Kollegen und Freunden. Ihre Thematik bestimmt Fechner als respektierte Autorität. Das Spektrum seines Wissens, seiner fachlichen Interessen und ihrer interdisziplinären Verflechtung ist erstaunlich breit: Medizin, Physik, Mathematik, Astronomie, Philosophie, Pädagogik, Psychologie, Theologie, Ästhetik und Kunstgeschichte, Maschinen und Fortschritt, Arbeiter und Industrie.

Oft lösen kleine, zunächst belanglos erscheinende Notizen aus der Tageszeitung oder Mitteilungen aus dem Familien- und Freundeskreis Gespräche über grundlegende Probleme der Wissenschaft aus (z.B. die eigenen und die berichteten Träume werden Anlässe zu psychologischen Überlegungen; der Auftritt eines Zauberers regt Gespräche über die Ästhetik an), die sich dann weiter entfalten und manchmal auch an einem der folgenden Tage fortgesetzt werden. Solche Diskussionen sind in der Zeit des Augenleidens, als Fechner nicht lehren kann, besonders häufig.

Mit großer Wissbegierde nimmt er Reiseberichte seiner Freunde auf, um Einzelheiten über ihm unbekannte Länder, Menschen und Städte zu erfahren. Nach dem Abklingen der Erkrankung wird die wissenschaftliche Arbeit (Fertigstellung, Drucklegung und Verkauf der Schriften, Anlegung eines Verzeichnisses der Publikationen) einer ständigen kritischen

Rechenschaft unterzogen. Dabei gibt es immer wieder Klagen über seine, wie er meint, mangelnde Produktivität.

Universitätsangelegenheiten (Rektoratsübergabe, Dozentenverein, Berufungen, Konkurrenz im Kollegium, Reformüberlegungen, Entwicklung der Studentenzahlen), fehlen im Tagebuch des Hochschullehrers nicht. Einen besonderen Raum nehmen die Bildbesprechungen im Kunstverein ein. Die ausgestellten historischen und zeitgenössischen Werke werden ausführlich besprochen, wobei sich die Wertung fast ausschließlich an der Überzeugungskraft der Inhalte und ihrer narrativen Darstellung orientiert. Auch die moralischen Maßstäbe des evangelischen Theologen fließen in die Beurteilungen ein. Hier zeigt sich eine ergiebige Quelle für die Diskussionen über bildende Kunst im 19. Jahrhundert.

Das Tagebuch enthält viele Anekdoten, teils von Besuchern erzählt, teils aus Zeitschriften entnommen, und Witze, die zwischen die Eintragungen gestreut sind. Beide haben offenbar einen großen Unterhaltungswert gehabt. Es werden immer wieder Rätsel notiert, die zum Teil Fechner (meist in Gedichtform) selbst erdacht hat. Sie sind oft, wie er sagt, aus Langeweile entstanden und beziehen sich auf aktuelle Situationen. Dagegen wirken die eigenen Gelegenheits*gedichte* und die für festliche Anlässe verfassten und dort ausgebrachten Toasts, die im Tagebuch nicht ohne eitlen Stolz festgehalten werden, aus der zeitlichen Distanz heraus bemüht, manieriert und längst nicht so lustig, wie sie vermutlich gemeint waren. Außerdem werden Nachrichten und vor allem volkstümliche Kuriositäten (Aberglauben, Gruselgeschichten, bedeutungsvolle Koinzidenz von Unfällen, volkstümliche Heilrezepte, Traumdeutungen etc.) aus der täglichen, stets aufmerksam gepflegten Zeitungs- und Zeitschriftenlektüre vorgetragen und besprochen. Man möchte »über Nichts und Alles sprechen, wobei man sich wohl befindet« (30.9. 1842). Aus dieser Vielfalt wird verständlich, dass Fechner in jungen Jahren zur Bestreitung seines Lebensunterhaltes ein 8-bändiges Hauslexikon hat herausgeben können. Besondere Merkwürdigkeiten aus der täglichen Lektüre notiert Fechner als Lesefrüchte; manchmal werden sie mit einer kritischen Anmerkung versehen.

Es verwundert, dass dieser so vielseitig interessierte, hoch begabte und kontaktfreudige Gelehrte, der sich weder über einen versiegenden Ideenreichtum noch über mangelnde Geselligkeit beklagen kann, immer wieder über Langeweile klagt und sich Übungen ausdenkt, um diese zu bekämpfen.

Bei dieser wachen Beobachtung, Registratur und Beschreibung auch unbedeutender Details aus dem Tagesablauf fällt auf, dass politische Ereignisse von erheblicher Tragweite, an denen die Zeit wirklich nicht arm gewesen ist, kaum oder gar nicht aufgezeichnet und kommentiert werden. Auf jeden Fall spielen sie keine nennenswerte Rolle. Es fällt weder ein Wort zu 1848 noch zu den beiden Kriegen 1864 und 1866. Und der Krieg 1870/71 gegen Frankreich wird nur kurz erwähnt.

Im Zusammenhang damit fallen einzelne Bemerkungen über die Kriege Napoleons. Die Nachrichten über den 1870er-Krieg beschränken sich auf einige pathetische Siegesmeldungen, auf die Diskussion, ob man sich für die Flaggenfarben schwarz-weiß-rot oder schwarz-rot-gold entscheiden sollte und auf Karrikaturen und Verspottung der Franzosen. Über Zerstörungen, den Tod junger Menschen, die Konsequenzen einer kriegerischen Auseinandersetzung oder die Auswirkung auf die Wirtschaft fällt kein Wort. Liegt das an dem Bedürfnis, Unangenehmes auszublenden?

So wird im häuslichen Bereich z.B. der Streit zwischen Clara Fechner und Luise Härtel, der zum Auszug des Ehepaares Fechner aus dem Gartenhaus der Familie Härtel geführt hat (1862, Bl. 20), das Fechners viele Jahre bewohnt hatten, nicht thematisiert. Ärger, Zorn, Verstimmungen, menschliche Enttäuschungen, kurz Negativa, die zum Alltag gehören und die es bei den engen Kontakten mit einem so großen Personenkreis von Zeit zu Zeit gegeben haben muss, finden keinen Eingang in das Tagebuch.

Mir liegt der bisherige Computerausdruck im Umfang von etwa 1000 Seiten vor; die geplante Buchfassung dürfte mehr Raum beanspruchen, da sie vermutlich einen kleineren Satzspiegel hat. Da die Seitenzahlen noch nicht festliegen, werden die Belege mit dem Datum des Tagebuches fixiert. Die Angaben können leider nicht punktgenau sein; denn die Tageseintragungen umfassen des öfteren mehrere Seiten. Um die Auffindung der Belegstellen zu erleichtern, wird bei besonders umfangreichen Eintragungen noch die Nummerierung der Faszikelseiten in der handschriftlichen Druckvorlage hinzugefügt, die im geplanten Druck angegeben ist.

Die Aufzeichnungen reichen von 1828 bis 1879. Sie beginnen sporadisch und setzen erst regelmäßig mit dem Beginn des Augenleidens 1842 ein, als die Sehschwäche die wissenschaftliche Arbeit ernstlich zu behindern beginnt. Mir ist es ein Rätsel, wie Fechner mit einer solchen Einschränkung der Sehkraft, die bis zur Erblindung geführt hat, die umfangreichen Tagebucheintragungen hat schreiben können. Er hat einen Schreibapparat zur Verfügung gehabt, der mit einem Rahmen die schreibende Hand stabilisiert zu haben scheint (eine handleitende Vorrichtung, 13.10. 1842) Er schreibt am gleichen Tage:

> Den Zustand meiner Augen anlangend, so ist nicht zu verkennen, daß ich nach meiner Krankheit etwas mehr Licht vertragen kann als vorher; aber die Besserung scheint keine Fortschritte machen zu wollen; auch dauert das Lichtflakkern noch continuirlich fort und ich kann das Auge weder zum Lesen noch Schreiben gebrauchen. Wenn ich schreibe, geschieht es immer noch, ohne auf das Blatt zu sehen, mit Hülfe einer besonderen, die Richtung der Zeilen regulirenden und ihre Trennung sichernden Rahmenvorrichtung. (13. 10. 1842)

Die Abgabe der Schreibmaschine wird nach dem Ende der Erkrankung (am 29. September 1844) mit großer Erleichterung berichtet.

Ich kenne das der Edition zugrunde liegende Manuskript nicht. Aber kleine eingefügte Faksimileproben zeigen eine zittrige, nicht immer kontrollierte alte deutsche Schreibschrift, deren Entzifferung nicht leicht gewesen sein dürfte.

1862 schreibt Fechner, seine Erkrankung habe vom Frühjahr 1840 bis zum Herbst 1843 gedauert (1862, Bl. 1). Nach den Aufzeichnungen ist allerdings ein längerer Zeitraum anzusetzen. Als das Augenleiden sich bessert (1.9. 1845) und die Forschungsarbeit wieder möglich wird, lassen die fortlaufenden Einträge nach. Es gibt mehrere monatelange Pausen; die längste ohne Notizen dauert 10 Jahre von 1850 bis 1860; auch zwischen dem 1.1. 1863 und dem 30.3. 1864 gibt es keine Eintragungen. Diese zeitlichen Abstände machen Fechners Bemerkungen zum resümierenden Rückblick. Die Erinnerungen aus einem größeren zeitlichen Abstand verändern den Bericht über die Ereignisse.

Versuchen wir nun, einige sprachliche Eigentümlichkeiten zu erkennen, die – wie ich meine – für die deutsche Bildungssprache des 19. Jahrhunderts charakteristisch sind und diese von der heutigen unterscheiden. Bei den Unterschieden zum heutigen Sprachgebrauch wird auch auf die Eigentümlichkeiten verwiesen, die uns heute selbstverständlich sind, die es aber damals noch nicht gegeben hat. Es werden also außer den Besonderheiten auch Leerstellen genannt.

Dabei stütze ich mich auf eigene Analysen der Sprachverwendung im 19. Jahrhundert, die ich an Briefen, Postkarten, Bittschriften, Beschwerden und Berichten der lokalen Presse aus der zweiten Hälfte des 19. Jahrhunderts (Grosse 1989, 1990) und an einem Schiedsmannbuch aus dem Beginn des 20. Jahrhunderts, dessen Autoren vor 1860 geboren sind, vorgenommen habe (Grosse 1993). Die untersuchten Texte stammen aus Westfalen. Nach Sachsen gehören die Bände der Familienzeitschrift »Die Gartenlaube« aus den 1880er- und 90er-Jahren, deren Sprachform ich beobachtet habe (Grosse 1998). So ist mir neben literarischen Werken aus dieser Zeit auch die Diktion (Syntax, Vokabular, Wortbildung und Stil) expositorischer und trivialer Texte gut bekannt.

Das 19. Jahrhundert darf nicht als die kleinbürgerliche, biedermeierliche Idylle friedfertiger Beschaulichkeit, wie sie uns in den Zeichnungen Ludwig Richters oder in den Karikaturen Wilhelm Buschs entgegen tritt, missverstanden werden. Es war eine politisch unruhige, ereignisreiche Zeit, in der die industrielle Revolution eine Vielzahl von Erfindungen und technischen Errungenschaften hervorgebracht und zugleich den Alltag des sozialen Gefüges mit tiefen Einschnitten radikal verändert hat. Die entstehenden Großstädte und Ballungszentren haben die Bevölkerung gemischt und umgeschichtet. Das hat zu einem komplexen Sprachwandel geführt, der in Kürze nicht beschrieben werden kann: neben der genormten überregionalen Hochsprache und den regional gebundenen Dialekten entsteht die Umgangssprache als Medium des alltäglichen Verkehrs.

Es fällt uns heute nicht schwer, Texte zu lesen und zu verstehen, die 150 Jahre alt sind. Wir brauchen für ihr Verständnis nur selten ein Wörterbuch als Dolmetscher. Aber zugleich wirkt die stilistische Diktion dieser Sprache auf uns antiquiert, zumindest würden wir so nicht sprechen wollen und können. Auf dieser Stilebene liegen viele Wörter und Wendungen, die zwar dem heutigen Sprach- und Ausdrucksvermögen angehören, aber in anderem Kontext verwendet werden. Ich kann für die Einzelerscheinungen jeweils nur wenige Beispiele aus dem umfangreichen Textkorpus bringen. Deshalb sind Angaben von Mengen und Relationen nicht möglich.

Fechners Sprache besitzt zwei Kennzeichen der deutschen Gegenwartssprache nicht: Sie hat weder Abkürzungen (selbst *Bahnhof* wird in der Ausgangsform *Eisenbahnhof*, 28.7. 1842, verwendet) noch Anglizismen. Die Texte weisen überhaupt relativ wenig Fremdwörter auf. Diese sind entweder griechisch-lateinische Termini der wissenschaftlichen Fachvokabularien, oder beim alltäglichen Gebrauch sind es heute nicht mehr gebräuchliche Entlehnungen aus dem Lateinisch/Französischen: z.B. *sautiren* (kurz braten, 9.9. 1842), *auf eine solenne Weise* (eine feierliche Weise, 2.10. 1842), *remonstrieren* (widersprechen, 2.10. 1842), *conversiren* (sich unterhalten, 13.10. 42), *sich ennuyiren* (sich langweilen, 17.10. 1842), *Bücherrepositorien* (Bücherregale, 23./25.10. 1842), *geistige Versabilität* (geistige Beweglichkeit, 21.5. 1845).

Beginnen wir mit der Orthographie. Sie zeigt die Schreibsituation der Gebildeten, wie sie vor der von Konrad Duden geprägten Reform Jahres 1901 im deutschen Sprachgebiet üblich gewesen ist. Sie war nicht einheitlich, so dass es Varietäten von Schule zu Schule und von Region zu Region gegeben hat. Deshalb ist zum Nutzen des überregionalen Schrifttums und seiner Wirkung das jahrzehntelange Bestreben des erfahrenen Schulmannes Konrad Duden um eine Vereinheitlichung der Schreibung verständlich. Es macht einem heutigen Leser keine Mühe, die damalige inkonsequente Schreibung zu lesen und zu verstehen.

Die 1901 getilgte *th*-Schreibung hält Fechner gleichmäßig ein: z.B. *anthun, Thee, Vortheil, Werth, gothische Baukunst.* Ebenso konsequent wird die *k*- und die *z*-Aussprache des Buchstaben *c* nicht markiert: *Citrone, Consultation, Succession.* Sehr viel häufiger als heute ist der Gebrauch des *ß*: *Verhältniß/Verhältniße, Anerkenntniß, Preiß, blos* und *bloß* stehen nebeneinander. Bei *dieß* und *indeß* könnte man sich das *ß* aus der Aufeinanderfolge von zwei *s* entstanden erklären: *dieses* und *indessen.* Unsicherheit besteht in der Wiedergabe der Vokallängen z.B. des langen *i*-Lautes: *bornirt, copiren, fixiren, interessiren, scandiren;* aber *spaziren/spazieren/spatziren, bankrottieren, zuwieder, erwiedern* und *er giebt, wir giengen; hieher und hiezu* wechseln mit *hiran.* Die *Bescheerung* hat ein doppeltes *ee.* Für das *i* wird oft *y* gebraucht: *seyn, Styl.* Ein Wechsel der Schreibung auf engem Raum ist nicht selten (*Brot/Brod*). Es stehen *nach dem Todte* und *bei dem Tode* dicht beieinander. *Die Aeltern* werden etymologisch geschrieben, wovor die jüngsten Reformer bei ihrer sonstigen Neigung zur Etymologie (*Stange/Stängel*) zurückgeschreckt sind. Das *ä* begegnet auch in *Gränze.* Ob *Hülfe, die Gehülfin, der Reuter, die gescheutesten Männer* damals noch üblich oder schon Archaismen oder aber Merkwürdigkeiten einer hyperkorrekten gelehrten Ausdrucksweise gewesen sind, vermag ich nicht zu sagen. *Göthe* wird stets mit Umlaut geschrieben.

Diese wenigen Beispiele ließen sich erweitern; nur müsste man dafür den in deutscher Schrift mit der Hand geschriebenen Ausgangstext einsehen. Die orthographischen Schwankungen und Inkonsequenzen handhabt Fechner souverän. An ihnen hat man zu seiner Zeit weder Anstoß genommen noch sie gar für Indizien einer mangelnden Intelligenz oder Bildung gehalten. Denn so sind die Verstöße gegen die verbindlichen Regeln von 1901 jahrzehntelang in der Schule bewertet und bestraft worden. Die jüngste Rechtschreibreform öffnet einen Freiraum für individuelle Varianten, und diese Liberalisierung, die in Großbritannien seit langem üblich ist, sollte die bisher normengläubige Schreibgemeinschaft nutzen und nicht verstört von sich weisen.

Fechner stammt aus Groß Särchen bei Muskau in der Lausitz. Nach dem Tod seines Vaters (1806) wuchs er zusammen mit seinem Bruder

Eduard Clemens bei seinem Vormund, dem Bruder seiner Mutter Pfarrer Gottlob Eusebius Fischer, in Wurzen und von 1810 an in Ranis bei Pößneck (Thüringen) auf. 1817 hat er das Studium der Medizin in Leipzig begonnen, d.h. das Leipziger Sächsisch hat er nicht von früher Kindheit an aufgenommen.

In den Tagebüchern gibt es einige sächsische Spuren. Am 18. Mai 1845 zitiert er den Arzt Dr. Carl Heinrich Wagner mit den Worten »ja, lieber Fechner, das kannst Du mir globen, unsere Geschichte ist mit Drecke versiegelt« (1845, Bl. 44). Unter dem 3. Januar 1868 ist eine kleine Anekdote eingetragen. Bei einer Jagd sagt eine unbeteiligte Frau zu den Schießkünsten des ihr unbekannten Theodor Weber, der Mediziner in Halle ist: »Der Klene schießt gut [...] Ei, sagt ihr Nachbar, das ist der Director des Clinicum in Halle. I, erwiederte sie, das glob' ich noch lange nich, werden se so en Knirps zum Director vom Colinicum machen.« Und am 7. Juni 1869 heißt es in einem Zitat »es is nischt daran.«

Viel hat Fechner anscheinend nicht von der sächsischen Mundart gehalten. Am 20. August 1864 bemerkt er anerkennend zur Sprache einer Livländerin (Estin), die schon mehr als 20 Jahre in Dresden wohnt, dass sie immer noch ihren prononcierten fremdartigen Dialekt beibehalten habe. Und er fügt hinzu: »ein Sachse würde seinen Dialekt im Auslande bald ändern. Der sächsische Dialekt ist aber auch sehr charakterlos.« Diese beiden Aussagen sind nicht die einzigen, die wissenschaftlich unhaltbar sind.

Häufiger, aber gemessen an der großen Textmenge doch selten, kommen sächsische Vokabeln im Wortschatz vor. Dabei nehmen die Verben die größte Zahl ein: z.B. *globen* (glauben, 1845, Bl. 44), *titschen* (eintunken, einen Zwieback in den Kaffee eintauchen 15. 5. 1845), *ningeln* (weinerlich nörgeln, 2./3. 10. 1864), *an der Butter krabbeln* (naschen, 12. 9. 1867), *an der Plumpe manschen* (mit Wasser und Dreck spielen, 12. 9. 1867), *klatschen* (petzen, 21.11.67), *papeln* (reden, 14. 10. 1866), *schindern* (nach einem Anlauf mit den Schuhen über eine glatte Schnee- oder Eisfläche gleiten, 26. 10. 1866), *duseln* (vor sich hindösen, 19. 2. 1872). Ein gängiger sächsischer Phraseologismus ist *das ist alle* (zu Ende, aufgebraucht, 26. 10. 1862); Clara sagt sogar vom November *der ist bald alle* (zu Ende, 26. 10. 1862).

Im Sächsischen übliche Substantive sind: *Fackeball spielen* (den Ball werfen und facken, auffangen, 21. 10. 1842), *Sammtbabouschen* (Hausschuhe, die Fechner als Weihnachtsgeschenk bekommt, 1.1.44, Bl. 4), *das Pferd macht Mätzchen* (ist eigensinnig, 17.6. 1845, Bl. 6), *Bärlatschen* (Filzpantoffeln für die Besucher der Walhalla, 1869, Bl. 67), *die Bommel* (eine Quaste als krönender Abschluss einer gestrickten Mütze, 19.7. 1867), *die Plettfrau* (kommt zum Bügeln der Wäsche, besonders der Hemden, ins Haus, 26.12. 1866), *der Abstreicher* (Abtreter vor der Haustür, 3.9. 1864), *die Butterbemme, Butterbemmchen* (mit Butter bestrichene Brotschnitte, 10.3. 1845), *die Büschekinder* (Kleinkinder im Wickelbett, 2.1. 1870). Die *Gose* (1.5. 1864) ist ein Leipziger Getränk. Ob die an jedem Weihnachtsfest als besonderes Geschenk für die Damen genannten *Magenmorsellen* (25.12. 1844) eine ähnliche sächsische Spezialität sind wie der Stollen, vermag ich nicht zu sagen. – An Namen ist *Hans* oder verdoppelt *Hans, Hans* zu nennen als in Sachsen üblicher Lockruf für Schwäne, die man füttern möchte (13.10. 1866).

An Adjektiven fallen auf: *der Thee ist zu lätschig* (nicht kräftig genug, Winter 30/31), *quabbelich* (umgangssprachlich: schwabbelich, 19.1.65), *baumlich* (beim Gehen hin und her wanken, wacklig laufen, 22.7.67) und *langstilig* (langweilig, 28.10.62). Die einzige belegte Interjektion ist *plautz*. Häufig werden die in direkter Rede wiedergegebenen Antworten nach einer Frage mit *ei* (3.1.68) oder *ei, ja* (1.12.67) eingeleitet. Auch dieser Satzbeginn ist mir aus meiner Jugendzeit als *echa* (* 1924 in Grimma) sprechsprachlich genauso vertraut wie alle anderen genannten Belege.

Ein Blick auf die Morphologie zeigt, dass es seit 150 Jahren einige Veränderungen gegeben hat. Von den Deklinationen der Substantive ist der Genitiv besonders betroffen. Ich glaube nicht, dass der Genitiv zahlenmäßig im Sprachgebrauch immer weiter zurückgegangen und heute seltener zu finden ist. Aber es hat eine Fluktuation der Funktionen gegeben: alte sind verschwunden und andere hinzugekommen. Von den neuen Verwendungsweisen ist z.B. die attributive Verbindung mit einem Verbalabstraktum zu nennen, die besonders in der Verwaltungs- und Rechtssprache häufig ist und im gegenwärtigen Deutsch die verlorene Anzahl der verschwundenen genitivischen Rektionskasus zahlenmäßig ausgeglichen haben dürfte: z.B. *die Anordnung des Stadtrates, die Fertigstellung der Straße, die Behinderung des Verkehrs, das Ereignis der Woche.* Diese Genitivkopplungen an Verbalsubstantive, besonders an solche auf *-ung* findet man bei Fechner nicht.

Dagegen ist der Genitiv als Objektskasus vor oder nach Verben häufig: *sich der Gabe freuen* (heute: sich über die Gabe freuen, 1.1. 1844), *völliger Achtung genießen* (völlige Achtung genießen, 20.10. 1844), *seiner Leistungen gedenken* (an seine Leistung denken, 22.5. 1845), *er rühmte sich seiner Erdbepflanzung* (er brüstete sich mit s. E. oder er gab mit seiner E. an, 22.5. 1845), *es bedurfte einer solchen Arbeit* (man braucht eine solche Arbeit, 1862, Bl. 27), *ich warte meiner Zeit* (ich warte auf meine Zeit, 20. 11. 1862, Bl. 327), *es kam des Besuchs zu viel* (es kam zu viel Besuch, 27. 10. 1842).

Der Versuch, die Konstruktion in den heutigen Sprachgebrauch zu transferieren zeigt drei Möglichkeiten: 1. tritt an die Stelle der synthetischen Genitivkonstruktion eine analytische, präpositionale, 2. der Genitiv wird durch den Akkusativ oder Nominativ ersetzt, und 3. verschwindet zugleich mit der fremd gewordenen Konstruktion auch das Verb (*rühmen*), das wir als veraltet empfinden. Merkwürdig erscheint uns die Wendung *Denkens thätig sein* (21. 5. 1845). Ist es eine Verlaufsform in Verbindung mit dem Genitivus Partitivus? Für welche Übersetzung soll man sich entscheiden, wenn man nicht das Simplex *denken* wählt, das Fechner ja nicht genommen hat? Es kann sich auch um eine Stilblüte handeln, wie sie in ähnlicher Form heute des öfteren zu hören und zu lesen ist: *wir müssen eine Verabredung tätigen.*)

Wenn die Genitivkonstruktion nach einer saloppen, umgangssprachlichen Wendung steht, dann könnte sie auch damals schon gespreizt wirken sollen:

> [...] wir kamen indeß bald überein, diese Lecktüre ganz aufzugeben, da uns die naturphilosophische Sauce nicht schmeckte und uns des Fleisches zu wenig dünkte. (27. 7. 1842)

Wir finden das vorangestellte Genitivattribut merkwürdig, weil es heute nicht mehr üblich ist: *ihres Bruders Kinder* (heute: die Kinder ihres Bruders, umgangssprachlich ist auch die analytische Verbindung möglich: die Kinder von ihrem Bruder, 12. 9. 1867). Das Relativpronomen im Genitiv ist heute ebenfalls selten: *10 000 Bäume, derer jeder nicht über 1000 Blatt hat* (von denen jeder nicht mehr als 1000 Blätter hat, 20. 2. 1872).

Der Dativ im Mask./Neut. Singular endet auf *-e*. Diese Form ist heute nur noch in festen Wendungen erhalten (zu Buche schlagen, zu Kreuze kriechen, bei Hofe, am Fuße des Berges). Fechner schreibt also: *beim Lichte, zum großen Theile, mit rothem Gesichte, nach seinem Tode, im Dorfe*. Das Verb *dünken* kann sowohl den Dativ als den Akkusativ regieren: *das dünkte mir* (1. 1. 1844) und dann heißt es *es wird mich bedünken, es dünkt mich* (13. 10. 1844, Bl. 97). Vornamen werden dekliniert: *daß wir Mathilden eine Last abnehmen* (13. 10. 1844).

Manche Akkusativverbindungen sind uns fremd, weil das Verb heute kaum noch gebräuchlich ist: *den Zustand meiner Augen anlangend* (was den Zustand meiner Augen betrifft, 13.10. 1842), *als wir die Anstalten gewahr wurden* (13.10. 1844).

Bei der Pluralbildung fallen die *Geburtstäge* (1.10. 1864) auf; drei Pluralbildungen, die auf *-s* enden: *daß die Bräutigams dumme Esels und erbärmliche Kerls seyen* (14., ohne Monatsangabe, 1828?)) und die Nichtbeachtung einer Kongruenz, die heutzutage in den schriftlichen Arbeiten der Studierenden oft zu beobachten ist, *es bewarben sich eine große Anzahl Candidaten* (14.10. 1862). Es gibt einen merkwürdigen pronominalen Plural: die Sänger bei den Kanarienvögeln sind die *Sieen,* das sind die Weibchen (Plural vom Singular Femininum *sie,* 28.9. 1842, Bl.187).

Die Morphologie des Verbs zeigt folgende Abweichungen vom heutigen Sprachgebrauch: Im Präsens fallen die Form *fodern* auf (für fordern, 8.1. 1844; es handelt sich nicht um einen Schreibfehler, das erste *r* fehlt in allen Belegen) und die finite Form *es erlöscht* (statt es erlischt, 14.10. 1866). Das präsentische Partizipialadjektiv lässt in der Bedeutung etwas von der Aktionsart der Veränderung anklingen in *das erwachsende Kind* (das erwachsen werdende Kind, 11.2. 1870), und als Superlativ *die vortretendsten Puncte* (2.1. 1865).

Im Präteritum gebraucht Fechner bei *werden* den alten Singular der dritten Person: *dabei ward erzählt* statt des heute dem Plural angeglichenen wurde. Die Form *ward* findet sich in den Grimm'schen Märchen und in den Fabeln Spekters, an deren Lektüre sich Fechners, besonders Clara, gern erfreut haben. Die Vergangenheitsbildung *sie rufte* (statt rief, 13.12. 1866) könnte ein Versehen sein. Merkwürdig ist das Endungs-*e* bei Präteritalformen, deren Singular auf *-ah* endet: *daß es greulich aussahe* (1.1. 1844), *als es geschahe* (8.1. 1865), *er sahe* (13.5. 1845). Beim Partizip Präteriti finden sich zwei Kuriositäten: *genachtwandelt* (27.10. 1866) und *ein aus einer Droschke ausgestiegener Herr* (6.6. 1870). Eine, vom heutigen Gebrauch abweichende Bildung des Genus Verbi ist *er wurde applaudiert* (6.11. 1844). Die Fügung eines ersten Funktionsverbs begegnet mit *in Verfall geraten* (19.3. 1870).

Das Adjektiv kann in flektierter Form nachgestellt werden: *die Reise war eine sehr heitere* (heute ist diese Form unflektiert: die Reise war sehr heiter, 21.5. 1864). Die Zusammensetzung und die Suffigierung lassen Adjektive entstehen, die wir nicht mehr kennen: *borgweise* (leihweise, 13.1. 1865), *kühlig* (27.10. 1866, Bl. 214), *laulich* (27.10. 1866, Bl. 214), *wurmfräßig* (20.12. 1866), *ein baumelicher Gang* (jemand, der unsicher geht, 19.7. 1867). Das heutige Modesuffix *-mäßig* ist bereits mit einem Beleg vertreten; *lazarettmäßig* (15.10. 1866). Auch die Zusammensetzung *belachenswerth* (14.5. 1831) erscheint uns fremd.

Das Relativpronomen *welcher* wird, wie in vielen Texten des 19. Jahrhunderts, auch in Fechners Tagebuch häufiger gebraucht als heute. In der zweiten Hälfte des Jahrhunderts ist es, wie etwa bei Gustav Freytag, zur Mode geworden, die Relativsätze mit *welcher* einzuleiten, also zu *welchern*. Auch die häufige Verwendung von *derselbe* als Demonstrativ- und Bezugspronomen (z.B. 1.10. 1866), kennen wir nicht mehr.

Merkwürdig erscheint uns der Gebrauch der Präposition *gegen* in den Wendungen: *ich hatte gegen sie geäußert* (ihr gegenüber, 13.4. 1844), *sie erwähnte gegen Jettchen* (25.10. 1866). – Unter den Konjunktionen ist mir nur eine begegnet, die wir heute nicht verwenden, nämlich *ungeachtet:* »ungeachtet sie blos den Unterricht der Dorfschule genossen, ist sie doch nicht ohne Kenntnisse« (20.10. 1844). Wir würden dafür obgleich oder obwohl einsetzen, aber eine Bedeutungsdifferenz bleibt bei dieser Übersetzung bestehen.

Von den Adverbien sind heute nicht mehr gebräuchlich: *fortgehends* (laufend, 29.7. 1845), *wir giengen 3 zusammen spazieren* (zu dritt, 13.10. 1844), *mittewochs* (8.10. 1862).

Die Tagebücher sind eine Fundgrube für Phraseologismen; denn es gibt eine Menge fester Wendungen, die wir nicht mehr verwenden: *im Allgemeinen beifallen* (zustimmen, 22.7. 1842), *als sie ganz wach im Bette aufsaß* (28.7. 1842), *der nachbarlich wohnende Dr. S.* (7.8. 1842), *sich ums Essen bekümmern* (für das Essen sorgen, sich um die Mahlzeit kümmern, 11.9. 1842), *einen überlästigen Charakter annehmen* (unerträglich werden 17.9. 1842), *Aufputz der Küche durch blankes Geschirr* (die Verschönerung der Küche mit glänzendem Kupfergeschirr, 22.9. 1842), *eine Partie Erdbeeren* (eine Portion Erdbeeren, 28.9. 1842), *alle aufgestoßenen Begegnisse* (alle auffallenden Ereignisse, 13.10. 1842), *es kann Dir ja nichts verschlagen, ob ich auf dem Sopha oder im Bette schlafe* (es kann dir nichts ausmachen, 18.10. 1842. Bl. 355), *unmuthig über etwas werden* (Nov. Sonntags 1842, Bl. 643), *zu Bette liegen* (1.1. 1844), *wir legten uns zu Bett* (1.1. 1844), *einen ausgespannten Regenschirm zuklappen* (aufgespannt, 14.9. 1844), *meine Frau war abgeschlagen gewesen* (abgespannt, überanstrengt 13.10. 1844), *Blutegel setzen lassen* (14.10. 1844), *den dortigen Brunnen brauchen* (das Brunnenwasser trinken, 28.8. 1842), *eine Cur brauchen* (machen, 14.10. 1844), *Sturzbäder brauchen* (anwenden, 14.10. 1844), *jemanden katholisch machen* (dumm machen, 7.10. 1862), *Emilie räth ein Pflaster an* (16.10. 1862), *eine An-*

rede halten (Rede oder Ansprache, 11.12. 1864), *ein stehendes Weihnachtsgeschenk* (kehrt als festes Präsent an jedem Weihnachtsfest wieder, wie z.B. für Fechner ein halber Eimer Wein von einem Verwandten oder Stollen von der Schwester Mathilde, 24.12. 1862), *auf ganz gemüthlichem Fuß stehen* (in herzlicher Freundschaft [= im Gemüt] verbunden sein, 25.11. 1866), *der Braten hatte seinen Umlauf gemacht* (die Runde gemacht, war herumgereicht worden, 25.11. 1866, Bl. 225), *Damen aufziehen* (zum Tanz auffordern, 13.1. 1867), *als wir abgegessen hatten* (das Essen beendet hatten, 25.2. 1867, Bl. 42). – Es zeigt sich, dass Studien zu einer historischen Phraseologie ergiebig sein dürften; denn ein Teil der Phraseologismen ist bis heute nicht stabil geblieben. Sie verursachen den verfremdenden altertümlichen Ton der Diktion. Es hat sich hier während der letzten 150 Jahre, wie man an den genannten Beispielen sieht, viel geändert. Einen Regenschirm kann ich nicht mehr ausspannen und zuklappen, obwohl sich weder an der Richtigkeit des Bildes noch am Mechanismus des Schirmes etwas geändert hat, sondern nur aufspannen und zu machen. Und der Präsident hält heute keine Anrede, sondern entweder eine Rede oder eine Ansprache. Diese Phrasen erscheinen uns fest, aber vielleicht ändern sie sich wieder und man hält künftig eine *Vorsprache.*

In der Wortbildung gibt es feminine Formen, zu denen wir uns heute in der Gleichberechtigungsdebatte noch nicht entschlossen haben: *die Verwandtin* (25.12. 1844, Bl. 265), *die Bekanntin* (16.10. 1842), *die Zöglingin* (15.11. 1864, Bl. 273). Das Suffix *-in* begegnet auch am Ende eines Familiennamens zur Bezeichnung der Frau: *die Schubertin* (24.12. 1862).

Weitere uns fremde Lemmata im Vokabular sind z.B. die Iterativa *sie ständerten in der Stube* (sie standen längere Zeit in der Stube herum, 6.10. 1842), *sie hatten zu packen und zu schäftern* (sie machten sich immer wieder zu schaffen, 6.10. 1842), Fremd sind uns: *der Kalbsstoß* (die Kalbskeule, 11.9. 1842), *das Kopfleiden* (Kopfschmerzen, 13.9. 1842), *die Beinkleiderrolle* (Hosenrolle, Leonore im Fidelio, 5.3. 1845, Bl. 9), *wegen Unterschleifes* (wegen Unterschlagung, 16.6. 1845), die mit einem negativen Präfix versehenen Substantive *Ungeneigtheit* (25.11. 1862), *Nichtarzt* (8.11. 1867) und *Unbekanntschaft* (8.11. 1867). In *der Aufenthalt hatte nicht sonderlich gefrommt* (6.10. 1842) ist noch die ursprüngliche Bedeutung von *fromm* (nützlich) erkennbar. *Auch ich habe sie allmählich überwachsen* (ich bin allmählich größer geworden als sie, 21.11. 1868, Bl. 277) würden wir heute nicht sagen, obwohl wir den Ausdruck verstehen. Öfter begegnet das nicht mehr geläufige Adjektiv *zierlich*: z.B. *das wenig Zierliche im Behaben* (die mangelnde Anmut, Feinheit im Benehmen, 28.9. 1842). Die wenigen Beispiele zeigen die unerschöpfliche Elastizität der deutschen Wortbildung und die Ausdrucksvielfalt auch in der Vergangenheit. Es kann sich in einigen Fällen durchaus um individuelle Schöpfungen Fechners handeln, die keinen Eingang in das Lexikon und den allgemeinen Sprachgebrauch gefunden haben.

Fechners, ihre Verwandten und Freunde reisen gern mit dem *Dampfwagen* (mit der Bahn, 20.8. 1864) in die Sommerfrische. Ihre Ziele sind nicht renommierte Bäder wie Karlsbad oder Kissingen, sondern kleine Ortschaften z.B. in Thüringen, wo man in einfachen Privatquartieren wohnt, sich in bescheidenen Gasthäusern verpflegt und vor allem die Touren- und Wandermöglichkeiten nutzt. Fechner notiert aus dieser Zeit des beginnenden Fremdenverkehrs:

> Im Interesse der Curgäste sind alle Punkte, von welchen die Aussicht lohnend ist, durch bequeme Wege zugänglich gemacht; [...] außerdem begegnet man auf allen Wegen Ruhebänken, Denksteinen, gefaßten Quellen, welche irgend einer Person durch irgend einen Verehrer geweiht sind oder den Namen des Liebhabers des Platzes und Stifters der Anlage tragen, also: Marienbrunnen, Bernhardsbrunnen, Jenny-Quelle, Fannyquelle, Clementinen-Quelle, Carolinen-Quelle, Alexandriner Höhe, Tonyruhe, usw. usw. (5.9. 1864, Bl. 132).

An anderer Stelle notiert er *den Preußenstein, die Lilihöhe, die Allerseelenbank, den Todtenstein* und *den Philosophenweg* (15.9. 1864, Bl. 119). Diese Namen sind für die Feriengäste zu wichtigen Ziel- und Orientierungspunkten im Netz der Wanderwege geworden. Sie prägen die Atmosphäre der Erholungsgebiete und sind in allen Kurorten über die Jahre hinweg von erstaunlicher Beständigkeit, und eine Besonderheit in der Wortbildung der Namenkunde.

Zum Schluss noch einige Bemerkungen zur Syntax und zum Textverlauf: Eine syntaktisch-stilistische Eigenart gibt es häufig in deutschen literarischen Texten des 18. und 19. Jahrhunderts: das ist der abhängige Satz, dessen zusammengesetzter Verbform am Ende das finite Hilfsverb (in der Regel eine Form von haben oder sein) fehlt: z.B. *ein fremder Officier, mit dem er hier öfters zusammen gespeist, verlangte* [...] (13.10. 1844, Bl.101). Nach *gespeist* fehlt das finite Hilfsverb *hat* oder *hatte*. Oder *als Laura bei Augusten gewesen, hat er sich nicht blicken lassen, ungeachtet er sonst immer großes Interesse an Laura genommen*. Fechner verwendet diese Satzform oft. Selten gibt es für den Versuch, das fehlende Finitum zu ergänzen, nur eine temporale oder modale Lösung: wie z.B. *es schien uns noch immer am wahrscheinlichsten, daß hiebei eine verborgene äußere Vermittlung statt gefunden, welche den Erzählern entgangen.* Ich würde hier ergänzen *statt gefunden habe* und *entgangen ist.* Diese Konstruktionen finden sich sehr oft in Relativsätzen, aber auch in anders eingeleiteten abhängigen Sätzen, die z.B. beginnen mit *als* (13.10. 1844, Bl. 107), *indem* (17.10. 1844, Bl. 117), *daß* (13.10. 1844, Bl. 105), *obschon* (27.11. 1867) *ungeachtet* (13.10. 1844, Bl. 107), *was* (17.10. 1844, Bl. 117), *weil* (30.10. 1844), *wenn* (22.11. 1867), *wie* (17.8. 1870), *wo* (18.10. 1844). Erläuterungen für die Entstehung dieser unvollständigen Nebensätze habe ich in den zeitgenössischen Grammatiken nicht gefunden. Es sind sprachliche Verbindungen, die zwischen einem abhängigen Satz und einer Partizipialkonstruktion stehen. Stichwortartige Notizen sind selten. Am 25. Juli 1842 schreibt Fechner:

> Gegen 9 Uhr aufgestanden, im Garten spaziert; dann bis Mittag an Aesthetik geschrieben. Nachm. Härtels zum Kaffee bei uns; dann im Garten spazirt; dann meine Frau abschreiben lassen. Nach dem Abendessen mit ihr in das Johannisthal gegangen.

Jedes Notat, bis auf das zweite (*im Garten spaziert*), beginnt mit einer Zeitangabe, welche die Reihenfolge der Handlungen verdeutlicht. Personalpronomina fehlen. Die finiten Hilfsverben werden ausgelassen wie in den im vorigen Abschnitt gezeigten Nebensätzen. *Härtels Kaffeebesuch* käme ohne jedes Verb aus. Diesen Platz sparenden Telegrammstil erwartet man im Tagebuch. Fechner verwendet ihn selten; denn seine Diktion orientiert sich an der Rede des freien Vortrags.

Vollständige Sätze von oft beträchtlicher Länge konstituieren die meisten Texte. Sie sind eingängig, da sie wenige in sich geschachtelte Hypotaxen enthalten, sondern eine Reihung abhängiger Sätze, wie man an dem folgenden Beispiel einer absurden Überlegung aus einer Diskussion im Kränzchen sieht:

> Haupt schlug vor, der Bundestag solle, um die Schweizer wegen ihrer Ausschweifung in liberalen Ideen zu bestrafen, die Abtragung ihrer Berge anordnen; dann würden nicht nur keine Fremden mehr ihr Land besuchen, sondern sie würden auch den Verdienst durch Fertigung von Käse verlieren. Ich erweiterte diesen Vorschlag dahin, die Berge sollten dann an die einzelnen Bundesstaaten vertheilt oder verlost werden, da jetzt eine unbillige Vertheilung der schönen Gegenden statt fände; wogegen jedoch das Bedenken geltend gemacht wurde, wie man mit den Bergen auch die Aussichten an die betreffenden Orte bringen könne. Auch machte Klee darauf aufmerksam, wenn der Montblanc

durch Loos einem kleinen Ländchen, wie dem Fürstenthum Lichtenstein zufiele, so könne dieses ganz davon zugedeckt werden. (5.8. 1842)

Die Gespräche sind stilistisch nicht so gestaltet, dass sich die Sprechenden mit einer jeweils individuellen Diktion voneinander unterscheiden. Die einzelnen Redeteile stimmt Fechner inhaltlich aufeinander ab, aber er gibt ihnen keine stilistische Eigenfärbung. Die Partner schließen sich der Meinung des Vorredners an oder sie widersprechen ihr, so dass der Einzelbeitrag im Gefüge der Konversation verständlich wird. Das sieht man z.B. an dem ausführlichen Gespräch über Luthers Bibelübersetzung, das am 24. Oktober 1866 am Frühstückstisch geführt wird und sich über mehrere Seiten erstreckt. Daran nehmen außer dem Ehepaar Fechner Pfarrer Allwill Volkmann, Claras Stiefbruder, und der Jurist Emil Kuntze, ältester Sohn von Fechners Schwester Emilie, teil. Das Gespräch ist vermutlich vor oder bei der Niederschrift sorgfältig redigiert, vielleicht auch von Fechner ergänzt worden. Dass dabei nicht die schwächsten Argumente von seiner Seite kommen, dürfte, falls es nicht stimmen sollte, verzeihlich sein. Mit der Verwendung von Demonstrativa und kontrastierenden Partikeln wie *aber, doch* und Zustimmungsfloskeln *so wird es sein, das mag sein, nun ja* wird das Bemühen um Spuren gesprochener Sprache erkennbar.

Die Sprache der Tagebuchtexte zeigt, dass während der letzten 150 Jahre mehr Veränderungen in der Grammatik, im Lexikon und in der Stilistik eingetreten sind, als man bei der Lektüre bemerkt. Das wird besonders an den Phraseologismen deutlich, die aus uns geläufigen Wörtern bestehen, aber in der festen Bindung einer Redensart nicht mehr gebräuchlich sind oder eine andere Bedeutung haben. Unsere Beobachtungen müssen eine Art Negativbilanz bleiben. Denn es lassen sich nur die damaligen Abweichungen aus der heutigen Sicht feststellen und nicht zugleich die hinzu gewachsene Andersartigkeit der gegenwärtigen Sprachverwendung erfassen und darstellen.

Literatur:

Cherubim, D.; Mattheier, K.J. (1989): Voraussetzungen und Grundlagen der Gegenwartssprache. Berlin; New York.

Cherubim, D.; Grosse, S.; Mattheier, K.J.(1998): Sprache und bürgerliche Nation. Beiträge zur deutschen und europäischen Sprachgeschichte des 19. Jahrhunderts. Berlin; New York.

Grosse, S. (1989): Sprachwandel und Sprachwachstum im Ruhrgebiet in der zweiten Hälfte des 19. Jahrhunderts. In: Voraussetzungen und Grundlagen der Gegenwartssprache. Hg. von D. Cherubim; K.J. Mattheier. Berlin; New York, 281–295.

Grosse, S. (1990): Zu Syntax und Stil in der deutschen Sprache des 19. Jahrhunderts. In: Neuere Forschungen zur historischen Syntax des Deutschen. Referate der Internationalen Fachkonferenz Eichstätt 1989. Hg. von A. Betten. Tübingen, 300–309. (= Germanistische Linguistik, RGL 103).

Grosse, S. (1990): Überlegungen zur deutschen Sprache im 19. Jahrhundert. In: Deutsche Sprachgeschichte. Grundlagen, Methoden, Perspektiven. Festschrift für Johannes Erben zum 65. Geburtstag. Hg. von W. Besch. Bern, 323–328.

Grosse, S. (1991): Arbeitersprache im Ruhrgebiet. In: Das 19. Jahrhundert. Sprachgeschichtliche Wurzeln des heutigen Deutsch. Hg. von R. Wimmer: Berlin; New York, 202–222. (=Institut für deutsche Sprache. Jahrbuch 1990).

Grosse, S. (1993): Spuren gesprochener Sprache in den Protokollen eines Schiedsmannbuches (1902–1918). In: Sprachgeschichte und Sprachkritik. Festschrift für Peter von Polenz zum 65. Geburtstag. Hg. von H.J. Heringer; G. Stötzel. Berlin; New York, 89–99.

Grosse, S. (1998): Morphologische und syntaktisch-stilistische Eigentümlichkeiten in deutschen Texten aus dem letzten Drittel des 19. Jahrhunderts. In: Sprache und bürgerliche Nation. Beiträge zur deutschen und europäischen Sprachgeschichte des 19. Jahrhunderts. Hg. von D. Cherubim; S. Grosse; K.J. Mattheier. Berlin; New York, 444–456.

Horst-Peter Brauns

G. Th. Fechners Studium als interdisziplinäres Unternehmen. »Wie es überhaupt seine Art war, sich in allen Richtungen des Geistes strebsam zu versuchen«[1]

Ein diachronisches Konzept von Studium im Sinne einer bildungsintensiven Lebensphase, in der sich sowohl Effekte früherer Entwicklung niederschlagen als auch für später bedeutsame Determinanten hinzukommen, dient als äußerer Rahmen dieser individualhistorischen Untersuchung. Intern strukturierender Leitbegriff dagegen ist ein zeitgenössischer Begriff von Studium mit einem eher institutionell-formalen sowie einem eher personenbezogenen-motivationalen Bedeutungsaspekt. Seine Anwendung auf den jungen Fechner führt auf der institutionellen Seite zu den Fächern Medizin, Mathematik und Philosophie sowie zu Austauschbeziehungen mit zentralen Mediatoren wie E.H. Weber, Mollweide und Krug. Diese drei Interaktionsbereiche werden beispielhaft abgehandelt. Mit ihnen zeigt sich in personal-motivationaler Hinsicht ein vielfältigeres Bild verknüpft. Es herrscht ein innerer »Zwiespalt« (Fechner o.J.) zwischen Kunst und Wissenschaft vor, den vor allem die Schulze-Episode dynamisiert. In dem Maße nun, in dem dieser Konflikt sich löst, füllt Fechner zunehmend die Rolle eines monodisziplinären akademischen Lehrers, Forschers und Autors aus. Momente aus dem interdisziplinären Studium werden erst in späteren Lebensphasen stärker in den Vordergrund treten.

1. Einleitung

Bedeutende Wissenschaftler werden oft mit überraschenden Gegensätzen kolportiert. Von Einstein heißt es gelegentlich, der Schöpfer der Relativitätstheorie sei kein allzu guter Schüler gewesen. Wundt, einer der sog. Gründungsväter der experimentellen Psychologie, soll zeitlebens mit der Mathematik auf Kriegsfuß gestanden haben. Auch wenn derartige Plakatierungen irgendwo ein Stück historischer Wirklichkeit enthalten mögen, so dürften sie dennoch kaum tauglich sein, die dynamische Vielfältigkeit

---

[1] Siehe Kuntze 1892, 29.

einer schöpferischen Persönlichkeit einzufangen. Das gilt in besonderem Maße für G. Th. Fechner, wie neuere Studien gezeigt haben.[2] Gleichwohl blieb Fechner von plakativen Kurzcharakteristiken nicht ausgenommen. Über den Urheber der Psychophysik ist mitunter zu hören, er sei zunächst Mediziner gewesen, später habe er dem *Spiritualismus* in scharfem Gegensatz zum Materialismus angehangen. Seriöse psychologiegeschichtliche Werke stellen bisweilen sein Forscherleben in sich überschneidenden Periodisierungen dar, die inhaltlich kaum miteinander zu vereinbaren sind. Danach war Fechner beispielsweise gleichzeitig Invalide und Philosoph, um nur ein Beispiel zu nennen.[3] Seine früheren Lebensabschnitte erscheinen bisher allerdings nahezu tabuisiert. Um weniger zutreffenden Kurzcharakteristiken darüber von vornherein entgegen zu arbeiten, dürfte Fechners 200. Geburtstag eine passende Gelegenheit sein, eine frühere Bildungsphase dieser eminenten Forscherpersönlichkeit eingehender auszuleuchten. Gemeint ist jener Entwicklungsabschnitt vom Jugendlichen- zum Erwachsenendasein, zwischen Schule und Berufstätigkeit, der nach akademischer Ausbildung ausläuft, indem der höchste erworbene Abschluss zum Eintritt in die wissenschaftliche Gemeinschaft berechtigt. Hinter dieser Konzentration auf die Studienzeit steht auch der Gedanke, dass für ein umfassenderes historisches Verstehen einer Forscherpersönlichkeit gerade frühere Lebensphasen wesentliche Voraussetzungen liefern und deren Offenlegung allzu vereinfachende Plakatierungen mit ihrer stark verallgemeinernden Dimensionalität erschweren können. Dies um so mehr, wenn deutlich gemacht wird, dass Lebensabschnitte – wie die hier im Mittelpunkt stehende Zwischenphase – einerseits Folgen vorausgehender Entwicklung und andererseits zugleich Bedingungen für spätere beinhalten. Für den Historiographen erwächst daraus u.a. die Forderung, nach Kontinuitäten und Spätfolgen, aber auch nach Diskontinuitäten, Brüchen sowie echten Neuerungen Ausschau zu halten.

Diese Studie unternimmt es daher, zunächst Fechners *familiären* Hintergrund und seine frühe Studienzeit zu skizzieren. Dazu werde ich einen Begriff von *Studium* aus der ersten Hälfte des 19. Jhs. einführen, diesen um den neueren Ausdruck *Interdisziplinarität* ergänzen und beide auf eine Auswahl aus jenem Quellenmaterial anwenden, das Fechner mit einer autobiographischen Darstellung seines Studiums liefert. Im einzelnen möchte ich versuchen, nicht nur Studiengebiete zu sondieren, sondern

---

[2] Siehe Gundlach 1993; Heidelberger 1993; Arendt 1999.

[3] Siehe Kuntze 1892; Boring 1957; 1961.

auch dort rezipierte Inhalte herauszustellen, welche ihrerseits lebensgeschichtliche und von Fall zu Fall auch wissenschaftshistorische Bedeutsamkeit erlangen. Teils kann ich mich dabei auf Selbstaussagen Fechners stützen, teils werden nicht unmittelbar zutage liegende Querverbindungen aufgespürt, über die sich Austauschbeziehungen manifestieren. Die ursprünglich beabsichtigte stärker persönlichkeitspsychologische Ausrichtung dieser Studie sowie speziellere Ausführungen zur Methodik habe ich nicht mehr in wünschenswerter Weise verwirklichen können.

2. Der junge Fechner und sein familiärer Hintergrund

Allseits bekannt ist die Herkunft aus einem evangelischen Pfarrhause mit entsprechenden Traditionen bei beiden Elternteilen. Der Fechner-Biograph Kuntze bemerkt hierzu: »Fechners Jugenderziehung ruhte auf dem Rationalismus des vorigen Jahrhunderts« (Kuntze 1892, 151). Diese Geisteshaltung äußert sich in Gestalt von Fechners früh verstorbenem Vater mehr in progressiven als konservativen Zügen. Ihr besonderes Gepräge findet die Familie in der zeichnerisch-malerischen Tätigkeit des Bruders und der sprachlich-dichterischen der Mutter. Sie »war« nach Kuntze, »mit einer poetischen Ader ausgestattet«, so dass »[ihr] leicht die Verse flossen« (Kuntze 1892, 30). Darf man wagen, die Hypothese einer entsprechenden *Heretabilität* bei Fechner selbst in den Raum zu stellen?

In das künstlerische Ambiente passt der einmal von der Mutter geäußerte Wunsch, der junge Fechner möge Klavierunterricht erteilen, ebenso wie sein freiwilliges Auswendiglernen von Tassos »Befreitem Jerusalem« und seine Teilnahme an einem Zeichenkurs auf der Akademie in Dresden, noch neben der Kreuzschule. Allem Anschein nach blieb es jedoch bei diesem frühen kurzen Ausflug in die bildende Kunst (Kuntze 1892, 30).

Wenn Kuntze zusammenfassend feststellt: »es war überhaupt seine Art, sich in allen Richtungen des Geistes strebsam zu versuchen« (Kuntze 1892, 29), dann dürften dem nicht allein die soeben angeführten Verhaltensproben des jungen Fechner zugrunde gelegen haben. Dazu beigetragen hat sicherlich die mehrfach bezeugte Tendenz zum *Autodidakten*. Sie zeigt sich bereits in einem Brief des Gymnasiasten auf der Dresdner Kreuzschule – vermutlich aus dem Jahre 1816 – an seinen Onkel Fischer, bei dem er mit seinem Bruder aufwächst. Darin bittet der 15-jährige Fechner, die Schule verlassen zu dürfen, um Privatstudien für den Übergang auf die Universität betreiben zu können. Ein Jahr später erfolgt schon die

Zustimmung zum Studium der *Medizin* nach großem Lob seiner Kenntnisse und Fähigkeiten durch den Leiter seiner Schule. Anzumerken ist, dass sich über die Gründe dieser Fächerwahl bisher kaum etwas Handfestes in Erfahrung bringen ließ. Von daher wäre derzeit noch als offen anzusehen, ob die Wahl des Studienfaches aus einem spezifischen Interesse heraus geschah oder eher aufgrund der damit verbundenen Berufschancen zustande kam.

3. Fechners Studium

3.1. Zum zeitgenössischen Begriff des Studiums

Wie oben gesagt, möchte ich bei dem folgenden Versuch, Fechners Studienphase auszuleuchten, einen zeitgenössischen Begriff von *Studium* zugrunde legen. Dazu entnehme ich seine allgemeine Bedeutung der 10. Auflage der Allgemeinen deutschen Realencyklopädie von 1854, speziellere Bedeutungsvarianten den »Grundlinien der Hodegetik oder Methodik des akademischen Studiums und Lebens« von K.H. Scheidler 1839, in 2. Aufl., seines Zeichens ordentlicher Honorarprofessor zu Jena (s. Tab. 1).

Dem in der Realenzyklopädie festgestellten allgemeinen Sprachgebrauch nach ist unter *Studium* »jede ernste Beschäftigung mit einer Wissenschaft oder Kunst« zu verstehen. Auf dem akademischen Felde begegnen vornehmlich zwei Varianten, eine eher personenspezifische, näher bestimmt durch eifriges, anhaltendes, sorgfältiges Forschen oder Nachsinnen infolge eines inneren Dranges oder Triebes. Die zweite, eher formale Variante meint Beschäftigung mit Wissenschaft auf der Universität, vor allem mit dem Ziel, den wissenschaftlichen Geist zu wecken und auszubilden (Scheidler 1839, 204).

Obzwar es sich nicht um völlig trennscharfe Nuancierungen handelt, möchte ich nun im weiteren versuchen herauszustellen, ob und inwieweit sich Fechners Lebensphase nach dem Schulabgang bis zu seinem *akademischen Abschluss* mit dem soeben erläuterten Gesamtbegriff von Studium zur Deckung bringen lässt. In diesem Kontext wird auch das neuere, im 19. Jh. offenbar noch nicht vorkommende Attribut »interdisziplinär« zu benutzen sein, und zwar vor allem im Sinne von *disziplinüberschreitend* (Brauns et al. 2000b). Es hat in dieser *idiographischen* Studie u.a. die Funktion, unsere Aufmerksamkeit auf die divergierende Breite von Fechners Begegnung mit der Wissenschaft (und übrigens auch einem Teil der Kunst) zu lenken (s. Tabelle 1).

Tabelle 1:

Zeitgenössischer Begriff von Studium
(siehe AdRE 1854)

»Jede ernste Beschäftigung mit einer Wissenschaft oder Kunst«
↑
Allgemeine Bedeutung

⇑
Studium
⇓

Speziellere Bedeutungsvarianten:
↓
↓ ↓

1.	2.
Eifriges, anhaltendes, sorgfältiges Forschen oder Nachsinnen infolge eines inneren Dranges oder Triebes personspezifische Variante	Beschäftigung mit Wissenschaft auf der Universität vor allem mit dem Ziel, den wissenschaftlichen Geist zu wecken und auszubilden formale Variante (Siehe Scheidler 1839, 203f.).

3.2. Fechners autobiographischer Studiumsbericht

Über den Fortgang der akademischen Ausbildung in Leipzig unterrichtet uns eine bei Kuntze o.J. eingerückte umfangreiche Selbstaussage:

> Ich hörte Collegia bei Krug (Logik), Schwägrichen (Botanik und Zoologie), Gilbert (Physik und Chemie), Eschenbach (Pharmacie), Rosenmüller (Anatomie), Kühn und Ernst Heinr. Weber (Physiologie), Jörg (Geburtshülfe), Mollweide(r) (Algebra); besuchte jedoch die meisten dieser Collegien nur zu Anfang oder unterbrochen, indem ich fand, dass ich mich aus Büchern bequemer und besser unterrichten konnte: nur die Vorlesungen von Weber über Physiologie – nach den geistlosen von Kühn – und von Mollweide(r) über Algebra, wodurch

> ich zuerst zum Studium der Mathematik geführt wurde, machten eine Ausnahme in dieser Beziehung und gewährten Anregungen, die in der Folge fruchtbar wurden. Auch famulirte ich einige Jahre bei Mollweide(r), habe es aber mit aller Mühe in der Mathematik wegen mangelnden Talentes dazu nicht weit bringen können. Pathologie und Therapie habe ich gar nicht gehört, sondern bloß aus Büchern studirt (Fechner in: Kuntze 1892, 37).

Eine so detaillierte Selbstbeschreibung gibt im Grunde ein umfangreicheres Forschungsprogramm auf, wenn man zu einer umfassenden Interpretation kommen will. Im Augenblick genügt indes eine erste, von unserem soeben facettierten Begriff von *Studium* geleitete Bestandsaufnahme. Neben Standardveranstaltungen zur Ausbildung des wissenschaftlichen Geistes für Mediziner fallen zunächst folgende Momente auf:

- das Studium zumindest eines nicht zur Medizin gehörenden Faches, nämlich der *Mathematik*;
- offenbar in Verbindung hiermit eine *mehrjährige Famulatur* bei Mollweide, der Mathematiker und Astronom war, und nicht bei einem Mediziner, was eigentlich von der Fächerwahl her zu erwarten gewesen wäre;
- der Besuch der *Logik-Veranstaltung* des Philosophen Krug;
- die *autodidaktische* Haltung, wenn es heißt, dass Selbstunterricht an Hand von Büchern »besser und bequemer sei« und schließlich
- die mehr zwischen den Zeilen stehende *kritische Haltung* zu dem geringen subjektiven Nutzen universitärer Lehrveranstaltungen, verbunden mit ausdrücklicher Anerkennung nützlicher Anregungen durch den Mediziner Weber und den Mathematiker Mollweide.

Es zeigt sich, dass man Fechners akademischer Ausbildung nicht allein mit der formalen Bedeutungsnuance gerecht werden kann, indem man einfach sagt, hier studiert jemand, der Mediziner werden will und sich zur Erlangung entsprechender Kenntnisse mit akademischen Lehrern austauscht. Denn zudem wird der *personspezifische Aspekt* von Studium im Sinne anhaltenden, eifrigen Forschens und Nachsinnens infolge eines inneren Triebes erfüllt. Er ist zumindest teilweise Ausdruck der bereits mehrfach diagnostizierten *autodidaktischen* Neigung bzw. der dieser entsprechenden Motivationslage.

Im Hinblick auf *Interdisziplinarität* ist unmittelbar keine monodisziplinäre, sondern vielmehr eine fächerübergreifende Anlage des Studiums erkennbar. Und zwar in dem Maße, in dem Fechner sich mit Disziplinen befasst, welche *nicht* zum institutionellen Fächerkanon seiner Medizinausbildung gehören. Das gilt zunächst und vor allem für die Nennung von Mollweide und das mit diesem Namen verbundene Fach Mathematik. Inwieweit sich Gleiches für Physik und Chemie bei Gilbert behaupten läßt, sei nur der Vollständigkeit halber als Frage angemerkt.

Einen vor allem in unserem Kontext wichtigen Hinweis liefert Fechners Feststellung über erhaltene Anregungen, die selbst späterhin noch wirksam wurden.

Während die diesbezügliche Nennung des Mediziners Weber kaum überraschend sein dürfte, ist die Mollweide zugeschriebene Anregungsfunktion die eines Nichtmediziners und somit als eine *interdiszplinäre* zu werten. Bei diesen Beschreibungen an der Oberfläche soll es aber nicht bleiben. Vielmehr gilt es weiterführend zu untersuchen, was sich hinter »fruchtbaren Anregungen« verbergen könnte. Denn es handelt sich schließlich um Momente, die für Fechners weiteres Forscherleben aus seiner Sicht relevant geworden sind, d.h., die ihn geprägt haben und ihn insoweit auch ein Stück charakterisieren. Mit dieser Vorgabe verfolge ich, formal betrachtet, *idiographische Hypothesen* über Austauschbeziehungen zwischen Fechner und seinen akademischen Lehrern, die jeweils anhand von Quellen zu belegen sind.[4] Der Übersichtlichkeit halber werde ich sie gesondert behandeln.

Ohne Zweifel können auf diesem Wege nicht erschöpfend alle auf den Studenten fruchtbar einwirkende Faktoren aufgespürt werden – zumal auch Fechners flottierende *autodidaktische* Neigung ins Kalkül zu ziehen und jene Skepsis angebracht ist, welche stets autobiographischen Äußerungen gegenüber besteht. Überdies sind Fechners Aussagen – selbst wenn es veridicale, d.h. zutreffende Feststellungen über die spätere Relevanz früherer Austauschbeziehungen zu seinen akademischen Lehrern sind – von seinem individuellen Standpunkt aus erfolgt, in Selbstsicht gleichsam. Auf einer kollektiven Analyseebene wie der der wissenschaftlichen Gemeinschaft etwa, d.h. in Fremdsicht, könnten noch andere Querbeziehungen – etwa durch Zitationsanalysen – aufscheinen und sich darin ebenfalls Anregungen geltend machen.

Um auch auf dieser Analyseebene zu explorieren, soll aus dem von Fechner benannten Ensemble akademischer Lehrer noch ein dritter herausgegriffen werden, der jedoch von Fechner weder zu seinen »Anregern« gezählt wird noch Mediziner gewesen ist. Auf diese Weise ließe sich in Fremdsicht auf der Ebene der wissenschaftlichen Gemeinschaft unter-

[4] Siehe Buksinski 1985.

suchen, ob nicht auch andere akademische Lehrer spätere Anregungsfunktion ausgeübt haben. Daran kann sich die Frage anschließen, inwieweit Fechner sich vielleicht noch stärker *interdisziplinär* orientiert hat. Formal ginge es erneut darum, eine auf Fechners Aussage fußende *idiographische Hypothese* zu verfolgen. Wird sie vom beigebrachten Quellenmaterial nicht gestützt, wäre die Alternativhypothese höher zu gewichten.[5] Beispielhaft werde ich die Exploration an Fechners akademischen Lehrer Krug, einem Philosophen, durchführen. Zunächst aber gehe ich auf E.H. Weber und K.B. Mollweide ein.

3.3. Fechner und der Anatom und Physiologe Ernst Heinrich Weber

Es handelt sich um die Begegnung des noch nicht einmal 25-jährigen Weber mit dem um sechs Jahre jüngeren Studenten der Medizin, die zugleich der Anfang einer etwa 60-jährigen Freundschaft werden sollte. Da diese Beziehung nicht nur bekannt ist, sondern bereits vielfach untersucht, fasse ich mich kurz, indem ich mich auf den paradigmatischen Konsens beschränke, der zwischen beiden Forscherpersönlichkeiten längerfristig in diachronischer Perspektive besteht. Er betrifft vor allem die paradigmatischen Komponenten Genauigkeit, Mathematisierung von Gesetzesaussagen sowie quantitativ-metrisches Experimentieren, welche insbesondere in der *Psychophysik* (Fechner 1860) zur Geltung kommen.[6] Als autodeskriptiver Beleg für die von Weber tatsächlich ausgeübte Anregungsfunktion lässt sich übrigens Fechners Nachruf auf den Freund vom 30. Januar 1878 anführen. Ich komme zu Fechners Austauschbeziehungen mit Mollweide.

3.4. Fechner und der Astronom und Mathematiker Karl Brandan Mollweide

Mollweide (1774–1825) kommt über Halle 1811 als a.o. Professor der Astronomie und Observator der Sternwarte nach Leipzig, wird 1812 Ordinarius und erhält zudem nach von Prasses Tod 1814 das Ordinariat für Mathematik. Vielleicht war es die Mehrfachbelastung durch pro Semesterwoche bis zu sechzehnstündigen astronomischen Beobachtungskursen in dem auf der Pleissenburg eingerichteten Observatorium, durch den

[5] Siehe hierzu Buksinski 1985.

[6] Siehe Brauns 2000a.

Lehrauftrag für Physik sowie mathematische Lehrveranstaltungen (u.a. über das »Wahrscheinlichkeitscalcul«), zu deren Verringerung der Student Fechner als Famulus beizutragen hatte.

Die Einschätzung der rezeptiven und zugleich *interdisziplinären* Austauschbeziehung zwischen beiden hängt insbesondere von der Beantwortung der Frage ab, ob Fechner der Autor eines 1825 erschienenen, mit F. unterzeichneten Nachrufs ist. Dort heißt es u.a: Jeder, der mit Neigung sich der *Mathematik* zugewandt habe, »konnte sicher seyn« in Mollweide »einen eifrigen Beförderer seiner Fortschritte zu finden. Er hat deshalb die Liebe aller seiner Schüler, die ihn näher kannten, genossen« (F., Anonymus, 1825, 548).

Im Hinblick auf uns interessierende Anregungen liegt mithin im Bereich des Möglichen, dass der Mathematikstudent Fechner über astronomische und mathematische Arbeiten seines Lehrers von Euler, La Place und Biot (Wolf 1890) hörte und Einblick in neueste mathematisch-naturwissenschaftliche Publikationen aus Frankreich, die sich der des Französischen mächtige Mollweide kommen ließ, nehmen konnte.

Darüber hinaus wären die Rezeption von Wissen aus der Geschichte der Optik und des Farbensehens (Mollweide 1812) ebenso anzunehmen wie das Kennenlernen der vom Newton'schen Standpunkt aus geführten, überaus kritischen Auseinandersetzung Mollweides mit Goethes Seh- und Farbenlehre (Mollweide 1804; 1810).

In Zeitschriftenartikeln demonstriert Mollweide anhand von Textstellen nicht nur, dass »man sich nicht überall auf die Uebersetzertreue des Hrn. von Göthe verlassen darf« (Mollweide 1810, 92). Sondern er äußert auch die Vermutung, dem Poeten sei »der Fundamentalsatz der ganzen Newton'schen Lehre nicht klar geworden« (Mollweide 1811) – obgleich dieser sehr wahrscheinlich am 12. 7. 1802 in Halle einer von Mollweide abgehaltenen optisch-physikalischen Unterrichtsstunde beiwohnte (vgl. Grumach 1985, 287). Das in dieser Stunde nicht ganz geglückte Demonstrationsexperiment mit einem drehbaren »Farbenkreis« hat Goethe wiederum in seinem Gedicht, »Dem Weißmacher«, verarbeitet und sicherlich nicht ohne Genugtuung in die Sammlung »Invectiven« seiner Werke aufgenommen:

> Dem Weißmacher.
> Newtonisch Weiß den Kinder vorzuzeigen,
> Die pädagogischem Ernst sogleich sich neigen,
> Trat einst ein Lehrer auf, mit Schwungsrads Possen,
> Auf selbem war ein Farbenkreis geschlossen.

> Das dorlte nun. »Betracht' es mir genau!
> Was siehst du, Knabe?« Nun, was seh' ich? Grau!
> »Du siehst nicht recht! Glaubst du, dass ich das leide:
> Weiß, dummer Junge, Weiß! so sagt's Mollweide.«
> (Goethe 1840; 6; 166)

Mollweide seinerseits gesteht dem Dichter zu, dass man »ohne Mathematik manche interessante Beobachtung von den Farben machen, auch viel Wahres und Schönes über Farben sagen könne« (Mollweide 1811, 234). Recht zu verstehen aber seien physikalische Optik und Newtons Theorie nur durch versierten Einsatz von *Mathematik*. »In metaphorische Redensarten eingekleidete Darstellung der Erscheinungen selbst« lieferten keine Erklärung (Mollweide 1804, 330).

Wahrscheinlich ist demnach, dass Fechner über dieses Spezialgebiet seines akademischen Lehrers schon so frühzeitig mit quasiexperimentellen optischen Demonstrationen aus der *Farbenlehre* bekannt geworden ist. Neben Nachbildern verweist Goethe u.a. auf helle Gegenstände, die auf dunklem Grund »etwa um ein Fünftel« größer erscheinen als gleich große dunkle auf hellem Grund. Zum Nachweis dieses Phänomens heißt es: »Man mache das schwarze Bild um so viel größer, und sie werden gleich erscheinen« (Goethe 1840*, 6; Fechner 1829, 473). Als Instruktion zur Manipulation eines Reizes bis zu seinem Gleicherscheinen mit einem zweiten verstanden, ist das eben jenes Angleichungsverfahren, welches uns unter den sog. *psychophysischen* Methoden als die der mittleren Fehler begegnen wird.[7] In einem Zwischenresümee ist somit festzuhalten:

Auch späterhin noch entwicklungswirksame *interdisziplinäre* Anregungen durch Mollweide beziehen sich auf Beschäftigung mit Mathematik, subjektive Nachbilder, Hochschätzung der aktuellen französischen Naturwissenschaften, paradigmatische Komponenten wie Genauigkeit, methodische Strenge, die sich »gegen den in neuern Zeiten herrschend gewordenen Hang zu unbestimmten Deductionen und unklaren mystischen Darstellungen auflehnte« (Fechner 1825, 546f.). Dazuzurechnen ist die Gegnerschaft zu der u.a. von Kant vertretenen Variante sog. dynamischer *Naturphilosophie*, die, wie die vorgenannten Momente, in Fechners späterem Forscherleben wieder präsent sein werden.

---

[7] Siehe Fechner 1858; Fechner 1860, 1, 74 und passim.

Die aufgewiesene Übereinstimmung zwischen dem bei Goethe vorfindbaren experimentellen *Angleichungsverfahren* und der *psychophysischen Methode* der mittleren Fehler ist wohl zweifelsfrei über Mollweide vermittelt. Ob indes Fechner sie in seiner Feststellung der Mollweide'schen Anregungen explizit mit gemeint hat, muss offen bleiben. Wir könnten daher auf ein typisches Beispiel für jene fruchtbaren Querbeziehungen gestoßen sein, welche sich auf der Analyseebene der wissenschaftlichen Gemeinschaft mittels *Zitationsanalyse* erschließen, d.h., nicht aus Fechners Selbstsicht, sondern aus späterer, wissenschaftshistorischer Fremdsicht.

Kommen wir nun zu der angekündigten zusätzlichen Untersuchung eines Vertreters der akademischen Lehrer Fechners, von denen er sagt, er habe ihnen keine längerfristig wirksamen Anregungen zu verdanken.

3.5. Fechner und der Philosoph Wilhelm Trautgott Krug

Eingangs erinnern wir an Fechners Selbstaussage, er habe Krugs Logik-Collegium gehört.

Mit an Sicherheit grenzender Wahrscheinlichkeit hat Fechner Krugs Logik nicht nur, wie autobiographisch kundgetan, in dessen Vorlesung kennen gelernt, sondern sich mit ihr und verwandten Schriften im Selbststudium befasst. Denn für seinen 1823 wohl wegen des finanziellen Ertrages publizierten knapp zweihundertseitigen »Katechismus der Logik oder Denklehre bestimmt zum Selbst= und Schulunterricht mit erläuternden Beispielen« hat zweifellos Krugs »Logik oder Denklehre« (Krug 1819) als Vorlage gedient.

Eine Zitationsanalyse zeigt nicht nur, dass sich eine der ganz wenigen Namensnennungen im Katechismus auf Krug bezieht,[8] sondern es dürften auch noch andere Veröffentlichungen Krugs, in denen Teile seiner *Logik* enthalten sind, wie etwa der »Versuch einer systematischen Enzyklopädie der Wissenschaften« (1796/97) und das »Handbuch der Philosophie und der philosophischen Literatur« (Krug 1820), von unserem jungen Autor herangezogen worden sein.

Die inhaltlichen Übereinstimmungen zwischen der Krug'schen Vorlage und Fechners logischem Katechismus sind so zahlreich und durchgängig, dass sie hier aus Raumgründen gar nicht als Parallelstellen einzeln aufgeführt werden können.

---

[8] Siehe Fechner 1823, 33.

Aus einer ausführlicheren Untersuchung ergibt sich zusammenfassend: Fechners autobiographischem Hinweis folgend, er sei allein Hörer des Krug'schen Logik-Collegiums gewesen, lässt sich zeigen: Der junge Fechner verfasst, aufs engste Krugs »Denklehre« verpflichtet, eine *Logik*, in die mit Sicherheit nicht nur bei Krug Gehörtes eingearbeitet wurde. In diesem Zusammenhang sind ihm nicht nur dieser Ausschnitt traditioneller und aktueller Philosophie, sondern übrigens auch eine Vermögenspsychologie bekannt geworden. Selbst wenn man in Durcharbeitung und Darstellung der Krug'schen Logik keine fruchtbringende Beschäftigung erblicken will, ist keineswegs von der Hand zu weisen, dass Krug nicht noch in anderer Weise für Fechner fruchtbar geworden ist. Krug hat das Fach Philosophie in seiner ganzen Breite vertreten, er war mehr als bloß Logiker. Quantität wird von ihm als Kategorie gesetzt. *Mathematik* ist auf eine Vielfalt von Gegenständen der Erfahrung anzuwenden. Intensive und extensive Größen sind fundamental für sie. Als selbstverständlich gilt, empfindungsmäßig graduell gegebene Realität metrisch-quantitativ zu bestimmen. Ferner sieht Krug eine ganze Wissenschaft, die des Maßes und der Maßeinheit zwecks Größenbestimmung von Empfindungen und anderer mentaler Phänomene sowie einer diesbezüglichen Theorie bedürfe.

Innerer und äußerer Sinn wie auch Sprachgebrauch begründen die *Leib-Seele*-Dichotomie. Deren Glieder, wie auch die Relation zwischen ihnen, haben sich wissenschaftlicher Bearbeitung zu stellen. Auf die empirische Psychologie käme damit u.a. die Befassung mit Intentionsgraden seelischer Zustände zu. Genau das ist, allgemein gesagt, ein Hauptanliegen der Fechner'schen *Psychophysik* der fünfziger Jahre.

Ohne allzu scharfe Überspitzung kann man nach alledem Fechners Philosophielehrer Krug als Programmatiker einer *Psychometrie* oder einer mathematischen Sensometrik charakterisieren, welche sein Schüler später mit seiner *Psychophysik* in die Tat umsetzt.

Mit der gebotenen Zurückhaltung ließe sich demnach – aus Fremdsicht – eine *interdisziplinäre*, späterhin wirksame gewordene Anregung konstatieren – obzwar Fechner, wie gesagt, Krug nicht zu jenen akademischen Lehrern rechnet, welche ihn inhaltlich zu motivieren vermochten. Demgegenüber stellt aber Fechners *Logik* unter Beweis, dass er sich eingehend zumindest mit diesem Teilbereich der Krug'schen Philosophie befasst und er damit generell und langfristig ein einsetzbares methodologisches und methodisches Rüstzeug erworben hat.

3.6. Fechners Studienabschlüsse in Medizin und Philosophie

Fechner absolviert sein *Medizinstudium* 1822 bis auf die Doktorpromotion. Ärztliche Praxis folgt u.a. deshalb nicht, weil er sich »auch des praktischen Talents baar [fühlte]« (Fechner in: Kuntze 1892, 38). In entgegengesetzter, theoretischer Richtung gibt es jedoch spätestens im Jahr 1823 eine intensivere Beschäftigung mit Philosophie zu verzeichnen, möglicherweise in Verbindung mit der m.E. oftmals zu stark pointierten, geradezu stilisierten Oken-Episode von 1820. Konkret plant Fechner, »naturphilosophische Ideen im Schelling-Oken'schen Geiste, der mich damals noch gefangen hielt, vorzutragen [...]« (Fechner in: Kuntze 1892, 72). Vermutlich in diese Zeit fällt bereits in ihren Anfängen, worauf hier nur hingewiesen sei, das Befassen mit exakter Naturwissenschaft. Bevor wir dazu kommen, haben wir Fechners Weg in die Philosophie noch weiter zu verfolgen.

Sein *Philosophiestudium* endet formal 1823 mit dem Magisterexamen vom Februar sowie der Habilitation vom September, mit der er vor dem Hintergrund seiner *Logik-Schrift* in die wissenschaftliche Gemeinschaft der Philosophie, zu der selbstredend Krug zu zählen ist, einzutreten beabsichtigt. Die rund 24-seitige lateinische Habilitationsarbeit trägt bekanntlich den Titel »Praemissae ad theoriam organismi generalem«.

Aus Raumgründen sei darauf nur zusammenfassend eingegangen. Kaum Zweifel dürfte es an der systematischen Zugehörigkeit der Schrift zur *Metaphysik* geben. Das Thema wird mehrfach als ein nur dort abzuhandelndes deklariert. Was rechte Metaphysik sei, wird bestimmt. Sie kommt jener Krug'schen aus dessen Metaphysik (Krug 1820a) nahe, wo es heißt: Diese habe die »Begriffe und Grundsätze, welche die ursprüngliche Erkenntnisform ausmachen« aufzustellen (Krug 1820b, 13).

Was nun das Vorgehen Fechners anlangt, so zeigt die Gedankenentwicklung der Prämissen insgesamt einen fortschreitenden logischen Aufbau, der offenkundig Resultat einer Selbstanwendung dessen ist, was der Katechismus lehrt. So bietet Fechner, seinen auf Krug basierenden *Wissenschaftsbegriff* realisierend, mit seiner Habilitationsschrift, »eine Mannichfaltigkeit von Erkenntnissen, die ein, nach logischen Regeln zusammenhängendes Ganze ausmachen« (Fechner 1823, 133).

Insgesamt erscheint die Schrift von paradigmatischen Komponenten, vor allem Werten der wissenschaftlichen Gemeinschaft der Philosophie, geformt, in die Fechner mit seiner erfolgreichen Habilitation einzutreten gedenkt – »[...] woraus aber nichts wurde«, wie er lakonisch bemerkt (Fechner in: Kuntze 1892, 72).

Dennoch ist hierin ein zweites Mal die Erfüllung der formalen Variante des oben eingeführten Begriffs von *Studium* zu erblicken, im Unterschied zur Medizin – jetzt mit Ableistung aller erforderlichen Formalitäten – zudem verbunden mit einem Abschluss, der Eintritt in die Tätigkeit in der wissenschaftlichen Gemeinschaft gestattet. Gleichzeitig hat Fechner mit der Verlagerung seines Studienschwerpunkts von der Medizin zur Philosophie abermals eine *interdisziplinäre* epistemische Bewegung vollzogen, die in Umfang und Tragweite der früheren zur Mathematik kaum nachstehen dürfte.

3.7. Zwischenresümee und Fechners Weg in die Physik sowie sein Eintritt in die wissenschaftliche Gemeinschaft

Fechner war für das *Studium* der Medizin eingeschrieben. Da »[...] es überhaupt seine Art war, sich in allen Richtungen des Geistes strebsam zu versuchen« (Kuntze 1892, 29), bilden die Grenzen dieses Faches weder Grenzen seines Erkenntnisinteresses noch die seiner Studieninhalte. Mathematik und Philosophie kennzeichnen seinen über die Medizin hinausgehenden *interdisziplinären* Studiengang (s. Tabelle 2).

Fechners Aufnahme in die wissenschaftliche Gemeinschaft führt über Studienabschlüsse der Medizin und Philosophie mit Habilitation in letzterer. Doch kommt es, wie wir gehört haben, weder zu praktischer ärztlicher Tätigkeit noch zu eigenständiger philosophischer Lehre, trotz der dafür erworbenen formellen Voraussetzungen. Mit entscheidend für diese pragmatische Diskontinuität sind die zur Sicherung des Lebensunterhalts gefertigten Übersetzungen medizinischer und naturwissenschaftlicher Fachliteratur aus dem Französischen (Fechner in: Kuntze 1892, 38f.; Gundlach 1993, 21f.). Dadurch qualifiziert er sich – ob sein *Mathematikstudium* nebst Famulatur bei Mollweide dem förderlich waren, lässt sich allenfalls mutmaßen – »nach dem im J. 1824 erfolgten Tode des Prof. Gilbert [...] bis zur Anstellung des Prof. Brandes die Vorlesungen über Physik« zu übernehmen (Fechner in: Kuntze 1892, 72). Freimütig bekennt Fechner, »dazu« nicht »sonderlich vorbereitet zu sein«. Ihn habe »die Uebersetzung des Biot etwas« in dieses Fach eingeführt (Fechner in: Kuntze 1892, 72).

Aus *interdisziplinärer* Perspektive auf Fechners wissenschaftlichen Werdegang blickend können wir, in einem relativ kurzen Zeitraum – nach Medizin, Mathematik und Philosophie – mit Physik ein viertes fachliches Engagement des jungen Gelehrten feststellen, das nach dem kaum abge-

Tabelle 2: Fechners interdisziplinärer Studiengang

	1819	1823	1824	1825
Medizin: Vorlesungen u.a. bei E.H. Weber	1.Examen	Veröffentlichung: »Katechismus oder Examinatorium über die Physiologie des Menschen«; Magisterexamen	Übersetzung: »Untersuchungen über die Erweichung des Gehirns« von Rostan	
Mathematik: Vorlesungen bei Mollweide				
Philosophie: Vorlesungen bei Krug		Habilitation; Veröffentlichung: »Katechismus der Logik oder Denklehre bestimmt zum Selbst- und Schulunterricht«		
Physik/ Chemie: Vorlesungen bei Gilbert			Übersetzung: »Lehrbuch der Experimental-Physik oder Erfahrungs-Naturlehre« von Biot; Übersetzung: »Handbuch der dynamischen Elektrizität« von Demonferrand; eigene Physik-Vorlesungen	Übersetzung: »Lehrbuch der theoretischen und praktischen Chemie« von Thénard

klungenen spekulativen naturphilosophischen Enthusiasmus keineswegs vorgezeichnet erscheint – und dennoch pragmatisch umgesetzt wird.

Haben wir damit nun endlich alle Nuancen des weiter vorn eingeführten zeitgenössischen Begriffs von *Studium* durch den jungen Fechner repräsentiert finden können? Genau besehen noch nicht ganz. Zwar gelang es, im wissenschaftlichen Bereich wesentliche Bestimmungsstücke aufzuweisen. Es fehlt indes noch jener Aspekt von Studium, der sich auf »ernste Beschäftigung mit Kunst« richtet. Im folgenden möchte ich zeigen, dass Fechners staunenswerte geistige Aktivität auch in dieses Gebiet eingedrungen ist. Ich stelle diesen letzten Abschnitt unter die Überschrift:

4. Fechners »Poetische Ader« und sein »Umgang mit« M.G. Schulze, »einer Art verdorbenen Genies«[9]

Die *interdisziplinäre* Breite der akademischen Ausbildung Fechners in Verbindung mit seiner *autodidaktischen* Neigung hat naheliegenderweise bisher überwiegend den Anschein erweckt, als ob Fechner, der angehende Mediziner, voll und ganz in seinem wissenschaftlichen Werdegang aufginge. Folglich lag darauf auch das Hauptaugenmerk der Fechner-Forschung. Indes wurde hierdurch, wie mir scheint, einem viel zu einseitigen Bild der Fechner'schen Persönlichkeit Vorschub geleistet. Das wiederum hat den Blick sowohl auf ihre frühe Dynamik als auch auf möglicherweise länger andauernde bzw. wiederkehrende *Konflikte* fast völlig verstellt u.a. mit der Konsequenz, dass im späteren Leben eintretende bedeutsame Ereignisse von der bisherigen Biographie isoliert erscheinen mussten.

Im folgenden werde ich daher auf die künstlerische Seite von Fechners Persönlichkeit etwas ausführlicher eingehen, genauer die des Dichters oder Poeten, nicht die des experimentellen Ästheten. Es ist das, was seine Mutter in seiner Familie repräsentierte und Kuntze so treffend mit *poetischer Ader* bezeichnet hatte.

Hierdurch wird nicht allein erkennbar, wie vielseitig engagiert Fechner während seines *Studiums* war, und zugleich ein Beitrag zum Verständnis seiner dichterisch-literarischen Produktionen geliefert. Vielmehr gewinnen wir auch Einblick in Fechners Welt- und Selbstsicht der 1820er-Jahre. Dabei werden wir gewahr, wie stark der Wissenschaftler eigentlich in seiner wissenschaftlichen Existenz gefährdet wurde. Jede These von einer

---

[9] Fechner in: Kuntze 1892, 44.

besonderen Harmonie in der Fechner'schen Persönlichkeit, die sich etwa bei Wundt (1887) und Becher (1927) findet, hat sich damit auseinander zu setzen.

Die bisher eher verdeckte *poetische* Seite, Fechners dichterisches Interesse, tritt mit allen ihren Begleiterscheinungen deutlich in der sog. Schulze-Episode hervor. Ihr wende ich mich nun zu.

Kuntze bemerkt, in Fechners Nachlass finde sich – ohne Jahresangabe – die ausführliche Charakterisierung eines ehemaligen Kommilitonen und späteren Mitbewohners, Reisegefährten und Freundes Martin Gottlieb Schulze. Dieser bricht sein Medizinstudium ab, beschäftigt sich mit lebensnäheren Dingen wie Geschichte, Memoiren, Dichtung, selbst Verse schreibend, geht fast mittellos auf Reisen. Mit Fechner brieflich Kontakt bis Mitte der 1840er-Jahre haltend, besucht er ihn letztmalig 1836. Schulze endet schließlich in einer psychiatrischen Anstalt. Kuntze hat diesen Lebensweg, um den Begriff des Dämonischen kreisend, im Geist seiner Zeit, des ausgehenden 19. Jhs., detailliert nachgezeichnet. Sein aufwendig facettiertes Genrebild ist seinerseits eine eigene Studie wert. Jedoch kann hierauf nicht näher eingegangen werden. Blicken wir stattdessen wieder auf Fechner:

Nach allem, was wir bisher wissen, ist kaum zu erwarten, dass er, der nach eigener Aussage aus dem Jahre 1825 »ein tägliches Leben wie ein Uhrwerk führt« (Kuntze 1892, 66), für Personen dieses Schlages näheres Interesse aufbringt. Das Gegenteil jedoch ist der Fall. Mehr noch. Man kann Fechners Beschreibung seines ehemaligen Stubenburschen Schulze vom Winter 1823/24 dazu nutzen, um aus ihr zurück zu schließen auf beträchtliche Teile seiner Selbst- und Weltsicht der zwanziger Jahre. Dafür lassen sich einige Belege anführen. Schulze wird von Fechner wie folgt beschrieben:

> Ueberall war es die poetische, naturwüchsige Seite der Dinge, die er gegenüber der Convention und verstandesmäßigen Betrachtung der Dinge hoch hielt, den Dingen absah und abfühlte, und zu einem verführerischen Ausdruck im Reden brachte. (Fechner in: Kuntze 1892, 47)

Auf Reisen aus der Rolle des Studenten, des Gebildeten heraustretend, sich dem Bauern und Fuhrmann zugesellend, kurzzeitig das nicht »cultivirte Leben« lebend, dabei zugleich offen für »das Schöne und Herrliche, was sich in den höheren Offenbarungen des Geistes und der Seele kundgibt«, wird Schulze empfänglich für empathisches Natur- und Kunsterleben (Fechner in: Kuntze 1892, 49). Hierin erblickt Fechner »die Freiheit

[...] von allem vergeblichen Sehnen und Streben, aller Angst und Zerstreuung des Denkens, die das Gemüth des Gebildeten nie zur Ruhe kommen lassen« (Fechner in: Kuntze 1892, 48).

Was läge näher als die Hypothese, wonach Fechner hier entsprechende selbst durchlebte, ja vielleicht sogar selbst durchlittene Erfahrungen und vielfach durchgespielte Gedanken hineingelegt hätte. Darin träte unverstellte Naturoffenheit konventionellem Rationalismus gegenüber und stellte ihn in Frage. Kultur verbildete äußere und innere Natur. In der Öffnung zu ihr läge jene *Freiheit*, über die der Wissenschaftler als Gebildeter – mit seinem angstbesetzten motus animi continuus – gerade nicht verfügte.

Über seine Beziehung zu Schulze bekennt Fechner ohne Scheu, »hauptsächlich in den 1820er-Jahren ist mein Verkehr mit ihm für mich sehr einflussreich gewesen« (Fechner in: Kuntze 1892, 46). Weiter heißt es:

> Der Einfluß, den er auf mich während unseres früheren jahrelangen Verkehrs geübt hat, war der, dass er mich der Neigung für die Wissenschaft, für die ich allein Talent habe, gänzlich entfremdete und mir die Beschäftigung damit, an die ich doch gebunden war, zur Last machte. Seine, mit allen realen Grundlagen des Lebens unverträglichen Grundansichten haben mir zwar nie als haltbar und für mich brauchbar imponirt und doch mich in einem inneren Zwiespalt erhalten, und erst allmählich habe ich angefangen, wieder Geschmack an der Thätigkeit, auf die ich allein angewiesen war, zu finden. Einen solchen fascinierenden Einfluß übte er nicht bloß auf mich, sondern auf die meisten jungen Leute aus, mit denen er näher verkehrt, und nicht alle haben diesen Einfluß überwunden (Fechner in: Kuntze 1892, 50).

In diesen Worten Fechners kommen wir einer grundlegenden Problematisierung wissenschaftlicher Tätigkeit sowie der damit verknüpften Existenzform auf die Spur. Dass es sich dabei im Kern um die beiden Komponenten eines *Konflikt* zwischen Wissenschaft und Kunst handelt, wird vollends deutlich in Fechners Wortwahl in seinem Schreiben an Jean Paul vom Oktober 1825. Proben eigener Poesie liegen bei. Einmal mehr bezeugt sich darin nicht allein Unentschiedenheit zwischen beiden Bereichen. Vielmehr bekennt sich Fechner auch zu seiner Vorliebe für die Kunst, zu der er aber nur geringeres Talent besitze. Gleichwohl möchte er hier wie dort »im Einzelnen gern ein Ganzes finden oder es dazu verarbeiten« (Fechner in: Kuntze 1892, 66).

Dazu sei angemerkt: indem Fechner poetisch, d.h. in seinen Augen künstlerisch tätig wird, wird nunmehr auch jener allgemeinere Begriff von *Studium* erfüllt, den wir weiter oben eingeführt haben. Erstaunlich dabei ist die für Kunst persönlichkeitsspezifisch geäußerte Präferenz. Wissenschaft bedeutet daher Verzicht. Aber damit nicht genug: Fechners dichterische Produktionen seit 1821 sind als Ausdruck seiner relativ stärksten Motivation hervor zu heben. Seine Zeit hat sie ihm – was bisher anscheinend noch kaum gewürdigt wurde – auch gedankt, denn Fechners »poetischer Ader« ist explizite Anerkennung in seiner Zeit nicht versagt geblieben.

Ein unübersehbares Indiz dafür findet sich unter Fechners Namen in der 10. Aufl. der »Allgemeinen deutschen Real-Encyklopädie« von 1854. »Verdienter Physiker, Dichter und philos. Schriftsteller« lautet dort seine erste Allgemeincharakteristik. Des näheren werden die Produktionen des Dichters Fechner für den Empfängerkreis der »gebildeten Stände« wie folgt ausgezeichnet:

1821 heißt es: »Beweise eines reichen und glücklichen, von treffendem Witze und gründlichen Kenntnissen gleichmäßig unterstützen Humors«. Später zeige sich eine dichtende »Phantasie [mehr] im geistreichem Spiele und schließlich werden ihm u.a. in einem Gedichtband »viele wahrhaft poetische und sinnige Stücke« attestiert. Für 1824 nennt die »Real-Encyklopädie« eine »Sammlung humoristischer Aufsätze«, die Jean Paul auffielen.

Nach alledem wage ich die zugegebenermaßen vielleicht doch etwas zu griffige Hypothese: Fechner war nicht nur zum einen (nach seinem Zeugnis) romantischer *Naturphilosoph*, sondern auch romantischer *Lebensphilosoph*. Erinnert nicht etwa sein in der Schulze-Episode wiederholt zutage tretendes Lebensgefühl – worauf wohl schon Heidelberger (1993) hinwies – an das des Eichendorff'schen Taugenichts? Und könnte sein vielgestaltiger Humor überdies nicht auch ein Stück romantische Ironie enthalten? Ich hoffe, einem Zirkelschluss zu entgehen, wenn hinzugefügt wird: in eben dieser romantischen Komponente der Fechner'schen Persönlichkeit liegt eine Voraussetzung für seine Anerkennung als *Dichter* in seiner Zeit.

Kehren wir nochmals zu Fechners Persönlichkeit zurück. Fechner hat nicht nur sein Wissenschaftlersein und -dasein rational in Frage gestellt. Den *Konflikt* zwischen »Kunst« und »Wissenschaft« sowie die damit verbundenen alternativen Lebensformen hat er auch intensiv gelebt. Somit ist Wundts und Bechers These von der inneren Harmonie der Fechner'schen Persönlichkeit zumindest während seiner zwanziger Lebensjahre nur schwer zu halten. Ferner wird man die Frage an Kuntze richten müssen, ob jener selbst erkannte »Zwiespalt« (Fechner in: Kuntze 1892,

50) tatsächlich je gelöst worden ist. Der Duktus von Kuntzes Darstellung – wenn auch mit Fechner'schen Selbstaussagen unterlegt – erweckt den Eindruck, erst durch »die Bekanntschaft und den mehrjährigen Umgang mit einer Art verdorbenen Genies, Schulze, in den 20er-Jahren« (Fechner in: Kuntze 1892, 44), erst durch dieses abschreckende Beispiel eines dämonischen, schließlich die Grenze zum Irrsinn überschreitenden Unbürgers, sei Fechner der Weg zur rechten Lebensordnung gewiesen worden.

Gewiss fand eine Umwertung der Präferenz, Kunst geht vor Wissenschaft, statt. Die Wissenschaft obsiegte. Aber wann schälte sich die Entscheidung heraus, war sie je eindeutig und durchgreifend? Und wenn ja, um welchen Preis wurde sie gefällt? Ein einmal erreichtes Gleichgewicht zwischen relativ gleich starken Motiven ist oft nicht von Dauer. Es gerät in Bewegung, beginnt, sich zu verschieben, wenn eine der beteiligten Komponenten ihre Stärke ändert – etwa in Reaktion auf bestimmte Ereignisse im sozialen Lebensfeld. So besehen bricht Fechners *Krankheit* nach einer intensiven physikalischen Arbeitsphase bei gleichzeitig starker Unterdrückung des künstlerischen Motivs auf. Und konkludent damit steht nach der Genesung nicht mehr die Naturwissenschaft im Vordergrund. Das Gegenteil trat – nach Kuntzes zutreffendem Urteil – lange vordem, beschleunigt durch die Reise im Jahre 1827 nach Paris ein, wo Fechner die persönliche Bekanntschaft u.a. von Thénard, Biot und Ampère machte. Seine naturwissenschaftliche Tätigkeit erfährt eine wesentliche Bekräftigung, seine künstlerischen Ambitionen verlieren an Valenz. Damit zeichnet sich mehr und mehr das Ende jener Lebensphase ab, die wir unter den Leitbegriff des *Studiums* gestellt hatten. Versuchte man für sie in Anlehnung an die hier herangezogenen Quellen eine Kurzcharakteristik zu finden, dann sollte darin vom jungen Fechner als einem Künstler aus Neigung die Rede sein, der sich – *konflikt*beladen – zunehmend *interdisziplinär* studierte Wissenschaft zur Lebenspflicht machte.

Literatur:

AdRE (1852; 1854): Allgemeine deutsche Real-Encyclopädie für die gebildeten Stände. Bd. 5.; Bd. 14. Leipzig.

Anonymus, F. (1825): Beitrag zur Biographie des verst. Professors Mollweide zu Leipzig. In: Neuer Nekrolog der Deutschen 3, 370–378.

Arendt, H.-J. (1999): Gustav Theodor Fechner. Ein deutscher Wissenschaftler im 19. Jahrhundert. Hg. von Gustav-Theodor-Fechner-Gesellschaft e.V. Leipzig.

Becher, E. (1929): Gustav Theodor Fechner. In: Deutsche Philosophen. München, 33–45.
Boring, E. (1957): A history of experimental psychology. New York.
Brauns, H.-P. (2000a): Gustav Theodor Fechner. Elemente der Psychophysik I/II (1860). In: Klassiker der Psychologie. Hg. von H.E. Lück, R. Miller & G. Sewz-Vosshenrich. Stuttgart 36–45.
Brauns, H.-P.; Mayer, S.; Miller, D. (2000b): Einheit und Interdisziplinarität in der Psychologie des 19. Jahrhunderts. Vortrag 42. Kongress der DGPS Jena. (im Druck).
Buksinski, T. (1985): Die Begründung historischen Wissens. In: Zeitschrift für allgemeine Wissenschaftstheorie 16, 1–18.
Fechner, G .Th. (1823): Katechismus der Logik oder Denklehre. Leipzig.
Fechner, G. Th. (1825): Nekrolog (Carl Brandan Mollweide). In: Zeitung für die elegante Welt 69, 545–547.
Fechner, G. Th. (1829): Kurze Darstellung der Goethe'schen Farbentheorie. In: Lehrbuch der Experimental-Physik. Hg. von J.B. Biot. Bd. 4. Schaltcapitel 12. Leipzig 486–488.
Fechner, G. Th. (1858): Das psychische Maß. In: Zeitschrift für Philosophie und philosophische Kritik. 32, 1–24.
Fechner, G. Th. (1860): Elemente der Psychophysik. 2 Bde. Leipzig.
Goethe, J. W. (1840a): Dem Weißmacher. In: Invectiven. Sämmtliche Werke. Bd. 6. Stuttgart 166.
Goethe, J. W. (1840b): Zur Farbenlehre. Sämmtliche Werke. Bd. 37. Stuttgart.
Grumach, R. (1985): Goethe. Begegnungen und Gespräche. 1800–1805. Bd. 5. Berlin.
Gundlach, H. (1993): Entstehung und Gegenstand der Psychophysik. Berlin.
Heidelberger, M. (1993): Die innere Seite der Natur. Gustav Theodor Fechners wissenschaftlich-philosophische Weltauffassung. Frankfurt a.M.
Krug, W. (1796/98): Versuch einer Systematischen Enzyklopädie der Wissenschaften. Wittenberg.
Krug, W. (1819): Logik der Denklehre. Königsberg.
Krug, W. (1820a): Handbuch der Philosophie und der philosophischen Literatur. Leipzig (2. Aufl. 1822; 3. Aufl. 1828).
Krug, W. (1820b): Metaphysik oder Erkenntnislehre. Königsberg.
Kuntze, J.E. (1892): Gustav Theodor Fechner (Dr. Mises). Ein deutsches Gelehrtenleben. Leipzig.
Mollweide, K. (1804): Ueber einige prismatische Farberscheinungen ohne Prisma, und ueber die Farbenzerstreuung im menschlichen Auge. In: Annalen der Physik. 17, 328–337.
Mollweide, K. (1810): Auszug aus einem Schreiben des Herrn Doctor Mollweide. In: Zachs monatliche Correspondenz. Juli , 91–93.
[Mollweide, K.] (1811): Rez.: »Zur Farbenlehre« von Goethe. 2 Bde. 1810. In: Allgemeine Literatur-Zeitung. Halle; Leipzig. Nr. 30, Sp. 233–239, 241–247, 249–251.
Mollweide, K. (1812): Einige Zusätze und Berichtigungen in der unter II. mitgetheilten Notiz, des Ptolemäus Optik betreffend. In: Annalen der Physik 40, 460–470.
Scheidler, K.H. (1839): Grundlinien der Hodegetik oder Methodik des akademischen Studiums und Lebens. Jena.
Wolf, R. (1890): Handbuch der Astronomie, ihrer Geschichte und Litteratur. 2 Bde. Zürich.
Wundt, W. (1887): Zur Erinnerung an Gustav Theodor Fechner. In: Philosophische Studien 4, 1888, 471–478.

Hans-Jürgen Arendt

Gustav Theodor Fechner und Hermann Härtel – eine lebenslange Freundschaft

Die Buchstadt Leipzig und ihr umfangreiches Verlagswesen, das sie im 19. Jahrhundert zum Zentrum der graphischen Industrie Europas machte, war von wesentlicher Bedeutung für Fechners publizistische Tätigkeit. Neben dem Philosophen Christian Hermann Weiße und dem Physiologen Ernst Heinrich Weber gehörte Hermann Härtel, der Mitinhaber des Buch- und Musikalienverlages Breitkopf & Härtel, zu den engsten Freunden Fechners. Von dieser Freundschaft gingen wesentliche geistige Anregungen für Fechner vor allem auf ästhetischem Gebiet aus. Härtel und seine bürgerlich liberalen Umgebung beeinflussten zweifellos auch Fechners Ansichten zu Politik und Gesellschaft; vor allem aber vermittelte ihm das gesellschaftliche Leben im Härtel'schen Hause zahlreiche weitere Beziehungen zu Persönlichkeiten aus dem Bürgertum der Messestadt, zu Künstlern, Musikern und Gelehrten, die Härtels Gäste waren. Durch die Freundschaft mit Hermann Härtel gewann Fechner im Verlag Breitkopf & Härtel seinen »Hausverlag«, in welchem seit 1834 der Großteil seiner Schriften erschien.

Es sei eine glückliche Fügung gewesen, schreibt Fechners Neffe und erster Biograph Johannes Emil Kuntze,

> das Fechner gleich in der ersten Zeit, wo seine Schwingen sich regen und entfalten konnten, in einen Lebenskreis versetzt ward, wo Poesie und Wissenschaft, kühne Spekulation und ernste Forschung sich berührten und vermählten und der tatkräftige Buchhandel über der literarischen Arena ein Schutzdach wölbte. (Kuntze 1892, 340)

Von Leipzig ist die Rede. Die Messe- und Universitätsstadt war das Buchhandelszentrum schlechthin. Es war die Stadt, die im 18. Jahrhundert den modernen Buchhandel hervorgebracht hatte und die sich im 19. Jahrhundert zum Zentrum der graphischen Industrie Europas entwickelte. 1832 gab es hier 79 Buchhandlungen, unter ihnen 49, die Verlag, Kommission und Sortiment gleichzeitig betrieben.[1] An keinem Ort der Welt wurde um

[1] Vgl. Schulze 1925, 79.

diese Zeit so viel Gedrucktes produziert und gehandelt, namentlich wissenschaftliche Literatur, für deren Entwicklung in Leipzig die Beziehungen zwischen den an der Universität tätigen Gelehrten und den Verlegern – wie auch Fechners Beispiel zeigt – von wesentlicher Bedeutung waren. Hinzu kommt, dass der *Leipziger Buchhandel* sich – vor allem in der Vormärzzeit – in enger Wechselwirkung mit den geistigen und politischen Strömungen entwickelte, besonders in Verbindung mit dem politischen Liberalismus, mit dem das Bürgertum seinen Führungsanspruch in der Gesellschaft erhob. Die Buchhändler gehörten in hohem Maße zu den Trägern der liberalen Bewegung, und etliche von ihnen gaben Schriften und Presseorgane von unverkennbar oppositioneller Tendenz heraus, zumal nach 1830, als in *Sachsen* die Zensur vergleichsweise locker gehandhabt wurde.

Fechner veröffentlichte seine Schriften – von wenigen Ausnahmen abgesehen – fast ausschließlich in *Leipziger Verlagen*. Das hing nicht zuletzt mit den persönlichen Beziehungen zusammen, die er als junger Wissenschaftler und später erst recht als Universitätsprofessor zu einigen Leipziger Verlagsbuchhändlern zu entwickeln vermochte. Das gilt zunächst vor allem für Friedrich Gotthelf Baumgärtner und Leopold Voß, die beide als Auftraggeber für die »literarischen Lohnarbeiten« des jungen Fechner fungierten. Bei Baumgärtner erschienen die beiden Katechismen Fechners zur Physiologie bzw. zur Logik (1823), bei Voß, den Fechner wohl durch seinen Chef Heinrich Brandes kennenlernte, alle Übersetzungen und selbständigen Schriften, die Fechner zwischen 1824 und 1833 veröffentlichte, wenn wir von den »Massbestimmungen über die galvanische Kette« absehen, die 1831 bei Brockhaus erschienen. Auch mehrere satirische Schriften sowie »Nanna« (1848) und »Zend-Avesta« (1851) veröffentlicht Fechner bei Voß, der – was letztere anbelangt – allerdings daran wenig Freude hatte, denn beide Werke wurden keine buchhändlerischen Erfolge und fanden bekanntlich auch in der wissenschaftlichen Welt wenig Anklang. Aber Voß dürfte – im Zusammenhang mit den Übersetzungen der Lehrbücher von Biot (1824/25) und Thénard (1825–1833) sowie der Monographie Rostans über das Gehirn (1824) – Fechners ausgezeichnete Französischkenntnisse ebenso geschätzt haben wie dessen physikalische und chemische Sachkunde sowie seine Bereitschaft, neuere wissenschaftliche Erkenntnisse in die teilweise schon veralteten Schriften der französischen Naturforscher einzuarbeiten.

Fechner publizierte noch bei anderen Leipziger *Verlegern*. Aber seinen »Hausverlag« hatte er seit 1834 in dem bekannten Buch- und Musikalienverlag Breitkopf & Härtel. Mit Hermann Härtel, einem der beiden Chefs des Verlages, war Fechner von etwa 1828 bis zu Härtels Tod 1875 aufs engste freundschaftlich verbunden. Diese Freundschaft war neben der zu dem Philosophen Christian Hermann Weiße und der zu dem Physiologen Ernst Heinrich Weber zweifellos die wichtigste unter den reichen persönlichen Beziehungen, die Fechner mit dem Leipziger Bürgertum verband. Von ihr sind bedeutende geistige Anregungen für Fechner vor allem auf ästhetischem und kunstwissenschaftlichem Gebiet ausgegangen. Härtels und Weißes Einfluss prägte zweifellos auch Fechners Ansichten zu Politik und Gesellschaft, vor allem aber vermittelte das Härtel'sche Haus ihm zahlreiche weitere Beziehungen zu Persönlichkeiten aus dem Bürgertum der Messestadt, zu Buchhändlern und anderen Kaufleuten, zu Künstlern und Musikern.

Fechner lebte etwa ein Jahrzehnt schon in Leipzig, hatte sein Studium abgeschlossen, sich habilitiert und auch seine bekannte Studienreise nach Paris schon hinter sich, als er in jenen aus jungen Akademikern bestehenden *Freundeskreis* eingeführt wurde, der sich »Eranion« (griechisch Mahlzeit) nannte. Zu ihm gehörten der Philologe und Philosoph Christian Hermann Weiße und Franz Eduard Raschig, der Mediziner Alfred Volkmann und sein Bruder Julius, ein Jurist, die Theologen Gustav Friedrich Billroth, Christian Friedrich Grimmer und Karl Hase (der ehemalige Leipziger Burschenschaftler und spätere bekannte Jenaer Kirchenhistoriker) sowie der Jurist Hermann Härtel.[2] Härtel bildete – wie wir aus den Erinnerungen Karl Hases wissen – den Mittelpunkt des Freundeskreises. Er wurde hier der »Armenadvokat« genannt, »wohl in Bezug auf den Jean Paul'schen Armenadvokaten Siebenkäs, und weil ihm nachgesagt wurde, dass er lieber Prozesse für die Armen führe als für die Reichen« (K. Hase 1890, 199).[3] So war es in der Tat, doch Härtel selbst entstammte einer der wohlhabendsten Familien Leipzigs. Sein Vater Gottfried Christoph Härtel, der aus Schneeberg im sächsischen Erzgebirge stammte, war der Universalerbe des bekannten Buch- und Musikalienverlegers Gottlieb Christoph Breitkopf, und die Erbschaft bestand in nichts Geringerem als dem bedeutendsten Musikalienverlag der damaligen Welt, den Breitkopf 1719 in Leipzig gegründet hatte, dem Verlag Bachs, Händels, Mozarts und Beethovens. Der 1803 in Leipzig, in dem berühmten Haus

---

[2] Zum Freundeskreis »Eranion« vgl. Arendt 1999, 46–51.

[3] Zu H. Härtel vgl. O. von Hase 1919, 2, 5–20; Volkmann 1937, 103–140; Arendt 1996, 100–113.

»Zum goldenen Bären« geborene Hermann Härtel, der älteste Sohn des Verlagsinhabers, erhielt Privatunterricht, besuchte ein Jahr auch die Nikolaischule, studierte Jura in Leipzig und Göttingen, ließ sich in der Messestadt als Advokat nieder und promovierte 1828 an der Leipziger Universität zum Dr. jur. Ein Jahr später trat er – gemeinsam mit Karl Hase – eine Reise nach Italien an, von der er 1831 mit einer geradezu enthusiastischen Begeisterung für die Antike und die Kunst der italienischen Renaissance zurückkehrte. Bildungshungrig und beseelt vom Geiste der deutschen Romantik, zog es ihn auch später immer wieder nach Italien, und die letzte dieser Reisen unternahm er in Gesellschaft des Ehepaars Fechner im Herbst 1874.

Härtel lernte auf seiner ersten Italienreise Künstler kennen, darunter Bonaventura Genelli, Friedrich Preller, Christian Rauch und Bertel Thorvaldsen. Er selbst brachte Zeichnungen von eigener Hand mit, die seine künstlerische Begabung ausweisen; von ihm stammt ja auch ein Porträt Fechners, das diesen im Alter von wohl etwa 40 Jahren zeigt. Was Härtel aus Italien mitbrachte, war der Plan, in Leipzig eine römische Villa bauen und mit Fresken ausstatten zu lassen. Fechner und seine Frau, die Tochter des Leipziger Ratsherrn Volkmann, waren zweifellos unter den Gästen, als am 9. Februar 1834 am Peterschießgraben »Hauskirchweih« gefeiert wurde. Härtels *Römisches Haus* war der wohl eleganteste Bau der Stadt, errichtet von dem Dresdener Architekten Woldemar Hermann im Stile des Spätklassizismus, für einige Jahre ein Treffpunkt der wohlhabenden bürgerlichen Gesellschaft der Stadt und für das Fechner'sche Ehepaar gleichermaßen »der Salon neben der Wohnstube« (Kuntze 1892,101), denn Fechners wohnten 1838 bis 1850 auf dem gleichen Grundstück, und Härtel war fortan nicht nur Freund und Verleger, sondern auch Hauswirt des Ehepaares Fechner. Das Erlebnis des blühenden Gartens mit den in eigentümlicher Klarheit leuchtenden Blumen, das Fechner in seinem Buch über das Seelenleben der Pflanzen beschreibt – unter Bezugnahme auf die Genesung von seiner schweren Krankheit –, ist mit dem Härtel'schen Garten hinter dem Römischen Haus verbunden.[4] Das Haus selbst gehörte Härtel zu dieser Zeit schon lange nicht mehr. Aus finanziellen Gründen hatte er es schon 1837 verkaufen müssen.

Aber einige Jahre hatten hier zahlreiche Abendgesellschaften und Konzerte stattgefunden, zu denen oft auch Fechner und seine Frau eingeladen waren. Dabei blieb es auch im nächsten Härtel'schen Haus, das sich auf

[4] Vgl. Fechner, Nanna, 1848, 391.

dem gleichen Grundstück befand. Aus Fechners Tagebüchern und Kuntzes Biographie erfahren wir, wem die Fechners hier begegneten: Robert und Clara Schumann – letztere war bekanntlich Fechners Stiefnichte – sowie den Gewandhauskapellmeistern Felix Mendelssohn Bartholdy und Niels Wilhelm Gade, dem Thomaskantor Moritz Hauptmann, den Sängerinnen Livia Frege, Jenny Lind und Anastasia Novello, dem Maler Friedrich Pecht, den in der liberalen Bewegung aktiven Gelehrten Karl Georg Waechter und Theodor Mommsen und vielen anderen.

Acht Jahre nach dem Tode seines Vaters trat Härtel in die Firma ein, die bisher allein sein Bruder Raymund geleitet hatte. Das war im August 1835. Hermann Härtels innovative Mitwirkung an der Spitze des Verlages war zweifellos ein bedeutender Faktor der weiteren Entwicklung des Unternehmens, das in den sechziger Jahren in seinen Werkstätten etwa 400 Arbeitskräfte beschäftigte, etwa 260 mehr als zu Beginn der dreißiger Jahre.

1836 verheiratete sich Härtel mit Louise Baumeister, der Tochter eines wohlhabenden Hamburger Kaufmanns. Vier Töchter wurden geboren. Clara Fechner war für sie eine Art zweite Mutter; ihr und ihrem Gatten waren die Kinder mehrfach anvertraut, wenn Härtels verreisten. Aus Fechners Tagebüchern erfahren wir, wie er sich mit den Kindern beschäftigte. Er erzählte ihnen sog. *Traumgeschichten* und brachte auch den kleinen märchenhaften Erzählungen der Mädchen, die sie sich zumeist in Anlehnung an bekannte Märchenmotive erdachten und als ihre Träume ausgaben, Interesse entgegen.[5]

Was Fechners publizistische Tätigkeit anlangte, so kann gesagt werden, dass Härtel und der Verlag Breitkopf & Härtel eine überaus wichtige Rolle bei der Veröffentlichung von Fechners Schriften seit 1834 spielten. Am Anfang stand die Edition des achtbändigen *Hauslexikons* (1834–1838) von dessen Text – auf immerhin 7032 Druckseiten – Fechner etwa ein Drittel selbst verfasste. Für den Verlag wurde es ein geschäftlicher Erfolg, und so erschien 1841 – drei Jahre nach dem Erscheinen des letzten Bandes der ersten Auflage – eine mit dieser textlich völlig identische zweite Auflage des Werkes.[6] Aber Härtel sorgte auch für die Veröffentlichung der Gedichte Fechners (1841) und einer Auswahl aus allen belletristisch-satirischen Schriften des »Dr. Mises« (1875). Bei Breitkopf & Härtel erschienen 1860 in zwei Bänden Fechners Hauptwerk »Elemente der Psy-

---

[5] Vgl. Fechner, Tagebuch 1845, Blatt 23–32 (Hs.), UB Leipzig.

[6] Zu Fechners Hauslexikon vgl. Arendt 1994.

chophysik« und später die beiden anderen Bücher Fechners zur Verteidigung seiner Psychophysik, außerdem »Die drei Motive und Gründe des Glaubens« (1863), die »Ideen zur Schöpfungs- und Entwicklungsgeschichte der Organismen« (1873) und andere.

Gerade bei den Schriften zur *Psychophysik* sollte sich zeigen, dass Härtel bzw. der Verlag durchaus geschäftliche Risikobereitschaft zeigte. Vom ersten Band der »Elemente« ließen sich z.B. bis September 1862 nur 310, vom zweiten Band nur 264 Exemplare verkaufen, womit – wie Fechner von Härtel erfuhr – gerade die Herstellungskosten des ersten Bandes ungefähr gedeckt waren.[7] Fechner selbst hatte bis dahin keinen Pfennig Honorar erhalten. Etwa 30 Taler jährlich brachten dem Autor die »Elemente der Psychophysik« in den letzten fünf Jahren des Verkaufs der ersten Auflage, d.h. in der ersten Hälfte der siebziger Jahre, ein.

Das Härtel'sche Haus war in Leipzig in den Jahren des Vormärz und auch in den Jahren zwischen der Revolution von 1848/49 und der Reichsgründung ein Kommunikationszentrum, ein Zentrum der künstlerisch-ästhetischen und auch der politischen Diskussion. Hier trafen sich z.B. die führenden Persönlichkeiten des *Leipziger Kunstvereins*, dessen spiritus rector Härtel quasi war. Härtel gehörte zu den Initiatoren der Vereinsgründung (1837) und auch der Gründung des Leipziger Museums der Bildenden Künste (1848). Fechner wurde im November 1837 Mitglied des Kunstvereins und nahm – vor allem in den sechziger Jahren – engagiert an dessen lebhafter Diskussion zu ästhetischen und anderen kunstwissenschaftlichen Problemen teil. Die bekannte »Madonnen-Frage« wurde u.a. hier erörtert.[8] Und in mannigfaltiger Weise wurde Fechner hier auch zum Widerspruch in grundlegenden Fragen des ästhetischen Urteils angeregt, was dann bekanntlich bei Fechner die Untersuchungen und das theoretische Konzept seiner experimentellen Ästhetik zur Folge hatte. Unter den Gesprächspartnern im Härtel'schen Haus und in Weißes Rittergut in Stötteritz dominierten natürlich die Vertreter der traditionellen, vom deutschen Idealismus herkommenden ästhetischen Ansichten bzw. jener, die Fechner die »Ästhetik von oben« nannte. Auch Härtel selbst gehörte zu deren Jüngern, war aber für Fechners Auffassungen aufgeschlossen und sorgte 1876 auch dafür, dass Fechners »Vorschule der Aesthetik« in zwei Teilen im Verlag Breitkopf & Härtel erscheinen konnte.

---

7 Vgl. Fechner, Tagebuch 1862, Bl. 128 (Hs.).

8 Vgl. dazu Arendt 1999, 174–183.

Was die *politische Diskussion* im Härtel'schen Haus anbelangt, so stand dieses – wie konnte es auch anders sein – der großbügerlich-liberalen Bewegung nahe. In den Jahren nach der französischen Julirevolution von 1830 und in der Vormärzzeit traten Härtel und seine Freunde – unter ihnen namentlich Heinrich Brockhaus – für liberale Reformen ein, vor allem auf gewerberechtlichem und pressegesetzlichem, aber auch auf staatsrechtlichem Gebiet und natürlich für die Überwindung der kleinstaatlichen Zersplitterung Deutschlands. Interessant ist, dass der Verlag Breitkopf & Härtel ein Zentrum der Publikation polnischer Literatur war; Härtel teilte die gerade für die dreißiger und vierziger Jahre des 19. Jahrhunderts charakteristische Begeisterung großer Teile des deutschen Volkes für die nationale Unabhängigkeit Polens. Sympathien für die *demokratische Bewegung*, die in Leipzig ihren Repräsentanten in Robert Blum besaß, brachte Härtel nicht auf. Offen trat er selbst politisch überhaupt wenig in Erscheinung, aber sein Bruder und Kompagnon in der Verlagsleitung, Raymund Härtel, gehörte im April 1848 zu den Mitbegründern des liberalen *Deutschen Vereins* in Leipzig, der die Märzerrungenschaften der Revolution begrüßte, vor einer weitergehenden revolutionären Entwicklung aber warnte und im übrigen das Projekt unterstützte, die Einigung Deutschlands durch Übertragung der Kaiserkrone an den preußischen König zu vollenden. Sein führender Kopf war der Historiker Karl Biedermann, der spätere Mitbegründer der Nationalliberalen Partei in Sachsen.

Auch Fechner wurde im April 1848 Mitglied des *Deutschen Vereins*, seine publizistischen Äußerungen zur Verfassungsfrage im »Leipziger Abendblatt« bewegen sich auf der Linie eines unverkennbaren liberalen Antidemokratismus, und es ist nicht zu übersehen – das zeigen auch zahlreiche Äußerungen in seinem Tagebuch, dass Fechner in seinen *politischen* Ansichten vom politischen Klima des Härtel'schen und übrigens auch des Weiße'schen Hauses stark geprägt wurde.[9] Demokratisch-revolutionäre Ideen lehnte er entschieden ab, und später teilten er und auch Härtel die Auffassungen jener gerade auch in Leipzig einflussreichen Kreise, die die Politik Bismarcks und den preußischen Weg zur nationalstaatlichen Einigung Deutschlands unterstützten, wobei Fechner interessanterweise noch 1870 die großdeutsche Lösung der nationalen Frage – also die unter Einschluss Österreichs – für möglich hielt.

---

[9] Vgl. Fechner 1848, Leipziger Abendblatt, 15.4.; 1.5. und 16.5.

Wenn wir festgestellt haben, dass Härtel auf großbürgerlich-liberalen Positionen stand, so bedeutet das nicht, dass er der sozialen Frage verständnislos gegenüberstand. Er war vielmehr der – bei ihm auch ethisch tief verwurzelten – Auffassung, dass sich gerade aus Wohlhabenheit und repräsentativer Stellung in der Gesellschaft soziale Verantwortung ergab, und es war keine Phrase, wenn Fechner in seinem Nachruf auf den am 4. August 1875 verstorbenen Freund sagte, dass dieser von seinen Untergebenen Pflichterfüllung verlangt habe, ihnen dafür aber auch mehr gewährte, als wozu er verpflichtet war, dass jedes tüchtige Unternehmen auf seine Unterstützung rechnen konnte und viele unbekannte Wohltaten von ihm ausgegangen seien.[10] Härtel begleitete nicht nur zahlreiche Ehrenämter und engagierte sich für Leipzigs Kunst- und Musikleben sowie für die Interessen des Buch- und Musikalienhandels.[11] Er gehörte auch zu denen, die 1837 einen finanziellen Fonds für die gemaßregelten »Göttinger Sieben« ins Leben riefen und die 1851 drei aus politischen Gründen aus der Universität Leipzig entlassenen Professoren – unter ihnen Theodor Mommsen – ein Jahr das Gehalt weiterzahlten.[12] Und durch ein Legat Härtels erhielt bei seinem Tode die Sächsische Gesellschaft der Wissenschaften, die spätere Sächsische Akademie der Wissenschaften zu Leipzig, 30 000 Taler. Nicht zu vergessen: Seine Unterstützung des Fechner'schen Ehepaares. Härtel finanzierte 1874 die gemeinsame Italienreise, und ein Jahr später hinterließ er Fechner und seiner Frau durch sein Testament 1000 Taler.[13]

Fechner brachte seinem Freund stets große Wertschätzung entgegen. Er bewunderte Härtels berufliche Tätigkeit, seine vielseitige Bildung, seine mit Engagement für die Mitbürger verbundenen künstlerischen Interessen, seinen ehrlichen und aufrechten Charakter. Doch Härtels Charakterschwächen blieben Fechner, der ein ausgezeichneter Beobachter und

---

[10] Vgl. Fechner 1875.

[11] Von 1836 bis 1838 gehörte Härtel dem Leipziger Stadtrat an und fungierte während dieser Zeit auch einige Monate als Bürgermeister. Er war schon 1829 maßgeblich an der Gründung des Vereins der deutschen Musikalienhändler beteiligt. Ferner gehörte er der Direktion des Leipziger Gewandhauses und dem Direktorium des Leipziger Kunstvereins an. 1850 gehörte er gemeinsam mit Robert Schumann, dem Thomaskantor Moritz Hauptmann und dem Universitätsprofessor Otto Jahn zu den Gründern der Bach-Gesellschaft. Auch im Vorstand des Vereins der Buchhändler zu Leipzig war Härtel 1839–1843 Mitglied, und aktiv wirkte er auch im Börsenverein der deutschen Buchhändler.

[12] Vgl. Wickert 1969, 3, 186–187.

[13] Vgl. Fechner, Tagebuch 1875, Bl. 64 (Hs.).

Menschenkenner war, dabei keineswegs verborgen. In einer außerordentlich interessanten Charakteristik Härtels in Fechners Tagebuch vom November 1844 finden sich u.a. Feststellungen zu Härtels herrischem Charakter und seinem gleichzeitigen Mangel an Selbstbeherrschung. »Er ist geboren«, so heißt es da, »ein reicher Mann zu seyn; Armuth würde ihm schwerlich gut stehen, sie würde ihn beugen, und schon seine jetzigen Verhältnisse, die einem Andern behaglich erscheinen möchten, erscheinen ihm drückend, weil sie die Mittel zur Befriedigung der zum Theil kostspieligen Ansprüche, die er an das Leben zu stellen gewöhnt ist, nicht vollständig enthalten. Er liebt die Geselligkeit und den Aufwand der Geselligkeit und hat nicht gelernt, sich Bequemlichkeiten des Lebens zu versagen« (Bl. 173). Es war das sicher treffende Urteil eines bescheidenen und den materiellen Gütern nahezu gleichgültig gegenüberstehenden Menschen über Charakterschwächen eines in vielerlei Hinsicht typischen Vertreters jener sozialen Schicht, die im 19. Jahrhundert nach Macht und Geltung strebte, des liberalen Bürgertums.

Anlage:

Fechners Charakteristik Hermann Härtels. Aus Fechners Tagebuch vom 7. November 1844.[14]

Zum Zeitvertreib entwarf ich heute beiligende Charakteristik Härtels: d. 7ten Oct. 1844[15]Hermann Härtel: Wenn es am zweckmäßigsten ist, um jemand zu charakterisiren, mit der vorstechendsten Eigenschaft desselben den Anfang zu machen, so werde ich sagen: Härtel ist ein grundnobler Charakter, daneben lang, blond, mit geraden Zügen in Gestalt, Gesicht und Sinn. Er ist, bei richtig blickendem Verstande, doch wesentlich Gefühlsmensch, und eben vermöge seines Tacts praktischer Natur, so weit nicht Vergeßlichkeit, und Unfähigkeit, sich consequent einem festen Berufe hinzugeben, im Wege stehen. Wo es etwas anzufassen, zu ordnen, anzuordnen giebt, ist er am Platze. Er hat einen warm und fein ausgebildeten Sinn für {das}[16] alles Schönste und Beste, was die Welt hat, er denkt, fühlt und

---

[14] Universitätsbibliothek Leipzig, Abt. Sondersammlungen, Nachlass G. Th. Fechner, Tagebuch 1844, Bl. 171–175 (Hs.). Der Abdruck erfolgt mit freundlicher Genehmigung der Leipziger Universitätsbibliothek. Für die Transkription ist Frau Irene Altmann und Frau Dr. Anneros Meischner-Metge (Leipzig) zu danken.

[15] Fechner nennt als Datum den 7. Oktober, nach der Reihenfolge des Tagebuches ist aber offensichtlich der 7. November 1844 gemeint.

[16] »das« – von Fechner gestrichen.

handelt wesentlich im Sinn desselben, nur um Keime eines Neuen hervorzubringen, fehlt es ihm an schöpferischem Talente. Seine Betrachtungs- und Handlungsweise fußt auf den gegebenen guten Normen, in denen er erzogen worden ist und in denen er reisend, lesend, schauend sich ferner selbst erzogen hat. Bei allem Gutem fehlt es ihm an Selbstherrschaft; er vermag keine hypochondrische Stimmung zu bezwingen; er folgt nur seinem, fast überall zum Guten überwiegenden, Triebe; vermag ihn aber doch nicht auf eine feste Richtung zu lenken, so daß seine Thätigkeit als ein Ganzes auch Früchte im Ganzen trüge. Aber auch Unterordnung unter Andre ist nicht seine Sache; er hat einen herrischen Charakter, fodert von seinen Untergebenen Gehorsam aufs Wort, bezahlt sie aber dafür freigebig und sorgt bei vorkommender Noth für sie aufs Beßte. Dabei ist er in sich selbst[17] der bescheidendste Mensch von der Welt, hat eine ausnehmende Achtung und selbst Demuth vor jedem fremden Verdienste, was er als ächt anerkennt; aber tritt mit einer Art Hochmuth des Gefühls jedem gegenüber, von dem er nichts hält, und giebt sich eben keine Mühe, ihm die Zeichen seiner Nichtachtung zu verbergen. Nie macht er sich gemein mit dem Gemeinen, sondern wendet sich mit Ekel davon ab oder zieht sich mit einer Art jungfräulicher Verschämtheit davor zurück. Er ist der gefälligste, treueste, ja aufopferndste Freund, wenn man Aufopferung nennen kann, wozu ihn die Natur drängt; dabei doch verschlossen; geht nicht leicht in Worten mit seinen Stimmungen gegen irgend jemand heraus, obwohl sie sich von selbst, oft nur zu deutlich, auf seine Stirn schreiben. Er ist geboren, ein reicher Mann zu seyn; Armuth würde ihm schwerlich gut stehen, sie würde ihn beugen und schon seine jetzigen Verhältnisse, die einem Andern behaglich erscheinen möchten, erscheinen ihm drückend, weil sie die Mittel zur Befriedigung der zum Theil kostspieligen Ansprüche, die er an das Leben zu stellen gewöhnt ist, nicht vollständig enthalten. Er liebt die Geselligkeit und den Aufwand der Geselligkeit, und hat nicht gelernt sich Bequemlichkeiten des Lebens zu versagen. Und noch mehr als auf die Bequemlichkeiten ist sein Sinn auf die Zierlichkeiten desselben gestellt. Er ist freigebig und großmüthig, schenkt gern Vielen und Viel. Und alles, was er schenkt, wie Alles, was er sich selbst schafft, soll zugleich den Stempel innerer Güte und den Vorzug äußerer Form an sich tragen. Nächst dem allgemein Menschlichen, für das er in hohem Grade empfänglich ist, interessirt ihn vor Allem die Kunst, besonders bildende Künste, Malerei, Sculptur, Baukunst; aber auch die Poesie. Lesen, sprechen, sammeln, anschauen, föderlich eingreifen in diesen Bezirken sind seine Lieblingsbeschäftigungen, nur productives Talent besitzt er nicht darin. Er zeichnet bewunderswürdig nett und sauber, hat im Sinne guter Muster(?)[18] das schönste Haus in Leipzig[19] gebaut, schreibt im klarsten, präcise-

[17] »er in sich selbst« – am Rand hinzugefügt.

[18] Nicht eindeutig lesbar; könnte auch »Meister« lauten.

[19] Gemeint ist das 1832 bis 1836 von dem Dresdener Architekten Woldemar Hermann

sten, saubersten Style, steht überall an der Spitze, wo in Leipzig von Angelegenheiten der Kunst die Rede ist, aber eigne Erfindung fehlt ihm. Hätte er mehr Vermögen, so würde er {gewiß einen großen Teil}[20] gewiß viel sammeln und viel bauen. Er dirigirt jetzt mit seinem Bruder Raimund[21] das Härtelsche Geschäft[22], und hat denselben durch seine Weise, immer die großartigen und liberalern Gesichtspunkte vorwalten zu lassen, eben so wohl große Vortheile als mitunter Verluste zugezogen. Aber er dirigirt es, mit Unlust, und nur weil es die Verhältnisse nothwendig so mit sich bringen; lieber möchte er sich der Liebhaberei für die Kunst ganz widmen. Was seine Freunde an ihm tadeln, ist, daß er überhaupt an keine regelmäßigen Beschäftigung recht zu fesseln ist; er kann nicht lange still sitzen; dann treibt es ihn wieder, einen Gang, oder wo möglich eine Reise, und zwar wo möglich nach Italien, zu machen. Ferner, daß er seine Stimmungen nicht recht beherrschen kann. In der Stadt zollt man ihm große Achtung, die er selbst bei Personen von ganz entgegengesetztem Charakter durch sein nobles Benehmen zu erzwingen vermag; doch haben viele auch Scheu vor ihm, und die Zerstreutheit, mit der er oft sein Geschäft verwaltet, ist Gegenstand manches harten Tadels. In Rücksichten der Gesundheit, sowohl eigner als fremder, soweit es ihn angehende Personen betrifft, ist er übertrieben ängstlich. Ohne recht entschiedene Krankheit hat er doch allerhand Unpäßlichkeiten. Er ist jetzt {glaube ich}[23] 41 Jahre alt.[24]

Literatur:

Arendt, H.-J. (1994): Gustav Theodor Fechner und sein Hauslexikon 1834 bis 1838. Ein Beitrag zur Fechner-Biographie und zur Geschichte der enzyklopädischen Literatur in Deutschland. Hg. von der G.-Th.-Fechner-Gesellschaft e.V., Leipzig.

Arendt, H.-J. (1996): Gustav Theodor Fechners soziale Beziehungen. Studien zur Biographie des Mitbegründers der modernen Psychologie. Leipzig.

Arendt, H.-J. (1999): Gustav Theodor Fechner. Ein deutscher Naturwissenschaftler und Philosoph im 19. Jahrhundert. Frankfurt a.M. (DAEDALUS. Europäisches Denken in deutscher Philosophie. Hg. von V. Caysa u.a. Bd. 12).

Fechner, G. Th. (1848): Nanna oder Über das Seelenleben der Pflanzen. Leipzig.

Fechner, G. Th. (1848): Ueber directe und indirecte Wahlen der Volks-Abgeordneten. In: Leipziger Abendblatt. 15.4.1848, Nr. 1.

---

errichtete Römische Haus am Leipziger Peterschießgraben. – Vgl. dazu Vogel 1903; Lammel 1986, 282–284.

20 »gewiß einen großen Teil« – von Fechner gestrichen.

21 Raymund Härtel (1810–1888), Verlagsbuchhändler in Leipzig.

22 Gemeint ist der Buch- und Musikalienverlag Breitkopf & Härtel in Leipzig, zu dieser Zeit im Haus »Zum goldenen Bären« in der Universitätsstraße.

23 »glaube ich« – von Fechner gestrichen.

24 Hermann Härtel wurde am 27. April 1803 geboren.

Fechner, G. Th. (1848): Ueber Volkssouverainetät. In: Leipziger Abendblatt. 1.5.1848, Nr. 37.

Fechner, G. Th. (1848): Noch ein paar Worte in Sachen der Volkssouverainetät. In: Leipziger Abendblatt. 16.5.1848, Nr. 32.

Fechner, G. Th. (1875): Nachruf für Dr. H. Härtel. In: Leipziger Tageblatt und Anzeiger. 10.8.1875, Nr. 222.

Hase, K. (1890): Ideale und Irrtümer. Leipzig.

Hase, O. von (1919): Breitkopf & Härtel. Gedenkschrift und Arbeitsbericht. 2.Bd. Leipzig.

Kuntze, J.E. (1892): Gustav Theodor Fechner (Dr. Mises). Ein deutsches Gelehrtenleben. Leipzig.

Lammel, G. (1986): Deutsche Malerei des Klassizismus. Leipzig.

Wickert, L. (1969): Theodor Mommsen. Eine Biographie. 3. Bd. Frankfurt a.M.

Schulze, F.(1925): Der deutsche Buchhandel und die geistigen Strömungen der letzten hundert Jahre. Leipzig.

Vogel, J. (1903): Das Römische Haus in Leipzig. Ein Beitrag zur Kunstgeschichte des neunzehnten Jahrhunderts. Leipzig.

Volkmann, L. (1937): Hermann Härtel als Kunstfreund und Künstler. In: Kunst und ihre Sammlung in Leipzig. Festschrift zum 100jährigen Jubiläum des Leipziger Kunstvereins und Museum der Bildenden Künste. Hg. von W. Teubser. Leipzig, 103–140.

Hanna Krajewska

Rezeption Fechners in Polen

Die Person Gustav Theodor Fechner wird in Polen nur in Lexika, besonders in denen des 20. Jahrhunderts, behandelt. Die besondere Rolle, die diese Lexika spielten und spielen, soll kurz behandelt werden. In der polnischen philosophischen Literatur wird über Fechner im Zusammenhang mit der zeitgenössischen deutschen Philosophie der Zeit geschrieben. Dies wirkt sich auf die Hochschulliteratur, zu der Skripten, Quellenbücher und Philosophiegeschichten gehören, aus. Philosophiegeschichte wird als Hintergrund für die Erklärung neuer Auffassungen herangezogen. Polnische Philosophen, vor allem K. Ajdukiewicz, K. Twardowski, W. Tatarkiewicz, haben sich zu Fechner geäußert. Auch auf Fechnerübersetzungen und die Fechner-Rezeption in der polnischen Philosophie wird in dem Beitrag eingegangen.

Die ersten schriftlichen Zeugnisse in Polen über Gustav Theodor Fechner finden sich in Lexika. Es sind Informationen über seinen Geburtsort, gelegentlich unter Angabe seines Geburtsdatums, Einzelheiten seines privaten und wissenschaftlichen Lebens und Auskünfte über seine Lebensanschauungen. Die Lexika beschreiben außerdem das *Weber-Fechner'sche Gesetz* und bieten eine umfangreiche Bibliographie.

Die meisten der Texte nennen als seinen Geburtsort Groß Särchen, das sich in der Lausitz – oder genauer – in der Niederlausitz bei Muskau befindet. Muskau befindet sich heute auf polnischen Territorium. Fechner wird dennoch immer als deutscher Philosoph bezeichnet und unter anderem beschrieben als Physiker, Dichter, Psychologe, Arzt und Physiologe. Alle Lexika geben auch über seine Studien in Leipzig Auskunft; einige gehen dabei sogar auf seine galvanischen Forschungen ein. Als Grund dafür, dass Fechner sich der Philosophie widmete, wird seine schwere Krankheit angeführt, die ihn an der Ausübung seines Lehramtes hinderte.[1] Dass es eine Augenkrankheit war wird nicht erwähnt, wie auch überhaupt der größte Teil der Lexika Fechners Erkrankung übergeht.

[1] Siehe Orgelbrandt 1864, 8, 705.

In allen Lexika wird über Fechner gesagt, dass er als Begründer der experimentellen Psychologie gilt. Aus der Reihe seiner Publikationen werden immer »Die Elemente der Psychophysik« (1860), »Die Revision der Hauptpunkte der Psychophysik« (1882), »Die Vorschule der Ästhetik« (1876), »Nanna oder über das Seelenleben der Pflanzen« (1844), »Die Seelenfrage« (1861) sowie »Die Tagesansicht gegenüber der Nachtansicht« (1879) genannt.

Einige Lexika geben Hinweise auf Fechners *humoristische Schriften* und sein Pseudonym als Dr. Mises: Er [sei] »ein ausgezeichneter und ungewöhnlicher Humorist« (Orgelbrandt 1899, 5, 319) bzw. ein »Schriftsteller mit poetischer Begabung und Talent zum Humor« (Orgelbrandt 1899, 8, 705). Bilder von Fechner finden sich nur selten in den Lexika.

Die frühesten Informationen über Fechner, die man in Lexika findet, stammen aus dem Jahr 1854. Sie finden sich in der »Encyklopedia Powszechna« (Allgemeines Lexikon). Dieses Lexikon umfasst 28 Bände, die in den Jahren 1859 bis 1868 erschienen sind. Verleger war der Warschauer Buchhändler Samuel Orgelbrandt. Dieser hatte es ausgezeichnet verstanden, berühmte polnische Wissenschaftler zur Mitarbeit am Lexikon zu gewinnen. Die »Encyklopedia Powszechna« war das beste Lexikon seiner Zeit in Polen und ist Dank seiner ausführlichen Details auch heute noch interessant. Der Artikel über Fechner ist breit gefächert und auch der Umfang der bibliographischen Angaben wurde in der Zukunft nicht übertroffen.

Orgelbrands Verlag hatte während der Jahre von 1872 bis 1876 ein neues »Allgemeines Lexikon« in 14 Bänden publiziert; später erschien in den Jahren 1898 bis 1912 eine weitere Ausgabe von 18 Bänden. Die Informationen über Fechner sind in diesen Ausgaben etwas knapper als in der Erstausgabe und in der letztgenannten Edition wird nur sein ungefähres Todesdatum angegeben.

In den 70er-Jahren des 19. Jahrhunderts erschien auch ein dreibändiges »Allgemeines Handlexikon« (Podręczna Encyklopedia Powszechna) unter der Redaktion des berühmten Schriftstellers A. Wiślicki. Ein Artikel über Fechner ist im zweiten Band des »Handlexikons« enthalten.

Das beste und größte *polnische Lexikon* war und ist das »Große Allgemeine Illustrierte Lexikon« (Wielka Powszechna Ilustrowana Encyklopedia), herausgegeben und begründet von dem Journalisten Saturnin Sikorski. In seinem Redaktionskomitee befanden sich stets die besten Wissenschaftler und Schriftsteller aus ganz Polen. Viele Artikel dieses Lexikons haben einen monografischen Charakter, weshalb es bis heute eine hervorragende und verdienstvolle Quelle ist. In den Jahren von 1892 bis 1914 sind 55 Bände dieses Lexikons erschienen. Der Erste Weltkrieg hatte die Arbeiten des Lexikons beim Buchstaben *P* unterbrochen. Das im Grossformat herausgegebene Lexikon widmet Gustav Theodor Fechner drei Seiten und ist damit die umfangreichste Darstellung Fechners in allen polnischen Lexika. Sie enthält Detailangaben zu Fechners physischen Forschungen, zeigt sehr ausführlich seine philosophischen Anschauungen auf und behandelt auch das *Weber-Fechner'sche Gesetz*. Allerdings ist die Bibliographie nicht so umfangreich wie in Orgelbrands Lexikon.

In der Zwischenkriegszeit nach 1918 gehörte die »Illustrierte Enzyklopädie« (Encyklopedia Ilustrowana) von Trzaska, Evert und Michalski, die von 1925 bis 1928 fünfbändig erschien, zu den populärsten Lexika der damaligen Zeit. Über Fechner wird darin gesagt, dass

> [...] sein philosophisches System nahe bei der Philosophie Schellings angesiedelt ist. Es geht von der atomistisch-mechanistischen Naturanschauung aus, erhebt sich aber über sie und mündet in der methaphysischen Konzeption, dass das Weltall geistig ist. (Trzaska u.a. 1927, 2, 26)

Alle polnischen Lexika der Zwischenkriegszeit enthalten Angaben über die Fechner'sche Lehre.[2] Nach dem zweiten Weltkrieg war die »Mała Encyklopedia Powszechna« (Kleine Allgemeine Enzyklopädie) sehr populär. Als einbändige Enzyklopädie erreichte sie eine Auflagenhöhe von mehr als 500.000 Exemplaren und brachte es auf 29 Ausgaben. In einigen Ausgaben fehlt allerdings ein eigener Artikel über Fechner; andere Ausgaben enthalten nur eine sehr kurze Information zum Stichwort.

In der »Wielka Encyklopedia Powszechna« (Grosse Allgemeine Enzyklopädie des Staatlichen Wissenschaftlichen Verlags), die in den Jahren 1962 bis 1968 13bändig erschien, wird Fechner gut beschrieben; auch seine Fotographie wird gezeigt.[3]

Die anderen in diesen Jahren erschienenen polnischen Lexika berücksichtigen Fechner ebenfalls.[4] Auf Fechners Geburtsort gehen die Lexika jedoch nicht weiter ein. In den verschiedenen polnischen Darstellungen der Geschichte der Philosophie wird Fechners Nähe zu Polen ganz ver-

---

[2] Siehe Encyklopedia Powszechna Ultima Thule, Bd. 3. Warszawa 1930, 523; Świat i Życie. 1937 5, 78.

[3] Siehe PWN (1962–1968).

[4] NEP 1995, 2, 173; Nowy Leksykon 1998,132; PEP 1995, Bd. Krakow, 167.

schwiegen. Fechner wird dort immer mit der deutschen Philosophie in Zusammenhang gebracht, die sich in Polen einer großen Popularität erfreut. Im »Lausitzer Biographischen Lexikon« (Serbski Biografiski Slownik, 1969) wird Fechner hingegen nicht erwähnt. Ebenso nicht erwähnt wurde Fechner in dem von Zwahr herausgegebenen Buch »Meine Landsleute. Die Sorben und die Lausitz im Zeugnis deutscher Zeitgenossen« (1984).

Im 19. Jahrhundert und bis 1918 war Polen aufgeteilt in drei von den Preussen, Russen und Österreichern annektierten Länder.

Im preußischen wie im russischen Teil gab es keine polnische Universität. In Warschau arbeiteten jedoch viele Polen an der russischen Universität. Hier wirkte zum Beispiel Henryk Struwe (1840–1912). Er hatte in Tübingen, Erlangen, Göttingen, Halle, Leipzig und Jena studiert. Adam Mahrburg (1855–1913), der ebenfalls an der russischen Universität in Warschau lehrte, hatte in Leipzig bei Wilhelm Wundt studiert. Eine eigene polnische Wissenschaft wurde am Ende des 19. und zu Beginn des 20. Jahrhundert zumeist im österreichischen Teil Polens betrieben. Nach der Reform im Jahre 1868 unter der österreichischen Monarchie erhielten polnische Wissenschaftler weitgehende Autonomie in ihren Forschungen. In Galizien, wie der polnische Landesteil damals hieß, hatten die Gelehrten viele Kontakte zu deutschen Wissenschaftlern. Die Verbindung zu Deutschland war sehr gut. Viele Polen studierten an deutschen Universitäten oder unternahmen Bildungsreisen nach Deutschland. Die allgemein anerkannte große Bedeutung der deutschen Philosophie, Kultur und Literatur führte zu vielfältigen institutionellen Kontakten zwischen der österreichischen und preussischen Wissenschaft in Polen.

Im österreichischen Teil Polens gab es in Krakau und Lemberg zwei polnische Universitäten. Eine neue Periode der originär polnischen Philosophie begann sich mit Kazimierz Twardowski zu entwickeln, der seit 1895 einen Lehrstuhl an der Universität Lemberg inne hatte. Twardowski (1866–1938) nimmt einen besonderen Platz in der polnischen Philosophie ein. Er wurde in Wien geboren und verbrachte seine Schulzeit am Theresianum. An der Universität Wien studierte er Philosophie und hörte dort auch Vorlesungen bei Franz Brentano (1838–1917). Seine Doktorarbeit legte Twardowski 1891 zum Thema »Idee und Perzeption. Eine erkenntnis-theoretische Untersuchung zu Descartes« vor. Später studierte er in Leipzig bei Wilhelm Wundt und in München bei Karl Stumpf. Im Jahre 1894 schrieb er seine Habilitationsarbeit in Wien zum Thema »Zur Lehre von Inhalt und Gegenstand der Vorstellungen«. Im Jahr darauf folgte er einem Ruf an die Universität Lemberg. Seine wissenschaftlichen Schriften wurden auch unter den deutschen Gelehrten bekannt und sehr geschätzt. Die philosophischen Gedanken Twardowskis leiten sich aus der österreichischen Schule, aus Elementen der Lehren F. Brentanos, dessen Schüler er war, und aus der Phänomenologie Edmund Husserls ab. Im Jahre 1901 veranstaltete Twardowski an der Universität Lemberg Übungen zur experimentellen Psychologie und richtete dort das erste *psychologische Institut* in Polen ein. Twardowski war der Begründer der philosophischen Schule, die in die polnische Wissenschaftsgeschichte als *Lemberger-Warschauer Schule* eingegangen ist. Die Zielsetzung des Kreises um Twardowski war die Pflege der Philosophie als Wissenschaft und deren wissenschaftlicher Methodik. Hervorgegangen aus den Lehren Twardowskis sind viele bedeutende Institutionen, wie die 1904 gegründete »Polnische Philosophische Gesellschaft«, die polnischen philosophischen Konferenzen und die seit 1911 erscheinende Zeitschrift »Ruch Filozoficzny« (Philosophische Bewegung).[5]

Twardowski war auch der erste polnische Philosoph, der die Fechner'schen Gedanken in Polen verbreitete. Er brachte den polnischen Lesern und Studierenden Fechners Gedankenwelt nahe. Es handelt sich um die *Übersetzung* der 2. Auflage der Fechner'schen Schrift »Das Büchlein vom Leben nach dem Tod« (1905), aber ohne das in der deutschen Ausgabe erschienene Vorwort und ohne einen zusätzlichen Kommentar. Wahrscheinlich ist es auch ihm zu verdanken, dass die Biographie Fechners von Kurt Laßwitz in polnischer Sprache erscheinen konnte.[6]

1907 erschien dann die *Übersetzung* der 6. deutschen Auflage des »Büchleins« ins Polnische.[7] Diese Übertragung wurde von Twardowski überprüft, der auch ein erweitertes Vorwort verfasste. Den Entschluss, ein eigenes Vorwort zur Übersetzung des Fechner'schen Werkes zu schreiben, begründete Twardowski mit folgenden Worten:

> Überall erweitert sich der Kreis der Denker von Fechners Philosophie und damit nehmen auch Fechners Bedeutung für die Philosophie und sein Ansehen zu. Verschiedene Diskussionen über Fechners Philosophie zeigen die besondere Bedeutung Fechners für die gegenwärtige Lehre der Philosophie, insbesondere populär ist sie in Deutschland. Friedrich Paulsen, der bekannte philosophische Schriftsteller, hat dort sogar wörtlich gefordert: »Auf zu Fechner«. Bei uns ist

---

[5] Siehe Sloniewska, Twardowski usw. 1959; Zamecki 1977.

[6] Siehe Lasswitz 1903.

[7] Siehe Fechner 1907.

> Fechner nur aus zweiter Hand bekannt, nur aus der Biographie, die Lasswitz über ihn geschrieben hat. Wir haben aber keine Übersetzung der Fechnerschen Schriften. Der Fachmann muss aber zum Original greifen. Fechners Originalschriften zeigen mir wie er denkt und schreibt. Seine Gedankenwelt zieht immer mehr neue Leser in ihren Bann. In seiner Heimat fördern sie sein Ansehen und seine Bedeutung. Sie sollen aber zum Eigentum einer gemeinsamen Kultur werden. Ich wünsche allen, dass dieses Büchlein, welches mit wissenschaftlichen Methoden den Glauben an das Leben nach dem Tod erklärt, auch der polnischen Philosophie die Gedankenwelt dieses hervorragenden Denkers und Forschers des 19. Jahrhunderts näher bringen möge.[8] (Twardowski in: Fechner 1907, 17–18)

Twardowski verweist in seinem Vorwort auf die wichtigsten Gedanken Fechners, auf den *psychophysischen Parallelismus* und auf seine Theorie der Bewusstseinsschwellen, bei denen Fechner den psychophysischen Wellen ein eigenes *Schwellenschema* zuweist.

Ein anderes Werk Fechners, dessen Übertragung ins Polnische einer Initiative Twardowskis folgte, ist das 1861 erschienene Buch »Ueber die Seelenfrage. Ein Gang durch die sichtbare Welt, um die unsichtbare zu finden«. Im Jahre 1915 war diese *Übersetzung* fertig gestellt, jedoch war es während des Ersten Weltkrieges unmöglich, die Übersetzung zu publizieren. Sie konnte erst 1921 erscheinen.[9] Im Vorwort schreibt Twardowski zur Bedeutung Fechners für die gegenwärtige Philosophie:

> Dieser Philosoph verbindet aussergewöhnlich geschickt Naturalismus mit Idealismus, Spekulation mit Empirismus, Religionsglauben mit Wissenschaft. Er eröffnet eine Ebene auf der verschiedene aber gleich starke Kräfte Erfüllungen der Bedürfnisse menschliches Sinnens verlangen. (Twardowski in: Fechner 1921, 15)

Twardowski schätzte Fechners Formulierungen sehr, wie etwa diese:

> Wer seine Bedürfnisse befriedigen und seine Meinung kund tun will, wer erobern oder seine Weltanschauung ergründen will, muss die wissenschaftlichen, religiösen und künstlerischen Leidenschaften des menschlischen Geistes ergründen. Dieser Geist geht in den Gedanken durch die sichtbare Welt zur unsichtbaren, er wird keine Mühe scheuen und davon überzeugt sein, dass sein Weg einem guten Führer folgt. (Fechner 1921, 21)

---

[8] Diese und die folgenden Übersetzungen aus dem Polnischen stammen von H. Krajewska.

[9] Siehe Fechner 1921.

Beide erwähnten Bücher Fechners sind gut übersetzt. Sie sind bis heute die einzigen Schriften Fechners, die in polnischer Sprache vorliegen.

Nachdem Polen 1918 seine staatliche Souveränität und damit seine Freiheit wieder erlangt hatte, entstanden bald neue polnische Universitäten, so in Warschau, Posen, Wilna und die Katholische Universität in Lublin.

Der später sehr berühmt gewordene Philosoph Kazimierz Ajdukiewicz (1891–1963) lehrte nach seiner Rückkehr nach Polen an der Warschauer Universität. Er war einer der bekanntesten Schüler Twardowskis, hatte an der Lemberger Universität studiert und später in Göttingen, wo er an Husserls Vorlesungen teilnahm. Ajdukiewicz war mit der Tochter Twardowskis verheiratet. Er beschäftigte sich in seinen Forschungen mit der Logik der Semantik, mit reiner Logik, mit Epistemologie sowie mit der Theorie und Methodologie der Wissenschaft an sich. Ajdukiewicz' Anschauungen beruhen auf Antirationalismus und Empirismus. Dank seiner Sprachforschungen konnte Ajdukiewicz die wechselseitige, feststehende Anschauungsstruktur konzipieren und damit zur philosophischen Theorie des Konventionalismus gelangen. Die Resultate seiner Forschungen über die Sprachsyntax und die kategoriale Grammatik werden heute von Übersetzungssystemen der Computer benutzt. Ajdukiewicz' Forschungen wurden in Handbücher für Studenten, in populär-wissenschaftlichen Publikationen und in zahlreichen wissenschaftlichen Aufsätzen veröffentlicht. In seinem Handbuch »Probleme und philosophische Richtungen«, das die Hauptdisziplinen der Philosophie enthält, schreibt Ajdukiewicz über Fechner:

> Fechner hat als Vertreter des Psychovitalismus gezeigt, dass die Natur eine lebendige Einheit ist, in der alles eine eigene Seele hat. (Ajdukiewicz 1949, 180)[10]

Dieses Handbuch wurde 1949 veröffentlicht und diente viele Jahre lang den Studenten nicht nur der verschiedenen philosophischen Lehrrichtungen als Grundlage eines allgemeinen Humanismus. Heute wird Ajdukiewicz immer mehr gelesen. Seine Präsentation der Fechner'schen Philosophie in diesem so wichtigen Handbuch zeigt, dass Fechner für Ajdukiewicz attraktiv und interressant war.

Ein anderer bekannter Schüler von Twardowski war Władysłw Tatarkiewicz (1886–1980). Schon zu Beginn seiner Karriere war Tatarkiewicz

---

[10] Vgl. auch Ajdukiewicz 1949, 180–181, 207–209, 211–215, 219–220, 226–227.

eine außergewöhnliche Persönlichkeit. Er studierte in Warschau, Zürich, Paris, Berlin und Marburg. Tatarkiewicz beschäftigte sich mit Philosophie, Geschichte der Philosophie, Ästhetik, Geschichte der Ästhetik und Kunstgeschichte. In seinen Büchern zeigte er Folgerichtigkeit, Klarheit und ein großes sprachliches Geschick. Sein Motto war: »leicht schreiben ist nicht leicht«. Zu den bekanntesten seiner Bücher gehört eine dreibändige, von 1931 bis 1955 erschienene Geschichte der Philosophie. In diesem Werk beschrieb er seine Methode als eine »Unstetige Repräsentation von Fakten (non-continuos representation of facts)«. Nach dieser Methode kann jeder Philosoph das Leben in seinen verschiedenen Abschnitten in die Komponenten Arbeitsaspekte, Vorbilder, Oppositionelles in Einrichtung, Chronologie, Terminologie und Kritik zerlegen. Tatarkiewiczs »Geschichte der Philosophie« gehört zu den am weitesten verbreiteten Lehrbüchern in Polen. Viele Generationen von Studenten haben nach dem Handbuch dieses hervorragenden Gelehrten studiert. Im 3. Band des Lehrbuchs wird unter dem Titel »Philosophie des 19. Jahrhunderts und der Gegenwart« der Name Fechners 15 Mal erwähnt. Fechners philosophisches Hauptanliegen sei *Metaphysik* im *Positivismus*; er lehne sich an Wundt und an die deutsche Metaphysik sowie an andere Philosophen an. Fechner wird auch im Zusammenhang mit Hermann Lotze (1817–1881) und Eduard von Hartmann (1842–1906) erwähnt. Tatarkiewicz schreibt über wichtige Werke Fechners und bezeichnet ihn als Metaphysiker und Empiriker. Bei seinen Beschreibungen befindet sich auch ein Foto von Fechner.[11]

In der zweiten Hälfte des 20. Jahrhunderts sind in Polen viele Handbücher zur Geschichte der Philosophie erschienen. Manche sind fragmentarisch, andere enthalten ausführliche oder auch kurze Beschreibungen der Philosophiegeschichte. Fechner wird aber immer erwähnt und seine Schriften werden zum Studium empfohlen, wenn auch nicht so intensiv wie die anderer Philosophen.[12]

Auch in den Übersetzungen von russischen oder englischen Darstellungen der Geschichte der Philosophie ins Polnische wird Fechner erwähnt. In der *russischen Philosophie* wird Fechner stark kritisiert, auf ähnliche Weise wie die ganze Metaphysik und der deutsche Idealismus überhaupt.[13]

---

[11] Siehe Tatarkiewicz Bd. 3; 9, 12, 16, 99, 115, 116, 120, 121, 122, 151–152, 153, 248, 495.

[12] Siehe Propedeutyka filozofii 1982; Cackowski 1977.

[13] Siehe Fuller 1967.

In Wörterbüchern der Philosophen und philosophischen Abhandlungen wird der Name Fechners selten erwähnt; er findet sich nur in den umfangreicheren und grösseren Wörterbüchern häufiger.

Heute gibt es in Polen fünfzehn Universitäten und mehr als 100 private und staatliche humanistische Hochschulen. Die von mir angeführten Handbücher dienten den Studenten bis heute als Lehrbücher. So ist dank dieser Bücher Fechner auch in Polen bekannt. Leider wird Fechner ausschließlich in Verbindung mit der deutschen *metaphysischen* Schule dargestellt. Dieses Faktum hat dazu geführt, dass aus dem umfangreichen Werk Fechners nur zwei seiner Schriften in *polnischen Übersetzungen* vorliegen. Das ist ein Grund, warum Fechners Werke vor allem den Spezialisten und nicht der Allgemeinheit bekannt sind.

Die Historiker sind davon überzeugt, dass man die besten Erkenntnisse nur aus den Originalen gewinnen kann. Wer Fechners Gedankenwelt näher kennen lernen will, wird in polnischen Bibliotheken eine Auswahl seiner Werke in der Originalsprache finden. Die Bücher sind verstreut und befinden sich in verschiedenen Bibliotheken. Die größte Auswahl ist in den Universitätsbibliotheken und in der Nationalbibliothek zu finden.

Ich habe die Hoffnung, dass das Fechner-Jahr das Interesse der polnischen Historiker und Philosophen an Theodor Gustav Fechner wieder weckt und zur größeren Verbreitung seiner originellen Ideen und Anschauungen beitragen wird.

Literatur:

Ajdukiewicz, K. (1949): Zagadnienia i kierunki filozofii. Warszawa 180–181, 207–209, 211–215, 219–220, 226–227.

Brankock, A. (Hg.) (1969): Serbski Biografiski Slownik. Budiszin.

Cackowski, Z. (1977): Główne zagadnienia i kierunki filozofii. Warszawa.

Fechner, G. Th. (1905): Książeczka o życiu pośmiertnym. (Übers. der 2. Aufl.) Hg. von K. Twardowski. Lwów.

Fechner, G. Th. (1907): Książeczka o życiu pośmiertnym. Mit e. Vorwort von K. Twardowski. Lwów.

Fechner, G. Th. (1907): Książeczka o życiu pośmiertnym. Lwów.

Fechner, G. Th. (1921): O zagadnieniu duszy. Wedrówka przez swiat widzialny ku niewidzialnemu. Lwów.

Fuller, G.A.G. (1967): Historia filozofii. Warszawa.

Lasswitz, K. (1903): Gustaw Teodor Fechner. Warszawa.

Lempicki, Z. (Hg.) (1937): Świat i życie. Zarys encyklopedyczny współczesnej wiedzy i kultury. Bd. 5. Lwów.

Mała Encyklopedia Powszechna (1994): Warszawa.
Michalski, S. (Hg.): Encyklopedia Powszechna Ultima Thule. Bd. 3. 1930. Warszawa.
NEP (1995): Nowa Encyklopedia Powszechna PWN Bd. 2. Warszawa.
Nowy Leksykon (1998): (PWN) Warszawa.
Orgelbrandt S. (1859–1868): Encyklopedia Powszechna. 28 Bde. Warszawa.
Orgelbrandt, S. (1872–1876): Encyklopedia Powszechna. 14 Bde. Warszawa.
Orgelbrandt, S. (1898–1912): Encyklopedia Powszechna. 18 Bde. Warszawa.
PEP (1995): Popularna Encyklopedia Powszechna. Bd. Kraków.
Jadacki J. (Hg.) (1982): Propedeutyka filozofii. Warszawa.
Słoniewska, Twardowski w psychologii polskiej. In: Ruch Filozoficzny. Nr 1–2, XIX, 1959, 17–24.
Sikorski S. (1892–1914): Wielka powszechna ilustrowana Encyklopedia. 55 Bde. Warszawa.
Tatarkiewicz, W. (1931–55): Historia filozofii. 3 Bde.Warszawa.
Trzaska, Evert, Michalski (1925–1928): Ilustrowana Encyklopedia. 5 Bde. Warszawa.
Wiślicki, A. (1873–1875): Podręczna Encyklopedia Powszechna. 3 Bde. Warszawa.
PWN (1962–1968): Wielka Encyklopedia Powszechna. 13 Bde. Warszawa.
Zwahr, H. (Hg.) (1984): Meine Landsleute. Die Sorben und die Lausitz im Zeugnis deutscher Zeitgenossen. Von Spencer und Lessing bis Pieck. Bautzen.
Zamecki, S. (1977): Koncepcja nauki w szkole lwowsko-warszawskiej. Wroclaw.

Irene Altmann

Fechners Beziehungen zu Literaten. Einige bisher unveröffentlichte Briefe

Die vorliegenden Briefe sollen Fechners Beziehungen zu Literaten im Zeitraum von 1825 bis 1879 aufzeigen, soweit die Briefe allein das zu leisten vermögen. Seine eigene literarische Tätigkeit ist dabei das verbindende Element. Am bemerkenswertesten ist die Beziehung zu Bettine von Arnim, mit der Fechner eine langjährige Freundschaft verband. Über Bettines Tochter Gisela machte Fechner auch die Bekanntschaft mit deren Ehemann Hermann Grimm. Dieser, jüngster Sohn des Sprachforschers Wilhelm Grimm, war Kunst- und Literaturhistoriker. Er wurde u.a. bekannt durch den Gesprächsroman »Unüberwindliche Mächte« (1859) sowie durch mehrere Künstlerbiographien wie das »Leben Michelangelos« (1860/1863), »Das Leben Raphaels« (1872) und ein Goethe-Buch (1877) in Essay-Form mit »Fülle« und »Überblick«, mit »Esprit und Stil« (Fontane 1979, 291).[1]

Die Veröffentlichung der unten genannten Briefe Fechners erfolgt mit freundlicher Genehmigung der Bibliotheken bzw. Archive, in deren Besitz die Autographen sind.[2] Die Antwortbriefe sind bis auf eine Ausnahme (Adelaide von Gottberg) nicht mehr existent.

1. Jean Paul Friedrich Richter, Leipzig, den 6. October 1825
2. Varnhagen von Ense, Leipzig, den 3.ten Jan. 1833
3. Wolfgang Menzel, Leipzig, d. 4ten Aug. 1834
4. Adelbert von Chamisso, Leipzig, d. 2t. Jan. 1838
5. Theodor Mundt, Leipzig, d. 30sten May, 1838
6. Gottfried Hermann, Leipzig, d. 13. Febr. [18]48
7. Bettine von Arnim, Leipzig, d. 8. September 1840

---

[1] Grimms Buch »Vorlesungen über Goethe« in 2 Bdn. (1877) erlebte 1923 die 12. Aufl.

[2] In der Transkription deuten eckige Klammern Auslassungen oder Ergänzungen an; die Originalblattzahl wird in runden Klammern angezeigt, z.B. (1), (2) usw.

8. Bettine von Arnim, Leipzig, d. 24 April 1841
9. Bettine von Arnim, [Leipzig, 1846]
10. Bettine von Arnim, Leipzig, d. 15 Mai [18]53
11. Gisela von Arnim, Leipzig, d. 14. 12. [18]55
12. Gisela Grimm, Leipzig, d. 14. Aug. 1862
13. Gisela Grimm, Leipzig, d. 7. Oct. [18]64
14. Hermann Grimm, Leipzig, d. 5. 8. [18]67
15. Hermann Grimm, Leipzig, d. 18. Juni [18]72
16. an Unbekannt, Leipzig, d. 6. Juli [18]49
17. Friedrich Zarncke, [Leipzig, etwa 1852]
18. an Unbekannt, Leipzig, d. 13. Sept. [18]55
19. Adelaide von Gottberg, Leipzig, 2. Juli [18]79.

1. Brief vom 6. Oktober 1825 (6 Blatt) an Jean Paul Friedrich Richter (Pseudonym: Jean Paul), Schriftsteller; Autograph: Preußischer Kulturbesitz – Staatsbibliothek zu Berlin, ausgelagert nach Kraków, Bibliotheka Jagiellónska, Sammlung Autographa:[3]

Hochgeehrtester Herr Legationsrath,

Sie haben Ihren Neffen zu schelten, wenn ich Ihnen durch die Uebersendung dieses Briefs und der beifolgenden Schriftchen beschwerlich falle, was ich nie gewagt haben würde ohne seine Aufmunterung dazu.[4] Dieselbe ergieng zwar schon vor einiger Zeit an (2) mich, und wenn ich ihr nicht früher folgte, ungeachtet sie mir eine außerordentliche Freude erregte, so geschah es, ich weiß selbst nicht, halb aus einer gewissen Schüchternheit, halb wohl auch aus einer Scheu, Ihnen, dessen Urtheil ich so hoch, so sehr hochachte, Schriften zuzusenden, die Ihr Urtheil über mich vielleicht ungünstig stimmen werden, da ich jetzt selbst gar Manches daraus ausgestrichen wünschte. Indeß konnte ich doch zuletzt dem Verlangen nicht widerstehen, mit Ihnen in eine nähere Berührung zu kommen, den ich so lange Zeit aus der Ferne (3) mit einer Art Staunen betrachtet habe, und dem ich so manche schöne Stunde verdanke, worüber ich mich gern weiter ausspräche, wenn ich mir nicht dächte, daß Sie die Ausdrücke der Bewunderung schon zu gewohnt seyn müssen, um noch von meiner Seite irgend eine Bedeutung darauf zu legen. Mich selbst anlangend, so werden Sie, wenn Sie die große Mühe bemerken, die ich mir

---

[3] Erstveröffentlichung: Nationalzeitung, Berlin, 26.11. 1887, Nr.22, Morgenausgabe. Die nochmalige Veröffentlichung im Rahmen des Aufsatzes erfolgt der Vollständigkeit halber.

[4] Es handelt sich um Fechners *satirische Schriften*: »Beweis, daß der Mond aus Jodine bestehe« (1821), »Panegiricus der jetzigen Medizin und Naturgeschichte« (1822) und »Stapelia mixta« (1824), die er unter seinem Pseudonym Dr. Mises herausgab.

wenigstens manchmal gegeben habe, pikant und witzig zu seyn, ja sogar zuweilen ein großes Muster nachzuahmen – ich gestehe das Alles, weil's Ihnen ohnehin sogleich in die Augen (4) [fallen] würde, und ich mir schwerlich durch ähnliche Arbeiten die *Minerva* wieder zur Feindin machen werden – vielleicht nicht denken, daß ich eigentlich das harmloseste Geschöpf auf Gottes Erdboden bin, der ein tägliches Leben wie ein Uhrwerk führt, wenigstens im Außern, und im Innern vielleicht selbst manchmal nicht recht weiß, was er will, es sey denn, was ich mir in der That bewußt bin, daß ich überall im Einzelnen gern ein Ganzes finden, oder es dazu verarbeiten möchte, nur daß ich zu letzterem leider in der Kunst, die meine Neigung der (5) Wissenschaft vorziehen würde, der innern Bedingungen ermangele. Verzeihen Sie, daß ich schon so lange bei einem so unbedeutenden Gegenstande, als meine Persönlichkeit ist, verweile, aber ich gestehe, daß ich jetzt wirklich so verzweifelt arm an äußerm Stoffe bin, von dem ich nichts zu sehen bekomme, und an innerm, dessen ohnehin nicht ergiebiger Quell bei der Art mechanischer Geistesarbeit, auf die ich meine materielle Subsistenz zu basiren genöthigt bin, leicht vollends versiegen dürfte, daß ich mich fast unfähig fühle, einen leidlichen Brief zu schreiben, zumal an Sie. Nehmen Sie daher diese Zeilen (6) nur als einen Beweis an, daß ich mich, was wirklich in hohem Grade der Fall ist, gefreut habe, überhaupt an Sie habe schreiben zu dürfen. Noch füge ich die Bitte hinzu, Sie möchten keine ungünstigen Folgerungen für meinen Charakter aus beiliegenden Schriftchen ziehen, deren Verurtheilung im Allgemeinen mich weder befremden noch kränken wird, da ich hierüber mit mir selbst hinlänglich im Reinen bin. Ihr Wohlwollen ist mir zu schätzbar, um nicht diesen Wunsch mit besonderm Nachdruck auszusprechen. Ich schließe mit der Versicherung der aufrichtigsten Verehrung, womit ich verharre

Leipzig, den 6. October 1825 — Ew. Wohlgeboren
ergebenster
M. Gustav Theodor Fechner

Der Überbringer des Briefes und der Mises-Schriften war der Neffe des Dichters, Richard Otto Spazier, mit dem Fechner befreundet war. Eine Antwort hat Fechner auf seinen Brief nicht erhalten, denn Jean Paul verstarb einen Monat später, am 14. November 1825. Spazier, der seinen Onkel bis zu seinem Tode pflegte, berichtet, dass Fechners *satirische Schriften* Jean Paul Friedrich Richter »einige frohe heitre Stunden am Abend seines Lebens verschafft« haben (Spazier 1826, 59f.).[5]

In jungen Jahren hatte Fechner mit Begeisterung die Werke von Jean Paul gelesen und Lebensweisheiten daraus geschöpft;[6] z.B. zitiert Fechner

[5] Vgl. Arendt 1999, 34.
[6] Vgl. Fechner Tagebuch 1867, Bl. 159 (Hs.), UB Leipzig, Nachlass Fechner.

ihn bei einem Treffen mit Freunden: »Inzwischen bemerkt schon Jean Paul richtig in der Levana, daß alles Große langsam geht, Elephanten, Frachtwagen also auch große Philosophen« (Tagebuch 1831, Bl. 4). Gemeint ist Jean Pauls pädagogische Schrift »Levana oder Erziehlehre« (1807).

2. Brief vom 3. Januar 1833 (4 Blatt) an Karl August Varnhagen von Ense, preußischer Diplomat, Schriftsteller, Chronist; Autograph: Preußischer Kulturbesitz – Staatsbibliothek zu Berlin, ausgelagert: Kraków, Bibliotheka Jagiellónska, Sammlung Varnhagen:[7]

[Schreiben des Verlages an K.A. Varnhagen von Ense]

Leipzig, den 3ten. Jan. 1833

Sr. Hochwohlgeb.

Hrn. geh. Legationsrath Ritter Varnhagen v. Ense in Berlin.

Ew. Hochwohlgeb. laden wir hierdurch ergebenst ein, an der im Breitkopf- und Härtelschen Verlage erscheinenden Leipziger Literatur-Zeitung Antheil zu nehmen, und im Fache der schönen Wissenschaften zu recensiren. Als Honorarium, welches pünktlich halbjährig ausgezahlt wird, haben wir Ihnen 15 Thaler für den gedruckten Bogen anzubieten. Auf erhaltene geneigte Antwort werden wir sogleich den Contract zu übersenden die Ehre haben, und verharren

Ew. Hochwohlgeb.
ganz ergebenste
Die Redaction der Leipz. Lit. Zeitung.

[G. Th. Fechner an K.A. Varnhagen von Ense]

Als künftiger Specialredakteur obengenannten Faches füge ich vorstehender Einladung noch den Ausdruck meines persönlichen Wunsches hinzu, Ihre Unterstützung für ein Unternehmen gewinnen zu können, was durch ein tüchtigeres Zusammenwirken von Kräften, als bisher großentheils daran thätig waren, sich neu zu gestalten versucht. Im Falle Ihrer Zusage würde es mir besonders angenehm seyn, wenn Sie selbst diejenigen Bücher, deren Beurtheilung Sie am liebsten übernehmen würden, bestimmen und nur zu Vermeidung von Collisionen durch eine an die Verlagshandlung gerichtete Notiz mir über Ihre getroffene Wahl jedesmal Kenntniß geben wollten. Sollten Sie noch außerdem eine directe Zusendung von Schriften, von denen ich voraussetzen könnte, daß Ihnen eine Beurtheilung derselben zusagen würde, oder wenigstens den Vorschlag derselben von meiner Seite ge-

---

[7] Dem Brief geht ein Schreiben des Verlages Breitkopf und Härtel voraus, in dem Varnhagen von Ense die Mitarbeit als Rezensent am »Leipziger Literaturblatt« angeboten wird. Fechner fügt als Redaktionsmitglied des Verlages der »Leipziger Literaturzeitung« einige persönliche Worte bei.

statten, so würde dieß allerdings um so wünschenswerther für mich seyn. Ich würde mich jedenfalls sehr freuen, wenn ich solchergestalt Gelegenheit erhielte, in speciellere Beziehung zu einem Manne zu treten, dessen Sachkenntniß und gediegenes Urtheil ich so oft schon hochzuschätzen Gelegenheit fand und wenn ich im Stande wäre, in seiner Mitwirkung der Literaturzeitung einen der kräftigsten Hebel für ihren neuen Aufschwung zu verschaffen. Genehmigen Sie den Ausdruck größter Hochachtung, womit ich verharre

Ew. Hochwohlgeb.
ergebenster
G. Th. Fechner, Prof.

N.S. Die Recensionen werden künftig, mit einer vom Re. selbst zu wählenden Chiffre unterzeichnet; doch ist auch Namensunterschrift gestattet, und von Männern, deren Name wie der Ihrige nur zum Glanze der Literaturzeitung beitragen kann, sogar erwünscht.

Eine Durchsicht der *Leipziger Literaturzeitung* ergab, dass Varnhagen von Ense als Mitarbeiter nicht gewonnen werden konnte. Es erschien lediglich die Ankündigung der Neuauflage von dessen Novelle »Die Sterner und die Psitticher« (Januar 1833).

3. Brief vom 4. August 1834 (2 Blatt) an Wolfgang Menzel, Schriftsteller, Literaturhistoriker, Redakteur; Autograph: Berlin-Brandenburgische Akademie der Wissenschaften, Akademiearchiv, Nachlass Menzel 234:

Leipzig, d. 4ten Aug. 1834.

Hochgeehrter Herr,

Ich benutze die Gelegenheit der Uebersendung der ersten Hefte des, meiner Redaction untergebenen, Hauslexicons, von dem ich recht sehr wünschte, daß es sich seiner Tendenz und Ausführung noch Ihres Beifalls und nachsichtigen Urtheils erfreuen möge, Ihnen meinen Dank für die so äußerst freundliche und aufmunternde Weise zu sagen, mit welcher Sie einige, pseudonym von mir herausgegeben, Schriftchen beurtheilt haben; und Sie werden gar glauben, daß ich bei dem großen Interesse, mit welchem ich von jeher Ihr literarisches Blatt in die Hand nahm, Ihre gütigen Aeußerungen darin in Bezug auf diese kleinen Productionen nur mit doppeltem Vergnügen finden konnte. Liegt es weder in der Statur meines Talents noch meiner Verhältnisse, Ihre Aufmerksamkeit (2) fortgehends in Anspruch nehmen zu können, so wünsche ich doch, Ihrem persönlichen Wohlwollen bleibend empfohlen zu seyn, und unterzeichne auch mit Hochachtung als

Ihr
ergebenster
G. Th. Fechner (Mises)

Menzel übernahm 1825 die Redaktion des dem Morgenblatt beigegebenen »Literatur-Blattes« der Cotta'schen Buchhandlung in Stuttgart und führte es in der Zeit von 1829–1846 sowie 1852–1869 unter seinem Namen weiter.[8]

Das von Fechner herausgegebene *Hauslexikon* wurde von Menzel im »Literatur-Blatt« angezeigt. Dieses von Breitkopf & Härtel verlegte Lexikon erschien von 1834 bis 1838 »regelmäßig in monatlichen brochirten Lieferungen« (Menzel 1834, 100 Beil). Es enthielt alphabetisch geordnete Artikel über allgemein Brauchbares und Nützliches aus allen Bereichen der Wissenschaft und Kunst.[9]

Fechner bezieht sich im Brief an Menzel auf zwei *Rezensionen* seiner kleinen Schriften: »Beweis, daß der Mond aus Jodine bestehe« und »Schutzmittel für die Cholera«.[10] Menzel bezeichnet 1832 Fechners »Cholerabüchlein« als »eine sehr geistreiche Schrift, die vor der Sündfluth der Choleraschriften warnt«, denn bis dahin wurden etwa 200 Schriften über die Cholera publiziert. Ferner heißt es in der Anzeige: »Der Verfasser, den man den Jean Paul der Naturphilosophie nennen könnte, ist einer unsrer besten Köpfe, einer unsrer liebenswürdigsten humoristischen Schriftsteller, obgleich er noch wenig bekannt zu seyn scheint. Im Jahr 1822 schrieb er einen *Panegyrikus* der jetzigen Medicin und Naturgeschichte, voll beißender Satyre gegen die Unvernunft der Aerzte; im Jahr 1824 *Stapelia Mixta*, eine Sammlung humoristischer Aufsätze, worin eine Symbolik der Kegelschnitte das Meisterhafteste war, endlich 1825 eine *vergleichende Anatomie der Engel,* voll der originellsten Gedanken. Auch die vorliegende jüngste Schrift ist durchaus humoristisch *für* die Cholera *gegen* die Aerzte geschrieben« (Menzel 1832, 97–100).

4. Brief vom 2. Januar 1838 (1 Blatt) an Adelbert von Chamisso, Schriftsteller und Naturforscher, Herausgeber des »Deutschen Musenalmanach«; Autograph: Preußischer Kulturbesitz – Staatbibliothek zu Berlin, Sign. Nachlass Chamisso:

Leipzig, d. 2t. Jan. 1838

Ew. Hochwohlgeb.

Gestatte ich mir, beifolgende Kleinigkeiten für den *Musenalmanach* von 1838, unter meinem gewöhnlichen pseudonymen Namen anzubieten. Für den Fall der

---

[8] Vgl. ADB 1885, 21, 382–383.

[9] Siehe Fechner 1834–1838; Arendt 1992.

[10] Vgl. Menzel 1832, 97–100, 104; Menzel 1833, 29–30.

Aufnahme dürfte ich wohl eines Freiexemplars des betreffenden Jahrgangs gewärtig seyn.

Mit vollkommner Hochachtung
unterzeichnet sich
Prof. G. Th. Fechner.

Zu einer Aufnahme von poetischen »Kleinigkeiten« des Dr. Mises in den »Deutschen Musenalmanach« kam es nicht, da Chamisso zu dieser Zeit bereits »ein alter, müder, kranker Mann, schier unfähig aller Arbeit« war.[11] Die Kürze des vorliegenden Briefes von Fechner an Chamisso lässt darauf schließen, dass Fechner ihn persönlich kannte. Chamisso war im Herbst 1837 mit der Schnellpost nach Leipzig gekommen, um den ersten bereits fertiggestellten Abschnitt der *Leipzig-Dresdner Eisenbahn* (Leipzig – Sellerhausen – Paunsdorf – Engelsdorf – Althen) zu befahren zusammen mit Karl August Reimer, Gustav Theodor Fechner, Christian Hermann Weiße und Hermann Härtel.[12] Letzterer war Mitglied der Leipzig-Dresdner-Eisenbahn-Kompagnie und Reimer, Sohn des mit Chamisso befreundeten Berliner Verlegers Georg Andreas Reimers, hatte 1831 eine Gesamtausgabe von Chamissos Gedichten in der Leipziger Weidmann'schen Buchhandlung verlegt. Trotz seiner erschütterten Gesundheit hat Chamisso dieses Erlebnis mit der neuen Eisenbahn ausgekostet. Er schrieb an Friedrich de la Motte-Fouqué: »ich hätte nicht ruhig sterben können hätte ich nicht vom Hochsitz dieses Triumphwagens in die sich entrollende Zukunft hinein geschaut« (Brief, 13. 1. 1838).[13] Eine längere Beziehung zwischen Fechner und Chamisso konnte sich nicht entwickeln, da Chamisso im August 1838 starb. Chamissos Ratschlag »Werden Sie nur nicht blos Dichter!«, den er jungen Literaten gewöhnlich gab, die ihm Gedichte für seinen »Musenalmanach« zusandten, behielt Fechner im Gedächtnis. Bei einer Diskussion über Dichter und ihren Lebensberuf meinte Fechner zu Chamissos Satz: »Das ist freilich ein sehr guter Rath«, denn er kannte persönlich »mehr als ein trauriges Beispiel von jungen Leuten, die blos Dichter werden wollten« (Fechner Tagebuch 1867, Bl. 170). Fechner nannte in diesem Zusammenhang die Schriftsteller Ernst Ortlepp, der durch seine »Polenlieder« 1831 bekannt wurde, Karl Herloßsohn, der Herausgeber der belletristischen Zeitschrift

---

[11] Zitat aus einem Brief Chamissos an Friedrich de la Motte-Fouqué vom 13. 1. 1838; siehe Pfeiffer 1902, 677.

[12] Vgl. Feudel 1980, 185; Kuntze 1892, 88.

[13] Vgl. Pfeiffer 1902, 677.

Abb. 1: Eisenbahnfahrt von Leipzig nach Althen, 1837 (aus: Eröffnung der Leipzig-Dresdener-Eisenbahn, Leipzig 1887).

»Komet« (1830–1848), und Ludwig v. Alvensleben, der Begründer der »Sachsenzeitung« (1830) und der »Allgemeinen Theaterchronik (1832). Ortlepp wurde wegen seiner politischen Gesinnung 1836 aus Leipzig ausgewiesen und 1864 in einem Wassergraben bei Schulpforta tot aufgefunden; Alvensleben beteiligte sich 1848 am Oktoberaufstand, lebte zuletzt in Wien in Not und Elend; auch Herloßsohn verstarb in großer Armut. Diese Lebensläufe bestätigten Fechner, dass er – in jungen Jahren selbst am Scheideweg zwischen Wissenschaft und Kunst stehend – als Wissenschaftler den richtigen Weg gewählt hatte.

5. Brief vom 30. Mai 1838 (2 Blatt) an Theodor Mundt, Prof. Dr. phil., Schriftsteller, Literaturhistoriker und Kritiker; Autograph: Preußischer Kulturbesitz – Staatsbibliothek zu Berlin, ausgelagert nach Krakow, Biblioteka Jagiellónska, Sammlung Varnhagen:

Leipzig, d. 30sten May, 1838

Geehrtester Herr Doctor,

blos um Ihnen meine Bereitwilligkeit zu zeigen, an der Fortsetzung Ihres Freihafens ferner Antheil zu nehmen, übersende ich Ihnen, da ich eben nichts in Prosa vorräthig habe, einige poetische Kleinigkeiten, es Ihnen jedoch gänzlich anheim stellend, ob Sie dieselben aufnehmen wollen; da vielleicht schon der Stoff hinreicht, sie nicht ganz passend für Ihre Zeitschriften scheinen zu lassen. Da ich Rücksichten dieser Art bei jedem Redacteur ehre, und keinen Werth auf diese Sachen lege, so werden Sie mich durch Zurücklegung derselben nicht im Mindesten verletzen. Vielleicht auch finden Sie etwa blos die ersten 7 Nummern zur Aufnahme geeignet, die übrigen aber theils gar zu unbedeutend theils im Tone unpassend, und es bliebe Ihnen dann gänzlich überlassen, diese sämtlich oder (2) beliebige daraus wegzulassen, ja es wird mir recht lieb seyn, wenn Sie Ihre Kritik der meinigen substituiren wollen, da von eigenen Producten niemand recht weiß, wie sie sich objectiv darstellen. Mich Ihrer Gewogenheit bestens empfehlend unterzeichnet sich

mit vollkommner Hochachtung
Prof. Fechner

Theodor Mundt gab u.a. von 1838–1844 die Zeitschrift »Der Freihafen, eine Gallerie von Unterhaltungsbildern aus den Kreisen der Literatur, Gesellschaft und Wissenschaft« in Altona heraus.[14] Fechner veröffentlichte im »Freihafen« unter seinem Pseudonym zwei Beiträge: einmal »Gedich-

[14] Brümmer o.J., 5, 84–85.

te aus den Bergen« und zum andern einen Aufsatz über »Deutsche Lyrik und Wilhelm Müller«.[15] Müller wurde bekannt als Autor der »Griechen-Lieder« (1821–1824) sowie der Liederzyklen »Die schöne Müllerin« (1821) und »Die Winterreise« (1823/24). Theodor Mundt lebte von 1832 bis 1839 als Mit-Redakteur der »Blätter für literarische Unterhaltung« in Leipzig. Fechner veröffentlichte in dieser Zeitschrift als Dr. Mises Aufsätze über »Friedrich Rückert« und »Heinrich Heine als Lyriker« (s. Fechner 1835).[16] Fechner kannte Th. Mundt vermutlich aus dessen Leipziger Zeit.

6. Brief vom 13. Febr. 1848 (3 Blatt) an Gottfried Hermann, klass. Philologe, Autograph: Preußischer Kulturbesitz – Staatsbibliothek Berlin, ausgelagert nach Krakow Biblioteka Jagiellónska:

Leipzig, d. 13. Febr. [18]48

Hochgeehrter Herr,

Die Jablonowskische Gesellschaft giebt sich die Ehre, Ihnen die, am 10ten dieses [Monats] auf Sie gefallene Wahl als Mitglied an die Stelle des verewigten Prof. Hasse anzuzeigen,[17] wobei ich die Verspätung dieser Anzeige durch einen Irrthum über meine Competenz zu derselben entschuldigt zu halten bitte. Da die Theilnahme an dieser, blos für die Stellung von Preisfragen und materielle Unterstützung wissenschaftlicher Zwecke aus gegebenen Fonds bestimmten Gesellschaft weder bedeutende Geschäfte noch Verpflichtungen auferlegt, so hegt die Gesellschaft die Hoffnung, daß Sie dieselbe durch Zusage Ihres Beitrittes erfreuen und durch Ihren ruhmwürdigen Namen einen neuen Glanz derselben zufügen werden. Den Ausdruck persönlicher innigster Verehrung hinzufügend unterzeichnet sich

Ihr ergebenster
Prof. Fechner,
d. z. Secretär.

Fechner wurde 1839 Ehrenmitglied und 1844 ordentliches Mitglied der Fürstlich *Jablonowskischen Gesellschaft.* Gottfried Hermann, seit 1803 ordentlicher Professor der »Beredsamkeit« und seit 1809 auch der »Poesie« an der Universität Leipzig, nahm die Wahl als Mitglied der Jablo-

---

[15] Siehe Fechner 1838.

[16] Vgl. den Aufsatz von Ritzer in vorliegendem Buch.

[17] Christian August Hasse, Historiker, war seit 1840 Präses der Fürstlich Jablonowskischen Gesellschaft.

nowskischen-Gesellschaft dankend an.[18] Seine Mitgliedschaft endete im gleichen Jahr, mit seinem Tod am 31.12. 1848.[19] Er hatte 1809 Pläne für eine Universitätsreform beim Oberkonsistorium in Dresden eingereicht, die in den Jahren 1830 bis 1832 verwirklicht wurden. Als eines ihrer Ergebnisse richtete Fechner, für dessen Berufung sich Hermann eingesetzt hatte, im Februar 1835 das »Physikalische Cabinet« im noch nicht vollendeten *Augusteum* am Augustusplatz ein. Es war auch Hermann, der bei der Einweihung des Augusteums am 3. August 1836 die Aula in einem feierlichen Promotionsakt ihrer akademischen Bestimmung symbolisch übergab. Er »gedachte in seiner Rede der Umbildung der Universität, welche auch die Landesuniversität erfahren habe« (Hasse 1836, 54).

Hermann kannte Fechner persönlich aus dem Alt-Volkmann'schen Haus. Er war ein früherer Kommilitone und enger Freund von Fechners Schwiegervater, des Juristen Johann Wilhelm Volkmann. Zeugnis dieser Freundschaft sind »Gottfried Hermann's lateinische Briefe an seinen Freund Volkmann«, herausgegeben von Allwill Volkmann (1882), seinem Sohn. Hermann besuchte Fechner wiederholt während dessen mehrjähriger *Krankheit*. Er nahm auch gelegentlich am sog. Fechner-*Kränzchen* teil, zu dessen Mitgliedern um 1842 außer Fechner der Germanist Moriz Haupt, der Philosoph Christian Hermann Weiße, der Philologe Julius Ludwig Klee, der Physiologe Hermann Lotze und der Verleger Hermann Härtel zählten. Es wurden aktuelle Tagesfragen aus dem Geschehen an der Universität erörtert, auch viel über Persönlichkeiten aus Politik, Wissenschaft und Literatur gescherzt sowie Anekdoten erzählt. Bei einem »Kränzchen«, das bei dem Germanisten Moriz Haupt am 9. September 1842 stattfand, sprach man u.a. über den Stand des Scharfrichters, den man in diesem Kreis zum Doktor ernennen wollte, wenn er »eine gewisse Anzahl Hinrichtungen« vollstreckt habe. Dabei kam die Frage auf, welcher Fakultät er angehören solle. Fechner meinte, es käme doch wohl die medizinische in Frage. Hermann erwiderte: »es könnte auch in der juristischen seyn, da das Köpfen doch eine Rechtssache« sei. Fechner entgegnete: »es könnte wohl auch in der philosophischen seyn, da das

---

[18] Vgl. Brief Hermanns vom 13.2. 1848 an Fechner, Sekretär der Gesellschaft, Nachlass 251. 2.3, UB Leipzig.

[19] Über Fechner und die Fürstlich Jablonowskische-Gesellschaft sowie deren Rolle bei der Entstehung der königlich sächsischen Gesellschaft der Wissenschaften, der heutigen Sächsischen Akademie der Wissenschaften zu Leipzig, siehe Brožek; Gundlach 1988, 92–94 und Arendt 1999, 93–100.

Köpfen als eine Kopfarbeit, als eine Art Kopfzerbrechen« anzusehen sei. Zuletzt fand die Meinung Lotzes den größten Beifall, »daß er nicht zum Doktor der Medicin im Allgemeinen, sondern blos der Chirurgie zu ernennen sey« (Fechner Tagebuch 1842, Bl. 115).

Im Haus von Hermann Härtel, mit dem Fechner in enger freundschaftlicher und verwandtschaftlicher Beziehung stand,[20] verkehrte G. Hermann ebenfalls. Hermann gilt als der Begründer der *Metrik*; zu nennen sind hier seine wissenschaftlichen Veröffentlichungen: »Demetris poetarum qraecorum et romanorum (1796); »De metris Pindari« (1798), »Das Handbuch der Metrik« (1799). »Besonders Goethe, der damals mit der [sic!] Achilles und der Helena beschäftigt war und genauer in das Wesen der antiken Versmasse einzudringen strebte, nahm den regsten Antheil daran« (Jahn 1849, 18). Goethe reiste im Jahr 1800 nach Leipzig und besuchte eines Abends Gottfried Hermann. In dem Gespräch über »Verskunst«, das sich zwischen ihnen entwickelte, schlug Goethe ihm vor, eine »deutsche Metrik« zu schreiben. Dies lehnte Hermann mit der Bemerkung ab: »es sei Goethe's Aufgabe« (Jahn 1849, 18). Die so geknüpfte freundschaftliche Beziehung wurde sowohl durch Briefe als auch persönliche Begegnungen, namentlich in Karlsbad, wo sie sich 1820 trafen, fortgesetzt. Hermanns Gedichte, die sich durch »ein sicheres Gefühl für Tonfall und Wortstellung« sowie »die feinsten Schattierungen des Ausdrucks« (Jahn 1849, 19) auszeichnen, sind gesammelt in den »Opuscula« erschienen (7 Bde. 1827–39; Bd. 8 1877). Bedeutend sind Hermanns kritische Editionen der Werke griechischer und lateinischer Dichter, z.B. Homer, Sophokles, Aristophanes, Plautus, deren Handschriften er sorgfältig prüfte, die er aber in »freier Kunstausübung« (Jahn 1849, 20) meisterhaft bearbeitete. Moriz Haupt (Hermanns Schwiegersohn) veröffentlichte posthum die Dramen des Aischylos (1852), die Hermann zu seinen Lebzeiten nicht vollenden konnte.

7. Brief vom 8. September 1840 (3 Blatt) an Bettine von Arnim, Schriftstellerin;[21] Autograph: Preußischer Kulturbesitz – Staatsbibliothek Berlin, ausgelagert nach Kraków, Bibliotheka Jagiellónska, Sammlung Varnhagen:[22]

---

[20] Vgl. den Aufsatz von Arendt in vorliegendem Buch.

[21] Eigentlich Elisabeth Catharina Ludovica Magdalene von Arnim, geb. Brentano.

[22] Von Clara Fechners Hand.

Leipzig, d. 8. September [18]40

Hochgeehrte gnädige Frau!

Ich sehe nun wohl daß meine Unart mir nun zu Haus und Hof kommt. Sie sind bös mit mir, denn Sie haben mir Ihren Briefwechsel mit der Günderode nicht geschickt;[23] das ist eine schwere Kränkung für mich und doch muß ich mir sagen, daß ich sie nur zu sehr verdient habe, denn ich habe Ihnen auf Ihr letztes Geschenk nicht einmal eine Zeile des Dankes erwiedert. Aber Sie müssen es nicht so genau mit mir nehmen. Ich habe jedes Zeichen Ihrer Freundlichkeit immer mit der freudigsten Dankbarkeit empfangen und der Grund meines langen Schweigens mit Ihnen lag doch nur in dem Gefühl, daß ich, um mich mit Ihnen zu unterhalten eigentlich in einer Stimmung seyn müßte, in der ich mich seit lange nicht befinde. Theils Beschäftigungen, die meiner geistigen Organisation zuwieder sind, theils körperliche Mißstimmungen haben mir die Freiheit des Geistes genommen und mir nur die Sehnsucht, aber nicht die Möglichkeit übrig gelassen, aus einem Zustande herauszukommen, der mich eben sowohl für mich, als für Andere, ungenießbar macht. Seit länger als einem halben Jahr ist mir außerdem die schwere Prüfung einer Augenkrankheit auferlegt, die mich durch Verhinderung eigenen Lesens und Schreibens zum gänzlichen Müßiggang verdammt und zwar Geduld und Ergebung, aber keine heitere Stimmung lehren kann, wie ich sie Ihnen entgegen bringen möchte. Endlich habe ich mein Versäumniß schon lange und schwer genug durch das Bewußtseyn gebüßt, die natürliche Folge davon müsse endlich das seyn, was ich nun wirklich erfahren, das Zurücklegen meiner in Ihrem Gedächtniß. Seyn Sie daher nicht hart gegen mich und geben Sie mir ein Zeichen Ihrer Versöhnlichkeit. Geister, reich wie der Ihrige, sind ja ohnehin gewohnt immer nur zu schenken ohne einen entsprechenden Entgelt erwarten zu dürfen und mein Fehler war nur der, daß ich dieses mein Verhältniß zu Ihnen zu lebhaft empfunden habe.

Empfehlen Sie mich vielmals Ihren Fräulein Töchtern, von deren Liebenswürdigkeit ich Wunderdinge höre. Auch meine Frau, durch deren Hand Sie diese Zeilen empfangen grüßt Sie und die Ihrigen herzlich.

Ganz der Ihrige
Fechner

Fechner ist vermutlich auf Bettine von Arnim durch die positive Rezension ihres Buches »Goethes Briefwechsel mit einem Kinde« (1835) im »Literatur-Blatt« aufmerksam geworden.[24]

Um Bettine von Arnim kennen zu lernen, sandte er ihr 1836 sein »Büchlein vom Leben nach dem Tode« zu. Emil Kuntze berichtet, dass

---

[23] Bettine von Arnim: Die Günderode. Ein Briefwechsel. 2 Bde. Grünberg 1840.

[24] Vgl. Menzel 1835, 127, 505–511.

Bettine von dem »Büchlein« begeistert war.[25] Fechner hingegen verfolgte mit großem Interesse deren literarischen Werke. So ließ er sich die »Günderode« (1840), Bettines Briefwechsel mit der romantischen Schriftstellerin Karoline von Günderode, gleich zweimal vorlesen. Beim Lesen des zweiten Abschnittes »Die Manen«, ein Dialog über die Sehnsucht »nach der unmittelbaren Verbindung mit den Manen der großen Vorzeit« (Bettine 1840, 8) bemerkt Fechner, »wie die darin ausgedrückten Ideen so ganz mit denen übereinstimmten« (Fechner Tagebuch 1842, Bl. 385), die er in seinem »Büchlein vom Leben nach dem Tode« bereits entwickelt hatte.[26] Fechner vermutet sogar, dass der Dialog über die Seelen der Verstorbenen später in Bettines Buch eingeflossen ist.

Nach der ersten Begegnung Fechners mit Bettine im Herbst 1836 in Leipzig entwickelte sich eine über zwei Jahrzehnte währende Freundschaft, die sich bis in die nächste Generation fortsetzte. Dem Neffen Fechners Emil Kuntze haben wir es zu verdanken, dass ein Brief Fechners an Bettine, den er unmittelbar nach der ersten Begegnung mit ihr geschrieben hatte, erhalten ist.[27] In diesem Brief kommt der nachhaltige Eindruck, den Bettine auf Fechner hinterlassen hatte, zum Ausdruck:

[Fechner an Bettine] [6. November 1836]

[...] Sie sind wie ein Meteor bei uns vorübergegangen, das uns mit einem steten geistigen Feuerregen beträufelt hat; aber wir haben es kaum recht betrachten und uns seiner erfreuen können, so ist es schon vorbei. [...] Immer kommen wir wieder auf Sie zurück. [...] Wären Sie nicht so unerschöpflich, und durch die Unerschöpflichkeit des Schöpferischen und Eigenthümlichen eben so merkwürdig, so würden Sie längst abgenutzt und durch das Hin- und Herrollen in unseren Betrachtungen kugelrund sein. Man hat Sie umgewandt nach allen Seiten, Sie anatomisch zerlegt, Sie beleuchtet von außen und von innen, von oben bis unten, Sie mit dem Fernrohr und der Lupe angeschaut, hat sich um Sie vertragen und ist sich in die Haare über Sie gerathen. Jedes hat Sie anders gesehen, weil Jedes sich selbst Ihnen als Spiegel vorgehalten, selbst das blindeste Glas hat Ihren Glanz empfunden, obwohl nicht jedes den ungewohnten ganz vertragen, wir aber preisen uns glücklich, die mit dem Glanz auch die Wärme empfunden haben. Unter den Damen haben Sie jedenfalls die enthusiastischsten Verehrerinnen an meiner und Weiße's Frau gewonnen, wie natürlich, da sie das Glück hatten, am meisten in Ihrer Nähe zu sein (Kuntze 1892, 91).

---

[25] Vgl. Kuntze 1892, 89.

[26] Manen (lat.): Bezeichnung für die guten Geister der Verstorbenen im antiken Rom.

[27] Vgl. Kuntze 1892, 90–93.

Bettine von Arnim besuchte Fechner mehrmals im Gartenhaus, worüber Emil Kuntze ausführlich berichtet.[28] Am 28. August 1842 stattete Bettine auf der Durchreise nach Kreuznach Fechner einen kurzen Besuch ab. Sie erzählte ihm von ihrem in Arbeit befindlichen Buch, das sie dem »König von Preußen didicirt« habe, »obschon das ganze Buch gegen ihn gerichtet« sei (Fechner Tagebuch 1842, Bl. 63).[29] Es enthalte »einige Briefe und Erinnerungen an Frau Rath«, Goethes Mutter, sowie »verschiedene Papiere, die auf ihre Zeit Bezug haben« (ebda., Bl. 63). Außerdem habe sie der »Frau Rath eine Menge Sachen in den Mund gelegt, die auf die jetztige Zeit passen« (ebda., Bl. 63); wobei es ihr »vortrefflich gelungen« sei, »ihren eigenthümlichen Ton dabei zu treffen« (ebda., Bl. 63). Bettine verkehrte auch im *Freundeskreis* von Fechner, namentlich bei dem Philosophen Christian Hermann Weiße in Stötteritz (bei Leipzig), bei dem Germanisten Moriz Haupt, bei dem Verleger Karl Reimer und dem Juristen Hermann Härtel im *Römischen Haus*.[30] Letzterer wurde 1842 auf Anregung von Fechner der Verleger ihrer Lieder-Kompositionen, die Bettine dem Komponisten Gasparo Spontini gewidmet hat (vgl. Brief 8).

8. Brief vom 24. April 1841 (2 Blatt) an Bettine von Arnim; Autograph: Preußischer Kulturbesitz – Staatsbibliothek Berlin, ausgelagert nach Kraków, Bibliotheka Jagiellónska Kraków, Slg. Varnhagen, von Clara Fechners Hand:

Leipzig, den 24.4. 1841

Hochverehrte gnädige Frau!

Da der selbst Begabteste am Wenigsten von Andern zu fordern pflegt, so darf ich auch hoffen, daß Sie mit Nachsicht das Büchlein, was ich Ihnen hierbei sende, aufnehmen werden. Betrachten Sie dasselbe als einen Zeitvertreib eines Halbblinden,[31] so werden Sie um so weniger Ansprüche daran machen, da ja Niemand besser als Sie selbst weiß, daß man, um Dichten zu können, eigentlich dem Leben frei und offen ins Auge schauen muß. Ich benutze zugleich diese Gelegenheit, Ihnen für die Freundlichkeit zu danken, mit der Sie bei mehreren Gelegenheiten meiner gedacht und mir dieß durch Gruß und Rath, den Sie mir sandten, bestätigt haben. Ich habe diesen Rath befolgt, nicht aus Ueberzeugung, indeß eine dämoni-

---

[28] Vgl. Kuntze 1892, 88.

[29] »Dies Buch gehört dem König« erschien 1843 in Berlin.

[30] Vgl. Fechner Tagebuch 1842 (Hs.); vgl. Drewitz 1999, 212.

[31] Es handelt sich um das kleine Bändchen »Gedichte« des Dr. Mises, Leipzig 1841.

sche Stimme zwingt uns ja wohl auch wieder Willen ihr zu folgen. Aber so ist es: wem der Rath, den ihm eine solche Stimme giebt, fruchten soll, der muß selber noch Theil am guten Dämon haben. Dann ist es gleichgültig, was ihm gerathen wird; und wenn ihm Kieselsteine eingegeben werden, so werden seine blöden Augen davon gesund werden; wen aber die guten Geister zu verlassen anfangen, den mag man die schönsten Pferde vor den Wagen spannen, und der Wagen wird mit den Pferden rückwärts durchgehen. Gewiß ist, daß ich trotz Kampfer, Schierling und Kieselerden, welche die Homöopathen bei mir vorgespannt hat, noch in meiner finstern Stube sitze. Ich wundere mich nicht, daß Sie den poetischen Irrthum der Homöopathie den prosaischen der Allopathie vorziehen; ich kann aber beide doch nur für ein paar Blinde halten, die sich in meinem Falle darum streiten, welche von beiden dem dritten Blinden helfen soll. – Daß Sie Ihre Lieder-Compositionen herauszugeben beabsichtigen, hat unter uns eine freudige Sensation erregt. Da bei Ihnen Alles aus dem Ganzen kommt, so wissen wir zum Voraus, was wir an den Tönen haben werden (2) nachdem Sie uns so schön gezeigt haben, was Sie durch die Worte vermögen; es werden doch nur Theile derselben Blüte seyn. Und Sie können ja Alles was Sie wollen; warum wollen Sie nur so selten was Sie können! Härteln würden Sie eine große Freude gemacht haben, wenn Sie ihn hätten zum Verleger wählen wollen; er wagte es aber nicht sich Ihnen selbst dazu anzubieten, da ihm Ihr Brief keine Aufforderung dazu zu enthalten schien. Und Sie haben wohl schon darüber disponirt? jedenfalls weiß er die Güte zu schätzen, mit welcher Sie die Zusendung, die er sich Ihnen zu machen erlaubte, aufgenommen haben, und er würde Ihnen dieß selbst schriftlich ausgedrückt haben, wenn er sich zu einer ferneren Correspondenz mit Ihnen berechtigt gehalten.[32] Sie sehen, ich bin nicht so bedenklich; erlange und verlange ich auch durch meine paar Worte Geschreibsel keine Antwort von Ihnen, so weiß ich doch kein anderes Mittel mich in Ihrem vielbeschäftigten Andenken zu erhalten, und ich wünschte nicht ganz darin zu erlöschen. So erhalten Sie denn etwas von Ihrer Theilnahme

Ihrem treuen Verehrer
Fechner

9. Brief aus dem Jahr 1846 (6 Blatt) an Bettine von Arnim;[33] Autograph: Universitätsbibliothek Leipzig, Nachlass 42.1 (Fechner):

[Leipzig, 1846]
An Bettine von Arnim, bei Übersendung der Schrift vom höchsten Gute.

So viel Ursach ich auch habe, Ihnen für Ihre mir so vielfach bewiesene Güte und Theilnahme dankbar zu sein, weiß ich doch anderseits, daß große und reiche Pa-

---

[32] Vgl. den Beitrag von Arendt in vorliegendem Buch; vgl. Drewitz, 1999, 233.
[33] Eine Abschrift; vgl. auch Lipps 1905, Nr. 3.

läste auch große Rumpelkammern haben und brauchen, und kann mich also nicht wundern, wenn ich mit der Zeit auch dahinein wandre. Zumal Sie schreiten immer so geradeswegs mit Elfenschritt über Blumen oder (2) mit eisernem Schritt durch Gestrüpp, was Ihnen im Wege liegt; nun bleibt entweder dahinter, wer nicht mit fort kann, oder wird niedergetreten, wer Ihnen nicht selbst als eine Blume im Wege erscheint oder gar mit einem Dorne den gar zu übermüthigen Fuß ritzen möchte. Inzwischen, wenn es Ihnen leicht sein wird, Jemand zu vergessen, (3) dessen Sie sich immer nur aus Güte erinnert haben, wird es dagegen nicht möglich sein, Ihnen dieß zu erwiedern für den, der so oft von Ihrem Geist und Ihrer Güte zugleich gezehrt hat. Nachdem meine Augen wieder etwas Kraft gewonnen, habe ich Ihr erstes immergrünes Buch wieder einmal zur Hand genommen und geistige Frische daraus gesogen, und noch vorigen Sonntag, am schönsten Morgen (4) dieses Jahres, saß ich mit meiner Frau und Jemand, der sich in Ihrer Verehrung mit uns verschwisterte, draußen im Grünen und am Wasser mit Ihrem Buche, und das Alles paßte so schön zusammen, als wenn Ihr Buch kein Buch, sondern selbst nur das schönste Wort aus der schönsten Natur wäre.[34]

Das kleine Schriftchen, was ich Ihnen übersende, benutze ich als Anlaß, wenigstens eine flüchtige Erinnerung meiner (5) Ergebenheit für Sie wieder einmal hervorzurufen. Was ich darin geschrieben, ist ernst gemeint, und ich wünschte, daß es bei Ihnen, da Sie immer den Wert wie der Sache nach die Verknüpfung des Guten mit dem Schönen vertreten haben, auch eine gute Statt finden möge. Sie werden ja leicht erkennen, daß diese Verknüpfung, wenn auch das Schriftchen nicht direct auf ihre Darlegung gerichtet ist, doch die nächstliegende (6) Ausgeburt der darin enthaltenen Lehre sein würde.

Ich füge die letzten Grüße von meiner Frau bei, welche die Erinnerung an Sie und die Ihrigen immer noch den Charakter eines festlichen Glanzes hat.

Ihr treuer Verehrer
Th. Fechner

10. Brief vom 15. Mai 1853 (10 Blatt) an Bettine von Arnim; Autograph: Preußischer Kulturbesitz – Staatsbibliothek Berlin, ausgelagert: Biblioteka Jagiellónska, Krakow, Sammlung Varnhagen:

---

[34] Gemeint ist Bettines Buch »Clemens Brentanos Frühlingskranz« (1844), eine Briefsammlung, zusammengestellt aus dem Briefwechsel der jungen Bettine mit ihrem Bruder Clemens.

Leipzig, d. 15 Mai [18]53

Hochgeehrte gnädige Frau,

Alle Welt macht Pfingstausflüge, gewiß kann ich nichts Besseres thun, als einen solchen zu Ihnen machen, zumal Sie mir selbst dazu Anlaß gegeben haben. Eben bekommt meine Frau aus dem Garten einer Freundin, die vorige Woche nach Stuttgart gereist ist, einen großen Strauß aus Maienzweigen mit Kaiserkronen und Tulpen dazwischen, womit diese Auftrag gegeben, sie am Pfingstmorgen zu grüßen; könnte ich Ihnen doch auch aus der Ferne mit etwas so Anmuthigem am Pfingstmorgen begegnen; doch Ihnen nähert man sich immer mehr, um zu empfangen, als um zu geben, und trägt nicht Blumen in den Garten, sondern hohlt sie aus demselben.

Mit welchem Interesse wir die Verlobung Ihrer Max gehört und die Bestätigung davon durch Sie selbst erhalten haben, können Sie sich wohl denken.[35] Freilich gewinnt nicht so leicht Jemand, ohne daß ein Anderer verliert, und so können wir nur von Herzen wünschen, daß der Verlust, den Sie selbst in gewisser Hinsicht durch die Entfernung und die neue Wendung der Interessen Ihrer Frl. Tochter erfahren werden, durch einen um so größeren Gewinn von (2) Seiten derselben im Sinne der Wünsche, die Sie selbst für sie hegen müssen, ausgeglichen werden möge. Bringen Sie uns alle, die wir uns ihrer liebenswürdigen Erscheinung von früheren Zeiten her noch so gern erinnern, mit diesen unsern beßten Wünschen bei dieser Gelegenheit ihr wieder in Erinnerung; und möchte uns die Freude werden, sie einmal in ihren neuen Verhältnissen begrüßen zu können.

Wir erhielten die Nachricht von diesem Ereigniß in Ihrem Familienkreise zuerst durch die kleine Frau Musikdirektor Hauptmann, die Ihnen ja bekannt ist.[36] Dabei fällt mir ein, daß vom Manne derselben vor kurzem eine Schrift erschienen ist, von der ich mir nach dem Titel, einer Anzeige im literar. Centralblatt und einigen mündlichen Notizen wohl denken könnte, daß sie Ihr Interesse in Anspruch zu nehmen verdiente; daher ich die Anzeige in Abschrift beilege; ich selbst kenne die Schrift nicht, und würde sie vielleicht auch bei meiner großen Unwissenheit in musikalischen Dingen nicht verstehen.[37] Jedenfalls scheint es mir eine schöne Aufgabe, die Einigung von Natur und Geist in Melodie und Harmonie aus lichtvollen Gesichtspunkten darzustellen, und die geheimnißvolle Weise, wie die Musik des Menschen Herz und Sinne zugleich (3) rührt, auch seinem Verständniß aufzuschließen, zumal, wenn es von einem so feinen Geiste geschieht, wie Hr. Hauptmann, den ich übrigens nicht persönlich kenne, sein soll. Namentlich aber dünkt mich, haben dergleichen Bestrebungen, selbst wenn sie das Ziel nicht ganz

---

[35] Gemeint ist Maximiliane von Arnim, Tochter von Bettine.

[36] Die Malerin und Graphikerin Susette Hummel war seit 1841 mit dem Komponisten und Musiktheoretiker Moritz Hauptmann verheiratet.

[37] Gemeint ist Hauptmanns Schrift »Die Natur der Harmonie und der Metrik«, Leipzig 1853.

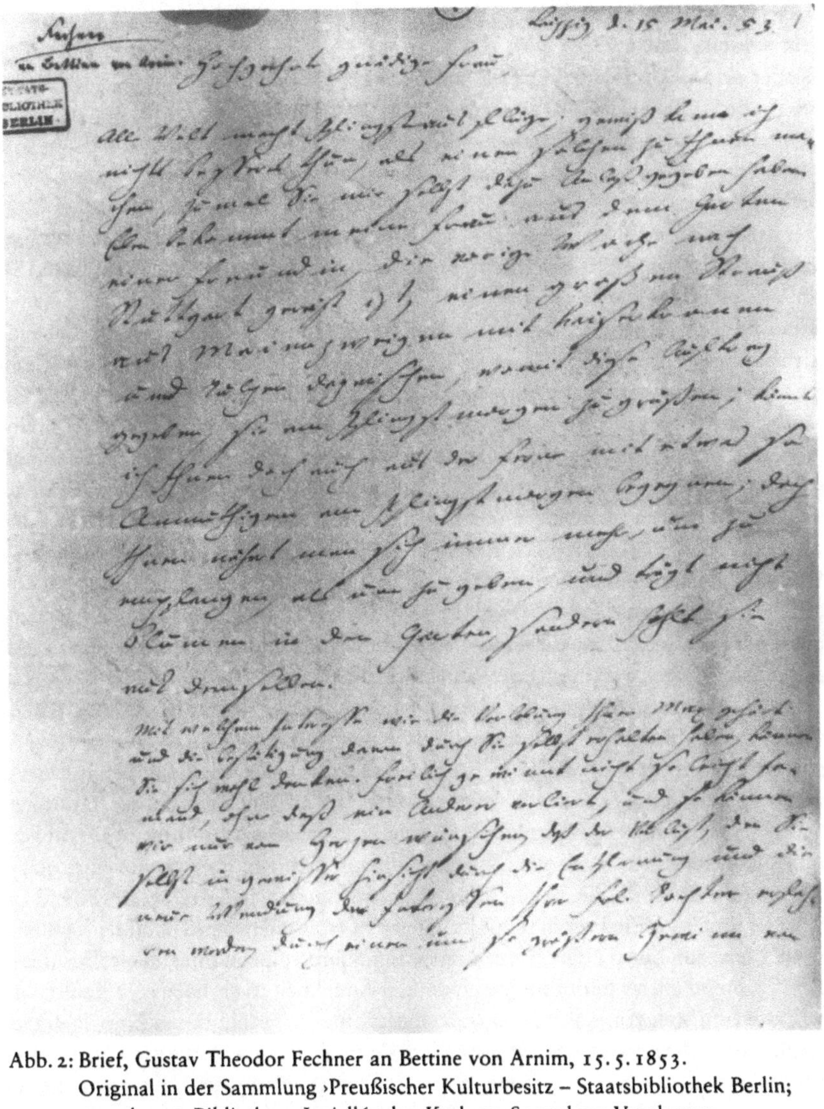

Abb. 2: Brief, Gustav Theodor Fechner an Bettine von Arnim, 15.5.1853.
Original in der Sammlung ›Preußischer Kulturbesitz – Staatsbibliothek Berlin;
ausgelagert: Bibliotheca Jagiellónska, Krakow, Sammlung Varnhagen‹.

erreichen sollten, etwas Erfreuliches, Erbauliches und Wohlthuendes gegenüber dem wüsten und wirren Spuk, der jetzt mit den Kräften und Beziehungen von Körper und Geist theoretisch und praktisch getrieben wird, und dämonische Nebel an die Stelle der alten Klarheit heraufbeschwören möchte. Da Sie selbst diesen Gegenstand angeschlagen haben, und mir das Beispiel v. Humboldt's ironisch vorhalten, der einem Feinde, dessen Luftstreichen und Phantasmagorieen mit den festen Waffen seiner Wissenschaft nicht zu begegnen vermochte, lieber den Rükken kehrte, so muß ich wohl eine Auffoderung darin sehen, auch einige Worte darüber zu sagen, und meinerseits Front zu machen, so gut es eben geht, sollten es auch nur Luftstreiche seyn, mit denen ich den Luftstreichen zu begegnen suche. Was übrigens Ihre eigne Ansicht anlangt, so bin ich in der That nicht recht klar darüber geworden, ob Ihre Ironie sich mehr gegen die Naturforscher oder gegen die Geisterforscher wendet, von denen jeder die Augen nur in andrer Weise zumacht, und denke mir, Sie haben im Grunde die Neigung, von dem, was jetzt umgeht, so viel als möglich zu glauben, da im Dunkeln gut munkeln ist und Niemand schöner als Sie zu munkeln weiß, nur daß Sie doch das Unmögliche eben nicht möglich finden, zu glauben, indeß sich's für mich gerad' umkehrt; ich habe die Neigung, so wenig als möglich davon zu glauben, und muß doch auch von dem Unmöglich scheinenden Einiges für möglich halten; denn Thatsachen, sagen Sie mit Recht, sind unwiderstehlich, und selbst die der (4) Hölle muß man ja anerkennen. Indessen, wenn man die Thatsachen anerkennen muß, kann man sich mit der Auslegung helfen, und das thue ich denn auch.

In der Welt, sage ich mir, sind Umkehrungen fast allwegs möglich, nur daß es zugleich auch immer Verkehrungen sind. Bisher tanzte der Mensch nach hölzernen Instrumenten; nun macht sich der Mensch zum Instrumente, Holz tanzen zu lassen; bisher schrieb man auf Tischen seine vernünftigen oder unvernünftigen Gedanken nieder; nun läßt man von Tischen sich seine vernünftigen oder unvernünftigen Gedanken zuklopfen. Warum sollte es nicht gehen? was vorwärts geht, geht auch rückwärts; die Tische thun Alles, was man sich einbildet, daß sie thun werden; und je verrückter die Einbildungen der Menschen werden, desto verrückter werden sich künftig die Tische unter ihren Händen benehmen, die selbst unter dem Einflusse dieser Einbildung stehen; das kann sich noch bis ins Unglaubliche wechselseitig steigern oder hat es vielmehr schon. So las ich dieser Tage in einem Artikel der sächsischen constitutionellen Zeitung, dessen Verfasser von der Redaction als ein durchaus achtbarer, zuverlässiger unbefangener Gelehrter bezeichnet wird, in dessen Aussagen nicht der mindeste Zweifel zu setzen sey, Beobachtungen über das Tischklopfen, hinsichtlich deren auf Zeugen provocirt und zur Constatirung an Ort und Stelle beim Verf. eingeladen wird, worin sich u.a. (5) findet, daß die Klopfgeister in den Tischen, wenn man sie fragt, was ihnen nicht recht ist, gern schimpfen, als z.B. Igel, Hund, Ochse, Esel, Schwein, dumme Gans und noch viel gemeiner, daß zwar nicht alle, aber die meisten auch lügen, daß sie *b* und *p*, *d* und *t* in der Orthographie, wie die Sachsen zu thun pflegen, verwechseln, u.s.w. Diese Thatsachen sind nun in der That so gut verbürgt, als das Beßte, was man von diesen Dingen weiß, und so glaube ich auch, daß es damit seine volle Richtigkeit hat, daß die Geister in den Tischen genau so schimpfen, fluchen, lügen, schreiben, wie es die Geister an den Tischen auch ohne den Tisch gethan haben würden.

Obwohl nicht ohne Besorgniß, Sie zu ermüden, da Sie mit dergleichen Dingen unstreitig so gut, als wie jetzt hier überschwemmt werden, will ich doch noch eines Berichtes darüber gedenken, der gerade Wasser auf meine Mühle schüttet. In einer kleinen Brochüre des Privatdozenten Dr. C.H. Schauenburg aus Bonn (Tischrücken und Tischklopfen, eine Thatsache, Düsseldorf, 1853) werden ähnliche Dinge als im obigen Artikel erzählt, nur daß die Tische sich der, unstreitig gebildeten Gesellschaft gemäß, in der sie sich befanden, auch gebildeter benommen haben, und Zeugnisse von K. Simrock, Hoffmann v. Fallersleben, Dr. O. Schade, I. Neusser für die Richtigkeit der Thatsachen hinten (6) beigedruckt.[38] Die letztern nun beschränken sich auf die einfache Bezeugung, daß sie Alles so gesehen und gehört, wie es vom Verf. beschrieben worden, nur K. Simrock äußert sich wie folgt:

Geehrtester Herr Doctor!

Daß die Erscheinungen, welche wir gesehen haben, nicht auf Täuschungen beruhten, wie sollte ich das bezeugen können? Auf absichtlichen Täuschungen beruhen sie gewiß nicht, davon sind wir wohl beide gleich sehr überzeugt, aber ob nicht auf unwillkührlichen Selbsttäuschungen? Wer kann glauben, daß ein unvernünftiger Tisch in die Zukunft schaue? Wären die Prophezeiungen und Wahrsagen, das Klopfen u.s.w. nicht neuerdings hinzugekommen, so hätte man das Bewegen wohl noch für eine Wirkung magnetischer Kräfte halten können. Aber das Wahrsagen bricht der ganzen Erscheinung den Hals. So gut es auf Täuschung beruhen muß, daß ein Tisch wahrsage, so gut wird es auch wohl auf Täuschung beruhen, daß er sich bewege. Ein wichtiges Phänomen wird jedenfalls durch diese Versuche erwiesen, das Phänomen, daß unsere Gliedmaßen unwillkührliche Vollstrecker unsers Willens sind. Mit freundlichem Gruß Ihr K. Simrock.«

(7) Ich gestehe Ihnen, daß mir dieß wie aus der Seele geschrieben ist und denke mir nach Allem, daß in der Einbildung und einem dadurch unbewußt gerichteten Willensantriebe und Phantasieerzeugniß der Haupthebel aller Erscheinungen beim Tischrücken, Geisterklopfen, Geistersehen, sympathetischen Curen, Vorsehen und was dergl. mehr ist, liegt. Nun freilich mag in jenen Momenten selbst eine Gewalt liegen, die nicht durch das, was in den Psycholologien[39] darüber steht, erschöpft ist, und die man immerhin magisch nennen mag, weil man noch nicht

[38] Carl Hermann Schauenburg (geb. 23.4. 1819), Arzt, Schriftsteller; Oskar Schade (1826–1906), Germanist; Karl J. Simrock (1802–1876), Schriftsteller und Germanist.

[39] Offensichtlich ein Schreibfehler Fechners, gemeint ist »Psychologien«.

weiß, wie mächtig, tief und eigenthümlich sie, namentlich in abnormen Fällen, ins Gebiet des Körperlichen im Menschen und von hier aus auf die Außenwelt übergreifen kann, und wie weit ihm dadurch aus der Außenwelt rückgespiegelt werden kann, was er erst in unbewußten Wirkungen in sie übertragen hat. Und sollten Sie sich nicht auch mit solcher Auffassung vertragen können, ja es nicht im Grunde von vorn herein die Ihrige seyn, und nur vielleicht die poetische Wendung, die sie bei Ihnen nimmt, eine etwas andre seyn, als sie bei Jemand nehmen kann, der nicht wie Sie mit der Muttermilch der Poesie, sondern der schweren Erdkluster der Naturwissenschaften groß gezogen worden ist.[40]

Wenn ich nach dieser langen Auseinandersetzung, die ich nur dadurch zu entschuldigen weiß, daß Sie dieselbe gewissermaßen herausgefodert haben, erst zuletzt auf Frau (8) von Marenholz zu sprechen komme, ist es gewiß nicht deßhalb, weil ihre Erscheinung an uns spurlos vorüber gegangen wäre, da sie vielmehr unser Interesse lebhaft in Anspruch genommen hat.[41] Zwar können wir nicht leugnen, daß wir uns nach dem Briefe, den Sie uns von ihr beilegten, einigermaßen vor ihrer Ankunft scheuten, da er uns Ansprüche an ein, uns doch gar zu fremd gebliebenes, Interesse einzuschließen schien; auch dürfte sie schwerlich in dieser Hinsicht ganz zufrieden mit uns abgereist seyn, indem wir ihrem Enthusiasmus für die Fröbelsche Sache doch nicht in der Weise nachzukommen vermochten, wie er in ihr selbst lebendig ist. Sie ist uns aber um so lieber geworden, je mehr wir das, was Sie selbst von ihr sagten, bestätigt fanden, daß Güte und eine edles ideales Streben der Kern ihres Wesens ist, worin sie ja doch abgesehen von dem mindern Umfange und der mindern Productivität und Selbstständigkeit ihres Geistes, ganz Ihre Verwandte ist; ja die feine Auslegung ihrer Persönlichkeit und der Enthusiasmus für die Idee, die sie vertritt und ihre Züge begeistert, können sie wahrhaft liebenswürdig erscheinen lassen, wenn auch die Einseitigkeit, mit der es geschieht, die fast den Charakter einer fixen Idee trägt, das feste und stete Anklammern an diese Idee und die übergewaltige Bedeutung, die sie hineinlegt, (9) zu keinem ganz harmonischen Eindruck kommen läßt. Die Nachklänge eines hart geprüften Lebens, die sich dazu in ihrer Erscheinung gelten machen, erwecken eine Art tragischen Eindruck. Von Fröbel und seiner Erziehungsmethode haben wir früher nicht viel gewußt, außer durch unbestimmtes Hörensagen. Die Weise, wie sie ihn selbst schildert, muß aber einen Jeden für diese urkräftige Persönlichkeit einnehmen, der im Kleinsten das Größte sah und erstrebte; und die Begeisterung, die er so vielfach einzuflößen gewußt hat, beweist wohl mehr als alles Andre für die lebendige

40 »Kluster« nach Grimms »Deutschem Wörterbuch« 1873, 5, 1307 im Sinne von: Kloß, Klumpen, Scholle.

41 Berta von Marenholtz geb. Bülow (1811–1893), pädagogische Schriftstellerin, seit 1830 verh. mit Geheimrat v. Marenholtz aus Hannover, von dem sie sich jedoch später trennte. Sie lernte 1850 den Pädagogen Friedrich Fröbel (1782–1852) persönlich kennen und widmete sich dann der literarischen und praktischen Verbreitung der *Fröbel'schen Erziehungsweise*.

Triebkraft seiner Ideen. Wer möchte ihm auch nicht beipflichten, wenn er darauf ausgeht, die Anlagen, die Gott und Natur in den Menschen gelegt haben, auf harmonischste und naturgemäßeste Weise zu Religiosität, Sittlichkeit und praktischen Lebenstüchtigkeit zu entwickeln, in den Kindern schon die Mutter und durch die Mutter wieder die Kinder zu erziehen und überall Anfang und Ende bezugsreich an einander zu knüpfen. Nur gerade in dem, wofür Frau v. M.[arenholz] wohl die meiste Theilnahme bei mir voraussetzte, wüßte ich mich am wenigsten damit einzuverstehen, in dem naturphilosophischen Ausdruck und den naturphilosophischen Tendenzen, die sie den Fröbelschen Ideen vielleicht mehr noch als er selbst unterlegt, und eine Art Symbolik abstracter allgemeiner Ideen, die mit dem Anspruch, etwas Tiefes zu bedeuten und vorzubereiten, in die ersten Kinderspiele gelegt wird, da mir scheint, daß die Naturphilosophie mit ihren Ideen noch viel zu schwankend, (10) in sich unklar, vieldeutig und strittig ist, um einen festen Ausgang, eine Stütze oder einen Zielpunct für eine praktische Erziehungsmethode darbieten zu können, und alle ausgeklügelten Symbole nur künstliche Eier sind, aus denen nichts herauskommt. Inzwischen ist das doch wohl nur das Unwesentliche der Sache und der Sinn der Dinge zulezt immer mehr werth, als ihr Verstand.

Schreiben Sie es dem Vergnügen zu, was ich nur darin finden kann, mich mit Ihnen zu unterhalten, wenn dieser Brief Sie länger als recht in Anspruch genommen hat, ein Vergnügen, das freilich für mich viel größer seyn würde, wenn ein so langer Brief von Ihnen als von mir herrührte. Die besten Grüße von uns darin auch an die Ihrigen. Weiße (der nicht abgeneigt scheint, zur Geisterfahne zu schwören), ist eben nach Dresden gereist, aber seine Grüße und Wünsche vereinigen sich immer mit den unsrigen. Wenn doch der letzte Sylvesterabend, den wir mit Ihnen zubrachten, eben nicht der letzte dieser Art wäre; er wird immer eine unsrer liebsten Erinnerungen bleiben. Erhalten Sie Ihre freundliche Gewogenheit

Ihrem treuergebenen
Fechner.

11. Brief vom 14. Dezember 1855 (4 Blatt) an Gisela von Arnim, Schriftstellerin, Tochter von Bettine von Arnim; Autograph: Hess. Staatsarchiv Marburg, Bestand 340 Grimm:

Leipzig, d. 14. Dec. [18]55

Gnädiges Fräulein,

dem Briefe, den Sie Eingangs des beifolgenden Buches finden, füge ich nur noch den Wunsch einer freundlichen Aufnahme mit der Bemerkung hinzu, daß die Widmung blos einer kleinen Anzahl meiner Freiexemplare vorgedruckt worden ist, da der Buchhändler sich in den Kopf gesetzt hatte, das gelehrte Publicum, auf das er hauptsächlich rechnete, möchte (2) durch eine, an eine Dame gerichtete,

Dedication mißtrauisch gegen den Ernst des Inhalts werden.[42] Ich sahe meinerseits in Betracht des Gegenstandes derselben nur eine kleine Zierde des Buches darin, womit ich es gern öffentlich geschmückt hätte, und hoffe, daß Sie nicht ungehalten darüber werden würden; habe aber doch (3) nachgeben müssen. Wie lange haben wir nichts von Ihnen gesehen; auch nur Weniges und nicht ganz Erfreuliches gehört. Wie dankbar würde ich Ihnen seyn, wenn Sie mich, zum Beweise, daß Sie mir meine frühere Unart nicht nachtragen, mit einigen Zeilen erfreuen wollten, die wo möglich eine ganz beruhigende Nachricht über das Befinden Ihrer Frau Mutter enthielten, worüber wir nichts Bestimmtes wissen. Mit der Bitte, sie und Ihre Fräulein Schwester, von mir und meiner Frau, die Ihnen mit wahrer Zärtlichkeit zugethan ist, beßtens und schönstens zu grüßen

der Ihrige
Fechner

12. Brief vom 14. August 1862 (3 Blatt) an Gisela Grimm geb. von Arnim; seit 1859 verh. mit Hermann Grimm; Autograph: Hess. Staatsarchiv Marburg, Bestand 340 (Grimm):[43]

Verehrteste Frau!

Sie haben uns schon so viel Freundlichkeit bewiesen, daß ich hoffe, Sie werden den Gruß, den ihnen die Ueberbringerin dieser Zeilen von uns mitbringt, so wie sie selbst mit ihrer hübschen Tochter auch freundlich empfangen; da sie eine Empfehlung von uns für Berlin wünschten; und eine Schönere als an Sie wüßte ich ihr freilich nicht zu geben. Möchte ich Ihnen nur nicht unbequem damit fallen. Es ist Frau Dr. Seiler, geb. Diernf, Enkelin des berühmten Chemikers Strotmeyer,[44] an einen Arzt in der Schweiz verheirathet gewesen, aber von ihm (durch Schuld des Mannes) geschieden, und jetzt einen neuen vortheilhaften Boden in Berlin zur Ausübung von Gesangsunterricht suchend, worin sie wie ich glaube tüchtiges leistet, wie sie denn auch ein hübsches Schriftchen darüber herausgegeben hat, und von anders her gut empfohlen ist. Eine wegen der Mannigfaltigkeit ihrer Schicksale und Vielseitigkeit ihrer Talente gewiß merkwürdige, wegen des Muthes, mit dem sie sich und die ihrigen durch schwere Verhältnisse durchgekämpft hat, so wie im Uebrigen nach meinem besten Wissen achtbare, durch die Lebhaftigkeit ihres Geistes und die unverwüstliche Heiterkeit ihres Temperamentes interessi-

[42] Nach H.-J. Arendt geht es offenbar um das Buch »Prof. Schleiden und der Mond«, in dem in einigen Exemplaren tatsächlich diese Widmung enthalten ist. Es kam schon im Dezember 1855 auf den Markt, obwohl es erst 1856 offiziell erschienen ist.

[43] Von Clara Fechners Hand, die Unterschrift von Fechner persönlich.

[44] Gemeint ist Friedrich Stromeyer (1776–1835), Professor der Chemie und Pharmazie in Göttingen.

rende, Frau; und eine vorzüglich schöne Eigenschaft derselben ihre große Gutmüthigkeit, Wichtigkeit und Freudigkeit, andern hilfreich zu sein und Freude zu machen. Damit hat sie es so weit gebracht, daß wir nicht umhin gekonnt haben, sie lieb zu gewinnen, ungeachtet ihre etwas zurückhaltslose Weise (2) der Darstellung und ihre Neigung andere um jeden Preis etwas Angenehmes zu sagen von vorn[h]erein mehr abstoßend als anziehend wirkte, Fehler, welche ich am liebsten gleich selbst bemerke, weil sie einen feinen Sinn wie dem Ihrigen freilich am wenigsten werden entgehen können.[45] Ich wünschte nur, daß diese doch nicht gar zu wesentlichen, wenn auch etwas auffälligen Schwächen ihrer Selbstdarstellung und den wirklich liebenswürdigen und braven Seiten ihres Charakters auch bei Ihnen überwogen werden möchten; sie hat diesen Wunsch wohl um uns verdient, da sie bei ihrem ungefähr zweijährigen Aufenthalt in Leipzig uns immer die größte Anhänglichkeit gezeigt, jede dankbare Gefälligkeit erwiesen hat, und mir noch in letzter Zeit bei meinem rückfälligen Augenleiden eine unermüdliche Vorleserin gewesen ist, so daß es Neigung und Pflicht zu gleich ist, was mich veranlaßt, mich für sie zu verwenden. Sollten Sie nun ihr gestatten wollen, ihre guten Eigenschaften auch bei Ihnen geltend zu machen, und Neigung und Gelegenheit finden ihr hiernach zu ihren Zwecken förderlich zu sein, so würde dies mich sehr erfreuen. Gerne erinnere ich mich dabei, wie sehr ich und die Meinigen Ihnen schon von früher her verpflichtet sind, was mich freilich abhalten sollte, neue Ansprüche zu machen. Meine Nichte zählt die Stunden die sie bei Ihnen in Berlin zubrachte, zu ihren liebsten Erinnerungen und wird die geistige Erquickung, die Sie ihr boten, gewiß jetzt um so mehr vermissen, da sie nach Wechsel ihrer Stellung in ein hocharistokratisches Haus in London, wo dergleichen nicht zu Hause ist, in das des Herzog's von Somerset als Gouvernante eingetreten ist.[46] Sie hat uns kürzlich einen Brief nicht ohne Interesse über ihren Eintritt darin geschrieben, und schreibt Ihnen auch noch selbst einmal darüber, (3) da es sie wie ich weiß glücklich macht, die Verbindung mit Ihrem Hause fortzuerhalten.[47] Um Ihnen auch ein paar Worte von uns zu sagen, so sind wir eben im Begriffe, nach Interlaken in der Schweiz zu gehen, hauptsächlich damit meine Frau die Molkencur daselbst wegen eines Halsleidens gebrauche was sie sich durch zu vieles Vorlesen zugezogen; eine Besserung für den sehr geschwächten und mich wieder ganz zur Unthätigkeit verurtheilenden Zustand meiner Augen wage ich freilich nicht von diesem Aufenthalte zu hoffen.[48] Gewiß wählen Sie selbst jedes Jahr einen andern schönen Sommer-

---

45 Vgl. Fechner Tagebuch 1864, Bl. 303 und 1869 Bl. 55 (Hs.).

46 Gemeint ist Malwine Kuntze, Tochter von Emilie Fechner verw. Kuntze.

47 Vgl. Brief von Malwine Kuntze: Fechner Tagebuch 1862, Bl. 289–293 (Hs.).

48 Die Reise nach Interlaken kam zustande (14.8.- 8.9. 1862). Fechner fuhr von Leipzig aus über Köln, Heidelberg, Basel nach Interlaken, zusammen mit seiner Frau, dem Schwager Alfred Volkmann und dessen Sohn Wilhelm. Adele und Anna Volkmann, Pauline und Karl Hase waren schon vorausgegangen. Härtels sowie Richard Volkmann

aufenthalt; sollten wir Sie nicht zufällig dort treffen können; viel lieber würde ich dann mündlich die Unterhaltung mit Ihnen fortsetzen, die mir schriftlich wie ich gestehe sehr unbequem wird, da ich mich der fremden Feder dazu bedienen muß. Lassen Sie mich also noch mit dem Danke für das, so hübsche Einfälle enthaltende, Märchen was Sie so freundlich waren, meiner Nichte für uns mitzugeben, und mit der Bitte meine Bitte durch mein Vertrauen zu Ihnen zu entschuldigen schließen. Meine Frau grüßt Sie herzlich und Ihrerseits bitte ich Sie mich Ihrem Herrn Gemahl bestens zu empfehlen.

Mit freundschaftlicher Hochachtung

der Ihrige
Prof. G. Th. Fechner

Leipzig, d. 14 Aug. 1862

13. Brief vom 7. Oktober 1864 (4 Blatt) an Gisela Grimm; Autograph: Hess. Staatsarchiv Marburg, Bestand 340 (Grimm):

Leipzig, d. 7. Oct. [18]64

Verehrteste Freundin,

Ich war immer gewohnt, Ihrer Frau Mutter meine neu erschienenen kleinen Schriften zuzuschicken, falls sie nicht ein blos gelehrtes Interesse in Anspruch nahmen, da ich einer freundlichen Aufnahme derselben sicher war, und gern die dadurch gebotene Gelegenheit benutzte, die Beziehung, in die sie uns gestattete, zu ihr zu treten, fortzuerhalten, die uns bei ihrem Leben so lieb war, und sich nach ihrem Hingange immer mehr verklärte. Gern trage ich diese Gewohnheit auf Sie über, die Sie die Freundlichkeit Ihrer Mutter auf uns übertragen haben, und meine, indem ich es thue, in der Beziehung zu Ihnen auch (2) die Beziehung zu ihr noch ferner fortzuerhalten, deren Tochter und Erbin Sie ja in mehr als einer Hinsicht sind. Das Räthselbüchlein habe ich Ihrer Frau Mutter wohl schon früher geschickt; die eben erschienene neue Auflage desselben findet bei seiner Kleinheit wohl noch ein Plätzchen in Ihrer Bibliothek.[49] Die »Motive« hatte ich Ihnen schon früher geschickt, aber Sie waren gerade in Italien, als das Büchlein erschien;[50] zudem leben Sie so ganz im Element der Poesie und die Schrift lebt so gar nicht darin! Auch scheint sie beim Publicum noch leichter vergessen als bekannt worden zu sein; indeß weiß sich ein Philosoph immer zu trösten, und we-

kamen später dazu. Insgesamt waren vierzehn Familienmitglieder zusammengekommen. Vgl. Fechners Reisebericht im Tagebuch 1862 Bl. 46–71 (Hs.).

49 Gemeint ist die 3. verm. Aufl. des »Räthselbüchleins« (1865), dass unter dem Pseudonym Dr. Mises erschien.

50 G. Th. Fechner: Die drei Motive und Gründe des Glaubens. Leipzig 1863.

nigstens hierin bin ich Philosoph genug. (3) Als Gegenstück dazu muß ich Ihnen doch eine Stelle aus einem Briefe abschreiben, den meine Frau neulich von ihrem Bruder, Prof. Volkmann in Halle, empfieng, da ich nicht zweifle, daß Sie als eine gute Frau Theil an den Erfolgen Ihres Mannes nehmen und sich des Beifalls freuen, den seine Werke finden. Mein Schwager ist ein Mann von Geschmack, und wenn ich es Ihnen nicht sagte, würden Sie es gewiß aus seiner Anerkenntniß eines, unstreitig noch mehr als blos geschmackvollen, Werkes schließen:[51] »Wir haben angefangen, Grimm's Werk über Michel Angelo zu lesen und sind ganz voll davon.[52] Nach den ersten Abschnitten zu urtheilen ist Stoff und Darstellung gleich prächtig.«

Ich selbst muß nun zu meiner Schande gestehen, daß ich das Werk noch nicht gelesen habe. Aber ich kann überhaupt wegen des Zustandes meiner Augen nichts in größerem (4) Zusammenhange selbst lesen; meine Frau kann wegen des Zustandes ihrer Stimme nicht vorlesen und mit dem Gebrauche fremder Augen und Stimmen muß ich sparen; so bleibt vieles Gute und Schöne ungelesen oder im Rückstand. Aber es muß doch einmal Zeit dazu werden, ein nach Stoff und Form gleich prächtiges Werk zu lesen; zumal mir ästhetische Interessen doch nicht fremd sind.

Wie man Jemanden eine Lectüre empfiehlt, empfiehlt man auch wohl einen Ort zum Ausfluge. Wir haben bei unserm jährlichen Ferienausfluge überall Berliner in Menge nur Sie nirgens getroffen. Wo mögen Sie immer gewesen sein? Sollten Sie sich einmal nach Thüringen wenden wollen, so können wir Ihnen Elgersburg empfehlen, gewiß der reizendst gelegene Ort Thüringens mit vortrefflicher Wald- und Bergluft, wo man noch ländlich leben und vergessen kann, daß es Staub giebt. Wir haben dießmal mit Weiße's einen Monat sehr gemüthlich da zugebracht.[53]

Meine Nichte Malwine ist mit ihrer Mutter und Schwester nach Dresden gezogen, um eine Pensionsanstalt zu etabliren; mein Neffe Emil wohnt noch bei uns.[54]

---

[51] Gemeint ist der Physiologe Alfred Volkmann (1801–1877); lebte seit 1843 in Halle.

[52] Grimms Werk »Das Leben Michelangelo« in 2 Bdn. (1860/63) erlebte 1922 die 19. Auflage.

[53] Christian Hermann Weiße (1801–1866), Philosoph, seit 1828 a.o. Professor an der Universität Leipzig; er zog sich 1837 auf mehrere Jahre von der akademischen Tätigkeit zurück und beschäftigte sich mit philosophischen Studien; wurde 1845 zum ordentlichen Professor berufen; Enkel des Dichters Christian Felix Weiße, Erbe des Rittergutes Stötteritz bei Leipzig (1910 eingemeindet).

[54] Emil und Malwine sind die Kinder von Fechners Schwester Emilie verw. Kuntze. Emil Kuntze (1824–1894), Jurist, seit 1856 Professor an der Leipziger Universität, lebte insgesamt 35 Jahre im Fechner'schen Haushalt; er war einer der kontinuierlichsten Vorleser Fechners und ein wichtiger Gesprächspartner in Sachen Literatur, Philosophie und Recht (vgl. Fechner Tagebuch 1862 Bl. 27–40; 1866, Bl. 140 (Hs.).

Wären sie eben gegenwärtig, würden sie mir gewiß die herzlichsten Grüße an Sie auftragen, da sie sich der freundlichen Aufnahme, die sie bei Ihnen gefunden, so gern erinnern. Jedenfalls die beßten Grüße von meiner Frau. Mit der Bitte, mich Ihrem Herrn Gemahl zu empfehlen

der Ihrige
Fechner.

Hermann Grimm und seine Frau Gisela besuchten Fechner am 19. Juni 1865 in seiner Wohnung in der Dresdner Straße. Fechner reflektiert darüber in seinem Tagebuch:

»Doch hatten wir heute Abend einen Besuch von Berlin, den wir nicht wohl ablehnen konnten und nicht gern abgelehnt hätten, nämlich von Hermann Grimm und seiner Frau. Ihn kannte ich noch nicht persönlich, sondern nur aus der Lectüre seines »Michel-Angelo«, die ich vor nicht langer Zeit mit meinem Vorleser v. Lindgreen beendigt hatte.[55] Sie hatte ich das letztemal vor Jahren gesehen, als sie mit ihrer Mutter Bettine und dem Klavier-Virtuosen v. Bülow einen Sylvesterabend bei uns zubrachte und seitdem nur im Schriftenwechsel mit ihr gestanden.[56] Sie selbst ist mir freilich viel lieber als ihre Trauerspiele; und da ich ihr nichts Willkommenes darüber sagen konnte, sprach ich gar nicht davon. An ihrer natürlichen Liebenswürdigkeit haben wir uns wieder sehr erfreut. [...] Er gehört zu den, sich über das gewöhnliche Literatenthum erhebenden, Berliner Autoren, die ich als Vertreter einer, mit Geist dem Kern der Dinge nachstrebenden, Richtung gern anerkenne, ohne zu ihrer etwas selbstbewußten, gesellschaftlich geriebenen, Persönlichkeit einen besondern Zug zu empfinden. Auch kam ich mit ihm in keinen recht nachhaltigen Fluß des Gesprächs, und hauptsächlich führte Weiße, den ich dazu eingeladen, die Unterhaltung mit ihm« (Tagebuch 1865, Bl. 126–128 (Hs.).

Wenn auch Fechner mit Hermann Grimm nicht in ein flüssiges Gespräch kam, boten dessen Schriften ihm dennoch reichlich geistige Berührungspunkte. Fechner und Grimm waren durch kunsthistorische Fragen verbunden (vgl. Brief 14 und 15).

---

[55] Der Vorleser v. Lindgreen ist im »Biographischen Index« nicht verzeichnet.

[56] Hans von Bülow (1830–1894), Pianist und Dirigent, erhielt seinen ersten Klavierunterricht bei Friedrich Wieck (Fechners Schwager); war ein Schüler von Richard Wagner und Franz Liszt; infolge seiner engen Verbindung zu Wagner wurde er u.a. zum Bahnbrecher für die Wagner'sche Musik (vgl. Ehrlich 1898, 56–61).

14. Brief vom 5. August 1867 (2 Blatt) an Hermann Grimm, Kunst- und Literaturhistoriker, Professor für Kunstgeschichte an der Universität Berlin; Autograph: Hess. Staatsarchiv Marburg, Bestand 340 Grimm:

Leipzig, d. 5. Aug. [18]67

Verehrtester Freund,

Herr Dr. v. Zahn hat seine Mittheilung über die betreffende Inschrift nebst Zeichnung derselben Herrn His-Heusler zur Publication übergeben, erklärt aber, nicht zu wissen, wann dieselbe erfolgen wird.[57] Inzwischen wird er seine Beistimmung zu Ihrer Ansicht über die Inschrift mit Bezugnahme auf seine Autopsie derselben (2) in einer demnächst erscheinenden Recension Ihres Schriftchens im liter. Centralblatt aussprechen. Mit freundlichsten Grüßen an die Ihrige.

Ihr ergebenster
Fechner.

Meine Frau hat sich so eben an dem Tongemuschel der Gletscherstille höchlichst amüsirt.

Es geht um Grimms kleine Schrift »Holbein's Geburtsjahr, kritische Beleuchtung der von den neuesten Biographen Holbeins gefundenen Resultate« (1867), rezensiert im »Literarischen Centralblatt« 1867 von dem Kunsthistoriker Albert von Zahn, Kustos des Städtischen Museum in Leipzig, den Fechner persönlich aus seinen Kontakten zum Museum und auch aus Zusammenkünften im Rittergut Weißes in Stötteritz kannte.

15. Brief vom 18. Juni 1872 (3Bl.) an Hermann Grimm; Autograph: Hess. Staatsarchiv Marburg, Bestand 340 (Grimm):

Leipzig, d. 18. Juni [18]72

Geehrtester Herr Doctor,

Es ist zwar sonst nicht eben Stil, daß sich Autoren für Werke, die sie sich wechselseits zuschicken, bedanken, und Manchem möchte der Dank für manche Zusendung ziemlich sauer werden, wenn er nicht humboldtsche Leichtigkeit darin besitzt. Indessen machen doch bedeutende Werke, für die man sich gern bedankt, eine Ausnahme, und so nehmen auch sie meinen beßten Dank (2) für die Zusendung eines Werkes, das, wenn es nicht von Ihnen selbst herrührte, es schwer genug finden würde, das Interesse und den Gehalt des vorausgegangenen Pararell-

---

[57] Eduard His-Heusler (1820–1905), Kunsthistoriker, Fachautor, Seidenbandfabrikant.

werkes zu erreichen. Bis jetzt hat sich erst meine Frau darin vertieft, denn meine Augen sind schlecht geworden, daß ich auf jede zusammenhängende Lectüre verzichten muß und dieselben wahrscheinlich im Herbst einer (3) Operation unterziehen werde; mein Vorleser ist mir aber eben abhanden gekommen; ich freue mich aber auf die Lectüre, wenn ich derselben wieder mächtig sein werde. Mit der Bitte, Ihre Frau Gemalin freundlichst zu grüßen hochachtungsvoll und ergebenst

der Ihrige
Fechner

Fechner bedankt sich im Brief für Grimms Buch »Das Leben Raphaels von Urbino« (1872). Als Parallelwerk ist Grimms Roman »Das Leben Michelangelos« (1860/63) gemeint, dass 1922 die 19. Auflage erlebte.

Mit der *Rezension* des Buches durch den Kunsthistoriker Anton Springer war Fechner nicht einverstanden. Sie erschien ihm »unbillig hart«, da Springer »nur« das hervorhob, »was er an dem Grimmschen Werke auszusetzen« fand. Der vom Rezensenten erhobene Vorwurf »literarischer Unredlichkeit« trage »den Charakter der Gehässigkeit« und schade »Springer'n selbst«; »von ein paar einzelnen Ungenauigkeiten, welche Grimm begangen« habe, »hätte Springer nicht so viel Wesens zu machen brauchen«, [...] »da es in einem Werke, welches unzählige Einzelnheiten zu verarbeiten« habe, »nie an solchen ganz fehlen« werde (Fechner Tagebuch 1873, Bl. 21). Springer missfiel, »daß Grimm das von ihm [Grimm] selbst als ganz unzuverlässig erklärte Leben Raphaels von Vasari als Faden für die Betrachtung der Werke und der gesammten Geschichte Raphaels« (ebda., Bl 21- 22) benutzt habe.[58] Er war der Meinung: »Raphael lebe für uns in seinen Werken und es wäre besser gewesen, wenn Grimm sich an diese [die Werke Raphaels] gehalten und den Faden der Betrachtung darin gesucht hätte« (ebda., Bl. 22).

Fechner erschien dagegen der »Plan von Grimm's Werk ein glücklicher«, da es für das Leben Raphaels keine andere »zusammenhängende Quelle als Vasari« gebe. Auch wenn sie »ungenau« sei, fände man sie »überall zu Grunde gelegt« (ebda., Bl. 22). Er stimmte auch dem Urteil Springers, mit dem dieser seine Rezension schließt, nicht zu: »Grimm hätte besser vorbereitet an seine Arbeit gehen sollen« (ebda., Bl 23). Nach Fechner war das Gegenteil der Fall: Er habe nicht nur »alles irgend belangreiche, was früher über Raphael geschrieben worden ist«, studiert, »sondern auch Alles, was von zerstreuten Notizen über Raphael vorliegt,

---

[58] Gemeint ist Giorgios Vasaris Schrift »Künstler der Renaissance« in 2 Bdn. von 1550.

gesammelt, mit Vasari und unter einander verglichen, sondern auch von den Handzeichnungen und Bildern Raphaels sich eine möglichst vollständige Kenntniß erworben, dazu auch auf die Vorgänger und Zeitgenossen Raphaels, welche etwa auf seine Kunstweise im Allgemeinen oder bestimmte Werke im Besondern Einfluß geübt haben konnten, die eingehendste Rücksicht genommen« (ebda., Bl. 23–24). Grimm habe das »ganze Material, was bei der Construction von Raphaels Leben und Genesis seiner Werke in Betracht« kam, manchmal in seinem Buche zu sehr ausgebreitet, es »nach verschiedenen Richtungen« diskutiert und die Möglichkeit gegeben, »sich selbst ein eigenes Urtheil zu bilden«. Daraus folgert Fechner, dass »die Grimmsche Arbeit immer einen erheblichen Werth« behalten werde, »der von Springer wohl hätte anerkannt werden« (ebda. Bl. 24) können. Die Tatsache, dass Grimms »Leben Raphaels« 1972 die 6. Auflage erlebte, spricht dafür.

16. Brief vom 6. Juli 1849 (4 Bl.) an Unbekannt;[59] Autograph: Bibliothek des Deutschen Museums München, Signatur: HS 1953–15:

Leipzig, d. 6. Juli [18]49

Geehrtester Herr,

Für das Zutrauen, was Sie mir durch Ihr Schreiben und die Zusendung Ihres Mährchens beweisen, sage ich Ihnen meinen beßten Dank, und ich wünschte nur, daß ich im Stande wäre, demselben auf eine für Sie selbst befriedigendere Weise zu entsprechen. Ihr Mährchen ist in einem sehr reichen und blühenden Style geschrieben, ja der eine gewisse berauschende Kraft hat; aber da Sie Offenheit von mir verlangen und ich mir dieselbe allerdings zur Pflicht mache, so kann ich nicht umhin, Ihnen zu gestehen, daß meine Aufmerksamkeit bei jeder lang durchgeführten Allegorie dermaßen erschlafft, daß ich nicht im Stande bin, derselben achtsam bis aufs Ende zu folgen und die Schönheiten (2) derselben in dem Maße zu würdigen, als es von Andern geschehen mag, die in dieser Beziehung anders gestimmt sind. Obschon ich in der That besorge, daß diese Abneigung allgemeiner ist, als für die günstige Aufnahme Ihres Mährchens erwünscht seyn kann. Indeß soll es mir lieb seyn, wenn Sie diesen Bemerkungen so wenig Gewicht als möglich beilegen. Ich bin ein viel trocknerer Physiker, als Sie vielleicht nach einigen Anläufen, die ich in Richtung der Poesie genommen, und wobei es doch nicht leicht allein auf Poesie abgesehen war, meinen, dessenungeachtet ist es mir bei meiner

---

[59] Verfasser eines Märchens.

Nanna begegnet,[60] nachdem ich glaubte, ich hätte Manches recht Ueberzeugende (3) darin gesagt, daß die Männer vom Fach sagten: »recht schön, es sind ganz gemüthliche Phantasieen, aber was ist damit bewiesen!« Sollte es Ihnen nicht mit Ihrem Mährchen eben so gehen? Freilich, es ist nicht für Männer vom Fach geschrieben. Aber wer blos Poesie will, will sie nun eben nicht leicht in Form einer gebundenen Allegorie. Doch, wie gesagt, halten Sie mein Urtheil in dieser Beziehung nicht maßgebend, da ich mir hier überhaupt kein Urtheil anmaße. Sie werden Andre finden, die in dieser Hinsicht andern Sinnes sind. Um Ihrem Wunsche zu entsprechen, habe ich Ihr Manuskript der Härtelschen und Voßschen Buchhandlung vorgelegt, den einzigen, mit denen ich in näherer (4) Verbindung stehe, und wenn dieselben Bedenken getragen, auf den Verlag desselben einzugehen, so schreiben Sie es wenigstens keiner ähnlichen Offenheit zu, als ich Ihnen schuldig zu seyn glaubte, da ich denselben das Manuskript zu ganz freien eignen Beurtheilung übersandt. Zugleich wird dieß die Verzögerung der Rücksendung entschuldigen. Es sollte mir sehr leid thun, wenn nach den so freundlichen Aeußerungen, die Sie gegen mich gethan, dieser Brief beitragen könnte, Ihr Wohlwollen gegen mich zu vermindern. Seyn Sie jedenfalls überzeugt, daß ich nicht unempfindlich dafür bin, und daß, wenn es blos auf meinen Wunsch ankäme, mir dasselbe erhalten zu können, es gewiß der Fall seyn würde.

Hochachtungsvoll
der Ihrige
Fechner.

Der Verfassers des Märchens ist Ed. Ferdinand Hauschild.[61] Fechner kommt mit der im Brief genannten Schrift einige Jahre später durch seine *Rezensententätigkeit* am »Literarischen Centralblatt« nochmals in Berührung (vgl. Brief 17).

17. Brief, vermutlich aus dem Jahr 1852 bzw. 1853 (2 Bl.), an Friedrich Zarncke, Begründer und Herausgeber des »Literarischen Centralblattes«, seit 1854 Professor der deutschen Sprache und Literatur an der Universität in Leipzig; Autograph: Universitätsbibliothek Leipzig, Nachlass 249:

Herrn Dr. Zarncke, Wohlgeb. [ohne Ort, ohne Datum]

Lange ist mir nichts so possierlich Abgeschmacktes vorgekommen, als das kleine Schriftchen von Hauschild, doch dauert mich der Verf. (der mir schon vor einem

60 Gemeint ist Fechners Schrift »Nanna oder Ueber das Seeleben der Pflanzen« (Leipzig 1848).

61 Der Vorname Hauschilds ist nicht vollständig auflösbar.

Jahre sein Manuscript einmal zugeschickt hat), da an seiner Einbildung, etwas Wunderschönes geschrieben zu haben, sein Glück zu hängen scheint. Versuchsweise habe ich daher die Anzeige so eingerichtet, daß ich mir denke, es kann höchstens ein leiser heilsamer Zweifel in ihm entstehen, ob man ihn nicht ironisch behandle, während der Unbefangene dieß nach den mitgetheilten Proben sofort übersehen wird. Ich habe aber auch gar nichts dagegen, wenn Sie die ganze Anzeige oder die letzten Sätze (über die Nase) unterdrücken; die Länge derselben kann natürlich blos durch das Amüsante, was die mitgetheilten Proben darbieten, motivirt seyn. Auch die Anzeige von Drossbach ist in Verhältniß zur Bedeutung des Schriftchens etwas lang gerathen; doch ließ sie sich nicht wohl kürzer einrichten, falls wirklich der, immerhin in eine originelle Ansicht auslaufender Gedankengang desselben dargelegt werden sollte; (2) und gerade in diesem Gebiete giebt es so wenig des Originalen.[62] Doch wäre ich auch gern erbötig, falls Ihnen die Anzeige zu viel Raum wegnehmen sollte, dieselbe blos auf ein allgemeines Urtheil zusammen zuziehen. – Unter einem größern Haufen Schriften, die ich durch Avenarius bekommen habe, finde ich auch »Perthy[,] über die Bedeutung der Anthropologie«, kann mich aber nicht mehr erinnern, ob sie mir zur Anzeige für Ihr Centralblatt oder zur Benutzung für meins zu geschickt worden ist, und bitte ergebenst darüber um eine Notiz.

Fechner.

[von fremder Hand]

Obiges Schriftchen von Perthy ist dem Herrn Prof. uns in der Erwartung geschickt worden, daß er es schnell zurückgeben werde, noch bevor Sie wieder etwas verschickten.

Es grüßt
Av. M.[63]

Hauschilds Schrift hatte den Titel »Psyche, oder der Becher Giamschids. Ein persisches Märchen« (Muskau 1852). Fechner übernahm ein Jahr später, trotz seiner kritischen Haltung, die *Rezension* des »Schriftchens« im »Literarischen Centralblatt«. Er leitet diese wie folgt ein:

Der Vf. schildert in einer sorgfältigst durchgeführten, höchst bilderreichen Allegorie, im blühendsten Style, mit den originellsten Wendungen, in der Form eines persischen Mythus (doch so, daß das Ganze in der That sein geistiges Eigenthum ist) das Verhältniß der Seele zum Körper [...] zu einander (Fechner 1853, 427).

---

[62] Vgl. Fechners Rezension der Schrift von Drossbach: Die individuelle Unsterblichkeit. Im: Literarischen Centralblatt 1853, 426–427.

[63] Eduard Avenarius gründete 1853 in Leipzig mit Hermann Mendelsohn ein Verlagsgeschäft unter der Fa. Av. und M. Von Georg Wiegand erwarben sie u.a. die Verlagsrechte des »Literarischen Centralblattes«, hg. von Zarncke.

Fechner zitiert dann den Verfasser an einigen Stellen, bemerkt, dass es unmöglich sein würde, »den reichen Schmuck und kühnen Schwung dieses Schriftchens in einzelnen Proben wiederzugeben«, richtet an den Verfasser die Frage, warum er bei seinen »auf alle Einzelnheiten eingehenden Schilderungen [...] des menschlichen Antlitzes die Nase ganz übergangen« habe, die nach seinem »Dafürhalten diese poetische Vernachlässigung schwerlich verdient«; er gibt dem Verfasser letztlich zu bedenken: »ein Gesicht ohne Nase!« (Fechner 1853, 428). Hauschild blieb als Literat unbekannt, obwohl sein Märchen 1853 eine zweite Auflage erlebte.

18. Brief vom 13. September 1855 (5 Bl.) an Unbekannt;[64] Autograph: Universitätsbibliothek Leipzig, Nachlass 249 (Zarncke):

Leipzig, d. 13. Sept. [18]55

Hochgeehrter Herr,

Es thut mir aufrichtig leid, daß ich nicht mehr im Stande bin, meine bisherige Thätikgeit für das Centralblatt fortzusetzen. Ich habe mich derselben nicht ungern unterzogen und namentlich ist es mir erwünscht gewesen, dadurch *au courant* der Literatur zu bleiben.[65] Aber meine Augen haben sich fortgehends verschlechtert; ich sehe voraus, daß es bald ganz aus mit dem Gebrauche derselben seyn wird, und muß das, was noch von Gebrauchsfähigkeit übrig ist, auf das Aeußerste sparen, um wo möglich noch ein paar Schriften, mit deren Abfassung ich beschäftigt bin, zu Stande zu bringen und das nöthige Material dazu einzusehen. Am Schreiben bin ich noch nicht gehindert, aber ich kann nur satzweis und unterbrochen lesen und verderbe mir dabei noch einmal über das andre die Augen so, daß ich sie tage- und wochenlang ganz außer Thätigkeit setzen muß. Die Anzeigen für das Centralblatt erfodert eine schnelle Durchsicht und ein (2) rasches Hin- und Herblicken, um das Wesentliche herauszufinden; nichts aber strengt gerade meine Augen mehr an als diese Gebrauchsweise desselben. Mit Vorlesen ist hier wenig auszurichten, es födert für den Zweck solcher Anzeigen viel zu wenig, und ist auch für andere Zwecke in Anspruch genommen. Ich wünschte Herrn Prof. Zarncke einige Vertreter für die Fächer, die mir bisher hauptsächlich übertragen worden sind, vorschlagen zu können, und erlaube mir in dieser Hinsicht nur einige ganz unmaßgebliche Bemerkungen. Ich würde meinen, daß Prof. Weiße in Stötteritz und Prof. Schaller in Halle das Meiste davon wohl decken könnten. Zwar bin (3) ich selbst in philosophischen Dingen ganz entgegengesetzter Ansicht

---

[64] Vermutlich an einen Mitarbeiter der Redaktion des »Literarischen Centralblattes« (Hg. Friedrich Zarncke).

[65] au courant (franz.): auf dem Laufenden.

als beide; aber hierauf kommt nichts an; in diesen Dingen ist ja überhaupt Niemand derselben Ansicht als der andre. Prof. Weiße ist ein sehr gewissenhafter, sehr gründlicher Beurtheiler von den umfassendsten literarischen und historischen Kenntnissen, in welcher Beziehung ich ihm nicht das Wasser reiche.[66] Nun ist zwar das streng philosophische Fach im Centralblatt schon vertreten, aber auch Schriften über Psychologie, über die allgemeine Beziehung von Leib und Seele, über die Unsterblichkeitsfrage würden ganz in sein Bereich passen. Das einzige Bedenken könnte seyn, daß es ihm vielleicht nicht immer ganz leicht werden wird, sich in den Gränzen der, für das Centralblatt gefoderten, Kürze zu halten; indeß ist er zu (4) einsichtig, um nicht den Foderungen der Verhältnisse Rechnung zu tragen. Prof. Schaller anlangend, so ist derselbe Naturphilosoph von Fach, und hat sich namentlich in letzter Zeit ernsthafter mit den Naturwissenschaften beschäftigt. Alles, was auf der Gränze zwischen Philosophie und Naturwissenschaft liegt, dürfte daher in sein Bereich gehören; auch der Beurtheilung populär naturwissenschaftlicher Schriften möchte er wohl gewachsen seyn. – Ich selbst würde, wie es jetzt mit mir steht; in der That nur die alleroberflächlichsten Anzeigen nach dem, was mir gerade auffällt, wenn ich einmal hier und da in ein Buch sehe, zu liefern im Stande seyn, was natürlich weder Sie noch ich wollen können. So sehr ungern es (5) geschieht, befinde ich mich daher doch in der einfachen Nothwendigkeit, Ihnen die übersandten Bücher wieder zurückzustellen, und habe mir zwei kleine Schriften (Richers und Frauenstädt) zurückbehalten, in der Absicht, Ihnen wenigstens den guten Willen zu beweisen, die Verbindung mit dem Centralblatt fortzuerhalten. Sollte sich wieder Erwarten der Zustand meiner Augen bessern, so werde ich der Erste seyn, meine Thätigkeit dafür wieder anzubieten. Mit der Bitte, mich Hrn. Prof. Zarncke zu empfehlen, und in der Hoffnung, daß Sie meine Motive so nehmen werden, wie sie sind, hochachtungsvoll und ergebenst

der Ihrige
Fechner.

Im Nachlass Zarnckes befinden sich insgesamt dreizehn Briefe Fechners; sie enthalten Mitteilungen bezüglich seiner *Rezensententätigkeit* am »Literarischen Centralblatt« in der Zeit von 1850 bis 1855. Von Bedeutung sind diese Briefe durchaus, da aus ihnen ersichtlich wird, dass Fechner durch seine Rezensententätigkeit am »Literarischen Centralblatt« wesentliche Impulse für seine schöpferische Arbeit erhielt. So rezensierte er 1854 Adolf Zeisings Schrift die »Neue Lehre von den Proportionen des menschlichen Körpers«. Die Hauptidee von Zeisings Schrift – das Verhältnis des »goldenen Schnittes« stelle das »architectonische Princip der

[66] Vgl. Anmerkung 40; Fechner war mit Christian Hermann Weiße seit 1824 befreundet; vgl. Fechner 1866.

Schönheit« dar – veranlasste bekanntlich Fechner, dessen Lehre experimentell zu bestätigen.[67] In seinem Tagebuch äußert sich Fechner sehr knapp zu diesem Thema. Es heißt dort, dass Zeising »bis zu gewissen Gränzen Recht, darüber hinaus Unrecht hat« (Tagebuch 1865, Bl. 18) und dass er »solchen Verhältnissen überhaupt nur eine sehr untergeordnete Bedeutung für das Zustandekommen der Schönheit« beilege. Die Hauptsache schien Fechner »in der Association der Bedeutung zu liegen« (ebda., Bl. 18).

19. Briefkonzept vom 2. Juli 1879 (3 Blatt) an Adelaide von Gottberg, Schriftstellerin; Autograph: Universitätsbibliothek Leipzig, Nachlass 42.2:

An Fr. v. Gottberg 2. Juli [18]79

Verehrtes Fräulein,

Beßten Dank dafür, die Freundlichkeit die Sie gehabt haben, einen Wunsch, den ich gegen meine Schwester Clementine in Betreff Ihrer Lieder aussprach, mit eigner Hand zu erfüllen, und schon eher würde ich Ihnen diesen Dank gebracht haben, wenn mich Ihre liebliche Sendung nicht gerade in eine trockne mathematische Untersuchung verwickelt gefunden hätte, die natürlich eine Einmischung von Poesie nicht verträgt, also vor Wendung dazu erst fertig gestellt sein wollte. Nun aber darf eine junge Dichterin von einem 78jährigen Gelehrten, der sich mit Dingen jener Art beschäftigt, überhaupt keine Kritik ihrer Lieder verlangen, das wäre, wie wenn ein Schmetterling, der sich seines eignen Fluges oder eine Blume, die sich ihres eignen Blühens erfreut, freiwillig in eine Hand geben wollten, in der ihre bunten Flügel oder Blätter die Gefahr des (2) Rupfens oder Ausrupfens unterlägen. Die beßte Kritik bleibt da die, welche Ihre Lieder schon erfahren haben, daß sie andre junge Herzen erfreut, erbaut und für die Dichterin selbst begeistert haben. Und auch ich mit meinem alten Herzen bin nicht unempfänglich geblieben für den Ausdruck inniger Empfindung, in dem reizenden Flusse Ihrer Lieder, möchte ich schon zweifeln, ob in einer so prosaischen und auf starke und wechselnde Erregungen erpichten Zeit, wie der jetzigen, der durchgehends zarte und gleichförmige Charakter der Lieder einer allgemeinern (3) Empfänglichkeit des Publicum[s] begegnen wird; denn Ihre ganze Gedichtsammlung ist so zu sagen nur Ein Gedicht. Nach meiner Altersstimmung vielmehr, als vergleichender Werthschätzung, die überhaupt in diesen Dingen möglich ist, möchte ich mir am liebsten etwa no. 4 (Ein Regen ist niedergefallen), no. 11 (Wann ich sterben möch-

[67] Vgl. Rezension der Schrift von A. Zeising durch Fechner in: Zarncke 1854, 555.

te), no. 12 (Vergessen) und no. 14 (Deingedenken), aneignen; aber Sie gestatten mir wohl, wenn Sie es nicht zu unbescheiden finden, die ganze Sammlung zurückzubehalten. Da ich Ihnen ein Blatt für Ihr Album schicken soll, lege ich, um es weder mit etwas Philosophischem noch Mathematischem zu belästigen, eine Kleinigkeit, frei nach Anakreon, bei. Meine Photographie schickte ich Ihnen lieber nicht, sie sieht so böse aus, ich bin aber nicht so. Bitte, meine Schwester zu grüßen, wenn Sie sie sehen, und Ihnen selbst, für die Freude, die Sie mir gemacht haben, den freundlichsten Gruß von

Ihrem ergebensten
Fechner.

Adelaide von Gottberg, geboren 1850, lebte seit 1872 in Dresden. Sie ließ ihre Sopranstimme bei Friedrich Wieck (Fechners Schwager) und später bei Marie Wieck ausbilden.[68] Die ersten Gedichte von Gottberg erschienen 1873 im »Pantheon«; sie übernimmt 1891 die Redaktion der »Dresdner Frauenzeitung«; 1895 wird sie alleinige Eigentümerin und Leiterin der Zeitung.[69]Gottberg – eine Verehrerin Fechners – kannte ihn aus seinen Schriften. Das geht aus ihrem Brief an Fechner hervor: »Mit höchstem Interesse habe ich durch Frau Wieck verschiedene Ihrer geistvollen Schriften kennengelernt, mir viele der Schriften, Räthsel, ja aus dem schönen Buch »Nanna«, (Seelenleben der Pflanzen) da ich die Blumen so liebe, viele viele Seiten abgeschrieben«.[70]

Fechner wurde auf sie durch seine Schwester Clementine Wieck aufmerksam, die – 1879 zu seinem Geburtstag in Leipzig weilend – von ihrer Bekannten, Fräulein von Gottberg, erzählte, »daß dieselbe Gedichte in allerlei Zeitungen gesetzt und damit außerordentlichen Beifall geerntet, ja in Folge dessen außer schmeichelhaftesten Zuschriften von verschiedensten Seiten sogar Heiratsanträge von jungen Leuten erhalten habe. Mit einem sei es sogar wirklich zur Verlobung gekommen, die jedoch später wieder zurückgegangen sei« (Fechner Tagebuch 1879, Bl. 63f.). Daraufhin äußerte Fechner gegenüber der Schwester den Wunsch, dass sie ihm »einmal von diesem Phönix der Poesie ein paar der hübschesten Gedichte zu kommen lassen« solle, worauf Adelaide von Gottberg ihm 26 Gedich-

---

[68] Marie Wieck (1832–1916), Pianistin, Konzertsängerin, Tochter von Friedrich Wieck aus zweiter Ehe mit Clementine Fechner, Schülerin ihres Vaters, trat bereits als Elfjährige öffentlich mit ihrer Halbschwester Clara auf; spielte in vielen europäischen Städten; lebte danach als Klavier- und Gesangslehrerin in Dresden, erhielt 1914 den Professorentitel verliehen; vgl. Ehrlich 1898, 372–373, 326–329.

[69] Pataky 1898, 1, 274–275.

[70] Vgl. Brief, Gottberg an Fechner, 19.6. 1879, UB Leipzig, Nachlass 42.2 (Hs.).

te zur Beurteilung übersandte. Fechner konnte »nicht viel an den Gedichten finden«; er stellte »einen leichten Fluß des Verses und einen Ausdruck zarter Empfindung« fest und notiert in sein Tagebuch:

Große Verlegenheit, in dem dankenden Antwortschreiben die Worte recht zu setzen, um weder unartig noch unwahr zu sein. (1879, Bl. 63)

Adelaide von Gottberg war erfreut, dass Fechner »einen so gütigen, der jungen Dichterin so nachsichtig kritisierenden Brief sandte« und erwiderte ihm:

Ich glaube gern, daß Ihnen alle die doch durchgängig lyrischen Ergüsse ein wenig einförmig vorgekommen sind, es ist anders, wenn man sie zu verschiedenen Zeiten in Journalen verstreut findet. [...] Ihr freundliches Uhrteil macht mich glücklich und da ich Ihnen meinen Dank doch nicht mündlich aussprechen kann, so will ich mich Ihnen wenigstens persönlich im Bilde vorstellen, (das eben gemacht wurde) in der Hoffnung, daß es gütige Aufnahme findet. (Brief, Gottberg an Fechner, 8.7. 1879, UB Leipzig)

Das Foto der jungen Adelaide von Gottberg befindet sich im Nachlass Fechners.

Literatur und Quellen:

ADB (1885): Allgemeine Deutsche Biographie. Hg. von Hist. Com. d. Akademie der Wiss. Bd. 21, 22, 24. Leipzig.

Arendt, H.-J. (1992): Gustav Theodor Fechner und sein Hauslexikon. 1834- 1838. Ein Beitrag zur Fechner-Biographie und zur Geschichte der enzyklopädischen Literatur in Deutschland. Hg. von der Fechner-Gesellschaft e.V. Leipzig.

Arendt, H.-J. (1999): Gustav Theodor Fechner. Ein deutscher Naturwissenschaftler und Philosoph im 19. Jahrhundert. Frankfurt a.M.; Berlin; Bern.

Arnim, Bettine von (1840): Die Günderode. Ein Briefwechsel. Grünberg; Berlin.

Brožek, J.; Gundlach H. (Hg.) (1988): G.T. Fechner und die Psychology. International Gustav Theodor Fechner Symposium Passau, 12. to 14. June 1987. Passau.

Brümmer, Franz (.o.J.): Lexikon der deutschen Dichter und Prosaisten vom Beginn des 19. Jahrhunderts bis zur Gegenwart. 6. Aufl. Leipzig.

DBE (1995): Deutsche Biographische Enzyklopädie. Hg. von W. Killy. München; New Providence; London; Paris.

Drewitz, I. (1999): Bettine von Arnim. München.

Ehrlich, A.(1893): Berühmte Klavierspieler der Vergangenheit und Gegenwart. Leipzig.

Fechner, G. Th. (1866): Erinnerungen an Ch. H. Weiße. In : Leipziger Zeitung. Wiss. Beil., 7. Oktober, Nr. 222.

Fechner, G. Th. (1835): Friedrich Rückert. In: Blätter für literarische Unterhaltung. Leipzig 245–247; 249–250; 253–254; 257–258 (Nr. 60–63).
Fechner, G. Th. (1835): Heinrich Heine als Lyriker. In: Blätter für literarische Unterhaltung. Leipzig 749–750; 753–754; 757–758; 761–762 (Nr. 182–185).
Fechner, G. Th. (1834–1838): Das Hauslexicon, ein vollständiges Handbuch praktischer Lebenskenntnisse für alle Stände. 8 Bde. Leipzig.
Fechner, G. Th. (1838): Gedichte aus den Bergen. In: Freihafen, eine Gallerie von Unterhaltungsbildern aus den Kreisen der Literatur, Gesellschaft und Wissenschaft. Altona 152–164.
Fechner, G. Th. (1838): Deutsche Lyrik und Wilhelm Müller. In: Freihafen. Altona 186–183.
Fechner, G. Th. (1853): Rez. Psyche, oder der Becher Giamschids. Ein persisches Märchen. (Ed. F. Hauschild). In: Literarisches Centralblatt. Hg. von F. Zarncke. Leipzig, 427–428.
Fechner, G. Th. (1850): Rez. Ueber Spinos Grundgedanken. (Trendelenburg). In: Literarisches Zentralblatt. Hg. von F. Zarncke. Leipzig, 226–227.
Fechner, G. Th. (1854): Rez. Neue Lehre von den Proportionen des menschlichen Körpers (Zeising). In: Literarisches Centralblatt. Hg. von F. Zarncke. Leipzig, 555–556.
Fechner, G. Th. (1865): Ueber die Frage des goldenen Schnittes. Exkurs zu einer künftig erscheinenden Schrift über die Holben'sche Madonna. In: Archiv für die zeichnenden Künste. Hg. von Naumann; Weigel. Leipzig 11, 100–112.
Feudel, W. (1980): Adelbert von Chamisso. Leben und Werk. Leipzig.
Fontane, Th. (1979): Hermann Grimm. Goethe. In: Theodor Fontane. Werke und Schriften. Hg. von W. Keitel; H. Nürnberger. Bd. 28: Theodor Fontane. Aufsätze und Aufzeichnungen. Hg. von J. Kolbe. Frankfurt a.M., 283–292.
Grimm, J. und W. (Hg.) (1873): Deutsches Wörterbuch. Bd. 5. Leipzig.
Hasse, Ch. A. (1836): Das Augusteum und dessen Übergabe an die Universität Leipzig am 3. Aug. 1836. Leipzig.
Jahn, O. (1849): Gottfried Hermann. Eine Gedächtnisrede, gehalten am 28. 1. 1849 in der Akademischen Aula zu Leipzig. Leipzig.
Korn, Th. (1999): Leben und Werk des Juristen Emil Kuntze. Leipzig (Diss., Univ. Leipzig).
Killy, W.; Vierhaus (Hg.) (1998): Deutsche Biographische Enzyklopädie (DBE). Bd. 7. München.
Kuntze, J.E. (1892): Gustav Theodor Fechner (Dr. Mises). Ein deutsches Gelehrtenleben. Leipzig.
Lipps, G.F. (1905): Bericht über das Fechner-Archiv. In: Berichte über die Verhandlungen der Kgl. Sächs. Gesell. der Wiss. zu Leipzig, Math.-phys. Cl. Bd. 57. Leipzig, 247–312.
Menzel, W. (Hg.) (1832, 1833, 1834): Literatur-Blatt. Stuttgart.
Mundt, Th. (Hg.) (1838): Freihafen. Altona.
Mundt, Th. (Hg.) (1835): Blätter für literarische Unterhaltung. Leipzig.
Pataky, S. (Hg.) (1898): Lexikon deutscher Frauen der Feder. 2 Bde. Berlin *Pfeifer, W. (1989):* Etymologisches Wörterbuch des Deutschen. H-P. Berlin.
Pfeiffer, W. (1902): Drei Briefe an Fouqué. In: Euphorion 9, 674–677.
Poggendorff's (1898): Biographisch-literarisches Handwörterbuch. Bd. 3: Teil 2. Leipzig.
Steig, R. (1904): Grimm, Hermann Friedrich. In: Biographisches Jahrbuch und Deutscher Nekrolog. Hg. von A. Bettelheim. Bd. 6. Berlin, 97–111.

Personenregister

Sachregister

Kolibri 360 GmbH
Ferdinand-Jühlke-Straße 7
99095 Erfurt, Deutschland
produktsicherheit@kolibri360.de